MAU

Fod

Switzerland

by Nancy Coons

"

"When it comes to information on regional history,
what to see and do, and shopping, these guides are
exhaustive."

—*USAir Magazine*

"Usable, sophisticated restaurant coverage, with an
emphasis on good value."

—Andy Birsh, *Gourmet Magazine* columnist

"Valuable because of their comprehensiveness."

—*Minneapolis Star-Tribune*

"Fodor's always delivers high quality...thoughtfully
presented...thorough."

—*Houston Post*

"An excellent choice for those who want everything
under one cover."

—*Washington Post*

"

Fodor's Travel Publications, Inc.
New York • Toronto • London • Sydney • Auckland
http://www.fodors.com/

Fodor's Switzerland '97

Editor: Amy McConnell

Editorial Contributors: Steven Amsterdam, Robert Andrews, David Brown, Nancy Coons, Audra Epstein, Laura M. Kidder, Heidi Sarna, Helayne Schiff, Linda Schmidt, Mary Ellen Schultz, M. T. Schwartzman (Gold Guide editor), Dinah Spritzer, Lito Tejada-Flores, James Wade, Stuart Wade

Creative Director: Fabrizio La Rocca

Associate Art Director: Guido Caroti

Photo Researcher: Jolie Novak

Cartographer: David Lindroth

Cover Photograph: ITTC Productions/Image Bank

Text Design: Between the Covers

Copyright

Special Sales

Fodor's Travel Publications are available at special discounts for bulk purchases for sales promotions or premiums. Special editions, including personalized covers, excerpts of existing guides, and corporate imprints, can be created in large quantities for special needs. For more information, contact your local bookseller or write to Special Markets, Fodor's Travel Publications, 201 East 50th Street, New York, NY 10022. Inquiries from Canada should be directed to your local Canadian bookseller or sent to Random House of Canada, Ltd., Marketing Department, 1265 Aerowood Drive, Mississauga, Ontario L4W 1B9. Inquiries from the United Kingdom should be sent to Fodor's Travel Publications, 20 Vauxhall Bridge Road, London SW1V 2SA, England.

PRINTED IN THE UNITED STATES OF AMERICA

10 9 8 7 6 5 4 3 2 1

CONTENTS

ON THE ROAD WITH FODOR'S

WE'RE ALWAYS THRILLED to get letters from readers, especially one like this:

It took us an hour to decide what book to buy and we now know we picked the best one. Your book was wonderful, easy to follow, very accurate, and good on pointing out eating places, informal as well as formal. When we saw other people using your book, we would look at each other and smile.

Our editors and writers are deeply committed to making every Fodor's guide "the best one"—not only accurate but always charming, brimming with sound recommendations and solid ideas, right on the mark in describing restaurants and hotels, and full of fascinating facts that make you view what you've traveled to see in a rich new light.

About Our Writers

Our success in achieving our goals—and in helping to make your trip the best of all possible vacations—is a credit to the hard work of our extraordinary writers and editors.

Nancy Coons has been following ancestral trails in Switzerland since moving to Europe in 1987. Having grown up in Michigan and worked as a writer and editor in New York, Chicago, and Little Rock, she contributes regularly to Fodor's publications and has written features on European topics for *National Geographic Traveler,* the *Wall Street Journal, Opera News,* and *European Travel & Life.*

Brothers **James** and **Stuart Wade** are the publishers of "The Switzerland Advisor" (http://www.swisstravel.com/), an on-line newsletter devoted to insider tips on Swiss travel and tourism. James has lived in Switzerland since 1982; he is currently the Director of Marketing at the Ecole hôtelère de Lausanne. Stuart, a Texas resident, is a publicist and freelance writer.

New this Year

This year we've reformatted our guides to make them easier to use. Each chapter of *Switzerland '97* begins with brand-new recommended itineraries to help you decide what to see in the time you have; a section called When to Tour points out the optimal time of day, day of the week, and season for your journey. You may also notice our fresh graphics, new in 1996. More readable and more helpful than ever? We think so—and we hope you do, too.

On the Web

Also check out Fodor's Web site (http://www.fodors.com/), where you'll find travel information on major destinations around the world and an ever-changing array of travel-savvy interactive features.

How to Use this Book

Organization

Up front is the **Gold Guide.** Its first section, **Important Contacts A to Z,** gives addresses and telephone numbers of organizations and companies that offer destination-related services and detailed information and publications. **Smart Travel Tips A to Z,** the Gold Guide's second section, gives specific information on how to accomplish what you need to in Switzerland as well as tips on savvy traveling. Both sections are in alphabetical order by topic.

Chapters in *Switzerland '97* are arranged roughly by canton, starting with Zürich and moving clockwise. Each city chapter begins with an Exploring section, which is subdivided by neighborhood; each subsection recommends a walking or driving tour and lists sights in alphabetical order. Each regional chapter is divided by geographical area; within each area, towns are covered in logical geographical order, and attractive stretches of road and minor points of interest between them are indicated by the designation En Route. Throughout, Off the Beaten Path sights appear after the places from which they are most easily accessible. And within town sections, all restaurants and lodgings are grouped together.

To help you decide what to visit in the time you have, all chapters begin with recommended itineraries; you can mix and match those from several chapters to create a complete vacation. The A to Z section that ends all chapters covers getting there, getting around, and helpful contacts and resources.

At the end of the book you'll find Portraits, wonderful essays about Swiss cheese, hiking, and skiing in Switzerland, followed by suggestions for pretrip reading, both fiction and nonfiction, and movies on tape with Switzerland as a backdrop.

Icons and Symbols

★   Our special recommendations
✕   Restaurant
🏠   Lodging establishment
✕🏠   Lodging establishment whose restaurant warrants a detour
⚠   Campgrounds
🕑   Good for kids (rubber duckie)
☞   Sends you to another section of the guide for more information
✉   Address
☎   Telephone number
FAX   Fax number
🕐   Opening and closing times
💰   Admission prices (those we give apply only to adults; substantially reduced fees are almost always available for children, students, and senior citizens)

Numbers in white and black circles that appear on the maps, in the margins, and within the tours correspond to one another.

Restaurant and Hotel Criteria and Price Categories

The restaurants and lodgings we list are the cream of the crop in each price range. Price categories are indicated at the start of Dining and Lodging sections in city chapters and in the Pleasures and Pastimes sections of regional chapters. In all restaurant charts, costs are based on a three-course meal, including sales tax and 15% service charge.

Lodging prices are based on *average* prices for a standard double room with bathroom. Prices may vary radically, depending on room size, view, whether there's a bathtub or walk-in shower, and, in resorts, whether it's high or low season. Though resorts often include half board in the price, resort hotel prices have been averaged and categorized without pension. Thus, a hotel classed in the $$ category (120 SF–180 SF) may average 150 SF— while you spend 200 SF for its best double with tub and Matterhorn view and 80

SF for the former broom closet down the hall with access to a public bathroom.

Restaurant Reservations and Dress Codes

Reservations are always a good idea; we note only when they're essential or when they are not accepted. Book as far ahead as you can, and reconfirm when you get to town. Unless otherwise noted, the restaurants listed are open daily for lunch and dinner. We mention dress only when men are required to wear a jacket or a jacket and tie. Look for an overview of local habits under Dining in the Pleasures and Pastimes section that follows each chapter introduction.

Hotel Facilities and Meal Plans

We always list the facilities that are available—but we don't specify whether they cost extra: When pricing accommodations, always ask what's included.

Particularly in ski resorts or in hotels where you've opted to stay for three days or more, you may be quoted a room price per person including *demipension* (half board). This means you've opted to eat either lunch or dinner in the hotel, selecting from a limited, fixed menu. Unless you're holding out for gastronomic adventure, your best bet is to take half board. Most hotels will be flexible if you come in from the slopes craving a steaming pot of fondue, and they will subtract the day's pension supplement from your room price, charging you à la carte instead.

Credit Cards

The following abbreviations are used: **AE,** American Express; **DC,** Diners Club; **MC,** MasterCard; and **V,** Visa.

Please Write to Us

You can use this book in the confidence that all prices and opening times are based on information supplied to us at press time; Fodor's cannot accept responsibility for any errors. Time inevitably brings changes, so always confirm information when it matters—especially if you're making a detour to visit a specific place. In addition, when making reservations be sure to mention if you have a disability or are traveling with children, if you prefer a private bath or a certain type of bed, or if you have specific dietary needs or any other concerns.

Were the restaurants we recommended as described? Did our hotel picks exceed your expectations? Did you find a museum we recommended a waste of time? If you have complaints, we'll look into them and revise our entries when the facts warrant it. If you've discovered a special place that we haven't included, we'll pass the information along to our correspondents and have them check it out. So send your feedback, positive *and* negative, to the Switzerland editor at 201 East 50th Street, New York, New York 10022—and have a wonderful trip!

Karen Cure

Karen Cure
Editorial Director

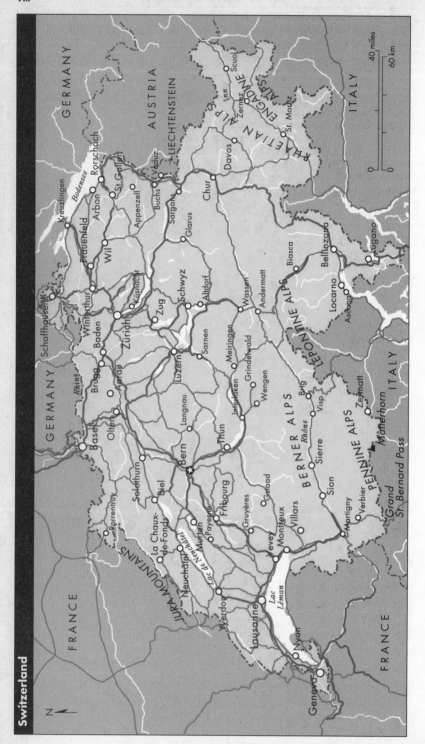

Switzerland

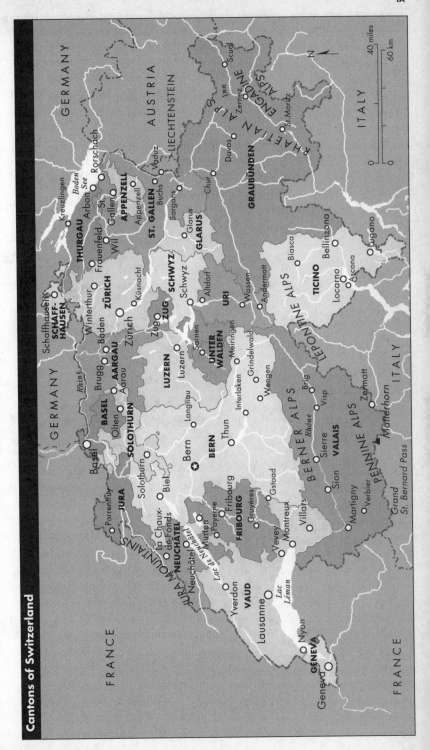

Cantons of Switzerland

Europe

Reykjavik
ICELAND

NORWAY
Bergen

SCOTLAND
NORTHERN
IRELAND
Edinburgh

North
Sea

Skagerrak

Belfast

IRELAND
Irish
Sea
Dublin

DENMARK

UNITED
KINGDOM

WALES

Hamburg

Cardiff
ENGLAND
NETHERLANDS
Amsterdam

London
The Hague
Rotterdam

GERM

ATLANTIC
OCEAN

English Channel

Brussels
BELGIUM

Bonn

Paris
LUXEMBOURG

Frankfurt

FRANCE
Zürich
Bern
SWITZERLAND

Munich

Lyon
LIECHTENSTEIN

Milan
Venic

PORTUGAL

Madrid
ANDORRA

Marseille

Nice
Monte
Carlo
MONACO

Florence

Lisbon

Barcelona

Corsica

SPAIN

Seville
Granada

Balearic
Islands

Sardinia

Tyrrhenia

Gibraltar

Mediterranean Sea

MOROCCO

ALGERIA

0   400 miles

0   600 km

TUNISIA

IMPORTANT CONTACTS A TO Z

*An Alphabetical Listing of Publications,
Organizations, and Companies that Will Help You
Before, During, and After Your Trip*

A

AIR TRAVEL

The major gateways to Switzerland include Zürich's **Kloten Airport** (☎ 1/157–10–60) and Geneva's **Cointrin International Airport** (☎ 22/799–31–11).

FLYING TIME

Flying time is seven hours from New York, 10 hours from Chicago, and 14 hours from Los Angeles.

CARRIERS

To GENEVA➤ Contact **Air Canada** (☎ 800/263–0882), **Continental** (☎ 800/231–0856), **Delta** (800/221–1212), **Swissair** (☎ 800/221–4750), and **United Airlines** (☎ 800/241–6522).

To ZURICH➤ Contact **Air Canada** (☎ 800/263–0882), **American Airlines** (☎ 800/433–7300), **Continental** (☎ 800/231–0856), **Delta** (800/221–1212), **Swissair** (☎ 800/221–4750), **TWA** (☎ 800/892–4141), and **United Airlines** (☎ 800/241–6522).

FROM THE U.K.➤ **British Airways** (☎ 0181/897–4000; outside London, 0345/222–111) flies directly to Zürich from London Heathrow (with flights averaging 1 hour 35 minutes), as does **Swissair** (☎ 0171/434–7300). There are nine flights daily. **Crossair** (☎ 0171/439–4144

offers direct service from London and Birmingham, **Swissair** and **Aer Lingus** (☎ 0181/899–4747) from Manchester.

Service to Geneva has greatly improved. There are now six nonstop flights daily by **BA** and four by Swissair from Heathrow. The flying time is 1 hour 30 minutes. There are **BA** flights from Gatwick, also. Basel airport (Basel/Freiburg) has two **British Airways** flights from Heathrow on weekdays and Sunday and one on Saturday; **Crossair** also offers two flights daily from Heathrow.

COMPLAINTS

To register complaints about charter and scheduled airlines, contact the U.S. Department of Transportation's **Aviation Consumer Protection Division** (✉ C-75, Washington, DC 20590, ☎ 202/366–2220). Complaints about lost baggage or ticketing problems and safety concerns may also be logged with the **Federal Aviation Administration (FAA) Consumer Hotline** (☎ 800/322–7873).

CONSOLIDATORS

For the names of reputable air-ticket consolidators, contact the **United States Air Consolidators Association** (✉ 925 L St., Suite 220, Sacramento, CA 95814,

☎ 916/441–4166, FAX 916/441–3520). For discount air-ticketing agencies, ☞ Discounts & Deals, *below.*

PUBLICATIONS

For general information about charter carriers, ask for the Department of Transportation's free brochure **"Plane Talk: Public Charter Flights"** (✉ Aviation Consumer Protection Division, C-75, Washington, DC 20590, ☎ 202/366–2220). The Department of Transportation also publishes a 58-page booklet, **"Fly Rights,"** available from the Consumer Information Center (✉ Supt. of Documents, Dept. 136C, Pueblo, CO 81009; $1.75).

For other tips and hints, consult the Consumers Union's monthly **"Consumer Reports Travel Letter"** (✉ Box 53629, Boulder, CO 80322, ☎ 800/234–1970; $39 1st year) and the newsletter **"Travel Smart"** (✉ 40 Beechdale Rd., Dobbs Ferry, NY 10522, ☎ 800/327–3633; $37 per year).

B

BETTER BUSINESS BUREAU

For local contacts in the hometown of a tour operator you may be considering, consult the **Council of Better Business Bureaus** (✉ 4200

Wilson Blvd., Suite 800, Arlington, VA 22203, ☎ 703/276–0100, FAX 703/525–8277).

C
CAR RENTAL

The major car-rental companies represented in Switzerland are **Alamo** (☎ 800/327–9633; in the U.K., 0800/272–2000), **Avis** (☎ 800/331–1084; in Canada, 800/879–2847), **Budget** (☎ 800/527–0700; in the U.K., 0800/181181), **Dollar** (☎ 800/800–4000; in the U.K., 0990/565656, where it is known as Eurodollar), **Hertz** (☎ 800/654–3001; in Canada, 800/263–0600; in the U.K., 0345/555888), and **National InterRent** (sometimes known as Europcar InterRent outside North America; ☎ 800/227–3876; in the U.K., 01345/222–525). Rates in Switzerland begin at $28 a day and $142 a week for an economy car with unlimited mileage. This does not include tax on car rentals, which is 6.5%.

RENTAL WHOLESALERS

Contact **Auto Europe** (☎ 207/828–2525 or 800/223–5555), **Europe by Car** (☎ 800/223–1516; in CA, 800/252–9401), and the **Kemwel Group** (☎ 914/835–5555 or 800/678–0678).

CHILDREN & TRAVEL
FLYING

Look into **"Flying with Baby"** (✉ Third Street Press, Box 261250, Littleton, CO 80163,

303/595–5959; $4.95 includes shipping), cowritten by a flight attendant. **"Kids and Teens in Flight,"** free from the U.S. Department of Transportation's Aviation Consumer Protection Division (✉ C-75, Washington, DC 20590, ☎ 202/366–2220), offers tips on children flying alone. Every two years the February issue of *Family Travel Times* (☞ Know-How, *below*) details children's services on three dozen airlines. **"Flying Alone, Handy Advice for Kids Traveling Solo"** is available free from the American Automobile Association (AAA) (✉ send stamped, self-addressed, legal-size envelope: Flying Alone, Mail Stop 800, 1000 AAA Dr., Heathrow, FL 32746).

KNOW-HOW

Family Travel Times, published quarterly by Travel with Your Children (✉ TWYCH, 40 5th Ave., New York, NY 10011, ☎ 212/477–5524; $40 per year), covers destinations, types of vacations, and modes of travel.

The *Family Travel Guides* catalog (✉ Carousel Press, Box 6061, Albany, CA 94706, ☎ 510/527–5849; $1 postage) lists about 200 books and articles on traveling with children. Also check *Take Your Baby and Go! A Guide for Traveling with Babies, Toddlers and Young Children,* by Sheri Andrews, Judy Bordeaux, and Vivian Vasquez (✉ Bear Creek Publications, 2507 Minor Ave. E,

Seattle, WA 98102, ☎ 206/322–7604 or 800/326–6566; $5.95 plus $1.50 shipping).

LODGING

For listings of family hotels throughout the country, contact the **Swiss Hotel Association** (SHA, ✉ Monbijoustrasse 130, Box 3001, Bern, ☎ 031/50–71–11) or **Switzerland Toursim** (☞ Visitor Information, *below*).

TOUR OPERATORS

Contact **Grandtravel** (✉ 6900 Wisconsin Ave., Suite 706, Chevy Chase, MD 20815, ☎ 301/986–0790 or 800/247–7651), which has tours for people traveling with grandchildren ages 7–17.

CUSTOMS
U.S. CITIZENS

The **U.S. Customs Service** (✉ Box 7407, Washington, DC 20044, ☎ 202/927–6724) can answer questions on duty-free limits and publishes a helpful brochure, "Know Before You Go." For information on registering foreign-made articles, call 202/927–0540 or write U.S. Customs Service, Resource Management, 1301 Constitution Ave. NW, Washington DC, 20229.

COMPLAINTS> Note the inspector's badge number and write to the commissioner's office (✉ 1301 Constitution Ave. NW, Washington, DC 20229).

CANADIANS

Contact **Revenue Canada** (✉ 2265 St. Laurent Blvd. S, Ottawa, Ontario K1G 4K3, ☎ 613/993–

0534) for a copy of the free brochure **"I Declare/Je Déclare"** and for details on duty-free limits. For recorded information (within Canada only), call 800/461–9999.

U.K. CITIZENS

HM Customs and Excise (⊠ Dorset House, Stamford St., London SE1 9NG, ☎ 0171/202–4227) can answer questions about U.K. customs regulations and publishes a free pamphlet, **"A Guide for Travellers,"** detailing standard procedures and import rules.

D

DISABILITIES & ACCESSIBILITY

COMPLAINTS

To register complaints under the provisions of the Americans with Disabilities Act, contact the U.S. Department of Justice's **Disability Rights Section** (⊠ Box 66738, Washington, DC 20035, ☎ 202/514–0301 or 800/514–0301, FAX 202/307–1198, TTY 202/514–0383 or 800/514–0383). For airline-related problems, contact the U.S. Department of Transportation's **Aviation Consumer Protection Division** (☞ Air Travel, *above*). For complaints about surface transportation, contact the Department of Transportation's **Civil Rights Office** (⊠ 400 7th St., SW, Room 10215, Washington DC, 20590 ☎ 202/366–4648).

LOCAL INFORMATION

Contact **Mobility International Schweiz** (⊠

Hard 4, CH-8408 Winterthur, ☎ 052/222–68–25, FAX 052/222–68–38) for information on special tours and travel. And contact Switzerland Tourism (☞ Visitor Information, *below*) for a copy of "Swiss Hotel Guide for the Disabled" (published by the Swiss Hotel Association in cooperation with the **Swiss Association for Disabled Persons** (⊠ Froburgstrasse 4, CH-4601 Olten, ☎ 062/212-12-62). A detailed guide to Swiss hotels offering facilities for guests with disabilities, it distinguishes between properties appropriate for visitors in wheelchairs and those suitable for visitors with walking impairments.

ORGANIZATIONS

TRAVELERS WITH HEARING IMPAIRMENTS➤ The **American Academy of Otolaryngology** (⊠ 1 Prince St., Alexandria, VA 22314, ☎ 703/836–4444, FAX 703/683–5100, TTY 703/519–1585) publishes a brochure, "Travel Tips for Hearing Impaired People."

TRAVELERS WITH MOBILITY PROBLEMS➤ Contact the **Information Center for Individuals with Disabilities** (⊠ Box 256, Boston, MA 02117, ☎ 617/450–9888; in MA, 800/462–5015; TTY 617/424–6855); **Mobility International USA** (⊠ Box 10767, Eugene, OR 97440, ☎ and TTY 541/343–1284, FAX 541/343–6812), the U.S. branch of a Belgium-based organization (☞ *below*) with affiliates in 30 countries; **MossRehab Hospital Travel**

Information Service (☎ 215/456–9600, TTY 215/456–9602), a telephone information resource for travelers with physical disabilities; the **Society for the Advancement of Travel for the Handicapped** (⊠ 347 5th Ave., Suite 610, New York, NY 10016, ☎ 212/447–7284, FAX 212/725–8253; membership $45); and **Travelin' Talk** (⊠ Box 3534, Clarksville, TN 37043, ☎ 615/552–6670, FAX 615/552–1182) which provides local contacts worldwide for travelers with disabilities.

TRAVELERS WITH VISION IMPAIRMENTS➤ Contact the **American Council of the Blind** (⊠ 1155 15th St. NW, Suite 720, Washington, DC 20005, ☎ 202/467–5081, FAX 202/467–5085) for a list of travelers' resources or the **American Foundation for the Blind** (⊠ 11 Penn Plaza, Suite 300, New York, NY 10001, ☎ 212/502–7600 or 800/232–5463, TTY 212/502–7662), which provides general advice and publishes "Access to Art" ($19.95), a directory of museums that accommodate travelers with vision impairments.

IN THE U.K.

Contact the **Royal Association for Disability and Rehabilitation** (⊠ RADAR, 12 City Forum, 250 City Rd., London EC1V 8AF, ☎ 0171/250–3222) or **Mobility International** (⊠ rue de Manchester 25, B-1080 Brussels, Belgium, ☎ 00–322–410–6297, FAX 00–322–410–6874), an international travel-information clearing-house for people with disabilities.

PUBLICATIONS

Several publications for travelers with disabilities are available from the **Consumer Information Center** (✉ Box 100, Pueblo, CO 81009, ☎ 719/948–3334). Call or write for its free catalog of current titles. The Society for the Advancement of Travel for the Handicapped (☞ Organizations, *above*) publishes the quarterly magazine **"Access to Travel"** ($13 for 1-year subscription).

The 500-page **Travelin' Talk Directory** (✉ Box 3534, Clarksville, TN 37043, ☎ 615/552–6670, FAX 615/552–1182; $35) lists people and organizations who help travelers with disabilities. For travel agents worldwide, consult the **Directory of Travel Agencies for the Disabled** (✉ Twin Peaks Press, Box 129, Vancouver, WA 98666, ☎ 360/694–2462 or 800/637–2256, FAX 360/696–3210; $19.95 plus $3 shipping).

TRAVEL AGENCIES & TOUR OPERATORS

The Americans with Disabilities Act requires that all travel firms serve the needs of all travelers. That said, you should note that some agencies and operators specialize in making travel arrangements for individuals and groups with disabilities, among them **Access Adventures** (✉ 206 Chestnut Ridge Rd., Rochester, NY 14624, ☎ 716/889–9096), run by a former physical-rehab counselor.

TRAVELERS WITH MOBIL-ITY PROBLEMS➤ Contact **Hinsdale Travel Service** (✉ 201 E. Ogden Ave., Suite 100, Hinsdale, IL 60521, ☎ 708/325–1335), a travel agency that benefits from the advice of wheelchair traveler Janice Perkins; and **Wheelchair Journeys** (✉ 16979 Redmond Way, Redmond, WA 98052, ☎ 206/885–2210 or 800/313–4751), which can handle arrangements worldwide.

TRAVELERS WITH DEVEL-OPMENTAL DISABILITIES➤ Contact the nonprofit **New Directions** (✉ 5276 Hollister Ave., Suite 207, Santa Barbara, CA 93111, ☎ 805/967–2841).

TRAVEL GEAR

The **Magellan's** catalog (☎ 800/962–4943, FAX 805/568–5406), includes a section devoted to products designed for travelers with disabilities.

DISCOUNTS & DEALS

AIRFARES

For the lowest airfares to Switzerland, call 800/FLY–4–LES.

CLUBS

Contact **Entertainment Travel Editions** (✉ Box 1068, Trumbull, CT 06611, ☎ 800/445–4137; $28–$53, depending on destination), **Great American Traveler** (✉ Box 27965, Salt Lake City, UT 84127, ☎ 800/548–2812; $49.95 per year), **Moment's Notice Discount Travel Club** (✉ 7301 New Utrecht Ave., Brooklyn, NY 11204, ☎ 718/234–6295; $25 per year, single or fam-

ily), **Privilege Card** (✉ 3391 Peachtree Rd. NE, Suite 110, Atlanta, GA 30326, ☎ 404/262–0222 or 800/236–9732; $74.95 per year), **Travelers Advantage** (✉ CUC Travel Service, 49 Music Sq. W, Nashville, TN 37203, ☎ 800/548–1116 or 800/648–4037; $49 per year, single or family), or **Worldwide Discount Travel Club** (✉ 1674 Meridian Ave., Miami Beach, FL 33139, ☎ 305/534–2082; $50 per year for family, $40 single).

HOTEL ROOMS

For hotel room rates guaranteed in U.S. dollars, call **Steigenberger Reservation Service** (☎ 800/223–5652).

PASSES

☞ Train Travel, *below*.

STUDENTS

Members of Hostelling International–American Youth Hostels (☞ Students, *below*) are eligible for discounts on car rentals, admissions to attractions, and other selected travel expenses.

PUBLICATIONS

Consult **The Frugal Globetrotter,** by Bruce Northam (✉ Fulcrum Publishing, 350 Indiana St., Suite 350, Golden, CO 80401, ☎ 800/992–2908; $16.95 plus $4 shipping). For publications that tell how to find the lowest prices on plane tickets, ☞ Air Travel, *above*.

DRIVING

AUTO CLUBS

The **Automobile Club de Suisse** (ACS, ✉ Wasserwerkegasse 39, Bern) and the **Touring Club Suisse** (TCS, ✉ Rue

THE GOLD GUIDE / IMPORTANT CONTACTS

Pierre Fatio 9, Geneva) have branches throughout Switzerland. In the U.K., the **Automobile Association** (AA, ⊠ Fanum House, Basing View, Basingstoke, Hampshire, RQ212 EA, ☎ 01256/20123) is affiliated with the TCS, while the **Royal Automobile Club** (RAC, ⊠ RAC House, Bartlett St., Box 10, Croydon, Surrey CR2 6XW, ☎ 0181/686–2525) is affiliated with both the ACS and the TCS.

G

GAY & LESBIAN TRAVEL

ORGANIZATIONS

The **International Gay Travel Association** (⊠ Box 4974, Key West, FL 33041, ☎ 800/448–8550, FAX 305/296–6633), a consortium of more than 1,000 travel companies, can supply names of gay-friendly travel agents, tour operators, and accommodations.

PUBLICATIONS

The premier international travel magazine for gays and lesbians is **Our World** (⊠ 1104 N. Nova Rd., Suite 251, Daytona Beach, FL 32117, ☎ 904/441–5367, FAX 904/441–5604; $35 for 10 issues). The 16-page monthly **"Out & About"** (☎ 212/645–6922 or 800/929–2268, FAX 800/929–2215; $49 for 10 issues and quarterly calendar) covers gay-friendly resorts, hotels, cruise lines, and airlines.

TOUR OPERATORS

Toto Tours (⊠ 1326 W. Albion Ave., Suite 3W, Chicago, IL 60626, ☎ 312/274–8686 or 800/565–1241, FAX 312/274–8695) offers group tours to worldwide destinations.

TRAVEL AGENCIES

The largest agencies serving gay travelers are **Advance Travel** (⊠ 10700 Northwest Fwy., Suite 160, Houston, TX 77092, ☎ 713/682–2002 or 800/292–0500), **Islanders/Kennedy Travel** (⊠ 183 W. 10th St., New York, NY 10014, ☎ 212/242–3222 or 800/988–1181), **Now Voyager** (⊠ 4406 18th St., San Francisco, CA 94114, ☎ 415/626–1169 or 800/255–6951), and **Yellowbrick Road** (⊠ 1500 W. Balmoral Ave., Chicago, IL 60640, ☎ 312/561–1800 or 800/642–2488). **Skylink Women's Travel** (⊠ 2460 W. 3rd St., Suite 215, Santa Rosa, CA 95401, ☎ 707/570–0105 or 800/225–5759) serves lesbian travelers.

H

HEALTH

FINDING A DOCTOR

For its members, the **International Association for Medical Assistance to Travellers** (⊠ IAMAT, membership free; 417 Center St., Lewiston, NY 14092, ☎ 716/754–4883; 40 Regal Rd., Guelph, Ontario N1K 1B5, ☎ 519/836–0102; 1287 St. Clair Ave. W., Toronto, Ontario M6E 1B8, ☎ 416/652–0137; 57 Voirets, 1212 Grand-Lancy, Geneva, Switzerland, no phone) publishes a worldwide directory of English-speaking physicians meeting IAMAT standards.

MEDICAL ASSISTANCE COMPANIES

The following companies are concerned primarily with emergency medical assistance, although they may provide some insurance as part of their coverage. For a list of full-service travel insurance companies, ☞ Insurance, *below.*

Contact **International SOS Assistance** (⊠ Box 11568, Philadelphia, PA 19116, ☎ 215/244–1500 or 800/523–8930; Box 466, Pl. Bonaventure, Montréal, Québec H5A 1C1, ☎ 514/874–7674 or 800/363–0263; 7 Old Lodge Pl., St. Margarets, Twickenham TW1 1RQ, England, ☎ 0181/744–0033), **Medex Assistance Corporation** (⊠ Box 5375, Timonium, MD 21094-5375, ☎ 410/453–6300 or 800/537–2029), **Traveler's Emergency Network** (⊠ 3100 Tower Blvd., Suite 3100A, Durham, NC 27702, ☎ 919/90–6065 or 800/275–4836, FAX 919/493–8262), **TravMed** (⊠ Box 5375, Timonium, MD 21094, ☎ 410/453–6380 or 800/732–5309), or **Worldwide Assistance Services** (⊠ 1133 15th St. NW, Suite 400, Washington, DC 20005, ☎ 202/331–1609 or 800/821–2828, FAX 202/828–5896).

I

INSURANCE

IN CANADA

Contact **Mutual of Omaha** (⊠ Travel Division, 500 University Ave., Toronto,

Ontario M5G 1V8,
☎ 800/465–0267(in
Canada) or 416/598-
4083).

IN THE U.S.

Travel insurance cover-
ing baggage, health,
and trip cancellation or
interruptions is avail-
able from **Access Amer-
ica** (✉ 6600 W. Broad
St., Richmond, VA
23230, ☎ 804/285–
3300 or 800/334–
7525), **Carefree Travel
Insurance** (✉ Box
9366, 100 Garden City
Plaza, Garden City, NY
11530, ☎ 516/294–
0220 or 800/323–
3149), **Near Travel
Services** (✉ Box 1339,
Calumet City, IL
60409, ☎ 708/868–
6700 or 800/654–
6700), **Tele-Trip** (✉
Mutual of Omaha
Plaza, Box 31716,
Omaha, NE 68131, ☎
800/228–9792), **Travel
Guard International** (✉
1145 Clark St., Stevens
Point, WI 54481, ☎
715/345–0505 or 800/
826–1300), **Travel
Insured International**
(✉ Box 280568, East
Hartford, CT 06128,
☎ 203/528–7663 or
800/243–3174), and
Wallach & Company
(✉ 107 W. Federal St.,
Box 480, Middleburg,
VA 22117, ☎ 540/
687–3166 or 800/
237–6615).

IN THE U.K.

The **Association of
British Insurers** (✉ 51
Gresham St., London
EC2V 7HQ, ☎ 0171/
600–3333) gives advice
by phone and publishes
the free pamphlet
**"Holiday Insurance and
Motoring Abroad,"**
which sets out typical
policy provisions and
costs.

L
LODGING

For information on
hotel consolidators, ☞
Discounts, *above.*

APARTMENT &
VILLA RENTAL

Among the companies
to contact are **Europa-Let**
(✉ 92 N. Main St.,
Ashland, OR 97520,
☎ 541/482–5806 or
800/462–4486, FAX 541/
482–0660), **Hometours
International** (✉ Box
11503, Knoxville, TN
37939, ☎ 423/588–
8722 or 800/367–
4668), **Interhome** (✉
124 Little Falls Rd.,
Fairfield, NJ 07004, ☎
201/882–6864, FAX 201/
808–1742), **Property
Rentals International** (✉
1008 Mansfield Cross-
ing Rd., Richmond, VA
23236, ☎ 804/378–
6054 or 800/220–3332,
FAX 804/379–2073),
**Rent-a-Home Interna-
tional** (✉ 7200 34th
Ave. NW, Seattle, WA
98117, ☎ 206/789–
9377 or 800/488–7368,
FAX 206/789–9379,
rentahomeinternational
@msn.com), and **Villas
International** (✉ 605
Market St., Suite 510,
San Francisco, CA
94105, ☎ 415/281–
0910 or 800/221–2260,
FAX 415/281–0919).
Members of the travel
club **Hideaways Interna-
tional** (✉ 767 Islington
St., Portsmouth, NH
03801, ☎ 603/430–
4433 or 800/843–4433,
FAX 603/430–4444,
info@hideaways.com;
$99 per year) receive
two annual guides plus
quarterly newsletters
and arrange rentals
among themselves.

FARM STAYS

Contact the **Schweiz-
erischer Bauernverband**

(Swiss Farmers Associa-
tion, ✉ CH-5200
Brugg, ☎ 056/462–
51–55, FAX 056/462–
22–12).

HOME EXCHANGE

Some of the principal
clearinghouses are
**HomeLink International/
Vacation Exchange Club**
(✉ Box 650, Key West,
FL 33041, ☎ 305/294–
1448 or 800/638–3841,
FAX 305/294–1148; $78
per year), which sends
members five annual
directories, with a
listing in one, plus
updates; and **Intervac
International** (✉ Box
590504, San Francisco,
CA 94159, ☎ 415/
435–3497, FAX 415/
435–7440; $65 per
year), which publishes
four annual directories.

M
MONEY

ATMS

For specific foreign
Cirrus locations, call
800/424–7787; for
foreign **Plus** locations,
consult the Plus direc-
tory at your local bank.

CURRENCY
EXCHANGE

If your bank doesn't
exchange currency,
contact **Thomas Cook
Currency Services**
(☎ 800/287–7362 for
locations). **Ruesch
International** (☎ 800/
424–2923 for locations)
can also provide you
with foreign banknotes
before you leave home
and publishes a number
of useful brochures,
including a "Foreign
Currency Guide" and
"Foreign Exchange
Tips."

WIRING FUNDS

Funds can be wired via
MoneyGram℠ (for

locations and information in the U.S. and Canada, ☎ 800/926–9400) or **Western Union** (for agent locations or to send money using MasterCard or Visa, ☎ 800/325–6000; in Canada, 800/321–2923; in the U.K., 0800/833833; or visit the Western Union office at the nearest major post office).

P
PASSPORTS & VISAS

U.S. CITIZENS

For fees, documentation requirements, and other information, call the State Department's **Office of Passport Services** information line (☎ 202/647–0518).

CANADIANS

For fees, documentation requirements, and other information, call the Ministry of Foreign Affairs and International Trade's **Passport Office** (☎ 819/994–3500 or 800/567–6868).

U.K. CITIZENS

For fees, documentation requirements, and to request an emergency passport, call the **London Passport Office** (☎ 0990/210410).

PHOTO HELP

The **Kodak Information Center** (☎ 800/242–2424) answers consumer questions about film and photography. The **Kodak Guide to Shooting Great Travel Pictures** (available in bookstores; or contact Fodor's Travel Publications, ☎ 800/533–6478; $16.50 plus $4

shipping) explains how to take expert travel photographs.

S
SAFETY

"Trouble-Free Travel," from the AAA, is a booklet of tips for protecting yourself and your belongings when away from home. Send a stamped, self-addressed, legal-size envelope to Trouble-Free Travel (✉ Mail Stop 75, 1000 AAA Dr., Heathrow, FL 32746).

SENIOR CITIZENS

EDUCATIONAL TRAVEL

The nonprofit **Elderhostel** (✉ 75 Federal St., 3rd Floor, Boston, MA 02110, ☎ 617/426–7788), for people 55 and older, has offered inexpensive study programs since 1975. Courses cover everything from marine science to Greek mythology and cowboy poetry. Costs for two- to three-week international trips—including room, board, and transportation from the United States—range from $1,800 to $4,500.

Interhostel (✉ University of New Hampshire, 6 Garrison Ave., Durham, NH 03824, ☎ 603/862–1147 or 800/733–9753), for travelers 50 and older, has two- to three-week trips; most last two weeks and cost $2,000–$3,500, including airfare.

ORGANIZATIONS

Contact the **American Association of Retired Persons** (✉ AARP, 601 E St. NW, Washington,

DC 20049, ☎ 202/434–2277; annual dues $8 per person or couple). Its Purchase Privilege Program secures discounts for members on lodging, car rentals, and sightseeing.

Additional sources for discounts on lodgings, car rentals, and other travel expenses, as well as helpful magazines and newsletters, are the **National Council of Senior Citizens** (✉ 1331 F St. NW, Washington, DC 20004, ☎ 202/347–8800; annual membership $12) and Sears's **Mature Outlook** (✉ Box 10448, Des Moines, IA 50306, ☎ 800/336–6330; annual membership $14.95).

PUBLICATIONS

A special guide to hotels that offer senior discounts, **Season for Seniors**, is available from the **Swiss Hotel Association** (✉ Monbijou-strasse 130, CH-3001 Bern, ☎ 031/370–41–11), or from **Switzerland Tourism** (☞ Visitor Information, *below*).

The 50+ Traveler's Guidebook: Where to Go, Where to Stay, What to Do, by Anita Williams and Merrimac Dillon (✉ St. Martin's Press, 175 5th Ave., New York, NY 10010, ☎ 212/674–5151 or 800/288–2131; $13.95 plus $4 shipping), offers many useful tips. **"The Mature Traveler"** (✉ Box 50400, Reno, NV 89513, ☎ 702/786–7419; $29.95), a monthly newsletter, covers all sorts of travel deals.

SPORTS

BOATING

Holders of the Swiss Pass or FlexiPass can go on boating excursions with Eurotrek's **Swiss Adventure** program (☎ 01/462–02–03, FAX 01/462–93–92).

CAMPING

Switzerland is ideal for campers, with approximately 450 sites throughout the country. All are classified with one to five stars according to amenities, location, and so on. The rates vary widely, but average around 15 SF per night for a family of four, plus car or camper. For further details see the **Swiss Camping Guide**, published by the Swiss Camping Association (at bookshops for 15 SF or from the **Camping and Caravaning Association** (✉ Box 24, CH-6004 Luzern, ☎ 041/210–48–22). Listings are also available from the **Touring Club of Switzerland** (Box 176, CH-1217 Meyrin, camping division ☎ 022/785–1333).

To stay in most European campsites you must have an **International Camping Carnet**, verifying your status as a bona fide camper. This is available from any national camping association within Europe, or from the **National Campers and Hikers Association** (✉ 4804 Transit Rd., Bldg. 2, Depew, NY 14043, ☎ 716/668–6242).

SKIING

Applications to the **Swiss Alpine Club** should be addressed to the club at Sektion Zermatt, Mr. Edmond F. Krieger, Postfach 1, CH-3920 Zermatt. Information on the application process is available from **Ruesch International** (☎ 800/424–2923). For a directory of mountain-club huts (38 SF), contact Swiss Alpine Club-Verlag S.A. (✉ Helvetia-platz 4, CH-3006 Bern, FAX 031/352–60–63).

STUDENTS

HOSTELING

In the United States, contact **Hostelling International–American Youth Hostels** (✉ 733 15th St. NW, Suite 840, Washington, DC 20005, ☎ 202/783–6161, FAX 202/783–6171); in Canada, **Hostelling International–Canada** (✉ 205 Catherine St., Suite 400, Ottawa, Ontario K2P 1C3, ☎ 613/237–7884); and in the United Kingdom, the **Youth Hostel Association of England and Wales** (✉ Trevelyan House, 8 St. Stephen's Hill, St. Albans, Hertfordshire AL1 2DY, ☎ 01727/855215 or 01727/845047). Membership (in the U.S., $25; in Canada, C$26.75; in the U.K., £9.30) gives you access to 5,000 hostels in 77 countries that charge $5–$40 per person per night.

ID CARDS

To be eligible for discounts on transportation and admissions, get either the **International Student Identity Card**, if you're a bona fide student, or the **GO 25: International Youth Travel Card**, if you're not a student but under age 26. Each includes basic travel-accident and illness coverage, plus a toll-free travel hot line. In the United States, either card costs $18; apply through the Council on International Educational Exchange (☞ Organizations, *below*). In Canada, cards are available for $15 each ($16 by mail) from Travel Cuts (☞ Organizations, *below*), and in the United Kingdom for £5 each at student unions and student travel companies.

ORGANIZATIONS

A major contact is the **Council on International Educational Exchange** (✉ mail orders only: CIEE, 205 E. 42nd St., 16th Floor, New York, NY 10017, ☎ 212/661–1450, info@ciee.org), with walk-in locations in Boston (✉ 729 Boylston St., 02116, ☎ 617/266–1926), Miami (✉ 9100 S. Dadeland Blvd., 33156, ☎ 305/670–9261), Los Angeles (✉ 10904 Lindbrook Dr., 90024, ☎ 310/208–3551), 43 other college towns in the U.S., and in the United Kingdom (✉ 28A Poland St., London W1V 3DB, ☎ 0171/437–7767). Twice per year, it publishes *Student Travels* magazine. The CIEE's Council Travel Service is the exclusive U.S. agent for several student discount cards.

The **Educational Travel Centre** (✉ 438 N. Frances St., Madison, WI 53703, ☎ 608/256–5551 or 800/747–5551, FAX 608/256–2042) offers rail passes and low-cost airline tickets, mostly for flights that depart from Chicago.

In Canada, also contact **Travel Cuts** (⊠ 187 College St., Toronto, Ontario M5T 1P7, ☎ 416/979–2406 or 800/667–2887).

PUBLICATIONS

Check out the *Berkeley Guide to Europe* (available in bookstores; or contact Fodor's Travel Publications, ☎ 800/533–6478; $18.95 plus $4 shipping).

T

TELEPHONES

The country code for Switzerland is 41. For local access numbers abroad, contact **AT&T** USADirect (☎ 800/874–4000), **MCI** Call USA (☎ 800/444–4444), or **Sprint** Express (☎ 800/793–1153).

OPERATORS AND INFORMATION

Anglo-Phone (☎ 1/575–014) is a 24-hour English-language information line giving details on hotels, restaurants, museums, nightlife, skiing, what to do in an emergency, and more. Calls cost 2 SF per minute.

TOUR OPERATORS

Among the companies that sell tours and packages to Switzerland, the following are nationally known, have a proven reputation, and offer plenty of options.

GROUP TOURS

SUPER-DELUXE➤ **Aber-crombie & Kent** (⊠ 1520 Kensington Rd., Oak Brook, IL 60521-2141, ☎ 708/954–2944 or 800/323–7308, FAX 708/954–3324) and

Travcoa (⊠ Box 2630, 2350 S.E. Bristol St., Newport Beach, CA 92660, ☎ 714/476–2800 or 800/992–2003, FAX 714/476–2538).

DELUXE➤ **Globus** (⊠ 5301 S. Federal Circle, Littleton, CO 80123, ☎ 303/797–2800 or 800/221–0090, FAX 303/795–0962), **Maupintour** (⊠ Box 807, 1515 St. Andrews Dr., Lawrence, KS 66047, ☎ 913/843–1211 or 800/255–4266, FAX 913/843–8351), and **Tauck Tours** (⊠ Box 5027, 276 Post Rd. W, Westport, CT 06881, ☎ 203/226–6911 or 800/468–2825, FAX 203/221–6828).

FIRST-CLASS➤ **Brendan Tours** (⊠ 15137 Califa St., Van Nuys, CA 91411, ☎ 818/785–9696 or 800/421–8446, FAX 818/902–9876), **Caravan Tours** (⊠ 401 N. Michigan Ave., Chicago, IL 60611, ☎ 312/321–9800 or 800/227–2826), **Collette Tours** (⊠ 162 Middle St., Pawtucket, RI 02860, ☎ 401/728–3805 or 800/832–4656, FAX 401/728–1380), **Gadabout Tours** (⊠ 700 E. Tahquitz Canyon Way, Palm Springs, CA 92262, ☎ 619/325–5556 or 800/952–5068), **Insight International Tours** (⊠ 745 Atlantic Ave., #720, Boston, MA 02111, ☎ 617/482-2000 or 800/582–8380, FAX 617/482–2884 or 800/622–5015), and **Trafalgar Tours** (⊠ 11 E. 26th St., New York, NY 10010, ☎ 212/689–8977 or 800/854–0103, FAX 800/457–6644).

BUDGET➤ **Cosmos** (☞ Globus, *above*) and

Trafalgar Tours (☞ *above*).

PACKAGES

Independent vacation packages are available from major airlines and tour operators. Contact **American Airlines Fly AAway Vacations** (☎ 800/321–2121), **Delta Dream Vacations** (☎ 800/872–7786), **DER Tours** (⊠ 11933 Wilshire Blvd., Los Angeles, CA 90025, ☎ 310/479–4140 or 800/782–2424), Swissair's **SwissPak** (☎ 800/221–4750), **TWA Getaway Vacations** (☎ 800/438–2929), and **United Vacations** (☎ 800/328–6877). **Funjet Vacations** based in Milwaukee, Wisconsin, and **Gogo Tours,** based in Ramsey, New Jersey, sell packages only through travel agents.

FROM THE U.K.➤ Varied tours and go-as-you-please packages are available from **Euro-break** (⊠ 10–18 Putney Hill, London SW15 6AX, ☎ 0181/780–7700), **Kuoni Travel** (⊠ Kuoni House, Dorking, Surrey RH5 4AZ, ☎ 01306/742–500), **Swiss Travel Service Ltd.** (⊠ Bridge House, 55-59 High Rd., Broxbourne, Herts. EN10 7DT, ☎ 01920/456–123), **Thomson Holidays** (⊠ Greater London House, Hampstead Rd., London NW1 7SD, ☎ 0171/707–9000), **Time Off Ltd.** (⊠ Chester Close, Chester St., London SW1X 7BQ, ☎ 0171/235–8070), and **Wallace Arnold Tours Ltd.** (⊠ Gelderd Rd., Leeds LS12 6DH, ☎ 01532/310–883; ⊠ 62 George St., Croydon

CR0 1AJ, ☎ 0181/ 686–2378).

THEME TRIPS

ADVENTURE➤ **Europeds** (✉ 761 Lighthouse Ave., Monterey, CA 93940, ☎ 800/321– 9552, FAX 408/655– 4501, Europeds@aol. com) has cycling, hiking, and skiing tours in the Swiss Alps. **Himalayan Travel** (✉ 112 Prospect St., Stamford, CT 06901, ☎ 203/ 359–3711 or 800/225– 2380, FAX 203/359– 3669) operates a range of adventure tours. **Horizons Adventures of a Lifetime** (✉ Box 670565, Marietta, GA 30066, ☎ 800/246– 3180, horizons@ horizadv.com, http:// www. horizadv.com) operates upscale biking, hiking, and white-water rafting trips.

BALLOONING➤ **Buddy Bombard European Balloon Adventures** (✉ 855 Donald Ross Rd., Juno Beach, FL 33408, ☎ 407/775–0039 or 800/862–8537, FAX 407/775–7008) offers dining and lodging packages with balloon rides in Switzerland.

BARGE/RIVER CRUISES➤ Contact **KD River Cruises of Europe** (✉ 2500 Westchester Ave., Purchase, NY 10577, ☎ 914/696–3600 or 800/346–6525, FAX 914/696–0833).

BICYCLING➤ Cycling between mountain inns is available from **Backroads** (✉ 1516 5th St., Berkeley, CA 94710-1740, ☎ 510/577– 1555 or 800/462–2848, FAX 510/527–1444, goactive@Backroads. com), **Classic Adventures** (✉ Box 153,

Hamlin, NY 14464-0153, ☎ 716/964– 8488 or 800/777– 8090, FAX 716/964-7297), and **Euro-Bike Tours** (✉ Box 990, De Kalb, IL 60115, ☎ 800/321–6060, FAX 815/758–8851).

HIKING/WALKING➤ For climbs in the Alps and through Swiss mountain villages, try **Above the Clouds Trekking** (✉ Box 398, Worcester, MA 01602-0398, ☎ 508/ 799–4499 or 800/233– 4499), **Alpine Adventure Trails Tours** (✉ 783 Cliffside Dr., Akron, OH 44313-5609, ☎ 216/867–3771), or **Europeds** (☞ Adventure, *above*). Hiking and camping trips are operated by **Adventure Center** (✉ 1311 63rd St., #200, Emeryville, CA 94608, ☎ 510/ 654–1879 or 800/227– 8747, FAX 510/654– 4200). Also contact **Abercrombie & Kent** (☞ Group Tours *above*), **Backroads** (☞ Adventure *above*), **Butterfield & Robinson** (✉ 70 Bond St., Toronto, Ontario, Canada M5B 1X3, ☎ 416/864–1354 or 800/ 678–1147, FAX 416/ 864–0541, info@ butterfield.com), **Country Walkers** (✉ Box 180, Waterbury, VT 05676-0180, ☎ 802/ 244–1387 or 800/464– 9255, FAX 802/244– 5661), **Euro-Bike Tours** (☞ Bicycling *above*), **Himalayan Travel** (✉ 112 Prospect St., Stamford, CT 06901, ☎ 203/359-3711 or 800/225–2380, FAX 203/ 359–3669), **Mountain Travel-Sobek** (✉ 6420 Fairmount Ave., El Cerrito, CA 94530, ☎ 510/527–8100 or 800/ 227–2384, FAX 510/

525–7710, Info@ MTSobek.com, http:// www.MTSobek.com), or **Smithsonian Study Tours and Seminars** (✉ 1100 Jefferson Dr. SW, Room 3045, MRC 702, Washington, DC 20560, ☎ 202/357–4700, FAX 202/633–9250) for an array of hiking and walking tours.

MOTORCYCLING➤ **Beach's Motorcycle Adventures** (✉ 2763 W. River Pkwy., Grand Island, NY 14072-2053, ☎ 716/773–4960, FAX 716/773–5227, robbeach@buffnet.net) will show you the natural beauty of the Alps.

SPAS➤ To stay at one of the top spas of Switzerland, contact **Custom Spa Vacations** (✉ 1318 Beacon St., Brookline, MA 02146, ☎ 617/ 566–5144 or 800/443– 7727, FAX 617/731– 0599), **Great Spas of the World** (✉ 211 E. 43rd St., #1404, New York, NY 10017, ☎ 212/599–0382 or 800/826–8062), **SpaFinders** (✉ 91 5th Ave., #301, New York, NY 10003-3039, ☎ 212/ 24–6800 or 800/255– 7727), and **Spa Trek Travel** (✉ 475 Park Ave. S, New York, NY 10016, ☎ 212/ 779–3480 or 800/272– 3480, FAX 212/779– 3471).

TENNIS➤ **Championship Tennis Tours** (✉ 7350 E. Stetson Dr., #106, Scottsdale, AZ 85251, ☎ 602/990–8760 or 800/468–3664, FAX 602/ 990–8744, mike@ tennistours.com, http:// www.tennistours.com) has packages to the Swiss Open.

VILLA RENTALS➤ Contact **Villas International**

(⊠ 605 Market St., San Francisco, CA 94105, ☎ 415/281–0910 or 800/221–2260, FAX 415/281–0919).

ORGANIZATIONS

The **National Tour Association** (⊠ NTA, 546 E. Main St., Lexington, KY 40508, ☎ 606/226–4444 or 800/755–8687) and the **United States Tour Operators Association** (⊠ USTOA, 211 E. 51st St., Suite 12B, New York, NY 10022, ☎ 212/750–7371) can provide lists of members and information on booking tours.

PUBLICATIONS

Contact the USTOA (☞ Organizations, *above*) for its **"Smart Traveler's Planning Kit."** Pamphlets in the kit include the "Worldwide Tour and Vacation Package Finder," "How to Select a Tour or Vacation Package," and information on the organization's consumer protection plan. Also get copy of the Better Business Bureau's **"Tips on Travel Packages"** (⊠ Publication 24-195, 4200 Wilson Blvd., Arlington, VA 22203; $2).

TRAIN TRAVEL

DISCOUNT PASSES

Swiss rail passes are sold by travel agents as well as **Rail Europe** (⊠ 226–230 Westchester Ave., White Plains, NY 10604, ☎ 914/682–5172 or 800/438–7245; 2087 Dundas East, Suite 105, Mississauga, Ontario L4X 1M2, ☎ 416/602–4195).

Eurail and EuroPasses are available through

travel agents and **Rail Europe** (⊠ 226-230 Westchester Ave., White Plains, NY 10604, ☎ 914/682–5172 or 800/438–7245; 2087 Dundas E., Suite 105, Mississauga, Ontario L4X 1M2, ☎ 416/602–4195, **DER Tours** (⊠ Box 1606, Des Plaines, IL 60017, ☎ 800/782–2424, FAX 800/282–7474), or **CIT Tours Corp.** (⊠ 342 Madison Ave., Suite 207, New York, NY 10173, ☎ 212/697–2100 or 800/248–8687 or 800/248–7245 in western U.S.).

FROM THE U.K.

The **Venice–Simplon–Orient Express** (⊠ 20 Upper Ground, London SE1 9PD, ☎ 0171/928–6000) runs from London to Zürich. Information is also available from Abercrombie & Kent (☞ Tour Operators, *below*).

TRAVEL GEAR

For travel apparel, appliances, personal-care items, and other travel necessities, get a free catalog from **Magellan's** (☎ 800/962–4943, FAX 805/568–5406), **Orvis Travel** (☎ 800/541–3541, FAX 703/343–7053), or **TravelSmith** (☎ 800/950–1600, FAX 415/455–0554).

ELECTRICAL CONVERTERS

Send a self-addressed, stamped envelope to the **Franzus Company** (⊠ Customer Service, Dept. B50, Murtha Industrial Park, Box 142, Beacon Falls, CT 06403, ☎ 203/723–6664) for a copy of the free brochure "Foreign

Electricity Is No Deep, Dark Secret."

TRAVEL AGENCIES

For names of reputable agencies in your area, contact the **American Society of Travel Agents** (⊠ ASTA, 1101 King St., Suite 200, Alexandria, VA 22314, ☎ 703/739–2782), the **Association of Canadian Travel Agents** (⊠ Suite 201, 1729 Bank St., Ottawa, Ontario K1V 7Z5, ☎ 613/521–0474, FAX 613/521–0805) or the **Association of British Travel Agents** (⊠ 55-57 Newman St., London W1P 4AH, ☎ 0171/637–2444, FAX 0171/637–0713).

U

U.S.

GOVERNMENT

TRAVEL BRIEFINGS

The U.S. Department of State's American Citizens Services office (⊠ Room 4811, Washington, DC 20520; enclose SASE) issues **Consular Information Sheets** on all foreign countries. These cover issues such as crime, security, political climate, and health risks as well as listing embassy locations, entry requirements, currency regulations, and providing other useful information. For the latest information, stop in at any U.S. passport office, consulate, or embassy; call the interactive hot line (☎ 202/647–5225, FAX 202/647–3000); or, with your PC's modem, tap into the department's computer bulletin board (☎ 202/647–9225).

V
VISITOR
INFORMATION

Contact **Switzerland Tourism** in the United States: ⊠ 608 5th Ave., New York, NY 10020, ☎ 212/757–5944, FAX 212/262–6116; ⊠ 222 N. Sepulveda Blvd., Suite 1570, El Segundo, CA 90245, ☎ 310/335–5980, FAX 310/335–5982; ⊠ 150 N. Michigan Ave., Suite 2930, Chicago, IL 60601, ☎ 312/630–5840, FAX 312/630–5848. In Canada: ⊠ 154 University Ave., Suite 610, Toronto, Ontario M5H 3Y9, ☎ 416/971–9734, FAX 416/971–6425. In the United Kingdom: ⊠ Swiss Centre, New Coventry St., London, W1V 8EE, ☎ 0171/734–1921, FAX 0171/437–4577.

WEB SITES

Switzerland Tourism (**www.switzerland-tourism.ch/na**) allows travelers to customize a vacation in Switzerland, and even to book it through an interactive travel planner.

Cross Publications (**http://www.swisstravel.com/**) contains insider tips on Swiss travel and tourism culled from the newsletter "The Switzerland Advisor."

Swiss Federal Railways (**www.sbb.ch**) broadcasts train schedules and time tables.

W
WEATHER

For current conditions and forecasts, plus the local time and helpful travel tips, call the **Weather Channel Connection** (☎ 900/932–8437; 95¢ per minute) from a Touch-Tone phone.

The *International Traveler's Weather Guide* (⊠ Weather Press, Box 660606, Sacramento, CA 95866, ☎ 916/974–0201 or 800/972–0201; $10.95 includes shipping), written by two meteorologists, provides month-by-month information on temperature, humidity, and precipitation in more than 175 cities worldwide.

THE GOLD GUIDE / IMPORTANT CONTACTS

SMART TRAVEL TIPS A TO Z

Basic Information on Traveling in Switzerland and Savvy Tips to Make Your Trip a Breeze

A

AIR TRAVEL

If time is an issue, **always look for nonstop flights,** which require no change of plane. If possible, **avoid connecting flights,** which stop at least once and can involve a change of plane, even though the flight number remains the same; if the first leg is late, the second waits.

For better service, **fly smaller or regional carriers,** which often have higher passenger satisfaction ratings. Sometimes they have such in-flight amenities as leather seats or greater legroom and they often have better food.

CUTTING COSTS

Scan the Sunday travel section of most newspapers for deals.

MAJOR AIRLINES➤ The least-expensive airfares from the major airlines are priced for round-trip travel and are subject to restrictions. Usually, you must **book in advance and buy the ticket within 24 hours** to get cheaper fares, and you may have to **stay over a Saturday night.** The lowest fare is subject to availability, and only a small percentage of the plane's total seats is sold at that price. It's smart to **call a number of airlines, and when you are quoted a good price, book it on the spot**—the same fare may not be available on the same flight the next day. Airlines generally allow you to change your return date for a $25 to $50 fee. If you don't use your ticket, you can apply the cost toward the purchase of a new ticket, again for a small charge. However, most low-fare tickets are nonrefundable. To get the lowest airfare, **check different routings.** If your destination has more than one gateway, **compare prices to different airports.**

FROM THE U.K.➤ To save money on flights, **look into an APEX or Super-Pex ticket.** APEX tickets must be booked in advance and have certain restrictions. Super-PEX tickets can be purchased right at the airport.

CONSOLIDATORS➤ Consolidators buy tickets for scheduled flights at reduced rates from the airlines, then sell them at prices below the lowest available from the airlines directly—usually without advance restrictions. Sometimes you can even get your money back if you need to return the ticket. Carefully read the fine print detailing penalties for changes and cancellations. If you doubt the reliability of a consolidator, **confirm your reservation with the airline.**

ALOFT

AIRLINE FOOD➤ If you hate airline food, **ask for special meals when booking.** These can be vegetarian, low-cholesterol, or kosher, for example; commonly prepared to order in smaller quantities than standard fare, they can be tastier.

JET LAG➤ To avoid this syndrome, which occurs when travel disrupts your body's natural cycles, try to maintain a normal routine. At night, **get some sleep.** By day, move about the cabin to **stretch your legs, eat light meals, and drink water—not alcohol.**

SMOKING➤ Smoking is not allowed on flights of six hours or less within the continental United States. Smoking is also prohibited on flights within Canada. For U.S. flights longer than six hours or international flights, **contact your carrier regarding their smoking policy.** Some carriers have prohibited smoking throughout their system; others allow smoking only on certain routes or even certain departures of that route.

WITHIN SWITZERLAND

The entire country of Switzerland is smaller in area than the state of West Virginia, so flying from one region to another is a luxury that, considering the efficiency of the trains, few travelers require—unless there's a convenient connection from your intercontinental arrival point (Geneva, Zürich) to a lesser airport (Basel, Bern, Lugano, St. Moritz). Crossair is Switzerland's domestic airline, flying between local airports and bringing in visitors from various Continental cities as well: Brussels, Düsseldorf, Florence, Nice, Paris, London, and Venice.

For 20 SF per bag round-trip, air travelers holding tickets or passes on Swiss Federal Railways can forward their luggage to their final destination, allowing them to make stops on the way unencumbered.

B

BOAT TRAVEL

All of Switzerland's larger lakes are crisscrossed by elegant steamers, some of them restored paddle steamers. Their café-restaurants serve drinks, snacks, and hot food at standard mealtimes; toilet facilities are provided. Service continues year-round, but frequency increases in summer. Unlimited travel is free to holders of the Swiss Pass. If you are not traveling by train, **consider the Swiss Boat Pass,** which for 40 SF allows half-fare travel on all lake steamers for the entire year (January 1–December 31).

BUS TRAVEL

Switzerland's famous yellow postbuses, with their stentorian tritone horns, link main cities with villages off the beaten track and even crawl over the highest mountain passes. Both postbuses and city buses follow posted schedules to the minute: You can set your watch by them. Free timetables can be picked up in post offices, from which the buses usually depart. Watch for the yellow sign with the picture of a hunting horn. The Swiss Pass (☞ Rail Travel, *below*) gives unlimited travel on the postbuses. Postbuses cater especially to hikers: Itineraries of attractive walks are available at postbus stops.

BUSINESS HOURS

Businesses still close for lunch in Switzerland, though this is changing, especially in larger cities. All remain closed on Sunday, and many stay closed through Monday morning as well. Banks are open weekdays from 8:30 to 4:30. Museums generally close on Monday. Many stores stay open late on Thursday. Stores in train stations often remain open to 9 PM; in Geneva and Zürich airports, shops are open on Sunday. See regional chapters for specifics.

C

CAMERAS, CAMCORDERS, & COMPUTERS

IN TRANSIT

Always **keep your film, tape, or disks out of the sun;** never put these on the dashboard of a car. Carry an extra supply of batteries, and **be prepared to turn on your camera, camcorder, or laptop computer for security personnel** to prove that it's real.

X-RAYS

Always **ask for hand inspection at security.** Such requests are virtually always honored at U.S. airports, and are usually accommodated abroad. Photographic film becomes clouded after successive exposure to airport X-ray machines. Videotape and computer disks are not harmed by X-rays, but **keep your tapes and disks away from metal detectors.**

CUSTOMS

Before departing, **register your foreign-made camera or laptop with U.S. Customs.** If your equipment is U.S.-made, call the consulate of the country you'll be visiting to find out whether it should be registered with local customs upon arrival.

CAR RENTAL

CUTTING COSTS

To get the best deal, **book through a travel agent who is willing to shop around.** Ask your agent to **look for fly-drive packages,** which also save you money, and **ask if local taxes are included** in the rental or fly-drive price. These can be as high as 20% in some destinations. Don't forget to find out about required deposits, cancellation penalties, drop-off charges, and the cost of any required insurance coverage.

Also **ask your travel agent about a company's customer-service record.** How has it responded to late plane arrivals and vehicle mishaps? Are there often lines at the rental counter, and—if you're traveling during a holiday period—does a confirmed reservation guarantee you a car?

Always **find out what equipment is standard** at your destination before specifying what you want; automatic transmission and air-conditioning are usually optional—and very expensive.

Be sure to **look into wholesalers**—companies that do not own their own fleets but rent in bulk from those that do and often offer better rates than traditional car-rental operations. Prices are best during off-peak periods; rentals booked through wholesalers must be paid for before you leave the United States.

INSURANCE

When driving a rented car, you are generally responsible for any damage to or loss of the rental vehicle. Before you rent, **see what coverage you already have** under the terms of your personal auto insurance policy and credit cards.

If you do not have auto insurance or an umbrella insurance policy that covers damage to third parties, purchasing CDW or LDW is highly recommended.

Collision policies that car-rental companies sell for European rentals typically do not cover stolen vehicles. Before you buy additional coverage for theft, find out if your credit card or personal

auto insurance will cover the loss.

LICENSE REQUIREMENTS

In Switzerland your own driver's license is acceptable—but **consider buying an International Driver's Permit,** available from the American or Canadian automobile associations, or, in the United Kingdom, from the AA or RAC (☞ Driving *in* Important Contacts A to Z). Some European rental firms will not lease to drivers over 70 years old.

SURCHARGES

Before you pick up a car in one city and leave it in another, **ask about drop-off charges or one-way service fees,** which can be substantial. Note, too, that some rental agencies charge extra if you return the car before the time specified on your contract. To avoid a hefty refueling fee, **fill the tank just before you turn in the car**—but be aware that gas stations near the rental outlet may overcharge.

CHILDREN & TRAVEL

BABY-SITTING

Supervised playrooms are available in some of the better Swiss hotels, and many winter resorts also provide lists of reliable baby-sitters. For recommended local sitters, **check with your hotel desk.**

CHILDREN'S CAMPS AND HOLIDAY COURSES

Every summer, some 120 private schools in Switzerland offer leisurely language study

and recreation courses for primary and secondary school-age children from around the world. Summer camps similar to those found in the United States are also available. Ask Switzerland Tourism for a copy of "Holiday and Language Courses," a list of camps and summer programs in Switzerland.

DRIVING

If you are renting a car, don't forget to **arrange for a car seat when you reserve.** Sometimes they're free.

FLYING

As a general rule, infants under two not occupying a seat fly at greatly reduced fares and occasionally for free. If your children are two or older **ask about special children's fares.** Age limits for these fares vary among carriers. Rules also vary regarding unaccompanied minors, so again, check with your airline.

BAGGAGE➤ In general, the adult baggage allowance applies to children paying half or more of the adult fare. If you are traveling with an infant, **ask about carry-on allowances** before departure. In general, for infants charged 10% of the adult fare you are allowed one carry-on bag and a collapsible stroller, which may have to be checked; you may be limited to less if the flight is full.

SAFETY SEATS➤ According to the FAA, it's a good idea to **use safety seats aloft** for children weighing less than 40 pounds. Airline policies vary. U.S. carriers allow FAA-approved models but usually require that you buy a ticket, even if your child would otherwise ride free, since the seats must be strapped into regular seats. However, some U.S. and foreign-flag airlines may require you to hold your baby during takeoff and landing—defeating the seat's purpose. Other foreign carriers may not allow infant seats at all, or may charge a child rather than an infant fare for their use.

FACILITIES➤ When making your reservation, **request children's meals or freestanding bassinets** if you need them; the latter are available only to those seated at the bulkhead, where there's enough legroom. If you don't need a bassinet, **think twice before requesting bulkhead seats**—the only storage space for in-flight necessities is in inconveniently distant overhead bins.

GETTING AROUND

Families traveling together in Switzerland should **buy a Family Card**, a special pass (20 SF, or free with the purchase of a Swiss Pass or Europass) that allows children under 16 to travel free on trains, postbuses, and boats when accompanied by ticket-holding parents or guardians. Adults must hold a valid Swiss Pass, Swiss Card, Swiss Transfer Ticket, or Eurail tariff ticket to obtain the Family Card, available at any Swiss train station, for their chil-

dren (☞ Train Travel, *below*).

LODGING

In many Swiss hotels, children six and under may stay in their parents' room at no extra charge; be sure to **ask about the cut-off age.** Some may charge extra for cribs, and cribs with sides are not always available. Children from six to 12 generally pay 50% of the adult rate, while those 13 to 16 pay 70%. Apartments, with separate rooms and full hotel services, are also available.

Many hotels offer special facilities and services for families with children. Provisions range from supervised children's playrooms to special children's menus and organized family walks and visits.

CUSTOMS & DUTIES

To speed your clearance through customs, **keep receipts for all your purchases abroad** and **be ready to show the inspector what you've bought.** If you feel that you've been incorrectly or unfairly charged a duty, you can **appeal assessments in dispute.** First ask to see a supervisor. If you are still dissatisfied, **write to the port director** at your point of entry, sending your customs receipt and any other appropriate documentation. The address will be listed on your receipt. If you still don't get satisfaction, you can take your case to customs headquarters in Washington.

IN SWITZERLAND

Entering Switzerland, a visitor 17 years or older may bring in 400 cigarettes, or 100 cigars, or 500 grams of tobacco; 2 liters of alcohol up to 15 proof; and a liter of alcohol over 15 proof. When entering from a European country, tobacco is restricted to 200 cigarettes or 50 cigars or 250 grams of tobacco. Medicine, such as insulin, is allowed for personal use only.

IN THE U.S.

You may bring home $400 worth of foreign goods duty-free if you've been out of the country for at least 48 hours and haven't already used the $400 allowance, or any part of it, in the past 30 days.

Travelers 21 or older may bring back 1 liter of alcohol duty-free, provided the beverage laws of the state through which they reenter the United States allow it. In addition, regardless of their age, they are allowed 100 non-Cuban cigars and 200 cigarettes. Antiques, which the U.S. Customs Service defines as objects more than 100 years old, are duty-free. Original works of art done entirely by hand are also duty-free. These include, but are not limited to, paintings, drawings, and sculptures.

Duty-free, travelers may mail packages valued at up to $200 to themselves and up to $100 to others, with a limit of one parcel per addressee per day (and no alcohol or tobacco products or perfume valued at more than $5); on the outside, the package must be labeled as being either for personal use or an unsolicited gift, and a list of its contents and their retail value must be attached. Mailed items do not affect your duty-free allowance on your return.

IN CANADA

If you've been out of Canada for at least seven days, you may bring in C$500 worth of goods duty-free. If you've been away for fewer than seven days but for more than 48 hours, the duty-free allowance drops to C$200; if your trip lasts between 24 and 48 hours, the allowance is C$50. You cannot pool allowances with family members. Goods claimed under the C$500 exemption may follow you by mail; those claimed under the lesser exemptions must accompany you.

Alcohol and tobacco products may be included in the seven-day and 48-hour exemptions but not in the 24-hour exemption. If you meet the age requirements of the province or territory through which you reenter Canada, you may bring in, duty-free, 1.14 liters (40 imperial ounces) of wine or liquor or 24 12-ounce cans or bottles of beer or ale. If you are 16 or older, you may bring in, duty-free, 200 cigarettes, 50 cigars or cigarillos, and 400 tobacco sticks or 400 grams of manufactured tobacco. Alcohol and tobacco must accompany you on your return.

An unlimited number of gifts with a value of up to C$60 each may be mailed to Canada duty-free. These do not affect your duty-free allowance on your return. Label the package "Unsolicited Gift— Value Under $60." Alcohol and tobacco are excluded.

IN THE U.K.

From countries outside the EU, including Switzerland, you may import, duty-free, 200 cigarettes, 100 cigarillos, 50 cigars, or 250 grams of tobacco; 1 liter of spirits or 2 liters of fortified or sparkling wine or liqueurs; 2 liters of still table wine; 60 milliliters of perfume; 250 milliliters of toilet water; plus £136 worth of other goods, including gifts and souvenirs.

D

DISABILITIES & ACCESSIBILITY

In Switzerland, most forms of public transportation offer special provisions, and accessible hotels are available in many areas of the country.

When discussing accessibility with an operator or reservationist, **ask hard questions.** Are there any stairs, inside or out? Are there grab bars next to the toilet and in the shower/tub? How wide is the doorway to the room? To the bathroom? For the most extensive facilities, meeting the latest legal specifications, **opt for newer accommodations,** which more often have been designed with access in mind. Older properties or ships must usually be retrofitted

and may offer more limited facilities as a result. Be sure to **discuss your needs before booking.**

DRIVING

Foreign visitors with either the Disabled Badge of their country or the International Wheelchair Badge mounted inside the windshield of their car are entitled to use parking spaces reserved for people with disabilities throughout the country. Motorists who cannot walk unaided can obtain a special permit for parking privileges, as well as the international badge mentioned above, from the local police authority.

TRAIN TRAVEL

Swiss Federal Railways are currently striving to adapt all stations and passenger trains to the needs of travelers with disabilities. Wheelchairs are often available; inform the stations ahead of time that you will need one. In addition, ramps or lifts and wheelchair-accessible toilets have been installed in more than 100 stations. All intercity and long-distance express trains and more than two-thirds of the country's regional shuttle trains now have wheelchair compartments.

DISCOUNTS & DEALS

You shouldn't have to pay for a discount. In fact, you may already be eligible for all kinds of savings. Here are some time-honored strategies for getting the best deal.

LOOK IN YOUR WALLET

When you **use your credit card to make travel purchases,** you may get free travel-accident insurance, collision damage insurance, medical or legal assistance, depending on the card and bank that issued it. Visa and MasterCard provide one or more of these services, so **get a copy of your card's travel benefits.** If you are a member of the AAA or an oil-company-sponsored road-assistance plan, always **ask hotel or car-rental reservationists for auto-club discounts.** Some clubs offer additional discounts on tours, cruises, or admission to attractions. And don't forget that auto-club membership entitles you to free maps and trip-planning services.

DIAL FOR DOLLARS

To save money, **look into "1-800" discount reservations services,** which often have lower rates. These services use their buying power to get a better price on hotels, airline tickets, and sometimes even car rentals. When booking a room, always **call the hotel's local toll-free number** (if one is available) rather than the central reservations number—you'll often get a better price. Ask the reservationist about special packages or corporate rates, which are usually available even if you're not traveling on business.

JOIN A CLUB?

Discount clubs can be a legitimate source of savings, but you must use the participating hotels and visit the participating attractions in order to realize any benefits. Remember, too, that you have to pay a fee to join, so determine if you'll save enough to warrant your membership fee. Before booking with a club, **make sure the hotel or other supplier isn't offering a better deal.**

GET A GUARANTEE

When shopping for the best deal on hotels and car rentals, **look for guaranteed exchange rates,** which protect you against a falling dollar. With your rate locked in, you won't pay more even if the price goes up in the local currency.

DRIVING

Swiss roads are usually well surfaced but wind about considerably—especially in the mountains—so **don't plan on achieving high average speeds.** When estimating likely travel times, look carefully at the map: There may be only 32 kilometers (20 miles) between one point and another—but there may be an Alpine pass in the way. There is a well-developed highway network, though some notable gaps still exist in the south along an east–west line, roughly between Lugano and Sion. A combination of steep or winding routes and hazardous weather means that some roads will be closed in winter. Signs are posted at the beginning of the climb. **Tune in to Swiss Radio 1** at around 7 PM for traffic updates in English, or dial 120 or 163 for bulletins and advance information in Swiss languages.

The CH on Swiss license plates refers to the country's Latin title: "Confoederatio Helvetica."

FROM THE U.K. BY CAR FERRY

There are many drive-on, drive-off car ferry services across the Channel, but only a few are suitable as a means of getting to Switzerland. The situation is complicated by the different pricing systems operated by ferry companies and the many off-peak fares, and by the fact that the French charge tolls on some of their motorways; these add up, particularly if you drive long distances. To avoid the tolls, **take a northerly route through Belgium or the Netherlands and Germany,** where motorways are free. The crossings for this route are Felixs-towe or Dover to Zeebrugge; Sheerness to Vlissingen; and Ramsgate to Dunkirk. All these Continental ports have good road connections, and Switzerland can be reached in one day's hard driving.

WITHIN SWITZERLAND

BREAKDOWNS➤ Breakdown assistance is available through the telephone exchange: Dial 140 and ask for "Autohilfe."

GAS➤ Unleaded (*sans plomb* or *bleifrei*) gas costs around 1.20 SF per liter, and super costs around 1.31 SF per liter. Leaded regular is no longer available. Prices are slightly higher in mountain areas. **Have some 10 SF and 20 SF notes available,** as many gas stations (especially in the mountains) offer vending-machine gas even when they're closed. Simply slide in a bill and fill your tank. You can get a receipt if you ask the machine for it.

PARKING> Parking areas are clearly marked. Parking in public lots normally costs 1.50 SF for the first hour, increasing by 0.50 SF every half hour thereafter.

RULES OF THE ROAD> Driving is on the right. In built-up areas, the speed limit is 50 kph (31 mph); on main highways, it's 80 kph (50 mph); on expressways, the limit is 120 kph (75 mph).

Children under 12 are not permitted to sit in the front seat. Driving with parking lights is prohibited. **Use headlights** in heavy rain or poor visibility and in road tunnels—they are compulsory. Always **carry your valid license and car-registration papers;** there are occasional roadblocks to check them. **Wear seat belts** in the front seats—they are required.

To use the main highways, you must display a disk or *vignette* in the lower left-hand corner of the windshield. You can buy it at the border (cash only; neighboring foreign currencies can be changed). It costs 40 SF, can be purchased from any post office, and is valid to the end of the year. Cars rented within Switzerland

already have these disks; if you rent a car elsewhere in Europe, ask if the company will provide the vignette for you.

Traffic going up a mountain has priority except for postbuses coming down. A sign with a yellow post horn on a blue background means that postbuses have priority.

In winter, **use snow chains,** which are compulsory in some areas and advisable in all. Snow-chain service stations have signs marked *Service de Chaînes à Neige* or *Schneekettendienst;* snow chains are available for rent.

If you have an accident, even a minor one, you must call the police.

H
HEALTH

Your trip to Switzerland is likely to be one of the most disease-free of any in your life: It's a country that has well earned its reputation for impeccable standards of cleanliness. But even at the foot of an icy-pure 2,000-meter (6,560-foot) glacier, you'll find the locals drinking bottled mineral water; you'll have to wrangle with the waiter if you want tap water with your meal. This is as much a result of the tradition of expecting beverages in a café to be paid for as it is a response to health questions. If you're traveling with a child under two years old, you may be advised by locals not to carry him or her on excursions above 2,000

meters (6,560 feet); check with your pediatrician before leaving home. Adults should limit strenuous excursions on the first day at extra-high-altitude resorts, those at 1,600 meters (5,248 feet) and above. Adults with heart problems may want to avoid all excursions above 2,000 meters (6,560 feet).

I
INSURANCE

Travel insurance can protect your monetary investment, replace your luggage and its contents, or provide for medical coverage should you fall ill during your trip. Most tour operators, travel agents, and insurance agents sell specialized health-and-accident, flight, trip-cancellation, and luggage insurance as well as comprehensive policies with some or all of these coverages. Comprehensive policies may also reimburse you for delays due to weather—an important consideration if you're traveling during the winter months. Some health-insurance policies do not cover preexisting conditions, but waivers may be available in specific cases. Coverage is sold by the companies listed in Important Contacts A to Z; these companies act as the policy's administrators. The actual insurance is usually underwritten by a well-known name, such as The Travelers or Continental Insurance.

Before you make any purchase, **review your existing health and** homeowner's policies to find out whether they cover expenses incurred while traveling.

BAGGAGE

Airline liability for baggage is limited to $1,250 per person on domestic flights. On international flights, it amounts to $9.07 per pound or $20 per kilogram for checked baggage (roughly $640 per 70-pound bag) and $400 per passenger for unchecked baggage. Insurance for losses exceeding the terms of your airline ticket can be bought directly from the airline at check-in for about $10 per $1,000 of coverage; note that it excludes a rather extensive list of items, shown on your airline ticket.

COMPREHENSIVE

Comprehensive insurance policies include all the coverages described above plus some that may not be available in more specific policies. If you have purchased an expensive vacation, especially one that involves travel abroad, comprehensive insurance is a must; **look for policies that include trip delay insurance,** which will protect you in the event that weather problems cause you to miss your flight, tour, or cruise. A few insurers will also sell you a waiver for preexisting medical conditions. Some of the companies that offer both these features are Access America, Carefree Travel, Travel Insured International, and Travel Guard (☞ Important Contacts A to Z).

FLIGHT

Think twice before buying flight insurance. Often purchased as a last-minute impulse at the airport, it pays a lump sum when a plane crashes, either to a beneficiary if the insured dies or sometimes to a surviving passenger who loses his or her eyesight or a limb. Supplementing the airlines' coverage described in the limits-of-liability paragraphs on your ticket, it's expensive and basically unnecessary. Charging an airline ticket to a major credit card often automatically provides you with coverage that may also extend to travel by bus, train, and ship.

HEALTH

Medicare generally does not cover health care costs outside the United States; nor do many privately issued policies. If your own health insurance policy does not cover you outside the United States, **consider buying supplemental medical coverage.** It can reimburse you for $1,000– $150,000 worth of medical and/or dental expenses incurred as a result of an accident or illness during a trip. These policies also may include a personal-accident, or death-and-dismemberment, provision, which pays a lump sum ranging from $15,000 to $500,000 to your beneficiaries if you die or to you if you lose one or more limbs or your eyesight, and a medical-assistance provision, which may either reimburse you for the cost of referrals,

evacuation, or repatriation and other services, or automatically enroll you as a member of a particular medical-assistance company. (☞ Health Issues *in* Important Contacts A to Z.)

TRIP

Without insurance, you will lose all or most of your money if you cancel your trip regardless of the reason. Especially if your airline ticket, cruise, or package tour is nonrefundable and cannot be changed, it's essential that you **buy trip-cancellation-and-interruption insurance.** When considering how much coverage you need, look for a policy that will cover the cost of your trip plus the nondiscounted price of a one-way airline ticket should you need to return home early. Read the fine print carefully, especially sections that define "family member" and "preexisting medical conditions." Also **consider default or bankruptcy insurance,** which protects you against a supplier's failure to deliver. Be aware, however, that if you buy such a policy from a travel agency, tour operator, airline, or cruise line, it may not cover default by the firm in question.

U.K. TRAVELERS

You can buy an annual travel insurance policy valid for most vacations during the year in which it's purchased. If you are pregnant or have a preexisting medical condition make sure you're covered before buying such a policy.

THE GOLD GUIDE / SMART TRAVEL TIPS

L

LANGUAGE

More than 70% of the population of Switzerland speaks one dialect or another of German. French is spoken in the southwest, around Lake Geneva, and in the cantons of Fribourg, Neuchâtel, Jura, Vaud, and most of the Valais. Italian is spoken in the Ticino. In the Upper and Lower Engadine, in the canton Graubünden, the last gasp of a Romance language called Romansh is still in daily use. There are several dialects of Romansh—five, in fact—so there's not much point in trying to pick up a few phrases. If you want to attempt communicating with the locals there, venture a little Italian. In the areas frequented by English and American tourists—Zermatt, the Berner Oberland, Luzern—people in the tourist industry usually speak English. Elsewhere, you might not be as lucky. Ask before you plunge into your mother tongue—the person you're addressing may run to fetch the staff member who can meet you on your own terms.

LODGING

Switzerland is as famous for its hotels as it is for its mountains, knives, and chocolates, and its standards in hospitality are extremely high. Rooms are impeccably clean and well maintained, and they are furnished with comforts ranging from the simplest to the most deluxe. Prices are accordingly high: You will pay more for minimal comforts here than in any other European country. Americans accustomed to spacious motels with two double beds, a color TV, and a bath/shower combination may be disappointed in their first venture into the legendary Swiss hotel: Spaces are small, bathtubs cost extra, and single rooms may have single beds. What you're paying for is service, reliability, cleanliness, and a complex hierarchy of amenities you may not even know you need.

ADDRESSES

Where no address is provided in the hotel listings, none was necessary: In smaller towns and villages, a postal code is all you need. To find the hotel on arrival, watch for the official street signs pointing the way to every hotel that belongs to the local tourist association.

APARTMENT & VILLA RENTAL

If you want a home base that's roomy enough for a family and comes with cooking facilities, **consider taking a furnished rental.** This can also save you money, but not always—some rentals are luxury properties (economical only when your party is large). Home-exchange directories list rentals—often second homes owned by prospective house swappers—and some services search for a house or apartment for you (even a castle if that's your fancy) and handle the paperwork. Some send an illustrated catalog; others send photographs only of specific properties, sometimes at a charge; up-front registration fees may apply.

BEDS

Some things to bear in mind when you check in: The standard double room in Switzerland has two prim beds built together with separate linens and, sometimes, sheets tucked firmly down the middle. If you prefer more sociable arrangements, ask for a "French bed" or *lit matrimoniale*—that will get you a single-mattress double. Note: Hotel listings in this edition count the total number of beds or places available rather than rooms. Some hotels may offer extra beds, for example to expand a double room to a triple.

FARM STAYS

An unusual option for families seeking the local experience: Stay on a farm with a Swiss family, complete with children, animals, and the option to work in the fields. Participating farm families register with the Schweizerischer Bauernverband (Swiss Farmers Association) listing the birth dates of their children, rooms and facilities, and types of animals your children can see. Prices are often considerably lower than those of hotels and vacation flats. Further information is available through Switzerland Tourism (☞ Visitor Information *in* Important Contacts A to Z, *above*).

HOME EXCHANGE

If you would like to find a house, an apartment, or some other type of vacation property to exchange for your own while on holiday, **become a member of a home-exchange organization,** which will send you its updated listings of available exchanges for a year, and will include your own listing in at least one of them. Arrangements for the actual exchange are made by the two parties involved, not by the organization.

HOTELS

When selecting a place to stay, an important resource can be the Swiss Hotel Association (SHA), a rigorous and demanding organization that maintains a specific rating system for lodging standards. Eighty percent of Swiss hotels belong to this group and take their stars seriously. In contrast to more casual European countries, stars in Switzerland have precise meaning: A five-star hotel is required to have a specific staff-guest ratio, a daily change of bed linens, and extended-hour room service. A two-star hotel must have telephones, soap in the room, and fabric tablecloths in the restaurant. But the SHA standards cannot control the quality of decor and the grace of service. Thus you may find a four-star hotel that meets these technical requirements but has shabby appointments, leaky plumbing, or a rude concierge; a good, family-run two-star may make you feel like royalty.

Some rules of thumb: If you are looking for American-style, chain-motel-level comfort—big beds, color TV, minibar, safe—you will probably be happiest in four-star, business-class hotels, many of which cater to Americans through travel agents and tour organizers; Best Western owns a number of four-star hotels in Switzerland. If you are looking for regional atmosphere, family ownership (and the pride and care for details that implies), and moderate prices, but don't care about TVs and minibars, look for three stars: Nearly all of their rooms have showers and toilets. Two stars will get you tidy, minimal comfort with about a third of the rooms having baths. One-star properties are rare: They have no baths in rooms and no phone available in-house, and generally fall below the demanding Swiss national standard. Several hotels in the SHA are specially rated *Landgasthof* or *relais de campagne,* meaning "country inn." These generally are rustic-style lodgings typical of the region, but they may range from spare to luxurious and are rarely set apart in deep country, as Americans might expect; some are in the midst of small market towns or resorts. The SHA distinguishes them as offering especially high-quality service, personal attention, and parking.

INNS

Travelers on a budget can find help from the *Check-in E & G Hotels* guide (E & G stands for *einfach und gemütlich*: roughly, "simple and cozy"), available through Switzerland Tourism. These comfortable little hotels have banded together to dispel Switzerland's intimidating image as an elite, overpriced vacation spot and offer simple two-star standards in usually very atmospheric inns.

Other organizations can help you find unusual properties: The Relais & Châteaux group seeks out manor houses, historic buildings, and generally atmospheric luxury, with most of its properties falling in the $$$ or $$$$ range. A similar group, Romantik Hotels and Restaurants, combines architectural interest, historic atmosphere, and fine regional food. Relais du Silence hotels are usually isolated in a peaceful, natural setting, with first-class comforts.

M
MAIL

POSTAL RATES

Mail rates are divided into first class (airmail) and second class (surface). Letters and postcards to the United States weighing up to 20 grams cost 1.80 SF first class, 0.90 SF second class; to the United Kingdom, 1.00 SF first class, 0.80 SF second class.

RECEIVING MAIL

If you're uncertain where you'll be staying, you can have your mail, marked *Poste Restante* or *Postlagernd*, sent to any post office in Switzerland. It needs the sender's name and address on the back, and you'll need proof of identity to collect it. You can also have your mail sent to American Express for a small fee, payable when you collect it. Postal codes precede the names of cities and towns in Swiss addresses.

MEDICAL ASSISTANCE

No one plans to get sick while traveling, but it happens, so **consider signing up with a medical assistance company.** These outfits provide referrals, emergency evacuation or repatriation, 24-hour telephone hot lines for medical consultation, cash for emergencies, and other personal and legal assistance. They also dispatch medical personnel and arrange for the relay of medical records.

MONEY

The unit of currency in Switzerland is the Swiss franc (SF), available in notes of 10, 20, 50, 100, 500, and 1,000. Francs are divided into centimes (in Suisse Romande) or rappen (in German Switzerland). There are coins for 5, 10, and 20 centimes. Larger coins are the ½-, 1-, 2-, and 5-franc pieces.

At press time (fall 1996) the exchange rate was about 1.17 SF to the dollar, 1.93 SF to the pound sterling, and .92 SF to the Canadian dollar.

ATMS

CASH ADVANCES➤ Before leaving home, **make sure that your credit cards have been programmed for ATM use** in Switzerland. Note that Discover is accepted mostly in the United States. Local bank cards often do not work overseas either; **ask your bank about a Visa debit card,** which works like a bank card but can be used at any ATM displaying a Visa logo.

TRANSACTION FEES➤ Although fees charged for ATM transactions may be higher abroad than at home, Cirrus and Plus exchange rates are excellent, because they are based on wholesale rates offered only by major banks.

COSTS

Despite increased competition across Europe, Switzerland remains one of the most expensive countries on the Continent for travelers, and with the dollar plummeting to near equality with the Swiss franc you may find yourself shocked by the price of a light lunch or a generic hotel room. If you are traveling on a tight budget, avoid staying in well-known resorts and the most sophisticated cities; Geneva, Zürich, Zermatt, and St. Moritz are exceptionally expensive. If you are traveling by car, you have the luxury of seeking out small, family hotels in villages, where costs are relatively low. Unless you work hard at finding budget accommodations, you will average more than 150 SF a night for two—more if you stay in business-

class hotels, with TV and direct-dial phone. Restaurant prices are standardized from region to region.

A cup of coffee or a beer costs about 2.50 SF in a simple restaurant; ordinary open wines, sold by the deciliter ("deci"), start at about 2.50 SF. All three beverages cost sometimes double that in resorts, city hotels, and fine restaurants. A plain, one-plate daily lunch special averages 14–18 SF. A city bus ride costs between 1.10 SF and 2.20 SF, a short cab ride 15 SF.

EXCHANGING CURRENCY

For the most favorable rates, **change money at banks.** You won't do as well at exchange booths in airports or rail and bus stations, in hotels, in restaurants, or in stores, although you may find their hours more convenient. To avoid lines at airport exchange booths, **get a small amount of the local currency before you leave home.**

TAXES

HOTEL➤ What you see is what you pay in Switzerland: Restaurant checks and hotel bills include all taxes.

VAT➤ On January 1, 1996, Switzerland introduced valued-added tax (VAT) of 6.5%, making it the 20th European country to adopt the measure. While the rate is the lowest in Europe, it can add a significant amount to already pricey bills. Culture vultures are one of the only groups not to be affected by the VAT, with theater and cinema tickets being exempt.

However, on any one purchase of 500 francs or more from one store, refunds are available for clothes, watches and souvenirs, but not for meals or hotel rooms. To **get a VAT refund,** request a form from the shopkeeper, and get it stamped at customs on departure. Then send the form in the provided envelope to Bern once you arrive back in the United States. The Swiss government will send the check to you in the United States in a few weeks.

TRAVELER'S CHECKS

Whether or not to buy traveler's checks depends on where you are headed; **take cash to rural areas and small towns, traveler's checks to cities.** The most widely recognized checks are issued by American Express, Citicorp, Thomas Cook, and Visa. These are sold by major commercial banks for 1%–3% of the checks' face value—it pays to **shop around.** Both American Express and Thomas Cook issue checks that can be countersigned and used by either you or your traveling companion, and they both provide checks, at no extra charge, valued in Swiss francs. So you won't be left with excess foreign currency, **buy a few checks in small denominations** to cash toward the end of your trip. Before leaving home, **contact your issuer for information on where to** **cash your checks** without a incurring a transaction fee. Record the numbers of all your checks, and keep this listing in a separate place, crossing off the numbers of checks you have cashed.

WIRING MONEY

For a fee of 3%–10%, depending on the amount of the transaction, you can have money sent to you from home through Money-Gram^{SM} or Western Union (☞ Money Matters *in* Important Contacts A to Z). The transferred funds and the service fee can be charged to a Master-Card or Visa account.

P
PACKING FOR SWITZERLAND

Switzerland is essentially sportswear country. Its cities are more formal, and men would be wise to include a jacket—and tie, as well, if you want to try one of the great restaurants. A tie and sweater are standard date-night wear. Women wear skirts more frequently here than in America, especially women over 50, though anything fashionable goes. Except at the most chic hotels in international resorts, you won't need formal evening dress.

Even in July and August, the evening air grows chilly in the mountains, so **bring a wool sweater.** And consider a hat or sunscreen, as the atmosphere is thinner at high altitudes. Sunglasses are important for high-altitude excursions, as glaciers can be blinding in the sun. Good walking shoes are a must, whether you're tackling medieval cobblestones or mountain trails.

If you need a washcloth to feel clean, bring your own: They are not standard equipment in Swiss hotels. Budget hotels occasionally do not provide soap. If you're planning on shopping and cooking, a tote bag will come in handy: Most groceries do not provide sacks, though sturdy, reusable plastic totes can be bought at checkout. Laundromats are rare, so laundry soap is useful for hand washing.

Bring an extra pair of eyeglasses or contact lenses in your carry-on luggage, and if you have a health problem, **pack enough medication** to last the trip or have your doctor write you a prescription using the drug's generic name, because brand names vary from country to country (you'll then need a duplicate prescription from a local doctor). It's important that you **don't put prescription drugs or valuables in luggage to be checked,** for it could go astray. To avoid problems with customs officials, carry medications in the original packaging. Also, don't forget the addresses of offices that handle refunds of lost traveler's checks.

ELECTRICITY

To use your U.S.-purchased electric-powered equipment, **bring a converter and an adapter.** The electrical current in Switzerland is 220 volts, 50 cycles alternating current (AC); wall outlets take Continental-type plugs, with two round prongs.

If your appliances are dual-voltage, you'll need only an adapter. Hotels sometimes have 110-volt outlets for low-wattage appliances near the sink, marked FOR SHAVERS ONLY; don't use them for high-wattage appliances like blow-dryers. If your laptop computer is older, carry a converter; new laptops operate equally well on 110 and 220 volts, so you need only an adapter.

LUGGAGE

Airline baggage allowances depend on the airline, the route, and the class of your ticket; ask in advance. In general, on domestic flights and on international flights between the United States and foreign destinations, you are entitled to check two bags. A third piece may be brought on board, but it must fit easily under the seat in front of you or in the overhead compartment. In the United States, the FAA gives airlines broad latitude regarding carry-on allowances, and they tend to tailor them to different aircraft and operational conditions. Charges for excess, oversize, or overweight pieces vary.

If you are flying between two foreign destinations, note that baggage allowances may be determined not by piece but by weight—generally 88 pounds (40 kilograms)

in first class, 66 pounds (30 kilograms) in business class, and 44 pounds (20 kilograms) in economy. If your flight between two cities abroad *connects* with your transatlantic or transpacific flight, the piece method still applies.

SAFEGUARDING YOUR LUGGAGE➤ Before leaving home, **itemize your bags' contents** and their worth, and label them with your name, address, and phone number. (If you use your home address, cover it so that potential thieves can't see it readily.) Inside each bag, **pack a copy of your itinerary.** At check-in, **make sure that each bag is correctly tagged** with the destination airport's three-letter code. If your bags arrive damaged—or fail to arrive at all—file a written report with the airline before leaving the airport.

PASSPORTS & VISAS

If you don't already have one, **get a passport.** It is advisable that you **leave one photocopy of your passport's data page** with someone at home and keep another with you, separated from your passport, while traveling. If you lose your passport, promptly call the nearest embassy or consulate and the local police; having the data page information can speed replacement.

U.S. CITIZENS

All U.S. citizens, even infants, need only a valid passport to enter Switzerland for stays of

up to three months. Application forms for both first-time and renewal passports are available at any of the 13 U.S. Passport Agency offices and at some post offices and courthouses. Passports, which are valid for 10 years, are usually mailed within four weeks; allow five weeks or more in spring and summer.

CANADIANS

You need only a valid passport to enter Switzerland for stays of up to three months. Passport application forms are available at 28 regional passport offices, as well as post offices and travel agencies. Whether for a first or a renewal passport, you must apply in person. Children under 16 may be included on a parent's passport but must have their own to travel alone. Passports are valid for five years and are usually mailed within two to three weeks of application.

U.K. CITIZENS

Citizens of the United Kingdom need only a valid passport to enter Switzerland for stays of up to three months. Applications for new and renewal passports are available from main post offices and at the passport offices in Belfast, Glasgow, Liverpool, London, Newport, and Peterborough. You may apply in person at all passport offices, or by mail to all except the London office. Children under 16 may travel on an accompanying parent's passport. All passports are valid for 10 years.

Allow a month for processing.

S

SENIOR-CITIZEN DISCOUNTS

Women over 62 and men over 65 qualify for special seasonal (and in some cases year-round) discounts at a variety of Swiss hotels. In the case of married couples, at least one spouse must fulfill these conditions. Prices include overnight lodging in a single or double room, breakfast, service charges, heating, and taxes. Arrangements can also be made for extended stays. Senior citizens are entitled to discounts at all movie theaters in Switzerland and, where posted, pay reduced admission prices at museums and attractions.

To qualify for age-related discounts, **mention your senior-citizen status up front** when booking hotel reservations, not when checking out, and before you're seated in restaurants, not when paying the bill. Note that discounts may be limited to certain menus, days, or hours. When renting a car, **ask about promotional car-rental discounts**—they can net even lower costs than your senior-citizen discount.

STUDENTS ON THE ROAD

To save money, **look into deals available through student-oriented travel agencies.** To qualify, you'll need to have a bona fide student ID card. Members of international student groups are also eligible (☞ Students *in* Important Contacts A to Z).

T

TELEPHONES

There is direct dialing to everywhere in Switzerland. For local and international codes, consult the pink pages at the front of the telephone book. To make a local call on the pay phone, pick up the receiver, put in a minimum of 0.50 SF, and dial the number. Digital readouts will tell you to add more as your time runs out. A useful alternative is the PTT phone card, available in 10 SF or 20 SF units. You can buy them at the post office or train station, and you slip them into adapted public phones. The cost of the call will be counted against the card, with any remaining value still good for the next time you use it. If you drain the card and still need to talk, the readout will warn you: You can either pop in a new card or make up the difference with coins.

LONG-DISTANCE

You can dial most international numbers direct from Switzerland, adding 00 before the country code. If you want a number that cannot be reached directly, dial 144 for a connection. Dial 191 for international numbers and information. It's cheapest to use the booths in train stations and post offices: Calls made from your hotel cost a great deal more. Rates are lower between 5 and 7 PM, after 9 PM, and on weekends. Calls to the United States cost about 1.80 SF a minute, to the United Kingdom about 1 SF a minute. If you're short on change and don't have a phone card, call from the phone cabins at the post office: Tell the clerk what country you want to call, then step in and dial. The cost is clocked behind the desk, and you may pay with a credit card. There's no difference in price between phone cabins and public phone booths.

Avoid making long-distance calls from hotel room, since many hotels charge up to 400% more than the calling card rate. Some hotels also block the access codes of long-distance carriers, so travel with more than one company's calling card—one of them might work. If the hotel operator claims that you cannot use any phone card, ask to be connected to an international operator, who will help you to access your phone card. You can also dial the international operator yourself. If none of this works, try calling your phone company collect in the United States. If collect calls are also blocked, call from a pay phone in the hotel lobby. Before you go, **find out the local access codes** for your destinations.

OPERATORS AND INFORMATION

All telephone operators speak English, and instructions are printed in English in all telephone booths. Precede the area-code number with 0 when dialing long-distance within Switzerland. Omit the 0 when using the international code to dial Switzerland from another country. Switzerland's country code is 41.

TIPPING

Despite all protests to the contrary and menus marked *service compris,* the Swiss *do* tip at restaurant meals, giving quantities anywhere from the change from the nearest franc to 10 SF for a world-class meal exquisitely served. Unlike American-style tipping, which is calculated by a percentage, usually between 10% and 20%, a tip is still a tip here: a nod of approval for a job well done. If, in a café, the waitress settles the bill at the table, fishing the change from her leather purse, give her the change on the spot—or calculate the total, including tip, and tell her the full sum before she counts it onto the table top. If you need to take more time to calculate, leave it on the table, though this isn't common practice in outdoor cafés. If you're paying for a meal with a credit card, try to tip with cash instead of filling in the tip slot on the slip: Not all managers are good about doling out the waiters' tips in cash. Tipping porters and doormen is easier: 2 SF per bag is adequate in good hotels, 1 SF per trip in humbler lodgings (unless you travel heavy).

TOUR OPERATORS

A package or tour to Switzerland can make your vacation less expensive and more hassle-free. Firms that sell tours and packages reserve airline seats, hotel rooms, and rental cars in bulk and pass some of the savings on to you. In addition, the best operators have local representatives available to help you at your destination.

A GOOD DEAL?

The more your package or tour includes, the better you can predict the ultimate cost of your vacation. Make sure you know exactly what is covered, and **beware of hidden costs.** Are taxes, tips, and service charges included? Transfers and baggage handling? Entertainment and excursions? These can add up.

Most packages and tours are rated deluxe, first-class superior, first class, tourist, or budget. The key difference is usually accommodations. If the package or tour you are considering is priced lower than in your wildest dreams, **be skeptical.** Also, **make sure your travel agent knows the accommodations** and other services. Ask about the hotel's location, room size, beds, and whether it has a pool, room service, or programs for children, if you care about these. Has your agent been there in person or sent others you can contact?

BUYER BEWARE

Each year a number of consumers are stranded or lose their money when operators—even very large ones with excellent reputations—go out of business. To avoid becoming one of them, take the time to **check out the operator**—find out how long the company has been in business and ask several agents about its reputation. Next, **don't book unless the firm has a consumer-protection program.** Members of the USTOA and the NTA are required to set aside funds for the sole purpose of covering your payments and travel arrangements in case of default. Nonmember operators may instead carry insurance; look for the details in the operator's brochure—and for the name of an underwriter with a solid reputation. Note: When it comes to tour operators, **don't trust escrow accounts.** Although there are laws governing those of charter-flight operators, no governmental body prevents tour operators from raiding the till.

Next, **contact your local Better Business Bureau and the attorney general's offices** in both your own state and the operator's; have any complaints been filed? Finally, **pay with a major credit card.** Then you can cancel payment, provided that you can document your complaint. Always **consider trip-cancellation insurance** (☞ Insurance, *above*).

BIG VS. SMALL➣ Operators that handle several hundred thousand travelers per year can use their purchasing power to give you a good price. Their high volume may also indicate financial stability. But some small companies provide more personalized service; because they tend to specialize, they may also be more knowledgeable about a given area.

USING AN AGENT

Travel agents are excellent resources. In fact, large operators accept bookings made only through travel agents. But it's good to **collect brochures from several agencies** because some agents' suggestions may be skewed by promotional relationships with tour and package firms that reward them for volume sales. If you have a special interest, **find an agent with expertise in that area**; ASTA can provide leads in the United States. (Don't rely solely on your agent, though; agents may be unaware of small-niche operators, and some special-interest travel companies only sell direct.)

SINGLE TRAVELERS

Prices are usually quoted per person, based on two sharing a room. If traveling solo, you may be required to pay the full double-occupancy rate. Some operators eliminate this surcharge if you agree to be matched up with a roommate of the same sex, even if one is not found by departure time.

Consider a first-class ticket only if the extra comfort is worth the price. The principal difference between first- and second-class is more space to yourself. **Make seat reservations** for trips during rush hours and in high season, especially on international trains.

Trains described as Inter-City or Express are the fastest, stopping only at principal towns. *Regionalzug* means a local train. If you're planning to use the trains extensively, get the official timetable ("Kursbuch" or "Horaire") for 14 SF; the portable, pocket version is called "Fribo" and costs 12 SF.

If your itinerary requires changing trains, **bear in mind that the average connection time is six to eight minutes.**

DISCOUNT PASSES

If Switzerland is your only destination in Europe, **consider purchasing a Swiss Flexipass,** which allows travel not just on the national rail network but aboard lake steamers, city transportation lines, and many private railroads. Prices begin at $132 for three days of second-class travel in a 15-day period and $264 for three days of first-class travel in a 15-day period. Passes are also available for additional days and in longer time periods. Other alternatives include rail-drive packages and family plans.

Switzerland is one of 17 countries in which you can **use EurailPasses,** which provide unlimited first-class rail travel, in all of the participating countries, for the duration of the pass. If you plan to rack up the miles, get a standard pass. These are available for 15 days ($522), 21 days ($678), one month ($838), two months ($1,148), and 3 months ($1,468). If your plans call for only limited train travel, **look into a Europass,** which costs less money than a EurailPass. Unlike EurailPasses, however, you get a limited number of travel days, in a limited number of countries, during a specified time period. For example, a two month Europass ($316) allows between five and fifteen days of rail travel, but costs $200 less than the least expensive EurailPass. Keep in mind, however, that the Europass is good only in France, Germany, Italy, Spain, and Switzerland, and the number of countries you can visit is further limited by the type of pass you buy. For example, the basic two-month Europass allows you to visit only three of the five participating countries.

In addition to standard EurailPasses, **ask about special rail-pass plans.** Among these are the Eurail Youthpass (for those under age 26), the Eurail Saverpass (which gives a discount for two or more people traveling together), a Eurail Flexipass (which allows a certain number of travel days within a set period), the Euraildrive Pass and the Europass Drive (which combines travel by train and rental car).

Whichever pass you choose, remember that you must **purchase your**

pass before you leave for Europe.

Many travelers assume that rail passes guarantee them seats on the trains they wish to ride. Not so. You need to **book seats ahead even if you are using a rail pass**; seat reservations are required on some European trains, particularly high-speed trains, and are a good idea on trains that may be crowded—particularly in summer on popular routes. You will also need a reservation if you purchase sleeping accommodations.

FROM THE UNITED KINGDOM

By combining the Hoverspeed rail/hovercraft-rail service to Paris, then the superb French *train à grande vitesse* (TGV), you can make it to Switzerland in less than 12 hours. Leave London (Victoria) in mid-morning on the CityLink service to Paris (Gare du Nord), then transfer by Métro/RER to the Gare du Lyon for TGV transit to Switzerland. You'll be in Geneva by nightfall. Reservations are essential.

TRAVEL GEAR

Travel catalogs specialize in useful items that can **save space when packing** and make life on the road more convenient. Compact alarm clocks, travel irons, travel wallets, and personal-care kits are among the most common items you'll find. They also carry dual-voltage appliances, currency converters and foreign-language phrase books. Some catalogs even carry miniature coffeemakers and water purifiers.

U

U.S. GOVERNMENT

The U.S. government can be an excellent source of travel information. Some of this is free and some is available for a nominal charge. When planning your trip, **find out what government materials are available.** For just a couple of dollars, you can get a variety of publications from the Consumer Information Center in Pueblo, Colorado. Free consumer information is also available from individual government agencies, such as the Department of Transportation or the U.S. Customs Service. For specific titles, see the appropriate publications entry in Important Contacts A to Z, *above.*

W

WHEN TO GO

In July and August, the best weather coincides with the heaviest crowds. June and September are still pleasant, and hotel prices can be slightly lower, especially in resorts. In May, the mountains are at their loveliest, with Alpine flowers blooming and the peaks capped with snow; however, as ski season is over, this is often considered low season, and many resort hotels close down.

Those that remain open reduce their prices considerably. A low-season disadvantage: Some cable-car and cogwheel train operations take a break between the midwinter and midsummer rushes. The most prestigious ski resorts charge top prices during the Christmas–New Year holidays but reduce them slightly in early January. February through Easter is prime time again. Many of the family-run, traditional hotels fill up a year ahead, and you'll have to settle for less appealing lodgings. Also, check with the resort for exact dates of high seasons: They vary slightly from region to region. Late autumn—from mid-October through early December—is the least appealing season for visiting the Alps, because there's usually little snow, no foliage, and a tendency toward dampness and fog. If you're sticking to the cities to shop and tour museums, you won't notice the doldrums that take over the resorts. The exception to the above rules of thumb: The Ticino, the only portion of Switzerland south of the Alps, boasts a Mediterranean climate and declares high season from April through October. Many of its hotels close down altogether from November through March.

CLIMATE

What follow are average daily maximum and minimum temperatures for major cities in Switzerland.

Climate in Switzerland

BERN

Jan.	36F	2C	May	65F	18C	Sept.	67F	19C
	25	− 4		47	8		50	10
Feb.	40F	4C	June	70F	21C	Oct.	56F	13C
	27	− 3		52	11		41	5
Mar.	49F	9C	July	74F	23C	Nov.	45F	7C
	34	1		56	13		34	1
Apr.	58F	14C	Aug.	72F	22C	Dec.	38F	36C
	40	48		56	13		29	− 2

GENEVA

Jan.	40F	4C	May	67F	19C	Sept.	70F	21C
	29	− 2		49	9		54	12
Feb.	43F	6C	June	74F	23C	Oct.	58F	14C
	31	− 1		56	13		45	7
Mar.	50F	10C	July	77F	25C	Nov.	47F	8C
	36	2		59	15		38	3
Apr.	59F	15C	Aug.	76F	24C	Dec.	40F	4C
	41	5		58	14		32	0

LUGANO

Jan.	43F	6C	May	70F	21C	Sept.	74F	23C
	29	− 2		50	10		56	13
Feb.	49F	9C	June	77F	25C	Oct.	61F	16C
	31	− 1		58	14		47	8
Mar.	56F	13C	July	81F	27C	Nov.	52F	11C
	38	3		61	16		38	3
Apr.	63F	17C	Aug.	81F	27C	Dec.	45F	7C
	45	7		59	15		32	0

ST. MORITZ

Jan.	29F	− 2C	May	50F	10C	Sept.	58F	14C
	11	−12		32	0		38	13
Feb.	34F	1C	June	59F	15C	Oct.	50F	10C
	13	−11		40	4		31	− 1
Mar.	38F	3C	July	63F	17C	Nov.	38F	3C
	18	− 8		41	5		22	− 6
Apr.	45F	7C	Aug.	61F	16C	Dec.	31F	− 1C
	25	− 4		41	5		14	10

ZÜRICH

Jan.	36F	2C	May	67F	19C	Sept.	68F	20C
	27	− 3		47	8		52	11
Feb.	41F	5C	June	74F	23C	Oct.	58F	14C
	29	− 2		54	12		43	6
Mar.	50F	10C	July	77F	25C	Nov.	45F	7C
	34	1		58	14		36	2
Apr.	59F	15C	Aug.	76F	24C	Dec.	38F	3C
	40	4		56	13		29	− 2

THE GOLD GUIDE / SMART TRAVEL TIPS

1 Destination: Switzerland

THE GOOD, THE BAD, AND THE TIDY

UP IN THE HOARY windswept heights and black fir forests of the Alps, an electric eye beams open a glistening all-glass door—and reveals the honey-gold glow of wood, the sheen of copper, the burnt-chocolate tones of ancient wooden rafters. Candles flicker, Sterno radiates blue-white flames under russet pots of bubbling fondue. The cheery *boomp-chick boomp-chick* of an accordion filters down from high-tech stereo speakers cleverly concealed behind oversize cowbells. Waitresses in starched black dirndls and waiters in bleached white ties scuttle briskly from kitchen to table, table to kitchen, while platters of gravy-laden veal, sizzling *Rösti* (hash brown potatoes), rosy entrecôte, simmer over steel trivets—preheated, electrically controlled—ready to be proudly, seamlessly served.

Coziness under strict control, anachronism versus state-of-the-art technology: strange bedfellows in a storybook land. Nowhere else in Europe can you find a combination as welcoming and as alien, as comfortable and as remote, as engaging and as disengaged as a glass cable car to the clouds. This is the paradox of the Swiss, whose primary national aesthetic pitches rustic Alpine homeyness against high-tech urban efficiency. Though they're proud, sober, self-contained, independent culturally and politically, disdainful of the shabby and the slipshod, painfully neat, rigorously prompt—the Swiss have a weakness for cuteness, and they indulge in incongruously coy diminutives: A German *Bierstube* becomes a *Stübli*, *Kuchen* (cake) becomes *Küchli*, *Wurst* becomes *Würstli*, *Pastete* (puff pastry) becomes *Pastetli*, and a *coupe* (glass) of champagne becomes a *Cüpli*.

It is lucky for tourists, this dichotomy of the folksy and the functional. It means your trains get you to your firelit lodge on time. It means the shower in your room runs as hot as a Turkish bath. It means the cable car that sweeps you to a mountaintop has been subjected to grueling inspections. It means the handwoven curtains are boiled and starched, and the high-thread-count bed linens are turned back with a chocolate at night. It means the scarlet geraniums that cascade from window boxes on every carved balcony are tended like prize orchids. It means the pipe smoke that builds up in the *stübli* at night is aired out daily, as sparkling clean, double-glazed windows are thrown open on every floor, every morning, to let sharp, cool mountain air course through hallways, bedrooms, and fresh-bleached baths.

Yet there is a stinginess that peeks around the apron of that rosy-cheeked efficiency. Liquor here is measured with scientific precision into glasses marked for one centiliter or two, and the local wines come in carafes reminiscent of laboratory beakers. Despite the fine linens and puffs of down that adorn each bed, double beds have separate mattresses with sheets tucked primly down the middle, sometimes so tightly you have to lift the mattress to loosen the barrier. And if you wash out your socks and hang them loosely on the shower rod in the morning, you may return at night and find them straightened, spaced, toes pointing the same direction, as orderly as little lead soldiers.

Nevertheless there is an earthiness about these people, as at ease with the soil as they are appalled by dirt. A banker in Zürich may rent a postage-stamp of land in a crowded patchwork outside town, sowing tight rows of cabbages and strawberries, weeding bright borders of marigolds, and on Sunday he may visit his miniature estate, pull a chair out from the tidy toolshed, and simply sit and smoke, like Heidi's Alm-Uncle surveying his Alpine realm. An elderly woman may don knickers and loden hat and board a postbus to the mountains, and climb steep, rocky trails at a brisk clip, cheeks glowing, eyes as icy-bright as the glaciers above her. A family of farmers—grandparents, schoolgirls, married sons—unite for the haycutting as if for Christmas dinner, standing shoulder to shoulder in the hip-high gold, swinging scythes from dawn to sunset.

HERE'S A 21ST-CENTURY counterpoint to this: the high-tech, jet-set glamour that splashes vivid colors across the slopes at St. Moritz, Gstaad, Zermatt, Verbier. Step out of a bulbous steel-and-glass cable car onto a concrete platform at 2,000 meters (6,560 feet) and see Switzerland transformed, its worker's blue overalls and good wool suits exchanged for Day-Glo ski suits—mango, chartreuse, swimming-pool blue. Wholesome, healthy faces disappear behind mirrored goggles and war-paint sunblock, and gaudy skis and poles bristle militarily, like the pikes and halberds in the Battle of Sempach.

The contradictions mount: While fur-clad socialites raise jeweled fingers to bid at Sotheby's on Geneva's quai de Mont-Blanc, the women of Appenzell stand beside their husbands on the Landsgemeindeplatz and raise their hands to vote—a right not won until 1991. While digital screens tick off beef futures in Zürich, the crude harmony of cowbells echoes in velvet mountain pastures. While a Mercedes roars down an expressway expertly blasted through solid rock, a horse-drawn plow peels back thin topsoil in an Alpine garden plot, impossibly steep, improbably high.

And on August 1, the Swiss national holiday, while spectacular displays of fireworks explode in sizzling colors over the cities and towns, the mountain folk build the bonfires that glow quietly, splendidly, on every hillside of every Alp, uniting Swiss citizens as they celebrate their proud independence, their cultural wealth, and above all their diversity. It's that diversity and those quirky contradictions that make Switzerland a tourist capital—the folksy, fiercely efficient innkeeper to the world.

WHAT'S WHERE

Zürich

Known as one of the leading financial centers of the world, Zürich is a surprisingly modest, small-scale city. Its old town, which straddles the River Limmat, has no more than three high-rise buildings, and Gothic guildhalls take the place of imperial palaces. In the distance, snow-clad peaks overlook the waters of the lake, dwarfing everything below.

Eastern Switzerland

Near Zürich, the cantons of Glarus, Schaffhausen, Thurgau, St. Gallen, and Appenzell, as well as the independent principality of Liechtenstein, are dominated by the Rhine River. With its obscure backcountry and thriving cities, the German-influenced region has everything from wood-shingle farmhouses to town houses adorned with oriel windows and frescoes. Still, the eastern cantons remain one of the most untouched regions of Switzerland.

Graubünden

Dominated by its trendy resorts—St. Moritz, Davos, Klosters, Arosa, Pontresina—Graubünden is nonetheless Switzerland's most culturally diverse and largest canton. German, Italian, and Romansh—the ancient dialect that is thought to date from 600 BC—are all spoken here, in a land where stalwart native farmers subsist alongside fur-clad tourists from abroad.

Ticino

Italian in language, culture, and spirit, Ticino is an irresistible combination of Mediterranean pleasures and Swiss efficiency. With its yacht-filled waterfront promenades of Locarno and Lugano, and its constantly sunny climate, Ticino is a canton set apart, a happy harbor for Switzerland's Italian-speaking minority.

Luzern and Central Switzerland

Endowed with a sophisticated transportation system that makes it one of the easiest regions to visit, Central Switzerland is full of neat little towns, accessible mountains, and modest resorts. Centered around the Vierwaldstättersee, "the lake of the four forest cantons," the region is steeped in history: It is where the Oath of Eternal Alliance is said to have been renewed, and it's also the birthplace of the legend of William Tell.

Basel

At the juncture of France and Germany, German-speaking Basel is a cultural capital with a sense of fun. Cultivated and yet down-home, it has 27 museums, Switzerland's oldest university, and some of the most diverse shopping in the country. All the same, beer and sausages are the snack of choice, and the annual Carnival is observed with a boisterousness that's unparalleled by other Swiss towns.

Fribourg, Neuchâtel, and the Jura

Unself-conscious and largely undiscovered, the cantons of Fribourg, Neuchâtel, and the Jura represent three very different worlds—even though they market themselves as a unit. Fribourg, part German and part French, is full of medieval villages; Neuchâtel, French in language and culture, is the center of watchmaking; and the isolated Jura Mountains, part German and part French, exist in a realm of their own.

Bern

Humble and down-to-earth, Bern is a city of broad medieval streets, farmers' markets, and friendly, slow-spoken people. It is also the federal capital of Switzerland and, more remarkably, a World Cultural Heritage city known for its sandstone arcades, fountains, and thick, sturdy towers.

Berner Oberland

The Bernese Alps concentrate the very best of rural Switzerland: panoramas of the Eiger and Jungfrau mountains; crystalline lakes, gorges, and waterfalls; and emerald slopes dotted with gingerbread chalets and cows with bells—not to mention world-class skiing. It's no secret, though: The Berner Oberland is among the most touristed cantons of Switzerland.

Valais

Alpine villages, famous peaks (the Matterhorn, most notably), world-class resorts (Zermatt, Saas-Fee, Crans, Verbier), and verdant vineyards are all reasons to visit the valley of the Rhone. This is the Switzerland of tumbledown huts, raclette eaters, and yodelers. Separated from the modern world by mountains, it feels like a land apart.

Vaud

Lausanne, Montreux, and the Vaudoise Alps comprise one of Switzerland's most diverse regions. Centered around Lac Léman (also known as Lake Geneva), this French-speaking canton harbors some of the country's most famous cathedrals and castles, as well as Alpine villages, balmy lake resorts, and above all, its most verdant vineyards.

Geneva

As the headquarters of the United Nations, the World Health Organization, and the International Red Cross; an international mecca for writers and thinkers of every stripe; and a stronghold of luxurious stores and extravagant restaurants, Geneva is Switzerland's most cosmopolitan city. This is a city of wealth and influence, where the rustic chalets of hilltop villages seem worlds away.

PLEASURES AND PASTIMES

Dining

If you're looking for diverse dining experiences, you can't do much better than Switzerland, where French, Italian, or German cuisine may dominate, depending on which cantons you visit. In French areas (roughly Vaud, Geneva, Jura, Neuchâtel, and western parts of Fribourg and Valais) the cuisine is clearly Gallic, and wine stews, organ meats, and subtle sausages appear alongside standard *cuisine bourgeoise:* thick, rare beef entrecôte with a choice of rich sauces, and *truite meunière* (trout dredged in flour and sizzled in butter). In the Ticino, the Italian canton, Italian cuisine appears virtually unscathed, particularly the Alpine-forest specialties of Piedmont and Lombardy (risotto, gnocchi, polenta, porcini mushrooms). The German cantons serve more pork than their neighbors and favor another standard dish that represents Switzerland though it vanishes in French-speaking or Italian-speaking areas: *Rösti,* a broad patty of hash-brown potatoes crisped in a skillet and often flavored with bacon, herbs, or cheese, is as prevalent in the German regions as fondue in the French. Beyond the obvious cultural differences, Swiss cuisine is also influenced by the terrain: Mountain farmers have traditionally subsisted on such basic foods as *raclette* (cheese melted over pickled vegetables and boiled potatoes), while cities nurtured wealthy burghers and noblemen with the cream of the crops of out-lying lands—milk-fed veal, fruits from low-lying orchards. Though fondue, Rösti, and veal are likely to be on any resort's menu these days, traces of these influences can still be found almost everywhere.

Hiking

When the snow melts and the mountain streams start to flow, Switzerland takes to the hills. That the Swiss Alps are the ultimate in hiking is no secret: On a sunny day in high season in the more popular vacation areas, footpaths can be almost as crowded as a line for Madonna tickets. On narrow trails, hikers walk in single file, and the more aggressive pass on the left as if on the Autobahns of Germany. However, there is an almost infinite quantity of quiet, isolated routes to be explored; if you prefer to hike in peace, head for one of the less inhabited Alpine valleys—in the Valais or Graubünden there are several—and strike out on your own. Each of the regional tourist departments publishes suggested hiking itineraries, and major map publishers distribute excellent topographical maps of wilderness trails. In the German-speaking region especially, hiking is a deeply rooted tradition, and people of all ages and in all physical conditions head for well-beaten paths in knickers, woolen stockings, and heavy boots; it's a sight to behold.

Regional Celebrations

Basel's extravagant pre-Lenten observance of *Fasnacht* (Carnival)—in which up to 20,000 costumed revelers fill the streets with the sounds of fifes and drums—is only one of the hundreds of festivals that the Swiss celebrate all year round. As if to prove that its spirit is vast despite its small size, almost every Swiss canton hosts its own popular celebration of one event or another. In Geneva, the Festival of the Escalade commemorates the heroic housewife who repelled the Savoyards by dumping hot soup on their heads. Lesser known festivals range from the frivolous—in the *Schlitteda Engiadinaisa,* young unmarried men and women ride decorated sleighs through the villages of the Engadine; to the symbolic—in the *Landsgemeinde,* the citizens of Appenzell pay homage to their country's democratic tradition by conducting a vote by public show of hands.

Shopping

Swiss Army knives, Swiss watches, Swiss chocolate—what could be more . . . Swiss? Though you won't find many bargains in Switzerland anytime soon, you will find some uniquely Swiss treasures. Some of the best souvenirs of this pragmatic country are typically practical, such as watches, clocks, and Swiss Army knives. Others are more luxurious, such as sweet milk chocolate: Lindt, Nestlé, and Tobler are major manufacturers. Marvelous music boxes from the watchmaking country around Lake Neuchâtel are sold in specialty shops all over the country. Linens and good cottons—dish and tea towels, aprons, sheets—are another Swiss specialty, as are pottery and ceramics—most of them dark-glazed and hand-painted with naive designs.

Skiing

Switzerland is Europe's winter playground, and its facilities are as technically advanced as its slopes are spectacular. Any level of skier can find a resort to meet his or her needs, from a cozy family-oriented village with easy and moderate slopes to the world-class challenges at Verbier, Wengen, and Zermatt. Most of the resorts publish an area map showing their slopes and rating the trails for difficulty. Familiarize yourself with the resort's signs, including those warning of avalanche zones, before you set out. For an analysis of the best ski resorts, *see* Skiing Switzerland *in* Chapter 14, Portraits of Switzerland. There's a comparison of each region's primary resorts at the end of each relevant chapter as well.

Spectator Sports

If awards were given to countries with the most unusual sports competitions, Switzerland would win hands down. In the winter, the action centers around St. Moritz, where a frozen lake provides a novel setting for golf, polo, dogsled races, and horse races: In the Winter Golf Tournament, red balls on white "greens" are a festive sight; in the Racing Hounds Competition, a motley crew of canines races across 480 meters (1,574 feet) of ice at an average speed of 55 miles per hour. Also in St. Moritz, the uniquely Swiss sport of Skijöring involves skiers being pulled by galloping horses. Cows are the players in another, non-winter event: In the "Combat de Reines" a particular breed of fighting cows battle each other; the winner, "La Reine," is decorated and awarded with the best grazing ground. Wrestling is a popular Swiss tradition: Men wear big baggy shorts of burlap and stand in sawdust rings; after the competition, costumed spectators sing and dance. Perhaps most unusual, stone-throwing competitions in Unspunnen (in the canton of Bern) take place every five years; 180-pound stones are used.

FODOR'S CHOICE

No two people will agree on what makes a perfect vacation, but it's fun and helpful to know what others think. We hope you'll have a chance to experience some of Fodor's Choices yourself while visiting Switzerland. For detailed information about each entry, refer to the appropriate chapters within this guidebook.

Lodging

★In Geneva's Old Town, **Les Armures** is an archaeological treasure with original stonework, frescoes, and stenciled beams. $$$$

★Lausanne's **Beau Rivage-Palace** stands apart in neoclassic grandeur, with manicured waterfront grounds and several first-class restaurants. $$$$

★**Tamaro,** a Romantik property on the Ascona waterfront, has a grand Mediterranean air and excellent lake views. $$$

★A 600-year old structure on the banks of the Limmat, **Zum Storchen** is one of Zürich's most atmospheric hotels. $$$

★In Château-d'Oex, the 18th-century **Bon Acceuil** has low wood-beam ceilings, creaking floors, antiques, and fresh flowers inside and out. $$

★A demure little inn on a hillside between Chillon and Montreux, **Masson** has offered peace and quiet to weary travelers since 1829. $$

★With lead-glass windows, homespun linen, and pewter pitchers, the all-wood chalet **Ruedihus** re-creates the atmosphere of the 1753 original. $$

Dining

★Called the chef of the century by his Parisian peers, Fredy Girardet draws

crowds who reserve at least a month in advance to eat at **Girardet,** in the small village of Crissier, of Lausanne. $$$$

★Inside what was once the Heuberg mansion in Basel, the **Teufelhof** has an inventive menu and chic, minimalist decor. $$$$

★The 20th-century-art collection is as plentiful as the food at Zürich's **Kronenhalle,** where robust cooking in hearty portions draws a genial crowd. $$$

★At **Wirtschaft zum Frieden,** in Schaffhausen, you can opt for a daily plate-lunch in an intimate stübli, a fancier meal in a tile-stove dining room, or selections from either menu in a private garden thick with wisteria. $$–$$$

★Authentic Lyonnaise cuisine is the specialty at Geneva's **Boeuf Rouge,** where *boudin noir* (blood sausage) and *tarte tatin* (caramelized apple tart) will make you think you've crossed the border. $$

★In a 1677 inn at the hub of Chur, **Stern** carries on the age-old tradition of Graubündner culture, complete with local wine served in pewter pitchers and waitresses in folk costume. $–$$

★Under a giant boar's head and century-old murals at **Bierhalle Kropf,** businesspeople, workers, and shoppers share crowded tables to feast on hearty Zürich cuisine. $

★Tucked in a tiny basement in an alleyway off Lugano's old town, **La Tinera** draws crowds of locals and tourists for its hearty meats, pastas, and local wine served in ceramic bowls. $

Views

★Perched high above town, Bern's **Rose Garden** overlooks the entire old town.

★From the top of the 3,474-meter (11,395-foot) **Jungfraujoch,** the Aletsch Glacier looks like a vast sea of ice.

★The terrace café of the Disneyland-like **Château Gütsch** affords an idyllic view of Luzern and the Vierwaldstättersee.

★From the summit station of **Gornergrat,** the snaggle-toothed Matterhorn steals the thunder from all surrounding peaks.

★With its mists, roaring water, jutting rocks, and bushy crags, the **Rheinfall,** from the Neuhausen side, appears truly Wagnerian.

★The sunset from the south-facing hilltop resort of **Wengen** is a sublime way to end a day of skiing.

Picturesque Villages and Towns

★Clinging vertiginously to a hillside, its flower-filled balconies overlooking the sea, tiny **Gandria** retains the ambience of an ancient fishing village.

★In the Lower Engadine, **Guarda** is a federally protected hamlet of architectural photo-ops, with cobblestone streets and flower boxes filled with red geraniums.

★An eagle's-nest town set on a precarious 1,000-meter (3,280-foot) slope in the Rhône Valley, **Isérables** is full of stone-shingled *mazots* (barns typical of the Valais) and narrow, winding streets.

★**Morcote,** an old resort village below Lugano, has clay-color Lombard-style houses and arcades that look out on the waterfront.

★In Western Switzerland near Avenches, the ancient town of **Murten** (known in French as Morat) is a popular lake resort with a superbly preserved medieval center.

★In the vineyard region of the Vaud, the cobblestone village of **St-Saphorin** is worth a stop, if only for a glass of the fruity local wine and a view of the lake from Café du Raisin.

★On the Rhine River in Eastern Switzerland, **Stein-am-Rhein** is a nearly perfectly preserved medieval village, replete with shingled, half-timber town houses boasting ornate oriels and flamboyant frescoes.

Perfect Moments

★Fireworks burst and mountain-farm bonfires smolder on the **Swiss National Holiday** (August 1).

★For a festive, outdoorsy evening, bring a lap blanket to a summer night's outdoor performance of the **Tellspiel** at Interlaken.

★Counting the waterfalls around the **Oeschinensee,** above Kandersteg, is a perfect way to celebrate spring.

★Feeding swans and ducks by the **Kapellbrücke** in Luzern is a favorite pastime of locals and tourists alike.

★When the sound of fife-and-drum music drifts from upstairs windows of guild houses in **Basel's old town,** you'll think the Middle Ages have dawned once again.

★A herd of male red deer, antlers silhouetted, in the **Parc Naziunal Svizzer** (Swiss National Park), is a memorable sight.

★Drinking **steaming-fresh milk** in an Alpine barn, you'll understand why Heidi loved Switzerland.

GREAT ITINERARIES

In a country as diverse as Switzerland, it makes sense to visit with a theme in mind. Below, we have outlined itineraries for culinary adventures and exploring historic castles. Bon appétit and happy exploring.

Swiss Gastronomy

This food-intensive itinerary offers aficionados an opportunity to travel from one great dining experience to another, sampling the very finest *haute gastronomie* at one stop, the most authentic regional classics—even the earthiest peasant cuisines—at another. Incidental pleasures—wandering in the Alps, for example, or strolling through medieval town centers in Switzerland's greatest cities—can be squeezed in between meals. We'll start in Geneva, sampling its Lyon-influenced cuisine, then head east toward Lausanne and Crissier, where the legendary chef Fredy Girardet holds forth. Then it's northward to Basel, where his rival Hans Stucki competes for culinary stars. From Basel, it's an hour's journey to Zürich, where the third of the Swiss triumvirate—Horst Petermann—reigns. After that, take a dip south to Luzern for regional cuisine. Now it's time for a little exercise: crossing the Alps into the Valais (the Rhône Valley), resting at Saas-Fee for a mountain-inn getaway, and following the Rhône back toward Geneva, stopping at Verbier, another mountain resort, for a gastronomic feast to tide you over for the journey home.

DURATION➣ Depending on your capacity for stellar meals—one or two per day—

you can concentrate the highlights of this trip into nine marathon days or stretch it out over two weeks or more. If you're planning to pack it all into a few days, check opening days carefully—and always book ahead. Many restaurants in Geneva close weekends, and many elsewhere close Monday or Tuesday.

GETTING AROUND➤ Each of the stopovers is accessible by train, though some of the restaurants may require cabs or tram rides; a rental car will give you more flexibility for reaching country inns.

THE MAIN ROUTE➤ **One night: Geneva.** Your first night, indulge in a hearty Lyonnaise bistro meal at Le Boeuf Rouge. For lunch the next day, head for the elite country-club atmosphere in the suburb of Cologny to rub shoulders with jet-set diners over bouillabaisse at Le Lion d'Or. Back in Geneva, have a relatively light Ticinese supper at La Favola. Incidental distractions to fill time between meals: world-class museums (especially the International Red Cross Museum), old-town antiques shops, or the early Christian diggings under the cathedral.

One night: Lausanne. Lunch at Girardet in nearby Crissier may be the crowning glory of the trip—but reserve judgment for after Basel and Zürich. At night, head down to the waterfront at Ouchy and have a chic, light supper at the Café Beau-Rivage.

One night: Basel. Two hours north, compare Stucki with Girardet at lunch. Then, after visiting, say, the Münster and the history museum, relax in the downstairs bistro at the Teufelhof: The light specialties are prepared by Michael Baader, who is chef for the top-notch restaurant upstairs as well.

Two nights: Zürich. Have lunch at Petermann's Kunststuben, in the suburb of Küsnacht, where the gastronomy vies for the title "best in Switzerland." Then, after a thorough walking tour of Zürich's old town, you can settle in for an atmospheric, old-world evening at the Kronenhalle, or an outdoor meal of fresh lake fish on the terrace of the Fischstube.

One night: Luzern. For a total contrast, and perhaps the most authentically *Swiss* meal of your tour, head for Galliker and a lunch of real farm food. Having taken in the Lion Monument, crossed the Kapellbrücke,

and toured the history museum, you can think about the evening meal: A light, sophisticated river-fish meal at Des Balances takes in waterfront views.

One night: Saas-Fee. From Luzern, allow for a full day's scenic mountain drive south over the Brünigpass, then on over the Grimselpass and down the Rhône Valley to Brig and the spectacular little resort of Saas-Fee. Once there, retreat to the isolated Waldhotel Fletschhorn for a sophisticated dinner and a bare minimum of one night to take in the mountain air.

One night: Verbier. Following the Rhône back west toward Geneva, take one more Alpine side trip up to this famous ski resort to feast and sleep at Rosalp, the popular rustic-chic inn in the village center.

INFORMATION➤ *See* Chapters 2 (Zürich), 6 (Luzern and Central Switzerland), 7 (Basel), 11 (Valais), 12 (Vaud), and 13 (Geneva).

Castles and Cathedrals

Romantics, history buffs, and architecture fans will enjoy a circle tour that takes in some of the best of western Switzerland's medieval and Gothic landmarks. Start at Geneva, where the cathedral covers Christian history from Gallo-Roman times through Calvin. At Montreux, you'll visit the famous waterfront castle of Chillon, where Lord Byron signed the pillar where his "Prisoner of Chillon" was manacled. In the green Fribourg countryside, the Gruyères castle perches at the top of a tiny preserved village. The bilingual capital Fribourg is the last Catholic stronghold of the west, rooted in its single-towered cathedral, and a stronghold for the Dukes of Zähringen as well. A jog down to the Berner Oberland and Thun takes you to the mighty Zähringen castle along the waters of the Thunersee. Then head up to Bern, entirely fortified by the Zähringen dukes, with its spectacular Münster, and on to Basel, where its own Münster dominates the old town.

DURATION➤ Six days.

GETTING AROUND➤ All stops are easily accessible by expressway and connecting roads.

The complete itinerary works by rail, with most sites accessible on foot from the station; Gruyères offers bus connections to the elevated castle and old town.

Language Regions of Switzerland

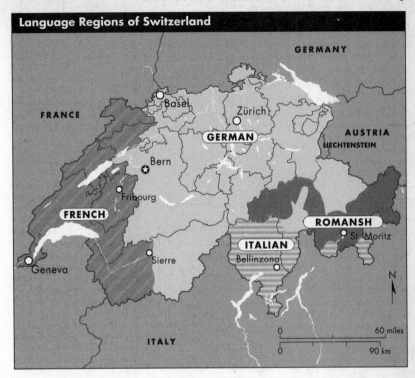

GERMANY

FRANCE

Basel

Zürich

GERMAN

AUSTRIA

LIECHTENSTEIN

Bern

Fribourg

FRENCH

ROMANSH

St. Moritz

ITALIAN

Sierre

Bellinzona

Geneva

N

0   60 miles

0   90 km

ITALY

THE MAIN ROUTE➤ **One night: Geneva.** The Cathédrale St-Pierre, begun during the 12th century, sinks roots into early Christianity: Immediately below its current structure, you'll find the *site archéologique,* where 3rd- and 5th-century ruins have been exposed.

One night: Montreux. The Château de Chillon, partially surrounded by the waters of Lac Léman (Lake Geneva), may be the most completely and authentically furnished in Switzerland, with tapestries, carved fireplaces, ceramics, and painted wooden ceilings.

One night: Gruyères. This craggy castle-village draws crowds to its ancient central street, souvenir shops, quaint inns, and frescoed castle, complete with dungeon and spectacular views.

One night: Fribourg. The Last Judgment tympanum and art nouveau stained-glass windows of the Cathédrale St-Nicholas deserve attention—but leave time to explore the old town, with its multilevel fortifications constructed for the ubiquitous Zähringens.

One night: Thun. If you're driving, cut across the rolling verdure of canton Fribourg toward Thun (by train, connect through Bern), where you'll see the Bernese Alps looming in all their splendor. Zähringen Castle, which dates from 1191, features a knight's hall, tapestries, local ceramics, and an intimidating collection of weapons.

One night: Bern. The Zähringens fortified this gooseneck in the River Aare; its 14th-century Münster features an unusually restored (full-color, painted) main portal.

One night: Basel. In this historic, cosmopolitan city, the Münster has a lovely Romanesque portal and the tomb of the great humanist Erasmus.

INFORMATION➤ ☞ Chapters 13 (Geneva), 12 (Vaud), 8 (Fribourg), 10 (Berner Oberland), 9 (Bern), and 7 (Basel).

FESTIVALS AND SEASONAL EVENTS

Top seasonal events in Switzerland include Fasnacht celebrations (carnival) in February and March, the Landsgemeinde open-air vote in Appenzell in April, the Montreux International Jazz Festival in July, the Menuhin Festival in Gstaad in August, the Knabenschiessen (Boys' Shooting Contest) in Zürich in September, and the Escalade festival in Geneva in December. Events are named below as publicized by the host region, usually in the local language.

EARLY DEC.➤ **Geneva Escalade** commemorates the defeat of the Duke of Savoy, whose invading troops were repelled by a local woman dumping hot soup on their heads from atop the city walls.

MID-JAN.➤ **Vogel Gryff Volksfest** is a colorful Basel tradition, with a costumed Griffin, a Lion, and a Wild Man of the Woods floating down the Rhine and dancing on the Mittlere Rheinbrücke.

LATE JAN.➤ **Schlittedas Engiadinaisa** is a winter Engadine tradition in which young unmarried men and women ride decorated sleighs from village to village. **Châteaux-d'Oex Hot Air Balloon Week** showcases the Vaud resort's specialty.

EARLY FEB.➤ **Hom Strom** at Bad Scuol in the Lower Engadine observes the burning of Old Man Winter.

LATE FEB.–EARLY MAR.➤ **Fasnacht** is observed throughout Switzerland, but nowhere more festively than in Basel, where it begins at 4 AM on the Monday after Ash Wednesday, with a drum-roll and a costume parade. Luzern celebrates on the Thursday before Ash Wednesday, with a traditional **Fritschi** procession, distributing oranges to children. On the same day, Schwyz celebrates **Blätzli** with a mummers' procession of harlequins. Lugano celebrates Carnevale with a **Festa del Risotto,** with risotto and sausages served in the streets.

EARLY MAR.➤ **Good Friday** (March 5) processions take place in several southern villages, including Mendrisio in the Ticino, where the procession derives from a medieval Passion Play that is performed on Maundy Thursday as well.

MID-MAR.➤ **Engadine Ski Marathon** covers the 42 kilometers (26 miles) between Zuoz and Maloja.

MAR.–MAY➤ **Primavera Concertistica** music festival takes place in Lugano.

APRIL➤ **Sechseläuten** in Zürich shows all its medieval guilds on parade and climaxes in the burning of the Böögg, a straw scarecrow representing winter.

APRIL➤ **Landsgemeinde** takes place in the town of Appenzell, with all citizens voting by public show of hands. Women voted for the first time in 1991.

APR.–MAY➤ The **International Jazz Festival—Bern** lasts five days in the federal capital.

MID-JUNE➤ **Grindelwald Country-Festival** brings American country-and-western groups to this mountain resort.

LATE JUNE–MID-SEPT.➤ **Wilhelm Tell** outdoor theater production, in Interlaken, has an epic-scale cast of locals.

JULY➤ **Montreux International Jazz Festival** hosts world-class artists.

JULY–AUG.➤ **Engadiner Concert Weeks** bring outdoor classical music events to resorts throughout the region. **Festival International de l'Orgue Ancien** at Valère in Sion honors the 13th-century instrument within, the oldest functioning organ in the world.

AUG. 1➤ **Swiss National Holiday** celebrates the confederation's birth in 1291 with fireworks and bonfires.

EARLY AUG.➤ **Geneva Festival** celebrates with folk processions and fireworks.

MID-AUG.➤ **Grächen Country Festival** imports American C&W music to the Alps. Vevey **International Festival of Film Comedy** honors comic classics on the outdoor screen.

MID-AUG.–MID-SEPT.➤ **Internationale Musikfestwochen** in Luzern combines concerts, theater, and art exhibitions. Davos **Young Artists in Concert** features tomorrow's classical music stars.

AUG.➤ Locarno's **International Film Festival** unveils top new movies in the Piazza Grande.

AUG.–MID-SEPT.➤ **Yehudi Menuhin Festival** in Gstaad showcases world-class musicians. Lugano's **Blues to Bop Festival** brings authentic blues to the lakefront.

LATE AUG.➤ **Zürich's Theaterspektakel** showcases avant-garde and mainstream playwrights as well as theater troupes from around the world.

LATE AUG.–OCT.➤ **Vevey–Montreux Music Festival** invites important artists to these twin lake resorts.

AUTUMN

EARLY SEPT.➤ **Knabenschiessen** takes place in Zürich with a folk festival and fair.

LATE SEPT.➤ The **Neuchâtel Wine Festival** is the biggest in the country.

LATE SEPT.➤ **Etivaz Cheese Sharing** celebrates the division of spoils from the cheese cooperative with yodeling, wrestling, and other activities. **Fribourg Braderie** combines a citywide sidewalk sale, folk festival, and onion market.

LATE OCT.➤ **Olma Schweizer Messe für Land- und Milchwirtschaft** (agricultural and dairy fair) in St. Gallen gathers representatives of the farming industry from across Switzerland.

LATE NOVEMBER➤ Bern's **Zwiebelemärit** (Onion Market) celebrates the open market established for area farmers in gratitude for aid they gave Bern after the great fire of 1405.

2 Zürich

*Known as one of the leading financial
centers of the world, Zürich is a
surprisingly modest, small-scale city. Its
old town, which straddles the River
Limmat, has no more than three high-
rise buildings, and Gothic guildhalls
take the place of imperial palaces. In
the distance, snow-clad peaks overlook
the waters of the lake, dwarfing
everything below.*

WHEN THE POUND STERLING sagged in the 1960s, the English coined the somewhat disparaging term "the Gnomes of Zürich," which evoked images of sly little Swiss bankers rubbing their hands and manipulating world currencies behind closed doors. Yet the spirit that moves the Züricher doesn't come out of folkloric forests but rather from the pulpit of the Grossmünster, where the fiery Reformation leader Huldrych Zwingli preached sermons about idle hands and the devil's playgrounds. It's the Protestant work ethic that has made Zürich one of the world's leading financial centers and that keeps its workers on their toes. One Zwingli lesson stressed the transience of wealth, and Zürichers show native caution in enjoying their fabulous gains. Nor have they turned their backs on their humbler heritage: On a first visit, you might be surprised to see a graceful jumble of shuttered Gothic buildings instead of cold chrome-and-glass towers.

Zürich is, in fact, a beautiful city, sitting astride the River Limmat where it flows into the Zürichsee. Its charming old town, comprising a substantial part of the city center, is full of beautifully restored historic buildings and narrow, hilly alleys. In the distance, snow-clad peaks overlook the waters of the lake, and the shores are dominated by turn-of-the-century mansions. Only three high-rise buildings disturb the skyline, and even they are small by U.S. standards. There are not even any dominating palaces to haunt the Züricher with memories of imperialism: In keeping with its solid bourgeois character, Zürich has always maintained a human scale.

The earliest known Zürichers lived around 4500 BC in small houses perched on stilts by the lakeside. Primarily hunter-gatherers, they also planted wheat and kept cattle and pigs. Underwater archaeologists have discovered a wealth of prehistoric artifacts dating back thousands of years, from Stone Age pottery and Bronze Age necklaces to charms made from boar fangs, bear teeth, and animal skulls; many relics are on display at the Schweizerisches Landesmuseum (Swiss National Museum) near the main station. The remains of 34 Stone Age and Bronze Age settlements are thought to be scattered around the lake.

During the 1st century BC the Romans, attracted by Zürich's central location, built a customs house on a hill overlooking the Limmat. In time, the customs house became a fortress, the remains of which can be seen on the Lindenhof, a square in the center of the city. The Romans also were accommodating enough to provide Zürich with its patron saints. Legend has it that the Roman governor beheaded the Christian brother and sister Felix and Regula on a small island in the river. The martyrs then picked up their heads, waded through the water, and walked up a hill before collapsing where the Grossmünster now stands.

When the Germanic Alemanni, ancestors of the present-day Zürichers, drove out the Romans during the 5th century, the region gradually diminished in importance until the Carolingians built an imperial palace on the Limmat four centuries later. Louis the German, grandson of Charlemagne, then founded an abbey here, making his daughter the first abbess; it was built on the site of what is now the Fraumünster, near the Bahnhofstrasse.

By the 12th century, Zürich had already shown a knack for commerce, with its diligent merchants making fortunes in silk, wool, linen, and leather. By 1336 this merchant class had become too powerful for an up-and-coming band of tradesmen and laborers who, allied with a charismatic aristocrat named Rudolf Brun, overthrew the merchants' town council and established Zürich's famous guilds. Those 13 original guilds never really lost their power until the French Revolution—and have yet to lose their prestige: Every year prominent Zürich businessmen dress up in medieval costumes for the guilds' traditional march through the streets, heading for the magnificent guildhalls that still dominate the old town.

If the guilds defined Zürich's commerce, it was the Reformation that defined its soul. From his pulpit in the Grossmünster, Zwingli galvanized the region, and he ingrained in the Zürichers their devotion to thrift and hard work—so successfully that it ultimately has led them into temptation: the temptations of global influence and tremendous wealth. The Zürich stock exchange, fourth in the world, after those of New York, London, and Tokyo, turns over 636 billion Swiss francs a year. The city's extraordinary museums and galleries, and the luxuries available in shops along the Bahnhofstrasse, Zürich's Fifth Avenue, attest to the city's position as Switzerland's spiritual, if not political, capital.

Pleasures and Pastimes

Dining

On German menus, the cuisine is called *nach Zürcher Art,* meaning cooked in the style of Zürich. What that means to Germans and to the rest of the world as well is meat, mushrooms, potatoes, butter, cream—and heartburn. Zürich's cuisine is one of the richest in the world, perfectly suited to the lead-glass and burnished-oak guild houses—ancient business organizations—that serve these dishes in their natural element. The signature dish, and one you'll encounter throughout both French and German Switzerland, is *geschnetzeltes Kalbfleisch* or, in French, *émincé de veau:* bite-size slices of milky veal (and sometimes veal kidneys) sautéed in butter and swimming in a rich, brown sauce thick with cream, white wine, shallots, and mushrooms. Its closest cousin is *geschnetzeltes Kalbsleber* (calves' liver) in similar form. Both are served at the table from broad copper chafing dishes with hot, fresh plates standing by to be filled when you've cleaned the first one. The inevitable accompaniment is *Rösti* (hash brown potatoes), in portions of equal scale—often the full 8-inch-diameter patty is served for one. An even more masculine tradition is the *Zouftschrübertopf* (sometimes known as the city councillor's platter), a straightforward spread of grilled meats: veal, calves' liver, beef, sweetbreads, kidneys, and thick smoked bacon.

The flip side of Zürich's penchant for rich meats and heavy sauces is its sweet tooth: Prestigious cafés draw crowds for afternoon pastries, and chocolate shops vie for the unofficial honor of making—and selling, by the thousands—the best chocolate truffles in town.

Museums

The wealth of Zurich bankers and industrialists gave rise to private art collections that are now part of the public art scene. Among the best is the Kunsthaus, with one of the world's best collections of Swiss art; the Rietberg Museum is famous for its East Asian collections. Many local museums are devoted to design, since Zurich was one of the centers of the graphic design industry as it grew earlier in the 20th century.

EXPLORING ZÜRICH

At the northern tip of the Zürichsee, where the Limmat River starts its brief journey to the Aare and, ultimately, to the Rhine, Zürich is neatly bisected by the river, which is crisscrossed with lovely low bridges. On the left bank are the Hauptbahnhof and the Bahnhofplatz, a major urban crossroads and the source of the world-famous luxury shopping street, Bahnhofstrasse. The right bank constitutes the younger, livelier old town, also known as Niederdorf.

Scattered throughout the town are 13 medieval guildhalls, or *Zunfthausen,* that once formed the backbone of Zürich's commercial society. Today most of these house atmospheric restaurants where high ceilings, lead-glass windows, and coats of arms evoke the mood of the merchants at their trade.

Great Itineraries

IF YOU HAVE 1 DAY

Start with a walking tour of the small but luxuriously gentrified old town, including time for window-shopping along the Bahnhofstrasse. Catch a temporary exhibition of Swiss art at the Kunsthaus; admire the Asian art and beautiful grounds at the Rietberg; learn about Swiss history and culture at the Swiss National Museum; or if weather permits, stroll along the scenic Limmat and watch the boats. Then cross over to the younger, livelier Niederdorf to see the Grossmünster, the Rathaus City Hall, and—farther up the hill—the Kunsthaus (Art Museum).

IF YOU HAVE 3 DAYS

After exploring the city itself, take a boat trip on Lake Zürich, followed by a trip to the outstanding Zürich Zoo. Consider a day-long side trip to well-preserved medieval Rapperswil, in the neighboring region of Eastern Switzerland (☞ Chapter 3).

IF YOU HAVE 5 DAYS

For a taste of backcountry Switzerland, drive north through the scenic countryside up to Schaffhausen (☞ Chapter 3), passing the Rhine Falls and a slew of wood-shingle farmhouses. If art is more your calling, visit the "Am Römerholz" Oskar Reinhart art collection in the nearby reputed art town of Winterthur (☞ Off the Beaten Path, *below*).

Bahnhofstrasse and the Old Town

Zürich's old town is home to several of Zürich's most important landmarks—the Lindenhof, Peterskirche, the Fraumünster, and the Stadthaus—as well as its luxury shopping street, the world-famous Bahnhofstrasse.

A Good Walk

Numbers in the text correspond to numbers in the margin and on the Zürich exploring map.

Begin at the **Hauptbahnhof** ① (Main Railway Station), a massive 19th-century edifice that was recently renovated. Directly behind the Hauptbahnhof is the **Schweizerisches Landesmuseum** ② (Swiss National Museum), housed in an enormous 19th-century neo-Gothic mansion; behind that, in turn, is the **Museum für Gestaltung** ③ with its impressive collection of 20th-century graphic arts. If you look across the Bahnhofplatz, you'll see traffic careening around a statue of **Alfred Escher,** the man who brought Zürich into the modern age.

Don't attempt to cross the square; instead take the escalators down to a convenient underpass and emerge on the **Bahnhofstrasse,** Zürich's principal business and shopping boulevard. A quarter of the way up the street—about five blocks—veer left into the Rennweg and left again on Fortunagasse, an atmospheric medieval street well removed from the contemporary elegance of the Bahnhofstrasse. Climb up to the **Lindenhof** ④, a quiet square that contains the remains of the city's original Roman customs house and fortress. From here a maze of medieval alleys leads off to your right. Nestled among them, in one of the loveliest medieval squares in Switzerland, is the **Peterskirche** ⑤, whose 13th-century tower has the largest clock face in Europe.

From Peterskirche bear right on Schlüsselgasse and duck into a narrow alley, Thermengasse, which leads left; you'll walk directly over recently excavated ruins of **Roman baths,** visible through gratings and accompanied by explanatory placards on the dig itself. You'll arrive at **Weinplatz,** which is lined with good shops and opens toward the riverbank. Turn right on Storchengasse, where some of the most elite boutiques are concentrated, and head toward the delicate spires of the **Fraumünster** ⑥, whose stained-glass windows are the work of Marc Chagall.

In the same square, you'll see two of Zürich's finest guildhalls. The **Zunfthaus zur Waag** ⑦, which dates from 1637, was the meeting place of the linen weavers and hat makers. The baroque **Zunfthaus zur Meisen** ⑧, erected for the city's wine merchants in the 18th century, houses the Landesmuseum's exquisite ceramics collection.

Wind left up Waaggasse past the Hotel Savoy to the **Paradeplatz** ⑨, the hub of Bahnhofstrasse and a major tram crossroads. Continue south on Bahnhofstrasse, which, as it nears the lake, opens onto a vista of bright-colored boats, wide waters, and distant peaks. At the Bürkliplatz, look to your right: Those manicured parks are the front lawn of the **Hotel Baur au Lac,** the hoary old aristocrat of Swiss hotels. Beyond, you'll see the modern structure of the **Kongresshaus** and the **Tonhalle,** where the Zürich Tonhalle orchestra holds forth.

Turn left and cross the **Quai Brücke** (Bridge), for one of the finest views in town: On one side, you'll see the wide sweep of the lake; on the other, the medieval town. At night, the image can be memorable: The floodlit spires reflect in the inky river, whose surface is disturbed only by drifting, sleeping swans.

TIMING
Zürich's old town is surprisingly compact; half a day is enough time for a cursory visit. The streets flood with businesspeople early and late, and lunch hour can be busy, but never exceedingly so. Afternoons during summer and the Christmas season bring crowds of sightseers and shoppers to Bahnhofstrasse all day long. If you're planning on museumhopping, the Kunsthaus, Landesmuseum, and Rietberg merit at least one or two hours apiece.

Sights to See

Alfred Escher. Leave it to Zürich to have a statue that honors, not a saint, not a poet or artist, but rather the financial wizard who single-handedly dragged Zürich into the modern age during the mid-19th-century. Escher established the city as a major banking center, championed the development of the federal railways and the city's university, and pushed through the construction of the tunnel under the St. Gotthard Pass. Today his statue stands proudly in the middle of the Bahnhofplatz.

Bahnhofstrasse. Zürich's principal boulevard, this famous street boasts luxury shopping that grows more and more extravagant and, proportionately, more and more discreet as the street heads south toward the lake. It's discreet not only in matters of consumerism: Though you won't see particular evidence of it, much of the banking business takes place along this street, behind upstairs windows where the only clue to the activities within is a digital trail of market statistics.

Below the Bahnhofstrasse, vaults under your feet house one of the world's great treasure troves: Zürich is a leading international precious-metals market, rivaled only by London, and much of the gold and silver lies heaped under this, its most glamorous boulevard.

★ ❻ **Fraumünster.** Of the church spires that are Zürich's signature, the Fraumünster's is the most delicate, a feminine sweep to a narrow spire; it was added to the Gothic structure in 1732. (The remains of Louis the German's original 9th-century abbey are below.) Its Romanesque, or pre-Gothic, choir has stained-glass windows by the Russian-born Marc Chagall, who loved Zürich; the Swiss sculptor Augusto Giacometti's father executed the fine painted window in the north transept. ⊠ *Stadthausquai.* ⊘ *Daily 9–noon and 2–6.*

OFF THE BEATEN PATH

MUSEUM RIETBERG – Here a wonderful gathering of art from India, China, Africa, Japan, and Southeast Asia is displayed in the neoclassic Villa Wesendonck, where Richard Wagner once lived (as in *Wesendonck Songs*). From the city center, follow Seestrasse about 1 mile until you see signs for the museum; or take the Kunsthaus–Rietberg Museum bus, which connects the two museums and stops at Bürkliplatz. ⊠ *Gablerstrasse 15,* ☎ *01/202-45-28.* ☞ *5 SF.* ⊘ *Tues. and Thurs.–Sun. 10–5.*

❶ **Hauptbahnhof** (Main Railway Station). Buzzing with activity from morning till night, this immaculate 19th-century edifice arguably could be the heart of Switzerland's obsession with order, cleanliness, and punctuality. Beneath it lies a better shopping mall than you'd find above ground in most cities, with everything from grocery stores to clothing and shoe boutiques, bookshops, and craft stores. When the Bahnhof first opened a century ago, one awestruck witness reported: "An admiring crowd wandered through the huge halls and brightly lit waiting rooms, with their heavily upholstered seats, mirrors, bouquets, and splashing fountains, and marveled not least at the luxury of the buffets and the noble appearance of the toilets." It doesn't quite match that description today, but the post-renovation Bahnhof still serves as a most welcome entry port.

❹ **Lindenhof.** On this quiet square, overlooking the old town on both sides of the river, are the remains of the original Roman customs house and fortress, and the imperial medieval residence. There's also a fountain here, put up in 1912, commemorating the day in 1292 when Zürich's women saved the city from the Hapsburgs. As the story goes, the town was on the brink of defeat as the imperial Hapsburg aggressors moved in. Determined to avoid this humiliation, the town's women donned armor and marched to the Lindenhof. On seeing them, the enemy thought they were faced with another army and promptly beat a strategic retreat. Today, the scene could hardly be less martial, as young mothers sit with their babies in the sun and locals play chess on a giant board.

❸ **Museum für Gestaltung.** Zürich's Museum of Design specializes in 20th-century graphic arts, including typography and poster and advertising design. ⊠ *Ausstellungstrasse 60, CH-8031,* ☎ *01/446–22–11.* ☞ *5 SF.* ⊘ *Tues., Thurs., and Fri. 10–6; Wed. 10–9; weekends 10–5.*

❾ **Paradeplatz.** The hub of the Bahnhofstrasse and a major tram crossroads, this square is ideal for people-watching. Always full of shoppers, it's one of the few spots in Zürich that doesn't hum with financial activity—even though the Union Bank of Switzerland and many other financial institutions are headquartered close by.

NEED A BREAK?

Fortify yourself at **Sprüngli** (⊠ Paradeplatz, ☎ 01/221-17-22), a landmark chocolatier and café for the rich Bahnhofstrasse habitués. If you need more than sweets, there's a short menu of good, plain, hot lunches and salads.

18

Zürich

0 — 200 yards
0 — 200 meters

Lagerstrasse

Militärstrasse

Gessner-Allee

Gessner Br.

Löwen-pl.

Zeughausstrasse

Rotwandstrasse

Müllerstr.

Bäckerstr.

Stauffacherstr.

Kasernenstrasse

Militär Br.

Gessner- Allee

Schanzengraben

Löwenstrasse

Uraniastrasse

Sihlstrasse

Seiden g.

Sihl

Sihl-Br.

Werdstr.

Stauffacher-Quai

Sihlstrasse

St. Annag.

Nüschelerstrasse

Talacker

Weberstr.

Stauff-Br.

Selnaustrasse

Selnau-Br.

Pelikanstrasse

Talstrasse

Bärengasse

Bärengasse

Flössergasse

Brandschenkestr.

Todistrasse

Am Schanzengraben

Bären Br.

Sihlhölzli-Br.

Freigutstrasse

Gartenstrasse

Bleicherweg

Claridenstr.

N

Tunnelstrasse

Stockerstrasse

Beethovenstrasse

Dreikönigstrasse

Gotthardstrasse

KEY

🛈 Tourist Information

Tram Line

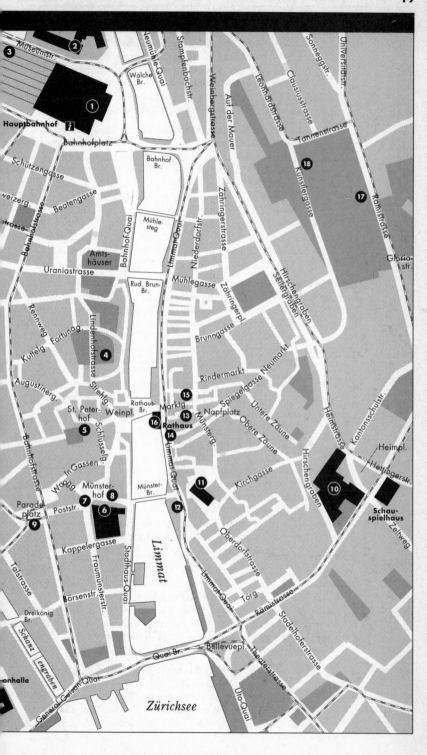

Museumstr. ②
③
Walche Br.
Neumühle-Quai
Stampfenbachstr.
Weinbergstrasse
Auf der Mauer
Sonneggstr.
Universitätsstr.
Clausiusstrasse
Teichhardtstrasse

① Hauptbahnhof 🛈
Bahnhofplatz

Schützengasse
Beatengasse
weizerg.
strasse

Bahnhof Br.
Bahnhof-Quai
Mühle-steg

Zähringerstrasse
Kunstlergasse
Tannenstrasse
⑱
⑰
Rämistrasse
Gloria-str.

Amts-häuser
Uraniastrasse
Rud. Brun-Br.
Mühlegasse
Niederdorfstrasse
Zähringerpl.
Mühlegasse
Hirschengraben
Seilergraben

Rennweg
Fortunag.
Lindenhofstrasse
Brunngasse
Brunngasse

Kuttelg.
Strehlg.
④
Rindermarkt
Spiegelgasse
Neumarkt
Untere Zäune
Obere Zäune

Augustinerg.
St. Peter-hof
Weinpl.
Rathaus-Br.
⑮
Marktg.
⑬
Napfplatz
Münsterg.

Bahnhofstrasse
⑤
Schlüsselg.
⑯ **Rathaus**
⑭
Heimlistrasse
Kantonsschulstr.

In Gassen
Limmat-Quai
Kirchgasse
⑩
Heimpl.
Hettingerstr.

Wogg.
Münster-hof
⑦ ⑧
Münster-Br.
⑪
Schau-spielhaus
Zeltweg

Parade-platz
⑨
Poststr.
⑥
⑫
Oberdorfstrasse

Kappelergasse
Stadthaus-Quai
Limmat
Kirchgasse

Talstrasse
Fraumünsterstr.
Börsenstr.
Limmat-Quai
Torg.
Rämistrasse
Stadelhoferstrasse
Theaterstrasse

Dreikönig Br.
Schanz
engraben
onhalle
General-Guisan-Quai
Quai Br.
Bellevuepl.
Uto-Quai

Zürichsee

★ ❺ **Peterskirche.** Zürich's oldest parish church, the Peterskirche is further distinguished by its 13th-century tower, whose clock face is the largest in Europe. Though the present building dates only from the early 13th century, there's been a church on this site since the 9th century. The existing building has, however, been considerably expanded over the years. The tower, for example, was extended in 1534, when the clock was added; the nave was rebuilt in 1705. Plays are often performed on the steps during the summer. ✉ *St. Peterhofstatt.* ⊙ *Daily 9–noon and 2–6.*

★ ❷ **Schweizerisches Landesmuseum** (Swiss National Museum). Housed in a gargantuan neo-Gothic building opened in 1889, the Landesmuseum possesses an enormous collection of objects dating from the Stone Age to modern times. In addition, the museum contains costumes, furniture, early watches, and a great deal of military history, including thousands of toy soldiers reenacting battle scenes. In the hall of arms there's a splendid mural, painted by the late-19th-century Bernese artist Ferdinand Hodler, *Retreat of the Swiss Confederates at Marignano*—depicting a defeat in 1515 by the French that set Zürich back considerably after generations of prosperity. ✉ *Museumstrasse 2,* ☎ *01/218–65–65.* 🎫 *Free.* ⊙ *Tues.–Sun. 10–5.*

❽ **Zunfthaus zur Meisen.** This aristocratic edifice, erected for the city's wine merchants in the 18th century, today houses the Landesmuseum's exquisite ceramics collection; the selection of 18th-century porcelain is particularly strong and includes works by Zürich and Nyon makers. Enter on the Fraumünster side. ✉ *Münsterhof 20,* ☎ *01/211– 21–44.* 🎫 *Free.* ⊙ *Tues.–Fri. and Sun. 10–noon and 2–5, Sat. 10– noon and 2–4.*

❼ **Zunfthaus zur Waag.** This circa-1637 guildhall was the meeting place for linen weavers and hat makers. Today it houses an elegant restaurant whose beautiful facade is adorned with Christmas decorations in season. ✉ *Münsterhof 8.*

The Niederdorf and the Kunsthaus

As soon as you step off the Quai Bridge on the east bank of the Limmat, you'll notice a difference: The atmosphere is livelier and more casual. The area is also the center of Zürich's nightlife—both upscale and down, with the city's opera house and its historic theater. Other major attractions here are the Kunsthaus, with its fine collection of art; and two architectural icons: the Grossmünster and the Town Hall.

A Good Walk

Start at Rämistrasse and walk to Heimplatz, where you'll find the **Schauspielhaus** (Theater), built in 1884. Across Heimplatz, you'll find the **Kunsthaus** ⑩, with a varied and high-quality permanent collection of medieval, Impressionist, and Swiss paintings. Return to Bellevueplatz and follow Limmatquai downstream to the gaunt, imposing **Grossmünster** ⑪, whose plump twin towers (1781) are one of Zürich's most distinctive sights.

Head back down the steps to the banks of the Limmat, where you'll find the 18th-century **Helmhaus** ⑫, the open court of which once served as a linen market. Now an art museum, the Helmhaus is attached to the late-15th-century **Wasserkirche** ⑫ (Water Church), one of Switzerland's most delicate late-Gothic structures, with stained glass by Giacometti.

Along the Limmatquai, a series of guildhalls today house popular and atmospheric restaurants. At No. 42, the 13th-century **Gesellschaftshaus zum Rüden** ⑬ was the noblemen's hall. No. 40 is **Zunfthaus zur Zim-**

merleuten ⑭; built in 1708, it originally served as the carpenters' guild. No. 54 is **Zunfthaus zur Saffran** ⑮, dating in various forms from as early as 1389, when it was a meeting point for haberdashers.

Across the Limmatquai from the Zunfthaus zur Saffran, the striking Baroque **Rathaus** ⑯ (Town Hall) seems to rise up from the river. From here, head back across the Limmatquai and up into the old-town streets, which meander past tiny houses, galleries, antiques shops, and new-wave (or post-punk) boutiques. Follow Marktgasse to **Rindermarkt,** site of the historic home of the Swiss poet and novelist Gottfried Keller, as well as the restaurant where he used to eat. The Rindermarkt joins the picturesque Neumarkt and Spiegelgasse streets at a tiny medieval square where you'll see a fine early Gothic tower, the Grimmenturm. There's another Gothic tower farther down Siegelgasse at Napfplatz, used during the 14th century by Zürich bankers.

From Napfplatz, take Obere Zäune up to **Kirchgasse,** a broad medieval thoroughfare packed with antiques shops, galleries, and bookstores. No. 13 was Zwingli's last home before he was killed in battle (1531) while defending the Reformation. From here you can either return to the Grossmünster or venture north to see the **Graphische Sammlung** ⑰, with its woodcuts, etchings, and engravings; or the more naturalistic wonders of the **Zoologisches Museum** ⑱.

If you want to explore the **Niederdorf** neighborhood, head north again along Münstergasse to Marktgasse and walk parallel to the river, where the entertainment has a less Calvinistic bent. Marktgasse quickly becomes Niederdorfstrasse. The latter eventually empties onto the Central tram intersection, opposite the Hauptbahnhof; from there it's easy to catch a tram down the Bahnhofstrasse or up the Limmatquai.

TIMING

Exploring the Niederdorf won't take more than a half day, and pedestrian traffic is sparse in comparison with Bahnhofstrasse. Again, leave yourself extra time if you'd like to window shop or invest up to an hour in each of the interesting museums and galleries.

Sights to See

★ ⑪ **Grossmünster.** Literally translated as "large church," this impressive cathedral is distinguished by plump twin towers (circa 1781) whose classical caricatures of Gothic forms are almost comical. The core of the structure was built during the 12th century on the site of a Carolingian church dedicated to the memory of martyrs Felix and Regula, who allegedly carried their severed heads to the spot. Charlemagne supposedly founded the church after his horse stumbled over their burial site. (On the side of the south tower, an enormous stone Charlemagne sits enthroned; the original statue, carved during the late 15th century, is protected in the crypt.) In keeping with what Zwingli preached from its pulpits during the 16th century, the interior is spare, even forbidding, with all luxurious ornamentation long since stripped away. The only artistic touches are modern: stained-glass windows by Augusto Giacometti, and ornate bronze doors, in the north and south portals, dating from the late 1940s. ✉ *Zwingliplatz,* ☎ *01/252–61–44.* ⏱ *Apr.–Sept., daily 9–6; Oct.–Mar., daily 1–4.*

⑬ **Gesellschaftshaus zum Rüden.** Now housing one of Zürich's finest restaurants, (☞ Dining, *below*), this 13th-century structure was the noblemen's guildhall. Peek inside at the barrel-vaulted ceiling and 30-foot beams; or better yet, stay for a meal.

⑰ **Graphische Sammlung.** The impressive collection of the Federal Institute of Technology includes a vast library of woodcuts, etchings, and engravings by European masters such as Dürer, Rembrandt, Goya, Picasso. Take tram no. 8 from the city center. ✉ *Rämistrasse 101*, ☎ *01/632–40–46.* 🎫 *Free.* ⊘ *Mon., Tues., Thurs., and Fri. 10–5; Wed. 10–8.*

🔟 **Helmhaus.** The open court of this museum once served as a linen market. Inside, there are changing exhibitions of contemporary art, as well as a bookstore specializing in art, design, and photography. Don't miss the neighboring ☞ **Wasserkirche.** ✉ *Limmatquai 31*, ☎ *01/251–61–77.* 🎫 *Free.* ⊘ *Tues., Wed., and Fri.–Sun. 10–6; Thurs. 10–9.*

★ 🔟 **Kunsthaus.** With a varied and high-quality permanent collection of paintings—medieval, Dutch and Italian Baroque, and Impressionist, the Kunsthaus is Zürich's best art museum. The impressive Swiss collection includes nearly 100 works by Hodler, as well as pieces by Füssli, Böcklin, and Zürich masters from the 15th century to the present. There also are representative works from the origins of Dadaism, conceived in Zürich by French exile Hans Arp, who in the 1920s proclaimed the new movement one that could "heal mankind from the madness of the age." ✉ *Heimplatz 1*, ☎ *01/251–67–55.* 🎫 *Admission varies with exhibition.* ⊘ *Tues.–Thurs. 10–9, weekends 10–5.*

<table>
<tr><td>OFF THE
BEATEN PATH</td><td>**STIFTUNG SUMMLUNG E. G. BÜHRLE** – One of Switzerland's best private collections is owned by the E.G. Bührle Foundation. Though it's known especially for its Impressionist and post-Impressionist paintings and sculptures, the collection also includes religious sculpture as well as Spanish and Italian paintings from the 16th to 18th centuries. ✉ *Zollikerstrasse 172*, ☎ *01/422–00–86.* 🎫 *6.60 SF.* ⊘ *Tues. and Fri. 2–5, Wed. 5–8.*</td></tr>
</table>

Niederdorf. This is Zürich's nightlife district, with cut-rate hotels, strip joints, and bars crowding along Marktgasse (which becomes Niederdorfstrasse). Each of the narrow streets and alleys that shoot down to the left offers its own brand of entertainment, but even the most wholesome stroller can feel comfortable walking in the district. The bars close early here: Zwingli hasn't lost his hold altogether.

★ 🔟 **Rathaus.** Zürich's striking Baroque Town Hall dates from 1694–98, and its interior remains as well preserved as its facade: There's a richly decorated stucco ceiling in the Banquet Hall and a fine ceramic stove in the government council room. Though it's not usually open to the public, you may attend the meetings of the cantonal and city parliaments on Monday morning and Wednesday afternoon, respectively. ✉ *Limmatquai 55.*

Rindermarkt. Fans of Gottfried Keller, commonly considered Switzerland's national poet and novelist, will want to visit this street. The 19th-century writer's former home, at No. 9, became famous in his novel *Der Grüne Heinrich* (*Green Henry*). Opposite is the restaurant, **Zur Oepfelchammer,** where Gottfried used to eat.

<table>
<tr><td>NEED A
BREAK?</td><td>Set back from the street in its own tiny courtyard is **Cafe Schober,** a Victorian sweetshop with homemade hot chocolate and cakes. ✉ *Napfgasse 4*, ☎ *01/251-80-60.*</td></tr>
</table>

Schauspielhaus. During World War II this was the only German-language theater in Europe that wasn't muzzled by the Berlin regime, and it attracted some of the Continent's bravest and best artists. It's been dishing out entertainment ever since it was built in 1884; today its productions aren't always so risky, but they are stunningly mounted and performed, of course, in German. ✉ *Rämistrasse 34*, ☎ *01/265-58-58.*

Wasserkirche. One of Switzerland's most delicate late-Gothic structures, this church has stained glass by Giacometti. Both the church and the

☞ **Helmhaus** once stood on the island on which Felix and Regula supposedly lost their heads. ⊠ *Limmatquai 31.* ⊙ *Apr.–Sept., daily 9–6; Oct.–Mar., daily 1–4.*

🖐 ⑱ **Zoologisches Museum.** Engaging and high tech, the Zoologisches Museum gives an even closer look in its accessible displays on Swiss insects, birds, and amphibians. You can examine butterflies and living water creatures through microscopes, and listen to birdcalls as you compare avian markings. ⊠ *Künstlergasse 16,* ☎ *01/257–38–38.* ▨ *Free.* ⊙ *Tues.–Fri. 9–5, weekends 10–4.*

⑮ **Zunfthaus zur Saffran.** This guildhall for haberdashers dates in various forms from as early as 1389. It is now a highly acclaimed restaurant, with beautiful old rooms and a facade facing the river. ⊠ *Limmatquai 54.*

⑭ **Zunfthaus zur Zimmerleuten.** Dating from 1708, this was the carpenters' guild. ⊠ *Limmatquai 40.*

OFF THE BEATEN PATH

ZÜRICH ZOO – This is one of Europe's outstanding zoos, with more than 1,500 animals and some 250 species, including Asian elephants, black rhinos, seals, and big cats. The naturalistic habitats must keep them happy: The Zürich Zoo enjoys an international reputation for successfully breeding wild animals. Set in a tree-filled park, it's a little out of the center of the city but easily reached by trams 5 and 6. ⊠ *Zürichbergstrasse 221,* ☎ *01/252–71–00.* ▨ *12 SF.* ⊙ *Mar.–Oct., daily 8–6; Nov.–Feb., daily 8–5.*

OSKAR REINHART COLLECTION "AM RÖMERHOLZ" – The textile town of Winterthur boasts a wealth of fine art donated to the city by prosperous local merchants. One such denizen was Oskar Reinhart, whose splendid home now contains a huge, high-quality collection of paintings from five centuries, including works by Rembrandt, Manet, Renoir and Cézanne. Winterthur is a half hour from Zürich by train, on the main rail route to St. Gallen. Fast trains leave daily from the Hauptbahnhof, about every half hour. By car, follow the Autobahn signs for Winterhur–St. Gallen. ⊠ *Stadthausstrasse 6, CH-8400,* ☎ *052/84-51-72.* ⊙ *Tues.–Sun. 10-5.*

DINING

The price categories listed below are slightly higher than those applied in other regional chapters, except in Geneva, which shares Zürich's inflated cost of living. Though there's a shortage of suggestions in the least expensive category, you can always choose soup for a first course, which costs about 8 SF, and save by skipping dessert. It's important to note that daily fixed-price menus are considerably cheaper, and even the flossiest places have business-lunch menus at noon—your best bet for sampling Zürich's highest cuisine at cut rates. For tight-budget travel, watch posted daily *Tagesteller* listings: Cheap daily plates, with meat, potatoes, and possibly a hot vegetable, can still be found in the Niederdorf for under 15 SF; sometimes you even get soup to boot.

CATEGORY	COST*
$$$$	over 90 SF
$$$	50 SF–90 SF
$$	30 SF–50 SF
$	under 30 SF

per person for a three-course meal (except in $ category), including sales tax and 15% service charge

$$$$ ✕ **Baur au Lac Grill Room.** Expected to reopen late in fall '96, this is
★ a traditional clubhouse-style institution popular among businesspeople, who are drawn to its Gothic woodwork, leather, stone fireplace,
and American high-stool bar. Despite a handful of token grilled meats,
the name is a bit of a figure of speech: The menu (shared with the more
formal and discreet Restaurant Français) features conservative but refined French cooking: breast of duck with glazed pearl onions, or
émincé of turbot with mushrooms and green beans. Diners can also
enjoy the same fare in the adjoining Pavillon Restaurant, a glassed-in
conservatory with views of the canal. ⊠ *Hotel Baur au Lac, Talstrasse
1,* ☎ *01/220–50–20. Reservations essential. AE, DC, MC, V.*

$$$$ ✕ **La Rotonde.** Even when not illuminated by candlelight, the Dolder
★ Grand's haute cuisine restaurant is one of Zürich's most romantic
spots. Housed in a great arc of a room, La Rotonde provides sweeping
park views that lure even the business crowd at lunchtime, even though
the hotel is well out of the way of the business district. The atmosphere
is formal, the staff attentive to a fault, the culinary style traditional French
with a fashionably light touch—sweetbreads on a bed of gnocchi with
asparagus and truffles, for instance, or grilled salmon with finely diced
lobster, scallops, and shrimp in a hazelnut oil sauce. The 75 SF prix-
fixe dinner is a particularly good value. Those who love hors d'oeuvres
will enjoy the Sunday afternoon buffet, which consists of nothing but
starters. ⊠ *Kurhausstrasse 65,* ☎ *01/251–62–31. AE, DC, MC, V.*

$$$$ ✕ **Petermann's Kunststuben.** This is one of Switzerland's gastronomic
★ meccas, and while it's south of the center, in Küssnacht on the lake's
eastern shore, it's more than worth the investment of time and effort.
Chef Horst Petermann, a German from Hamburg, never rests on his
laurels: The ever-evolving menu may include lobster with artichoke and
almond oil; grilled turbot with lemon sauce and capers; or Tuscan dove
with pine nuts and herbs. There are great wines available by the glass,
and a pleasant little garden. ⊠ *Seestrasse 160, Küsnacht,* ☎ *01/910–
07–15. Reservations essential. AE, DC, MC, V. Closed Sun. and Mon.*

$$$$ ✕ **Piccoli Accademia.** Upscale, urban, and patrician, this is one of the
best Italian restaurants in Switzerland, offering classic homemade filled
pastas (ravioli, *agnolotti*), several veal dishes, and a distinctly local range
of calves' liver and kidneys. The menu is vast, and the wine list includes
a broad range of great Italian choices. ⊠ *Rotwandstrasse 48,* ☎ *01/241–
62–43. Reservations essential. AE, DC, MC, V. Closed weekends.*

$$$$ ✕ **Tübli.** Tucked on a back alley in the colorful Niederdorf neighborhood, this intimate little Züricher secret continues to draw insiders for
some of the best—and most innovative—cuisine in the city center. Es-
chewing à la carte standbys for ever-changing, weekly seven-course
menus, chef Martin Surbeck experiments with almost indiscriminate
pleasure with literally far-fetched ingredients: Portuguese chocolate for
his fish carpaccio, Norwegian reindeer with mulberry flower mousse-
line, or passion-fruit soufflé. An Italian wine list adds to the multicul-
tural air. ⊠ *Schneggengasse 8,* ☎ *01/251–24–71. AE, DC, MC, V.
Closed weekends.*

$$$ ✕ **Blaue Ente.** Part of a chic shopping gallery in a converted mill south
★ of the center, this modern bar-restaurant draws well-dressed crowds
from the advertising and arts scene. In a setting of white-washed brick
and glass, with jazz filtering through from the adjoining bar, guests sam-
ple a pot-au-feu of clams, prawns, and saffron, or lamb with eggplant
and potato pancakes. Take the No. 2 tram toward Tiefenbrunnen. ⊠
Seefeldstrasse 222, ☎ *01/422–77–06. AE, DC, MC, V.*

$$$ ✕ **Haus zum Rüden.** The most culinarily ambitious of Zürich's many
Zunfthaus dining places, this fine restaurant—dating in part from
1295—is also the most architecturally spectacular, combining river views
with a barrel-vaulted ceiling and 30-foot beams. Slick modern im-

provements—including a glassed-in elevator—manage to blend intelligently with the ancient decor, and by combining the upgraded ambience with chic graphics, damask, and sophisticated cuisine, its management keeps it a cut above its staid competitors. Specialties include pigeon in cornmeal with Pinot sauce, and snapper in a "potato coat." ⊠ *Limmatquai 42,* ☎ *01/261–95–66. AE, DC, MC, V.*

$$$ ✕ **Hummer-und Austernbar.** In a fin de siècle setting of polished wood, candles, and rich scarlet, you can have your fill of impeccably fresh lobsters and oysters (*Hummer* means lobster; *Austern,* oysters), or sample Brittany lobsters poached in champagne sauce and St. Pierre (a large, cold-water sea fish known in England as John Dory) flambéed with fennel. In August, the city's expatriate Swedes flock here for crayfish, a late-summer Nordic favorite. There's depth to the wine list, but champagne seems to be the beverage of choice with Zürichers, who come here in hordes. ⊠ *Hotel St. Gotthard, Bahnhofstrasse 87,* ☎ *01/ 211–83–15. AE, DC, MC, V.*

$$$ ✕ **Kronenhalle.** From Stravinsky, Brecht, and Joyce to Nureyev, Deneuve,
★ and St-Laurent, this beloved landmark has always drawn a stellar crowd. The atmosphere is genial, the cooking hearty, and the collection of 20th-century art astonishing. Every panel of gleaming wood wainscoting frames works of Picasso, Braque, Miró, or Matisse, collected by patroness-hostess Hulda Zumsteg, who owned the restaurant from 1921 until her death in 1985. Her son, Gustav, carries on the tradition, serving robust cooking in hefty portions: herring in double cream, tournedos with truffle sauce, duck *à l'orange* with red cabbage and spaetzle. Despite linens and chafing-dish service, there's no shame in ordering the sausage and Rösti just to take in the animated scene. And be sure to have a cocktail in the small adjoining bar: *Le tout* Zürich drinks here. ⊠ *Rämistrasse 4,* ☎ *01/251–66–69. AE, DC, MC, V.*

$$$ ✕ **Veltliner Keller.** Though its rich, carved-wood decor borrows from Graubündner Alpine culture, this ancient dining spot is no tourist-trap transplant: The house, built in 1325 and functioning as a restaurant since 1551, has always stored Italian-Swiss Valtellina wines, which were carried over the Alps and imported to Zürich. There is a *Zunfthaus*-like stress on the heavy and the meaty, but the kitchen is flexible and reasonably deft with more modern favorites as well: grilled salmon, veal steak with Gorgonzola, and dessert mousses. If you're not heading on to Graubünden, try the house version of *schoppa da giuotta,* the traditional barley soup. ⊠ *Schlüsselgasse 8,* ☎ *01/221–32–28. AE, DC, MC, V.*

$$ ✕ **Oepfelchammer.** This was once the haunt of Zürich's beloved writer
★ Gottfried Keller, and, recently restored, it still draws unpretentious literati. One room is a dark and heavily graffitied bar, with sagging timbers and slanting floors; the other is a welcoming little dining room, with a coffered ceiling and plenty of carved oak and pink damask. Traditional meat dishes—calves' liver and veal Geschnetzeltes, tripe in white wine sauce—come in generous portions; salads are fresh and seasonal. The place is always packed, and service can be slow, so stake out a table and plan to spend the evening. ⊠ *Rindermarkt 12,* ☎ *01/251–23– 36. MC, V. Closed Sun.*

$$ ✕ **Zunfthaus zur Schmiden.** Alone, the sense of history and the decor—a magnificent mix of Gothic wood, lead glass, and tile stoves—justify a visit to this popular landmark, the guild house of blacksmiths and barbers since 1412. All the Zürich meat classics are available in enormous portions, and there's a considerable selection of alternatives—fish among them. The guild's own house-label wine is fine. ⊠ *Marktgasse 20,* ☎ *01/251–52–87. AE, DC, MC, V.*

$$ ✕ **Zunfthaus zur Waag.** Another, airier guildhall, its woodwork whitewashed, its Gothic windows looking out to the Fraumünster, this lovely

Dining

Lodging

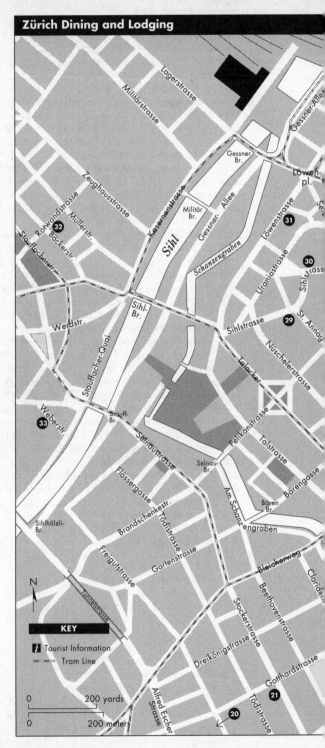

Zürich Dining and Lodging

KEY

ℹ️ Tourist Information

🚋 Tram Line

0   200 yards

0   200 meters

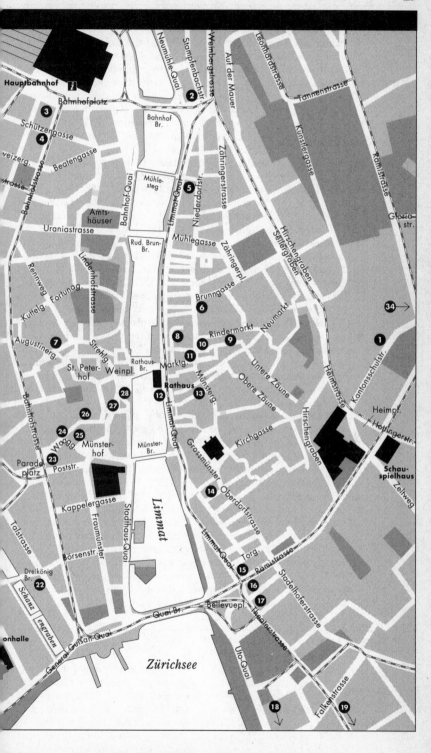

Hauptbahnhof **i**
Bahnhofplatz
Neumühle-Quai
Stampfenbachstr.
Wernbergstrasse
Auf der Mauer
Leonhardstrasse
Tannenstrasse
2
3
Schützengasse
Beatengasse
Bahnhof Br.
Künstlergasse
Rämistrasse
4
sweizerg.
strasse
Mühle-steg
Zähringerstr.
Niederdorfstr.
Zähringerpl.
Hirschengraben
Sefftelgraben
Gloria str.
Bahnhof-Quai
Limmat-Quai
Amts-häuser
Uraniastrasse
Mühlegasse
Rud. Brun-Br.
5
Brunngasse
Rennweg
Lindenhofstrasse
Fortunag.
6
Neumarkt
34
Kuttelg.
8
Rindermarkt
9
1
Augustinerg.
7
Strehlg.
10
Untere Zäune
Kantonsschulstr.
11
St. Peter-hof
Weinpl.
Rathaus-Br.
Marktg.
Münsterg.
Obere Zäune
Heimstrasse
Heimpl.
Hottingerstr.
28
Rathaus
13
Kirchgasse
Bahnhofstrasse
26
12
Hirschengraben
27
24
25
Münster-hof
Münster-Br.
Grossmünster
Schau-spielhaus
Zellweg
Woog.
23
Parade platz
Poststr.
Kappelergasse
Fraumünster
Stadthaus-Quai
Oberdorfstrasse
14
Talstrasse
Börsenstr.
Limmat
Limmat-Quai
Torg.
Rämistrasse
Stadelhoferstrasse
Drekönig Br.
22
Schanz
engraben
Quai Br.
Bellevuepl.
15
16
17
Theaterstrasse
onhalle
General-Guisan-Quai
Uto-Quai
Zürichsee
18
Falkenstrasse
19

dining spot offers generous portions of the local classics, somewhat formally served. ⊠ *Münsterhof 8,* ☏ *01/211–07–30. AE, DC, MC, V.*

$ ✕ **Bierhalle Kropf.** Under the giant boar's head and restored century-
★ old murals, businesspeople, workers, and shoppers crowd shared tables to feast on generous hot dishes and a great selection of sausages. The *Leberknödli* (liver dumplings) are tasty, *Apfelküchli* (fried apple slices) tender and sweet, and the bread chewy and delicious—though you pay for every chunk you eat. The bustle, clatter, and wisecracking waitresses provide a lively, sociable experience: You'll get to know your neighbor here, and most of them are locals. ⊠ *Gassen 16,* ☏ *01/ 221–18–05. AE, DC, MC, V.*

$ ✕ **Hiltl Vegi.** As the German world takes its cholesterol count, more and more vegetarian restaurants are catching on, including this popular old landmark, founded in the late 19th century. The atmosphere these days is all contemporary, with posted color photos of daily specials, which include soups, curries, and variations on ratatouille. ⊠ *Sihlstrasse 28,* ☏ *01/221–38–70. AE, DC, MC, V.*

$ ✕ **Mère Catherine.** This is a popular French-style bistro, with dark and unself-conscious old-style decor and specials listed on the blackboard. You can have onion soup, duck liver terrine, seafood, and a few meat dishes—even *steak de cheval* (horse steak). The clientele is young, bohemian, and sociable. On warm evenings, opt for courtyard seating. ⊠ *Nägelihof 3,* ☏ *01/262–22–50. No credit cards.*

$ ✕ **Odéon.** This historic café-restaurant, as Parisian as this town ever
★ gets, was once frequented by the prerevolutionary Lenin, who nursed a coffee and read the house's daily papers. Now the crowd is just as intense, and a tonic air of countercultural chic mixes with the nonfilter cigarette smoke. You can nurse a coffee, too, or have a plate of pasta, a sandwich, or dessert from the limited menu. ⊠ *Am Bellevue,* ☏ *01/ 251–16–50. AE, DC, MC, V.*

$ ✕ **Rheinfelder Bierhaus.** Dark and smoky, with every wooden table squeezing in mixed parties of workers, bikers, shoppers, and tourists, this solid old institution in the Niederdorf area serves a rich *Rindspfeffer* (preserved beef stew) with homemade Spätzli, sausage standbys, and the chef's pride: an incongruous but freshly homemade paella, served once a month. ⊠ *Marktgasse 19,* ☏ *01/251–29–91. No credit cards.*

$ ✕ **Zeughauskeller.** Built as an arsenal in 1487, this enormous stone-
★ and-beam hall offers hearty meat platters and a variety of beers and wines in comfortable and friendly chaos. Waitresses are harried and brisk, especially at lunchtime, when crowds are thick. Unlike the shabbier beerhalls in Niederdorf, this is clean and bourgeois, and it reflects its Paradeplatz location—but you can roll up your sleeves and dig in. They're not unaccustomed to tourists—menus are posted in English, Japanese, and at least 10 other languages—but locals consider this their home away from home. ⊠ *Bahnhofstrasse 28, at Paradeplatz,* ☏ *01/ 211–26–90. No credit cards.*

LODGING

Spending the night in Zürich is as expensive as eating out, though its options are no more outlandishly priced than those in the prestigious ski resorts. Deluxe hotels—the five-star landmarks—average between 450 SF and 600 SF per night for a double, and you'll be lucky to get a toilet in your room for less than 120 SF. Yet a full (if top-heavy) range of choices is available in the city center, so even if you're flying into Zürich-Kloten on your way to a mountain retreat, don't shy away from a day or two stopover.

CATEGORY	COST*
$$$$	over 430 SF
$$$	300 SF–430 SF
$$	160 SF–300 SF
$	under 160 SF

All prices are for a standard double room, including breakfast, tax, and service charge.

$$$$ 🏨 **Baur au Lac.** This is the hoary, high-browed patrician of Swiss ho-
★ tels, with luxury facilities but none of the glitz associated with flashier
upstarts in prestige resorts. Its broad back is turned to the commercial
center, and its front rooms overlook the lake, the canal, and the manicured lawns of its own private park. The decor is posh, discreet, and
firmly fixed in the Age of Reason. Lakeside corner junior suites (priced
as deluxe doubles) represent a relatively good value. In summer, meals
(including breakfast) are served in the glassed-in pavillon along the canal;
in winter, in the glowing Restaurant Français. The Grill Room is a business tradition. ⊠ *Talstrasse 1, CH-8022,* ☎ *01/221–16–50,* 🖷
*01/211–81–39. 210 beds. Restaurant, bar, café, grill, beauty salon,
dance club. AE, DC, MC, V.*

$$$$ 🏨 **Dolder Grand.** A cross between Camp David and Maria Theresa's
★ summer palace, this sprawling Victorian fantasy-manse sits high on a
hill over Zürich, quickly reached by funicular railway (free for guests)
from Römerhof and offering splendid views. A picturesque hodgepodge
of turrets, cupolas, half-timbers, and mansards, it was opened in 1899
as a summer resort; the uncompromisingly modern wing was added
in 1964, but from inside the connection is seamless. The garden and
forest views from the rear rooms nearly match the beauty of those of
the golf course, the park, and the city itself. Guest rooms, with Em-
pire-cum-Euro-modern decor, are distinguished by their spaciousness
and high ceilings. Restaurant La Rotonde serves excellent traditional
French haute cuisine (☞ Dining, *above*). ⊠ *Kurhausstrasse 65,* ☎ *01/
251–62–31,* 🖷 *01/251–88–29. 300 beds. Restaurant, bar, café, pool,
beauty salon, 9-hole golf course, tennis court, jogging, ice-skating, parking. AE, DC, MC, V.*

$$$$ 🏨 **Savoy Baur en Ville.** The oldest hotel in Zürich, built in 1838, this
★ luxurious downtown landmark was gutted in 1975 and solidly reconstructed as an urban gem. It's directly on the Paradeplatz and thus
at the hub of the banking, shopping, and sightseeing districts. Rooms
have a warm, postmodern decor, with pear-wood cabinetry, brass, and
chintz, and there are two fine restaurants—one French, one Italian—
as well as a city-slick café-bar. ⊠ *Am Paradeplatz, CH-8022,* ☎ *01/
211–53–60,* 🖷 *01/221–14–67. 150 beds. 2 restaurants, café. AE, DC,
MC, V.*

$$$$ 🏨 **Widder.** This is the newest addition to Zürich's pantheon of five-
star hotels, and architecturally the most interesting, as it combines
the ancient and contemporary as only the Swiss can do. Eight adjacent houses dating from the Middle Ages were gutted to create the
Widder; from the outside, the beautifully restored facades are fully
intact, while inside, the design is modern and high tech. The location at the edge of the old town is a plus. The Widder Bar is a popular spot for live jazz. ⊠ *Rennweg 7, CH-8001,* ☎ *01/224–25–26,*
🖷 *01/224–24–24. 49 rooms with bath. 2 restaurants, bar. AE, DC,
MC, V.*

$$$ 🏨 **Central-Plaza.** Despite its landmark-quality exterior—it was built
in 1883—this hotel aims to please a young and often American crowd,
with slick, universally appreciated comforts and a fresh (if hotel-chain-
style) decor: brass, bamboo, palms. The piano bar, champagne bar, and

theme restaurants all appear to have been contrived to appeal to habitués of shopping malls. Its location is ideal, directly on the Central tram crossroads on the Niederdorf side, a two-minute walk from the Bahnhof. ⊠ *Central 1, CH-8001,* ☎ *01/251–55–55,* FAX *01/251– 85–35. 135 beds. 2 restaurants, 2 bars. AE, DC, MC, V.*

$$$ ⊞ **Neues Schloss.** Headed by Bernard Seiler, an heir to the Zermatt
★   hotel dynasty, this small, intimate hotel in the business district, southeast of Paradeplatz, shows its bloodlines, offering a warm welcome, good service, and the inviting decor of a tastefully furnished private home. Its airy, floral restaurant, Le Jardin, is popular at lunch. ⊠ *Stockerstrasse 17, CH-8022,* ☎ *01/201–65–50,* FAX *01/201–64–18. 89 beds. Restaurant. AE, DC, MC, V.*

$$$ ⊞ **Schweizerhof.** This is one of the first landmarks you see when you leave the train station, and traffic surges around it night and day. But the windows are triple glazed, the brass-and-marble decor is soothing and classic, and the staff is welcoming. Although renovations have modernized it a bit, the choices in color and furnishings were already discreet, so you'll be comfortable in old rooms as well as in the refurbished ones. ⊠ *Bahnhofplatz 7, CH-8001,* ☎ *01/211–86–40,* FAX *01/211– 35–05. 150 beds. Restaurant, bar, 2 cafés. AE, DC, MC, V.*

$$$ ⊞ **Splügenschloss.** Constructed at the turn of the century as luxury apartments, this Relais & Châteaux property maintains an ornate and historic decor, with antiques in guest rooms as well as public spaces. Some rooms have been paneled completely in Graubünden-style pine; others are done in fussy florals. The location—in a spare banking district—may be a little out of the way for sightseeing, but if you yearn for atmosphere you'll find this hostelry worth the effort. No-smoking rooms are available. ⊠ *Splügenstrasse 2, CH-8002,* ☎ *01/201–08– 00,* FAX *01/201–42–86. 75 beds. Restaurant, bar. AE, DC, MC, V.*

$$$ ⊞ **Zum Storchen.** The central location of this airy 600-year-old struc-
★   ture—tucked between the Fraumünster and Peterskirche on the gullstudded banks of the Limmat—is stunning, and the hotel is modern and impeccable. It has warmly appointed rooms, some with French windows that open over the water, and a terrace restaurant as well as a cozy, guild-houselike dining room. ⊠ *Weinplatz 2, CH-8001,* ☎ *01/ 211–55–10,* FAX *01/211–64–51. 110 beds. Restaurant, bar, café, snack bar. AE, DC, MC, V.*

$$ ⊞ **City.** Close to the Bahnhofstrasse, the train station, and the Löwenstrasse shopping district, this is a hotel in miniature, with small furnishings and baths and a high proportion of single rooms. The whole place has a chic pastel polish. ⊠ *Löwenstrasse 34, CH-8021,* ☎ *01/ 211–20–55,* FAX *01/212–00–36. 100 beds. AE, DC, MC, V.*

$$ ⊞ **Glockenhof.** This centrally located Best Western property, two blocks from the Bahnhofstrasse, hasn't kept its decor up to the level of other business-class hotels, but ask for one of the few new rooms: They're in fresh pastels. The back rooms overlook a garden court. There's an inexpensive restaurant (Glogge-Egge) on the ground floor, with cheap daily plates, and a terrace café. ⊠ *Sihlstrasse 31, CH-8023,* ☎ *01/211–56– 50,* FAX *01/211–56–60. 170 beds. Restaurant, café. AE, DC, MC, V.*

$$ ⊞ **Rössli.** Young, trendy, and completely high tech, this hip new spot
★   in Oberdorf, near the Grossmünster, offers a refreshing antidote to Zürich's medievalism. Decor is white on white with vivid lithos, splashy fabrics, and metallic-tile baths; hair dryers, robes, and in-room outlets for guests' fax machines keep services above average, especially for the price. For a real treat, ask the director, Frau Traber, for the penthouse, which gives you private access to the roof; she'll even allow you to grill your own steaks overlooking the rooftops. The adjoining bar is very popular with young locals, but it's not uncomfortably noisy. ⊠

Rössligasse 7, ☎ *01/252–21–21,* FAX *01/252–21–31. 23 beds. Breakfast rooms, bar. AE, DC, MC, V.*

$$ 🏨 **Wellenberg.** Though the effort at high style is less effective than at the Rössli, this new hotel makes a definite postmodern retro statement with its burled wood, black lacquer, Deco travel posters, and Hollywood photos. Guest rooms are relatively roomy, if occasionally garish, and the central location—on Niederdorf's Hirschenplatz—is superb. Some rooms are more expensive. ✉ *Niederdorfstrasse 10,* ☎ *01/262–43–00,* FAX *251–31–30. 63 beds. Breakfast room. AE, DC, MC, V.*

$$ 🏨 **Zürichberg.** This newly opened hotel is the Dolder Grand's "stepsister": Both hotels share the same view from atop the prestigious hill that gave its name to both the neighborhood and the hotel. However, where the Dolder is flashy and urbane, the Zürichberg is down-to-earth—especially the room rates. Decor is modern and airy; next door is an annex called the Schneckenhaus ("snail house") where rooms radiate outward from a central, oval-shape atrium. Run by the Zürich Women's Association, the hotel is alcohol-free, but this restriction doesn't prevent the chef from concocting memorable meals in the popular restaurant. Tram 6 heads straight to the hotel from the Hauptbahnhof. ✉ *Orellistrasse 21, CH-8044,* ☎ *01/268–35–35,* FAX *01/268–35–45. 111 beds. Restaurant, café. AE, DC, MC, V.*

$ 🏨 **Limmathof.** This austere and dormlike city hotel inhabits a handsome, historic shell and is ideally placed, minutes from the Bahnhof on the edge of the Niederdorf nightlife district. Despite the no-frills decor, all rooms have tile baths. There's a wood-paneled Weinstube with a limited menu and wines by the glass. ✉ *Limmatquai 142, CH-8023,* ☎ *01/261–42–20,* FAX *01/262–02–17. 100 beds. Restaurant. No credit cards.*

$ 🏨 **St. Georges.** While this simple former pension has a fresh, bright lobby and breakfast room, rooms and corridors are considerably more spare, with mint-green walls, red linoleum floors, and '60s pine furniture. Rooms with showers—half are without—cost 40% more. Take tram 3 or 14 from the station to Stauffacher; it's another five minutes on foot. ✉ *Weberstrasse 11,* ☎ *01/241–11–44,* FAX *01/241–11–42. 44 rooms. Breakfast room. AE, DC, MC, V.*

$ 🏨 **Vorderer Sternen.** On the edge of the old town and near the lake,
★ this plain but adequate establishment takes in the bustle (and noise) of the city. It is steps from the opera house, theaters, art galleries, cinemas, and a shopping area, and it's also close to one of Zürich's main tram junction's, Bellevue. There's a dependable and popular restaurant downstairs with moderate standards; none of the rooms has a bath. ✉ *Theaterstrasse 22,* ☎ *01/251–49–49,* FAX *01/252–90–63. 17 beds. Restaurant. AE, DC, MC, V.*

NIGHTLIFE AND THE ARTS

Nightlife

Of all the Swiss cities, Zürich has the liveliest nightlife, with bars, clubs, discos, and even jazz.

Bars and Lounges

The **Jules Verne Panorama Bar** (✉ Uraniahaus, ☎ 01/211–11–55) offers cocktails with a wraparound view of downtown Zürich. The narrow bar at the **Kronenhalle** (✉ Rämistrasse 4, ☎ 01/251–15–97) draws mobs of well-heeled locals and internationals for its prize-winning cocktails. **Champagnertreff** in the Hotel Central (✉ Central 1, ☎ 01/251–55–55) is a popular Art Deco piano bar with several champagnes available by the glass. Serving a young, arty set until 4 AM, **Odéon**

(✉ Am Bellevue, ☎ 01/251–16–50) is a cultural and historic land-mark (Mata Hari danced here) and a gay bar by night. At **Bierhalle Kropf** (✉ Gassen 16, ☎ 01/221–18–05), locals and tourists alike have been sipping draft beers under the boar's head for more than a century. **Zeughauskeller** (✉ Bahnhofstrasse 28, ☎ 01/211–26–90) spe-cializes in *Stangen* (draft beers), with more than 70 to choose from. **The James Joyce Pub** (✉ Pelikanstrasse 8, off Bahnhofstrasse, ☎ 01/221–18–28) fills with bankers at happy hour, when whiskey and Guinness on tap flow freely.

Cabarets and Nightclubs

There's a variety show with dancers and magicians at **Polygon** (✉ Markt-gasse 17, ☎ 01/252–11–10).

Zwingli didn't get to everyone here: There are strip shows all over town. One of the most well known is at **Le Privé** (✉ Stauffacherstrasse 106, ☎ 01/241–64–87). **Moulin Rouge** (✉ Mühlegasse 14, ☎ 01/262–07–30), true to its namesake, is good for a thrill. **Terrasse** (✉ Limmatquai 3, ☎ 01/251–10–74) has one of the more sophisticated shows.

Discos

Mascotte (✉ Theaterstrasse 10, ☎ 01/252–44–81) is popular with all ages on weeknights, with a young crowd on weekends. **Le Petit Prince** (✉ Bleicherweg 21, ☎ 01/201–17–39) attracts a chic crowd. **Raspu-tine's** (✉ Schützengasse 16, ☎ 01/211–50–58) offers 40 different va-rieties of vodka. The most exclusive club is **Diagonal** at the Hotel Baur au Lac (✉ Talstrasse 1, ☎ 01/211–73–96), where you must be a hotel guest—or the guest of one. **Joker** (✉ Gotthardstrasse 5, ☎ 01/206–36–66) has live bands—folk, rock, and tango.

Jazz Clubs

Casa Bar (✉ Münstergasse 30, ☎ 01/261–20–02) is, arguably, Zürich's most famous. The popular **Widder Bar** (✉ Widdergasse 6, ☎ 01/224–24–11), in the recently restored five-star Hotel Widder, attracts local celebrities with its 800-count "library of spirits."

The Arts

Despite its small population, Zürich is a big city when it comes to the arts; it supports a top-ranked orchestra, an opera company, and a the-ater. Check *Zürich News,* published weekly in English and German, or "Züri-tip," a supplement to the Friday edition of the daily German-language newspaper *Tages Anzeiger.* For tickets to opera, concert, and theater events, contact **BiZZ** (✉ Billettzentrale Zürich, Kulturpavillon, Werdmühleplatz, ☎ 01/221–22–83) and sometimes, depending on the event, **Musik Hug** (✉ Limmatquai 26, ☎ 01/251–68–50) or **Jecklin** (✉ Rämistrasse 30, ☎ 01/261–77–33).

The music event of the year is the **Zürich International Festival,** when, for four weeks in June, orchestras and soloists from all over the world perform, and plays and exhibitions are staged. Book well ahead. De-tails are available from Präsidialabteilung der Stadt Zürich (✉ Post-fach, CH-8001, ☎ 01/216–31–11). During July or August, the **Theaterspektakel** takes place, with circus tents housing avant-garde the-ater and experimental performances on the lawns by the lake at Mythenquai.

Film

Movies in Zürich are serious business, with films presented in the orig-inal language. Check *Zürich News* and watch for the initials E/d/f, which means "English version with German (Deutsch) and French subtitles."

Music
Tonhalle. The Zürich Tonhalle Orchestra, named for its concert hall, was inaugurated by Brahms in 1895 and enjoys international acclaim. There are also solo recitals and chamber programs here. They sell out quickly, so try to book ahead; contact the Tonhalle directly. ⊠ *Claridenstrasse 7,* ☎ *01/206–34–34.*

Opera
Opernhaus. The permanent company here is widely recognized and, understandably, difficult to drop in on if you haven't booked well ahead. Try anyway, at the ticket office. ⊠ *Theaterplatz,* ☎ *01/262–09–09.*

OUTDOOR ACTIVITIES AND SPORTS
Golf
The nine-hole **Dolder Golf Club** (☎ 01/261–50–45) is near the Dolder Grand Hotel. **Zumikon Golf Club** (☎ 01/918–00–50) is near the city center in Zumikon, with 18 holes.

Health and Fitness Clubs
Luxor (⊠ Glärnischstrasse 35, ☎ 01/202–38–38) offers visitors four squash courts, StairMasters, saunas, and a steam bath, but no pool. At the Hotel Zürich's **Atmos** club you can use the big pool and the steam bath, sauna, and sundeck, for 25 SF per day.

Jogging
The Vita-Parcours track closest to the center is at **Allmend Sportplatz** (take Tram 13 to the last stop).

The **Dolder Grand Hotel** (☞ Lodging, *above*) has a jogging path that winds through the forest.

SHOPPING
Auctions
Sotheby's (☎ 01/202–00–11) holds forth at 20 Bleicherweg.

Department Stores
Globus (⊠ Bahnhofstrasse and Löwenplatz, ☎ 01/221–33–11) is one of the city's best. **Jelmoli** (⊠ Bahnhofstrasse and Seidengasse, ☎ 01/220–44–11) has top-notch merchandise. **ABM** (⊠ Bellevueplatz, ☎ 01/261–44–84) is known for good value. **Vilan** (⊠ Bahnhofstrasse 75, ☎ 01/229–51–11) has an affordable selection of department-store goods.

Flea Markets
At **Bürkliplatz** at the lake end of the Bahnhofstrasse, there's a flea market open Saturday from 6 to 3:30 from May to October. There's a curio market on the **Rosenhof** every Thursday and Saturday between April and Christmas.

Shopping Streets
The glittering **Bahnhofstrasse** concentrates much of Zürich's best shopping, with the most expensive and exclusive goods offered at the Paradeplatz end. The west bank's **old town,** along Storchengasse near the Münsterhof, is a focal point for high-end designer goods. The old town on the east bank, around **Niederdorf,** offers less expensive, younger fashions, as well as antiques and old bookshops. There's another pocket of good stores around **Löwenstrasse,** southwest of the Hauptbahnhof.

Specialty Stores

CHOCOLATE

Teuscher (⊠ Storchengasse 9, ☎ 01/211–51–53; ⊠ Globus, Lowen-platz, ☎ 01/211–33–11); ⊠ Cafe Schober, Napfgasse, 4, ☎ 01/251–80–60) specializes in champagne truffles. **Sprüngli** (⊠ Paradeplatz, ☎ 01/224–46–46; ⊠ Hauptbahnhof, ☎ 01/211–84–83; ⊠ Löwen-platz, ☎ 01/211–96–12) offers truffes du jour.

FOOD

Even if you're not in the market for coffee beans, dried fruits, or nuts, visit **H. Schwarzenbach** (⊠ Münstergasse 19, ☎ 01/261–13–15); you'll find old-style open-bin shopping in an aromatic store with oak shelves.

GIFTS AND SOUVENIRS

Heimatwerk (⊠ Rennweg 14, Bahnhofstrasse 2, ☎ 01/211–57–80) carries a broad range of good ceramics, linens, wood carvings, and toys, all handmade in Switzerland. There are additional branches on the Brun-Brücke and at the train station.

LEATHER GOODS

Leder Locher (⊠ Bahnhofstrasse 91, ☎ 01/211–70–82; ⊠ Münster-hof 18, ☎ 01/211–18–64) has luxurious assortments. **Fendi** (⊠ Pa-radeplatz, ☎ 01/221–02–34) has a central location and an appealing selection.

MEN'S CLOTHES

Giorgio Armani (⊠ Zinnengasse 6, ☎ 01/221–23–48) is in the west bank's old town. **Gianni Versace** (⊠ Storchengasse 23, ☎ 01/221–06–21) is not far from its arch-rival, Armani. **Trois Pommes** (⊠ Storchen-gasse 6/7, ☎ 01/211–02–39) carries men's designer wear.

WATCHES

It goes without saying that the shops of the finest watchmakers in Switzer-land are worth visiting. However, there are fine jewelers on practically every street corner, and relatively inexpensive watches—ideal as sou-venirs or gifts—can be found at department stores.

One of the broadest assortments in all price ranges is available at **Bucherer** (⊠ Bahnhofstrasse 50, ☎ 01/211–26–35). **Gübelin** (⊠ Bahn-hofstrasse 36, ☎ 01/221–38–88) is a world-class watch purveyor. **Beyer** (⊠ Bahnhofstrasse 31, ☎ 01/221–10–80) has one of Switzerland's finest selections.

WOMEN'S CLOTHES

Trois Pommes (⊠ Storchengasse 6/7) represents Jil Sander, Alaïa, and Comme des Garçons. **Beatrice Dreher Presents** (⊠ Gassen 14, ☎ 01/211–13–48) carries Chloë and Krizia. **Weinberg** (⊠ Bahnhofstrasse 11, ☎ 01/211–29–54) sells a wide variety of top names. For last year's cutting edge at severely reduced prices, go to **Trois Pommes Checkout** (⊠ Tödistrasse 44, ☎ 01/202–72–26). **A Propos** (⊠ Lim-matquai 36–38, ☎ 01/252–37–37) carries progressive Zürich-made designs.

ZÜRICH A TO Z

Arriving and Departing

By Car

Until the new expressway is finished between Basel (Bâle) and Zürich, your best bet for approaching from the northwest frontier is by way of N2 from Basel to N1, south of Olten, which leads directly into the city. N1 continues east to St. Gallen. Approaching from the south and the St. Gotthard route, take N14 from Luzern (Lucerne); after a brief break of highway (E41) it feeds into N3 and approaches the city along the lake's western shore. You can take N3 all the way up from Chur in Graubünden.

By Plane

AIRPORTS AND AIRLINES

Kloten (☎ 01/812–71–11) is Switzerland's most important airport and the 10th busiest in the world. It is served by some 60 airlines, including **American, United,** and, of course, **Swissair.** You also can catch domestic and European flights out of Kloten on **Crossair,** Switzerland's domestic airline.

BETWEEN THE AIRPORT AND CENTER CITY

It's easy to take a **Swiss Federal Railway feeder train** directly from the airport to Zürich's main station (☎ 01/157–22–22). Tickets cost 5 SF one way, and trains run every 10–15 minutes, arriving in 10 minutes. **By Taxi.** Taxis cost dearly in Zürich. A ride into the center costs 50 SF–60 SF, and takes 20–40 minutes, depending on traffic. **By Shuttle. Welti-furrer Limo** (☎ 01/444–14–44) works through hotel concierges and charges about 18 SF per person for a one-way trip. Its minivan shuttles run between the airport and various hotels about every 45 minutes. **By Limousine. Welti-furrer** rents chauffeured limousines by the hour, half day, or full day.

By Train

There are straightforward connections and several express routes leading directly into Zürich from Basel Geneva (Genève), Bern (Berne), and Lugano. All roads lead to the **Hauptbahnhof** in the city center.

Getting Around

By Bus and Tram

VBZ-Züri-Linie, the tram service in Zürich, is swift and timely. It runs from 5:30 AM to midnight, every six minutes at peak hours, every 12 minutes at other times. All-day passes cost 6.40 SF and can be purchased from the same vending machines that post legible maps and sell one-ride tickets; you must buy your ticket before you board. Free route plans are available from VBZ offices, located at major crossroads (Paradeplatz, Bellevue, Central, Klusplatz).

By Taxi

Taxis are very expensive, with an 8 SF minimum but no additional charge per passenger.

Guided Tours

Orientation

Three introductory **bus tours** are offered by the tourist office. The daily "Sights of Zürich" tour (27 SF) gives a good general idea of the city in two hours. "In and Around Zürich" goes farther and includes an aerial cableway trip to Felsenegg. This is also a daily tour; it takes 2½ hours and costs 35 SF for adults, 20 SF for children. "Zürich by Night," offered May through October, takes in everything from folklore to striptease in 3½ hours (69 SF). All tours start from the main station.

Walking

Daily from May to October, two-hour conducted **walking tours** (16 SF) start from the tourist office.

Opening and Closing Times

Banks are open Monday–Wednesday and Friday 8:15–4:30, Thursday 8:15–6.

Museums are usually open Tuesday–Friday and Sunday 10–noon and 2–5, Saturday 10–noon and 2–4; there are many variations, so check listings.

Stores are open weekdays 9–6:30, Saturday 8–4. On Thursday, some central shops stay open to 9. Some close Monday morning.

Important Addresses and Numbers

Consulates
United States: ⊠ Zollikerstrasse 141, ☎ 01/422–25–66. **United Kingdom:** ⊠ Dufourstrasse 56, ☎ 01/261–15–20.

Emergencies
Police (☎ 117). **Ambulance** (☎ 144). **Hospital** (⊠ Zürich Universitätsspital, Schmelzbergstrasse 8, ☎ 01/255–11–11). **Doctors and dentists** can be referred in case of emergency by the English-speaking operators who man the *Notfalldienst* phones (☎ 01/261–61–00).

English-Language Bookstores
Payot (⊠ Bahnhofstrasse 9, ☎ 01/211–54–52) carries a good stock of English fiction despite the store's French focus. **Stäheli** (⊠ Bahnhofstrasse 70, ☎ 01/201–33–12) specializes in English publications.

Pharmacies
Bellevue Apotheke (⊠ Theaterstrasse 14, ☎ 01/252–56–00).

Travel Agencies
American Express (⊠ Bahnhofstrasse 20, ☎ 01/211–83–70). **Kuoni Travel** (⊠ Bahnhofplatz 7, ☎ 01/221–34–11).

Visitor Information
The **tourist office** is at Bahnhofplatz 15 (⊠ CH-8023, ☎ 01/211–4000). For **hotel reservations,** call 01/211–31–11.

3 Eastern Switzerland

Near Zürich, the cantons of Glarus, Schaffhausen, Thurgau, St. Gallen, and Appenzell, as well as Liechtenstein, are dominated by the Rhine River. With its obscure backcountry and thriving cities, the German-influenced region has everything from wood-shingle farmhouses to town houses adorned with oriel windows and frescoes. Still, the eastern cantons remain one of the most untouched regions of Switzerland.

DESPITE ITS PROXIMITY TO ZÜRICH, this Germanic region, bordered on the north by Germany and on the east by Austria, maintains a personality apart— a personality that often plays the wallflower when upstaged by more spectacular touristic regions. Lush with orchards and gardens, its north dominated by the romantic Rhine, with a generous share of mountains (including Mt. Säntis, at roughly 2,500 meters/8,200 feet) and lovely hidden lakes as well as the enormous Bodensee (popularly known as Lake Constance), it's a region that doesn't lack for variety—only tourists. Because the East draws fewer crowds, those who do venture in find a pleasant surprise: This is Switzerland sans kitsch, sans hard sell, where the people live out a natural, graceful combination of past and present. And, while it's a prosperous region, with its famous textiles and fruit industry, its inns and restaurants cost noticeably less than those in regions nearby.

Comprising the cantons of Glarus, Schaffhausen, Thurgau, St. Gallen, Appenzell, and (administratively) the principality of Liechtenstein, the region covers a broad sociological spectrum, from the thriving city of St. Gallen, with its magnificent Baroque cathedral, to the most obscure, Ozark-like backcountry of Appenzell, where women couldn't vote in cantonal elections until the federal court in Lausanne intervened on their behalf in 1990. (Federal law granted women the national vote in 1971.) On alternating years in Glarus, Appenzell city, and Trogen/Hundwil, you still can witness the *Landsgemeinde,* an open-air election counted by a show of hands.

Architecture along the Rhine resembles that of old Germany and Austria, with half-timbers and rippling red-tile roofs. In cities like Schaffhausen, masterpieces of medieval frescoes deck town houses, many of which have ornate first-floor bays called *oriels.* In the country, farmhouses are often covered with fine, feathery wooden shingles as narrow as Popsicle sticks and weathered to chinchilla gray. Appenzell has its own famous architecture: tidy narrow boxes painted cream, with repeated rows of windows and matching wood panels. The very countryside itself—conical green hills, fruit trees, belled cows, neat yellow cottages—resembles the naive art it inspires.

Pleasures and Pastimes

Dining
Your plate will feel the weight of German and Austrian influence in this most Teutonic of Swiss regions: Portions are on a Wagnerian scale, and pork appears often on the menu. A side of *Spätzli* (little sparrows), *Knöpfli* (little buttons) or *Hörnli* (little horns) adds further heft: These are flour-egg dough fingers, either pressed through a sieve or snipped, gnocchi-style, and served in butter. You also can order a full-meal portion of *Käseknöpfli* (cheese dumplings), which come smothered in pungent cheese sauce.

All across Switzerland you'll find the St. Gallen bratwurst, called Olmabratwurst on its home turf. (Olma is the name of an annual autumn agricultural exhibition here.) In restaurants it's served with thick onion sauce and *Rösti* (hash brown potatoes), but in St. Gallen itself the locals eat it on the hoof, queuing up at lunchtime at one of two or three outdoor stands, then holding the thick, white-veal sausage in a napkin with one hand and a round, chewy chunk of whole-grain *Bürli* bread in the other. They never add mustard.

In the quirky region of Appenzell, the famous Appenzeller cheese deserves its stardom, as among the fine hard cheeses of Switzerland it has the most complex, spicy flavor, with traces of nutmeg. Other Appenzeller treats include a variation of Graubünden's famous air-dried beef, here called *Mostbröckli* and steeped in sweet apple cider before drying. It is served in translucent slices, its moist, mildly sweet flavor countered with bites of pickled onion. *Bauernschublig* are dark, dried blood sausages. Appenzeller *Biber* are honey cakes filled with almond and stamped with a design. *Birnebrot* is a thick, dried pear puree wrapped in glazed dough. *Chäsemagarone* is a rich, plain dish of large macaroni layered with butter, grated Appenzeller cheese, and butter-fried onions. It is often eaten with *Apfelmousse* (applesauce).

Eastern Switzerland is the country's orchard region, especially the Thurgau area. There are several fine fruit juices made here, as well as *Most* (sweet cider) and some good fruit schnapps. Among area wines, Berneck comes from the Rhine Valley, Hallau from near Schaffhausen, and crisp whites from Stein-am-Rhein.

CATEGORY	COST*
$$$$	over 70 SF
$$$	40 SF–70 SF
$$	20 SF–40 SF
$	under 20 SF

per person for a three-course meal, including sales tax and 15% service charge

Hiking
Uncrowded hiking trails lead through all kinds of terrain, from rolling vineyards along the Rhine to isolated, rugged mountain wilderness above the Toggenburg Valley. This is a region of unspoiled nature, well-preserved villages, and breathtaking scenery.

Lodging
More and more hotels in this, one of Switzerland's least touristic regions, are throwing away their Formica and commissioning hand-painted furniture to complement the beams they've so carefully exposed. However, bargain renovations tend toward the crisp, if anonymous, look of light tongue-in-groove pine paneling and earthtone ceramic baths. The prices are somewhat lower on average here, with only slight variations from high to low season. Half board is rarely included.

CATEGORY	COST*
$$$$	over 250 SF
$$$	180 SF–250 SF
$$	120 SF–180 SF
$	under 120 SF

All prices are for a standard double room, including breakfast, tax, and service charge.

Exploring Eastern Switzerland

With their obscure backcountry and thriving cities, the German-influenced cantons of Glarus, Schaffhausen, Thurgau, St. Gallen, and Appenzell are some of the most untouched in Switzerland. In the northern part of the region are the old Rhine city of Schaffhausen, the dramatic Rheinfall, and the preserved medieval town of Stein-am-Rhein. The Bodensee occupies the northwestern corner of Switzerland, just below Germany. Farther south are the textile center of St. Gallen, the quirky Appenzell region, and the resort area of the Toggenburg Valley. The

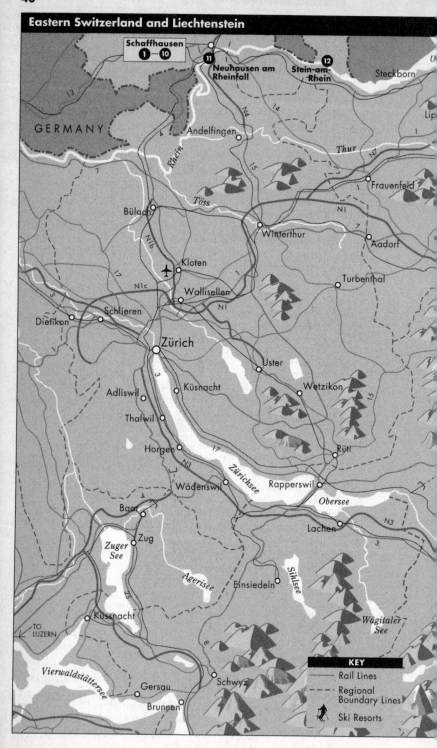

40

Eastern Switzerland and Liechtenstein

Schaffhausen
1 — **10**

11

Neuhausen am
Rheinfall

12 Stein-am-
Rhein

Steckborn

GERMANY

13

Andelfingen

Rhein

N4

14

Thur

N7

Lip

1

Frauenfeld

4

15

Töss

N1

Bülach

N1b

Winterthur

1

7

Aadorf

Kloten

1

Turbenthal

Wallisellen

N1c

N1

17

3

Schlieren

Diefikon

Zürich

3

Uster

Küsnacht

Wetzikon

Adliswil

15

Thalwil

Horgen

17

Zürichsee

Rüti

N3

Wädenswil

Rapperswil

Obersee

Baar

A

N3

Zug

Lachen

3

Zuger
See

Ägerisee

Einsiedeln

Sihlsee

Küssnacht

TO
LUZERN

Wägitaler
See

8

Vierwaldstättersee

Gersau

Schwyz

Brunnen

KEY	
——	Rail Lines
- - -	Regional Boundary Lines
🎿	Ski Resorts

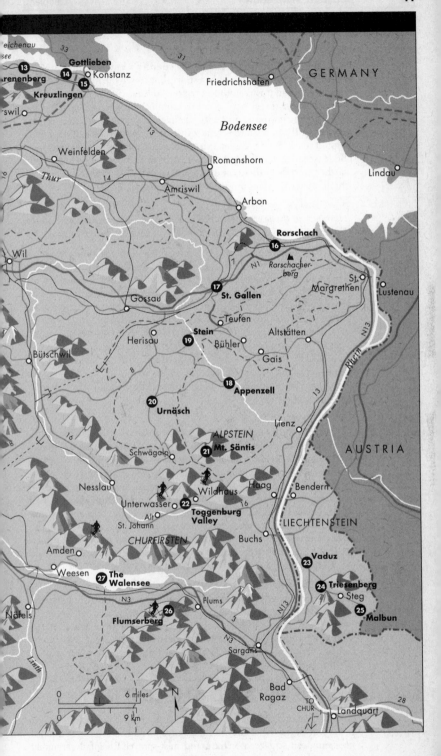

tiny principality of Liechtenstein lies just across the eastern border, within easy driving distance.

Great Itineraries

Although Eastern Switzerland is the country's lowest region, it's still fairly rugged. It will take only a short time to see the major sights, but they are spread throughout the region, so leave time each day to be in transit. Train travel here is more complicated than in neighboring areas, requiring more intercity changes, so plan your itinerary accordingly. If you want to get back into the Appenzell hills, though, you should rent a car. St. Gallen is a good excursion center for visiting the Bodensee, Appenzell, Mt. Säntis, and the principality of Liechtenstein; farther west, Schaffhausen offers easy access to the magnificent Rheinfall, medieval Stein-am-Rhein, and the Bodensee, as well.

IF YOU HAVE 1 OR 2 DAYS

Numbers in the text correspond to numbers in the margin and on the Eastern Switzerland and Liechtenstein and Schaffhausen maps.

If you are coming from Zürich, enter the region at its northernmost tip and start with the old Rhine city of ⬚ **Schaffhausen** ①–⑩, known for its medieval frescoes and baroque oriel windows. From there it's an easy excursion to the nearby **Neuhausen am Rheinfall** ⑪, the city that's known for its broad, dramatic series of falls utterly different from those in more mountainous regions. Just on the other side of Schaffhausen, spend your second day visiting ⬚ **Stein-am-Rhein** ⑫, a wholly preserved medieval gem reflected in the river. Then dip south to old ⬚ **St. Gallen** ⑰, a busy textile center with an active old town beside its grand baroque cathedral. From St. Gallen you explore the picture-pretty ⬚ **Appenzell** ⑱ region where both the cuisine and folklore are quirky.

IF YOU HAVE 3 OR 4 DAYS

With a little more time, you can spend your first two days in the northernmost areas, visiting ⬚ **Schaffhausen** ①–⑩, **Neuhausen am Rheinfall** ⑪, and ⬚ **Stein-am-Rhein** ⑫; then make your way south, starting below Germany's Konstanz and following the southern coast of the Bodensee, a popular spot for local resorters. See the twin cities of **Kreuzlingen** ⑮ and Konstanz (in Germany) and ⬚ **Gottlieben** ⑭. Visit ⬚ **St. Gallen** ⑰ and ⬚ **Appenzell** ⑱, then trace the **Toggenburg Valley** ㉒, which runs in a great curve between Mt. Säntis and Wil and draws Swiss tourists to its resorts and spas. Finally, head to the tiny principality of Liechtenstein, to see the royal castle and explore its art and stamp museums, and then west to the isolated Walensee.

When to Tour Eastern Switzerland

Summers in Eastern Switzerland provide the best weather but also the greatest traffic both on roads and in towns; spring and fall are good alternatives. Stein-am-Rhein alone receives enough coach tours to virtually paralyze the village with pedestrians during high season; if you go, arrive earlier in the day or come on a weekday when crowds are thinner.

SCHAFFHAUSEN AND THE RHEIN

Known to many Swiss at Rheinfallstadt (Rhine Falls city), Schaffhausen is the seat of the Swiss canton that shares its name, also the country's northernmost. To gaze upon the grand, mist-sprayed Rheinfalls, arguably the most famous waterfall in Europe, is to look straight into the romantic past of Switzerland. Goethe and Wordsworth were just two of the world's best-known wordsmiths to immortalize the Falls' powerful grandeur.

Bicycles can be rented at the federal rail station in Schaffhausen.

Schaffhausen

★ **❶**–**❿**   *48 km (29 mi) northeast of Zurich, 20 km (12 mi) east of Stein-am-Rhein.*

A city of about 35,000, Schaffhausen was, from the early Middle Ages, an important depot for river cargoes, which—effectively stopped by the rapids and waterfall farther along—had to be unloaded there. The name Schaffhausen is probably derived from the "skiffhouses" ranged along the riverbank.

❶   The **Münster zu Allerheiligen** (All Saints' Cathedral) and its adjoining cloister and grounds dominate the lower city. Founded in 1049, the original cathedral was dedicated in 1064, and the larger one that stands today was built in 1103. Its interior has been restored to Romanesque austerity with a modern aesthetic (hanging architect's lamps, Scandinavian-style pews). The **cloister,** begun in 1050, offers a better opportunity to dip into the past, combining Romanesque and later Gothic elements. Memorial plates on the inside wall honor the noblemen and civic leaders buried in the cloister's central garden. The enormous **Schiller bell** in the courtyard beyond was cast in 1486 and hung in the cathedral tower until 1895. Its inscription, "*vivos—voco/mortuos—plango/fulgura—frango*" ("I call the living, mourn the dead, stop the lightning"), supposedly inspired the German poet Friedrich von Schiller to write his *Lied von der Glocke* (*Song of the Bell*). You also will pass through the aromatic **herb garden** (⊠ Klosterplatz 1, ☎ 052/625–43–77); it's re-created so effectively in the medieval style that you may feel you've stepped into a unicorn tapestry.

❷   The **Museum zu Allerheiligen** houses an extensive collection of ancient and medieval history, as well as information on Schaffhausen industry. There are temporary exhibitions of international caliber as well. ⊠ *Klosterplatz 1,* ☎ *052/625–43–77,* 🖭 *Free.* ☉ *10–noon and 2–5; closed Mon. and holidays.*

❸   The Baroque **Gerberstube** (Tanners' Guild House) is known for its doorway framed by two lions stretching a two-handled tanner's knife.

❹   Dominating the old town of Schaffhausen is the **Munot,** built between 1564 and 1589 in full circle form, its massive stone ramparts serving as a fortress allowing the defense of the city from all sides. From its top are splendid Schaffhausen and Rhine Valley views. 🖭 *Free.* ☉ *May–Sept., daily 8–8; Oct.–Apr. 20, daily 9–5; closed Apr. 21–30.*

❺   **Zur Wasserquelle** and **Zieglerburg** are a Rococo duplex dating from 1738. Across the street are the **Tellenbrunnen,** a fountain-statue of William Tell copied from the 1522 original, and the **St. Johannkirche,** whose Gothic exterior dates from 1248. ⊠ *Pfarrhofgasse 2.*

❻   The **Schmiedstube** (Smith's Guild House), with its spectacular Renaissance portico and oriel, is an excellent example of Schaffhausen's state of suspended animation. Framed over the door are the symbol of the tongs and hammer for the smiths, and that of a snake for doctors, who depended on smiths for their tools and thus belonged to the guild.

❼   The city's finest mansion, **Haus zum Ritter** (Knight's House) dates from 1492. Its magnificent fresco facade was commissioned by the resident knight, Hans von Waldkirch. Tobias Stimmer painted all three

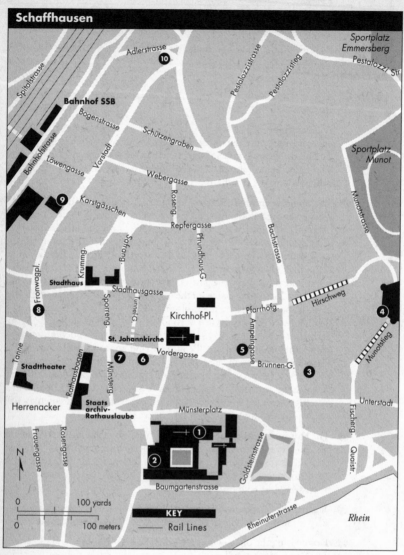

Schaffhausen

Fronwagplatz, **8**
Gerberstube, **3**
Haus zum Ritter, **7**
Munot, **4**
Münster zu
Allerheiligen, **1**
Museum zu
Allerheiligen, **2**

Neuturm, **10**
Schmiedstube, **6**
Zum Goldenen
Ochsen, **9**
Zur Wasserquelle/
Zieglerburg, **5**

stories of classical themes, which are now displayed in the Museum zu Allerheiligen (☞ *above*); the contemporary replacement was copied in the 1930s.

❽ The ancient marketplace **Fronwagplatz** is marked with the large Metzgerbrunnen, a 1524 fountain-statue of a prosperous burgher. The large clock tower over the square once held the market scales; its astronomical clock dates from 1564 and records not only the time but also eclipses, seasons, and the course of the moon through the zodiac. Across the square, a reproduction of the 1535 **Mohrenbrunnen** (Moor's Fountain) represents Kaspar of the Three Kings. The original fountain is stored in the Museum zu Allerheiligen (☞ *above*).

NEED A BREAK? The streets around the Fronwagplatz are lined with sidewalk cafés where shoppers stop for pastries, coffee and people-watching. Just off the Platz in the Vordergasse, try **Café Rohr** (⊠ Vordergasse 57, ☎ 052/625-40-21).

❾ Once a restaurant, **Zum Goldenen Ochsen** (At the Golden Ox) now houses offices and shops. The building was remodeled in 1608 to its current Renaissance style. Its exterior frescoes celebrate Greek and Babylonian history (you'll see the Hanging Gardens on the third level).

❿ At the far end of the Vorstadt, the **Neuturm** (New Tower), dates from 1370. It was once part of the city wall.

Dining and Lodging

$$-$$$ ✕ **Wirtschaft zum Frieden.** This unpretentious traditional restaurant, ★ in a wonderful old clubhouse at the base of the theater square, offers diners a variety of delightful settings: an intimate (read: tiny) stübli full of waxed and weathered wood, its walls decked with silhouettes of the club's current members; a graceful tile-stove dining room on the antiques-filled first floor; and a small private garden thick with wisteria and luxuriant trees. You can have a cheap, generous *Tagesteller* (daily-plate lunch) in the stübli, an ambitious and well-executed meal upstairs, or choices from both menus in the garden, where the locals crowd to drink in a summer evening with their carafe of local wine. The menu includes home-smoked salmon, homemade Knöpfli, the very local *Kutteln* (tripe), and poached plums. ⊠ *Herrenacker 11,* ☎ *052/625-47-15. AE, DC, MC, V.*

$$$$ ✕▥ **Rheinhotel Fischerzunft.** A complete renovation in 1990 gave this ★ Relais & Châteaux property a modern sheen that's a bit out of place in this medieval city on the Rhine. Of its 10 rooms—each one different, some in fussy florals, others in sleek jewel-tone solids—six have river views, but everyone shares the lovely Rhine view at breakfast. Gault Millaut rates the restaurant among the country's three best. Its mixed nautical and Oriental decor reflects the chef's Franco-Chinese leanings: He trained in Hong Kong and has married the two cuisines brilliantly with the help of his Chinese wife. ⊠ *Rheinquai 8,* ☎ *052/625-32-81,* FAX *052/624-32-85. 24 beds. Restaurant. AE, DC, MC, V.*

$$$ ✕▥ **Kronenhof.** This fine, quiet city hotel in the heart of Schaffhausen's ★ old town has a shutter- and flower-trimmed facade but an all-modern interior, with tidy, well-constructed rooms cheered by Oriental prints and cherry-stained paneling. The public areas are more dated but are trimmed with regional prints. The American-cafeteria look in the restaurant seems at odds with the excellent, refined versions of local dishes, including trout, herring, and rich soups. This is a logical choice for families and business travelers. ⊠ *Kirchhofplatz 7,* ☎ *052/625-66-31,* FAX *052/624-45-89. 58 beds. Restaurant, bar. AE, DC, MC, V.*

$$ ✕🛏 **Alte Rheinmühle.** A modern renovation has preserved the traditional atmosphere of this historic former mill built in 1674. The Rhine laps at its foundations and you can enjoy a view of the river while savoring good fish dishes by firelight. Büsingen, on the north shore of the Rhine just east of Schaffhausen, is a tiny German enclave where Swiss francs are accepted. ⊠ *D-78266, Büsingen, Germany,* ☎ *0049/7734–60–76,* FAX *0049/7734–60–79. 30 beds. Restaurant. AE, DC, MC, V.*

$$ ✕🛏 **Park-Villa.** Despite the no-nonsense elevator tacked onto the exterior, this Belle Epoque mansion, built by a local industrialist, has been transformed into a small hotel with surprisingly little disruption to its grand but familial style. Many of the original furnishings—inlaid pieces, chandeliers, Persian rugs—remain, even in some of the nicer guest rooms. The upper floors are modern but retain their eccentric shapes, and some have Rhine or fortress views. The fine old garden room is luxurious and a steal (the toilet is down the hall); all the other rooms have full baths. The Park-Villa sits slightly apart, and uphill, from the old town. ⊠ *Parkstrasse 18,* ☎ *052/625–27–37,* FAX *052/624–12–53. 36 beds. Restaurant, bar, tennis court. AE, DC, MC, V.*

$$ ✕🛏 **Promenade.** This solid, simple Edwardian hotel, on the same residential hill as the Park-Villa but with a pretty park walk to the viaduct and the old town, offers spare Formica-and-beige rooms, a garden restaurant, and modest fitness equipment. ⊠ *Fäsenstaubstrasse 43,* ☎ *052/624–80–04,* FAX *052/624–13–49. 64 beds. Restaurant, fitness center. AE, DC, MC, V.*

$ ✕🛏 **Löwen.** At the edge of suburban Herblingen, where the bedroom community seems to melt back into its origins as a half-timber country town, this quintessential old guest house still draws the locals to its pub and serves regional standards in its restaurant. Rooms, however, are all modern, with ceramic tile and modern pine paneling. ⊠ *CH-8207 Herblingen,* ☎ *053/643–22–08. 15 beds. Restaurant, pub. AE, DC, MC, V.*

Neuhausen am Rheinfall

★ ⓫ *3 km (1¼ mi) south of Schaffhausen.*

Adjacent to Neuhausen, on the north bank of the Rhine, a series of magnificent waterfalls powers the city's industry (arms, railroad cars, aluminum). The falls are 150 meters (492 feet) wide, drop some 25 meters (82 feet) in a series of three dramatic leaps, and are split at the center by a bushy crag straight out of a 19th-century landscape painting. The effect—mists, roaring water, jutting rocks—is positively Wagnerian; Goethe saw in the falls the "ocean's source." From Neuhausen there's a good view toward the Schloss Laufen.

Stein-am-Rhein

★ ⓬ *20 km (13 mi) east of Schaffhausen.*

Stein-am-Rhein, a nearly perfectly preserved medieval village and one of Switzerland's most picturesque towns, lies at the point where the Rhein leaves the Bodensee. Crossing the bridge over the river, you see the nearly perfectly preserved medieval village spread along the waterfront, its foundations and docks rising directly out of the water. Here, restaurants, hotels, and souvenir stands occupy 16th- and 17th-century buildings, and the Rhein appears to be a narrow mountain stream—nothing like the sprawling industrial trade route it becomes farther downstream.

The **Rathausplatz** and main street are flanked by tight rows of shingled, half-timber town houses, each rivaling the next for the ornateness of its oriels, the flamboyance of its frescoes. The elaborate decor usually illustrates the name of the house: *Sonne* (Sun), *Ochsen* (Ox), *Weisser Adler* (White Eagle), and so on. Most of the artwork dates from the 16th century. The **Rathaus** (Town Hall) itself was built between 1539 and 1542, with the half-timber upper floors added in 1745; look for its fantastical dragon waterspouts, typical of the region.

NEED A BREAK?   Have a lunch special or a glass of the local wine from the vineyards above town at the old-style **Weinstube zum Roten Ochsen** (⊠ Rathausplatz 9, ☎ 052/741–23–28) on the Rathausplatz.

At the edge of the old town, just upstream from the last bridge over the Rhine before the Bodensee, is the Benedictine **Kloster St. Georgen** (Monastery of St. George), a curious half-timbered structure built in 1005; it houses a small museum of woodwork and local paintings and also shelters a cloister.

Directly above the town atop vineyards and woods stands the 13th-century hilltop castle of **Hohenklingen,** which now houses a restaurant and offers broad views of the Rhine Valley and the lake beyond.

Dining and Lodging

$–$$$$ ✕ **Sonne.** Upstairs, you'll find a formal dining room (ceiling beams, ★   damask, and Biedermeier) where chef Philippe Combe's inventive, top-drawer cuisine—Rhine fish, crisp duck with cabbage—is served at top prices. Downstairs in the Weinstube, he offers a daily plate and simple light lunches, dished up in a spare, chic, gentrified pub: more beams, stone, stucco, parquet—and exposed pipes painted maroon. The Weinstube benefits from the kitchen upstairs; it offers homemade pastas, simple but sophisticated stews, and access to the fine wine list. ⊠ *Am Rathausplatz,* ☎ *052/741–21–28. AE, DC, MC, V. Closed Wed.*

$$$$ ✕🏠 **Chlosterhof.** Its all-new brick-and-angled-glass exterior seems utterly misplaced in this medieval gem of a village, but this hotel worked hard to face as many rooms as possible toward the Rhine. Inside, the look is modern, suburban, and business-class despite token vaulting in the lobby and scattered antiques; indeed, the focus is on entertaining conference groups and their spouses. The rooms feature sleek dark-pine cabinetry and some four-poster beds, but the creamy pastels and carpets say "upscale international chain." Suites claim the best Rhine views. ⊠ *Oehningerstrasse 201,* ☎ *052/742–42–42,* ℻ *052/41–13–37. 140 beds. 4 restaurants, bar, in-room VCR, indoor pool, sauna, fitness center, dance club. AE, DC, MC, V.*

$$ ✕🏠 **Rheinfels.** Even some of the bathrooms have ceiling beams in this ★   fine old waterfront landmark, built between 1508 and 1517. The public spaces have creaking pine plank floors and suits of armor on display, and every room—modernized in beige and rose tones, with all-tile baths—has a Rhine view. The restaurant specializes in top-quality freshwater fish at reasonable prices. ⊠ *Rhigasse 8,* ☎ *052/741–21–44,* ℻ *052/741–25–22. 38 beds. Restaurant. MC. Closed Jan. and Feb.*

$–$$ ✕🏠 **Adler.** With one of the most elaborately frescoed 15th-century fa-★   cades on the Rathausplatz, this hotel has a split personality: Its interior is airy, slick, and immaculate, with gray industrial carpet, white stucco, and blond wood throughout. The cabinetry is built-in, the baths are tile, and the windows are double glazed. The comfortable ambience comes from the young, local family who runs the hotel with pride; other families will fit right in. The pleasant restaurant serves good regional cooking, along with some French cuisine. ✉ *Rathausplatz 15,* ☎ *054/741–61–61,* FAX *054/41–44–40. 46 beds. Restaurant. AE, DC, MC, V.*

$ 🏠 **Bleiche.** This private farmhouse lodging, on a hill high over the Rhine
★   Valley, just a mile or so out of the village center, offers a chance to sleep
      under deep shingled eaves and wake to the sound of cowbells. The rooms
      are rock-bottom simple (linoleum, a mix of dormitory and collectible
      furniture), with showers down the hall, but the setting is surpassingly
      beautiful. A friendly German-speaking woman runs it and lives in a
      newer farmhouse next door. She serves breakfast only. ✉ *Bleicherhof,*
      ☎ *052/741–22–57. 10 beds. No credit cards.*

$ 🏠 **Mühlental.** On the road heading out of the center of Stein-am-
      Rhein, this pretty, 300-year-old guest house has been renovated, and
      its rooms, while creaky, are freshly clad in Formica, linoleum, and all-
      weather carpet. The ground floor is dominated by a tiled pizzeria. Not
      all rooms have a bath. ✉ *Oehningerstrasse 6,* ☎ *052/741–27–25. 31
      beds. Restaurant. AE, MC, V.*

$ 🏠 **Zur Rheingerbe.** Right on the busy waterfront promenade, this
      small inn has new wood-panel ceilings and big, Sears-catalog furnish-
      ings (sculptured carpet, spindle beds). All rooms have a bath, and
      some overlook the Rhine. The first-floor restaurant has a full-length
      bay window along the riverfront. ✉ *Schifflände 5,* ☎ *052/741–29–
      91,* FAX *052/741–21–66. 16 beds. Restaurant. AE, DC, MC, V.*

En Route   Fourteen kilometers (9 miles) east of Stein-am-Rhein, the town of
      Steckborn has some fine old houses, including the Baronenhaus and
      the Gerichtshaus; it's also home to Turmhof Steckborn, a half-timbered
      waterfront castle built in 1342 and now housing a small local museum
      containing ancient artifacts.

Arenenberg

⑬ *20 km (12 mi) east of Stein-am-Rhein; 40 km (25 mi) east of
   Schaffhausen.*

Just east of Steckborn, the Rhine opens up into the Untersee, the lower
branch of the Bodensee. In its center lies the German island of Reichenau.
Charles the Fat, great-grandson of Charlemagne, was buried here.

The villages on either side of the Untersee are dominated by castles.
On the Swiss side, behind the village of Mannenbach (nearly opposite
Reichenau), the **castle at Arenenberg** was once home to the future
Napoléon III and serves today as a museum with furnishings and art-
work from the Second Empire. ✉ *CH-8268,* ☎ *072/64–18–66.* 🚃 *5
SF.* ☉ *Apr.–Sept., Tues.–Sun. 9–noon and 1:30–6; Oct.–Mar., Tues.–Sun.
10–noon and 1:30–4.*

Gottlieben

⑭ *5 km (3 mi) east of Arenenberg; 45 km (28 mi) east of Schaffhausen.*

As the Untersee narrows to the east, the village of Gottlieben has a Do-
minican monastery-castle, where the Protestant reformers Jan Hus
and Jerome of Prague were imprisoned during the 15th century by order
of Emperor Sigismund and Pope John XXII. Pope John was himself
confined in the same castle a few years later. Today, though the castle
can be viewed only from the outside, Gottlieben offers a romantic, half-
timbered waterfront promenade—and two fine old hotels—before you
reach the urban complex of Kreuzlingen and Germany's Konstanz.

Dining and Lodging

$$$ ✕⊞ **Drachenburg und Waaghaus.** On the misty banks of the Rhine
★ between the Bodensee and the Zellersee, this half-timbered apparition
of onion domes, shutters, and gilt gargoyles was first built in 1702 and
retains its historic air despite modern expansion and ranks of Mercedes
in the parking lot. The original house, the Drachenburg, lies across a
walk from the old waterfront Waaghaus, and a third house was added
recently for overflow guests. The original Drachenburg is the most at-
mospheric by far: It has gleaming old staircases, four-poster beds, bro-
cade, chaises longues, and crystal sconces throughout the labyrinth of
rooms and parlors, where reproductions mix with authentic antiques.
The scale is grand but cozy, and Rhine-view rooms are furnished like
honeymoon suites. Three restaurants vary in ambience, the most so-
phisticated being in the original house; fish is a specialty. ✉ *CH-8274,*
☎ *071/669–14–14,* ℻ *071/669–17–09. 100 beds. 3 restaurants,*
bar. AE, DC, MC, V.

$$ ✕⊞ **Krone.** Immediately downstream from the Drachenburg, this
member of the Romantik chain is smaller, cheaper, and a tad more generic
than its flamboyant neighbor but dates from the same era. Its complete
renovation in the 1970s clad standard doubles in mild, classic beiges;
only the suites (which dominate river views) went baroque. Breakfast
is served in a beam- and herringbone-ceiling hall overlooking the
Rhine. The glowing dark-wood restaurant offers nouvelle-influenced
seafood as well as lake fish. ✉ *Seestrasse,* ☎ *071/669–23–23,* ℻ *071/*
669–24–56. 40 beds. Restaurant. AE, DC, MC, V.

FROM THE BODENSEE TO ST. GALLEN

Sometimes known as Lake Constance, the Bodensee is about 65 kilometers (40 miles) long and 15 kilometers (9 miles) wide, making it second in size in Switzerland only to Lac Léman (Lake Geneva). As it is
not protected by mountains, it is turbulent in stormy weather and even
on fine days is exposed to the wind. Compared with Switzerland's usual
crystalline lakes, the Bodensee is gloomy and brooding; nonetheless,
it draws European vacationers in summer for swimming, windsurfing,
and fishing. Many Swiss have built tidy homes along the lakefront.

Outdoor Activities and Sports

HIKING

As a summer resort destination, the area around the Bodensee is usually thronged with hikers. For timed hiking itineraries, topographical
maps, and suggestions on the areas best suited to your style of wandering, consult the **Tourismusverband Ostschweiz** (✉ Bahnhofplatz 1a,
CH-9001 St. Gallen, ☎ 071/222–62–62).

SWIMMING

People do swim the Bodensee; there are **public beaches** at Rorschach,
(☎ 071/841–16–84), Arbon (☎ 071/446–13–33), and Romanshorn
(☎ 071/463–11–47).

Kreuzlingen and Konstanz

⑮ *7 km (4 mi) east of Gottlieben; 46 km (28 mi) east of Schaffhausen.*

The big German city of Konstanz, with its Swiss twin of Kreuzlingen,
dominates the straits that open into the Bodensee. Though Kreuzlingen itself offers little of interest to travelers, Konstanz is easily accessible from the Swiss side, though your passport may be checked even
if you pass on foot. Konstanz belonged to Switzerland until 1805 but
offers a distinct cultural contrast to its neighbor today.

Outdoor Activities and Sports

The **Eissporthalle** in Kreuzlingen/Konstanz (⊠ Seestrasse 1b, ☎ 072/72–30–05) is a public skating rink.

En Route   About halfway between Kruezlingen and Rorschach (follow highway 13 east along the Bodensee), you'll come to the small town of **Romanshorn.** An industrial town and an important ferry port for Friedrichshafen in Germany, this is also a surprisingly pleasant resort with fine views of the Swiss and Austrian mountains.

Between Romanshorn and Rorschach on highway 13, **Arbon** (known to the Romans as Arbor Felix) lies on a little promontory jutting out into the Bodensee, surrounded by lovely meadows and orchards. It was a Celtic town before the Romans came in 60 BC and built military fortifications. Evidence of the Romans can be found in an interesting collection of relics in the late-Gothic St. Martinskirche.

Rorschach

⑯   *41 km (25 mi) southeast of Kreuzlingen; 80 km (49 mi) southeast of Schaffhausen.*

The lake resort of Rorschach, a port on the Bodensee, lies on a protected bay at the foot of the Rorschacherberg, an 883-meter (2,896-foot) mountain covered with orchards, pine forests, and meadows. For generations, Rorschach has carried on a thriving grain trade with Germany, as the imposing baroque **Kornhaus** (Granary), built in 1746, attests. There's a public beach here too.

Outdoor Activities and Sports

There are several sailing schools in Goldach. Try **Bruno Stadler** (☎ 071/35–11) or **Segelschule Rorschach** (☎ 071/41–35–11).

St. Gallen

⑰   *14 km (9 mi) southwest of Rorschach; 94 km (59 mi) southeast of Schaffhausen.*

Switzerland's largest eastern city, St. Gallen has been known for centuries as both an intellectual center and the source of some of the world's finest textiles. St. Gallus, an Irish missionary, came to the region in 612, to live in a hermit's cell in the Steinach Valley. In 720 an abbey was founded on the site where he died. Becoming a major cultural focus in medieval Europe, the abbey built a library of awesome proportions; its illuminated manuscripts are now more than 1,200 years old.

★   The abbey was largely destroyed in the Reformation and was closed down in 1805, but its magnificent Rococo **Stiftsbibliothek** (Abbey Library), built in 1758–67, still holds a collection of more than 100,000 books. The library hall itself is one of Switzerland's treasures. Visitors enter behind the cathedral, climb an institutional staircase (there's a boys' school in the same structure), and step into large, gray carpet slippers to protect the magnificently inlaid wood flooring. The hall is an explosion of gilt, frescoes, and undulating balconies, but the most striking aspect by far is the burnished woodwork, all luminous walnut and cherry. Its contents, including handwritten manuscripts and incunabula, comprise one of the world's oldest and finest scholarly collections. ⊠ *Klosterhof 6d, CH-9000,* ☎ *071/22–57–19.* 🎫 *5 SF.* ☉ *May and Sept.–Oct., Mon.–Sat. 9–noon and 1:30–5, Sun. 10:30–noon; June–Aug., Mon.–Sat. 9–noon and 1:30–5, Sun. 10:30–noon and 1:30–4; Dec.–Mar., Tues.–Sat. 9–noon and 1:30–4; Apr., Mon.–Sat. 9–noon and 1:30–4.*

★ The **Kathedrale** (Cathedral) is impressive in its own right. Begun in 1755 and completed in 1766, it is the antithesis of the library, though the nave and rotunda are the work of the same architect, Peter Thumb: The scale is outsize and the decor light, bright, and open, despite spectacular excesses of wedding-cake trim.

The grounds of the abbey and the cathedral border the **old town,** which demonstrates a healthy symbiosis between scrupulously preserved Renaissance and Baroque architecture and a thriving, modern shopping scene. The best examples of oriel windows, timbers, and frescoes can be seen along Gallusstrasse, Schmiedgasse, Marktgasse, and Spisergasse.

NEED A
BREAK?

As St. Gallen is known for its creaky old first-floor (second-floor to Americans) restaurants and guild houses, have coffee or a glass of wine at **Weinstube zum Bäumli** (⊠ Schmiedgasse 18), typical and convenient to the cathedral and old town.

St. Gallen's history as a textile capital dates from the Middle Ages, when convent workers wove linen toile of such exceptional quality that it was exported throughout Europe. The industry expanded into cotton and embroidery and today dominates the top of the market. To enjoy some marvelously ornate old embroidery, visit the **Textilmuseum** (Textile Museum). Its lighting is dim to protect the delicate fabrics and its captions are all in German, but the work speaks for itself. ⊠ *Vadianstrasse,* ☎ *071/223–17–44. ◻ 5 SF. ☉ Nov.–Mar., weekdays 10–noon and 2–5; Apr.–Oct., weekdays 10–noon and 2–5, Sat. 10–noon and 2–5.*

Dining and Lodging

$$$$ ✕ **Am Gallusplatz.** This is the grandest restaurant St. Gallen has to offer, serving its nouvelle-inspired classics (Scotch lamb Provençal, grilled rabbit with morels and polenta fritters) under deeply cross-vaulted ceilings and heavy chandeliers in a fine old half-timber building near the cathedral. Business travelers are often brought here to be impressed by the architecture, the formality, and the enormous wine list. A daily lunch menu offers fewer dishes, usually featuring *cuisine du marché,* home cooking based on the freshest ingredients possible. ⊠ *Gallusstrasse 24,* ☎ *071/223–33–30. AE, MC, V. Closed Mon.*

$$–$$$ ✕ **Zum Goldenen Schäfli.** Of the first-floor (second-floor to Americans) restaurants that are St. Gallen's trademark, this is the most popular, and its slanting floors groan under crowds of locals and tourists. The low ceiling and walls are all aged wood, and it's easy to imagine coach-and-four passengers lifting a pewter stein. The menu offers hearty standards with a special twist: sweetbreads in mushroom sauce, tripe in Calvados sauce, lake fish with almonds. The prices seem high considering the down-home setting, but this beloved landmark could probably double them and still thrive. ⊠ *Metzgergasse 5,* ☎ *071/223–37–37. AE, DC, MC, V. Closed Sun. No lunch Sat.*

$$ ✕ **Schlössli.** Tidy, bright, and modern despite its setting in a historic
★ building, this first-floor landmark has a less woody atmosphere than its peers, the Bäumli and the Schäfli, but better cooking. The Käse Spätzli are homemade and the salads fresh and good, especially the main-course salad with duck liver. Classics like Rösti with veal bits in cream sauce (Geschnetzeltes) are dependable. The café draws casual families and locals playing *Jass* at lunch; businessmen choose the only slightly more formal dining room that adjoins it. ⊠ *Am Spisertor, Zeughausgasse 17,* ☎ *071/222–12–06,* ☏ *071/223–12–06. AE, DC, MC, V. Closed weekends.*

$–$$ ✕ **Weinstube zum Bäumli.** All dark, glossy wood and lead glass, this 500-year-old first-floor beauty serves classic local fare (veal, bratwurst, Rösti) to tourists, businesspeople, and workers, who share tables comfortably in the midst of the noisy bustle. ⊠ *Schmiedgasse 18,* ☎ *071/222–11–74. No credit cards. Closed Sun.–Mon.*

$$$$ 🏨 **Einstein.** Tucked back into a slope at the edge of the old town, this former embroidery factory is now a sleek, upscale business-class hotel, with Hilton-like interiors (polished cabinetry, lacquered rattan, subdued florals), a uniformed staff, and a five-star attitude—which has its pros and cons. The generous breakfast buffet, laid out in the sky-lighted top-floor loft that serves as the à la carte restaurant by night, is not included in the room price. The bar is dark, leathery, and American business-style, appropriate to the clientele. ⊠ *Berneggstrasse 2,* ☎ *071/220–00–33,* ℻ *071/223–54–74. 117 beds. Restaurant, bar. AE, DC, MC, V.*

$$$ 🏨 **Gallo.** Now a relatively cheap business hotel, this graceful former apartment house is set beside a busy road but has double-glazed windows to shut out the roar. The location is not particularly convenient to the old town (Bus 3, named Heiligkreuz, stops at nearby Olma or carries you into the center), but interiors are fresh and attractive, with big tile baths and bright-color lacquer; two lovely attic doubles have beams and dormer windows. There is a first-class Italian restaurant on the ground floor. ⊠ *St. Jakobstrasse 62,* ☎ *071/245–27–27,* ℻ *071/245–45–93. 49 beds. Restaurant. AE, DC, MC, V.*

$$$ 🏨 **Im Portner & Pförtnerhof.** The original old Im Portner hotel, in the
★   old town, is comfortable but undistinguished with its gold carpet, Naugahyde, and mix-and-match rooms. But across the street, the annexed Pförtnerhof stands apart: The big, bay-window, half-timber house has been restored and updated with style. The rooms combine antiquity (lead glass, painted woodwork, stone niches) with high tech (halogen, lithos, Euro-style baths). The location is ideal for sightseeing. ⊠ *Bankgasse 12,* ☎ *071/222–97–44,* ℻ *071/222–98–56. 37 beds. Restaurant, café. AE, DC, MC, V.*

$–$$ 🏨 **Elite.** In the modern deco style of the 1950s, this old-town spot has a functional air and a friendly staff. Half the rooms have baths; the others have running water and cost less. The back rooms are quieter. ⊠ *Metzgergasse 9/11,* ☎ *071/222–12–36,* ℻ *071/222–21–77. 36 beds. Breakfast room. AE, DC, MC, V.*

$–$$ 🏨 **Vadian.** A narrow town house tucked behind half-timber landmarks in the old town, this is a discreet and tidy little place. Most of its tiny rooms have been updated with beige stucco and knotty pine and new tile baths. Rooms without bath cost less. ⊠ *Gallusstrasse 36,* ☎ *071/223–60–80,* ℻ *071/222–47–48. 28 beds. Breakfast room. AE, DC, MC, V.*

Shopping

For a region world-renowned for its textiles and embroidery, it's surprisingly difficult to find the real thing at a single store. The excellent exception: **Saphir** (⊠ Bleichestrasse 9, ☎ 071/223–62–63) carries a dense, high-quality collection of embroidered handkerchiefs, bed and table linens, and bolts of embroidered fabric and lace—all from the St. Gallen region.

Sturzenegger (⊠ St. Leonhardstrasse 12, ☎ 071/222–45–76), the better-known source, has branches in several major Swiss cities. Its stock includes its own line of linens and lingerie, designed and manufactured in the factory a block away; Sturzenegger, a major embroidery firm, was established in 1883.

An outstanding assortment of antique prints of Swiss landscapes and costumes is sold at a broad range of prices at **Graphica Antiqua** (⊠ Oberer Graben 46, near Hotel Einstein, ☎ 071/223–50–16). The pictures are cataloged alphabetically by canton for easy browsing.

Appenzell

⑱ *20 km (12 mi) south of St. Gallen; 98 km (60 mi) southeast of Schaffhausen.*

Isolated from St. Gallen by a ridge of green hills, Appenzell is one of Switzerland's most eccentric regions. Fellow Swiss think of its people as hillbillies, citing their quirky sense of humor and mode of dress. A small highway (No. 3) leads into the hills through Teufen; the quaint Appenzell–*Teufen*–Gais rail line, whose red cars have a bear printed on the side, also serves the region. Either way, the city of St. Gallen melts away into undulating hills spotted with doe-skinned cows, a steep-pastured, isolated verdure reminiscent of West Virginia or the Ozarks. Prim, symmetrical cottages inevitably show rows of windows facing the valley. Named Appenzell after the Latin *abbatis cella* (abbey cell), the region served as a sort of colony to the St. Gallen abbey, and its tradition of fine embroidery dates from those early days.

The town of Appenzell focuses some of the best and worst of the region, offering tourists a concentrated and somewhat self-conscious sampling of the culture. Its streets lined with bright-painted homes, bakeries full of *Birnebrot* (pear bread) and souvenir *Biber* (stamped honey cakes), and shops full of embroidery (which, on close examination, often is made in China), Appenzell seems to watch the tourists warily and get on with its life while profiting from the attention. Its **Landsgemeindeplatz** is the site of the famous open-air elections (until 1991, for men only), which take place the last Sunday in April. Embroidery has become big business here, and it's rare to find handmade examples of the local art; though women still do fine work at home, it's generally reserved for gifts or heirlooms. Instead, large factories have sprung up in Appenzell country, and famous, fine-cotton handkerchiefs sold in specialty shops around the world are made by machine here at the Dörig, Alba, and Lehner plants.

A completely renovated **Museum Appenzell** showcases regional lacework. ⊠ *Hauptgasse 4,* ☎ *071/788–96–31.* 🖀 *5 SF.* ☉ *Apr.–Oct., Mon.–Sun. 10–noon and 2–5; Nov.–Mar., Tues.–Sun. 2–4.*

Dining and Lodging

$$$ ✕🏠 **Appenzell.** Although it was built from scratch in 1983, this com-
★ fortable new lodging has all the gabled Gemütlichkeit of its neighbors, with rows of shuttered windows and a view over the Landsgemeindeplatz (which, except on picturesque voting days, functions as both a busy intersection and a parking lot). Homey rooms, warmed with polished wood, owe their airiness to the traditional multiple windows. With stained glass, new carved wood, and laminated menus, the popular restaurant downstairs has the look of an upscale American pancake house, but the cooking is right on the regional target, with Mostbröckli, *Pastetli* (miniature puff pastry shells filled with chicken and mushroom sauce), *Siedfleischteller* (pot-au-feu, or beef stew), and an Appenzeller cheese-and-onion salad. The breakfast room for guests features the woodwork and a buffet transplanted from the family home that stood here before. A pastry shop adjoins the hotel. ⊠ *Landsgemeindeplatz,* ☎ *071/787–42–11,* 🖷 *071/787–42–84. 31 beds. Restaurant, breakfast room, patisserie, café. AE, DC, MC, V.*

$$$ ✕⊞ **Löwen.** Wising up to the tourists' quest for "typical" local decor, the owners of this renovated 1780 guest house furnished several rooms in authentic Appenzeller styles, with embroidered linens and built-in woodwork (canopy bed, armoires) painted with bright designs and naive local scenes—some actually reflecting the view from the window. Standard rooms in dormitory-style oak also are available for a slightly lower price. The public spaces are quarry-tile and stucco modern. ⊠ *Hauptgasse 25,* ☎ *071/787–21–87,* ⨳ *071/787–25–79. 58 beds. Restaurant, sauna. AE, DC, MC, V.*

$$–$$$ ✕⊞ **Säntis.** As a member of the Romantik hotel group, this is the prestige hotel in Appenzell, and prices are slightly higher. The ambience is new and formal, though the earliest wing has been a hotel-restaurant since 1835. Old-style touches—inlaid wood furnishings, painted beams—mix comfortably with new Naugahyde in the reception and lounge areas; jewel-tone rooms have gleaming walnut cabinetry and some four-poster or canopy beds. The main first-floor restaurant serves regional specialties, slightly Frenchified, in either of two wood-lined dining rooms, one Biedermeier, the other a folksy Appenzeller style. A fresh, cherrywood stübli at street level attracts locals. ⊠ *Landsgemeindeplatz,* ☎ *071/787–87–22,* ⨳ *071/787–48–42. 60 beds. Restaurant. AE, DC, MC, V.*

$$ ✕⊞ **Adler.** This pleasant lodging, across the street from the roaring River Sitter but at downtown's edge, offers a variety of decor, from the mod avocado of the café and restaurant to some of the nicest versions of regional style in town. The rooms in the main building, dating from 1895, are spacious and beige-Formica spare, with the public areas trimmed in "Spanish" ironwork. The older wing, once a private home, has been partly renovated to include four rooms in Appenzeller style, with the repeated square paneling and colorful painted cabinetry loyally reproduced. Four no-shower rooms, also in the old wing, are creaky but well-priced. Two friendly brothers live upstairs and run the hotel, the restaurant, and an adjoining pastry shop. ⊠ *Adlerplatz,* ☎ *071/87–13–89,* ⨳ *071/787–13–65. 40 beds. Restaurant, café, patisserie. AE, DC, MC, V.*

$ ✕⊞ **Freudenberg.** This is a cookie-cutter modern chalet, but its setting on a velvety green hillside behind the train station and overlooking town is the most scenic and tranquil you'll find here. Built in 1969, it still has dormlike rooms and sculptured carpet in harvest gold, but some rooms have balconies, and the broad, shaded terrace café—festive in the evening with strings of yellow lights—lets you take in the picture-pretty views. Ten minutes from the center of town on foot, it is also easily accessible by car. ⊠ *CH-9050,* ☎ *071/787–12–40,* ⨳ *071/787–12–40. 18 beds. Restaurant, café. AE.*

$ ✕⊞ **Hof.** One of Appenzell's most popular restaurants, this serves
★   hearty regional meats and cheese specialties (*Käseschnitte, Käse Spätzli*) to locals and tourists who crowd elbow-to-elbow along shared tables, especially at lunch, and raise their voices to be heard over the clatter from the service bar. The all-modern rustic-wood decor and ladder-back chairs, the knotty pine, and the display of sports trophies add to the local atmosphere. Upstairs, groups can rent cheap summer-camp dormitory lodgings and play skittles after dinner. ⊠ *Engelgasse 4,* ☎ *071/787–22–10,* ⨳ *071/787–58–83. 58 beds. Restaurant. AE, DC, MC, V.*

$ ✕⊞ **Taube.** Behind its charming, shuttered facade lies a drab interior: The restaurant-café is dim and slightly shabby despite its wood, stained glass, and cowbells, and regular rooms are '50s mix-and-match. The *dépendence* (neighboring annex), however, is a cheery alternative and worth seeking out for families or groups: In this rose-trellised, weathered-wood cottage, each pair of rooms is divided by double-access baths.

(If there's space, these can be rented as simple doubles with bath, with the second room closed off.) Here the decor is warm and traditional, with painted armoires and a picket-fence yard. ⊠ *Hirschengasse 8,* ☎ *071/787–11–49,* [FAX] *071/787–56–33. 33 beds. Restaurant, café. AE, DC, MC, V.*

Shopping

Butchers, bakers, and liquor shops up and down the streets offer souvenir bottles of Appenzeller Bitter (Alpenbitter), a very sweet aperitif made in town, and a well-balanced eau-de-vie, made of blended herbs, called Appenzeller Kräuter. Cheese and embroidery are also specialties of the region. Picnickers can sample the different grades of Appenzeller cheese and its unsung mountain rivals at **Sutter** (⊠ Industriestrasse 2, ☎ 071/787–12–27). **Mösler** (⊠ Hauptgasse, ☎ 071/787–13–33) also has a good selection of local cheeses.

True locally made hand embroidery is rare in Appenzell, though from the rows of shops displaying embroidered blouses and handkerchiefs along the town's main streets, you would think the stuff was native material. Ask: Many handkerchiefs that beautifully reproduce the blinding close work that locals no longer pursue have been hand-stitched in Portugal. Though an odd souvenir, they capture the spirit of Appenzell handwork better than much of the pretty, though broad, machine work available in the stores. **Margreiter** (⊠ Hauptgasse 29, ☎ 071/787–33–13) carries a large stock of machine-made handkerchiefs from the local Dörig, Alba, and Lehner factories, many decorated with edelweiss or other Alpine flowers. **Trachtenstube** (⊠ Hauptgasse 23, ☎ 071/787–16–06) offers high-quality local handiwork—lace, embroidery, and crafts.

Stein

⑲ *13 km (8 mi) northwest of Appenzell; 94 km (58 mi) southeast of Schaffhausen.*

At the **Schaukäserei** in Stein (not to be confused with Stein-am-Rhein), modern cheese-making methods are demonstrated. ☎ 071/368–50–70. ⬚ *Free.* ☉ *Mar.–Oct., daily 8–7; Nov.–Feb., daily 9–6. Note: Cheese is made 9–3 only.*

The **Appenzeller Volkskunde Museum** (Folklore Museum) demonstrates Appenzell arts and crafts, local costumes, and hand-painted furniture. ☎ 071/368–50–56. ⬚ *7 SF.* ☉ *Nov.–March, Sun. 10–5; Apr.–Oct., Mon. 1:30–5, Tues.–Sat. 10–noon and 1:30–5, Sun. 10–6.*

Urnäsch

⑳ *10 km (6 mi) west of Appenzell; 110 km (68 mi) southeast of Schaffhausen.*

In this modest countryside town, the **Museum für Appenzeller Brauchtum** (Museum of Appenzeller Traditions) displays costumes, cowbells, a cheese wagon, and examples of farmhouse living quarters. ☎ 071/364–23–22. ⬚ *4 SF.* ☉ *May–Oct., daily 1:30–5; Apr., Wed. and weekends 1:30–5; winter, by appointment only.*

Mt. Säntis

㉑ *11 km (7 mi) south of Urnäsch; 121 km (75 mi) southeast of Schaffhausen.*

A pleasant high-altitude excursion out of Appenzell takes you west to Urnäsch, then south to the hamlet of Schwägalp, where a cable car carries you up to the peak of **Mt. Säntis,** at 2,502 meters (8,209 feet) the highest in the region and a source of fine views of the Bodensee as well as of the Graubünden and Bernese Alps. The very shape of the summit—an arc of jutting rock that swings up to the jagged peak housing the station—is spectacular. ☎ 071/365–65–65. ☞ 27 SF round-trip. ☉ July–Aug., daily 7:30–7; May, June, and Sept., daily 7:30–6:30; Oct.–Apr., 8:30–5; closed for 3 wks in Jan. Departures every 30 mins.

Toggenburg Valley

㉒ *Entrance 11 km (7 mi) south of Mt. Säntis; 132 km (82 mi) southeast of Schaffhausen.*

A scenic pre-Alpine resort area popular with locals but relatively unexplored by outsiders, this is an ideal place for skiers and hikers who hate crowds. In the rugged Upper Toggenburg, weather-boarded dwellings surround the neighboring resorts of Wildhaus (Zwingli's birthplace), Unterwasser, and Alt–St. Johann, all of which draw Swiss families for winter skiing and summer hiking excursions into the Churfirsten and Alpstein mountains. As they lie within shouting distance of each other, the ski facilities can be shared, and the jagged teeth of the mountains behind provide a dramatic backdrop.

If you are fascinated by the Reformation, you may want to make a pilgrimage to Wildhaus' **Zwinglihaus,** the farmhouse where Huldrych Zwingli was born in 1484. His father was president of the commune, and the house was used as a meeting place for their council. A small museum within displays some restored furniture from his time, though not from his family, and an impressive collection of period Bibles. The fire-and-brimstone preacher celebrated his first mass in the town's Protestant church and went on to lead the Protestant Reformation in Zürich. ✉ Wildhaus/Lisighaus, ☎ 071/999–21–78. ☞ Free. ☉ Tues.–Sun. 2–4; closed mid-Apr.–May and mid-Nov.–Dec.

Skiing

Equally popular with locals, the triplet ski resorts of Wildhaus, Unterwasser, and Alt–St. Johann combine forces to draw visitors into the Churfirsten "Paradise" in the Toggenburg Valley. Here you'll find altitudes and drops to suit even jaded skiers, the most challenging starting on the 2,076-meter-high (6,809-foot-high) Gamserrugg and winding down 1,000 meters (3,280 feet) to Wildhaus itself; a medium-difficult rival winds from Chäserrugg (2,262 meters/7,419 feet) all the way down to Unterwasser. A one-day pass for all three resorts costs 45 SF; a six-day pass costs 188 SF.

Unterwasser, at 910 meters (2,986 feet), has one funicular railway, one cable car, four T-bars, 50 kilometers (31 miles) of downhill runs, 45 kilometers (28 miles) of cross-country trails, and 27 kilometers (17 miles) of ski-hiking trails.

At 1,098 meters (3,601 feet), **Wildhaus** offers skiers four chairlifts, five T-bars, 50 kilometers (31 miles) of downhill runs, 45 kilometers (28 miles) of cross-country trails, and 27 kilometers (17 miles) of ski-hiking trails. Besides skiing you can go skating or curling.

Outdoor Activities and Sports

Wildhaus (☎ 071/999–12–11) has two outdoor **tennis courts.** Unterwasser has three outdoor tennis courts (☎ 071/999–12–05) at **Sport Sutter.**

PRINCIPALITY OF LIECHTENSTEIN AND THE WALENSEE

When you cross the border from Switzerland into Liechtenstein, you will be surrounded by license plates marked "FL": This stands for "Fürstentum Liechtenstein," or "Principality of Liechtenstein." You are leaving the world's oldest democracy and entering a monarchy that is the last remnant of the Holy Roman Empire—all 157 square kilometers (61 square miles) of it. If you blink, you may miss it entirely.

This postage-stamp principality was begun at the end of the 17th century, when a wealthy Austrian prince, Johann Adam von Liechtenstein, bought out two bankrupt counts in the Rhine Valley and united their lands. In 1719 he obtained an imperial deed from Kaiser Karl VI, creating the principality of Liechtenstein. The noble family poured generations of wealth into the new country, improving its standard of living, and in 1862 an heir named Prince Johann the Good helped Liechtenstein introduce its first constitution as a "democratic monarchy" in which the people and the prince share power equally.

Today the principality's 30,000 citizens enjoy one of the world's highest per-capita incomes and pay virtually no taxes. Its prosperous (though discreet) industries range from jam making to the molding of false teeth. Ironically, prosperity has built the lower reaches of Liechtenstein into a modern, comfortable, bourgeois community, full of big, new cream-color bungalows that hardly seem picturesque to tourists seeking traces of the Holy Roman Empire.

Vaduz (Leichtenstein)

㉓ *15 km (9 mi) southeast of the Toggenburg Valley; 159 km (98 mi) southeast of Schaffhausen.*

Arriving in downtown Vaduz (there are exits from the N13 expressway from both the north and the south), a visitor could make the mistake of thinking Liechtenstein's only attraction is its miniature scale.

Liechtenstein's small **Briefmarkenmuseum** (Stamp Museum) demonstrates the principality's history as a maker of beautifully designed, limited-edition postage stamps. ⊠ *Städtle 37,* ☎ *075/232–14–43.* ▣ *Free.* ☉ *Apr.–Oct., daily 10–noon and 1:30–5:30; Nov.–Mar., daily 10–noon and 1:30–5.*

The **Liechtensteinische Staatliche Kunstsammlung** (Liechtenstein State Museum of Art) displays an ever-changing fraction of the country's extraordinary art collection, including graphic art, paintings, and other works from the world-famous art collection of the Prince. Look for the 18th-century golden carriage. ⊠ *Städtle 37,* ☎ *075/232–23–41.* ▣ *3 SF.* ☉ *Apr.–Oct., daily 10–noon and 1:30–5:30; Nov.–Mar., daily 10–noon and 1:30–5.*

The **Liechtensteinisches Landesmuseum** (National Museum), in a former tavern and customs house, covers the geology, Roman history, and folklore of the principality. ⊠ *Städtle 43,* ☎ *075/232–23–10.* ▣ *2 SF.* ☉ *May–Sept., daily 10–noon and 1:30–5:30; Oct.–Apr., Tues.–Sun. 2–5:30.*

★ At the top of a well-marked hill road (you can climb the forest footpath behind the Hotel Engel) stands **Vaduz Castle.** Here, His Highness, Johannes Adam Pius, Reigning Prince of Liechtenstein, Duke of Troppau and Jaegerndorf, holds forth in a gratifyingly romantic fortress-home with striped medieval shutters, massive ramparts, and a broad perspective over the Rhine Valley. Originally built during the 12th century, the castle was burned down by troops of the Swiss Confederation in the Swabian Wars of 1499 and partly rebuilt during the following centuries, until a complete overhaul that started in 1905 gave it its present form. It is not open to the public, as Hans-Adam enjoys his privacy. He is the son of the late, beloved Franz Josef II, who died in November 1989 after more than 50 years' reign. Franz Josef's birthday is still celebrated as the Liechtenstein national holiday on August 15; Hans-Adam—the last living heir to the Holy Roman Empire—has been known to join the crowds below to watch the fireworks, wearing jeans.

Dining and Lodging

$ ★ ✕ **Wirthschaft zum Löwen.** Though there's plenty of French, Swiss, and Austrian influence, Liechtenstein has a cuisine of its own, and this is the place to try it. In a wood-shingle landmark farmhouse on the Austrian border, the friendly Biedermann family serves tender homemade *Schwartenmagen* (the pressed pork-mold unfortunately known as headcheese in English), pungent *Sauerkäse* (sour cheese), and Käseknöpfli, plus lovely meats and the local crusty, chewy bread. Try the region's wines and the automatic snuff machine. ⊠ *FL-9488,* ☎ *075/373-11-62. V.*

$$$$ ✕⊞ **Park-Hotel Sonnenhof.** A garden oasis commanding a superb view over the valley and mountains beyond, this hillside retreat offers understated luxury minutes from downtown Vaduz. Rooms are decorated in homey pastels; many open directly onto the lawns while others have balconies. The public areas are full of antiques, rugs, woodwork, and familial touches. This Relais & Châteaux property has an excellent French restaurant, exclusively for guests. ⊠ *Mareestrasse 29,* ☎ *075/232-11-92,* FAX *075/232-00-53. 50 beds. Restaurant, indoor pool, sauna. AE, DC, MC, V.*

$$$–$$$$ ★ ✕⊞ **Real.** Here you'll find rich, old-style Austrian-French cuisine in all its buttery glory, prepared these days by Martin Real, son of the unpretentious former chef, Felix Real—who, in his retirement, presides over the 20,000-bottle cellar. There's an abundance of game in season, rich-sauce seafood, soufflés, and a few new dishes inspired by the East. The ambience is old school, and generous seasonal salads are prepared at your table. The extraordinary wine list includes some rare (and excellent) examples of the local product. Downstairs, the more casual stübli atmosphere is just right for Geschnetzeltes mit Rösti (bits of meat with hash brown potatoes); upstairs, you'll find 11 small but airily decorated rooms with baths. ⊠ *Städtle 21,* ☎ *075/232-22-22,* FAX *075/ 232-08-91. 21 beds. Restaurant. AE, DC, MC, V.*

$$ ✕⊞ **Engel.** This simple hotel-restaurant on the main tourist street has a comfortable, local ambience despite the tour-bus crowds. The Schönauer family oversees the easygoing pub downstairs, where home cooking (*Gulasch Suppe*) and live music (synth and organ) draw Vaduzers to a sociable supper. Upstairs, the more formal restaurant features Chinese cuisine; in fine weather, you can eat on the balcony. The refurbished guest rooms are in fresh colors, with tile bathrooms. ⊠ *Städtle 13,* ☎ *075/232-03-13,* FAX *075/233-11-59. 30 beds. Restaurant, pub. AE, DC, MC, V.*

Outdoor Activities and Sports

In Vaduz, bikes and small motorcycles can be rented from **Hans Melliger** (☎ 075/232-16-06). Vaduz has covered **tennis courts** (☎ 075/ 232-77-20) on Schaanerstrasse.

Shopping

Though shops on the main street of Vaduz carry samples of the local dark-glazed pottery, painted with folksy flowers and figures, the central source is **Schaedler Keramik** in Nendeln, 8 kilometers (5 miles) north of Vaduz on the main highway. Simpler household pottery is available for sale as well as the traditional and often ornate hand-painted pieces. Pottery making is demonstrated daily. ⊠ *FL-9485 Nendeln,* ☎ *075/373–14–14.* ⊙ *Weekdays 8–noon and 1:30–6.*

Liechtenstein is sometimes called the unofficial, per capita world champion of stamp collecting. To buy some of its famous stamps, whether to send a postcard to a philatelist friend or to invest in limited issue commemorative sheets, you must line up with the tour-bus crowds at the popular **Post Office** (⊠ Städtle).

Triesenberg

㉔ *3 km (2 mi) southeast of Vaduz; 162 km (100 mi) southeast of Schaffhausen.*

Those looking for remnants of Roman times would do well to visit this cluster of pretty chalets clinging to the mountainside, with panoramic views over the Rhine Valley. Triesenberg was settled during the 13th century by immigrants from the Valais in southwest Switzerland. The **Walser Heimatmuseum** (Valais Heritage Museum) traces the culture of the people who emigrated from the Valais to Triesenberg during the 13th century. Furnishings and tools from farmers and craftsmen are displayed, and a 20-minute slide show illustrates their history. ☎ *075/262–19–26.* ⚞ *2 SF.* ⊙ *Tues.–Sat. 1:30–5:30; June–Aug., Sun. 2–5.*

Malbun (Liechtenstein)

㉕ *5 km (3 mi) southeast of Triesenberg; 167 km (103 mi) southeast of Schaffhausen.*

In winter, this 1,580-meter (5,182-foot) high mountain resort on the border of Austria draws crowds of local families who come for the varied slopes, many of which are well suited to beginners. (England's Prince Charles and Princess Anne learned to ski here while visiting the Liechtenstein royal family in Vaduz.) In summer, Malbun becomes a quiet, unpretentious resort with reasonable prices.

Skiing

Malbun is a sunny natural bowl with low, easy slopes and a couple of difficult runs as well; you can ride a chairlift to the top of the Sareiserjoch and experience the novelty of skiing from the Austrian border back into Liechtenstein. Facilities are concentrated at the center, including hotels and cafés overlooking the slopes. One-day lift tickets cost 32 SF; six-day passes cost 132 SF.

Dining and Lodging

$–$$ ✕⌂ **Alpenhotel.** This 85-year-old chalet, well above the mists of the Rhine in sunny, easygoing Malbun, has been remodeled and has added a modern wing. The old rooms are small, with creaky pine trim; the higher-priced new rooms are modern stucco. The Vögeli family's welcoming smiles and good food have made the establishment a Liechtenstein institution. ⊠ *FL-9497,* ☎ *075/263–11–81,* ⅲ *075/263–96–46. 50 beds. Restaurant, café, indoor pool. AE, DC, MC, V.*

Flumserberg

㉖ *25 km (15 mi) west of Malbun; 122 km (75 mi) southeast of Schaffhausen.*

On the windswept, timberless slopes overlooking the Walensee and the Churfirsten mountains, this resort is the site of one of the world's longest cableways: Over a distance of about 3 kilometers (1¾ miles), a procession of little four-seater cabins reaches up to the rocky summit at **Leist** (2,056 meters/6,743 feet).

Skiing

Flumserberg, at 540–1,390 meters (1,772–4,560 feet), has three cable cars, five chairlifts, 13 T-bars, 50 kilometers (31 miles) of downhill runs, 21 kilometers (13 miles) of cross-country trails, and 20 kilometers (12 miles) of mountain trails. You'll also find skating, ski bob, and night skiing. One-day lift tickets cost 45 SF; six-day passes cost 188 SF.

The Walensee

㉗ *5 km (3 mi) northwest of Flumserberg; 127 km (78 mi) southeast of Schaffhausen.*

Between Liechtenstein and Zurich, the spectacular, mirrorlike lake called the Walensee is a deep, emerald gash stretching 16 kilometers (10 miles) long through the mountains, and reflecting the jagged Churfirsten peaks.

At the western end of the lake, **Weesen** is a quiet, shady resort noted for its mild climate and lovely lakeside walkway. Six kilometers (4 miles) north of Weesen on a winding mountain road lies **Amden,** a major winter sports center despite its small size; tidy, up-to-date, and traditional, it is rarely penetrated by foreigners.

Skiing

Amden, perched above the Walensee in the relatively undiscovered region south of the Churfirsten mountains, offers modest, familial skiing opportunities in a ruggedly beautiful setting. Easy and medium slopes with unspectacular drops and quick, short lift runs provide good weekend skiing for the crowds of local Swiss who bring their children here. At 910 meters (2,986 feet)—highest trails start at 1,700 meters (5,576 feet)—it has one chairlift, five T-bars, one children's lift, 25 kilometers (16 miles) of downhill runs, and 11 kilometers (7 miles) of cross-country trails. There are also a ski school, skating on a natural ice rink, and walking paths. One-day lift tickets cost 29 SF; six-day passes cost 125 SF.

Outdoor Activities and Sports

SKATING

There's a public **skating rink** in Amden; call ☎ 055/611–14–13 for information.

SWIMMING

Schwimm-und Badeanstalt Mühleholz (☎ 075/232–24–77) offers heated outdoor swimming for Vaduz and the village of Schaan in Liechtenstein.

TENNIS

Amden has two outdoor **tennis courts** (☎ 058/46–12–92).

....

OFF THE
BEATEN PATH

RAPPERSWIL – Between the Walensee and Lake Zürich, this small town affords pleasant views and summertime waterfront strolls. Its forbidding 13th-century castle looks like part of a gothic novel, with a trio of grave towers. Its walkway faces a small deer park and affords a view of Zürich; from its terrace you'll see the Glarus Alps. Children will love the Knie's Kinderzoo (Children's Zoo). There are dolphin shows, 70 types of animals from around the world, elephant and pony rides, and plenty of creatures to feed and pet. (Elephant rides are not given on rainy days.)

Follow signs; it's near the train station. ⊠ *CH-8640,* ☎ *055/27-52-22.* 🖃 *7 SF.* ⊙ *Mid-Mar.–Oct., daily 9–6.*

EASTERN SWITZERLAND A TO Z

Arriving and Departing

By Car

The N1 expressway from Zürich heads for St. Gallen through Winterthur. To reach Schaffhausen from Zürich, take N1 to Winterthur, then head north on cantonal highway E41. You also can leave Zürich by way of the N4 expressway past Kloten airport, cross through Germany briefly, and enter Schaffhausen through Neuhausen am Rheinfall. From the south, the N13 expressway, shared with Austria, leads you from Chur along Liechtenstein to the eastern end of the Bodensee; from there, you take N1 into St. Gallen.

By Plane

Kloten airport in Zürich, the most important in Switzerland, lies about 48 kilometers (30 miles) south of Schaffhausen, about 75 kilometers (46 miles) west of St. Gallen, and 130 kilometers (81 miles) northwest of Liechtenstein.

By Train

A connection by train from the Zürich Hauptbahnhof into Schaffhausen takes about 40 minutes; into St. Gallen and Sargans, about an hour. Connections from the south (Graubünden) are more complicated, as both Austria and the Alps intervene.

Getting Around

By Boat

Swiss Federal Railways provide regular year-round service on the Bodensee, though fewer boats run in winter. There is also a cruise-ship route on the Walensee and a Rhine cruise between Schaffhausen and Kreuzlingen-Konstanz. The Swiss Boat Pass allows half-fare travel (☞ Smart Travel Contacts *and* Resources A to Z *in* the Gold Guide).

By Bus

Postbuses provide much of the public transport in areas not served by trains, particularly smaller towns and, of course, Liechtenstein, which has no rail service. The details of schedules are available from the PTT (post, telephone, and telegraph office).

By Cable Car

Although there are a few scattered across the region, the most popular and spectacular cable-car rides are up Mt. Säntis from Schwägalp and to the Ebenalp via Appenzell-Wasserauen.

By Car

Driving in Eastern Switzerland allows you to see the best of this region, with its highway along the Bodensee and pretty back roads in Appenzell. Neither St. Gallen nor Schaffhausen is a big enough city to warrant all-out panic, although you'll find it easiest to head directly for the center and abandon the car for the duration of your visit.

By Train

Rail connections are somewhat complicated in this area, especially if you want to visit more of Appenzell than its major towns. The only railroads into this unspoiled country are the narrow-gauge line between St. Gallen and the town of Appenzell, which passes Teufen and Gais;

and the Gossau–Appenzell–Wasserauen line. To see more of the territory, you may return to St. Gallen on this same line by way of Herisau.

Although there is no regional rail pass available for Eastern Switzerland, the general Swiss Pass includes St. Gallen and Schaffhausen city
transit as well as overall rail privileges. You cannot enter Liechtenstein
by rail; the international express train that passes between Switzerland
and Austria doesn't bother to stop. From the train stations at Buchs
or Sargans, you can catch a postbus into Vaduz.

Contacts and Resources

Emergencies
Police (☎ 117). **Ambulance** (☎ 144). **Medical assistance:** in St. Gallen
(☎ 071/226–11–11). **Doctor, dentist, late-night pharmacies** (☎ 111).

Guided Tours
The **Schaffhausen tourist office** (✉ Fronwegturm, ☎ 053/625–51–41)
gives guided walking tours of the old town, the monastery, and the
Munot.

You can take a free half-hour guided tour of an Appenzeller cheese factory in Stein (☎ 071/59–17–33).

The **Untersee und Rhein** ship company (✉ Freier Platz 7, 8202
Schaffhausen, ☎ 052/625–42–82) offers a winning combination of
a boat ride on the Rhine and romantic views of storybook castles, citadels,
and monasteries gliding past. There are bathrooms and meals on
board. Boats run regularly up- and downstream, docking at Schaffhausen,
Stein-am-Rhein, Gottlieben, Konstanz, and Kreuzlingen. Prices vary according to distance traveled. A one-way trip from Schaffhausen to Kreuzlingen takes about 4½ hours.

Visitor Information
The tourist office for all of Eastern Switzerland is based in St. Gallen
(✉ Bahnhofplatz 1a, CH-9001, ☎ 071/222–62–62).

There are small regional visitor information offices throughout Eastern
Switzerland. **Appenzellerland** (✉ Hauptgasse 4, CH-9050 Appenzell, ☎
071/87–96–41; CH-9063 Stein, ☎ 071/59–11–59). **St. Gallerland** (✉
Bahnhofplatz 1a, CH-9001 St. Gallen, ☎ 071/222–62–62). **Schaffhausen**
(✉ Fronwagturm 4, CH-8201 Schaffhausen, ☎ 053/625–51–41).
Liechtenstein (✉ Städtle 37, FL-9490 Vaduz, ☎ 075/232–14–43). **Thur-
gau** services the Bodensee (✉ Gemeindehaus, CH-8580 Amriswil, ☎
071/67–68–51).

4 Graubünden

Dominated by its trendy resorts—St. Moritz, Davos, Kloster, Arosa, Pontresina—Graubünden is nonetheless Switzerland's most culturally diverse and largest canton. German, Italian, and Romansh—the ancient dialect that is thought to date from 600 BC—are all spoken here, in a land where stalwart native farmers subsist alongside fur-clad tourists from abroad.

THOUGH THE NAMES OF ITS RESORTS strike a resonance of global recognition few in the world can match— St. Moritz, Davos, Klosters, Arosa, Pontresina—the region wrapped around them remains surprisingly unsung, untouched by the fur-clad poseurs who people its stellar sports centers, aloof to their glamorous trends—quirky, resilient, a land apart. Nowhere in Switzerland will you find sharper contrasts than those between the bronzed town-and-country people who jet into St. Moritz and the stalwart native farmers who nurse their own archaic dialects and gather their crops by hand, as their Roman-Etruscan forefathers did.

Graubünden is the largest canton in Switzerland, covering more than one-sixth of the entire country. As it straddles the continental divide, its rains pour off north into the Rhine and Inn rivers and south into the Italian River Po. The land is thus riddled with bluff-lined valleys, and its southern half is bathed in crystalline sun—except for the Italian Ticino, it receives the most sunshine in the country. These valleys are flanked by dense blue-black wilderness and white peaks, among them Piz Buin (3,313 meters/10,863 feet) in the north and Piz Bernina (4,050 meters/13,281 feet) in the south.

Of all the Swiss cantons, Graubünden is the most culturally diverse. Its northern flank borders Austria and Liechtenstein, and in the east and south, it abuts Italy. Dialects of both German and Italian are widely spoken. But the obscure and ancient language called Romansh (literally, "Roman") is spoken by a full third of the population, harking back to its days in the 1st century BC, when it was a Roman province called Rhaetia Prima. Some venture that the tongue predates the Romans and trace its roots back as far as 600 BC, when an Etruscan prince named Rhaetus invaded the region.

Though anyone versed in a Latin tongue can follow Romansh's simpler signs (*camara da vacanza* is vacation apartment; *il büro da pulizia,* the police office), it is no easy matter to pick it up by ear. Nor do the Graubündners smooth the way: Rhaetian Romansh is fragmented into five subdialects beyond its codified form, so that anyone living in one of the isolated valleys of the region might call the same cup a *cuppina,* a *scadiola,* a *scariola,* a *cuppegn,* a *tazza,* or a *cupina.* Even the name *Graubünden* itself comes in a variety of forms: In French it's Les Grisons; in Italian, I Grigioni; and in Romansh, Il Grischun. It dates from the 14th century, when its people formed a "gray confederation" to rebel against Hapsburg rule.

With so many tongues and dialects cutting one valley culture neatly off from another, it's no wonder the back roads of the region seem as removed from the modern mainstream as the once-a-century world of Brigadoon.

Pleasures and Pastimes

Dining

In this relatively exotic region of Switzerland, with its myriad dialects and potent mix of Latin and German blood, the cuisine is as novel and unexpected as its culture. Though you hear of little but the ubiquitous *Bündnerfleisch* (air-dried beef pressed into rectangular loaves and shaved into chewy, translucent slices), you will find a much broader range of delights—including variations on the theme as simple as air-dried ham or air-dried bacon. Italian influence is strong here, but— unlike the Ticinese to the southwest, who borrow from Italy wholesale—the Graubündners have evolved their own versions, and incorporate Germanic styles as well. Versions of gnocchi (potato-based pasta balls) and *Spätzli* (tiny flour dumplings) coexist here, with relatives of *Rösti* (hash brown potatoes) and polenta asserting their own local flavor.

Coming from an isolated, rural region, the cuisines of Graubünden are earthy and direct, with sausages, potatoes, cheese, and cabbage as staples, and onions, garlic, bacon, and dried fruits to provide the hearty flavors. You may feel you've stepped back to the Middle Ages when you sit down to *pizzoccheri neri* (little buckwheat Spätzli or dumplings swimming in garlic) or to *maluns* (grated potatoes stirred in pools of butter until they form crisp balls) served with tart applesauce. *Capuns* or *krutkapuna* are bundles of Swiss chard smothered in butter and cheese and flavored with dried meat, and *hexenpolenta* is nothing but cornmeal mush sweetened with raisins and apples.

Your problem will be finding these down-to-earth treasures. The average visitor to Graubünden will be hard-pressed to locate menus imaginative enough to incorporate them alongside the token regional specialties most offer: robust *Gerstensuppe* (barley soup), *Engadiner Nusstorte* (a chewy walnut-and-honey cake found in every bake shop and even packaged commercially), and the inevitable (but wonderful) variety of cold local meats offered as a *Bündnerplatte*. Nonetheless, a few fine restaurateurs work hard to maintain the region's culinary heritage, and if the trend toward reviving dialects is an indication, a revival of local cuisines can't be far behind.

Watch for the annual winter **Gourmet Festival,** when 10 world-renowned chefs serve their specialties in 10 host restaurants of St. Moritz. Friday evenings during the summer, the Engadine wunderkind, chef Roland Jöhri, serves a meal on a train ride from Chur to St. Moritz. The "Grand Gourmet Finale" is a gargantuan feast prepared by 30 chefs on the frozen St. Moritz lake. For reservations call the St. Moritz tourist office (☎ 081/837−33−33).

Graubünden has its own distinctive wines: red pinot noir, white Riesling x Silvaner, and pinot gris from the Bündnerherrschaft, the sunny region around Maienfeld, Jenins, and Malans; and the unique Veltliner, a hearty red Nebbiolo grown over the border in Valtellina, which, then known as the Veltlin, was ceded to Italy in 1815. The wine has always been carried into Graubünden, where it is aged and bottled as a product that is, at least in spirit, Swiss.

CATEGORY	COST*
$$$$	over 80 SF
$$$	50 SF–80 SF
$$	20 SF–50 SF
$	under 20 SF

per person for a three-course meal (except in $ category), including sales tax and 15% service charge

Farmhouse Vacations

If you want to go beyond the usual resort experience and live the Graubündner way, you can rent an apartment or a room on a working farm. The regional tourist office publishes a list of cooperating families along with inventories of their attractions: number of children and birth dates (helpful if you have kids looking for playmates); cows, horses, pigs, rabbits, and other animals; and farm-fresh food products available for sale. You can even join in with the chores if you're so inclined. A functioning knowledge of German (or Italian, depending on the region) makes a big difference in the degree of diplomatic exchange. For a copy of the booklet "Ferien auf dem Bauernhof" (Farm Vacations) contact the Graubünden Tourist Office (☎ 081/302–61–00); address written requests to the Chur Tourist Office (✉ Alexanderstrasse 24, CH-7001 Chur, ☎ 081/252–18–18).

Lodging

Of all the regions in Switzerland—each trading on its homeyness, its quaintness, its picture-book image—Graubünden is the one that delivers the most, as its hoteliers invest fortunes in preserving Alpine coziness inside and out. Unlike most regions, where hotels radiate warmth and history from their shuttered facades but have interiors as stark as hospital rooms, more and more Graubünden hotels are softened from within with wood. The source is *Arvenholz,* the prized Alpine pine (*Pinus cembra*), thick with knots and rich in natural color—a color that deepens from buff to burnished toffee over the decades. Where it was originally installed, it has been preserved; where it wasn't, it is being built in, and beds, armoires, end tables, and sometimes even ceilings are being made of the lovely material. But while they preserve it, they don't always leave it alone: Sometimes it's lavishly carved in Graubünden style. Whether it keeps company with rustic plaids, pristine whites, or contemporary chintz, the effect is welcoming and unmistakably Swiss.

Prices in this popular region are relatively high—even if you leave exorbitant St. Moritz out of the curve—and they remain so most of the year. Winter is the priciest, summer close behind.

CATEGORY	COST*
$$$$	over 300 SF
$$$	200 SF–300 SF
$$	120 SF–200 SF
$	under 120 SF

All prices are for a standard double room, including breakfast, sales tax, and 15% service charge. Resort hotels are without demipension.

Skiing and Snow Sports

With Davos as the site of the first ski lift in history, St. Moritz as the world's ritziest resort, and a host of other justifiably famous winter wonderlands within its confines, Graubünden easily earns its reputation as the ultimate winter destination. In addition to downhill skiing at all levels, Graubünden also offers cross-country and off-piste skiing, snowboarding and heli-skiing, and a host of other winter activities—from curling, skating, and tobogganing to more unusual spectator sports such as dogsled racing and ski joering, in which participants are pulled on skis by a horse. For those who prefer summer sports in the winter, St. Moritz offers ice polo and ice golf on its frozen lake.

Trains

The narrow-gauge, bright red trains of the Rhätische Bahn were designed with sightseeing in mind, and along with the legendary, panoramic Glacier Express to Zermatt, which takes you up and over the barren heart of Switzerland near Andermatt, trains throughout the region travel over spectacular glacial terrain, crossing bridges built unbelievably high over mountain gorges, and cutting through mountainsides by way of viaducts. Crossing between Andermatt and Disentis, you'll think you've landed on the moon; there's not a footprint in sight atop the glacier, yet tiny villages and train stops serve to remind you that the Swiss have yet again made "the impossible" routine.

Exploring Graubünden

The region is fairly neatly bisected, by a spine of 2,989-meters (9,800-foot) peaks, into two very different sections, connected only by the Julier Pass, the Albula Pass, and the Flüela Pass. In the northwest, the region's capital, Chur, is flanked by ancient villages and a few lesser-known ski resorts. Farther east is the wild and craggy Prättigau region, which includes the resorts of Klosters and Davos as well as the Flüela Pass. The other half of the canton is comprised of the famous Engadine region, home to sophisticated resorts and mountain-ringed lakes: Sils-Maria, Pontresina, and St. Moritz—as well as the magnificent Swiss National Park.

Great Itineraries

IF YOU HAVE 1 OR 2 DAYS

Numbers in the text correspond to numbers in the margin and on the Graubünden map.

Concentrate on ⌖ **St. Moritz** ⑭, where you can indulge in some of the world's most varied sports activities as well as sophisticated cuisine and exclusive nightlife (expect to pay dearly for all). To wind down afterwards, head to **Pontresina** ⑬, whose stately old hotels, sgraffitied buildings, and pine and larch forests form the ideal setting for those in search of a low-key resort.

IF YOU HAVE 3 OR 4 DAYS

Drive the mountain passes through "Heidi Country." Start at the region's capital **Chur** ③, then continue to ⌖ **Klosters** ⑤, where the British royal family vacations. Alternatively, head from Chur to ⌖ **Arosa** ④— whose isolated setting and old village character set it apart.

IF YOU HAVE 5 OR MORE DAYS

In addition to all of the above, visit the Upper and Lower Engadine. In the Upper Engadine Valley, the superior **Parc Naziunal Svizzer** ⑩ is a magnificent federally-protected preserve of virtually virgin wilderness. Climb the **Julier Pass** heading north to **Tiefencastel** ⑯ (if you're going that way, leave the region via the San Bernardino Pass), or simply take in a spa at **Bad Ragaz** ① on your way back to civilization.

When to Tour Graubünden

Though the tourism industry breathlessly awaits winter, when Graubünden's resorts fill to capacity, summer is becoming a popular season as well. Such warm-weather sports as hiking, climbing, cycling, golfing, boating, and even hot-air ballooning are transforming the area into a year-round destination. Avoid November and early December, when most resorts close for preparations and annual renovations. In late September to late October, the weather is beautiful and still quite warm, with fall colors and crisp, clear skies. Spring arrives late, in May; April is still usually muddy and cold.

HEIDI COUNTRY, CHUR, AND AROSA

Though it's the gateway to Graubünden, this region has a catchier claim to fame: It was here that the legendary Heidi enjoyed the fresh air and rustic pleasures of the Alps.

Bad Ragaz

❶ *20 km (12 mi) north of Chur.*

When Heidi's crippled friend Clara needed to take a cure, she came first to Bad Ragaz, the renowned thermal spa in the Rhine Valley. Its warm (37°C/98°F), abundant springs have been tapped for a thousand years for the treatment of rheumatism, circulation problems, and—as in Clara's case—paralysis. Nowadays you can take the cure at one of two indoor thermal pools, open to the public, though preferably a public with more stringent medical needs than a good, hot soak. The baths are open daily from 7 AM to 8:30 PM. The ambience in this old resort

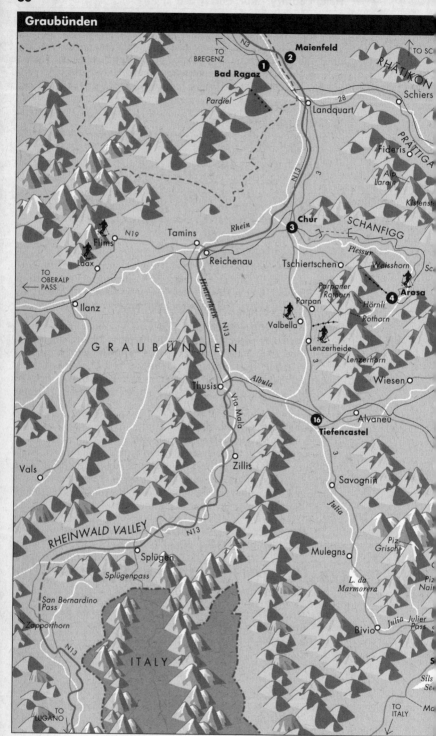

TO BREGENZ

N3

Maienfeld

2

RHÄTIKON

1

Bad Ragaz

Schiers

TO SC

Pardiel

Landquart

28

PRÄTIGA

N13

Fideris

Alp Larein

Kistenste

3

Chur

3

SCHANFIGG

Rhein

Tamins

Plessur

N19

Flims

Reichenau

Tschiertschen

Weisshorn

Sc

Laax

Parpaner Rothorn

4 **Arosa**

TO OBERALP PASS

Parpan

Hörnli

Valbella

Rothorn

Ilanz

Lenzerheide

3

Lenzerhorn

G R A U B Ü N D E N

Albula

Wiesen

Hinterrhein

N13

Via Mala

Thusis

16

Alvaneu

Tiefencastel

3

Vals

Zillis

Savognin

Julia

RHEINWALD VALLEY

N13

Mulegns

Piz Grischi

Splügen

Splügenpass

L. da Marmorera

Piz Nair

San Bernardino Pass

Zapporthorn

Julia *Julier Pass*

N13

Bivio

S

TO LUGANO

ITALY

Sils See

TO ITALY

Ma

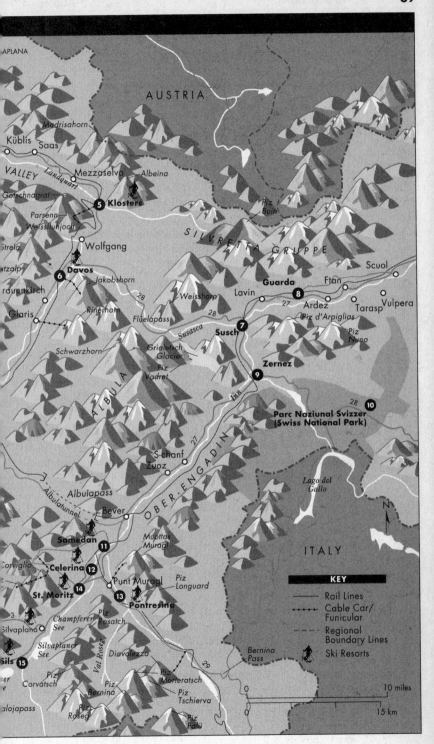

APLANA

AUSTRIA

Madrisahorn

Küblis   Saas

VALLEY   Landquart   Mezzaselva   Albeina

Gotschnagrat

5 Klosters

Parsenn
Weissfluhjoch

Wolfgang

Strela

SILVRETTA GRUPPE

atzalp

6 Davos

Jakobshorn

rauenkirch   Weisshorn   Lavin   **Guarda**   Ftan   Scuol

Glaris   Rinerhorn   28   **8**   27   Ardez   Tarasp   Vulpera

Flüelapass   28   Piz d'Arpiglias

Susasca   **Susch** **7**   Piz Nuna

Schwarzhorn   Grialetsch Glacier

Piz Vadret   **Zernez**

9

ALBULA   Inn   28   **10**

Parc Naziunal Svizzer (Swiss National Park)

27

Lago del Gallo

S-chanf

Zuoz

OBER ENGADIN

ITALY

Albulapass

Albulatunnel   Bever

Samedan   **11**   Muottas Muragl

Corviglia   **Celerina**   **12**

St. Moritz   **14**   Punt Muragl   Piz Languard

13   **Pontresina**

Silvaplana   Champferer See   Piz Rosatch

Silvaplaner See   Val Roseg   Diavolezza

15   Bernina Pass   29

Piz Corvatsch   Piz Bernina   Piz Morteratsch

alojapass   Piz Roseg   Piz Tschierva

Piz Palü

KEY
—— Rail Lines
••••• Cable Car/ Funicular
–– –– Regional Boundary Lines
⛷ Ski Resorts

0   10 miles

0   15 km

N

is more therapeutic than aesthetic, though the views of the mountains—
including the Falknis (2,562 meters/8,400 feet)—are lovely. There's a
fine golf course, and a cable car runs up to Pardiel (1,631 meters/5,350
feet), with a lift to Laufboden (2,226 meters/7,300 feet).

Maienfeld

❷ *5 km (3 mi) east of Bad Ragaz; 11 km (7 mi) north of Chur.*

Above this graceful little village full of fountains, vineyards, and old
stucco houses, the Zürich author Johanna Spyri set *Heidi*, the much-
loved children's story of an orphan growing up with her grandfather
on an isolated Alpine farm. Taken away to accompany the invalid Clara
in murky Frankfurt, she languishes until returning to her mountain home.
Spyri spent time in Maienfeld and hiked the mountains behind, but it's
questionable whether actual people inspired her tale. Nonetheless, you
can hike from the Heidihof hotel across steep open meadows and up
thick forest switchbacks to what have now been designated "Peter the
Goatherd's Hut" and "The Alm-Uncle's Hut"—and take in awesome
Rhine Valley views from flowered meadows that would have suited Heidi
beautifully.

Chur

❸ *27 km (17 mi) south of Maienfeld.*

Now the region's capital and a small city of 33,000 with a bustling
downtown and a busy rail crossroads, Chur is actually the oldest con-
tinuously settled site in Switzerland; there are traces of habitation
from as far back as 3000–2500 BC. The Romans founded Curia Rae-
torium on the rocky terrace south of the river; from here, they protected the Alpine routes that led to the Bodensee. By AD 284 it served
as the capital of the flourishing Roman colony Rhaetia Prima. Its heyday, however, evident throughout the old town even now, was during
the Middle Ages, when it was ruled by bishops and bishop-princes. Narrow streets, cobblestone alleys, hidden courtyards, and ancient shuttered buildings abound; towering over them all is the massive
12th-century Kathedrale (Cathedral).

Dominating the old town is the **Rathaus** (Town Hall), built as two structures in 1464 and connected in 1540. Its striking deep roof, topped
with a lantern tower, follows the odd form of the joined buildings—
one end is narrower than the other. Inside, the Grosser Ratsaal has a
timbered ceiling dating from 1493 and an 18th-century ceramic stove.
The Bürgerratskammer has Renaissance wall panels and another ceramic stove, this one from 1632. To visit either of these rooms, ask in
advance at the tourist office. Embedded in the wall beside the Reichs-
gasse door of the Rathaus, there's a rod of iron about a foot long—
the standard measure of a "foot" or shoe before the metric system was
introduced. Nearby, **Altes Gebäu** (literally, Old Building), is an early
18th-century mansion built for a Chur statesman.

The slender, spired **Kirche St. Martin** (Church of St. Martin) was built
in 1491 in the late-Gothic style after a fire destroyed the 8th-century
original. Since 1526, it has been a Protestant church. Three stained-
glass windows created in 1919 by the Graubünden sculptor Alberto
Giacometti's father, Augusto Giacometti, are on your right as you
enter. The steeple of the church dates from 1917; with permission from
the sacristan, you can climb to the top to see the bells.

The **Rätisches Museum** (Rhaetic Museum) is housed in the 1675 mansion of the wealthy von Buol family. Its collection includes not only

furnishings and goods from the period, but also archaeological finds from the region, both Roman and prehistoric. Across from the Rätishces Museum stands the **Oberer Spaniöl**, another luxurious mansion from the 1640s. ✉ *Hofstrasse 1,* ☎ *081/257–28–89.* ⓥ *Tues.–Sun. 10–noon and 2–5.*

The stone archway under the **Hof-Torturm** (Court Entrance Tower) leads into the residence of the strong bishop-princes of Chur, once hosts to Holy Roman emperors who passed through on their way between Italy and Germany—sometimes with whole armies in tow. The bishops were repaid for their hospitality by imperial donations to the people. The thick fortifications of the residence demonstrate the disputed powers of the bishops; by the 15th century, irate inhabitants who rebelled again and again were rebuffed and punished with excommunication. By 1526 the Reformation broke the domination of the Church—although the city remains a Catholic bishopric today.

NEED A BREAK?   Turn back the hands of time in the **Hofkellerei,** inside the Court Entrance Tower (☎ 081/252-32-30), an inn since the 14th century. Here you can dine in a room with Gothic windows and a timbered ceiling from 1522.

The centerpiece of Chur is the **Kathedrale St. Maria Himmelfahrt** (Cathedral of the Ascension of the Virgin Mary), built between 1151 and 1272 in a mix of styles that spanned the century and drew on influences across Europe. The capitals of the columns are worked in a distinctly Romanesque style, carved with fantastical, evil beasts; at their base are clustered less threatening animals, many recognizable from the region—including sheep and the humble mountain marmot. In the choir, a magnificent three-sided altar, elaborately carved in gilded wood, dates from the 15th century. The structure built on this site in prehistoric times was supplanted by a Roman castle, a bishop's house in 451, and a Carolingian cathedral in the 8th century. The marble panels under the altars of St. Laurentius and St. Fidelis have been preserved from this earliest church.

Obere Gasse, once the main street through Chur and a major route between Germany and Italy, is lined with small shops, cafés, and an open-air theater that draws local crowds. At the end stands the 16th-century **Obertor** (Upper Gate), guarding the bridge across the Plessur River.

At the **Kutschensammlung** (Coach Museum), a collection of turn-of-the-century carriages and sleighs, buffed to a picture-book high sheen, transports visitors back to the era of romance. One 1880 sleigh has a fur blanket and jingle bells straight out of Hans Christian Andersen's *The Ice Queen.* ✉ *Hotel Stern, Reichgasse 11,* ☎ *081/252–35–55.* ▱ *Free.* ⓥ *Daily 1:30–5 or by appointment.*

Dining and Lodging

$–$$ ✗ **Controversa.** With a sleek, modern look to match its forward-looking menu—at last, a salad bar with everything from lamb's lettuce to beets—this lively, young restaurant offers a dose of non-tradition in a very traditional town. In addition to the salad bar, eating options range from excellent carpaccio to such daring pasta dishes as tagliatelle with sliced chicken, mango, and hot curry sauce. The bar is a popular draw into the wee hours of the night. ✉ *Steinbruchstrasse 2,* ☎ *081/252–99–44. AE, DC, MC, V. Closed Sunday.*

$–$$$ ✗▱ **Stern.** This is a rare find: a historic inn at the hub of an excursion ★   center with a restaurant that serves authentic regional cooking—moderately priced. Built in 1677, this member of the Romantik group has modern, wood-warmed rooms, a fireplace lounge, and a lovely restau-

rant wrapped in seasoned Arvenholz. Owner Walter Brunner carries
on the long-standing Stern tradition of coddling and reviving Graubündner culture. His menus offer unusual dishes ranging from *Kalbsleber
"dolce brusco"* (breaded liver in sweet red wine sauce with raisin polenta and dried fruit compote) to air-dried beef with dried apples and
pears. All meals are served with anise bread and local wine in pewter
pitchers—by waitresses in folk costume. You'll see travelers and workers here as well as local businesspeople homesick for Grandma's cooking. ⊠ *Reichgasse 11, CH-7000,* ☎ *081/252–35–55,* ꜰᴀx *081/
252–19–15. 110 beds. Restaurant, stübli. AE, DC, MC, V.*

Outdoor Activities and Sports

Chur has an indoor **swimming pool** (☎ 081/254–42–88).

Arosa

★ ❹ *29 km (18 mi) east of Chur.*

The idyllic, high-altitude Arosa (1,830 meters/6,000 feet) can be
reached from Chur by rail or by car. Although it's one of the best known
and most popular of Graubünden's winter- and summer-sports centers, its modest size, isolation, and natural beauty set it apart. There
is none of the rush of Davos, nor the pretensions of St. Moritz: This
is a friendly, family-oriented spot staffed on all sides by upbeat, down-
to-earth people. There are a few grand hotels with social ambitions,
but their guests seem to keep a lid on it: Even the most well-heeled let
their hair down and rarely dress for dinner.

The village lies at the end of a spectacular, winding, 30-kilometer (19-
mile) road that cuts through a steep-walled valley and climbs through
tiny steepled towns on grades of more than 12%. The road empties
into a sheltered, sunny mountain basin at the end of the Schanfigg, the
valley source of the Plessur, a basin surrounded by white peaks and
centered on two broad, accessible lakes. Cars should be left in the lakeside lots when possible, as a convenient free bus shuttles through the
town, and traffic is forbidden between midnight and 6 AM.

Although the town has a slick, busy commercial center, it's strung along
a narrow shelf with broad southern views, and within moments you
can melt into the wilderness here on good mountain trails—some of
which are cleared for hikers even in winter. There are four skating rinks—
one indoors—and the skiing at all levels of difficulty is among the best
in Switzerland. The altitude ensures good snow, and pistes lead directly
down into the village. A good network of well-located ski lifts and linking runs make the broad, high fields easily accessible. Arosa's branch
of the Swiss Ski School is one of the largest.

From Arosa, you can take a cable car up to the Weisshorn (2,654 me-
ters/8,700 feet) for views over resorts, lakes, and a sweep of peaks. Gondola cars take you from Arosa to Hörnli (2,501 meters/8,200 feet) for
similar views from a different perspective.

Skiing

Open to ski tourism since 1877, Arosa is remote and humble in comparison to the worldly resorts of Gstaad and St. Moritz. Closely surrounded
by its screen of mountains, the 1,754-meter-high (5,750-foot) resort is
family-oriented, with runs suitable for every level of skier. Beginners and
children can enjoy the sunny and gentle slopes of Pratschli, while
maniacs who want a battering will find on Weisshorn (2,654
meters/8,700 feet) the black piste of their dreams. Most of the runs, however, are intermediate—even those of the Hörnli (2,460 meters/8,200 feet),
which is served by a cable car. These slopes are so broad and clear that

moonlight and torchlight skiing is organized regularly, generally following fondue or raclette and wine in a restaurant high on the mountain—to the tunes of a Ländlerkapelle, a musical ensemble typical of German Switzerland. For the local branch of Switzerland's official ski school, call 081/377–11–50.

Arosa's 16 lifts have an hourly capacity of 21,000 and cover 70 kilometers (43 miles) of trails. Its facilities don't match those of Davos, the neighbor that an unbreachable rock barrier renders light years away, but they are sufficient for the 8,000 guests that the resort welcomes in high season (end of December, February, and Easter). With the exception of one heavily trafficked strategic run, Arosa does not have snowmaking; nevertheless, it has often been possible to ski throughout an entire season despite a poor snowfall. A one-day lift ticket costs 52 SF; a six-day pass costs 219 SF.

Dining and Lodging

$$ ✕ **Grischuna.** Although most of the best food can be found in hotels in this accommodating resort, the Grischuna merits a stop for its comfortable ambience and regional decor—wood, ceramics, farm tools, game trophies. Its simple menu includes local cold meat and cheese dishes, as well as trout and plain bourgeois meats, including horse steak. ⊠ *Poststrasse,* ☎ *081/377–17–01. No credit cards.*

$$$$ ✕🏨 **Kulm.** For a luxury hotel with roots in 1882, this is refreshingly
★ young and sporty. Now completely renovated, it combines international trends to an almost confusing degree: Is this Vail? Santa Fe? Mikonos? Oslo? There are miles of curving stucco and glass, heavy beams and high-tech fixtures, chintz and primitive prints. The wraparound windows take in acres of green. Indeed, the hotel's position is its biggest draw, as it stands on the farthest edge of town at the base of the slopes: You can ski home at the end of the day. The atmosphere is suburban-golf-resort casual. ⊠ *CH-7050,* ☎ *081/377–01–31,* ℻ *081/377–40–90. 250 beds. 3 restaurants, 2 cafés, tennis court, fitness center, bowling, dance club, baby-sitting. AE, DC, MC, V.*

$$$$ ✕🏨 **Waldhotel National.** First a sanatorium, then a military hospital, this member of the Relais du Silence group became a hotel in 1965 and has been consistently upgraded and refined ever since. Its most recently decorated rooms mix rich colors and low, smooth-lined furniture, upholstered Euro-style; its oldest rooms bask in golden pine. Northern rooms look over the forest and southern ones have the spectacular Arosa view. Above the town and set on its own 50,000-square-foot wooded park, it offers a peaceful retreat. Rates are demipension only. ⊠ *CH-7050,* ☎ *081/377–13–51,* ℻ *081/377–32–10. 168 beds. Restaurant, bar, indoor pool, massage, sauna. AE, DC, MC, V.*

$$ ✕🏨 **Central.** Although it's set back slightly from the main street, Central lives up to its name, with neither the elevation nor the isolation of its competitors. Yet it's solid and slickly done, with pristine stucco and knotty pine, and good views on the south side. (The back rooms have neither balcony nor view.) The restaurant Arvenstube, all richly detailed knotty pine, offers some of the best food in town: The changing menu of updated French classics may include such specialties as flambéed rack of roe deer, poached trout in dill, or lamb fillets in mushroom puree; there are veal and beef standards as well. You can order cheaper daily plates, as well as fondues, in the Grotto. ⊠ *CH-7050,* ☎ *081/377–02–52,* ℻ *081/377–42–71. 85 beds. 2 restaurants, bar, hot tub, sauna. AE, DC, MC, V.*

$$ ✕🏨 **Hold.** This busy, happy family place—full of books and toys and
★ hikers—is just across the road from the luxurious Kulm and shares the advantages of its location beyond the crowds, near the slopes. The rooms

are simple, bright, and updated with blond wood and new carpet; the back rooms are larger, with big tile baths. The restaurant serves good bourgeois standards—fried fish, entrecôte, vegetarian dishes, and fondues. There's a cozy little outdoor terrace tucked in below the road. The owners are keen to please. ✉ CH-7050, ☎ 081/377–14–08, FAX 081/377–49–27. 30 beds. Restaurant, café. AE, DC, MC, V.

$$ 🏨 **Alpina.** This hotel just above the main street, with views over the Untersee and the mountains, strikes an appealing balance between old and new. Built in 1935, it was recently renovated and in 1985 added a new white stucco wing full of rustic touches—farm implements and antiques—to remind you of where you are. The rooms in the original wing combine old wood with new Euro-style furniture, while the new wing is done in bright blond pine; the old wing is higher, so its views are superior. ✉ CH-7050, ☎ 081/377–16–58, FAX 081/377–37–52. 55 beds. Restaurant, bar, café, stübli, sauna. AE, DC, MC, V.

$$ 🏨 **Panorama Raetia.** Among the bank of hotels on the shelf over the main street, this has the broadest sweep of view from both its original wing, which dates from the 1890s, and its new wing, built during the 1950s. As if they knew they couldn't top the beauty of its Bündnerstübli, with its original Arvenholz aged to burnished gold, its owners have left the newer portions untouched; perhaps the '70s-style avocado and shocking orange decor will acquire similar patina in years to come. The public rooms are wide open and sociable. ✉ CH-7050, ☎ 081/377–02–41, FAX 081/377–22–79. 70 beds. Restaurant, stübli. AE, DC, MC, V.

$ 🏨 **Vetter.** In a resort with generally high prices, this offers budget travelers spare quarters and a central location with a few additional rewards: Though most rooms have flea-market furnishings, there are three lovely old Arvenholz rooms and a few with forest views. (Front rooms face the street and the town.) Rooms without bath are relatively cheap even in high season. ✉ CH-7050, ☎ 081/377–17–02, FAX 081/377–49–19. 40 beds. Restaurant. No credit cards.

Nightlife and the Arts

To find out what's happening in Arosa, check its *Wochenbulletin*, published every two weeks.

BARS AND LOUNGES

There's a popular piano bar at **Hotel Carmenna** (☎ 081/377–17–66).

CASINOS

Arosa's **casino** (☎ 081/377–50–51) has a roulette wheel with the usual 5 SF gambling limit—but the casino's 75 slot machines, set up after their ban was withdrawn in 1994, are its prized novelty.

CLUBS

Crazy, a nightclub near the Bahnhof (☎ 081/377–01–21), has a strip show.

DANCING

For dancing and discos, **Nuts** (☎ 081/377–39–40) is open until 3 AM. The tiny **Tschuetta Dancing-Bar** (☎ 081/377–19–49) manages to squeeze a live band in front of a '70s-style, rainbow-color backdrop. **Gada Street** (☎ 081/377–17–66) has a Wild West theme and live music. The **Kitchen Club,** at the Hotel Eden (☎ 081/377–02–61), is a disco inside an original 1907 kitchen, where a young crowd dances among old pots, pans, and washing machines, while the disc jockey perches above antique aluminum refrigerators.

There are **organ concerts** in the mountain chapel from Christmas through mid-April, Tuesday at 5.

Outdoor Activities and Sports

HIKING

The tourist office offers an unusual hiking package with lodging included (☞ Guided Tours, *below*).

HORSEBACK RIDING

Call **Weierhof** (☎ 081/377–16–07).

PARAGLIDING

Contact **Flying School Arosa** (☎ 081/377–48–49).

SKATING

Arosa has no fewer than four skating rinks: the indoor Eissporthalle (☎ 081/377–17–45), Kunsteisbahn Obersee (☎ 081/377–17–45), Natureisbahn Hof Maran (☎ 081/377–01–85), and Natureisbahn Inner-Arosa (☎ 081/377–29–30); the last three are outdoors.

SWIMMING

There's a free bathing **beach** on the Untersee.

TENNIS

There are three public courts at the Hof Maran (☎ 081/377–01–85).

THE PRÄTTIGAU

Its name means "meadow valley," and it's just that—a lush landscape of alternating orchards, pastures, and pine-covered mountains. Here are the renowned ski resorts of Davos and Kloster, which attract skiers from all over the world. The predominant language is German, though most towns still have Romansh names that date from ancient times.

Klosters

5 *26 km (19 mi) southeast of Landquart.*

Once a group of hamlets, Klosters has become a small but chic resort town, nestled in the valley and framed between striking peaks. There's an aesthetic scattering of weathered-wood and white-stucco chalets and a clock-tower church, the only remnant of the medieval cloister that gave the town its name.

Klosters is famed for its **skiing**—the British royal family are faithful visitors—and makes the most of its access to the slopes of the Parsenn, which afford some of the finest skiing anywhere. The starting point for the best of the Klosters-Parsenn runs is the Weissfluhjoch, reached by a cable-car ride from the town to the Gotschnagrat, a short ski run, and then a second cable car. The run back to Klosters, almost 10 kilometers (6 miles), drops around 1,495 meters (4,900 feet). The variety of runs from the Weissfluhjoch and the Gotschnagrat is almost unlimited, but the best known are those that lead north all the way to Küblis or south to Wolfgang. The Madrisa slopes, reached by the Albeina gondolas, are popular with both skiers and sunbathers.

On a winter Friday, a brief outing to the **Nutli-Hüschi** folk museum will illustrate how far this resort has evolved from its mountain roots: A pretty wood-and-stone chalet, built in 1565, has been restored and fitted with the spare furnishings of its day, including kitchen tools and a children's bed that lengthens as the child grows. ⊠ *Monbielerstrasse,* ☎ *081/410–20–20.* 💷 *3 SF.* ⏱ *Jan.–mid-Apr., Fri. 4–6.*

Skiing

Along with its twin resort Davos, Klosters is known for its vast range of trails and facilities, with their hundreds of kilometers of downhill runs divided nearly equally among easy, moderate, and difficult pistes.

More rural than Davos, Klosters is favored by the royal family for its 315 kilometers (196 miles) of maintained runs and 55 lifts in a half-dozen ski areas. Lift tickets to the combined Davos/Klosters areas cost 56 SF for one day, 259 for six days.

Dining and Lodging

$$$ ✕ **Alte Post.** In this warm, woody local favorite, pleasantly cluttered with ceramics and game trophies, you can enjoy the straightforward cooking of John Ehrat, a Klosters native who specializes in game and salmon. There are token French classics and a few Swiss standards, but the old-style dishes are his forte: rabbit in thyme, *tête de veau* (veal head) vinaigrette, beef with Marsala and risotto, and lots of trout and lamb. If you like salmon, go for the *Lachsmenu* (fixed-price salmon menu) with salmon in every dish but the sorbet. The restaurant is slightly apart from the town center, but worth the trip. ✉ *Doggilochstrasse 136, CH-7250 Klosters-Aeuja,* ☎ *081/422–17–16,* FAX *081/422–38–07. DC, MC, V. Closed Mon. and Tues.*

$$ ✕ **Höhwald.** This is a friendly, touristy restaurant up the hill from Klosters in Monbiel, with a large, open terrace that takes in valley and mountain views, and a wood-panel café and restaurant that draws festive crowds. There are hearty soups, cheese specialties (such as *Chäsgatschäder,* bread soaked in milk with grated cheese, all fried like a big pancake), Bündner meats, and a local mix of Italian and country cooking, stressing game. The fruit tarts are fresh and homemade. More formal, the interior restaurant features game elaborately prepared and served. ✉ *CH-7250,* ☎ *081/422–30–45. AE, MC, V.*

$$ ✕ **Wynegg.** The English—including a few crowned heads—come
★ here to drink pints après-ski, eat enormous platters of local cold meats, and enjoy the cozy surroundings, slightly kitschy with all the checkered tablecloths and cuckoo clocks. ✉ *CH-7250,* ☎ *081/422–13–40. AE, MC, V.*

$$$–$$$$ ✕🏠 **Chesa Grischuna.** Although it's directly in the center of town at the main thoroughfare and crossroads, this creaky 1890 mountain farmhouse qualifies as a country inn—as well as one of the most popular places to stay and dine in ski season. Every room is full of old carved wood, and some have balconies to take in the sun. There are antiques and regional knickknacks throughout, and plenty of public spaces, as this is a sociable place: Whether you bowl in the vaulted cave, play cards, or dance to the piano music at happy hour, you'll be surrounded by Klosters regulars. Prices are high for the limited facilities (no elevator, some rooms without bath), but you pay for the coveted social mix. The popular restaurant serves straightforward meat and fish, including Klosters trout and grilled lamb chops. It's a Romantik property, and its name is Romansh for "Graubünden House." ✉ *CH-7250,* ☎ *081/422–22–22,* FAX *081/422–22–25. 42 beds. Restaurant, bar, bowling. AE, MC, V.*

$$$ ✕🏠 **Walserhof.** Of the high-end hotels in Klosters, this is the most so-
★ phisticated, having struck a smart balance between old and new. It was built in 1981 with the weathered materials from an old farmhouse. Its restaurant and café are paneled with ancient carved wood; stone, stucco, and quarry tile are used elsewhere. The only drawback is its location, on the main road through town; the best views take in either the street or fairly well developed fields behind. (Prince Andrew, a one-time guest, didn't seem to mind.) The superb restaurant specializes in sophisticated international fare as well as upscale regional cooking, and a menu from Prättigau, the Davos-Klosters region, is available every day, including such specialties as trout in cider, cabbage dumplings with wild mushrooms, game terrines, or lamb stew with polenta. ✉ *CH-*

7250, ☎ 081/422–42–42, ℻ 081/422–14–37. 24 beds. Restaurant, stübli. AE, DC, MC, V.

$$–$$$ 🏨 **Albeina.** This large and luxurious resort complex lies in the lower valley of Klosters-Dorf, with easy access to skiing—but it provides its own activities regardless of season or weather. The look is all new and very suburban, and polo shirts and Land Rovers are much in evidence. ✉ CH-7252, ☎ 081/423–21–00, ℻ 081/423–21–21. 120 beds. Restaurant, bar, indoor pool, tennis courts, boccie, Ping-Pong, playground. AE, DC, MC, V.

$$ 🏨 **Rätia.** Set in Klosters-Dorf, in the broad, quiet valley west of the
★ center, this Relais du Silence hotel lives up to the chain's name. It's a classic vacation lodge, with a great stone fireplace in the log-and-beam dining hall and balconies facing up toward the slopes. In summer, you can have tea on the broad porch under hanging geraniums; in winter, a schnapps by the fire after skiing to the doorstep from the Gotschnagrat. As a farmhouse, it started taking in guests and expanded to take in a neighboring home; in the 1970s a new wing was added. Most rooms are plain, with office-style furniture, but some have lovely aged wooden paneling. Unlike most hotels, the Rätia rents by the week to ensure low-key holidays for its loyal guests. ✉ CH-7252, ☎ 081/422–47–47, ℻ 081/422–47–49. 42 beds. Restaurant, bar. MC, V.

$$ 🏨 **Silvapina.** This delightful budget hotel, which enjoys the same val-
★ ley position as the Rätia, places emphasis on family, as the owners have three children of their own and the father was born under the very roof he now repairs. The weathered-wood Victorian-style chalet was built in 1931, with a new wing added in 1960; the rooms in the new wing are spare white with pine touches, while older rooms have lovely burnished wood everywhere. The sitting rooms and dining area are fresh and tidy. There's even a private tennis court. ✉ CH-7252, ☎ 081/422–14–68, ℻ 081/422–40–78. 30 beds. Restaurant, stübli, tennis court. AE, MC, V.

Nightlife and the Arts
Chesa Grischuna (☞ Dining and Lodging, *above*) is a popular after-dinner spot, with piano music and several intimate bars.

For dancing, try **Casa Antica** (☎ 081/422–16–21), in a 300-year-old converted barn.

Outdoor Activities and Sports
PARAGLIDING
Contact **Flugschulcenter Grischa** (☎ 081/416–55–46).

SKATING
There are two rinks for year-round skating (☎ 081/422–20–22).

SWIMMING
The local municipal heated outdoor swimming pool has a restaurant and table tennis (☎ 081/422–15–24).

TENNIS
Tennis Club Klosters (☎ 081/422–20–23) has eight outdoor clay tennis courts.

Davos

❻ 11 km (7 mi) south of Klosters; 37 km (23 mi) south of Landquart.

With a reputation nearly as far-flung as those of St. Moritz and Gstaad, Davos is one of Switzerland's most esteemed winter resorts—famed for its ice sports as well as its skiing. At 1,561 meters (5,117 feet), it's good for cold-weather sports even in the soggiest winter.

Davos lies at the end of the Davos Valley, which runs parallel to the Upper Engadine though they're separated by the vast Albula chain, at some points more than 2,989 meters (9,800 feet) high. On the opposite side of the valley stands the Strela chain, dominated by the Weissfluh. The open, sunbathed slopes of this range provide magnificent skiing. The Parsenn funicular railway runs from Davos up to Weissfluhgipfel, 2,664 meters (8,734 feet) high, and the upper end of the Parsenn run. From there you can ski down over vast, open snowfields to the town, a drop of around 1,000 meters (3,280 feet). Or, striking off to the northeast, you come to Davos's neighboring resort: Klosters. Another funicular, combined with a gondola, goes to Strela. There's a lift to Rinerhorn (2,046 meters/6,708 feet), and a couple of dozen other mountain railways, cable cars, and assorted lifts. On the opposite side of the valley you have direct access to the well-equipped Brämabüel-Jakobshorn ski area, reached by cable car and lift from Davos-Platz. In addition, there are more than 75 kilometers (47 miles) of prepared cross-country ski trails.

Vacationers, be warned: This is a capital for action-oriented sports lovers, and not for anyone seeking a peaceful, rustic mountain retreat. Davos-Dorf and its twin, Davos-Platz, are strung along the valley in one noisy urban strip, with thick traffic, timed parking, department stores, and trendy bars. But for a few token historic structures, most of Davos consists of awkward concrete-balcony hotels and apartment buildings. In town, the bracing mountain air that drew Davos's first visitors, tuberculosis sufferers taking sanatorium cures, can be offset by the exhaust of city traffic. Yet this Alpine metropolis is surrounded by dramatic mountain passes, green hillsides, and farms punctuated by weathered sheds and outbuildings. And no matter how densely populated and fast-paced the twin towns become, nothing changes on the magnificent slopes, and people return to them generation after generation.

Among the town's few architectural highlights, the late-Gothic **Hauptkirche St. Johann** (Church of St. John the Baptist) stands out with windows by Augusto Giacometti. Nearby is the 17th-century **Rathaus.**

The **Kirchner Museum** houses the world's largest collection of works and documents by and about Ernst Ludwig Kirchner, the German Expressionist artist who came to Davos in 1917 to cure his failing health and stayed to paint. ☎ 081/413–22–02, ✉ 7 SF. ☉ Tues.–Sun. 2–6.

Skiing

More urbane than its twin resort Klosters, Davos (1,562 meters/5,120 feet) extends more than 35 kilometers (22 miles) along a relatively sheltered valley floor, the Prättigau, which opens on a fantastic panorama at higher elevations. From Küblis (814 meters/2,670 feet) to Glaris (1,458 meters/4,780 feet), the commune of Davos is Switzerland's second largest and can accommodate some 22,000 visitors.

At the southeastern end of Davos, the west-facing easy pistes bask in afternoon sun. On the other side of the valley, the steep slopes of the Parsenn draw hordes of experts. Locals and others in the know often prefer to ski on the other side of the valley at Rinerhorn, where the slopes, less crowded but nearly as interesting, lead to the hamlet of Glaris, 7 kilometers (4½ miles) from the center of Davos. A must for the very good skier: the descent from Weissfluhgipfel (2,846 meters/9,330 feet) to Küblis (814 meters/2,670 feet). It's a 2,000-meter (6,560-foot) vertical drop and a magnificent piste 15 kilometers (9 miles) long. Lift tickets to the combined Davos/Klosters areas cost up to 52 SF for one day (depending on which areas you choose to ski in), 259 SF for six days.

Dining and Lodging

$$$$ ✕⊞ **Berghotel Schatzalp.** Isolated on a sunny shelf 300 meters (984
★ feet) above the noisy city of Davos, this gracious Belle Epoque mountain retreat stands aloof, the wicker lounge chairs of its full-length sun-
porch taking in up to four more hours of sun a day than can be had
in the valley below. By the fireplace under the stained glass in the art-
nouveau lounge are laden oak bookcases. Some rooms maintain museum-quality period decor, right down to the bath fixtures; others
have been updated and look quite ordinary. Ask for a room at the far
end, away from the funicular that brought you up from town; it also
brings up hordes of rowdy day-trippers heading for the slopes. The
frozen-in-time aspect isn't always a plus: The old swimming pool has
a grim, institutional air. Pension guests and those in the mood for a
formal meal dine with the grand view; the casual Schatzalp serves local
specialties in a wood-trimmed pavilion. This is a Relais du Silence property. ⊠ CH-7270, ☎ 081/413–83–31, ℻ 081/413–13–44. 173 beds.
2 restaurants, indoor pool, massage, sauna. AE, DC, MC, V.

$$$$ ✕⊞ **Davoserhof.** With lovely Jakobshorn views from its south side;
★ fresh, pretty rooms in taupe, paisley, and pine; and all-new, all-white
tile baths, this is one of the most welcoming little hotels in town—without taking into account its restaurants, which are two of the region's
finest. During the World Economic Forum conference that takes place
here every February, you'll be hard-pressed to find a table either in the
intimate old Davosstübli, with its burnished Arvenholz and ceramic
stove, or in the elegant, piney Jenatschstube. In spring and summer,
everyone eats on the broad terrace overlooking the green hills and mountains. Chef Kurt Jaussi, something of a wunderkind, creates innovative dishes that are strictly cosmopolitan. ⊠ CH-7270, ☎ 081/
415–66–66, ℻ 081/415–66–67. 46 beds. 2 restaurants, bar, dance
club. AE, DC, MC, V.

$$$$ ✕⊞ **Golfhotel Waldhuus.** Right at the edge of the Davos golf course,
with the leisurely *"pock-pock"* of a tennis game echoing next door, this
Relais du Silence property re-creates a suburban country club on the
outskirts of an Alpine city. Solid, sunny, and serene, with plenty of pine
and stucco to soften its prefab feel, it offers late sun on the terrace, a
fireplace in the lobby, and the soothing tunes of a pianist in its bar. The
rooms are decorated in country-casual miniature prints and pink linens,
public spaces in pink, lace, and dried flowers. The restaurant serves
standards with nouvelle twists (pike quenelles with black noodles,
quail salad with balsamic vinegar). ⊠ CH-7270, ☎ 081/416–81–81,
℻ 081/416–48–61. 100 beds. Restaurant, bar, indoor pool, sauna,
driving range, 2 tennis courts, fitness room. AE, DC, MC, V.

$–$$$$ ✕⊞ **Hubli's Landhaus.** Though on the busy mountain highway between
★ Davos and Klosters, this country inn is quiet as well as comfortable
and attractive with its somewhat modernized rustic decor (scarlet,
stucco, dark pine, and wrought iron). Its setting in gardens and valley
greenery is idyllic. But the strong point by far is the food: Chef Felix
Hubli prepares sophisticated international fare (turbot with wild mush-
rooms and ginger, pigeon with leeks and truffles) and serves it in two
lovely dining rooms: one for visitors, one for demipension guests,
who—considering the à la carte prices—are getting a terrific deal. ⊠
CH-7265 Davos-Laret, ☎ 081/416–21–21, ℻ 081/416–33–42. 40
beds. Restaurant. V.

$$$ ✕⊞ **Ochsen.** Central and urban, with a few upper rooms rising above
the street to take in Jakobshorn views, this modest hotel is now run
by an ambitious young team, who have spent the last few years redo-
ing the rooms in pastels and pine and perfecting Graubündner specialties
in the restaurant. The welcoming dining/breakfast room is wall-to-wall
Arvenholz, and the *stube* (tavern) is down-to-earth enough to draw lo-

cals. ⊠ *CH-7270,* ☎ *081/413–52–22,* FAX *081/413–76–71. 90 beds. Restaurant, bar, stübli. AE, DC, MC, V.*

$$$$ ⚏ **Steigenberger Belvedere.** With its neoclassic stone fireplace and plaster details, this is a grand hotel in the full sense of the word: It sweeps the length of a hillside with south-facing balconies, and its interiors are lavished with period detail. Rooms vary widely from Arvenholz rustic to warm pastels, with only an occasional touch of drab chenille: It's worth it to pay for "superior" class rooms, as north and end views (and decors) are distinctly inferior. ⊠ *CH-7270,* ☎ *081/415–60–00,* FAX *081/415–60–01. 238 beds. Restaurant, bar, café, indoor pool, sauna. AE, DC, MC, V.*

Nightlife and the Arts

BARS, LOUNGES, AND CASINOS

Hotel Europe (☎ 081/413–59–21) has two popular bars, the chic **Tonic Piano Bar,** serving until 3 AM; and the homey **Cabana Bar.** In addition, a **casino** has recently opened in the hotel, offering more than one hundred slot machines and boule table. After 3 AM, hipsters gather for live music and snacks at **X Bar** (☎ 081/413–56–45), open until 6 AM. **Casa Antica** (☎ 081/422–16–21) is a 300-year-old converted barn that is the focus of late nightlife.

DANCING

For dancing, **Pöstli** (☎ 081/414–11–61) is a winter-only institution. There's dancing in the cavelike **Cava Grischa** (⊠ Hotel Europe, ☎ 081/413–68–17). A popular dance club is the **Jakobshorn-Club,** in the Davoserhof (☎ 081/415–68–17). At 10:30 PM the Cabana Bar becomes the **Cabana Club** (☎ 081/413–59–21) whose techno decor and loud music attract a rowdy crowd.

Outdoor Activities and Sports

GOLF

There's an 18-hole golf course at **Golfplatz Davos** (☎ 081/416–56–34). **Golf Club Vulpera** has nine holes (☎ 081/864–96–88). **Golf Club Arosa** (☎ 081/377–42–42) is a nine-hole course.

HIKING

Davos offers an unusual hiking package with lodging included (☞ Guided Tours, *below*).

HORSEBACK RIDING

Try **Riding School Flüela** (☎ 081/416–38–88).

PARAGLIDING

Contact **Gleitschirmschule Davos** (☎ 081/413–60–43) or **Flugschulcenter Grischa** (☎ 081/416–55–46).

SAILING AND WINDSURFING

For sailing and windsurfing on the lake of Davos (☎ 081/416–15–05); for the sailing school, ☎ 081/416–31–30.

SKATING

Davos has long been reputed as an important ice-sports center, with its enormous speed-skating rink, skating tournaments, and curling facilities. **Eisstadion Davos** has one indoor and two outdoor rinks (☎ 081/413–73–54).

SPORTS CENTERS

The **Sports & High Altitude Centre Davos** (☎ 081/415–21–15) offer various facilities.

SWIMMING

Davos has an indoor-outdoor swimming pool complex (☎ 081/413–64–63); you can also swim from the **Strandbad** (open beach) on the Davoser See (☎ 081/416–15–05).

TENNIS

Tennis and Squash Center Davos has four indoor and five outdoor tennis courts, plus two squash courts (☎ 081/413–31–31).

En Route The main road from Davos leads into the Engadine by way of the spectacular **Flüelapass** (Flüela Pass). For 11 kilometers (7 miles) you climb southeast over mild grades and modest switchbacks. Dense larch forests give way to pine, then to fir, and finally, above the timberline, to a rocky, desolate waste of boulders and jutting cliffs, much of it snow-covered except in summer. Ahead, on the left, are the rocky slopes of the **Weisshorn** (3,086 meters/10,119 feet), with the **Schwarzhorn** (3,147 meters/10,319 feet) to the right. Toward the summit, even in August, you may drive through snow. You'll pass between two small lakes: the Schottensee and the Schwarzsee. At the summit (2,379 meters/7,800 feet), 14 kilometers (9 miles) from Davos, is the **Flüela Hospiz** (☎ 081/416–17–47), a picturesque wooden chalet with a windmill, where you can get refreshments and a night's lodging at reasonable rates.

The descent from the Flüela Pass into the Romansh region of the Lower Engadine takes you through a narrow valley and across the River Susasca, in sight of the 3,233-meters (10,600-foot) Piz Vadret, to the base of the great **Grialetsch** glacier—a spectacular mass of jagged ice and snow. The road winds, following the increasingly torrential river and its deep, rocky gash, down to Susch, where it flows into the River En or, in Romansh, Inn.

THE LOWER ENGADINE

Like Dorothy landing in Oz, you may find your sudden arrival in this, the most picturesque and novel of Graubünden's many valleys, something of a shock. The language abruptly dissolves into archaic Romansh; the terrain grows thick with dense, fairy-tale forests; and the houses—squat cream-color stucco bungalows, their doors deep Etruscan arches, their windows sunk into thick Mediterranean walls, every inch of facade scrawled with designs and images—bear testimony to an ancient Latinate culture unlike any of its neighbors'. The stucco decoration, called sgraffiti, is the signature of the Engadine: An underlayer of dark gray stucco is whitewashed; then designs are scraped into the paint to reveal the undercolor. The Lower Engadine—more enclosed and less developed than its Upper counterpart—shares the region's clear, sharp, dry air—a climate that protects the ornate facades and draws admirers from across Europe.

Susch

❼ *27 km (17 mi) east of Davos; 64 km (40 mi) southeast of Landquart.*

Susch guards the entrance to the Lower Engadine, guarded itself by the magnificent Piz d'Arpiglias (3,289 meters/9,930 feet). Here the River Susasca tumbles into the Inn, and the town seems to cling to the banks of the roaring, white-water torrent as it heads on its way to the Danube. Though Susch was partially burned in 1925, its houses remain stubbornly traditional in style, and the streets are lined with sgraffitied structures, their windows spilling geraniums, their heavy wooden doors often half-ajar to display interiors quirkily furnished with crockery, copper, antiques, and stuffed game.

At the **Kirche St. Jon** (Church of St. John) two towers stand high over the river, one Romanesque, the other—and the body of the church—dating from 1515. During a restoration in 1742, the late-Gothic style of the windows was changed, but in 1933, on the evidence of recently discovered fragments, they were restored to their original form.

Guarda

8 *7 km (4 mi) east of Susch; 71 km (44 mi) southeast of Landquart.*

Between Susch and the resort towns of Scuol, Vulpera, and Tarasp (follow the River Inn downstream), a scenic valley passes through several gorges and then emerges into flowered plains and a pleasant chain of hamlets: Lavin, Guarda, Ardez, and Ftan. Each offers another show of fine sgraffitied homes, but Guarda deserves a leisurely exploration among its steep, patterned-cobble streets. The federal government protects the architecture, and row upon row of the vivid dark-on-white etchings, contrasting sharply with the bright red geraniums lined up on the windowsills, draws pedestrians from one photogenic stop to another. As its name implies, Guarda sits high on a hillside looking out over the valley and the 3,001-meter (9,840-foot) peaks to the south.

Lodging

$$$$ **Meisser.** This comfortable lodge lives up to its picturesque setting, with sgraffiti and flower boxes outside, antiques and Arvenholz inside. There's a grand Victorian dining hall with pine wainscoting and parquet, and a more casual porch restaurant with spectacular valley views. Some rooms are simple and modern, though you can have a splendid old carved-pine room if you pay a little bit more. A recently renovated 17th-century farmhouse offers five new suites. The sitting rooms are welcoming, with books and corners for rainy days. ✉ CH-7545, ☎ 081/862–21–32, 🆄 081/862–24–80. 62 beds. Restaurant, playground. AE, DC, MC, V.

En Route Between Guarda and Scuol, a small back road leads through Boscha to **Ardez,** among whose botanical sgraffiti themes is an elaborate Adam-and-Eve fresco on the valley side of the main street. The back road continues through Ftan, with its fine view of Schloss Tarasp (☞ *below*).

Scuol, Vulpera, and Tarasp

13 km (8 mi) east of Guarda; 84 km (52 mi) southeast of Landquart.

Sometimes grouped under the name Bad Tarasp-Vulpera, the three towns of Scuol, Vulpera, and Tarasp effectively form a holiday and health resort complex whose waters are reputed to be highly beneficial to those who suffer from liver ailments. Beautifully located in the open valley of the Inn, whose grass-covered and wooded hillsides are backed on each side by mountains, all three towns have hitherto been highly popular summer resorts, frequented most often by Swiss and Germans. Now they fill up in winter as well, thanks to the network of gondola cars and ski lifts and the unobstructed south-facing slopes. Scuol, the most urban of the three, has a busy downtown; the other two lie across the river and valley from Scuol. Vulpera is draped along the valley floor and crowded with large hotels and the old cure house. Tarasp stands apart, little more than a cluster of hotels scattered over green hillsides.

From Scuol and Vulpera, a bus goes up to the historic **Schloss Tarasp** (Tarasp Castle) in 15 minutes; it's a scenic drive, and you can walk it in 1½ hours. Up close, as well as from across the valley, it's an impressive structure, a rambling fantasy perched 153 meters (500 feet) above the valley floor. Among the slit windows, turrets, and doubled walls is an

Austrian coat of arms. The main tower and chapel date from the 11th century, when the castle was the stronghold of the knights of Tarasp. Long a source of discord between the powerful Bishop of Chur and the Count of Tyrol, it was the seat of the Austrian governors until the early 19th century, when Graubünden joined the Swiss Confederation. Some years ago, it was sold to a toothpaste manufacturer who spent 3 million SF restoring it—and then gave it to the prince of Hesse.

Dining and Lodging

$$$ ✕🏨 **Chasté.** While many Swiss hoteliers are proud to claim a second
★ generation of family ownership, this hidden treasure has spent 500 years under Pazeller family care. It started as a farm, then housed builders for the castle Tarasp, which hovers on the hill above; its restaurant drew overnight guests, who eventually demanded modern plumbing—and today it's an impeccable, welcoming inn with every comfort. The Pazellers have preserved the bulging, sgraffitied stucco exterior, and within, the carved and aged Arvenholz has been protected and matched during modernization. Rudolf Pazeller himself is the chef and offers a small but sophisticated menu; his fish dishes are outstanding. ⊠ *CH-7553,* ☎ *081/864–17–75,* ℻ *081/864–99–70. 45 beds. Restaurant, bar, stübli, sauna, steam room. No credit cards.*

$$–$$$ ✕🏨 **Villa Maria.** This simple hillside retreat above the baths has an elite, genteel air, with flowers on the antique furniture and Oriental rugs on the quarry tile. The rooms are homey but fresh, and some have balconies overlooking the forested valley. A little restaurant downstairs has a fireplace and other rustic touches and serves good cuisine du marché; the chef grows his vegetables out back. ⊠ *CH-7552,* ☎ *081/864–11–38,* ℻ *081/864–91–61. 30 beds. Restaurant, bar, café. No credit cards.*

$$$ 🏨 **Guardaval.** This member of the Romantik chain, built in 1693, pre-
★ serves its original wing, with its stucco vaulting and heavy beams, but has altered the rest to keep rooms up-to-date. Now there's a modern terrace with views that stretch along the valley, and the rooms have spare new decor in white and pine. Despite additions like sliding glass doors, the public areas are dripping with atmosphere, in the form of carved and painted antique furniture, ibex antlers, and even a bear rug. Because the building is protected by historic preservation laws, a few rooms still don't have showers—but their vaulting and ancient wood compensate. ⊠ *CH-7550,* ☎ *081/864–13–21,* ℻ *081/864–97–67. 80 beds. Restaurant, bar, café, sauna, steam room. AE, DC, MC, V.*

$$ 🏨 **Engiadina.** This typical Engadiner house, with sgraffiti, oriels, vault-
★ ing, and beams, was built during the 16th century in the lower, older section of Scuol. There's a new wing, with pine paneling and modern Scandinavian-style furniture, but rooms in the original house have local Arvenholz and rustic furnishings. The pine-paneled *ustaria* (simple restaurant) serves local specialties, and another cozy pine Arvenstube (separate dining room) is used for breakfasts. ⊠ *CH-7550,* ☎ *081/864–14–21,* ℻ *081/864–12–45. 41 beds. Restaurant, breakfast room. No credit cards.*

$ 🏨 **Traube.** This fresh, friendly inn reflects the personal touch: The rooms
★ are all wood, the baths are all tile, and the public areas—in parquet and pine, with antiques and a ceramic stove—are pristine. Locals are drawn to the warmth of the pub and the candlelit restaurant. Although it's in town, there's a garden and a sun terrace with mountain views. ⊠ *CH-7550,* ☎ *081/864–12–07,* ℻ *081/864–84–08. 35 beds. Restaurant, stübli, sauna. AE, DC, MC, V.*

Outdoor Activities and Sports

For **paragliding,** call **Walter Schönauer** in Scuol (☎ 075/232–72–88).
Swissraft arranges rafting expeditions (☎ 081/911–52–50).

THE UPPER ENGADINE

Stretching from St. Moritz to Zernez and encompassing the vast Swiss National Park, this is one of the country's highest regions—with an elevation of 1,800 meters (5,904 feet)—and one of its most dazzling. Chains of mountains with names such as Piz Bernina and Piz Corvatsch afford not only world-class skiing, but also the chance to gaze down on the world from dizzying heights.

Engadine Concert Weeks, Switzerland's international chamber music festival, involves some 20 world-class concerts between mid-July and late August.

Zernez

★ ❾ *6 km (4 mi) south of Süsch.*

This friendly little crossroads is the last town before the higher valley of the Inn. Here, hordes of serious hikers sporting loden hats, knickers, warm knee socks, and sturdy boots come to stock up on picnic goods, day packs, and topographical maps before setting off for the Swiss National Park. A number of moderate hotels make Zernez a great overnight base for park goers.

Dining and Lodging

$$ ★ ✕🏨 **Il Fuorn.** This mountain inn was built in 1894 in the middle of what is now the Swiss National Park, and it is the only commercial property that remains there. It makes an ideal base for hikers tackling more than one route, and it's easily accessible from the park's only highway. There are big pine beams inside, a pretty wooden stübli, and a choice of either old-style rooms without bath or pine-and-stucco rooms with bath in the new wing, added in 1980. The plain, meaty Swiss cooking is augmented by a generous salad bar. ⊠ *CH-7530,* ☎ *082/8–12–26,* 🗏 *082/8–18–01. 55 beds. Restaurant, café, stübli. AE, DC, MC, V.*

$ ★ ✕🏨 **Bettini.** This solid old roadhouse is one of the town's best hotels: It's clean, bright, and thoroughly local. Game trophies hang on the knotty pine walls, rustic antiques stand in the hallways, and lovely valley views open from the dining hall, which serves dependable (if predictable) meals. A few back rooms have balconies with the same valley views; two rooms without bathrooms are a real bargain. ⊠ *CH-7530,* ☎ *082/8–11–35,* 🗏 *082/8–15–10. 50 beds. Restaurant, café. AE, DC, MC, V.*

$ ✕🏨 **Crusch Alba.** Next door to the Bettini, with the same advantageous views, this offers a pleasant alternative—and the policemen relax in its stübli, which speaks well for the local ambience. There's plenty of wood and stucco, and knickknacks in guest rooms add to the already homey atmosphere. The restaurant serves game year-round. ⊠ *CH-7530,* ☎ *082/8–13–30,* 🗏 *082/8–17–78. 32 beds. Restaurant, café. AE, DC, MC, V.*

$ ★ 🏨 **Piz Terza.** This garni hotel is completely modern behind its traditional facade; its rooms have slick, plain built-in cabinetry and a spare, utilitarian look. Yet the back rooms have balconies that look over the valley, and each has its own blooming geranium—an indication of the management's friendly, house-proud approach to bargain hotel service. The public pool is across the street; the National Park house, just a block beyond. ⊠ *CH-7530,* ☎ *082/8–14–14,* 🗏 *082/8–14–15. 46 beds. No credit cards.*

Parc Naziunal Svizzer

10 *Entrance 12 km (7 mi) east of Zernez; 18 km (11 mi) southeast of Susch.*

The Swiss National Park is a magnificent federal preserve of virtually
virgin wilderness. Although its 168 square kilometers (64 square miles)
cover only 1% or 2% of the territory of a U.S. or Canadian national
park, it has none of their developments: no campgrounds, no picnic
sites, no residents. It also has few employees: Three administrators and
five desk clerks staff the visitor center, and of 10 rangers, only five work
full-time—and they live outside the park. This is genuine wilderness,
every leaf and marmot protected from all but nature itself. Dead wood
is left to rot, insects to multiply, and only carefully screened scholars
are allowed to perform preapproved experiments. As a result, the park
contains large herds of ibex with long, curving horns; delicate, short-
horned chamois; huge red deer and tiny roe deer; and vast colonies of
marmots. They are wild animals, however, and are not likely to line
up for Twinkies by the road: Without binoculars (for rent at the visitor center), you're unlikely to get a good look.

The average person's natural urge to see wilderness tends to render the
wilderness less wild. Thus the zealous park staff and the tourists are
often at odds, and in high seasons, when the hiking hordes descend,
rangers watch grimly for visitors who miss the point. The intensity of
their philosophy of restriction is everywhere in evidence, as signs, fly-
ers, and brochures adopt a scolding tone in five languages: "Wastepa-
per and other residues disfigure natural beauty. Take them with you!
Don't pick a single flower! Leave your dog at home!" The list of pro-
hibitions includes hunting, fishing, camping, picking berries, collecting roots, grazing cattle, carrying guns, skiing, making commercial
movies, even making loud noises. Nonetheless, the wildlife gives a wide
berth to paths where, on fine summer days, foot traffic becomes so thick
that hikers have to walk in single file and ask permission to pass.

This is no African big-game preserve. Sighting a group of ibex on a
distant hill or great herds of male red deer, their antlers silhouetted above
a snowy ridge, you may feel more privileged than when petting a
dozen Yellowstone bison. If the big game makes no appearance, search
your greedy soul and try to follow the park's advice: "Appreciate a
butterfly or an ant as much as a herd of chamois."

The trails and settings themselves are magnificent. From small parking
lots off the park's only highway (visitors are encouraged to take postbuses in to their starting point), a series of wild, rough, and often steep
trails takes off into the coniferous forests. From Parking 7, the Il
Fuorn–Stabelchod–Val dal Botsch trail marks botanical and natural phenomena with multilanguage signs (some in English) and leads to a spectacular barren ridge at 2,340 meters (7,672 feet); the round-trip takes
about three hours.

Another three-hour route, from picturesque S-chanf (pronounced "sss-
chonpf") to Trupchun, takes the Höheweg, or high road, into a deep glacial
valley where ibex and chamois often gather; the return, by a riverside
trail, passes a handy log snack bar—just across the park border and thus
permitted. Visitors are restricted to the trails except at designated resting places, where broad circles are marked for hikers to collapse and have
lunch. The visitor center provides detailed maps and suggested routes,
including time estimates; it also has an introductory film, displays on
wildlife and geology, and a new edition of the scientific hiking guide. ⊠
Nationalpark-Haus, CH-7530, ☎ *081/856–13–78.* ⊡ *4 SF.* ☉ *June–
Oct., daily 8:30–6.*

NEED A   You can have a drink or a meal either on the terrace or in the carved-
BREAK?   wood stübli of the **Hotel Parc NazIunaI** at Il Fuorn hotel (☎ 081/856–
             12–26), the only commercial site in the National Park accessible by car.

Outdoor Activities and Sports

The **Swiss National Park** (☎ 081/856–13–78) charts out a series of
spectacular all-day or half-day ventures, for large groups only, into the
wilderness preserves, some of them covering steep and rough trails.

En Route   Drive south along the River Inn from the Swiss National Park toward
             its source, past S-chanf and Zuoz, both full of Engadine-style houses.
             The drive is lovely, a mild but steady climb past snowcapped peaks and
             the roaring river. You may notice an increase in Jaguars, Mercedes, and
             the occasional Rolls as you approach St. Moritz.

Samedan

⑪ *27 km (17 mi) south of Zernez; 33 km (20 mi) southeast of Susch.*

This small, cozy (if less prestigious) resort near St. Moritz has an impressive 18-hole golf course, is nearest to the Upper Engadine's airport,
and gives magnificent views of the awe-inspiring Bernina chain to the
south: **Piz Bernina** (4,057 meters/13,300 feet), **Piz Palü** and **Piz Roseg**
(3,935 meters/12,900 feet), **Piz Morteratsch** (3,752 meters/12,300
feet), **Piz Tschierva** (3,569 meters/11,700 feet), **Piz Corvatsch** (3,447
meters/11,300 feet), **Piz Rosatsch** (3,111 meters/10,200 feet), and
many others. An intricate network of funiculars, cableways, and lifts
carries the surrounding resorts' visitors up to overlooks, cafés, hiking
trails, and ski pistes that offer an infinite combination of views of these
peaks.

Celerina

⑫ *2 km (1 mi) south of Samedan; 3 km (1¼ mi) northeast of St. Moritz.*

Though it lies in the shadow of St. Moritz, Celerina (Schlarigna in Romansh) is a first-rate ski resort in its own right, with easy access to the
facilities of its glamorous neighbor. Although it has an attractive cluster of Engadine houses in its oldest neighborhood, its most striking landmark is the 15th-century Church of **San Gian** (St. John).

En Route   Between Celerina and Pontresina, in the direction of the Bernina Pass,
             you'll find **Punt Muragl,** the base of the funicular up to the summit of
             Muottas Muragl. A 15-minute ride takes you to an altitude of 2,455
             meters (8,050 feet), 702 meters (2,300 feet) above the valley floor. From
             the top you get an eagle's-eye view of St. Moritz, the nearby water-
             shed of **Piz Lunghin,** and the chain of lakes that stretches almost 16
             kilometers (10 miles) toward Maloja.

Pontresina

⑬ *4 km (2 mi) south of Celerina; 6 km (4 mi) east of St. Moritz.*

Lying on a south-facing elevated shelf along the Bernina Valley, Pontresina is an exceptionally picturesque resort. From here you can see
clear across to the Roseg Valley, once filled with the Roseg Glacier. (The
glacier has retreated, now, to the base of Piz Roseg itself.) To the left
and southeast, the Flaz River winds down the mountain-framed valley from its source, the Morteratsch glacier, which oozes down from
Piz Bernina. The altitude of Pontresina (1,830 meters/6,000 feet) ensures wintry weather, and its access to skiing on the slopes of Diavolezza (2,974 meters/9,751 feet) is convenient. It it is also a superb base
for hiking, either to the glaciers or into the heights around them, for

fine overviews—and for mountaineering as well. There are concerts presented here summer mornings, in the shaggy-pine Tais woods, and you can take a horse-drawn carriage up the Val Roseg anytime. Though the main streets are built up with shops and services, the dazzling resort still has the feel of a balanced vacation retreat.

Dining and Lodging

$$$$ ✕🏠 **Kronenhof.** Started on this scenic site as a coach stop for post horses
★ running Veltliner wine over the Bernina Pass, and developed in three graceful wings, this grandest of luxury structures was completed in 1898, and very little has been changed. If the views from the lobby bay don't dazzle you, the baroque splendor of the decor will, as the ceilings—already thick with elaborate moldings—are gilded and frescoed to the maximum with pink cherubs and blushing nymphs. Everywhere you'll find original parquet, darkened pine, and restored murals; the hotel stayed in one family for 136 years from its days as a coach stop, and the current manager stepped in from the loyal staff. The rooms have been steadily renewed, in colors and styles that last (discreet pastels, Biedermeier). The lawn that sprawls out toward the Roseg Valley views is a social center in summer and winter, with tennis courts becoming an ice rink, and a pavilion taking in winter sun. The Kronenstübli, all barrel-vaulted Arvenholz, serves international *cuisine du marché* (menus based on the freshest ingredients available in the local market)—such as lobster with ginger butter, and smoked foie gras—and the wine may come from the still-functioning Veltlinerkeller below. ✉ CH-7504, ☎ 081/842–01–11, FAX 081/842–60–66. *150 beds. 2 restaurants, bar, café, indoor and outdoor pools, beauty salon, massage, tennis, boccie, bowling, ice-skating. AE, DC, MC, V.*

$ ✕🏠 **Rosegggletscher.** Hike up the ruggedly beautiful Roseg Valley or
★ take a horse-drawn carriage to this isolated modern hotel in traditional style. The restaurant, where you can either be served or visit the cafeteria line, offers simple regional favorites except in fall, when the owner brings in game from the surrounding countryside; his trophies adorn the walls. This is a very popular lunch spot for hikers. The rooms are spartan but fresh. ✉ CH-7504, ☎ 081/842–64–45, FAX 081/842–68–86. *45 beds. 2 restaurants, cafeteria. No credit cards.*

$$$$ 🏠 **Walther.** If the elaborate Kronenhof is Dionysus, the Walther is Apollo,
★ strictly classical with its discreet pastels and sleek, unfussy wood. Though it was built in 1907, most of it has been renovated within the last decade, and while a few ornate moldings remain, the look is contemporary. The rooms have new built-in pine cabinetry; those with south-facing balconies are most in demand. The state-of-the-art pool is in a glass-and-pine pavilion that opens onto a wooded garden. The clientele is younger than at the Kronenhof. ✉ CH-7504, ☎ 081/842–64–71, FAX 081/842–79–22. *130 beds. Restaurant, bar, indoor pool, hot tub, massage, sauna, steam room, fitness center. AE, DC, MC, V.*

$$$ 🏠 **Bernina.** After a recent renovation, this comfortable sport hotel displays fresh floral prints, pine furniture, and new tile baths. Balconies and luxury corner doubles take in splendid views. The restaurant and Stube were updated, too, and there's a big sun terrace overlooking the mountains. The restaurant serves regional specialties. ✉ CH-7504, ☎ 081/842–62–21, FAX 081/842–70–32. *70 beds. Restaurant, café, stübli, sauna, steam room. AE, DC, MC, V.*

$$$ 🏠 **Schweizerhof.** Although its public areas, restaurant, and some older rooms are frozen in the '60s and '70s—the bold era of avocado stripes, big daisies, Formica, chenille—a number of rooms in this 1904 landmark have been updated recently with fresh white stucco and lovely Arvenholz cabinetry. Corner bay doubles—not all upgraded yet—have panoramic southwestern views. The public pool is across the street. ⊠ *CH-7504,* ☎ *081/842–01–31,* FAX *081/842–79–88. 120 beds. Restaurant, bar, café, hot tub, sauna. AE, DC, MC, V.*

Nightlife and the Arts

BARS AND LOUNGES
For piano music until 2 AM, try the **Sport-piano-bar** (⊠ Sporthotel, ☎ 081/842–63–31) or **Pöstli-Keller** (⊠ Hotel Post, ☎ 081/842–63–18).

DANCING
Dance club **Sarazena** (☎ 081/842–63–53), in a charming old Engadine house, is open to 2 AM.

MUSIC
Kurorchester Pontresina plays chamber concerts daily at 11 AM in the Taiswald (Tais Forest), free of charge.

Outdoor Activities and Sports

BICYCLING
You can rent both conventional and mountain bikes at Pontresina's **Fähndrich-Sport** (☎ 081/842–71–55), **Michel Massé** (☎ 081/842–68–24), and **Flück Sport** (☎ 081/842–62–62).

HIKING
Pontresina offers guided excursions to the Swiss National Park (☞ Guided Tours, *below*).

MOUNTAINEERING AND CLIMBING
Bergsteigerschule Pontresina (☎ 081/842–64–44) is the biggest school in Switzerland, with a staff of up to 70 in high season. They offer rock and ice instruction for beginners and advanced climbers, plus private guided tours.

RAFTING
The tourist office will arrange outings.

SKATING
There's a large natural ice skating rink by the indoor swimming pool (☎ 081/842–73–41 or 081/842–82–57 for both).

SWIMMING
Pontresina Hallenbad is a municipal indoor pool with sauna, solarium, and a sunbathing terrace (☎ 081/842–73–41). There are two public artificial grass-sand tennis courts and two sand courts at the **Sportpavilion Roseg** (☎ 081/842–63–49).

St. Moritz

★ ⑭ *5 km (3 mi) west of Pontresina; 85 km (53 mi) southeast of Chur.*

Who put the "ritz" in St. Moritz? The approach to this celebrated city may surprise newcomers who, having heard the glittering, musical name dropped in the same breath as Paris and Rome, expect either a supremely cosmopolitan Old World capital or a resort whose spectacular natural setting puts other resorts to shame. It is neither. What makes St. Moritz's reputation is the people who go there, who have been going, generation by generation, since 1864, when hotelier Johannes Badrutt dared a group of English resorters—already summer regulars—to brave the Alpine winter as his guests. They loved it, delighted in the novelty of snowy mountain beauty, until then considered something to be avoided, and told their friends. By the turn of the century, St. Moritz, Switzerland, and snow were all the rage.

Not that St. Moritz had been a stranger to tourism before that. Since 1500 BC, when Druidic Celts first passed through, people have made the pilgrimage here to take healing waters from its mineral springs. The Romans had a settlement here, and later a church was founded on the site, dedicated to Mauritius, an early Christian martyr. The first historical reference to the town dates from 1139, and in 1537 Paracelsus, the great Renaissance physician and alchemist, described the health-giving properties of the St. Moritz springs. It is said that during the late 17th century the duke of Parma led a retinue of 25 followers over the mountain passes to taste the waters, and an 18th-century visitor from Germany described the coveted experience: "It puckers lips and tongue like the sharpest vinegar, goes to the head, and is like champagne in the nose."

In fact, 70% of the latter-day pilgrims who visit St. Moritz come from abroad, still the cosmopolitan mix of socialites, blue bloods, and stars that made the resort's name. But despite the reputation, not all are glamorous. St. Moritz catches social fire around the winter holidays—some New Year's Eve events have guest lists closed a year in advance—but the glitter fades by spring. Very ordinary people fill the streets come summer—the same hikers you might meet in any resort—and hotel prices plummet.

Then visitors see St. Moritz for what it really is: a busy, built-up old resort city sprawled across a hillside above an aquamarine lake, surrounded by forested hills and by graceful, though not the region's most dramatic, peaks. Piz Rosatsch, with its glacier, dominates the view, with Piz Languard (3,263 meters/10,699 feet) on the east and Piz Güglia (2,285 meters/7,492 feet) on the west. St. Moritz-Dorf is the most "downtown," with busy traffic and competitive parking in the shopping district. St. Moritz-Bad, the original spa-resort at the base of the lake, now bristles with brutish modern housing more worthy of a Costa Moritza than a pedigreed watering place. The town shows its best face from a distance, especially at dusk: From the See promenade, the popular walk around the lake, modern edges soften and the lake reflects the darkening mountains, warm hotel lights, and the grace that first made St. Moritz a star.

Even a hundred years of hype have not exaggerated its attractions as a winter sports center. Host to the Olympics in 1928 and again in 1948, it offers excellent facilities for ice skating, bobsledding, ski jumping, riding, and even winter golf, polo, and horse racing on the frozen lake. But it does not have a corner on fine skiing: It shares a broad complex of trails and facilities with Sils, Silvaplana, Celerina, and Pontresina; only the slopes of Corviglia, Marguns, and Piz Nair are directly accessible from town. More complex connections are required to ski Corvatsch/Furtschellas, above Silvaplana, and Diavolezza, beyond Pontresina.

One of the few reminders that the now-contemporary St. Moritz was once an Engadine village is the **Engadine Museum,** a reproduction of the traditional sgraffitied home. It exhibits and explains the local way of life through tools, furniture, and pottery, all displayed in rooms restored in different styles. A visit can illuminate tours throughout the region. ⊠ *Via dal Bagn,* ☎ *081/833–43–33.* ⌨ *5 SF.* ☺ *June–Oct., weekdays 9:30–noon and 2–5, Sun. 10–noon; Dec.–Apr., weekdays 10–noon and 2–5, Sun. 10–noon.*

Skiing

As a resort of superlatives—it's the oldest (its thermal springs were known 3,000 years ago), the most snobbish, and the most chic—St. Moritz could not, obviously, be content with only one ski area. It has three: one on each side of the valley, Corviglia and Corvatsch, and another in reserve, 20 minutes away by car—Diavolezza-Lagalp. Piz Corviglia, Piz Nair, and Grisch, on the northwest slopes of St. Moritz, are ideal terrain for family skiing, with 80 kilometers (50 miles) of generally easy runs, wide and well groomed, restaurants here and there, and lift service more than sufficient except for several days in high season. Corviglia—where the principal ski competitions of the Winter Olympics were held in 1924 and 1948—offers, in spite of its exceptionally sunny location, all the conditions from which intermediate skiers can profit to the maximum during their stay. The elevation (1,647 meters/5,400 feet) and the snow-making machines at Corviglia and Marguns defy even calamitous snow seasons. Diavolezza and Lagalp do not offer the same possibilities. Each warrants a day (less for strong skiers), especially for the panorama, as well as an easy but awe-inspiring descent from Diavolezza to Morteratsch. Lift tickets cost 54 SF for one day, 258 for six.

Dining and Lodging

$$$$ ✕ **Jöhri's Talvò.** Chef Roland Jöhri has moved his highly respected kitchen from Ftan to Champfèr, just outside St. Moritz, and established himself in a charmingly renovated 350-year-old Engadine house, where he and his wife make resort guests as comfortable over afternoon tea as over his stellar meals. Both the cooking and decor reflect their philosophy: to marry the best of Graubünden tradition with classic French elegance, from the delicate linens softening weathered woodwork to the light sauces that curb the heartiness of local capuns, pizzocheri, and maluns. There's also a popular lobster menu, with one whole lobster divided and transformed into three or four inspired courses. Aim for a table in the open gallery overlooking the ground floor, reserve the cozy familial living room for an intimate meal, or head for the wind-sheltered terrace. ⊠ *CH-7512,* ☎ *081/833–44–55. AE, DC, MC, V. Closed Mon.*

$$$ ✕ **Chesa Veglia.** This 17th-century *Bauernhof* (farmhouse) retains its raw beams and naive carvings within a theme restaurant so self-consciously restored you may think you're in an American mall—an effect enhanced by the restaurant's fragmentation into three theme rooms (an upscale grill, a "stübli," and a pizzeria). Nonetheless, this could be the most authentic Graubündner experience you'll have in this cosmopolitan town, even if you choose a pizza or Greek salad instead of the platter of farmers' cheeses. Despite the rustic setting, the main menu aspires to international cuisine; you can order *côte de boeuf à la moelle et aux truffes* (beef with marrow and truffles), carpaccio, and *terrine de lièvre* (hare pâté), at prices that are St. Moritz–high. There are good fruit tarts at teatime, when the atmosphere is at its most convincing; later, you'll find dinner-dancing with live entertainment and piano music in the grill. ⊠ *CH-7500,* ☎ *081/833–35–96. AE, DC, MC, V.*

$$ ✕ **Engiadina.** With its very plain linoleum and pine, this could pass for a St. Moritz diner, though its raison d'être is fondue—which it serves to crowds of skiers in winter and tourists in summer. Champagne fondue is the house specialty. Other favorites are cheap *steak-frites* (steak with french fries), snails, and side orders of Spätzli. It's a popular oddity in this ritzy resort. ⊠ *CH-7500,* ☎ *081/833–32–65. AE, DC, MC, V.*

$$$$ ✕🔟 **Badrutt's Palace.** With its pseudo-Gothic stone and mismatched sprawl of architectural excess, the Palace is pure Hollywood, all glitz and conspicuous consumption. Winter is its prime time: Flagrant and showy, with Rolls-Royces and Learjets discharging guests willing to pay more per night than for a transatlantic flight, it fills with beautiful people and wealthy wannabes who made token appearances on the slopes before checking in at the hairdresser. A jacket and tie are required in all public spaces after 7 PM, though a *dark suit* is required only in the most formal area, the Restaurant and Grill-Room. And nowhere in Switzerland will you find more facilities—the hotel even has private ski instructors and a private cinema. The Restaurant is as vast as a mess hall, beswagged and chandeliered; the Grill-Room is a celadon jewel-box and enjoys a culinary reputation beyond the guest list. The rooms are surprisingly discreet, and rather like a lot of other hotel rooms at a third the price—but it's not the drapes you're paying for. ⊠ *CH-7500,* ☎ *081/837–10–00,* FAX *081/837–29–99. 420 beds. 3 restaurants, bar, indoor and outdoor pools, hot tubs, massage, sauna, 4 tennis courts, fitness center, squash, ice-skating, downhill ski school, cinema, dance club, nightclub, nursery. AE, DC, MC, V.*

$$$$ ✕⌂ **Carlton.** If you want luxury without the glitz, consider this un-sung hotel, which stands slightly above the city center and offers fine views. Built in 1913 and now completely renovated, it's slick, bright, and modern, with a white-marble lobby more like a performing-arts center than a Belle Epoque hotel. The luxurious bar–sitting room up-stairs has period decor, and there are grand stone fireplaces. The guest rooms are all modern—there's not a sliver of Arvenholz in sight—and the baths are state-of-the-art Euro-style. The beautiful glassed-in pool has views over the lake and a sun terrace. ⊠ *CH-7500,* ☎ *081/833– 11–41,* FAX *081/833–20–12. 180 beds. Restaurant, bar, indoor pool, beauty salon, massage, sauna, fitness center, nursery. AE, DC, MC, V.*

$$$$ ✕⌂ **Kulm.** Far from the bustle of St. Moritz society, you can hear a spoon stirring a cup of tea in the hushed, classical lobby of this lux-ury hotel. It's discreetly done with slightly old-fashioned good taste—cream, gold, scarlet—and pampers a more sedate clientele than its competitors. The facilities are top-quality, the breakfast room is pure Wedgwood, and the à la carte restaurant—Rôtisserie de Chevaliers—is a romantic vaulted space, serving (predictably enough) old-style haute cuisine. In winter, the outdoor terrace is usually dominated at lunchtime by hardy men just off the icy Cresta Run, St. Moritz's ex-clusive skeleton run up the road. ⊠ *CH-7500,* ☎ *081/833–11–51,* FAX *081/833–27–38. 300 beds. Restaurant, bar, pool, massage, sauna, 3 tennis courts, fitness center. AE, DC, MC, V.*

$$$$ ✕⌂ **Schweizerhof.** This big-city hotel, right in the center of town, was built in 1896 and is still very grand. Public areas are heavy with carved wood and moldings, and the Victorian splendor is almost oppressive. The older rooms are decorated in dated shades of gold and orange, but most have been brought up to date with slick postmodern burled-wood cabinets and chic color schemes with much taupe and pistachio. The fifth floor, added in the early 1970s, has been luxuriously renewed; this is where the suites and the best south-facing doubles are. There's a popular piano bar and a lively stübli that draws a young après-ski crowd. The Acla restau-rant, at street level, serves casual Italian and Austrian meals. ⊠ *CH-7500,* ☎ *081/833–21–71,* FAX *081/833–83–00. 150 beds. 2 restaurants, 4 bars, sauna, fitness center, nursery. AE, DC, MC, V.*

$$ ✕⌂ **Meierei.** On a winding, private forest road partway around the
★ lake, this *Landgasthof* (country inn) is a rural mirage, an incongruity in the city but spiritually allied to the mountains and lake. It started in the 17th century as a farm where the bishop stopped over when trav-eling; later, it became a dairy restaurant and—150 years ago—a hotel. The look today is generally modern, though pine, game trophies, and a stone fireplace warm the restaurant and reception area, and the sit-ting room is comfortably scattered with overstuffed chairs. The rooms, painted white, have simple pine trim, and the baths are all new and all tile; a few rooms have ancient wood ceilings and antique furnishings. There are horses, rabbits, and a donkey for children, and a lovely ter-race café that draws walkers working their way around the lake. The

restaurant serves light meals and updated standards (trout in tomato butter, calves' liver in raspberry vinegar sauce) and is worth a visit even if you're not a guest and even though you'll have to walk in, as only guests may drive in. ⊠ CH-7500, ☎ 081/833–32–42, ℻ 081/833–88–38. 18 beds. Restaurant, café. No credit cards.

$$ ✕⊞ **Waldhaus am See.** This is another world, a good hotel perched
★ on a peninsula overlooking the lake and mountains with a merely peripheral view of St. Moritz's urban turmoil (well filtered through double glass) across the highway. The location is a peninsula across the highway; the view is primarily of lake and mountains. People speak softly here, and the carpets absorb the sound. With the big, sunny balcony, the dining rooms with views, and the comfortable decor (pine, plush armchairs), it's a vacation lodge geared to leisurely stays of a week or two. There are group excursions and theme buffets. The reasonably priced restaurant, which serves good lake trout, is famous for its award-winning wine list, which boasts more than 1,500 wines. The rooms are plain, with pine trim and some dated plumbing, though many new bathrooms have been added in recent years. A new wing provides 20 new beds. Sunny corner doubles have tiny bays over the lake. You pay less by the week, and for rooms without bath. ⊠ CH-7500, ☎ 081/833–76–76, ℻ 081/833–88–77. 72 beds. Restaurant, sauna, fitness center. DC, MC, V.

$–$$ ✕⊞ **Veltlinerkeller.** One of the most popular spots in town, this draws
★ a healthy mix of resorters and local workers who love the regional food. The plain, bright, genial restaurant has nothing swanky about it—just lots of wood, ancient moldings in the form of grapes, a few outsize game trophies, and a welcoming wood fire where the meat is roasted while you watch. The owner mans the grill, and his touch with Italian-Romansh cooking is light, and straightforward. In addition to grilled meats and whole trout, there are good and varied homemade pastas served family-style from crockery bowls. The nine double rooms upstairs are finished in slick quarry tile and stucco, with cotton floral prints and all-tile baths. ⊠ CH-7500,, ☎ 081/833–40–09, ℻ 081/833–37–41. 25 beds. Restaurant, stübli, bar. No credit cards.

$$$$ ⊞ **Steffani.** A standard city business-class hotel, this landmark built in 1869 is owned by Best Western and thus tailored to meet American expectations. Despite its age, it now has a heavy, modern look, with some stylized local details but more stress on function and dependability than history. The facilities are ample, and the staff is welcoming. ⊠ CH-7500, ☎ 081/833–21–01, ℻ 081/833–40–97. 120 beds. 3 restaurants, 3 bars, indoor pool, hot tub, massage, sauna, bowling, dance club. AE, DC, MC, V.

$$$ ⊞ **Soldanella.** This slightly faded Belle Epoque lodging in the center of town offers spare but luxury-scale corner doubles with wraparound views, some with desks built into bay windows. The look is Victorian, with pillars, runners, and heavy upholstery, although beds in some rooms have vinyl-padded headboards with a flea-market feel. There are big, comfortable parlors and a sunporch, and the dining hall is grand, if a little past its prime. Prices are high for the modest style. ⊠ CH-7500, ☎ 081/833–36–51, ℻ 081/833–23–37. 65 beds. Restaurant, bar. AE, DC, MC, V.

$$ ⊞ **Eden.** Just up from the center of town, on a hilltop, this small hotel *garni* (without a restaurant) has been in the same family since it opened in the 1890s. Such personal touches as the buffed original Arvenholz in some guest rooms, the personal antiques collection on display in the public rooms, and the pretty blue-and-white china at breakfast reflect the owner's singular style. Some rooms have been updated with blond oak and modern furnishings, and the bathrooms may have peculiar color

mixes (red and green), but the ambience is genteel and the service personal. ⊠ *CH-7500,* ☎ *081/833–61–61,* ℻ *081/833–91–91. 50 beds. Breakfast room. No credit cards.*

$$ ⊞ **Landguard.** This delightful little hotel stands just above the Eden, ★ with lovely mountain views, and its young, energetic management is deservedly house-proud. A face-lift has restored regional details such as sgraffiti and wooden windows and preserves the best from its earlier days, including carved ceilings, antiques, warm Oriental runners, and fine darkened pine in some rooms. The big corner rooms deserve the top price they command; back rooms look over town. All-tile baths add modern sparkle. ⊠ *CH-7500,* ☎ *081/833–31–37,* ℻ *081/833-45–46. 40 beds. Breakfast room. AE, DC, MC, V.*

Nightlife and the Arts

To find out what's happening in the arts world, check *St. Moritz Aktuell* or the booklet "Engadin," which offers weekly events information for the Upper Engadine resorts.

BARS AND LOUNGES

The Hotel Schweizerhof **piano bar** (☎ 081/832–21–71) has a pianist in its bar and a champion bartender who serves exotic cocktails to upscale crowds in a tiny Jugendstil lounge. The hotel's pine **stübli,** open all year, draws casual young people après-ski with a live guitarist and snacks, including raclette in winter. The **Muli Bar,** in the Schweizerhof's former library, offers country music après-ski. The **Renaissance Bar** in the Palace (☎ 081/837–11–01), with American-style bar stools and tables, has an open fireplace; the awe-inspiring **lobby lounge,** also in the hotel, has a pianist evenings. The **Cava-Weinstube** in the Hotel Steffani (☎ 081/832–21–01) attracts a casual crowd. **Bobby's Pub** (⊠ Gallaria Badrutt, at Via dal Bagn 52, ☎ 081/833–47–67) has an English atmosphere.

CASINOS

The casino in **St. Moritz** (☎ 081/832–10–80) has inaugurated 75 slot machines to supplement its roulette.

CLUBS

La Volière (⊠ Suvretta House, ☎ 081/832–11–32) is a very formal nightclub, requiring evening dress. The **Grand-Bar Nightclub** (⊠ Palace, ☎ 081/837–11–01) has dancing to live music.

DANCING

King's Club of the Palace (☎ 081/837–10–00), with its urban-decay decor (graffiti, neon, dated Keith Haring look), attracts the jet set at holiday time; prepare for a massive cover charge. **Vivai** is a popular disco club in the Hotel Steffani (☎ 081/832–21–01). **Absolut** (⊠ Via Maistra 10, ☎ 081/833–66–57) also draws a crowd.

MUSIC

The **St. Moritz Kurorchester,** a 13-piece summer chamber group, plays free concerts summer mornings at 10:30 in the Heilbadzentrum concert hall—or outside, if the weather is fine.

Outdoor Activities and Sports

BICYCLING

Bicycles can be rented at the **Rhaetian Railway station,** though use of the vehicles is restricted to bike trails. Mountain bikes also are available, but they are rarely permitted on pedestrian trails. You can rent both conventional and mountain bikes at the **Corviglia Tennis Center** in (☎ 081/833–15–00).

CLIMBING

Bergführerverein school (☎ 081/833–77–14) designs special programs for you.

GOLF

St. Moritz and Samedan share Switzerland's oldest 18-hole golf course, **Engadine Golf Samedan** (☎ 081/852–52–26), along the River En.

HORSEBACK RIDING

Riding schools at St. Moritz-Bad offer escorted group trips (☎ 081/833–57–33).

PARAGLIDING

For hang gliding call ☎ 081/833–24–16; for paragliding call ☎ 081/833–81–67.

RAFTING

For white-water rafting expeditions on the River En, call **Swissraft Engadine** (☎ 081/842–68–24). Tours are run June–September.

SAILING AND WINDSURFING

Arnoud Missiaen heads a windsurfing school (☎ 081/833–44–49). The **Segelschule St. Moritz** (☎ 081/833–40–56) gives sailing lessons.

SKATING

Ludains, an artificial outdoor skating rink, is open all year (☎ 081/833–50–30).

SPORTS CENTERS

St. Moritz/Celerina has an **International Center for Training and Competition** with equipment for all Olympic sports (☎ 081/837–61–59).

SWIMMING

You can swim in **Lake Nair** by St. Moritz. For indoor swimming, try the **Hallenschwimmbad,** a municipal pool and sauna (☎ 081/833–60–25) with coed and sex-segregated hours.

TENNIS

St. Moritz's **Corviglia Tennis Center** has four outdoor and four indoor tennis courts, with staff instructors (☎ 081/833–15–00). The local tourist office can tell you about other available courts.

Sils, Sils Baselgia, and Sils-Maria

⑮ *13 km (8 mi) southwest of St. Moritz.*

Southwest of St. Moritz, the Lower Engadine valley broadens into green meadows punctuated by a series of crystalline lakes: the little Champferer See, just past St. Moritz; the larger Silvaplaner See, headed by the small hillside resort of Silvaplana, and the long sprawl of the Silser See, accessible from the land bar that separates the two bodies of water. On this green lowland 13 kilometers (8 miles) from St. Moritz stands the resort complex of Sils (Segl in Romansh), connecting Sils-Baselgia and, farther back against the mountains, Sils-Maria. From Sils the highway heads over the Maloja Pass (1,816 meters/5,953 feet) and crosses over into Italy.

Although the flat setting and expanding new housing make Sils-Maria look like an American suburban country club (despite vast plains of green grass, there is no golf course here), Sils-Maria is a resort with old-Engadine flavor and inspiring views. Nietzsche wrote *Also Sprach Zarathustra* in his house here, which is now a museum. ⊠ *Next to Hotel Edelweiss,* ☎ *081/826–53–69.* 🖃 *4 SF.* ⊙ *mid-Dec.–Apr. and June–Nov., Tues.–Sun. 3–6.*

Hotel Hauser (⊠ Via Traunter Plazzas 7, ☎ 081/833–44–02) has a
large sunny terrace where you can have the best strudel with hot vanilla
sauce or Engadiner Nusstorte (walnut and caramel cake) in town. The
Hauser has its own chocolate shop, resided over by Australian-Swiss
Marinda Hauser, who will ship parcels of goodies worldwide.

Dining and Lodging

$$$$ ✕🖾 **Waldhaus.** Hermann Hesse, Thomas Mann, C. G. Jung, Marc Cha-
★   gall, Albert Einstein, and Richard Strauss all found solace in this hilltop forest retreat, high above the meadow that separates Lake Sils and
Lake Silvaplana and offers spectacular views in all directions. You can
have tea on the terrace, surrounded by tall evergreen woods, or play
tennis on the courts just below; either way, you'll be accompanied by
the hotel's resident string trio, which adds to the sense of Wagnerian
idyll. Even the indoor pool, built of pine and rock, takes in forest views
on all sides. The building itself is steeped in tradition and full of creaky
grandeur, with its heavy marble pillars, burnished parquet, Oriental
runners, and richly weathered Arvenstube. The rooms range from
spare (chenille and parquet) to splendid (bay windows with fine panoramas), but the public areas are consistently gracious, warmed with
rugs, antiques, and books and enhanced by views into the surrounding pines. ⊠ CH-7514, ☎ 081/826–66–66, 🖷 081/826–59–92. 220
beds. Restaurant, stübli, bar, beauty salon, massage, steam room,
miniature golf, 4 tennis courts. MC, V.

$ ✕🖾 **Chesa Marchetta/Pensiun Andreola.** You won't find a more pleas-
★   ant and complete regional experience than here, in this tiny twin pension and restaurant, run by two sophisticated sisters; not only do they
decorate with taste but they also serve authentic local dishes. The
sgraffitied pension is furnished in pine and chic cotton prints, while
the neighboring restaurant is an Arvenholz gem, perfectly preserved
since 1671. The menu is limited to one main dish a night—homemade
pasta with lamb, perhaps, or polenta with veal—with permanent options of *plain in pigna* (potato gratin with homemade sausage) or fondue Chinoise; but there are always cold local meats and Engadiner
Nusstorte, the region's signature nut cake. Meals are served evenings
only, snacks from 3:30 on. In the hotel, three-day stays are preferred.
⊠ CH-7514, ☎ 081/826–52–32, 🖷 081/826–62–60. 20 beds, some
without bath. Restaurant, stübli. No credit cards.

$$ 🖾 **Chesa Randolina.** This sleek resort hotel in Sils-Baselgia, adjoining
Sils-Maria, sits back from the water on lush green plains. The archi-
tecture is low-slung but pure Engadine, with stucco vaulting, beams,
and pine in nearly every room; the best have long balconies facing south.
There's a broad, spacious lounge with a stone fireplace and a cozy restau-
rant (hotel guests only) with a sgraffitied ceiling. ⊠ CH-7515, ☎ 081/
826–51–51, 🖷 081/826–56–00. 65 beds. Restaurant, bar. No credit
cards.

$$ 🖾 **Privata.** Tucked into a green corner at the edge of the village, this
★   tidy, fresh little Engadine-style inn is full of personal touches: antiques,
books, comfortable parlors, and a lovely garden behind. Decorated in
white and pine, most rooms offer good views, though the hotel behind
spoils a few. Some upper rooms have tiny balconies with chairs. The
restaurant is open only to inn guests. ⊠ CH-7514, ☎ 081/826–52–
47, 🖷 081/826–61–83. Restaurant. No credit cards.

Nightlife and the Arts

Small **chamber ensembles** perform from late June through September
in Sils, at 4 or 4:30 on the Konzerztplatz in Sils-Maria; in bad weather,
they move to the schoolhouse.

Outdoor Activities and Sports

CLIMBING

Sils/Silvaplana has a climbing school, **Bergsteigerschule "La Margna,"** which offers guided tours (☎ 081/826–88–15).

PARAGLIDING

In Sils, contact instructor Andrea Kuhn (☎ 081/826–54–00).

SAILING AND WINDSURFING

Sils has a sailing school under Antonio Walther (☎ 081/826-53–50). **Malojawind** is a windsurfing school (☎ 081/826–58–77) in Sils. Silvaplana's **Water Sports Centre** has schools for sailing (☎ 081/828–85–95) and windsurfing (☎ 081/828–92–29).

SPORTS CENTERS

Silvaplana has the **Sportcentrum Mulets** (☎ 081/828–93–62), with two sand tennis courts, a soccer field, an ice rink, a playground, and a training room. Sils's **Muot Marias** (☎ 081/826–62–57) is a well-equipped sports center.

SWIMMING

You can swim in Sils near the Chastè peninsula.

TENNIS

Sils has two public tennis courts, booked through the Hotel Waldhaus (☎ 081/826–66–66).

THE JULIER ROUTE TO THE SAN BERNARDINO

The Julier Pass is one of the three great Alpine passes that are known to have been used by the Romans (the Grand St. Bernard and the Splügen are the other two)—though even in those days, the Julier was favored because of its immunity from avalanches. The present road, built between 1820 and 1826, is dominated by three mountains, Piz Julier, Piz Albana, and Piz Polaschin, and near the top it is marked by two pillars, about 1½ meters (5 feet) high, which are said to be the remains of a Roman temple. The terrain here is barren, windswept, and rocky—the perfect place to imagine an open stage for marching legions.

En Route About 16 kilometers (10 miles) beyond the summit of the Julier Pass is the village of **Bivio**: A former Roman settlement named Stabulum Bivio, it is Bivio in Italian and Swiss German, and Beiva in Romansh—and residents speak all three.

Tiefencastel

🔟 *44 km (27 mi) northwest of Sils; 29 km (18 mi) south of Chur.*

Where the Julia flows into the Albula, this valley town, buried deep in the mountain forests and accessible only by steep, winding roads, was entirely destroyed by fire in 1890. Above the rebuilt town, the tall white church of **St. Ambrosius** still stands out against the background of fir trees that cover the encroaching hills.

En Route From Tienfencastel, the road forks: You can drive north toward Chur through Lenzerheide (1,525 meters/5,000 feet), a winter and summer resort known for moderate slopes for beginning skiers and a good 18-hole golf course, or cut west to Thusis. The Thusis route is particularly spectacular via the Rhaetian Railway, as it passes through 16 tunnels, one of them more than 5 kilometers (3 miles) long, and across 27 bridges and viaducts. The most celebrated of these is the **Solis Viaduct,** the center arch of which is 42 meters (137 feet) across and 89 meters (293 feet) high.

Thusis, a town surrounded by high mountains and thick forest, has a late-Gothic church (1506) and the ruins of the old Schloss Hohenrhaetien, perched on rocky heights to guard the entrance to the ancient **Via Mala** road. Leading south from Thusis, the Via Mala writhes along the bottom of a deep ravine crisscrossed by bridges. It has been replaced by the new highway, but you can still see the old Via Mala by leaving the highway about 5 kilometers (3 miles) after Thusis and following the traffic signs marked "Via Mala," towards San Bernardino. On foot, you can descend 321 steps into the gorge to see the bridges that, in various epochs, man has strung across the treacherous water.

At Zillis, the Via Mala ends and N13 leads south and west toward the **Splügenpass** (the southbound entrance into Italy). Just west of the Splügenpass is **San Bernardino Pass** (Little St. Bernard Pass). There is an easy express tunnel through the pass these days, 8 kilometers (5 miles) long, but the tortuous climb up the old highway rewards drivers (and postbus passengers) with astonishing perspectives: As you begin to ascend, the Rheinwald Valley opens below, and you see the first currents of the Hinter or Lower Rhine; beyond looms its source, the glacier of the **Zapporthorn** (3,154 meters/10,340 feet).

GRAUBÜNDEN A TO Z

Arriving and Departing

By Bus
You can take the Swiss postbus system on the *Palm Express* from Ascona or Lugano in the Ticino over the Maloja Pass and into St. Moritz. For information, call 081/833–30–72.

By Car
As Graubünden is dense with mountains and thin on major throughways, drivers usually enter either by way of the San Bernardino Pass from the Ticino or from the north past Liechtenstein, both on N13, the region's only expressway; it traces the Rhine to its main source.

By Train
The only main Swiss Federal (SBB) trains to enter Graubünden come into Chur; from there, the fine local Rhaetian Railroad (RhB) takes over, with its broad network of narrow-gauge track. For general information on SBB and Rhaetian Rail connections, ☎ 081/21–91–21.

To make the most of the Rhaetian rail systems, you can take famous scenic train routes in or out of the region: the **Bernina Express** from Chur to St. Moritz via the Albula route and on to Italy past the spectacular Bernina peaks, and the glamorous **Glacier Express,** which connects St. Moritz with Zermatt via the Oberalp Pass and pulls a burnished-wood period dining car. During the 7½-hour trip, the *Glacier Express* crosses 291 bridges and 91 tunnels, covering spectacular Alpine terrain. To reserve a table, contact Schweizerische Speisewagen Gesellschaft (✉ CH-7000 Chur, ☎ 081/252–14–25). For seat reservations for the train (also compulsory), contact the tourist offices concerned or the railway itself.

Getting Around

By Bus
Postbuses are a dramatic way to lumber up Alpine switchbacks over the region's great passes—if you're not inclined to motion sickness. You

also can use them to make circle tours, with some careful studying of the schedule. Information is available at all post offices.

By Car

The N13 expressway cuts a swift north–south route through Graubünden. Fine valley highways connect the rest of the area, though to move from one resort to another you may have to crawl over a mountain pass. If you want to get back into the deep farmlands, you'll definitely need a car.

By Train

The Rhaetian Railway (☞ Arriving and Departing, *above*) consists of 375 kilometers (243 miles) of track and 116 tunnels and offers unusually thorough coverage of the terrain. Without resorting to cogwheel supports, some of the trains climb stiff mountain grades of up to 7%. Holders of the Swiss Pass travel free on all RhB lines.

Contacts and Resources

Emergencies

Police: in the Upper Engadine (☎ 081/832–27–27); in Arosa (☎ 081/377–19–38); in Klosters (☎ 081/422–12–36). **Ambulance:** in St. Moritz (☎ 081/837–41–41); in Klosters (☎ 081/422–17–13). **Hospital:** in the Upper Engadine (☎ 081/851–11–11); in Davos (☎ 081/414–12–12). **Doctors:** Upper Engadine referral (☎ 081/852–56–57). Available doctors, dentists, and emergency pharmacies are listed in local newspapers under "Notfalldienst" (emergency service) and in the city or resort's tourist periodical.

Guided Tours

The **Arosa** tourist office (☎ 081/377–16–21) offers guided tours and nature walks every morning and afternoon from June through October; you can visit a cheese maker, a regional museum, and a 15th-century chapel. **Pontresina** offers guided walking tours of its old town, full of typical Engadine houses, from mid-June to mid-October. It also offers guided botanical excursions, sunrise viewings, glacier tours, and hiking trips to the Swiss National Park, plus mushroom-picking outings in season (usually August–September). If you are staying in Pontresina, the tours are free of charge; day visitors pay a small fee (☎ 081/842–64–88). Arosa, Davos, and Lenzerheide-Valbella offer an unusual **hiking package:** They'll book your hotel and deliver your bags ahead. You can walk from Davos to Arosa one day, and from Arosa to Lenzerheide the next. A seven-day program lets you spend more time in each resort. Contact any of the tourist offices.

Visitor Information

Chur's tourist office, (☎ 081/252–18–18), the main office of the region, provides leaflets and colored footprints on its sidewalks to lead you around the old town at your own pace; it also offers personally guided tours, with departures from the Rathaus.

Arosa (☎ 081/377–16–21), **Davos** (☎ 081/415–21–21), **Klosters** (☎ 081/410–20–20, FAX 081/410–20–10), **St. Moritz** (☎ 081/837–31–47), **Zernez** (☎ 082/8–13–00). The tourist office for the "Heidiland" areas of the canton is in **Maienfeld** (⊠ Autobahn Raststaette Heidiland, CH-7304, ☎ 081/302–61–00).

5 Ticino

Italian in language, culture, and spirit, Ticino is an irresistible combination of Mediterranean pleasures and Swiss efficiency. With its yacht-filled waterfront promenades of Locarno and Lugano, and its constantly sunny climate, Ticino is a canton set apart, a happy harbor for Switzerland's Italian-speaking minority.

NEWCOMERS TO THE OLD WORLD, a little weak on their geography, might hear the names Lugano, Ascona, Locarno, Bellinzona and assume—quite naturally—they're in Italy. Color photographs of the region might not set them straight: Nearly every publicity shot shows palm trees and mimosa, red roofs and loggias, azure waters and indigo skies. Surely this is the Italian Mediterranean or the coast of the Adriatic. But behind the waving date palms are tell-tale signs: surgical neatness, fresh paint, geometric gardens, timely trains. There's no mistake about it: It's a little bit of Italy, but the canton of Ticino is pure Swiss.

For the German Swiss, it's a little bit of paradise. They can cross over the St. Gotthard or the San Bernardino Pass and emerge in balmy sunshine, eat gnocchi (potato-based pasta balls) and polenta in shaded *grotti* (rustic outdoor restaurants), drink Merlot from ceramic bowls, taste gelato (ice cream) overlooking the waters of Lago di Maggiore (Lake Maggiore)—and still know their lodging will be strictly controlled by the Swiss Hotel Association. They don't even have to change money. The combination is irresistible, and so in spring, summer, and fall they pour over the Alps to revel in low-risk Latin delights.

And the Ticinese welcome them, like rich distant cousins to be served and coddled and—perhaps just a bit—despised. For the Italian-speaking natives of the Ticino—a lonely 8% of the Swiss population—are a minority in their own land, dominated politically by the German-speaking Swiss, set apart by their culture as well as by their language. Their blood and their politics are as Mediterranean as their climate: In a battle over obligatory seat belts, the Ticinese consistently voted to reject the federal intrusion. They were voted down by their Germanic neighbors—a 70% majority—and they protested. It was brought to vote again, and again they were defeated. Nowadays the Ticinese defy the federal law—and their policemen, Ticinese themselves, of course, turn a blind and supportive eye.

Their Italian leanings make perfect sense: An enormous mountain chain cuts them off from the north, pushing them inexorably, glacier-like, toward their lingual roots. Most of the territory of the Ticino belonged to the pre-Italian city-states of Milan and Como until 1512, when the Swiss Confederation took it over by force. It remained a Swiss conquest—oppressed under the then-tyrannical rule of Uri, Schwyz, and Underwald, the very cantons now revered for forming the honorable Confederation of Switzerland—until 1798, when from the confusion of Napoléon's campaigns it emerged a free canton, and in 1803 it joined the confederation for good.

It remains a canton apart nonetheless, graceful, open, laissez-faire. Here you'll instantly notice differences in manner and body language among Ticinese engaged in conversation; you'll also notice fewer English-speaking Swiss. The climate, too, is different: There's an extraordinary amount of sunshine here—more than in central Switzerland and even in sunny Italy immediately across the border, where Milan and Turin often are haunted by a grim overcast of gray. Mountain-sports meccas aside, this is the most glamorous of Swiss regions: The waterfront promenades of Lugano and Locarno, lined with pollards, rhododendrons, and bobbing yachts, blend a rich social mix of jet-set resorters and olive-skinned gentlefolk, the men in Bordolinos, the women in heavy gold. A few miles' drive brings the canton's impoverished past into view—the foothill and mountain villages are still scattered with low-roof stone peasants' cabins, but nowadays those cabins often prove to be gentrified as chic vacation homes.

Although they're prosperous, with Lugano standing third in banking, after Zürich and Geneva, the Ticinese hold on to their past, a mountain-peasant culture that draws them into the heights to hike, hunt, and celebrate with great pots of risotto stirred over open outdoor fires. It's that contrast—contemporary glamour, bucolic past—that grants travelers a visit that's as balanced, satisfying, and unique as a good Merlot.

Pleasures and Pastimes

Dining

Of all the Swiss regions this can be the most pleasurable to eat in, as the stylish and simple cuisine of Italy has been adopted virtually intact. Because the Ticinese were once a poor mountain people, their everyday cooking shares the earthy delights of another once-poor mountain people, the Piemontese, whose steaming polenta and ribsticking gnocchi share the table with game and meaty porcini mushrooms. *Manzo brasato* (savory braised beef with vegetables) and osso buco are standards, as are polenta *con carne in umido* (with meat stew), *busecca* (vegetable soup with tripe), and any number of variations on risotto. If you look and ask, you might be lucky enough to find *trota in carpione* (trout marinated in red wine and vinegar and served as a cold hors d'oeuvre). Game offerings usually include *coniglio* (rabbit), *lepre* (hare), and *capretto* (roast kid).

As in the rest of Switzerland, local cold meats come in a broad variety, from myriad salamis to *prosciutto crudo,* the pearly-pink cured raw ham made famous in Parma. Any food product made locally is called *nostrano,* and the prosciutto crudo nostrano is worth asking for at the butcher, as you won't find a match for its forthright, gamey flavor back home. Eat it with bread and sweet butter to balance the salt.

Most cooks import Italian cheeses—Parma *Reggiano,* sharp *Pecorino*—though there are good, hard, white mountain varieties (*Piora, Gesero*) in most shops. The most local treat: tiny *formaggini,* little molds of ultrafresh goat cheese, still shining with whey and served whole as individual portions.

The best place to sample these down-to-earth delicacies is in a grotto, one of the scores of traditional country restaurants scattered across the region. Some of them are set deep in the mountains and forests, little more than a few rows of picnic tables and a string of festive lights. While some serve only cold meats, a few offer a daily hot dish or two. Wine is poured into an individual *boccalino,* a traditional ceramic pitcher, or a small ceramic bowl, to be drunk from like a cup. If the weather is steamy, you can have a beer to quench your thirst, but it's rarely consumed with food here. Or you can order *gazosa* (lemon-lime soda) and *vino nostrano* (the house red wine) and mix them, as the locals do. If you want a real Italian-style espresso, one-finger deep and frothing with golden foam, ask for *un liscio.* Otherwise they'll serve it with cream, Swiss-style—and might even charge you extra. If you want a shot of *grappa* (grape brandy) thrown in, ask for it *corretto*—literally, "correct." To experience an authentic grotto, avoid the ones with *ristorante* in their names; the categories of eating establishments are carefully regulated, so these will always be pricier—and not the real thing.

But the Ticino today isn't all simple pleasures. Its prosperous resorts draw the mink-and-Vuarnets set, and they in turn demand the best and the latest in international cooking—though inevitably with an Italian accent.

CATEGORY	COST*
$$$$	over 80 SF
$$$	50 SF–80 SF
$$	20 SF–50 SF
$	under 20 SF

per person for a three-course meal (except in the $ category), including sales tax and 15% service charge

Lodging

The hotel industry of this Mediterranean region of Switzerland capitalizes on its natural assets, with lakeside views of Lake Lugano and Lake Maggiore, and swimming pools and terraces that pay homage to the omnipresent sun. As the Ticino is at its temperate best in spring and fall, and packed with sunseekers in summer, many hotels close down for the winter. Tourist offices often publish lists of those remaining open, so if you're planning to come in low season—and even in January the lake resorts can be balmy—check carefully. Although these are vacation resorts, they do not depend on the demipension system as much as their mountain counterparts, but arrangements can be made.

CATEGORY	COST*
$$$$	over 300 SF
$$$	180 SF–300 SF
$$	120 SF–180 SF
$	under 120 SF

All prices are for a standard double room, including breakfast, tax, and service charge.

Mountain Valleys

Val Blenio, Val Maggia, Valle Verzasca, Val Leventina, and other mountain valleys just a short distance from the major cities are rugged reminders of the region's modest history. Stone-rendered peasant homes, called *rustici,* permeate the valleys, some cut so deeply into the lands that the sun never quite reaches bottom. Driving these valleys is a unique experience where time seems to have stopped; you'll encounter whole villages perched on craggy mountainsides, in apparent defiance of gravity.

Waterfront Promenades

Switzerland's sunniest waterfronts—with boating, swimming, charming cafés, fine dining, and shops of all sorts—are in Ticino. Palm-lined promenades in Lugano, Locarno and Ascona offer tremendous views overlooking rugged Italian alps. Evenings, harbor lights twinkle as the Ticinese stroll by, enjoying the balmy climate.

Exploring Ticino

The canton is divided into two geographic regions by the small mountain (554 meters/1,817 feet) called Monte Ceneri, which rises up south of the valley below Bellinzona. Radiating northeast and northwest of Monte Ceneri in the windswept region called Sopraceneri (whose name translates as "above Ceneri") are several mountainous valleys, including Val Blenio, Val Maggia, Valle Verzasca, Val Leventina (the approach from St. Gotthard and others), and the balmier resorts of Locarno and Ascona, which share a peninsula bulging into Lake Maggiore, Italy's famous northern lake.

Great Itineraries

While Lugano and Locarno alone provide an overview of the region, completing the picture requires forays to the less touristic waterfront village Ascona, the mountain stronghold Bellinzona, and the rural, rugged mountain valleys beyond.

Numbers in the text correspond to numbers in the margin and on the Ticino and Lugano maps.

Concentrate on 🏨 **Lugano** ⑦–⑭, exploring the waterfront shops, venturing east to the Villa Favorita, and riding a funicular up Monte Bre. Profit from the city's great restaurants and nighttime lake views from one of its many hotels. On the second day, take in the sights of the serene hillside city **Locarno** ② and the former fishing village of **Ascona** ⑥, both on the shores of Lake Maggiore.

In addition to all of the above, explore the medieval fortifications of **Bellinzona** ①, the canton's capital, and tiny **Campione** ⑰, perhaps the most Italian of all Swiss towns. Also take a drive through the wilds of Ticino, into any of the numerous valleys where peasant life has carried on virtually unchanged amid rugged terrain for centuries.

When to Tour the Ticino

Lush and Mediterranean, Ticino is gorgeous in springtime; the season starts as early as mid-March here, making the region a popular late winter escape. In summertime, lakeside activity surges, and the weather can at times be hot; warm summer nights are incredibly romantic, particularly on the Lago di Lugano. Crowds fill the promenades at Lugano and Locarno throughout summer, but neither waterfront becomes unpleasantly jammed.

SOPRACENERI

Radiating northeast and northwest of Monte Ceneri in the windswept region called Sopraceneri (whose name translates as "above Ceneri") are several mountainous valleys, including Val Blenio, Val Maggia, Valle Verzasca, Val Leventina, and the balmier resorts of Locarno and Ascona—which share a peninsula bulging into Italy's famous Lake Maggiore.

Bellinzona

★ ❶   *128 km (79 mi) south of Luzern; 150 km (93 mi) south of St. Mortiz.*

All roads lead to Bellinzona, the fortified valley city that guards the important European crossroads of the St. Gotthard and San Bernardino routes. Its importance through the ages makes itself evident: Massive fortified castles—no fewer than three—rise over its ancient center, each named for a strong force: Schwyz, Uri, and Unterwalden, the core cantons of the Swiss Confederation. They were built by the noble Sforza and Visconti families, the dukes of Milan who ruled northern Italy and environs for centuries and held this crucial juncture until 1422, when the Swiss Confederates began a violent century of battling for its control.

The three castles have been exceptionally well restored, and each merits a visit, but the city itself should not be overlooked: It is a classic Lombard town, with graceful architecture and an easy, authentically Italian ambience; it is relatively free of tourists and thus most revealing of the Ticino way of life.

Pick up a map in the tourist office in the **Palazzo Comunale,** a splendid Renaissance structure heavily rebuilt in the 1920s. Its courtyard is framed by two stacked rows of delicate vaulted arcades, with airy loggias at the top, and is decorated with murals of the old town painted in the mid-1920s. The Palazzo stands in the heart of the old town, where

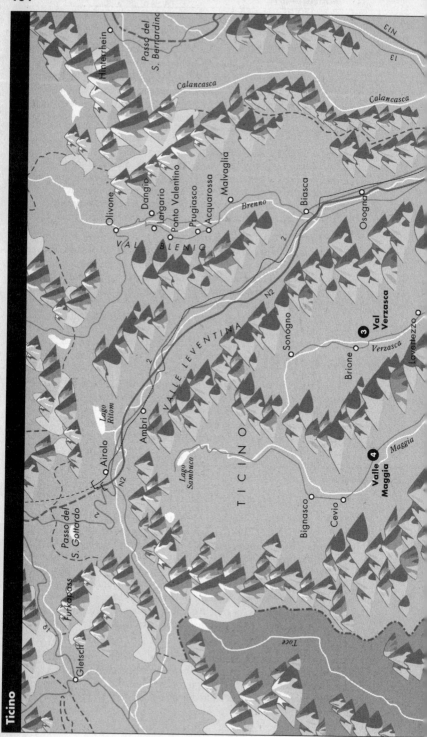

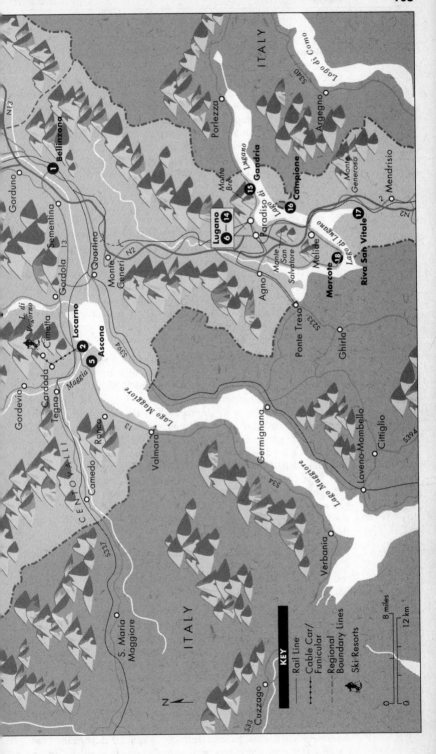

heavy columned arcades, wrought-iron balconies, and shuttered facades show the direct influence of medieval Lombardy.

Castelgrande, also called the Castle of Uri, is the oldest here, its origins dating from the 6th century, though the current structure traces to the 1200s. The massive exterior is dominated by two heavy, unmatched towers and the remaining portion of its crenellated wall, which once stretched all the way to the river. Renovations and modern additions have created an elaborate new complex of restaurants and museums, including art and archaeology exhibitions. The newly mounted 14th-century ceiling murals, created to embellish the wooden ceiling of a local villa (now demolished), offer a peek at privately commissioned decorative art. ☎ *091/826–23–53. ✉ 2 SF, multiple ticket for Castello di Montebello and Castello di Sasso Corbaro as well, 4SF. ☉ Winter, Tues.–Sun. 9–12:30 and 2–4:30; summer, Tues.–Sun. 9–11:30 and 2–5:30.*

The most striking of Bellinzona's three castles is the **Castello di Montebello.** Its oldest, center portion dates from the 13th century; there are a palace and courtyard from the 15th century, with spectacular walkways around the top of the encircling walls overlooking views worthy of a feudal lord. The center structure houses an attractive, modern **Museo Civico** (Civic Museum), with exhibits on the history and architecture of the area, including a striking collection of Gothic and Renaissance stone capitals. ☎ *091/825–13–42. ✉ 2 SF, multiple ticket for Castelgrande and Castello di Sasso Corbaro as well, 4SF. ☉ Oct.–May, Tues.–Sun. 10–noon and 2–5; June–Sept., Tues.–Sun. 9–noon and 2–6.*

The **Castello di Sasso Corbaro,** the highest of the three Bellinzona castles, is visible for most of the length of the valley. If you are an ambitious walker, you can reach it uphill from the Castello di Montebello along a switchback road through woods with lovely views (about 45 minutes on foot); if you are driving, follow the signs. This castle is a typical Sforza structure, designed by a Florentine military engineer and built in 1479 for the duke of Milan, who insisted that the work be completed in six months. In the dungeon, there's a branch of the **Museo dell'Arte e delle Tradizioni Popolari del Ticino** (Ticino Museum of Popular Arts and Traditions), displaying coins, stamps, historic photographs of Bellinzona, and a fine exhibit of Ticino folk costumes. *Castle and museum,* ☎ *091/825–55–32. ✉ 2 SF, multiple ticket for Castello di Montebello and Castelgrande as well, 4 SF. ☉ Apr.–Oct., Tues.–Sun. 9–noon and 2–5.*

The imposing late-Renaissance facade of the **Chiesa Collegiata** of Sts. Pietro and Stephano, begun during the 16th century, stands across from the Castelgrande. Chiesa Collegiata's interior is lavishly frescoed in Baroque style by late-18th-century Ticino artists.

Chiesa San Biagio (Church of St. Biagio), one of Bellinzona's two Italianate churches, is a spare, simple medieval treasure guarded on the exterior by an outsize fresco of a soldierly Christ. Built during the 12th century, its late-Romanesque structure suggests a transition into Gothic style. The natural alternating redbrick and gray stone complement fragments of exquisitely colored 14th-century frescoes. It's the humblest but possibly the most moving landmark in town.

Chiesa di Santa Maria delle Grazie (Church of the Holy Virgin Mary) was built at the end of the 15th century, about 300 years later than the Chiesa San Biagio. Its main feature is a split transept in the Franciscan style, with a dividing wall spectacularly frescoed by an unknown 15th-century Lombard artist. The central image is a crucifixion scene; the surrounding panels depict the life of Christ. Beside the church, on its left, a graceful 16th-century **cloister** now serves the adjoining home for the aged.

Villa dei Cedri, the city's art gallery, was founded in 1985; with a private collection donated to Bellinzona, it mounts worthwhile temporary exhibitions. Behind the villa's enclosed garden and grounds, the city grows its own tiny crop of local Merlot, available for sale inside. ☎ 091/826–28–27. ⊡ 5 SF. ⊙ Mar.–Dec., Tues.–Sun. 10–noon and 2–5.

Dining

$$–$$$ ✕ **Castelgrande.** Now that the oldest of Bellinzona's "grand castles" has been renovated, its chic, modern restaurant merits a visit along with ★ the new exhibitions, and it's a logical, central place for a serious dining stop. That is, don't expect a quick cafeteria lunch served to shorts-clad tourists: This is a real restaurant, with a daringly cool post-Memphis decor and sophisticated efforts from the Italian chef: goose liver with blueberries, quail with porcini mushrooms, pigeon and pearl onions in sweet-and-sour sauce. The wine list flaunts more than 70 Ticino Merlots. In contrast to the chic interior grotto, the great terrace has a lighter atmosphere, with views, sunshine, and meals served throughout the day. ⊠ Castelgrande, ☎ 091/751–23–53. AE, DC, MC, V. Closed Mon.

$$ ✕ **Osteria Sasso Corbaro.** From the heights of the ancient Castello Sasso Corbaro, the highest of Bellinzona's three castles, this atmospheric restaurant serves meals inside a beautifully restored hall or outside, at stone tables, in the shady, walled-in courtyard. The cooking is simple and regional, with cold and grilled meats, trout, and seasonal vegetables. There are good local wines and a holiday air, as the restaurant opens only in high season. ⊠ Castello Sasso Corbaro, ☎ 091/825–55–32. No credit cards. Closed Mon., and Nov.–Apr.

$–$$ ✕ **Montebello.** At this spot on a hill above the center in the adjoining suburb of Daro, you can relax under a grape arbor at linen-covered tables and enjoy an authentic meal in true Italian style: casual, elegantly simple, and served with easygoing flair. From a standing menu and list of daily specials, sample carpaccio, homemade pasta, and frothy zabaglione (egg whipped with sweet Marsala). ⊠ Via alla Chiesa 3, Bellinzona/Daro, ☎ 091/825–83–95. AE, DC, MC, V. Closed Sun.

Val Blenio

17 km (11 mi) north of Bellinzona; 80 km (49 mi) north of Lugano.

To see the deep countryside of the Ticino—despite its resorts and cities, it consists mostly of such terrain—follow the N2 expressway north from Bellinzona, toward St. Gotthard; after 17 kilometers (11 miles), exit at **Biasca,** a miniature Bellinzona itself as it guards two major access roads from the north.

Drive north from Biasca in the direction of Olivone and you'll soon find yourself in the Val Blenio, a characteristic Ticinese valley cutting deeper and higher into wild, rocky country. Its villages mingle tidy suburban cottages with the architectural signature of Ticino life: ancient stone houses, some little more than huts, with ramshackle roofs of odd-size slab and small windows taking in grand views. This is the *rustico* once inhabited by mountain peasants starving under the harsh rule of the Swiss-German confederates; today the heirs of both those ancient lines happily profit from a new twist: The Ticinese now rent their *rustici* to wealthy tourists—most of them Swiss-German—who hope to escape the pressures of urban prosperity.

It's a matter of a simple round-trip up Val Blenio, toward the Lucomagno Pass. On the main highway north, life remains fairly civilized, though the canyonlike hillsides are split by misting cascades. But about

23 kilometers (14 miles) in from Biasca, just past Olivone, the road
cuts sharply south. At the hairpin, a rough country road continues south
and leads down the wilder west side of the valley, high over the River
Brenno. In these villages—Largario, Ponto Valentino, Prugiasco—
you'll see the real, rural Ticino. By the time you reach tiny Acquarossa,
with its restaurants and hotels, 12 kilometers (7 miles) from Olivone,
it may seem as urban as Locarno.

Locarno

❷ *21 km (13 mi) west of Bellinzona; 39 km (24 mi) northwest of Lugano.*

Superbly placed on the sheltered curve of the northernmost tip of Lake
Maggiore and surrounded on all sides by mountains, Locarno is the
sunniest town in Switzerland. Here, subtropical flora flourishes, with
date palms and fig trees, bougainvillea, rhododendron, even aloe vera
burgeoning on the waterfront. Its fauna is no less colorful: Every
spring, summer, and fall the arcaded streets and cafés teem with exotic characters in fur coats and T-shirts, lamé, leather, neon short-shorts—
and sunglasses. One doesn't show one's face in Locarno without a stylish
set of shades.

In August, Locarno makes worldwide news with its film festival, which
showcases some of the latest cinema on an outdoor screen in the Piazza Grande. There's also opera outdoors, as well as international artists
in concert. Its facilities haven't just drawn culture hounds: Here, in 1925,
Briand, Stresemann, Mussolini, and Chamberlain signed the Locarno
Pact, securing the peace—albeit temporarily—in Europe.

Locarno's raison d'être is its waterfront, which has a graceful promenade curving around the east flank of the bay and a beach and public
pool complex along the west; its clear lake is often still as glass, reflecting the Tincinese alps across to the south. However, Locarno's Lombard-style shopping arcades and historic landmarks continually draw
visitors inland as well.

★ The **Piazza Grande** is the heart of the old town and its social center,
too: From under the crowded arcades shoppers spill onto open ground
to lounge in cafés and watch each other drink, smoke, and pose.

Chiesa Nuova (New Church) on via Cittadella is an exuberantly decorated Baroque church (1630) with an enormous statue of St. Christo-
pher on the facade. Down the street from Chiesa Nuova, the **Casa dei
Canonici** (House of the Canons) dates from the same period; note the
lovely interior courtyard.

The 17th-century **Chiesa di Sant'Antonio** (Church of St. Anthony) lies
at the end of **via Sant'Antonio**, a fine, narrow street lined with splendid old houses in both medieval and Flamboyant Baroque styles.

Immediately to the right of Chiesa di Sant'Antonio stands the **Casa Rusca**,
an 18th-century residence that now serves as the city art gallery. ☎
091/756–34–58. ☞ *5 SF.* ☉ *Tues.–Sun. 10–noon and 2–5.*

The heavy, frescoed **Chiesa di San Francesco** (Church of St. Francis)
and its convent date from the mid-15th century; legend has it that it
was founded by St. Anthony of Padua. The emblems on its Renaissance facade show Locarno's social distinctions of the era: The eagle
represents the aristocrats; a lamb, the countrymen; and the ox (un-
kind, surely), the citizens. In its sanctuary, concerts are performed every
spring and fall.

Built in 1300 as the stronghold of the dukes of Milan, **Castello Visconti** was soon virtually destroyed by the invading Swiss Confederates.

Today it contains a **Museo Archeologico** (Archaeological Museum), with Roman relics and Romanesque sculpture. ☎ *091/825–81–45.* ✉ *5 SF.* ⊙ *Apr.–Oct., Tues.–Sun. 10–noon and 2–5.*

NEED A BREAK?	Join the thirsty locals and trendy poseurs at the outdoor tables of the **Ravelli Tearoom** (✉ Piazza Grande, ☎ 091/751-12-05) for the Piazza Grande café scene.

★ You can get to the **Santuario della Madonna del Sasso** (Sanctuary of the Madonna of Sasso) via a five-minute funicular ride to a high plateau, with fine views over the city and the bay. The sprawling church complex is where, in 1480, Brother Bartolomeo da Ivrea saw a vision of the Virgin Mary; the sanctuary was begun seven years later and gradually enlarged to include a convent, a museum, and side galleries. Within the sanctuary, you'll find Bramantino's *The Flight to Egypt* (1520) and *Christ Carried to the Sepulcher,* a dramatic, Caravaggiesque procession scene painted in 1870 by Antonio Ciseri, from nearby Ascona. You'll also see naïve-art "thank yous" to the Madonna from peasants who've survived everything from family tragedies to fender-benders.

Dining and Lodging

$$$$ ✕ **Centenario.** Set back from the waterfront along the hotel row east
★ of the urban tangle, this gracious ristorante serves innovative Franco-Italian cuisine that is unashamedly nouvelle and absolutely top-quality, from its moderately priced business lunch to the all-out *menu de dégustation* (sampling menu). Specialties include risotto in Merlot with crayfish tails, rack of roe deer, and tangy lemon soufflé. You can have an aperitif on the lakefront terrace before sitting down to a meal amid quarry tile, Persian rugs, and gleaming silver. ✉ *Lungolago 17,* ☎ *091/743–82–22. AE, DC, MC, V. Closed Sun. and Mon.*

$$–$$$ ✕ **Cittadella.** This popular dining spot in the old town along a narrow, historic street offers inexpensive regional food—pizza, pastas, simple fish—in its casual downstairs trattoria, and fine fish dishes in the more formal restaurant upstairs. The preparation is light and Italian, the flavors subtle with oils and herbs. Since the restaurant opened hotel rooms upstairs, it has become more commercial and a mite self-promoting. ✉ *Via Cittadella 18,* ☎ *091/751–58–85. AE, DC, MC, V.*

$$$$ ✕▥ **Reber au Lac.** This richly landscaped oasis at the end of the waterfront row holds a roomy, comfortable holiday hotel with enough amenities—spacious garden, big pool, bathing beach, sheltered terrace dining—to make up for some bold and dated decor. Renovation has brought the building up to date, and awning-shaded balconies overlook lawn and pool, while interiors are done in tasteful pastels. Although demipension is stressed here, the Grill Room has a reputation with locals for the Franco-Italian cuisine it serves in a Spanish setting. ✉ *CH-6600,* ☎ *091/743–02–02,* ℻ *091/743–79–81. 120 beds. 2 restaurants, 2 bars, pool, sauna, tennis court, beach. AE, DC, MC, V.*

$$$ ✕▥ **Beau-Rivage.** Small and genteel in a row of ostentatious competitors,
★ this recently renovated lodging built in 1900 retains its gracious sitting rooms, low vaulting, and terrazzo floors. Although lakeside rooms can be spare and boxy, the views are picture-perfect; back rooms overlook a lush subtropical garden. More trees surround the dining room, which has picture windows that open toward the lake. Demipension is standard. ✉ *CH-6600,* ☎ *091/743–13–55,* ℻ *091/743–94–09. 90 beds. Restaurant. AE, DC, MC, V.*

$$–$$$ ✕▥ **Belvedere.** Well above the city and somewhat blocked from the
★ best lake views by other developments, this Belle Epoque hotel has gone all out, gutting and rebuilding all interiors in postmodern beech,

lacquer, and marble and adding a solid new wing. There's extra architectural interest in the building's historic core: It started as a private home in 1680, and its florid dining hall remains, with frescoes, elaborately trimmed vaults, and a massive stone fireplace. The combination of gracefully old and smartly new works well, and miles of glass bathe the public areas in sunlight; all rooms face south. L'Affresco, the formal restaurant, serves upscale Italian specialties in the frescoed dining room or on the balcony; the Palme has less expensive Italian fare. You can reach the Belvedere by funicular from the train station or on foot in five minutes (uphill). ⊠ CH-6601, ☎ 091/751–03–63, ℻ 091/751–52–39. 140 beds. 2 restaurants, bar, pool, hot tub, sauna, fitness center, playground. AE, DC, MC, V. Closed Jan.–mid-Feb.

$$ ✕🏨 **Dell'Angelo.** At the end of the Piazza Grande and the long row
★ of Lombardy arcades, this friendly downtown hotel fits right in: It was based on a 1674 structure but rebuilt in 1976, with ground-floor arches and iron-trim balconies. Walnut-grain Formica and beige stucco fill the hospital-spare rooms. A lively pizzeria at street level serves pizzas cooked in a wood-burning oven and grilled meats, and you can choose from the same menu in the restaurant upstairs, where you'll eat amid chintz and damask under the faded remains of frescoed vaulting. ⊠ Piazza Grande, CH-6601, ☎ 091/751–81–75, ℻ 091/751–82–56. 100 beds. Restaurant, pizzeria. AE, DC, MC, V.

Nightlife and the Arts

La Bussola (☎ 091/743–60–95) and **La Carbonara** (☎ 091/743–67–14) have piano bars.

The **Kursaal** (Casino) (☎ 091/751–03–33) offers 142 slot machines and boule (a casino game popular in Switzerland with a federally imposed 5 SF limit).

From March through July, Locarno hosts **Concerti di Locarno,** offering a series of classical concerts in the Chiesa San Francesco, the Sala Sopracenerina, and the castle courtyard.

The **Locarno International Film Festival,** gaining ground on Cannes for prestige because of the caliber of films it premieres, takes place every August in the Piazza Grande.

OFF THE   **CIMETTA** – A winter sports center with views of Monte Rosa, the Swiss
BEATEN PATH   Alps, and the Italian Apennines, Cimetta (1,672 meters/5,482 feet) can be reached only by chairlift; first you must take a cable car to Cardada, then a chairlift to the resort. But don't be put off; the ride is part of the fun: As the lake falls away beneath, you sail over flowery meadows and wooded hills. Cimetta is also a hiker's paradise.

Val Verzasca

❸ 12 km (7 mi) north of Locarno; 25 km (15½ mi) north of Lugano.

A short drive along a small highway through the wild and rugged mountain gorge of the Val Verzasca leads to **Corippo,** where a painterly composition of stone houses and a 17th-century church are all protected as architectural landmarks.

About 12 kilometers (7 miles) north of Corippo, in the town of **Lavertezzo,** you'll find a graceful double-arched stone bridge, **Ponte dei Salti,** dating from 1700. The mountain village of Sonogno lies at the end of the 26-kilometer (16-mile) valley.

Valle Maggia

❹ *4 km (2 mi) northwest of Locarno; 30 km (19 mi) northwest of Lugano.*

A drive through this rugged agricultural valley that stretches northwest from Locarno will give you a sense of the tough living conditions endured for centuries by Ticinese peasants who today mine granite. The valley is cut so far into the earth that the sun in winter never reaches bottom—a stark contrast to sunny Locarno only a short distance south. Until the 1920s many Val Maggia natives immigrated to the United States; many returned, bringing with them several English phrases that still pepper the local Ticinese dialect. As you pass through Gordevio, Maggia, Someo, and Cevio—the valley's main village—you'll feel as if you're in a time capsule: There's little commercialization, and the mostly 17th-century houses call to mind a movie set. Bignasco, just beyond Cevio, is the last village before the Val splits in two continuing north.

Ascona

❺ *3 km (1¾ mi) west of Locarno.*

Though it's only a few minutes from Locarno, tiny Ascona leads its own life. Little more than a fishing village until the turn of the century, the town was discovered and adopted by a high-minded group of northerners who arrived to develop a utopian, vegetarian artists' colony on **Monte Verità,** the hillside park behind the waterfront center. Influenced by Eastern and Western religions as well as the new realms of psychology, its ideals attracted thousands of sojourners, including Ruggiero Leoncavallo, Isadora Duncan, and C.G. Jung. You can visit the group of Monte Verità buildings, including the unusual flat-roof wooden Casa Anatta, and view papers and relics of the group's works. ☎ 091/791–03–27. ▨ 5 SF. ☉ Apr.–June, Sept., and Oct., Tues.–Sun. 2:30–6; July and Aug., Tues.–Sun. 3–7.

Monte Verità's influence spread through Ascona, its reputation grew throughout the world, and today the still-small village of 5,000 attracts artists, art restorers, and traditional bookbinders to its ancient, narrow streets. On the waterfront, however, it's a sun-and-fun scene, with the

★ **Piazza Motta** (isolated from traffic as a pedestrian zone) crowded with sidewalk cafés and the promenade at water's edge swarming with boats.

Just beyond the main street of Ascona, curving down the peninsula, a string of postwar hotels worthy of Acapulco vie for beachfront and marina space on the way to the public lido and, ultimately, the perfectly manicured golf course. Behind the Piazza Motta, a charming labyrinth of lanes leads uphill past artisan galleries (not all showing gallery-quality work) to the **via Borgo,** lined with contemporary shops and galleries.

The ideals that brought Isadora Duncan here still bring culture to Ascona: Every year it hosts a New Orleans jazz fest (late June–July), a series of world-class classical music concerts (August–October), and a festival of marionettes (September). The lakefront piazza serves as an open-air stage for almost daily summer entertainment, with mime, theater, and live pop bands. Locarno's film festival is only a cab ride away across the peninsula.

OFF THE
BEATEN PATH **BRISSAGO ISLANDS** – From Ascona, an easy excursion by car or bus leads to Brissago, a flowery lakefront resort at the lowest elevation in Switzerland. The main attraction, however, lies offshore: The Brissago Is-

lands, two floral gems floating in Lake Maggiore, have been federally preserved as botanical gardens, with more than 1,000 species of subtropical plants. Boats from Brissago, Porto Ronco, or all the way from Ascona or Locarno land at the larger of the two islands regularly. You can buy an admission ticket at the entrance gate when you arrive or when you buy your boat ticket (Swiss Boat Passes are valid within Swiss waters but do not apply on Lake Maggiore). Plaques identify the flora in Italian, German, and French; an English guide to the plants is for sale at the gate (2 SF). You may have lunch or drinks at the island's restaurant, in a beautifully restored 1929 villa that now doubles as a seminar center and offers lodging to groups. Individuals must leave with the last boat back to the mainland—usually around 6—so check schedules carefully when you plan your excursion.

Dining and Lodging

$$–$$$ ✕ **Da Ivo.** Run by the same family for nearly 30 years, with son Ivo replacing his father in the kitchen, this Ascona institution has something for everyone: fresh, straightforward regional standards as well as refined, nouvelle-influenced dishes. No matter how sophisticated the food you choose, you can relax in the knowledge that you won't be disappointed. In the cozy interior, you can dine near a huge fireplace, its flickering glow reflected in the copper pots hanging nearby; in the idyllic arbored garden, ladder-back chairs, checked pink linens, and fresh flowers set the informal, summery tone. Specials may include delicate leek tart, *linguetti neri* (pasta flavored with squid ink) with seafood, or Ticino-style lamb with rosemary. ⊠ *Via Collegio 11,* ☎ *093/791–10–31. No credit cards. Closed Mon. and late Dec.–mid-Mar.*

$$$$ ✕▣ **Giardino.** The Great Gatsby would feel in his element here, in this
★   Relais & Châteaux property that's as glamorous and atmospheric as a Mediterranean villa, despite its creation from thin air in 1986. Portuguese ceramics, Florentine floor tiles, Veronese marble, ceramic room-number plaques in della Robbia style, and even a Swiss-baroque carved wood conference chamber from Zürich's Bierhalle Kropf have been imported. The luxury borders on decadence: The sheets are pure linen, every room has the latest toilet-bidet combination, and there's a landscaped pool, not to mention a chauffeured Bentley, an antique bus-shuttle service, and pink bicycles for guest use. The restaurants are excellent: Giardino rates among the best in Switzerland for international cuisine; Aphrodite falls not far behind with its vegetarian and Italian specialties. Director Hans Leu started out at the Dolder Grand in Zürich, then managed Arosa's Kulm for 20 years; Giardino is his own idea of a luxury hotel. ⊠ *Via Segnale,* ☎ *091/791–01–01,* 🅵🅰🆇 *091/791–10–94. 144 beds. 2 restaurants, bar, pool, beauty salon, hot tub, steam room, cabaret, baby-sitting. AE, DC, MC, V. Closed mid-Nov.–mid-Mar.*

$$$–$$$$ ✕▣ **Ascolago.** This concrete monolith juts out toward the water at a curve in the bay, its rows of awninged balconies offering fine views of lake and lawns. Although some rooms have been upgraded to rosewood and pastel plush, many remain buried under the heavy style that can only be called Swiss Bourgeois. The pool lies between an indoor pavilion and the open lawn, and the terrace provides direct access to the lake and marina, which has a sailing school and moorings. The restaurant is elegantly alfresco, with linens and candles; its specialties include French-international standards with a few local twists: rabbit in thyme on a bed of leeks, rack of lamb roasted with rosemary and balsamic vinegar. ⊠ *CH-6612,* ☎ *091/791–20–55,* 🅵🅰🆇 *091/791–42–26. 40 beds. Restaurant, indoor-outdoor pool, massage, sauna, windsurfing. AE, DC, MC, V.*

$$$–$$$$ ✕🏨 **Castello Seeschloss.** Dating from 1250 and now completely re-
★ built within, this is a romantic enough hotel as is—not even taking into
account its garden setting and position across from the waterfront. Its
interior is rich with frescoes, beams, vaults, and heavy masonry; other-
wise the decor is light and contemporary—in some cases even indus-
trial-modern. There's an isolated courtyard for summer-night dining
and an isolated pool. Honeymooners, take note: Deluxe rooms in the
towers start at prices not much higher than standard doubles and offer
lavish—even baroque—appointments. ✉ CH-6612, ☎ 091/791–01–
61, ℻ 091/791–18–04. 75 beds. Restaurant, bar, outdoor pool. AE,
DC, MC, V. Closed mid-Nov.–mid–Mar.

$$$ ✕🏨 **Tamaro.** Occupying a vaulted and shuttered patrician house on
★ the waterfront, this Romantik property really earns the parent com-
pany's name: The sitting rooms are richly furnished with antiques, books,
and even a grand piano, and the restaurants have a sunny, Mediterranean air that isn't at all contrived. The rooms range from lavish corner doubles with lake views and reproductions of antiques to tiny,
bathless quarters that are an excellent value. Like the Piazza, it's right
on the waterfront, and its restaurant and café fill quickly on sunny days.
There's a private sun terrace high over the street with fine lake views;
you may feel you're on the beach. ✉ CH-6612, ☎ 091/791–02–82,
℻ 091/791–29–28. 78 beds. Restaurant, café. AE, DC, MC, V.

$$ ✕🏨 **Piazza.** This tidy, modest member of the familial Minotel chain,
in the middle of the Piazza Motta, looks first and foremost like a cof-
fee shop or café, and you have to wend your way through crowded ta-
bles to get to the reception area. The throngs are enjoying at ground
level what you'll see better from your room: the pollards, park benches,
and blue expanse of the waterfront. The rooms can be tiny, but they're
remarkably well planned, with carefully built-in amenities and all-tile
baths. (Cheaper rooms are available in the *dépendence*, or neighbor-
ing annex, just uphill, but they lack views and have a scarlet-and-gold
decor dating from the '70s.) ✉ CH-6612, ☎ 091/791–11–81, ℻
091/791–27–57. 44 beds. Restaurant, café. AE, DC, MC, V.

$$$–$$$$ 🏨 **Casa Berno.** This Relais du Silence hotel on a forest road far above
the town and lake is tucked into a hillside near the top, so the anony-
mous rows of concrete balconies offend no one but offer everyone
panoramic views—from the Islands of Brissago to Bellinzona. Its ab-
solute isolation and self-containment (there's even a magazine-and-to-
bacco shop in the lobby) and the aura of dated gentility, projected by
the avocado brocade and Picasso prints in cream frames, appeal to re-
laxed vacationers who want to laze by the big pool overlooking the
lake, have drinks and lunch on the broad roof terrace, and get away
from it all—completely. ✉ CH-6612, ☎ 091/791–32–32, ℻ 091/791–
11–14. 100 beds. Restaurant, bar, café, outdoor pool, massage, sauna,
fitness center. AE, DC, MC, V.

Nightlife and the Arts

Younger **disco** enthusiasts flock to **Happyville** (☎ 091/791–49–22),
Piccolo Porto (☎ 091/791–85–98), and **Cincillà** (☎ 091/791–51–71).
More sedate dancers go to **Lello Bar** (☎ 091/791–13–74) for live
music. **Al Lago** (☎ 091/791–10–65) is a discotheque for young peo-
ple, with a piano bar upstairs.

La Tana (☎ 091/791–13–81) has an orchestra and striptease acts.

Ascona hosts an **International Festival of Marionettes** every Septem-
ber, with a full schedule of plays—most of them for adults rather than
children—from around the world. Most performances take place in
the Teatro San Materno (☎ 091/791–85–66). The **Teatro di Locarno**

(☎ 091/751–03–33) hosts international theatrical companies year-round.

Ascona Festa New Orleans Music seeks out performers a cut above standard Dixieland and swing groups and brings them to its open-air bandstands in late June and early July. The **Settimane Musicali** (Musical Weeks) begin in late August and last into October, bringing in full orchestras, chamber groups, and top-ranking soloists.

SOTTOCENERI

The Sottoceneri ("below Ceneri") includes the more developed, business and resort towns of the south, the foremost being Lugano.

Lugano

❻–⓴ *45 km (28 mi) southeast of Ascona; 39 km (24 mi) southeast of Locarno.*

Strung around a sparkling bay like Venetian glass beads, with dark, conical mountains rising primordially out of its waters and icy peaks framing the scene, Lugano earns its nickname as the Rio of the Old World. Of the three world-class lake resorts that dominate the waterfront, Lugano tops Ascona and Locarno for architectural style, sophistication, and natural beauty.

This is not to say that it has avoided the pitfalls of a successful, modern resort: There's thick traffic right up to the waterfront, much of it manic Italian-style, and it has more than its share of concrete waterfront high-rise hotels with balconies skewed to produce "rooms with a view" regardless of aesthetic cost.

Yet the sacred *passeggiata*—the afternoon stroll to see and be seen that winds down every Italian day—asserts the city's true personality as a graceful, sophisticated Old World resort—not Swiss, not Italian . . . just Lugano.

The serious view-hound may want to take at least one **funicular** excursion, up either Monte San Salvatore or Monte Brè. (The latter's summit can be reached by car as well.) The San Salvatore funicular departs from Paradiso; Monte Brè, from Cassarate. Both afford stunning lakeward views.

Much of Lugano—and indeed much of the landscape beyond—can be seen in an afternoon's walk. The **waterfront promenade,** lined with pollarded lime trees, funereal cypress, and palm trees, affords stunning mountain views: straight ahead, the rocky top of **Monte Generoso** (1,702 meters/5,579 feet); flanking the bay at right and left, respectively, the dark wooded masses of **Monte San Salvatore** and **Monte Brè**. The waterfront is also home to another, less natural attraction: the **Casino,** where bets are limited by law to 5 SF.

❻ The **Parco Civico** (Town Park) has cacti, exotic shrubs, and more than 1,000 varieties of roses, as well as an aviary, a tiny deer zoo, and another fine view of the bay from its peninsula.

❼ In the Parco Civico, the canton's **Museo Cantonale di Storia Naturale** (Museum of Natural History) contains exhibits on animals, plants, and mushrooms, mostly those typical of the region. ✉ *Viale Cattaneo 4,* ☎ *091/923–78–27.* ⌷ *Free.* ☉ *Tues.–Sat. 9–noon and 2–5.*

OFF THE   **VILLA FAVORITA** – This splendid 16th-century mansion in Castagnola
BEATEN PATH   houses a portion of the extraordinary private art collection of the Baron von Thyssen-Bornemisza. (Take Bus 1 in the direction of Castagnola;

Lugano

Lago di Lugano

N

KEY

i Tourist Information

| 0 | 440 yards |
| 0 | 400 meters |

Cattedrale di San
Lorenzo, **11**
Chiesa di Santa Maria
degli Angioli, **13**
Giardino
Belvedere, **14**
Lido, **8**
Museo Cantonale di
Storia Naturale, **7**

Palazzo Civico, **9**
Parco Civico, **6**
Parco del Tassino, **12**
Piazza della
Riforma, **10**

otherwise, it's a 40-minute walk.) Although, after a scandalous international battle, portions of the collection were temporarily transferred to Spain, a significant display of 19th- and 20th-century paintings and watercolors from Europe and America remains, shown to better advantage than ever in the totally renovated space. Artists represented include Thomas Hart Benton, Giorgio de Chirico, Frederick Church, Lucien Freud, Edward Hopper, Franz Marc, Jackson Pollock, and Andrew Wyeth. ⊠ *Strada Castagnola,* ☎ *091/972-17-41.* ▣ *12 SF.* ☉ *Easter–Oct., Fri.–Sun. 10–5; during special exhibitions, Tues.–Sun. 10–5.*

CASTAGNOLA PARKS – For an idyllic daytime excursion, combine a trip to the Villa Favorita with one or both of the parks that neighbor it. (Take Bus 1 in the direction of Castagnola or walk 40 minutes on the road to Gandria.) The **Parco degli Ulivi** (Olive Park) spreads over the lower slopes of Monte Brè and offers a romantic landscape of silvery olive trees mixed with cypress, laurel, and wild rosemary; its entrance lies opposite the Fischer's Seehotel. **Parco San Michele** (St. Michael Park), also on Monte Brè, has a public chapel and a broad terrace that overlooks the city, the lake, and, beyond, the Alps (from Cassarate, walk up the steps by the lower terminus of the Monte Brè funicular).

❽ The city's **lido** is a stretch of sandy beach, with two swimming pools and a restaurant; to reach it, you'll have to cross the Cassarate River, follow the riverbank left to the main street, viale Castagnola, and then turn right; the main Lido entrance is just ahead on your right. ▣ *5 SF, changing cabins 3 SF.* ☉ *May and Sept., daily 9–6; June and mid–late Aug., daily 9–7; July–mid-Aug., daily 9–7:30.*

❾ Toward Lugano's center, the pompous **Palazzo Civico** (Town Hall) is a neoclassical structure dating from 1844. Across the street, steamers depart for Lake Lugano from the **Imbarcadero Centrale**.

★ ❿ The Luganese and their visitors spend endless hours in the lively piazzas that dominate the center of town. **Piazza della Riforma** is so nearly filled with tables it's as if the cafés owned it. Closer to the shore is **Piazza Rezzonico**.

NEED A BREAK? You may choose to spend the whole afternoon at the **Caffè Federale** (⊠ Piazza Riforma, ☎ 091/923–91–75), which offers light meals and daily plates as well as drinks to the diverse and often glamorous crowds who all face forward, as if an audience for the real-life theater passing by.

Via Luvini is the entrance to the **old town,** where narrow streets are lined with chic Italian clothing shops and small markets offering pungent local cheeses and porcini mushrooms. German-Swiss culture subtly asserts itself at lunch stands, where *panini* (small sandwiches) are made not only of prosciutto, tuna, or mozzarella but of sauerkraut and sausage as well.

⓫ The **Cattedrale di San Lorenzo** (Cathedral of St. Lawrence) has a Renaissance exterior and richly frescoed Baroque interior. At the bottom of the staircase leading down and west from the cathedral, a **funicular** mounts from Piazza Cioccaro to the train station.

⓬ The luxuriously manicured **Parco del Tassino** lies on a plateau behind the train station and offers lovely bay views from among its rose gardens. Children will enjoy its small deer park and playground.

★ ⓭ Via Nassa, Lugano's main shopping street, opens onto the **Piazza Luini,** where the **Chiesa di Santa Maria degli Angioli** (Church of St. Mary of the Angels), begun in 1455, merits a visit. It contains a magnificent fresco of the Passion and Crucifixion by Bernardino Luini (1475–1532).

An incongruous **statue of George Washington** stands across the Piazza Luini from Chiesa di Santa Maria degli Angioli. In fact, Washington never visited Lugano, though this image was erected in 1859 by a grateful Swiss engineer who had made his fortune in America.

⑭ The waterfront **Giardino Belvedere** (Belvedere Gardens) frames 12 modern sculptures with palms, camellias, oleander, and magnolias. At the far end there's public bathing. ⊠ *Riva Antonio Caccia,* ☎ *091/994–20–35.* 🖃 *3 SF.* ☺ *Mid-May–mid-Sept., daily 9:30–7:30.*

Dining and Lodging

$$$$ ✕ **Al Portone.** Silver and lace dress up the stucco and stone here, but
★ the ambience is strictly easy, never formal. Chef Roberto Galizzi pursues *nuova cucina* (nouvelle cuisine, Italian-style) with ambition and flair, and he rarely resorts to gimmickry while putting local spins on Italian classics. You might choose roast veal kidneys with balsamic vinegar, lobster salad, seafood carpaccio, or simple creamed potatoes with priceless white truffle. Or you could *lascia fare a Roberto* (leave it to Robert)—as he calls his menu de dégustation. ⊠ *Viale Cassarate 3,* ☎ *091/923–55–11,* 🄵🄰🄷 *091/971–65–05. AE, DC, MC, V. Closed Sun. and Mon.*

$$$ ✕ **Galleria.** Though the decor aspires to formal hauteur, with its contemporary appointments and very modern art, family warmth permeates the restaurant, making it a comfortable source of good traditional Italian cooking: pasta, veal favorites, and good, plain grilled fish, as well as a fine little list of local and Italian wines. ⊠ *Via Vegezzi 4,* ☎ *091/923–62–88. AE, DC, MC, V. Closed Sun.*

$$$ ✕ **Locanda del Boschetto.** The grill is the first thing you see in this no-
★ nonsense, low-key ristorante, a specialist in pure and simple seafood *alla griglia* (grilled). The decor is a study in linen and rustic wood, and the service is helpful and down-to-earth. ⊠ *Via Boschetto 8,* ☎ *091/994–24–93. AE, DC, MC, V. Closed Mon.*

$$$ ✕ **Santabbondio.** Ancient stone and terra-cotta blend with pristine pas-
★ tels in this upgraded grotto, where subtle, imaginative new Franco-Italian cuisine du marché—delicately sauced seafood, painterly desserts—is served in intimate, formal little dining rooms and on a shady terrace. Watch for lobster risotto, scallops in orange-basil sauce, or eggplant ravioli to confirm what locals assert: Chef Martin Dalsass is the canton's best. There's a good selection of open wines. Note that you'll need a cab to get here; it's worth the trip. ⊠ *Via ai Grotti di Gentilino,* ☎ *091/993–23–88,* 🄵🄰🄷 *091/994–32–37. AE, DC, MC, V. Closed Mon. and 1st wk of Jan. No lunch Sat., no dinner Sun.*

$$ ✕ **Al Barilotto.** Despite its generic pizzeria decor and American-style salad bar, this restaurant draws local crowds for grilled meats, homemade pastas, and wood-oven pizza. Take Bus 10 from the city center; the restaurant (inside Hotel de la Paix) is uphill from the main lakefront road. ⊠ *Hotel de la Paix, via Calloni 18,* ☎ *091/994–96–95. AE, DC, MC, V.*

$ ✕ **La Tinera.** Tucked down an alley off via Pessina in the old town, this
★ cozy basement taverna squeezes loyal locals, tourists, and families onto wooden benches for authentic regional specialties, hearty meats, and pastas. Regional wine is served in traditional ceramic bowls. ⊠ *Via dei Gorini 2,* ☎ *091/923–52–19. AE, DC, MC, V.*

$ ✕ **Sayonara.** There's nothing Japanese about this place: It's a modern urban pizzeria, with several rooms that fill at lunch with a mix of tourists and shoppers. The old copper polenta pot stirs automatically year-round, and polenta is offered in several combinations, sometimes with mountain hare. ⊠ *Via F. Soave 10,* ☎ *091/922–01–70. AE, DC, MC, V.*

$$$$ **⊡ Splendide Royale.** This landmark was first converted from a villa
★ to a hotel in 1887, and much of the Victorian luster of its public
spaces—with their marble, pillars, terrazzo, and antiques—has been
respectfully preserved. Since the new wing was added in 1983, you can
choose between solid, well-constructed lodgings decorated in sleek
beech, beige, and gold, or more florid period rooms in the original wing.
All rooms are air-conditioned, and there's an attractive S-shape indoor
pool. The restaurant serves classic French standards to live piano
music. ⊠ *Riva A. Caccia, CH-6900,* ☎ *091/985–77–11,* ⅟ᴬˣ *091/994–
89–31. 179 beds. Restaurant, bar, indoor pool, massage, sauna. AE,
DC, MC, V.*

$$$$ **⊡ Ticino.** In this warmly appointed 16th-century row house in the heart
★ of the old town, shuttered windows look out from every room onto a
glassed-in garden and courtyard, and there are vaulted halls lined with
art and antiques. The formal restaurant, full of dark-wood wainscoting and leather banquettes, serves Ticinese specialties. It's a Romantik property, only steps away from the funicular to the station. ⊠ *Piazza
Cioccaro 1, CH-6901,* ☎ *091/922–77–72,* ⅟ᴬˣ *091/923–62–78. 35
beds. Restaurant. AE, DC, MC, V.*

$$$$ **⊡ Villa Principe Leopoldo.** This extravagantly furnished garden man-
★ sion, located on a hillside high over the lake, is in a price range all its
own but offers Old World service and splendor to match. Its rooms
have been converted to 39 junior suites, and there's a stunningly arranged pool-and-terrace complex encircled by a double staircase—a
slightly baroque touch of Bel Air. Free transportation to the airport and
town is provided. ⊠ *Via Montalbano 5, CH-6900,* ☎ *091/985–88–
55,* ⅟ᴬˣ *091/985–88–25. 72 beds. 2 restaurants, bar, pool, hot tub, sauna,
fitness center. AE, DC, MC, V.*

$$$–$$$$ **⊡ De la Paix.** Slightly uphill from the main lakefront road, this busi-
ness-class property was completely renovated and redecorated, with a
new wing adding 43 rooms. They've kept the palm-encircled outdoor
pool and a choice of three restaurants. ⊠ *Via Cattori 18, CH-6902,*
☎ *091/994–23–32,* ⅟ᴬˣ *091/994–95–18. 266 beds. 3 restaurants,
bar, outdoor pool. AE, DC, MC, V.*

$$$–$$$$ **⊡ Du Lac.** This discreet and simple hotel offers more lakefront luxury
than does the glossier Eden down the same beach. Owned by one fam-
ily since it was founded in 1920, Du Lac was rebuilt in 1962, and its
walls are decked with needlework art reproductions handmade by its
owner. All rooms face the lake; those on the sixth floor are the qui-
etest, and have warm, sleek decor. The hotel has a private swimming
area on the lake. ⊠ *Riva Paradiso 3, CH-6902,* ☎ *091/994–19–21,*
⅟ᴬˣ *091/994–11–22. 87 beds. Restaurant, bar, pool, massage, sauna,
beach. AE, DC, MC, V.*

$$$ **⊡ Alba.** This solid little hotel, isolated on its own landscaped grounds
★ and lavish inside to the extreme, is ideal for lovers with a sense of camp
or honeymooners looking for romantic privacy. Mirrors, gilt, plush,
and crystal adorn the public areas, and the beds are all ruffles and
swags. The garden is studded with palms, a lovely place for a drink.
⊠ *Via delle Scuole 11, CH-6902,* ☎ *091/994–37–31,* ⅟ᴬˣ *091/994–
45–23. 52 beds. Restaurant, bar, outdoor pool. AE, DC, MC, V.*

$$$ **Belmonte.** Five minutes from Villa Favorita, this tall, sun-bleached
hotel has a Mediterranean facade of white stucco with tall, powder-
blue shutters framing some 40-odd individual balconies. Every room
offers a superb view over Lago di Lugano, which seems miles below.
The terrace in front of the hotel is shaded by a large yellow awning
and makes a good spot for lunch or afternoon drinks. ⊠ *Via Serenella
29, CH-6976, Lugano-Castagnola,* ☎ *091/971–40–33,* ⅟ᴬˣ *091/972–
61–39. Pool. Closed Dec.–Feb.*

$$$ ⊞ **International au Lac.** Just a stone's throw from the lake, this big, old-fashioned, friendly hotel offers many lake-view rooms. The interiors are floridly decorated with baroque reproductions, heavy plush furniture, and a Victorian dining hall in a tower bay. It's next to the Church of St. Mary of the Angels, on the edge of the shopping district and the old town. ⊠ *Via Nassa 68, CH-6901,* ☎ *091/922–75–41,* FAX *091/922–75–44. 120 beds. Restaurant, pool, free parking. AE, DC, MC, V.*

$$–$$$ ⊞ **Park-Hotel Nizza.** On the lower slopes of Monte San Salvatore and
★ well above the lake, this former villa offers panoramic views and an attractive mix of luxurious parlors and modern comforts. Most rooms are small, with mixed antique reproductions; lake views don't cost extra. An ultramodern bar (silver vinyl and glass) overlooks the lake, as does a good restaurant that serves vegetable dishes (and even wine) from the hotel's own garden. Summer meals are served in the garden, and there's a weekly barbecue in L'Hacienda grill. It's a hike into town but there's a shuttle service to Paradiso. ⊠ *Via Guidino 14, CH-6902,* ☎ *091/994–17–71,* FAX *091/994–17–73. 55 beds. Restaurant, bar, pool. AE, MC, V.*

$$ ⊞ **San Carlo.** Ideally located on the main shopping street, a block from the waterfront, and only 150 yards from the funicular, this friendly but no-frills hotel is clean, small, and freshly furnished; it's one of the better deals in town. ⊠ *Via Nassa 28, CH-6900,* ☎ *091/922–71–07,* FAX *091/922–80–22. 44 beds. Breakfast room. AE, DC, MC, V.*

$ ⊞ **Flora.** Though it's one of the cheapest hotels in town, this 70-year-
★ old family-run lodging has been reasonably maintained, with tile baths and double-glazed windows. The room decor is minimal, the taste decidedly '60s (red-and-orange prints, wood-grain Formica), and the once-elegant dining hall has seen better days. But some rooms have balconies, and there's a sheltered garden terrace for balmy nights. ⊠ *Via Geretta 16, CH-6902,* ☎ *091/994–16–71,* FAX *091/994–27–38. 85 beds. Restaurant, bar, pool. AE, DC, MC, V.*

$ ⊞ **Zurigo.** Ideally placed behind the tourist office, and handy to parks, shopping, and waterfront promenades, this spartan hotel near the Palais Congrès offers quiet comfort at affordable rates, even in high season. Several rooms have a full bath. ⊠ *Corso Pestalozzi 13, CH-6900* ☎ *091/923–43–43,* FAX *091/923–43–43. 28 rooms. Breakfast room. No credit cards.*

Nightlife and the Arts

BARS AND LOUNGES
There's a piano bar in the **Hotel Eden** in Paradiso (☎ 091/993–01–21). The **Splendide Royale Principe Leopoldo** (☎ 091/994–20–01) and **Ristorante Gambrinus** (☎ 091/923–19–55) on the Piazza Riforma both have piano bars.

CASINOS
The **Kursaal** (☎ 091/921–02–03) has a restaurant, dance club, bar, slot machines, and a gaming room. There also are Sunday tea dances.

CLUBS
Dancing Cécil (☎ 091/994-97–24) and **Europa 1001 Notte** (☎ 091/993-14–38) have orchestras, dancing, and show girls.

DANCING
Amadeus 200 (☎ 091/922–94–38), **B-52** (☎ 091/923–16–96), **Mitico Covo 3** (☎ 091/923–40–81), and **La Piccionaia** (☎ 091/923–45–46) have disco dancing. At **Bar 90** (☎ 091/922–93–33) there's traditional cheek-to-cheek dancing, including waltzes and tangos.

MUSIC

In April and June, Lugano hosts its **Primavera Concertistica di Lugano,** with top-level orchestras and conductors. Its **Estival Jazz** in July offers free outdoor concerts in the Piazza Riforma. There is a **Blues to Bop Festival** in the city's squares at the end of August and even a traditional **New Folk Worldmusic Festival** in mid-August.

OFF THE
BEATEN PATH

SWISSMINIATUR – Of infinite novelty and surprisingly high quality, this child's paradise is a detailed model of the architectural highlights of Switzerland, built in stone on a scale of 1 to 25. There's a tiny Chillon, the Cathedral of Lausanne, the Parliament buildings of Bern, a recent reproduction of the Lausanne Olympic Committee Museum, and exquisitely detailed reproductions of Swiss trains, boats, and cable-car systems—all fully functional. Carefully landscaped on the waterfront, the park offers a playground for kids who lose interest while Dad is still watching the trains. ⊠ *Melide, below Lugano,* ☎ *091/649–79–51.* ▧ *10.50 SF.* ◷ *Mid-Mar.–Oct., daily 9–6.*

Gandria

⓯ *7 km (4 mi) east of Lugano.*

Although today its narrow waterfront streets are crowded with tourists, the tiny historic village of Gandria merits a visit, either by boat from Lugano or by car, as parking is available just above the town. It clings vertiginously to the steep hillside, and its flower-filled balconies hang directly over open water. Souvenir and craft shops now fill its backstreet nooks, but the ambience of an ancient fishing village remains.

NEED A
BREAK?

For unobstructed views up and down the lakefront and across to Italy, stop in one of the many balconied cafés that, behind their restaurants, open out over the water.

OFF THE
BEATEN PATH

CANTINE DI GANDRIA – Across Lago di Lugano from Gandria—almost in Italy—this tiny village has a small **Museo Doganale** (Customs Museum), casually known as the "Smuggler's Museum." Here you'll learn the romantic history of clandestine trade with displays of ingenious containers, weapons, and contraband. You can catch a boat from the jetty (☎ 091/971–57–77 for schedules). ☎ *091/923–98–43.* ▧ *Free.* ◷ *Apr.–Oct., daily 1:30–5:30.*

Campione

⓰ *18 km (11 mi) south of Gandria; 12 km (7 mi) south of Lugano (take the Paradiso highway across the Melide causeway, then cut north via Bissone).*

In the heart of Swiss Italy lies Campione. Here, in this southernmost of regions, the police cars have Swiss license plates but the policemen inside are Italian; the inhabitants pay their taxes to Italy but do it in Swiss francs.

In the 8th century, the lord of Campione gave the tiny scrap of land to St. Ambrosius of Milan. Despite all the wars that passed it by, Campione remained Italian until the end of the 18th century, when it was incorporated into the Cisalpine Republic. When Italy unified in 1861, Campione became part of the new Kingdom of Italy—and remained so. There are no frontiers between Campione and Switzerland, and it benefits from the comforts of Swiss currency, customs laws, and postal and telephone services. Despite its miniature scale, it has exercised disproportionate influence on the art world: From Campione and the surrounding region, a school of stonemasons, sculptors, and architects emigrated during the Middle Ages to Milan and began working on the cathedrals of Milan, Verona, Cremona, Trento, Modena—and Hagia Sophia in Constantinople.

Today, Campione is a magnet for gamblers, as its large, glittering **casino** offers visitors to conservative Switzerland a chance to play for higher stakes than the usual 5 SF: Following Italian law, the sky's the limit here. The casino has a restaurant, dancing, and a show as well. ⊠ *Piazza Milano 1,* ☎ *091/649–79–21.*

Riva San Vitale

⑰ *9 km (5½ mi) south of Campione; 13 km (8 mi) south of Lugano.*

At the southern end of Lago di Lugano sits Riva San Vitale, where a 5th-century baptistery remains, still containing its original stone immersion font. Riva San Vitale rivals Campione for its odd history: In 1798 its people objected to new boundaries and declared themselves an independent republic. Their glory lasted 14 days before a small cantonal army marched in and convinced them to rejoin Switzerland.

Four kilometers (2 miles) south of Riva San Vitale, colorful **Mendrisio**— cradle of the Ticinese wine industry—is a colorful little town known for its medieval processions.

Morcote

★ **⑱** *6 km (4 mi) northwest of Riva San Vitale; 10 km (6 mi) south of Lugano.*

At the southernmost tip (10 kilometers/6 miles from Lugano) of the glorious waterfront of the Ceresio peninsula is the atmospheric old resort-village of Morcote, its clay-color Lombard-style houses and arcades looking directly over the waterfront. A steep and picturesque climb leads up to the **Chiesa di Madonna del Sasso** (Church of Madonna of Sasso), with its well-preserved 16th-century frescoes; its elevated setting affords wonderful views.

TICINO A TO Z

Arriving and Departing

By Bus
The Palm Express is a scenic postbus route that carries visitors from St. Moritz to Lugano or Ascona, via the Maloja Pass and Italy. It takes about four hours and is arranged through the appropriate tourist offices.

By Car
There are two major gateways into Ticino: the St. Gotthard Pass in the northwest and the San Bernardino Pass to the northeast. From the St. Gotthard, the swift N2 expressway leads down the Valle Leventina to Bellinzona, where it joins with N13, which cuts south from the San Bernardino. N2 directs the mingled traffic flow southward past Lugano to Chiasso and the Italian border, where the expressway heads directly to Como and Milan.

By Plane
The nearest intercontinental airport, **Malpensa,** is in **Milan,** Italy, as is the international **Linate** airport; you can continue into Ticino via rail, car, or taxi. **Crossair,** Switzerland's domestic airline, connects directly into Lugano's domestic airport from **Kloten** airport in **Zürich** and from

Cointrin in **Geneva** as well as from other European destinations. Call Lugano airport (☎ 091/610–12–12) for information.

By Train

The St. Gotthard route connects south from Zürich, cuts through the pass tunnel, and heads into Bellinzona and Lugano. Side connections lead into Locarno from Brig, crossing the Simplon Pass and cutting through Italy. Swiss Pass travelers do not have to pay Italian rail fares to cross from Brig to Locarno via Domodossola. Trains connect out of Zürich's airport and take about three hours; from Geneva, catch the Milan express, changing at Domodossola, Locarno, and Bellinzona. Trains do not go directly into Ascona but stop at Locarno: You must connect by taxi or local bus. For train information from Lugano, call 091/175–33–33.

Getting Around

By Boat

Like Switzerland's inland lakes, Lake Lugano and northern Lake Maggiore are plied by graceful steamers that carry passengers from one waterfront resort to another, offering excellent perspectives on the mountains. Steamer travel on Lake Lugano is included in the Regional Passes and the Swiss Pass; tickets can be purchased near the docks before departure. In Lugano, the Navigation Company of Lake Lugano (☎ 091/971–52–23) offers cruise-boat excursions around the bay to Gandria and toward the Villa Favorita. Note that Lake Maggiore's steamers belong to an Italian ship company and thus do not accept the Swiss Pass; Regional Passes are valid only on Swiss waters.

By Bus

There is a convenient postbus sightseeing system here that tourists can use—easily—to get around the region, even into the backcountry. The PTT (post, telephone, and telegraph office) publishes illustrated booklets with suggested itineraries and prices (3 SF through the **Generaldirektion PTT,** Schweizer Postautodienst, CH-3030 Bern) or through local tourist and post offices. Postbus excursion prices are reduced with the Locarno or Lugano Regional Pass and free with the Swiss Pass.

By Car

A car is a real asset here if you intend to see the mountain valleys—and a hindrance in the congested urban, lakeside resorts. Traffic between Bellinzona and Locarno can move at a crawl during high season.

By Train

Secondary rail connections here are minimal and can make all but the most mainstream rail sightseeing a complicated venture; most excursions will require some postbus connections. Nevertheless there are Regional Passes: Lugano's offers seven days' unlimited travel on most rail and steamer lines, with 50% reductions on various other excursions and modes of transit (92 SF); or three days' travel within seven consecutive days (70 SF). In Locarno/Ascona, the seven-day Regional Pass offers unlimited travel on local rail and steamer trips and 50% reductions on chairlift and funicular rides (76 SF, available through tourist offices). Compare the Locarno and Lugano passes carefully before choosing; many of their discounted facilities overlap. As the Swiss Pass doesn't cover all the transport facilities of the Lake Lugano region, Regional Passes are offered to its holders at a discount.

Guided Tours

Orientation

The *Wilhelm Tell Express* carries you by paddle steamer and rail from Luzern (Lucerne) over the St. Gotthard Pass and into Locarno and

Lugano with a guide and running commentary. The trip takes about six hours and includes lunch. Contact the Lake Luzern Navigation Company (⊠ Box 4265, CH-6002, Luzern, ☎ 041/4367–67–67) or rail stations.

Guided walks for a minimum of five persons tour the Monte Verità area of **Ascona,** departing from the tourist office. They last about three hours and cost 10 SF, including a one-way bus ride. A short tour in the old town of Ascona, with a cultural emphasis, lasts about 1½ hours, costs 5 SF, and leaves from the tourist office. **Bellinzona** offers guided tours of the city and castles on request, through the tourist office. Someone from the **Locarno** tourist office leads a walk; the office will also help you choose from among a wide range of guided bus excursions available through Lago Maggiore Tours. **Lugano** provides a guided walking tour of the city leaving from the Chiesa degli Angioli at Piazza Luini (free). Though it is sponsored by Danzas, reserve with the tourist office (☎ 091/921–46–64).

Important Addresses and Numbers

Emergencies
Police: Bellinzona, Ascona, Locarno, and Lugano (☎ 117).

Medical assistance: In Bellinzona (⊠ Ospedale San Giovanni, ☎ 091/820–91–11); in Locarno (⊠ La Carità, ☎ 091/751–01–21; ⊠ Santa Chiara, ☎ 091/751–02–52); in Lugano, the civic hospital (☎ 091/805–61–11). **Dental clinic:** In Lugano (☎ 091/935–01–80).

Visitor Information
The principal tourist authority for the Ticino is the **Ente Ticinese per il Turismo** (⊠ Villa Turrita, Via Lugano 12, Box 1441, Bellinzona, CH-6501, ☎ 091/825–70–56).

Other tourist offices are in **Ascona** (⊠ Casa Serodine, Box 449, CH-6612, ☎ 091/791–00–90), **Bellinzona** (⊠ Palazzo Civico, via Camminata, CH-6500, ☎ 091/825–21–31), **Biasca** (⊠ CH-6710, ☎ 091/862–33–27), **Blenio** (⊠ CH-6716, Acquarossa, ☎ 091/871–17–65), **Ceresio** (⊠ Via Pocobelli 14, CH-6815, Melide, ☎ 091/649–63–83), **Locarno** (⊠ Teatro di Locarno, Casino-Kursaal, Via Largozorzi, CH-6600, ☎ 091/751–03–33), **Lugano** (⊠ Palazzo Civico, CH-6901, ☎ 091/921–46–64), and **Mendrisiotto e Basso Ceresio** (⊠ via Angelo Naspoli 15, CH-6850, Mendrisio, ☎ 091/646–57–61).

6 Luzern and Central Switzerland

Endowed with a sophisticated transportation system that makes it one of the easiest regions to visit, Central Switzerland is full of neat little towns, accessible mountains, and modest resorts. Centered around the Vierwaldstättersee, "the lake of the four forest cantons," the region is steeped in history: it is where the Oath of Eternal Alliance is said to have been renewed, and it's also the birthplace of the legend of William Tell.

AS YOU CRUISE DOWN THE LEISURELY sprawl of the Vierwaldstättersee, mist rising off the gray waves, mountains—great loaflike masses of forest and stone—looming above the clouds, it's easy to understand how Wagner could have composed his *Siegfried Idyll* in his mansion beside this lake. This is inspiring terrain, romantic and evocative. When the waters roil up you can hear the whistling chromatics and cymbal clashes of Gioacchino Rossini's thunderstorm from his 1829 opera, *Guillaume Tell*. It was on this lake, after all, that William Tell—the beloved, if legendary, Swiss national hero—supposedly leapt from the tyrant Gessler's boat to freedom. And it was in a meadow nearby that three furtive rebels and their cohorts swore an oath by firelight and planted the seed of the Swiss Confederation.

The Rütli meadow, a national landmark on the western shores of the Vierwaldstättersee, is the very spot where the Confederates of Schwyz, Unterwald, and Uri are said to have met on the night of November 7, 1307, to renew the 1291 Oath of Eternal Alliance—Switzerland's equivalent of the U.S. Declaration of Independence. Through this oath, the world's oldest still-extant democracy was formed, as the proud charter territories swore their commitment to self-rule in the face of the oppressive Hapsburgs and the Holy Roman Empire. Every August 1, the Swiss National Holiday, citizens gather in the meadow in remembrance of the Oath of Eternal Alliance, and the sky glows with the light of hundreds of mountaintop bonfires.

William Tell played an important role in that early rebellion, and his story, especially as told by German poet and playwright Friedrich von Schiller in his play *Wilhelm Tell* (1805), continues to stir those with a weakness for civil resistance. Though there are no valid records to prove his existence, and versions of the legend conflict with historical fact, no one denies the reality of his times, when Central Switzerland—then a feudal dependent of Austria but, by its own independent will, not yet absorbed into the Holy Roman Empire—suffered brutal pressures and indignities under the rulers in residence. The mythical Gessler was one of those rulers, and his legendary edict—that the proud, resistant Swiss should bow before his hat, suspended on a pole in the village square at Altdorf—symbolizes much crueler oppressions of the time. Schiller's Tell was a hero through and through—brisk, decisive, a highly skilled helmsman as well as marksman—and, not one for diplomatic negotiations, he refused to kneel. Tell's famous punishment: to shoot an apple off his young son's head before a crowd of fellow townsmen; if he refused, both would be killed. Tell quietly tucked an arrow in his shirt bosom, loaded another into his crossbow, and shot the apple clean through. When Gessler asked what the arrow was for, Tell replied that if the first arrow had struck his child, the second arrow would have been for Gessler and would not have missed.

For this impolitic remark, Tell was sentenced to prison. While deporting him across the Vierwaldstättersee, the Austrians (including the ruthless Gessler) were caught in a violent storm (remember your Rossini) and turned to Tell, the only man on board who knew the waters, to take the helm. Unmanacled, he steered the boat to a rocky ridge, leapt free, and pushed the boat back into the storm. Later he lay in wait in the woods near Küssnacht and, as Gessler threatened to ride down a woman begging mercy for her imprisoned husband, shot him in the heart. This act of justified violence inspired the people to overthrow their oppressors, swear the Oath of Eternal Alliance around a roaring bonfire, and lay the groundwork for the Swiss Confederation.

Pretty romantic stuff. Yet for all its potential for drama, Central Switzerland and the area surrounding the Vierwaldstättersee is tame enough turf: neat little towns, accessible mountains, resorts virtually glamour-free—and modest, graceful Luzern (Lucerne) holding forth along the River Reuss much as it has since the Middle Ages.

An eminently civilized region, Zentralschweiz (Central Switzerland) lacks the rustic unruliness of the Valais, the spectacular extremes of the Berner Oberland, the eccentricity of Graubünden. But it's not too sophisticated either, and lacks both the snob appeal of jet-set resorts and the cosmopolitan mix of Geneva, Basel, and Zürich. The houses are tidy, pastel, picture-book cottages, deep-roofed and symmetrical, each rank of windows underscored with flowers. The villages, ranged neatly around their medieval centers, radiate tradition; and the wilderness is served by good roads. Luzern, the capital, hosts arts festivals and great shopping but little native industry. Serene and steady as the Reuss that laps at the piers of its ancient wooden bridges, it's an approachable city in an accessible region. Central Switzerland's popularity with tourists has spawned an infrastructure of hotels, restaurants, museums, excursions, and transportation that makes it one of the easiest places in Switzerland to visit, either by car or by rail—and one of the most rewarding. As Wagner exclaimed, perhaps carried away a bit by his own waterfront idyll: "I do not know of a more beautiful spot in this world!"

Pleasures and Pastimes

Dining

Rooted in the German territory of Switzerland and the surrounding farmlands, Central Switzerland's native cuisine is down-home and hearty, though its specialties offer some variety from the veal-and-*Rösti* (hash brown potatoes) found everywhere else. In the heights, there are Alpine cheese specialties (*Aelpler Magrone*—pasta, butter, cheese, and fried onions); in the orchard country around Zug, there are such cherry specialties as *Zuger Kirschtorte,* a rich yellow cake liberally soaked with cherry schnapps. Pears from the local orchards are dried, then spiced and poached in sweetened red Dole (wine). Luzern takes pride in its *Kügelipaschtetli,* puff-pastry nests filled with tiny veal meatballs, chicken or sweetbreads, mushrooms, cream sauce, and occasionally raisins.

But here the real *cuisine du marché,* based on the freshest ingredients available in local markets, focuses on lake fish. The Vierwaldstättersee and its neighboring Zugersee (Lake Luzern and Lake Zug) produce an abundance of *Egli* (perch), *Hecht* (pike), *Forellen* (trout), and *Felchen* (whitefish), and Zug produces its own exclusive *Röteln,* a red-bellied relation to the trout and Geneva's *omble chevalier* (a type of salmon trout found in Lac Léman). Restaurants—especially along waterfronts—trade heavily in these freshwater products, whether they come from the region or not. Ask, and you may get an honest answer: The sources vary, but the tradition and style of preparation remain local. In Zug, whole fish may be baked with sage, bay, shallots, cloves, and plenty of white wine and butter; a Luzern tradition has them sautéed and sauced with tomatoes, mushrooms, and capers.

CATEGORY	COST*
$$$$	over 70 SF
$$$	40 SF–70 SF
$$	20 SF–40 SF
$	under 20 SF

*per person for a three-course meal (except in $ category), including sales tax and 15% service charge

Hiking

Since Switzerland's 1991 septicentennial, celebrating the 700-year anniversary of its confederation, Central Switzerland has marked and developed a historic foot trail, the Swiss Path, which covers 35 kilometers (21½ miles) of lakefront lore along the southernmost branch of Lake Luzern and the Vierwaldstättersee. You'll trace the mythical steps of William Tell and the genuine steps of medieval forefathers and foremothers, climb through steep forests and isolated villages, and visit the holiday resort of Brunnen. Complete information and maps can be requested through the Central Switzerland Tourist Office (✉ Alpenstrasse 1, CH-6002); a videocassette, "Hiking the Swiss Path," is available through branches of Switzerland Tourism.

Lodging

Luzern provides a convenient home base for excursions all over the region, though villages are peppered with small shuttered guest houses, and you may easily find a spot as you drive through the countryside. As the terrain and climate vary radically between balmy lakefronts and icy heights, check carefully for high and low seasons before booking ahead. Water-sport resorts like Weggis and Vitznau cut back service considerably in winter, which is just when Engelberg comes alive. Luzern, unlike most Swiss urban areas, has high and low seasons, and drops its prices by as much as 25% in the winter, approximately November through March.

CATEGORY	COST*
$$$$	over 350 SF
$$$	250 SF–350 SF
$$	120 SF–250 SF
$	under 120 SF

All prices are for a standard double room, including breakfast, tax, and service charge.

Shopping

Although Luzern no longer produces embroidery or lace, one can find here a wide variety of Swiss handiwork of the highest quality, crafts, and watches in all price categories. High-end watch dealers Gübelin and Bucherer offer inexpensive souvenirs to lure shoppers into their luxurious showrooms; smaller shops carry Tissot, Rado, Corum and others—but prices are controlled by the manufacturers. Watch for close-outs on out-of-date models.

Exploring Luzern and Central Switzerland

Vierwaldstättersee means "lake of the four forest cantons," but its environs take in not only the four cantons that abut the lake—Luzern, Uri, Schwyz, and Unterwalden—but the canton of Zug as well. Unterwalden itself is divided politically into two half-cantons: Obwalden (upper) and Nidwalden (nether). It was the canton of Schwyz that gave Switzerland its name.

The narrow, twisting lake flows from Flüelen, where the Reuss opens into the Urnersee, its southernmost leg. This is the wildest end of the lake, where much of the Tell story was set. The north end of the lake is flanked by the region's highest points, Mt. Pilatus (2,121 meters/6,953 feet) and Mt. Rigi (1,798 meters/5,894 feet). Luzern lies in a deep bay at the lake's northwestern extreme and at the point where the Rivers Reuss and Emme part ways. Zug stands apart, on the northern shore of its own Zugersee, which is divided from the Vierwaldstättersee by the mass of Mt. Rigi.

Great Itineraries

Visiting this multiterrain area, you must change modes of transit frequently to see it in all its variety; part of the region's interest is the variety of boat trips, train rides, and drives you'll experience to reach the sights. Within the space of one to two days, you may walk through the lovely old town of Luzern, ascend Mt. Pilatus by cable car and descend by cogwheel train, take a lake steamer from Luzern around the eastern shore of the Vierwaldstättersee, and drive through the Rütli meadow.

IF YOU HAVE 1 OR 2 DAYS

Numbers in the text correspond to numbers in the margin and on the Central Switzerland and Luzern exploring maps.

Take in the old town sights of ⌖ **Luzern** ①–⑫, including the Verkehrshaus, which can be reached easily by car or boat. A boat trip on the **Vierwaldstättersee** gives you the opportunity to see the sights of the region from the lake itself; there are half-day excursions as well as longer ones. **Mount Pilatus** offers central Switzerland's best mountaintop panoramas. You can get there easily by boat or car; allow yourself a half day to ascend the mountain.

IF YOU HAVE 3 OR MORE DAYS

In addition to all of the above, take a longer boat trip to **Einsiedeln** ㉔, with its 9th-century Benedictine monastery. Or, following the course of a lake steamer from Luzern, drive to St. Gotthard along the lakefront highway (N2 road). A combined train and cable car trip will take you to the summit of ⌖ **Mt. Rigi**, where you can see as far as the Black Forest and Mount Säntis, and even spend the night in the hotel at the top.

When to Tour Luzern and Central Switzerland

If you don't mind negotiating heavy traffic, particularly in Luzern, summer is the ideal season for boat excursions on the lake and great views from the tops of Mt. Pilatus and Mt. Rigi. In fall, when the crowds thin, you'll find crisp, beautiful weather around the mountains and the lake.

LUZERN TO ENGELBERG

Luzern is a convenient home base for excursions all over central Switzerland, a region indelibly marked by William Tell's legend and Swiss national history. The countryside here is tame, and the vast Vierwaldstättersee offers a prime opportunity for a lake steamer cruise.

Luzern

①–⑫ *57 km (36 mi) southwest of Zurich.*

Where the River Reuss flows out of the Vierwaldstättersee, Luzern's old town straddles the narrowed waters with the greater concentration of city life lying on the river's right bank. The city's focal point is
★ the prominent **Kapellbrücker,** with its flanking water tower.

The main avenue of Luzern, Rathausquai, is lined with hotels and cafés. Facing the end of a modern bridge (the Rathaus-Steg) stands the **Altes Rathaus** (Old Town Hall), built between 1599 and 1606 in the late-Renaissance style. The Luzern town council held its first meeting here in 1606 and still meets here today.

① Just to the right of the Rathaus, the **Am Rhyn-Haus** (Am Rhyn House), also known simply as the Picasso Museum, contains an impressive collection of late paintings by Picasso. ⊠ *Furrengasse 21,* ☎ *041/410–17–73.* ☷ *6 SF.* ⊘ *Apr.–Oct., daily 10–6; Nov.–Mar., daily 11–1 and 2–4.*

Luzern is full of ancient guildhalls and market squares. Among the best is the ornately frescoed **Zunfthaus zur Pfistern,** a guildhall and restaurant dating from the late 15th and early 16th century, and still operating as an eatery today. Just across the square is the **Kornmarkt,** the former site of the local grain market.

The **Weinmarkt** is the loveliest of Luzern's several fountain squares. This former site of the wine market drew visitors from across Europe from the 15th to the 17th century to witness its passion plays. Its Gothic central fountain depicts St. Mauritius, patron saint of warriors, and its surrounding buildings are flamboyantly frescoed in 16th-century style.

② **Spreuerbrücke,** across the Mülenplatz from Weinmarkt, is a narrow, weathered, all-wood covered bridge, dating from 1408. Its interior gables hold a series of eerie, well-preserved paintings (by Kaspar Meglinger) of the *Dance of Death;* they date from the 17th century, though their style and inspiration—tracing to the plague that devastated Luzern and all of Europe during the 14th century—are medieval.

③ The **Natur-Museum** (Natural History Museum) uses unusually modern display techniques to bring nature lessons to life: There are model panoramas of early Luzern settlers, and live animals for children to meet. ⊠ *Kasernenplatz 6,* ☎ *041/228–54–11.* ☷ *4 SF.* ⊘ *Tues.–Fri. 10–noon and 2–5, weekends 10–5.*

④ The stylish **Historisches Museum** (Historical Museum), next to the Natural History Museum, exhibits city sculptures, Swiss arms, and flags; reconstructed rooms depict rural and urban life. The building itself was the late-Gothic armory, dating from 1567. ⊠ *Pfistergasse 24,* ☎ *041/228–54–24.* ☷ *4 SF.* ⊘ *Tues.–Fri. 10–noon and 2–5, weekends 10–5.*

NEED A BREAK?

Where Pfistergasse meets Baselstrasse beyond the Natural History Museum, a funicular (2 SF) carries you up to the **Château Gütsch** (☞ *Lodging, below*). There you can have a drink or a picnic on the panoramic terrace and take in a bird's-eye view of the old town. For photographers, this is a must.

On a charming fountain square (Franziskanerplatz) just off Münzgasse, **⑤** the **Franziskanerkirche** (Franciscan Church) is more than 700 years old and, despite persistent modernization, retains its 17th-century choir stalls and carved wooden pulpit. The barefoot Franciscans once held a prominent social and cultural position in Luzern, which took a firm Counter-Reformation stance and remains more than 70% Roman Catholic today.

★ ⑥ On the Bahnhoffstrasse stands the Baroque **Jesuitenkirche** (Jesuit Church), constructed in 1667–78. Its symmetrical entrance is flanked by two onion-dome towers, added in 1893. Do not fail to go inside: Its vast interior, restored to mint condition, is a rococo explosion of gilt, marble, and epic frescoes. Nearby is the Renaissance **Regierungs- gebäude** (Government Building), seat of the cantonal government.

⑦ **Kapellbrücke** (Chapel Bridge), the oldest wooden bridge in Europe, snakes diagonally across the water. When it was built in the early 14th century, it served as the division between the lake and the river. Its shingle roof and grand stone water tower are to Luzern what the Matterhorn is to Zermatt, but considerably more vulnerable, as a 1993 fire proved. News of the fire at this revered landmark sent the country into a sort

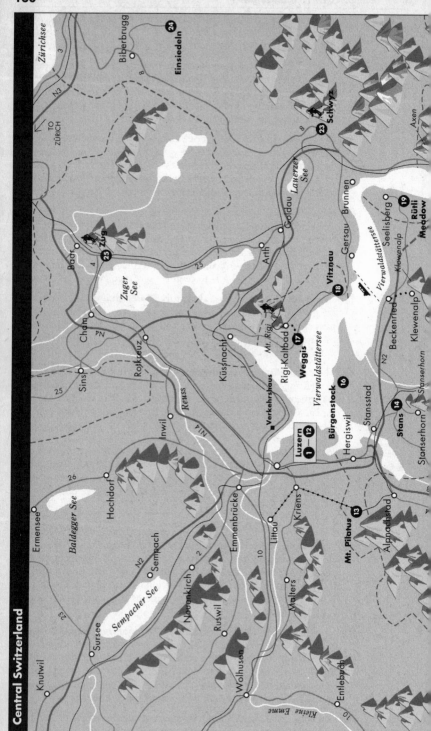

Tschamut

Bürglen
17

Altdorf
21
Erstfeld
Amsteg

20
Flüelen
Reuss
N2
2
Oberalppass
Andermatt
Göschenen
22

Urnersee

Wassen
TO ST.
GOTTHARD
PASS

Sustenhorn
Göscheneralp
See
Dammastock
Titlis
Engelberg
15
Trübsee
Aa
Grafenort
11
Gadmen
Guttannen
Innerkirchen
Sarnen
6
Sarner See
Kaiserstuhl
N
Lungern
See
4
Meiringen
Brienzwiler
Brienzer
Rothorn
TO
INTERLAKEN

KEY

	Rail Lines
	Cable Car/ Funicular
	Tunnels
	Regional Boundary Lines
	Ferry
	Ski Resorts

0   4 miles
0   6 km

Luzern

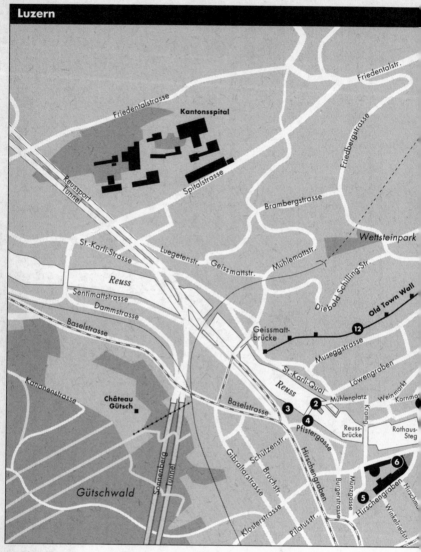

Am Rhyn-Haus, **1**
Bourbaki-
Panorama, **9**
Franziskanerkirche, **5**
Gletschergarten, **11**
Historisches
Museum, **4**

Hofkirche, **8**
Jesuitenkirche, **6**
Kapellbrücke, **7**
Löwendenkmal, **10**
Natur-Museum, **3**
Spreuerbrücke, **2**
Zytturm, **12**

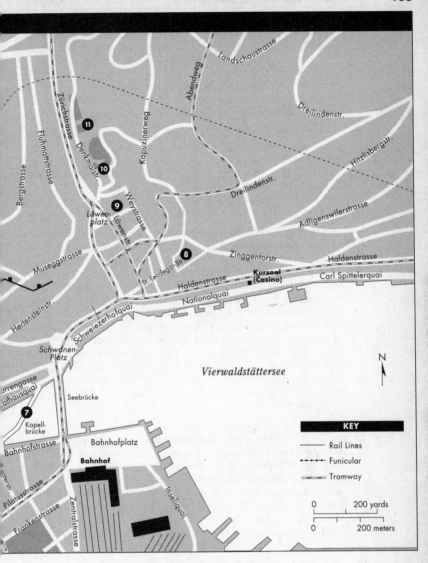

Landschaustrasse

Abendweg

Dreilindenstr.

Zürichstrasse

Denkmalstr.

Fluhmattstrasse

Bergstrasse

11

10

Kapuzinerweg

Weystrasse

9

Löwen-
platz

Löwenstr.

Dreilindenstr.

Hitzlisbergstr.

Adligenswilerstrasse

Museggstrasse

8

St.-Leodegar Str.

Zinggentorstr.

Haldenstrasse

Hertensteinstr.

Haldenstrasse

Nationalquai

**Kursaal
(Casino)**

Carl Spittelerquai

Schweizerhofquai

Schwanen-
Platz

Vierwaldstättersee

N

urrengasse
athausquai

Seebrücke

7

Kapell-
brücke

Bahnhofstrasse

Bahnhofplatz

Bahnhof

Inseliquai

KEY

——— Rail Lines

•••••• Funicular

≡≡≡ Tramway

Pilatusstrasse

Zentralstrasse

Frankenstrasse

| 0 | | 200 yards |
| 0 | | 200 meters |

of cultural mourning, and the accident made front page headlines as far away as Japan. Almost 80% of this fragile monument was destroyed, including many of the 17th-century paintings inside; restorations are still underway. However, a walk through this dark, creaky landmark will take you past polychrome copies of the 112 gable panels painted by Heinrich Wägmann during the 17th century, depicting Luzern and Swiss history, stories of St. Leodegar and St. Mauritius, Luzern's patron saints, and coats of arms from local patrician families.

8 The **Hofkirche** (Collegiate Church) of St. Leodegar was first founded in 750 as a monastery. Its Gothic structure was mostly destroyed by fire in 1633 and rebuilt in late-Renaissance style, so only the towers of its predecessor were preserved. The carved pulpit and choir stalls date from the 17th century, and the 80-rank organ (1650) is one of Switzerland's finest. Outside, Italianate loggias shelter a cemetery for patrician families of old Luzern. ⊠ *St. Leodegarstrasse 13.*

Dominating Löwenplatz like a remnant of a Victorian world's fair is **9** the **Bourbaki-Panorama,** an enormous conical wooden structure. It was created between 1876 and 1878 as a genuine, step-right-up tourist attraction and is, in its undiluted period form, as interesting for its novel nature as for its content. At the top of wide entry stairs, the conical roof covers a sweeping, wraparound epic painting of the French Army of the East retreating into Switzerland at Verrières—a famous episode in the Franco-Prussian War. It was painted by Edouard Castres of Geneva, who was aided by many uncredited artists, including Hodler. As you walk around the circle, the imagery seems to pop into three dimensions; in fact, with the help of a few strategically placed models, it does. There's a recorded commentary in English. ⊠ *Löwenplatz,* ☎ *041/410–99–42.* 🗐 *3 SF.* ☉ *May–Sept., daily 9–6; Mar., Apr., and Oct., daily 9–5.*

Just beyond the Bourbaki-Panorama, one of the world's most evocative public sculptures—the **Löwendenkmal** (Lion Monument)—com-
★ **10** memorates the 760 Swiss guards and their officers who died defending Louis XVI of France at the Tuileries in Paris in 1792. Mark Twain called it "the most mournful and moving piece of stone in the world." Designed by Danish sculptor Berthel Thorwaldsen and carved out of a sheer sandstone face by Lucas Ahorn of Konstanz, this 19th-century wonder is a simple image of a dying lion, his chin sagging on his shield, a broken stump of spear in his side. The Latin inscription translates: "To the bravery and fidelity of the Swiss."

11 The bedrock of the **Gletschergarten** (Glacier Garden), a 19th-century tourist attraction, was excavated between 1872 and 1875 and has been dramatically pocked and polished by Ice Age glaciers. A private museum on the site displays impressive relief maps of Switzerland. ⊠ *Denkmalstrasse 4,* ☎ *041/410–43–40.* 🗐 *7 SF.* ☉ *May–mid-Oct., daily 8–6; Mar., Apr., and mid-Oct.–mid-Nov., daily 9–5; mid-Nov.–Feb., Tues.–Sun. 10:30–4:30.*

Museggstrasse cuts through an original city gate and runs parallel to the watchtowers and crenellated walls of Luzern, constructed around **12** 1400. The clock in the **Zytturm,** the fifth of the towers, was made in Basel in 1385 and still keeps time.

Dining and Lodging

$$$$ ✕ **Mignon.** Among the dining rooms of the splendid lakefront Hotel Palace (☞ Lodging, *below*), this is the grandest, with its stretch of windows overlooking the lake, the reflected city, and the pollarded promenade. The Palace's up-to-date elegance also prevails in the kitchen; the cuisine tends toward the nouvelle—veal tenderloin in tarragon

with beet noodles—and is faultlessly prepared and formally presented, even in the garden court. ⊠ *Haldenstrasse 10,* ☎ *041/410–04–04. Reservations essential. AE, DC, MC, V.*

$$–$$$$ ✕ **La Vague.** This chic restaurant and bistro in the Hotel des Balances
★ (☞ Lodging, *below*) offers a combination as desirable as it is rare: soigné decor, a shimmering riverside view, and adventurous, worldly, informed cuisine that features (believe it or not) local fish. A standing fixed-price *menu de poissons du lac* (lake-fish menu) may offer crayfish soup, grilled omble chevalier in vegetable vinaigrette, and steamed perch in chive butter. Light, fresh fish fondue for two is a house specialty. The lean sweep of deco-postmodern burled wood takes in the more casual, less expensive bistro side as well, where a certain Italian influence can be detected in the delectable *fritto misto* (mixed batterfry) of perch, trout, and pike. ⊠ *Metzgerrainle 7 (Weinmarkt),* ☎ *041/ 410–30–10. AE, DC, MC, V.*

$$$ ✕ **Old Swiss House.** Conceived as self-consciously as its name implies and purpose-built in 1859, no doubt to satisfy the romantic expectations of the flood of English tourists heading for the Lion Monument, this popular establishment pleases crowds (and groups) with its beautifully contrived collection of 17th-century antiques, lead glass, and an Old World artifice now pleasantly burnished by 130 years of service. The standing menu includes specialties from around the country: cheese croquettes, veal and Rösti, lake fish, and Swiss chocolate mousse. (You also may order à la carte.) ⊠ *Löwenplatz 4,* ☎ *041/410–61– 71. AE, DC, MC, V. Closed Mon. and Feb.*

$$$ ✕ **Wilden Mann.** You may choose the ancient original Burgerstube, all
★ dark beams and family crests, which began as a rest stop for St. Gotthard travelers in 1517; or you may opt for the more formal adjoining Liedertafel restaurant, with wainscoting, vaulting, and candlelight. On either side, young chef Andreas Stübi strikes a fine balance between old-style local cooking and savvy French style: smoked salmon tartare wrapped in Rösti with dill sauce; duck breast with dandelion honey and balsamic vinegar; lamb glazed with mustard and horseradish. If you would like a lighter meal, try cheese-filled buckwheat ravioli with sage butter or roast chicken with risotto in the Burgerstube tavern; soup, salad, or *Würsli* (sausage) are available here as well. The pretty, new Geranium Terrace, which is sheltered, serves a menu alfresco, with the full linens-and-flowers treatment. ⊠ *Bahnhofstrasse 30,* ☎ *041/210– 16–66. AE, DC, MC, V.*

$$ ✕ **Galliker.** Step past the ancient facade into a room roaring with local
★ action, where Luzerners drink, smoke, and wallow in their culinary roots like puppies in mud. Brisk, motherly waitresses serve up the dishes Mutti used to make: fresh *Kutteln* (tripe) in rich white wine sauce with cumin seeds; real *Kalbskopf* (chopped fresh veal head) served with heaps of green onions and warm vinaigrette; authentic Luzerner *Chugelipastetli* (puff pastry filled with bite-size meatballs, mushrooms, cream sauce, and bits of pork, veal, or sweetbreads); and beef pot-au-feu. Desserts may include dried pears steeped in pinot noir. Occasional experiments in a more modern mode—such as ginger ice cream—prove that Peter Galliker's kitchen is no museum. The all-wood room is trimmed with chaste, flowered curtains, and the tables form elbow-to-elbow ranks where neighbors wish each other *Guten Appetit.* ⊠ *Schützenstrasse 1,* ☎ *041/240–10–02. AE, MC, V. Closed Sun., Mon., and mid-July–mid-Aug.*

$$ ✕ **Rebstock/Hofstube.** At the opposite end of the culinary spectrum from Galliker, this up-to-date kitchen offers modern, international fare, including rabbit and lamb, as well as East Asian and vegetarian specialties. But you're still in Switzerland: The chewy breads, baked up the street in loaves as big as couch cushions, are so beautiful that they're displayed as objets d'art. The lively bentwood brasserie hums with locals lunching by the bar, while the more formal, old-style restaurant glows with wood and brass under a low beam-and-herringbone parquet ceiling. In summer, opt for outdoor seating in the garden or on the terrace. ⊠ *St.-Leodegarstrasse 3,* ☎ *041/410–35–81. AE, DC, MC, V.*

$ ✕ **Zur Pfistern.** One of the architectural focal points of the old-town waterfront, this floridly decorated old guild house—its origins trace back to 1341—offers a good selection of moderate meals in addition to higher-priced standards. Lake fish and Pastetli are worthy local options. Inside, it's woody and publike, if slightly down-at-the-heels, but in summer the small first-floor balcony may provide the best seat in town for the postcard waterfront view and top-notch secluded people-watching. There are also chestnut-shaded tables directly along the waterfront, in the thick of the strolling crowds, though you'll be vulnerable to the hazards of open-air dining—passing dogs have been known to lift a leg inches from diners' chairs. ⊠ *Kornmarkt 4,* ☎ *041/410–36–50. AE, DC, MC, V.*

$$$$ 🏨 **Château Gütsch.** Any antiquity in this "castle" built as a hotel in 1888 is strictly contrived, but honeymooners, groups, gullible romantics, and other neophytes seeking out storybook Europe enjoy the Disneyland-like experience: the turrets and towers worthy of a mad Ludwig of Bavaria, the cellars, crypts, and corridors lined with a hodgepodge of relics, not to mention the magnificent hilltop site above Luzern, once a lookout point. An extravagant renovation, reducing the number of fantasy-style rooms but enlarging them considerably, has made this lodging-cum-attraction rather more luxurious. Theme bedrooms are decked out for romance, some with four-poster canopy beds, all with grand baths. The restaurant is known for its dramatic views of Luzern, and there are wine tastings in the atmospheric cellar. ⊠ *Kanonenstrasse,* ☎ *041/249–02–72,* 𝔽𝔸𝕏 *041/249–02–52. 62 beds. Restaurant, pool. AE, DC, MC, V.*

$$$$ 🏨 **National.** Although you might be put off by the modernized lobby, the inner sanctums of this monumental landmark have been restored to florid splendor, down to the last cupola, crown molding, and Corinthian column. Founded in 1870 and once home base to Cesar Ritz and August Escoffier, the hotel dominates the lakeside promenade—its mansarded facade stretches the length of two city blocks. The service matches the scale: They even stamp their logo in the sand of the big public-area ashtrays. Forty apartments take up some of the mass, but there's plenty of space. The rooms are French provincial with brass beds, the domed bar is decked with mahogany and aglitter with crystal, and the marble-column breakfast hall may be the most splendid in Switzerland—even without the lake view. ⊠ *Haldenstrasse 4, CH-6003,* ☎ *41/419–09–09,* 𝔽𝔸𝕏 *041/419–09–10. 130 beds. Restaurant, indoor pool, sauna, fitness center. AE, DC, MC, V.*

$$$$ 🏨 **Palace.** The general air of bankers' wealth here is just one aspect of this hotel's seamless, urbane polish. Brilliantly refurbished and modernized to take in the broadest possible lake views, it has a classic look with a touch of postmodern. Built in 1906 to share the waterfront with the National, it's lighter, airier, and altogether sleeker—with refurbished fifth-floor rooms and, in keeping with the rest of the building, an entirely new sixth floor. Rooms are large enough for a game of badminton between the beds and the writing desks, and picture windows afford sweeping views of the Vierwaldstättersee and Mt. Pilatus. The conductor Herbert von Karajan chose it for sojourns during the annual International Festival, as do a number of current stars. The Mignon is one of Luzern's best restaurants (☞ Dining, *above*). ⊠ *Haldenstrasse 10, CH-6002,* ☎ *041/410–04–04,* 𝔽𝔸𝕏 *041/410–15–04. 341 beds. Restaurant, bar, 2 saunas, steam room, health club, parking. AE, DC, MC, V.*

$$$$ ⊞ **Schweizerhof.** Built in 1844 and expanded during the 1860s, this imposing structure has hosted Napoléon III, Leo Tolstoy, and Mark Twain—and Richard Wagner lived here while his lakefront home at Tribschen was being completed. Rooms have a sweeping view of the lake and mountains. ⊠ *Schweizerhofquai 3, CH-6002,* ☎ *041/410–04–10,* FAX *041/410–29–71. 214 beds. Restaurant, café, bar, parking. AE, DC, MC, V.*

$$$ ⊞ **Des Balances.** Restored and renewed, outside and in, this riverfront
★ property built during the 19th century on the site of an ancient guild house gleams with style. State-of-the-art tile baths, up-to-date pastel decor, and one of the best sites in Luzern (in the heart of the old town, with idyllic Reuss views) make this the slickest in its price class. Go elsewhere for historic interiors (though the few unrenovated rooms are studies in Victorian plush), but nearly every window frames a period scene outdoors. Rear rooms look toward the Weinmarkt. The restaurant-bistro La Vague (☞ *Dining, above*) is so good that you may want to eat every meal in the hotel. ⊠ *Metzgerrainle 7, CH-6003,* ☎ *041/410–30–10,* FAX *041/410–64–51. 108 beds. 2 restaurants, piano bar. AE, DC, MC, V.*

$$$ ⊞ **Montana.** This neoclassic 1910 palace glows with musty, beeswaxed beauty, its luxurious original woodwork, parquet, and terrazzo in superb condition. The public rooms are parlor-fussy, but guest rooms are fresh and new. Those in back overlook a hillside, while the front doubles (slightly costlier) have balconies with views of the city and lake. The building is perched on a slope above town, accessible by funicular from the waterfront or by car. TV is available by request only. ⊠ *Adligenswilerstrasse 22, CH-6003,* ☎ *041/410–65–65,* FAX *041/410–66–76. 116 beds. Restaurant, bar. AE, DC, MC, V.*

$$$ ⊞ **Wilden Mann.** Living up to its reputation, the city's best-known hotel
★ offers its guests a gracious and authentic experience of Old Luzern. Joining several old houses that were once part of the town wall, and including the original 1517 tavern, the structure has been carefully renewed to Reformation polish, with stone, beams, brass, hand-painted tiles, and burnished wood everywhere. Standard rooms have a prim, 19th-century look; deluxe rooms have separate sitting areas and efficient modern bathrooms. Warm colors, rich fabrics, and antique furniture decorate the inviting public lounges. The location is convenient to the old town, though across the river, steps from the Franciscan church. This is, appropriately, a property of the Romantik chain. ⊠ *Bahnhofstrasse 30, CH-6003,* ☎ *041/210–16–66,* FAX *041/210–16–29. 80 beds. 2 restaurants, lounges. AE, DC, MC, V.*

$$ ⊞ **Des Alpes.** With a terrific riverfront location in the bustling heart of the old town, this historic hotel has an inside that makes it look like a laminate-and-vinyl chain motel. The rooms, however, are generously proportioned, tidy, and even sleek; front doubles, several with balconies, overlook the water and promenade. Cheaper back rooms face the old town; those on higher floors have rooftop views and plenty of light. The restaurant has balcony seating, a terrace, and a waterfront café. ⊠ *Rathausquai 5, CH-6003,* ☎ *041/410–58–25,* FAX *041/410–74–51. 90 beds. Restaurant, café. AE, DC, MC, V.*

$$ ⊞ **Diana.** This is a city hotel, on the Bahnhof side and off the main shopping street, but it's reached through a quiet park. Newly decorated rooms may have built-in fixtures in sleek beech or warm knotty pine; some have French windows that open onto balconies. In the oldest rooms, a bleak Formica look, a holdover from the '60s, prevails. Jugendstil touches remain in the corridors, and the public areas are modern but worn. ⊠ *Sempacherstrasse 16, CH-6003,* ☎ *041/210–26–23,* FAX *041/210–02–05. 74 beds. Breakfast room. AE, DC, MC, V.*

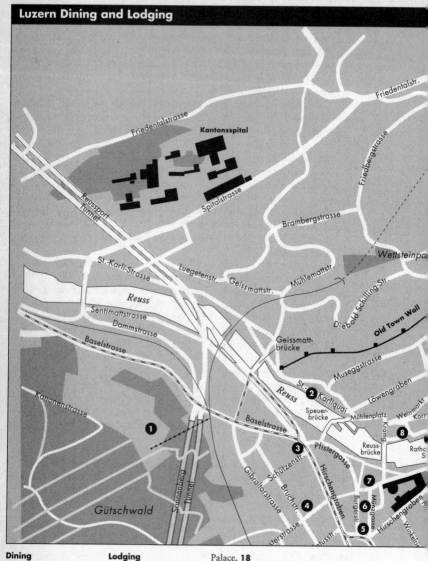

Dining
Galliker, **3**
La Vague, **8**
Mignon, **18**
Old Swiss House, **15**
Rebstock/
Hofstube, **14**
Wilden Mann, **7**
Zur Pfistern, **10**

Lodging
Château Gütsch, **1**
Des Alpes, **12**
Des Balances, **8**
Diana, **9**
Drei Könige, **4**
Goldener Stern, **5**
Montana, **17**
National, **16**

Palace, **18**
Schlüssel, **6**
Schweizerhof, **13**
SSR Touristen, **2**
Wilden Mann, **7**
Zum Weissen
Kreuz, **11**

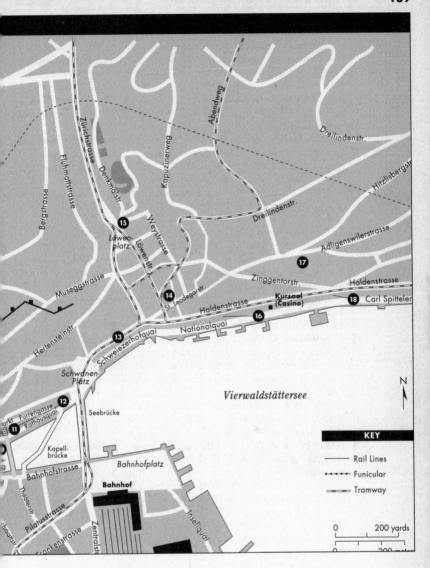

Bergstrasse

Fluhmattstrasse

Zürichstrasse

Denkmalstr.

Kapuzinerweg

Abendweg

Dreilindenstr.

Hitzlisbergstr.

Dreilindenstr.

Adligenswilerstrasse

15

Weystrasse

Löwen-platz

Löwenstr.

Museggstrasse

Zinggentorstr.

Haldenstrasse

17

14

St. Leodegarstr.

Haldenstrasse

Kursaal (Casino)

18 Carl Spitteler

Hertensteinstr.

16

Nationalquai

13

Schweizerhofquai

Schwanen-platz

Vierwaldstättersee

N

12

Furrengasse

Rathausquai

Seebrücke

arkt

11

Kapell-brücke

Bahnhofplatz

g

Bahnhofstrasse

Bahnhof

Theaterstr.

Pilatusstrasse

Zentralstr.

nmatstr.

Frankenstrasse

Inselquai

KEY
—— Rail Lines
•••• Funicular
⚎⚎ Tramway

0   200 yards

0   200 meter

$$ ⊞ **Drei Könige.** This urban inn, far from the Bahnhof but very handy to bridges to the old town, is in a noisy district and has little to offer of Old Luzern, though its restaurant claims roots in the 17th century. Renovated rooms are Scandi-bland and show their age. The higher floors are quieter; ask for a room in back. Bus 2 takes you from the station to the nearby Hirzenhof stop. Eat at the neighboring Galliker (☞ Dining, *above*) and waddle the short stretch home. ⊠ *Bruchstrasse 35, CH-6003,* ☎ *041/240–88–33,* 𝔽𝔸𝕏 *041/240–88–52. 110 beds. Restaurant. AE, DC, MC, V.*

$$ ⊞ **Zum Weissen Kreuz.** Now upgraded, this former bargain hotel on
★ the waterfront is slick, bright, and airtight; and tile, stucco, oak, and pine soften the modern edges. Some rooms face the lake, others the old town. You couldn't find a more convenient or atmospheric setting, off the Kornmarkt. The Italian restaurant Al Forno serves pasta and pizza. ⊠ *Furrengasse 19, CH-6003,* ☎ *041/410–40–40,* 𝔽𝔸𝕏 *041/410–40–60. 48 beds. Restaurant. AE, DC, MC, V.*

$–$$ ⊞ **Goldener Stern.** This clean, plain, and pleasant former wine cellar has restored its fine 17th-century exterior and redecorated its restaurant to present an upscale face to the world. Pretty, pristine linens soften the modern rooms; windows, some looking over the Franciscan church, are double-glazed. The stübli is popular with locals. A friendly family business, Goldener Stern is now managed by the second generation. ⊠ *Burgerstrasse 35, CH-6003,* ☎ *041/227–50–60,* 𝔽𝔸𝕏 *041/227–50–61. 30 beds. Restaurant. AE, MC, V.*

$ ⊞ **Schlüssel.** On the Franziskanerplatz, with several rooms overlooking the Franciscan church and fountain, this spare, no-nonsense little lodging attracts young bargain hunters. It's a pleasant combination of tidy new touches (quarry tile, white paint) and antiquity: You can have breakfast or a simple hot meal in a low, cross-vaulted "crypt" and admire the fine old beams in the lobby. ⊠ *Franziskanerplatz 12, CH-6003,* ☎ *041/210–10–61,* 𝔽𝔸𝕏 *041/210–10–21. 20 beds. Breakfast room. MC, V.*

$ ⊞ **SSR Touristen.** Despite its friendly, collegiate atmosphere, this cheery
★ dormlike spot is anything but a backpackers' flophouse. It has a terrific setting on the Reuss, around the corner from the old town. Its spare modern architecture is brightened with fresh, trendy colors and framed prints, and rooms that don't have the river view face greenery instead. The staff is young and helpful, and the coed four-bed dorms (sex-segregated in high season) draw sociable travelers with their rock-bottom prices. Rooms are available with or without bath; the shared baths are handy and well maintained. ⊠ *12 St. Karli Quai, CH-6003,* ☎ *041/410–24–74,* 𝔽𝔸𝕏 *041/410–84–14. 100 beds. AE, DC, MC, V.*

Nightlife and the Arts

BARS AND LOUNGES

The **Des Balances** hotel has a hip, upscale piano bar (⊠ Metzgerrainle 7, ☎ 041/410–30–10). **Château Gütsch** (⊠ Kanonenstrasse, ☎ 041/249–02–72) draws a sedate dinner-and-dancing crowd. The **Mr. Pickwick** (⊠ Rathausquai 6, ☎ 041/410–59–27) functions as an English pub. The **National Hotel** (⊠ Haldenstrasse 4, ☎ 041/419–09–09) serves drinks in both its glossy American-style bar and its imposing lobby lounge. The **Palace Hotel** (⊠ Haldenstrasse 10, ☎ 041/410–04–04), like the National, has two American-style bars.

CASINOS

The most sophisticated nightlife in Luzern is found in the **Casino** (⊠ Haldenstrasse 6, ☎ 041/51–27–51), on the northern shore by the grand hotels. You can play boule in the Gambling Room (5 SF limit, federally imposed), dance in the **Babilonia** club, watch a strip show in the

Red Rose, or have a Swiss meal in **Le Chalet** while watching a folklore display.

DISCOS

Flora-Club (✉ Seidenhofstrasse 5, ☎ 041/229–79–79) mixes dancing with folklore shows.

FOLKLORE

Besides the folklore shows at Flora-Club and the casino, there are performances at the **Stadtkeller** (✉ Sternenplatz 3, ☎ 041/410–47–33) that transport you to the Valais—cheese specialties, yodelers, dirndled dancers, and all. A phenomenon called the ***Night Boat*** (☎ 041/367–67–67), which sails from Landungsbrücke 6 every evening at 8:45 from May through September, offers meals, drinks, and a folklore show during a pleasant lake cruise.

MUSIC

Luzern, the cultural hub of Central Switzerland, hosts the **International Music Festival** for three weeks in August every year. Performances take place at the **Kunsthaus** (✉ Frohburgstrasse 6, ☎ 041/210–30–80). For further information on the festival, contact **International Musikfestwochen** (✉ Postfach, CH-6002, ☎ 041/210–94–64).

The **Allgemeine Musikgesellschaft Luzern** (AML), the local orchestra in residence, offers a season of concerts from October through June, at the Kunsthaus (☎ 041/210–50–50). For information on its concerts and other performances throughout the year, consult *Official Guidebook: Luzern,* published by the city seasonally.

THEATER

The **Stadttheater** (✉ Theaterstrasse 2, ☎ 041/21—66–18), directly on the waterfront on the Bahnhof side of town, is home to Luzern's principal theater group, which stages plays in German, and operas, usually in the original language. Current productions are detailed in *Official Guidebook.*

FILM

Movie theaters, concentrated on the Bahnhof side of town along Pilatusstrasse and Bahnhofstrasse, usually present films in their original language.

Outdoor Activities and Sports

BICYCLING

The standard Swiss practice of renting bicycles from the train station (☎ 041/21–31–11) comes in handy here, as the lake-level terrain offers smooth riding.

BOATING

Pedal, motor, and sailboats are available in Luzern through **Bucher & Co.** (☎ 041/410–92–30), **SNG Luzern** (☎ 041/368–08–08), and **Werft Herzog** (☎ 041/410–43–33).

GOLF

Golfplatz Dietschiberg outside Luzern (☎ 041/420–97–87) has an 18-hole course open to visitors.

SWIMMING

At the **lido,** past the casino, you can swim in the Vierwaldstättersee.

TENNIS

Tennisclub Carlton Tivoli (✉ Haldenstrasse, ☎ 041/410–31–37) has four outdoor courts available.

WINDSURFING

Contact Kempf Sport (☎ 041/210–10–57).

Shopping

The best shopping in the region is concentrated in Luzern, which, although it no longer produces embroidery or lace, still offers a wide variety of Swiss handiwork as well as the high-fashion and luxury goods appropriate to its high profile. Note: During the summer, most shops remain open in the evening until 9 and open on Sunday morning after 11. On Thursday night year-round, shops stay open until 9.

DEPARTMENT STORES

The main department store in town is **Jelmoli** (⌧ Pilatusstrasse 4, ☎ 041/211–22–11). **Migros** (⌧ Hertensteinstrasse 44 and Letzihof, Hirschengraben 41, ☎ 041/410–63–63) specializes in groceries and also has inexpensive stationery and office supplies. **Manor, Nordmann, & Co.** (⌧ Weggisgasse 5, ☎ 041/418–33–33) is the Swiss version of Woolworth or Kmart. **EPA** (⌧ Rössligasse 20, ☎ 041/410–19–77), like Manor, Nordmann, is an inexpensive, all-purpose store.

EMBROIDERY

The main producer of Swiss embroidery is **Sturzenegger** (⌧ Schwanenplatz 7, ☎ 041/410–19–58) of St. Gallen, which sells its own machine-made lace and embroidered goods as well as Hanro and Calida underwear. The store also stocks a conservative line of women's dresses and blouses. For fine handcrafted lace and embroidery, visit **Neff** (⌧ Löwenstrasse 10, ☎ 041/410–19–65), if not to buy, just to browse.

HANDICRAFTS AND GIFTS

Schmid-Linder (⌧ Denkmalstrasse 9, ☎ 041/410–43–46) carries an extensive line of Swiss embroidery and linen as well as cuckoo clocks, cowbells, and a large stock of wood carvings from Brienz, in the Berner Oberland. **Innerschweizer Heimatwerk** (⌧ Franziskanerplatz 14, Burgerstrasse, ☎ 041/210–69–44) sells nothing but goods—most of them contemporary rather than traditional Swiss—made in the region by independent craftspeople, from weaving to ceramics and wooden toys.

MARKETS

A **flea market** takes place every Saturday from 8 to 4 at Untere Burgerstrasse. For locally made crafts, there's a **Handwerksmarkt** on the Weinmarkt on the first Saturday of every month.

SHOES

Bally Coulin (⌧ Kapellplatz 8, ☎ 041/410–72–71) is the main source here for Swiss-made Bally shoes.

WATCHES

Competition is heavy, and the two enormous patriarchs of the watch business advertise heavily and offer inexpensive souvenirs to lure shoppers into their luxurious showrooms. **Gübelin** (⌧ Schweizerhofquai, ☎ 041/410–51–42) is the exclusive source for Audemars Piguet, Patek Philippe, and its own house brand. **Bucherer** (⌧ Schwanenplatz, ☎ 041/369–77–00) represents Piaget and Rolex.

WOMEN'S CLOTHING

The czarina of women's fashion in Luzern is **Christina De Boer,** who runs a group of boutiques. **De Boer** (⌧ Weggisgasse 29, ☎ 041/410–20–22) carries Max Mara, Escada, and Ferraud. **De Boer Rive Gauche** (⌧ Pilatusstrasse 14, ☎ 041/210–89–16), by the theater, carries Georges Rechs, Byblos, and Strenesse. **De Boer's Esprit** is for younger women (⌧ Kornmarkt, ☎ 041/410–27–76). The shop called simply **Christina De Boer** (⌧ Weggisgasse 29, Werchlaube, ☎ 041/410–62–39) carries Jil Sander and Lange.

McStore/Maglia Poletti (⌧ Furrengasse 7, ☎ 041/410–21–15) stocks such hip, upscale Eurodesigners as Apropos, Annex, Pink Flamingo (all

Swiss designers), and Paul Smith, as well as Poletti's own line of knits in wool, silk, and cotton.

Mühlebach & Birrer (☎ 041/410–66–73) on Kapellplatz carries a full line of traditional Austrian wools by Geiger as well as embroidered sweaters and Appenzeller handkerchiefs.

OFF THE
BEATEN PATH

VERKEHRSHAUS – The Swiss Transport Museum is one of Luzern's (if not Switzerland's) greater attractions. Easily reached by steamer, car, or Bus 2, it's almost a world's fair in itself, with a complex of buildings and exhibitions both indoors and out, including dioramas, live demonstrations, and a "Swissorama" (360° screen) film about Switzerland. Every mode of transit is discussed, from stagecoaches and bicycles to jumbo jets and space capsules. If you're driving, turn east at the waterfront and follow the signs. ⊠ *Lidostrasse 5,* ☎ *041/370–44–44.* 🎫 *15 SF.* ☉ *Mar.–Oct., daily 9–6; Nov.–Feb., weekdays 10–4, Sun. 10–5.*

Mt. Pilatus

⑬ *10 km (6 mi) southwest of Luzern.*

This 2,121-meter (6,953-foot) mountain was named either from the Latin *pileatus* (wearing a cap), to refer to its frequent cloud covering, or, more colorfully, for the ghost of Pontius Pilate, who supposedly haunts the summit: His body, it was said, was brought here by the devil. For centuries it was forbidden to climb the mountain and enrage the ghost, who unleashed deadly storms. Unlike Queen Victoria, who rode to the summit by mule in 1868, you can now reach it by cable car for a hefty 73 SF in summer, 42 SF in winter.

Take a trolley from the train station in Luzern to the suburb of Kriens, where you catch a tiny, four-seat cable car that flies silently up to Fräkmüntegg (1,403 meters/4,600 feet); then change to the 40-seat cable car that sails through open air up the rock cliff to the summit station (1,696 meters/5,560 feet). From here a 10-minute walk takes you to the **Esel** (2,123 meters/6,962 feet), at the center of Pilatus's multiple peaks, where views unfold over the Alps and the sprawling, crooked Vierwaldstättersee.

A pleasant variation for the return trip to Luzern from Mt. Pilatus involves riding a steep cogwheel train, often down gradients of nearly 18%, through four tunnels that pierce sheer rock face, to Alpnachstad. From there, take a train back to Hergiswil, where you can cross the track and climb aboard the small, private Stans-Engelberg train that heads up the Engelbergertal (Engelberg Valley). By car, simply head from Alpnachstad toward Stans and Engelberg. At lake level, you'll cross a brief neck of land that separates the Alpnachersee and the Vierwaldstättersee. If you are coming straight from Luzern, trains run every hour to Engelberg.

Stans

⑭ *10 km (6 mi) east of Mt. Pilatus; 10 km (6 mi) south of Luzern.*

In the heart of lush valley terrain and mossy meadows, Stans is an old village whose appealing old-town center is dotted with typical deeproof houses in the Central Swiss style. This was the home of the beloved Heinrich Pestalozzi, the father of modern education. When the French army invaded the village in 1798, slaughtering nearly 2,000 citizens, it was Pestalozzi who gathered the orphaned children in a school where he applied his progressive theories in the practice of the budding science of psychology.

The bell tower of Stans' early Baroque **parish church** is in Italian Romanesque style (with increasing numbers of arched windows as the tower rises), though the incongruous steeple was added during the 16th century; the church as it stands dates from the Renaissance period.

On the town square stands a 19th-century **monument to Arnold von Winkelried,** a native of Stans who martyred himself to lead the Swiss Confederates to victory over the Austrians at the battle of Sempach in 1386: The Austrians, armed with long spears, formed a Roman square so that the Swiss, wielding axes and halberds, couldn't get in close enough to do any damage. Shouting "Forward, Confederates, I will open a path!" von Winkelried threw himself on the spears, clasping as many of them as he could to his breast—creating an opening for his comrades.

Another native son, from the neighboring village of Flüeli, is Niklaus von Flüe, who saved the Confederation again, nearly 100 years after von Winkelried, through wise council at the Diet of Stans in 1481. He was canonized in 1947.

NEED A BREAK?	If the weather is fine, have a drink in the pleasant sheltered garden behind the chicly restored **Wirtschaft Höfli zur Rosenburg** (☎ 041/610–24–61) between the train station and the town center.

En Route   A two-part journey on a nostalgic 1893 funicular and an ultramodern cable car takes you to the **Stanserhorn** (1,891 meters/6,200 feet), from whose peak you can see the lakes; the Titlis, at 3,050 meters (10,000 feet) the highest point in Central Switzerland; and even the Jungfrau.

Engelberg

🟕 *12 km (8 mi) from Stans; 27 km (17 mi) south of Luzern.*

At the top of the village of Obermatt, Engelberg (1,000 meters/3,280 feet) is a popular resort for skiers from nearby Zurich, but its slopes are limited in comparison to St. Moritz, Wengen, and Zermatt. Engelberg clusters at the foot of its Benedictine **Kloster** (monastery) founded in 1120; until the French invaded in 1798, massacring thousands, this monastery ruled the valley. Now, numerous hotels cater to winter skiers and summer hikers.

OFF THE BEATEN PATH	**TITLIS** – This is perhaps the most impressive of the many rocky peaks that surround the Obermatt's long, wide bowl. Thanks to a sophisticated transportation system that benefits skiers, hikers, climbers, and tourists alike, it's possible to ride a small cable car up to the tiny mountain lake (and famous ski area) called **Trübsee** (1,801 meters/5,904 feet). From there change to a larger cable car, which rotates to give 360-degree panoramas, and ascend to Stand and ultimately to the summit station on the Titlis. There's an ice grotto (serving drinks from a solid-ice bar) and a panorama restaurant: Views take in the Jura Mountains, the Graubünden and Bernese Alps, and what, from this perspective, seems like the puny Pilatus. Round-trip cost is 75 SF.

Skiing

At the base of the 3,021-meter-high (9,906-foot-high) Titlis, Engelberg serves Central Switzerland as its most serious ski resort, offering limited but spectacular runs for all levels. The Titlis itself provides both medium and difficult runs from very near its peak, ending up at the 1,801-meter (5,904-foot) plateau called Trübsee; from there, easy trails lead all the way down the valley to Engelberg at 1,051 meters (3,445 feet)—a total run of 12 kilometers (7½ miles), dropping 2,001 meters (6,560 feet). Engelberg has two funicular railways, seven cable cars, 13 lifts, 45 kilometers (28 miles) of downhill runs, 34 kilometers (21 miles) of cross-country trails, 3½ kilometers (2 miles) of toboggan runs, and ice-skating.

Dining and Lodging

$$$ ✕🏠 **Regina Titlis.** In a resort haunted by fading grand hotels from a bygone Victorian boom, this centrally located high-rise, a little Dallas in the Alps, strikes a jarring note. Built in 1983 on the ashes of its predecessor, it has fresh, solid rooms with warm wood accents, balconies with views, and generous facilities. If you're looking for quiet, reserve a room at the back of the hotel, away from the street. ✉ *CH-6390,* ☎ *041/637–28–28,* FAX *041/637–23–92. 256 beds. 2 restaurants, café, bar, indoor pool, sauna, fitness center, parking. AE, DC, MC, V.*

$$ ✕🏠 **Hess.** Though it was gutted and rebuilt inside nearly a decade ago, this fine old mountain lodge retains the character you expect from a hotel run by the family that founded it in 1884. The pine-and-chintz rooms are fresher than those decorated in dark wood, and corner doubles are bright, with fine views. Southern mountain views look over the road. The public areas are rustic but grand, with parquet floors, a scattering of game trophies, and a grandly scaled fireplace in the main lounge. The restaurant, Tudor-Stübli, is known for good food; Mr. Hess does some of the cooking himself. ✉ *CH-6390,* ☎ *041/637–13–66,* FAX *041/637–35–38. 84 beds. Restaurant, piano bar, sauna, fitness center, dance club. AE, DC, MC, V.*

$$ ✕🏠 **Schweizerhof.** Though the exterior suggests a once-grand, this lovely
★ old fin-de-siècle structure has been attentively remodeled inside to combine fresh, light new knotty-pine looks with plush Edwardian comforts. The south-side views are fine, especially from rooms with balconies. Bay corner doubles are worth asking for. It's steps from the little train station but still quiet, and it has an air of being tended by a family that knows the business. ✉ *CH-6390,* ☎ *041/637–11–05,* FAX *041/637–41–47. 80 beds. Restaurant. AE, DC, MC, V.*

$ ✕🏠 **Alpenklub.** This is, ironically, a rare find in Switzerland: a cozy
★ little old-fashioned chalet, every square inch pine-paneled and dark-timbered, with down-quilted beds, a glowing fondue stübli, and a quiet sun terrace looking out on snowy peaks. It's lively, casual, and, above all, cheap. And it draws mobs of young skiers to its disco-bar and pizzeria, and families to its firelit restaurant, one of three in the hotel. (All serve à la carte only.) Though it stands slightly beyond the urbanized center, toward the monastery, it's not for quiet retreats, at least at ski time. There are only nine rooms, so book well in advance. ✉ *CH-6390,* ☎ *041/637–12–43,* FAX *041/637–03–37. 18 beds. Restaurant, bar, pizzeria, stübli. AE, DC, MC, V.*

$ ✕🏠 **Engel.** Its first wing built in 1778 on the foundations of a 1623 tavern, Engelberg's oldest structure has expanded over the years into a creaky sprawl of Victorian coziness. Labyrinthine corridors lead to simple old rooms, most trimmed in '50s-style wood, a handful updated in a spare '70s look. The plush parlors and pub, however, look as if Lincoln could have lived there, and the vaulted restaurant—in the oldest wing—displays ancient family seals. The grandiose ballroom has been converted to a billiards hall. ✉ *CH-6390,* ☎ *041/637–11–82,* FAX *041/637–47–16. 70 beds. Restaurant, pub. AE, DC, MC, V.*

Outdoor Activities and Sports

Rent mountain bikes in Engelberg through **Sportgeschäft Arndt** (☎ 041/637–49–39), **Bike 'n' Roll** (☎ 041/637–46–91), or **Amstutz** (☎ 041/ 637–27–14). There are five outdoor tennis courts at the **Hotel Bellevue**

(☎ 041/637–12–13) and two indoor courts at the **Sportcenter Erlen** (☎ 041/637–34–94).

THE VIERWALDSTÄTTERSEE TO ST. GOTTHARD AND EINSIEDELN

From Luzern, you can take a lake steamer all the way down to the Unersee (the southern leg of the leg); or you can drive the same route along the lakefront highway, continuing on to the historic pilgrimage town of Einsiedeln. Either trip will involve switching to train or cable car if you want to climb to Rigi Kulm.

If you choose to go by boat, depart at any convenient time (schedules are available at the ticket and tourist offices) from the main docks by the train station (or, by car, past the casino along the waterfront drive); the boat will be marked for Flüelen. First-class seats are on top; each level has a restaurant-café. The exterior seats are only slightly sheltered; if you want to sit inside, you may feel obligated to order a drink. Take advantage of the boat's many stops—you can get on and off at will.

Bürgenstock

16 *20 km (13 mi) from Luzern.*

Most Flüelen-bound boats go to Bürgenstock, from which visitors can take a funicular to the isolated resort at the top. Though the plateau isn't terribly high—only 458 meters/1,500 feet—it rises dramatically above the water and offers striking views over the lake region; that's why a small colony of luxury hotels has mushroomed, most of them owned by the Frey family. Bürgenstock also can be approached by car, up a narrow, steep road, from Stansstad, on the road between Luzern and Stans.

Weggis and Rigi-Kaltbad

★ **17** *25 km (15 mi) northeast of Bürgenstock; 20 km (12 mi) northeast of Luzern.*

Weggis is a summer resort town known for its mild, almost subtropical climate. There's a pretty waterfront park and promenade; and as it's far from the autoroute and accessible only by the secondary road, you get a pleasant sense of isolation.

The famed **Mt. Rigi** (1,800 meters/5,900 feet) is just a cable car ride away from Weggis: Follow signs for the Rigibahn, a station high above the resort (a 15-minute walk). From here you can ride a large cable car to Rigi-Kaltbad, a small resort on a spectacular plateau; walk across to the electric rack-and-pinion railway station; and ride the steep tracks of the Vitznau–Rigi line to the summit of the mountain. Take an elevator to the **Hotel Rigi-Kulm** to enjoy the views indoors or walk to the crest (45 minutes) to see as far as the Black Forest in one direction and Mt. Säntis in the other. Or consider climbing to the top, staying in the hotel, and pursuing what Mark Twain spoke of as the perfect sunrise. You have the option of returning to Luzern from Weggis by taking a different railway down, from Rigi to Arth-Goldau; the two lines were built by competing companies in the 1870s in a race to reach the top and capture the lion's share of the tourist business. The line rising out of the lakefront resort of Vitznau won, but the Arth-Goldau line gets plenty of business, as its base terminal lies on the mainstream St. Gotthard route.

Lodging

$$–$$$ **★** 🏨 **Beau-Rivage.** Built in 1908 but modernized inside over the past few years, this attractive business-class resort concentrates its comforts on a small but luxurious waterfront site, with an awning-shaded restaurant above the manicured lakeside lawn, a swimming pool with mountain views, and lounge chairs at the lake's edge. Its rooms glow with rosy wood, brass, and pastel fabrics. It's at the center of town, near the boat landing. ✉ CH-6353, ☎ 041/390–14–22, FAX 041/390–19–81. 75 beds. Restaurant, bar, pool. AE, DC, MC, V. Closed Nov.–Mar.

$$–$$$ 🏨 **Posthotel.** Management changes transformed this already modern establishment into a business-oriented hotel by expanding its restaurants, conference facilities, and services, and by adding a casino, which was slated to open in July 1996. All bedrooms face the street leading to the lakefront, and a wide range of fitness facilities is available. The old wooden stübli is still here—preserved intact from the original stagecoach café—but now you'll also find an ambitious Italian restaurant, a French brasserie with Sunset-Boulevard terrace, and an outdoor waterfront grill with live music. The hotel sits directly over the boat landing. ✉ CH-6353 Weggis, ☎ 041/390-23–23, FAX 041/390–12–77. 100 beds. 4 restaurants, 2 bars, café, indoor pool, sauna, fitness center, beach, dock, meeting rooms. AE, DC, MC, V. Closed Dec.–Feb.

$$ 🏨 **Du Lac Seehof.** Behind its magnificent classic waterfront facade you'll be welcomed on a humbler, homier scale: This is a family-owned-and-run resort hotel, with a comfortable woody café downstairs and an arbored terrace café-restaurant. The renovated rooms are bright and spare, with tile baths. Lake-view rooms with balconies cost more but are worth it; the back rooms look over the street and face storefronts. The hotel is near the boat landing. ✉ Gotthardstrasse 4, CH-6353, ☎ 041/390–11–51, FAX 041/390–11–19. 50 beds. Restaurant, café. AE, DC, MC, V.

$$ 🏨 **Rigi-Kulm.** If you find the novelty of mountaintop stopovers appealing, this high-altitude hotel is for you; built in 1950 and partly renovated (if in a rather generic style), it still has the air of a rugged but genteel lodge. Southern rooms have rustic decor, bathrooms, and great views. (Be warned, however: Mountainside transportation makes this an awkward home base for excursions, and if it's raining during your stay, the views disappear; you might as well be on the dark side of the moon.) A short walk from the summit, at 1,800 meters (5,900 feet), it is accessible by cable car from Weggis to Rigi-Kaltbad, then cogwheel rail; or by cogwheel from Vitznau or Arth-Goldau. Or you can climb up from Weggis, allowing either three hours or, as Mark Twain required, three days, depending on your penchant for resting. ✉ CH-6410, ☎ 041/811–65–26, FAX 041/811–11–14. 100 beds. Restaurant, café. AE.

Outdoor Activities and Sports

For **skiing,** Rigi, at 5,900 feet, has two funicular railways, three cable cars, seven lifts, 30 kilometers (19 miles) of downhill runs, 14 kilometers (9 miles) of cross-country trails, 14 kilometers (9 miles) of ski-hiking trails, and curling.

The tourist office at Weggis (☎ 041/390–11–55) rents **bicycles.** Weggis maintains several public **tennis** courts (☎ 041/390–11–55). **Windsurfer** lessons and rentals in Weggis are available through the Hotel Hertenstein, ☎ 041/390–14–44.

Vitznau

⑱ 4 km (2½ mi) southeast of Weggis; 26 km (16 mi) southeast of Luzern.

Any tour of the Vierwaldstättersee—by car or by boat—should include Vitznau, a tiny waterfront resort that competes with Weggis in balmy weather, although its main claim to fame is the palatial Park-Hotel, built in 1902.

En Route   From Vitznau, a boat tour will take you across the Vierwaldstättersee to **Beckenried,** from which a cable car leads up to **Klewenalp** (1,601 meters/5,250 feet), a small winter sports and summer resort in a wonderful position overlooking the lake.

If you're driving, follow the north shore until the boat rejoins it at **Gersau,** a tiny lake resort that from 1332 to 1798 was an independent republic—the world's smallest. From Gersau the boat snakes around the sharp peninsula of the Seelisberg; the 1980 completion of a 9¼-kilometer (6-mile) tunnel across the peninsula, south of the lake, opened the way for even swifter north–south travel between Luzern and points north and the St. Gotthard and points south.

Lodging

$$$$ ⊞ **Park.** This isolated but lavish retreat dominates the tiny lakefront
★   village of Vitznau like the castle of a feudal lord. Constructed in 1902 and enlarged in 1985 with an identical new wing painstakingly reproduced to the last detail, it's a vaulted and beamed Edwardian dream in impeccable modern form. Even the corridors are grand, with massive oak triple doors and Persian runners stretching over quarry tile. Rooms are varied but all have timeless pastels, and lakefront rooms command dreamy Alpine views. The back rooms overlook the slopes of the Rigi, dotted with grazing cows. Thoroughly self-contained, with a private landing dock that occasionally highjacks the public steamers, the Park offers a magnificent lakefront lawn and exceptional facilities. ⊠ *CH-6354,* ☎ *041/397–01–00,* ⍯ *041/397–01–10. 180 beds. 2 restaurants, café, indoor and outdoor pools, golf, tennis, beach, dock, waterskiing, playground. AE, DC, MC, V. Closed Nov.–Mar.*

$$ ⊞ **Rigi.** A modest alternative to the village castle and less than half the price, this solid lodging has modernized interiors and a welcoming stübli atmosphere in its public areas. The corner rooms have balconies with a lake view. The Rigibahn roars by during business hours only. The hotel is one block from the boat landing. Both the restaurant and the less formal stübli serve good, simple fish dishes, and there's a pleasant garden terrace. ⊠ *CH-6354,* ☎ *041/397–21–21,* ⍯ *041/397–18–25. 72 beds. Restaurant, stübli. AE, DC, MC, V.*

$ ⊞ **Schiff.** Commanding much the same view as the Park (though the
★   Park itself clouds some of its lakefront beauty), this plain old roadhouse perches on the hill across the street and offers cheap, no-bath rooms in '50s summer-cottage styles. The vine-trellised terrace restaurant, wide open to the water and mountain skyline, serves inexpensive lake-fish dishes. Private bathrooms will be added "someday," although not too soon, we hope; it's cozy as is. ⊠ *CH-6354,* ☎ *041/397–13–57. 12 beds. Restaurant. MC, V. Closed Oct. and Nov.*

Outdoor Activities and Sports

Motorboats and paddleboats are for rent through **Anker Travel** (☎ 041/397–17–07). Rent bikes through the Hotel Vierwaldstättersee (☎ 041/397–22–22). For tennis, the **Park-Hotel** (☎ 041/397–01–01) rents court time, as do the **Seehotel Vitznauerhof** (☎ 041/397–13–15) and **Camping Vitznau** (☎ 041/397–12–80). You can **swim** in the bay, which is naturally warmer than Luzern's lido.

En Route   At the south end of the Vierwaldstättersee, the narrow, majestic **Urnersee** is the wildest and most beautiful leg of the lake. Along its shores lie some of the most historic—or, at least, romantic—landmarks in the region. The **Schillerstein** (on the right as you cruise past the peninsula) is a natural rock obelisk extending nearly 26 meters (85 feet) up out of the lake; it bears the simple dedication: "To the author of *Wilhelm Tell*, Friedrich von Schiller. 1859."

Rütli Meadow

★ ⑲ *15 km (10 mi) north of Altdorf on Urnersee; 25 km (15 mi) southeast of Luzern.*

Perhaps the most historically significant site in Central Switzerland, the Rütli Meadow, just above the Rütli dock, is where the Confederates of Schwyz, Unterwald, and Uri are said to have met to renew the 1291 Oath of Eternal Alliance. **Tellsplatte,** on the eastern side of the lake, at the foot of the Axen mountain, is the rocky ledge onto which Tell, the rebellious archer, leapt to escape from Gessler's boat, pushing the boat back into the stormy waves as he jumped. There is a small chapel here, built around 1500 and restored in 1881; it contains four frescoes of the Tell legend, painted at the time of restoration.

Another monumental event took place here centuries later: Amid threats of a 1940 German invasion, General Guisan, Swiss Army Commander-in-Chief, summoned hundreds of officers to the meadow to reaffirm their commitment to the Swiss Confederation in a secret, stirring ceremony.

Altdorf

⑳ *20 km (12 mi) south of Rütli Meadow; 35 km (22 mi) southeast of Luzern.*

Schiller's play *Wilhelm Tell* combines and dramatizes chronicles of the period and sums up the tale for the Swiss, who perform his play religiously in venues all over the country—including the town of Altdorf, just up the road from the Rütli Meadow. Leave the steamer at Flüelen, the farthest point of the boat ride around the lake, and connect by postbus to Altdorf, the capital of the canton Uri and, by popular if not scholarly consensus, the setting for Tell's famous apple-shooting scene. There is a much-reproduced **Tell monument** in the village center, showing a proud father with crossbow on one shoulder, the other hand grasping his son's hand; it was sculpted by Richard Kissling in 1895.

Outdoor Activities and Sports

Rent bikes at the train station in **Altdorf** (☎ 041/870–10–08). Mountain bikes can be rented in Altdorf through **Mototreff** (☎ 041/870–97–37). You can rent pedal boats and motorboats in Flüelen at **Herr F. Kaufmann** (☎ 041/870–15–75).

Bürglen

㉑ *3 km (1¾ mi) southeast of Altdorf; 40 km (25 mi) southeast of Luzern.*

Tell was supposedly from the tiny town of **Bürglen,** just up the road from Altdorf; there's a museum devoted to him there with documents and art on the subject. ☎ *041/870–41–55. ⊙ June–Oct., daily 10–11:30 and 2–5; July and Aug., daily 10–5.*

Andermatt

㉒ *25 km (15 mi) south of Bürglen (exit the N2 expressway at Göschenen); 67 km (41 mi) southeast of Luzern.*

Andermatt serves as a crossroads for traffic arriving from the Furka Pass, the Oberalp Pass, and the St. Gotthard Pass. It also boasts exceptional skiing and fine winter resort facilities; from the top of **Gemsstock,** approached by cable car from the town, it is said you can see 600 Alpine peaks. Nonetheless, it's a relaxing little backwater with lovely valley hiking and, thanks to its level terrain, fine cross-country skiing. Mountain biking is popular here; to rent bikes, call **Christen Sport** (☎ 041/887–72–51).

Skiing

A high, sheltered plateau at the crossroads of three passes—the Gotthard, the Furka, and the Oberalp—Andermatt (1,449 meters/4,750 feet), is easily accessible from all directions. It offers three cable cars, 10 lifts, 55 kilometers (34 miles) of downhill runs, and 20 kilometers (12 miles) of cross-country trails.

OFF THE BEATEN PATH	**ST. GOTTHARD PASS** – This ancient passage started as a narrow path during the 13th century; a railway was not completed until 1882, and the new tunnel was finished in 1980. In these bleak and icy heights, the watershed source of the Rhine and the Rhône, you may spot eerie, partially concealed military facilities dug deep into the rock and see soldiers drilling in the snow: It's the Swiss Army, refining its Alpine defense skills.

Schwyz

㉓ *30 km (20 mi) north of Andermatt (via highway 8 or the N2 expressway—exit just past Altdorf); 44 km (27 mi) east of Luzern.*

This historic town is the capital of the Schwyz canton, root of the name Switzerland, and source of the nation's flag. Switzerland's most precious archives are stored here as well. Traces of an independent settlement at Schwyz have been found from as far back as the Bronze Age (2500–800 BC), but it was its inhabitants' aid in the 1291 Oath of Allegiance that put Schwyz on the map. You can see the beautifully scripted and sealed original document as well as battle flags and paintings of the period in Schwyz's **Bundesbrief-Archiv** (Archives of the Federal Charters), an impressively simple concrete building completed in 1936. ⊠ *Bahnhofstrasse 20,* ☎ *041/819–20–64.* ▨ *Free.* ☉ *Daily 9:30–11:30 and 2–5.*

Schwyz has several notable Baroque churches and a large number of fine old patrician homes dating from the 17th and 18th centuries, not least being the **Ital-Redinghaus,** with its magnificent interior, antique stoves, and fine stained glass. A visit to this grand house includes a peek inside the neighboring **Bethlehemhaus,** the oldest wooden house in Switzerland, dating from 1287. ⊠ *Rickenbachstrasse 24,* ☎ *041/811–45–05.* ▨ *2 SF.* ☉ *May–Oct., Tues.–Fri. 2–5, weekends 10–noon.*

Curiously, many of Schwyz's splendid houses owe their origin to the battlefield. The men of Schwyz had a reputation as fine soldiers and were in demand in other countries as mercenaries during the 16th and 17th centuries. They built many of the houses you can see today with their military pay.

Skiing

At 519 meters (1,700 feet), Schwyz has three cable cars, 11 lifts, and 32 kilometers (20 miles) of downhill trails.

En Route   From Schwyz, follow the local road past picturesque alpine pastures to historic Einsiedeln.

Einsiedeln

㉔ *27 km (18 mi) northeast of Schwyz; 69 km (43 mi) northeast of Luzern.*

A minor summer and winter resort, Einsiedeln has been a center for pilgrimage since AD 946 and is also the home of the **Black Madonna,** still on display after more than a thousand years. The Benedictine monastery was founded in Charlemagne's time—the 9th century—when Meinrad, a Hohenzollern count and monk, chose the remote site to pursue his devotions in solitude. The abbess of Zürich gave him an image of the Virgin Mary, for which he built a little chapel, and Meinrad lived in peace, fed—the story goes—by two ravens who brought him supplies. When he was murdered by brigands seeking treasure, the ravens followed the thieves to Zürich and shrieked over their heads until they were arrested. A monastery was built over Meinrad's grave. When it was completed the Bishop of Konstanz was invited to consecrate it, but as he began the ceremony a voice was heard crying out in the chapel three times, "Brother, desist: God himself has consecrated this building." A papal bull acknowledged the miracle and promised a special indulgence to pilgrims.

Through the ages the monastery of Einsiedeln has been destroyed many times by fire, but always the Black Madonna has been saved. When Napoléon's armies plundered the church, hoping to carry off the sacred image, it had already been taken to the Tirol in Austria for safekeeping. Today the Black Madonna is housed in a black marble chapel just inside the west entrance to the church. When seen from a distance its color appears to be a rich bronze, not black, and there is something quaint and gentle about the figure despite its jeweled splendor. The present structure of the abbey was built by Caspar Moosbrugger in 1735 and decorated by the famous brothers Egid Quirid and Cosmos Damian Asam; it is one of the finest late-Baroque churches of its kind, the impressive simplicity and grace of the exterior contrasting vividly with the exuberance of its ornate interior. In front of the church, a grand square surrounds a golden statue of the Virgin Mary with a large gilded crown. Around the base, water trickles from 14 spouts, and pilgrims, to be sure of good luck, traditionally drink from each one in turn.

Einsiedeln remains a center for religious pomp and ceremony and celebrates a Festival of the Miraculous Dedication every September 14. Every five years some 700 citizens, coached by the monks, perform *Das Grosse Welttheater* (*The Great World Theater*) before the abbey church. A religious drama on life and the problems of humankind, it was first performed before the Court of Spain in 1685. The next performance of this historic pageant takes place in summer 1998.

Einsiedeln is just off the autobahn that connects Zürich with Eastern Switzerland. You can take this autobahn to return to Luzern, but a more interesting route is back over the hills via Hütten to Zug, famous for its old town.

Outdoor Activities and Sports
At a mere 901 meters (2,953 feet), Einsiedeln has four lifts, 2½ kilometers (1½ miles) of downhill **ski** runs, 96 kilometers (60 miles) of cross-country trails, and ski-hiking trails. Due to its low elevation, conditions here are highly variable.

For **bicycle** rentals, call the train station (☎ 055/412–21–58). There are four outdoor tennis courts at **Grotzenmühle** (☎ 055/412–44–88).

Zug

❷⑤ *27 km (17 mi) from Einsiedeln; 28 km (18 mi) northeast of Luzern (via N14 and N4).*

On arriving at the train station in Zug, you may be surprised to find that it is bustling, modern, and full of multinational corporations. Its contemporary life unfurls around the remnants of ancient ramparts, and its lakefront neighborhood seems frozen in another century. From the train station area on Alpenstrasse you can head straight for the waterfront of the **Zugersee** (Lake Zug). This landscaped promenade and park offers fine views of Pilatus, Rigi, and the Bernese Alps—including the Eiger, the Mönch, and the Jungfrau.

Zug's old town is dominated by the **Rathaus,** which was completed during the early 16th century. Inside, there are exhibits of gold and silver work as well as embroideries, wood carvings, stained glass, and the flag Wolfgang Kolin held until he perished in the battle of Arbedo (1422), when 3,000 Swiss tried valiantly to hold off 24,000 Milanese soldiers. Unfortunately, you'll see these fine furnishings only if you dine in the **Rathauskeller,** one of the best—but most expensive—restaurants in Central Switzerland (☞ Dining and Lodging, *below*).

By passing through a gate under the Zytturm (Clock Tower), you'll come upon **Kolinplatz,** dedicated to Wolfgang Kolin and dominated by a fountain in his image.

Rising high above town are the delicate spires of the **Kirche St. Oswald** (Church of St. Oswald), built during the 15th and 16th centuries.

Burg, a former Hapsburg residence, has a half-timber exterior so heavily restored it looks like a Disney set for Snow White. It now houses the **Burg-Museum** of archaeology, art, and history from Zug. ⊠ *Kirchenstrasse 11,* ☎ *041/728-32-97.* ⊿ *5 SF, free Sun.* ⊙ *Tues.–Fri. 2–5, weekends 10–noon and 2–5.*

NEED A BREAK?	While waiting for your return train, stop at the patisserie-café **Meier** (⊠ Alpenstrasse 14, ☎ 041/711-10-49) for coffee and a slice of the famous Zug *Kirschtorte* (cherry cake)—though the only cherry you'll find is a heavily alcoholic essence that soaks the delicate yellow cake and butter cream.

Beyond the four towers and ruins of Zug's old city walls lies the **modern city.** The most atmospheric streets of Zug are the **Ober-Altstadt** and the **Unter-Altstadt,** tight lanes closed in on each side by narrow, shuttered 16th-century town houses now in the throes of early gentrification: The storefronts are full of arts and crafts, ceramics, jewelry, and a few trendy baby clothes and toys.

Dining and Lodging

$$$$ ✕ **Rathauskeller.** This culinary landmark, given all the more ballast by its location in one of Zug's historic landmarks, matches its imposing decor with serious cuisine du marché. Upstairs, though, you're surrounded by a museumlike collection of medieval regional treasures, and you're served nothing but cuisine from the cutting edge, with an emphasis on good fish (scallops marinated in olive oil and lemon juice), meats (tender rabbit filet with wild mushroom risotto), and a minimum of visual fuss. Downstairs, in the traditional, dark little stübli—and even at a handful of tables on the cobblestones outside—you can order simpler, cheaper dishes from the same kitchen. ⊠ *Oberaltstadt 1,* ☎ *041/ 711–00–58. AE, V. Closed Sun. and Mon.*

$–$$ ✕ **Aklin.** This 500-year-old Alstadt landmark offers *Grossmutters Küche* (Grandmother's cooking)—brains, Kalbskopf, *Siedfleisch* (boiled beef), and lake fish—on candlelit wooden tables by a ceramic-tile stove in the upstairs restaurant, or in the atmospheric, casual bistro downstairs. ⊠ *Off Kolinplatz,* ☎ *041/711–18–66. AE, DC, MC, V. Closed Sun.*

$$–$$$ ⊞ **Ochsen.** While the notch-gable facade has been preserved at this 16th-century landmark on the imposing Kolinplatz of Zug's old town, the interior is strictly upscale-chain. Hints of architectural detail have been sanded away, and the buffed wood of the restaurant looks more Scandi-sleek teak now than Swiss; it's hard to believe that Goethe was once a guest here. The rooms are high-tech chic; the best are at the far back (above a tiny courtyard) and—of course—looking over the Kolinplatz fountain, toward the lake. The restaurant deserves its good reputation for fine local dishes impeccably served: meats, Rösti, and its specialty, lake fish. ⊠ *Kolinplatz 11, CH-6301,* ☎ *041/711–32–32,* FAX *041/711–30–32. Restaurant. AE, DC, MC, V.*

Outdoor Activities and Sports

At 436 meters (1,430 feet), Zug has 9 kilometers (6 miles) of cross-country **ski** trails, 17 kilometers (11 miles) of ski-hiking trails, and curling.

You can rent bicycles from the train station (☎ 041/711–39–88). For windsurfing, telephone TNC Nautik-Sport (☎ 041/711–88–26).

LUZERN AND CENTRAL SWITZERLAND A TO Z

Arriving and Departing

By Car

It's easy to reach Luzern from Zürich by road, approaching from national expressway N3 south, connecting to N4 via the secondary E41, in the direction of Zug, and continuing on N4 to the city. A convenient all-expressway connection between the two cities won't be open before the end of the decade. Approaching from the southern, St. Gotthard Pass route, or after cutting through the Furka Pass by rail ferry, you descend below Andermatt to Altdorf, where a view-stifling tunnel sweeps you through to the shores of the lake. If you're heading for resorts on the north shore, leave the expressway at Flüelen and follow the scenic secondary route. From Basel in the northwest, it's a clean sweep by N2 to Luzern.

By Plane

The nearest international airport is **Kloten** in **Zürich,** approximately 54 kilometers (33 miles) from Luzern. **Swissair** flies in most often from the United States and the United Kingdom.

By Train

Luzern functions as a rail crossroads, with express trains connecting hourly from Zürich (49 minutes) and every two hours from Geneva (3½–4 hours, with a change at Bern). Trains enter from the south via the St. Gotthard Pass (from the Ticino) and the Furka Pass (from the Valais). For rail information, call the station (☎ 041/157–33–33).

Getting Around

By Boat

It would be a shame to see this historic region only from the shore; some of its most impressive landscapes are framed along the waterfront, as seen from the decks of one of the cruise ships that ply the lake. Rides on these are included in a Swiss Pass or a Swiss Boat Pass. Individual tickets can be purchased at the departure docks near the train station (☎ 041/367–67–67). Any combination of transportation can be arranged, such as a leisurely cruise from Luzern to Flüelen at the lake's southernmost point (about 3½ hours); a return by train, via the Arth–Goldau line, takes little more than an hour.

By Bus

The PTT postbus network carries travelers faithfully, if slowly, to the farthest corners of the region. It also climbs the St. Gotthard and the Furka passes. For schedules and prices, check at the post office nearest your home base or pick up a copy of the *Vierwaldstättersee Fahrplan,* a booklet that covers cruise ships and private railways as well (50 rappen).

By Car

Although Mt. Rigi and Mt. Pilatus are not accessible by car, nearly everything else in this region is. The descent from Andermatt past the Devil's Bridge, which once carried medieval pilgrims from the St. Gotthard and drew thrill-seekers during the 19th century, now exemplifies awe-inspiring Swiss mountain engineering: From Göschenen, at 1,106 meters (3,627 feet), to the waterfront, it's a full four-lane expressway.

By Train

The Swiss national rail system is enhanced here by a few private lines (to Engelberg, Pilatus, the Rigi Kulm) that make it possible to get to most sights. If you don't have a Swiss Pass, there's a Central Switzerland regional pass, called the **Tell-Pass,** available for 15 or 7 days. The 15-day pass grants you 5 days' unlimited free travel on main routes, 10 days at half fare. The 7-day pass gives you 2 days free, 5 at half fare. The ticket can be bought at rail or boat ticket offices, on a cruise boat, from travel agencies, or from the tourist office. At press time, the 15-day pass cost 170 SF second class, 190 SF first class; the 7-day pass cost 124 SF second class, 134 SF first class. Children under six travel free, and children under 16 accompanied by their parents can travel free if you have arranged for a Family Card from your stateside travel agent before leaving the United States; without it they pay half price. Note: Plan your itinerary carefully to take full advantage of all discount rates, and before you buy a regional pass, add up your excursions à la carte. Remember that many routes always charge half price. All boat trips and the private excursions to Rigi and Pilatus are free to holders of regional passes—but getting to the starting point may cost you half price. If you plan to cover a lot of ground, however, you may save considerably. Choose your free days in advance: You must confirm them *all* with the first inspector who checks your pass.

Guided Tours

Walking

The **Luzern tourist office** offers a guided walking tour of Luzern. They last about two hours and cost 15 SF, including a drink.

Contacts and Resources

Emergencies

Police (☎ 117). **Medical, dental, and pharmacy referral** (☎ 111). **Auto breakdown:** Touring Club of Switzerland (☎ 140), Swiss Automobile Club (☎ 041/210–01–55).

Guided Tours

The **Schiffahrtsgesellschaft des Vierwaldstättersees** (✉ Werftestrasse 5, CH-6002, ☎ 041/367–67–67) offers historic and Alpine theme cruises with commentary.

The **Wilhelm Tell Express,** a cooperative effort of Swiss federal railroads and lake steamers, operates daily from May through October, carrying passengers by steamship and rail to Lugano. The journey, without stopovers, takes six hours. For information contact the Luzern tourist office.

Visitor Information

The principal tourist office for the whole of Central Switzerland, including the lake region, is the **Zentralschweiz Tourismus** (⊠ Alpenstrasse 1, CH-6002, Luzern, ☎ 041/410–18–91, 🅵🅰🆇 041/410–72-60). The main tourist office for the city of **Luzern** is located near the Bahnhof (⊠ Frankenstrasse 1, ☎ 041/410–71–71). There's also an accommodations service. A new tourist office has opened at Schweizerhofquai 2.

Additional local tourist offices: **Altdorf** (☎ 041/870–28–88). **Andermatt** (☎ 041/887–14–54). **Engelberg** (☎ 041/637–11–61). **Schwyz** (☎ 041/819–19–19). **Stans** (☎ 041/61–88–33), and **Weggis** (☎ 041/390–11–55).

7 Basel

At the juncture of France and Germany, German-speaking Basel is a cultural capital with a sense of fun. Cultivated and yet down-home, it has 28 museums, Switzerland's oldest university, and some of the most diverse shopping in the country. All the same, beer and sausages are the snack of choice, and the annual Carnival is observed with a boisterousness that's unparalleled in other Swiss towns.

THOUGH IT LACKS THE GILT AND GLITTER of Zürich and the Latin grace of Geneva, in many ways quiet, genteel Basel (Bâle in French) is the most sophisticated of Swiss cities. At the frontier between Europe's two most assertive personalities, France and Germany, and tapped directly into the artery of the Rhine (Rhein in German), it has flourished on the lifeblood of two cultures and grown surprisingly urbane, cosmopolitan, worldly-wise. It is also delightfully eccentric, its imagination as well as its cultural grounding fed by centuries of intellectual input: Basel has been host to Switzerland's oldest university (1460) and patron to some of the country's—and the world's—finest minds. A northern center of humanist thought and art, it nurtured the painters Konrad Witz and Hans Holbein the Younger as well as the great Dutch scholar Erasmus. And it was Basel's visionary Lord Mayor Johann Rudolf Wettstein who, at the end of the Thirty Years' War, negotiated Switzerland's groundbreaking—and lasting—neutrality.

Every day 27,500 French and German commuters cross into Basel, and 10 million tonnes (11 million tons) of cargo pass through its ports. Banking activity here is surpassed only by that in Zürich and Geneva, and every month representatives of the world's leading central banks meet in secret in the city center at the Bank for International Settlements, the world's central bank clearinghouse. Yet Basel's population hovers around a modest 200,000, and its urban center lies gracefully along the Rhine, no building so tall as to block another's view of its cathedral's twin spires. Two blocks from the heart of the thriving shopping district you can walk 17th-century residential streets cloaked in perfect, other-worldly silence.

The disproportionate number of museums per capita reflects much on the Baslers' priorities: The city has 28, including the world-class Kunstmuseum (Museum of Fine Arts) and the new Jean Tinguely Museum. As high culture breeds good taste, Basel has some of the most varied, personal, even quirky shopping in Switzerland; antique bookshops, calligraphers, and artisans do business next to sophisticated designer shops and famous jewelers. But you can still get a beer and a sausage here: Baslers speak almost exclusively German, or their own local version of Schwyzerdütsch, called Baseldütsch. On Freie Strasse, the main shopping street, dense crowds of shoppers stand outside a local butcher's, holding bare *Wienerli* (hot dogs) and dipping the pink tips into thick gold mustard. They also indulge in *Kaffe und Kuchen*—the late-afternoon coffee break Germans live for—but Baslers do it differently. Instead of the large slices of creamy cake their neighbors favor, they select tiny sweet gems—two or three to a saucer, perhaps, but petite nonetheless—and may opt for a delicate China tea.

The Celts were the first to settle here, some 2,000 years ago, on the site of the Münster (cathedral). During the 1st century BC the Romans established a town at Augst, then called Colonia Augusta Raurica; the ruins and the theater can be visited today, 10 minutes by car outside town. By the 3rd century, the Romans had taken the present cathedral site in Basel proper, naming the town Basilia (royal stronghold). Germanic invaders banished them in 401, and it was not until Henry II, the Holy Roman emperor, took Basel under his wing during the 11th century that stability returned. His image and that of his wife, Kunegunde, adorn the cathedral and the Rathaus (Town Hall). Henry built the original cathedral—on the site of a church destroyed by a raiding band of Hungarian horsemen in 916—and established Basel as one of the centers of his court. In 1006 the bishop of Basel was made ruler of the town, and throughout the Middle Ages these prince-bishops gained and exerted enormous temporal, as well as spiritual, power. Today, Basel's coat of arms, with its black bishop's staff, is a potent reminder of the age of the cathedral's bishop-lords.

Yet Basel is first and foremost a Renaissance city in the literal sense of the word: a city of intellectual and artistic rebirth, its flourishing river commerce bringing with it the flow of ideas. In 1431 the Council of Basel, an ecumenical conference on church reform, was convened here, bringing in—over a period of 17 years—the great sacred and secular princes of the age. One of them, who later became Pope Pius II, granted permission for the founding of the university and established Basel as the cultural capital it remains today.

All this culture hasn't made Basel stuffy, however. The Baslers' pre-Lenten celebration of Fasnacht (Mardi Gras, or Carnival) turns the city on its ear, and beginning at 4 AM with a burst of drums and fifes, the streets are filled with grotesquely costumed revelers bearing huge homemade lanterns lampooning local politicians. You'll see masks, drums, and fifes displayed and sold everywhere, all year, and hear strains of fife-and-drum marches wafting from the guild houses' upper windows; they're rehearsing for Fasnacht. Even in Basel's most sedate and cultivated corners, there always seems to be a hint of Fasnacht, age-old and unpredictable.

Pleasures and Pastimes

Dining
When the Alemanni hordes sent the Romans packing, they brought their Germanic cuisine as well; despite persistent bombardment from international cultures, for the most part the German style stuck. When a Basler lets down his hair and eats home-style, it's inevitably sausage, schnitzel, *Spätzle* (tiny flour dumplings), and beer. The city is full of comfortable haunts lined with carved wood and thick with the mingled odors of cooking meat and cigar smoke.

Yet the proximity of the Rhine has left its *riverains* (riverside dwellers) with a taste for river fish, too, and if Basel could claim a regional specialty it would be salmon. Salmon made its way from the ocean to the Rhine during the Ice Age and became such a commonplace in Basel's golden age that some cooks refused to prepare it more than twice a week. Basel's better restaurants often feature the meaty pink fish (though it's likely imported, as the Rhine has suffered from pollution), served in a white-wine marinade with fried onions on top *nach Basler-Art* (in the Basel style). Try it with a bottle of the fruity local Riesling-Sylvaner.

Of course, Basel can't help but show the sophistication of generations of international and university influence, and has a surprising number of innovative French and international restaurants—some of them world-class (and priced accordingly). In fact, dining in Basel is a pricey venture, whether your sausage is stuffed with lobster and truffles or merely pork scraps. If you want to keep expenses down, stick to beer-hall fare, or watch posted menus for lunch specials.

Fasnacht
Originating in the Middle Ages, Fasnacht, Switzerland's best-known Carnival, is a must-see if Basel's on your springtime travel itinerary. Beginning at 4 AM the Monday morning before Ash Wednesday (Shrove Monday), the "Morgenstraich" opens the event with a blast of drums and fifes in the freezing darkness. To mark the beginning of Lent, young and old participants wearing colorful masks and costumes march through Basel's streets for two hours, after which the hungry revelers

pour into early opened restaurants to eat traditional Fasnact fare: onion pie and flour soup.

Museums

Home to the world's oldest public art collection, the Kunstmuseum (Museum of Fine Arts) is as impressive on the inside as its grand exterior heralds; alone it would qualify Basel as a city with great museums. But that's only the beginning: The city's 27 other museums cover such topics as design, ethnography, folklife, paper and printing, and pharmaceutical history.

EXPLORING BASEL

The Rhine divides the city of Basel into two distinct sections: The whole of the old town lies in Grossbasel (Greater Basel), the commercial, cultural, and intellectual center. The opposite, east, bank is Kleinbasel (Little Basel), a tiny Swiss enclave on the "German" side of the Rhine and the industrial quarter of the city. Unless you are visiting on business and meeting at the convention center east of the river, your time on the right bank will probably be limited to a waterfront stroll and a good night's sleep, as some hotels are located here.

Great Itineraries

IF YOU HAVE 1 OR 2 DAYS

Stroll through Basel's old town, making sure to stop in at its world-class art museum. Take in the city's medieval gates Spalentor and St. Alban-tor. Don't miss the Münster and the sweeping views from the church's Rhine terrace, the Pfalz. Beneath the Münster, take one of the little ferries across to the Kleinbasel side for a Rhine-side afternoon stroll along the Oberer Rheinweg.

On the following day, take in some of the city's smaller museums, including the Kirschgarten House, the Historical Museum, the Museum of Architecture, the Museum for Contemporary Art, the Pharmaceutical Museum, and the world-renowned Zoo. See some of the city's ancient ramparts (Mühlegraben), and cross the river to see the new Jean Tinguely Museum, honoring Switzerland's best-known 20th-century sculptor.

IF YOU HAVE 3 TO 5 DAYS

Given the luxury of several days, make sure to take a boat trip to the Roman ruins of Augusta Raurica east of Basel. Take a driving tour of the small villages scattered south of Basel among the gently rolling hills of the Jura: Balsthal, Holderbank, Oberer Hauenstein, Langenbruck, and Liestal.

The Old Town

Standing in the middle of the Marktplatz or even watching river traffic from the Mittlere Rheinbrücke, it's easy to envision the Basel of centuries ago. Situated on a bend of the Rhine, Basel's old town is full of majestic Gothic spires and side streets that have remained largely unchanged since the 1600s. Still, much of the delicately preserved architecture of the old town incorporates impressive, state-of-the-art museums and miles of pedestrian shopping.

A Good Walk

Numbers in the text correspond to numbers in the margin and on the Basel exploring map.

Six bridges link the two halves of the city, the most historic and picturesque being the **Mittlere Rheinbrücke** ① (Middle Rhine Bridge).

160

Blaues und Weisses
Haus, **4**

Drei Könige Hotel, **17**

Haus zum
Kirschgarten, **11**

Historisches
Museum, **12**

Kunsthalle, **10**

Kunstmuseum, **9**

Lällekönig, **2**

Leonhardskirche, **13**

Martinskirche, **3**

Mittlere
Rheinbrücke, **1**

Münster, **6**

Museum für
Gegenwartskunst, **8**

Naturhistorisches
Museum, **5**

Peterskirche, **14**

Pharmazie-Historisches
Museum, **15**

Rathaus, **16**

St. Alban-Tor, **7**

Tinguely Museum, **18**

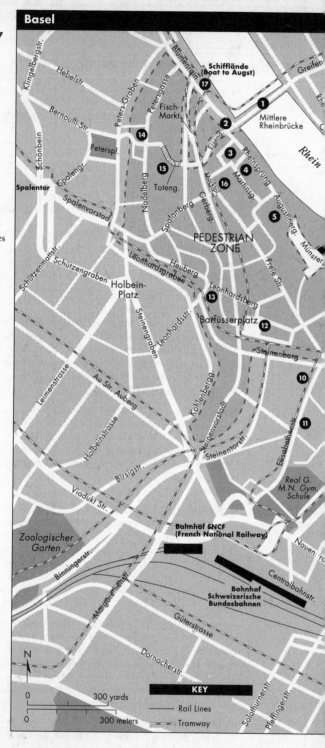

Basel

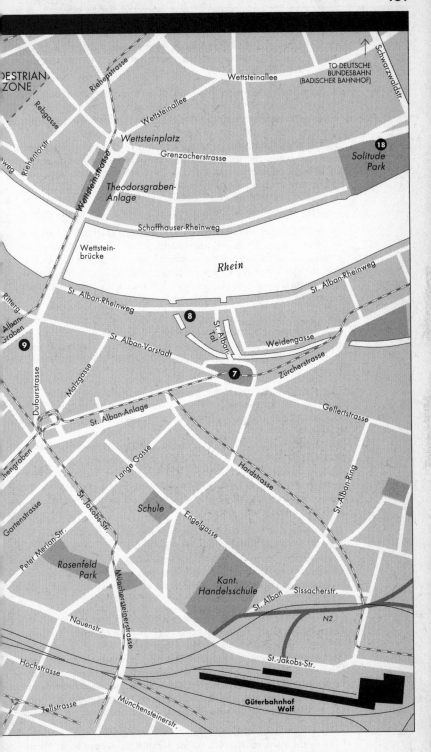

PEDESTRIAN ZONE

Riehenstrasse

Rebgasse

Wettsteinallee

TO DEUTSCHE
BUNDESBAHN
(BADISCHER BAHNHOF)

Schwarzwaldstr.

Riehentorstr.

Wettsteinallee

Wettsteinstrasse

Wettsteinplatz

Grenzacherstrasse

18

Solitude
Park

Theodorsgraben-
Anlage

Schaffhauser-Rheinweg

Wettstein-
brücke

Rhein

St. Alban-Rheinweg

St. Alban-Rheinweg

Ritterg.

8

St. Alban-
Graben

9

St. Alban-Vorstadt

St. Alban-
Tal

Weidengasse

Zürcherstrasse

Dufourstrasse

Malzgasse

7

St. Alban-Anlage

Gellertstrasse

...hengraben

Lange Gasse

Hardstrasse

St.-Alban-Ring

Gartenstrasse

St. Jakobs-Str.

Schule

Engelgasse

Peter Merian-Str.

Rosenfeld
Park

Münchensteinerstrasse

Kant.
Handelsschule

St. Alban

Sissacherstr.

Nauenstr.

N2

Hochstrasse

St.-Jakobs-Str.

Tellstrasse

Münchensteinerstr.

**Güterbahnhof
Wolf**

Start at its Grossbasel end, by the tourist office. On the corner of what is now a chain restaurant (Churrasco) at Schifflände you can see a facsimile of the infamous **Lällekönig** ②, a 15th-century gargoyle of a king mechanized by clockworks to stick out his tongue and roll his eyes at his rivals across the river.

Walking across the bridge, you'll encounter sweeping panoramic views of the riverfront. You'll also see Basel's peculiar little gondolalike ferry boats, attached to a high wire, angling silently from shore to shore, powered only by the swift current of the river. (You can ride one for 1 SF.) Across the Rhine, pause for a moment to take in one of Basel's many tongue-in-cheek artworks, a statue of Helvetia, the very symbol of Switzerland (the woman depicted on most Swiss coins), apparently taking a momentary break from standing on a pedestal all day long and now sitting atop the wall looking exhausted, her professional accoutrements leaning beside her: a spear, a shield . . . and a briefcase!

Across the Rhine, turn right before the Café Spitz and the Merian Hotel to follow Oberer Rheinweg, the peaceful, often sunny riverfront promenade. Follow the river upstream past a bank of shuttered houses, then take the first left on Riehentorstrasse to turn left again onto Rheingasse, a narrow old street that doubles back left toward the bridge. (At night, crowds of suspicious-looking youths clog this sidewalk.)

Back across the Mittlere Rheinbrücke in Grossbasel, turn left up a steep little alley called the **Rheinsprung,** banked with 15th- and 16th-century houses and curious shops. Turn right at Archivgässlein and you'll come to **Martinskirche** ③ (Church of St. Martin), the oldest parish church in town, dating from 1288.

Continue along Martinsgasse, on your left, to the elegant neighboring courtyards of the **Blaues und Weisses Haus** ④ (Blue House and White House), meeting place of kings. (There's another fine view of the houses from the Rheinsprung alley.) Just beyond, turn left and head for Augustinergasse. At No. 2 is the entrance to the **Naturhistorisches Museum** ⑤ (Natural History Museum), the **Schweizerisches Museum für Volkskunde** (Swiss Museum of Folklife), and the **Museum für Völkerkunde** (Museum of Ethnography). Under one roof, you will find one of the world's foremost natural history and prehistory collections, as well as European artifacts.

Augustinergasse leads onto the Münsterplatz, dominated by the striking red sandstone 12th-century **Münster** ⑥ (cathedral), burial place of Erasmus and Queen Anna of Hapsburg. When you've finished perusing the ancient interior, walk around to the church's riverside to a terrace called the Pfalz, which offers yet another scenic viewpoint of the river, the old town, and, on a clear day, the Black Forest.

From the Münsterplatz, head down Rittergasse, past its elegant villas and courtyards, to the first cross street. Ahead of you is St. Alban-Vorstadt, which leads to the **St. Alban-Tor** ⑦, one of the original 13th-century medieval city gates. St. Alban-Tal runs off St. Alban-Vorstadt and leads down to St. Alban-Rheinweg on the Rhine to the **Basler Papiermühle/Schweizer Papiermuseum und Museum für Schrift und Druck** (Basel Paper Mill/Swiss Museum of Paper, Writing and Printing) and **Museum für Gegenwartskunst** ⑧ (Museum of Contemporary Art).

Leaving the museum, turn left off St. Alban-Rheinweg onto St. Alban-Graben; here is the imposing **Kunstmuseum** ⑨ (Museum of Fine Arts), home of one of Europe's oldest public collections (owned by the city since 1661). Continue down St. Alban-Graben to the next cross street and veer right on Steinenberg, which leads to the **Kunsthalle** ⑩ (Basel Art Gallery), the first European gallery to show American abstract expressionists.

Just beyond the gallery in a comfortable open court on Theaterplatz, the whimsical Tinguely-Brunnen or **Fasnachts-Brunnen** (Carnival Fountain) is worth a peek. Rather than head down Steinenberg, you can turn left on Elisabethenstrasse to visit the **Haus zum Kirschgarten** ⑪ (Kirschgarten House), which houses the 18th- and 19th-century collections of the Basel Historical Museum. Then go on to the **Zoologischer Garten,** directly west of the SBB train station.

At the end of Steinenberg lies the bustling Barfüsserplatz, dominated by the Barfüsserkirche (Church of the Bare Feet), built during the mid-14th century. In 1894 this deconsecrated Franciscan church was converted into the **Historisches Museum** ⑫ (Historical Museum) containing medieval and Renaissance guild rooms and the Münster treasury.

From Barfüsserplatz, turn left up the narrow Leonhardsberg, then climb the stairs to the late-Gothic **Leonhardskirche** ⑬ (St. Leonard's Church). Continue along the street named Heuberg, the spine of one of the loveliest sections of old Basel. A network of small roads and alleys threads through the quarter, lined with graceful old houses from many periods: Gothic, Renaissance, Baroque, Biedermeier. Where Heuberg joins Spalenvorstadt stands the **Holbeinbrunnen** (Holbein Fountain), which depicts a group of dancing farmers—copied from a drawing by Holbein, hence the name.

The Spalenvorstadt leads to the 14th-century **Spalentor,** another of Basel's medieval city gates. Spalengraben leads from here past the buildings of the Universität (university), one of the six oldest universities in German-speaking Europe. Nearby Petersplatz is the site of the 13th-century **Peterskirche** ⑭ (St. Peter's Church) and the lively Saturday *Flohmarkt* (flea market).

Behind the Peterskirche lies an alley called Totengässlein, which leads past the **Pharmazie-Historisches Museum** ⑮ (Museum of Pharmaceutical History). Totengässlein leads down steep stairs into **Marktplatz,** the historic and modern heart of Basel. Towering over it all is the **Rathaus** ⑯ (Town Hall), a late-Gothic wonder decorated on its exterior by frescoes and a massive clock.

Leading off the south end of the Marktplatz, main shopping streets Freie Strasse and Gerbergasse are lined with international shops and department stores. The north end leads into Fischmarkt, site of the medieval city's fish market: Its tall fountain of the Virgin Mary, St. Peter, and John the Baptist dates from 1390. Marktgasse leads past the historic **Drei Könige Hotel** ⑰ (Three Kings).

TIMING

To see all the sights at a leisurely pace, give yourself at least 2½ hours. Allow more time if you want to see the museums in depth; the Kunstmuseum alone merits at least 45 minutes. Start your walk early so as to arrive just after 10 AM (opening time) at the three-museums-in-one building that houses the Naturhistorisches Museum (Natural History Museum), the Schweizerisches Museum für Volkskunde (Swiss Museum of Folklife), and the Museum für Völkerkunde (Museum of Ethnography).

Sights to See

Basler Papiermühle/Schweizer Papiermuseum und Museum für Schrift & Druck. Though its name sounds esoteric, the Basel Paper Mill and Swiss Museum of Paper, Writing, and Printing is surprisingly accessible, with a functioning waterwheel and live demonstrations of paper making, typesetting, and bookbinding. It's in a beautifully restored medieval mill house on the waterfront. ⊠ *St. Alban-Tal 35/37,* ☎ *061/272–96–52.* ⊠ *8 SF.* ☼ *Tues.–Sun. 2–5.*

④ Blaues und Weisses Haus (Blue House and White House). Built between 1762 and 1768 for two of the city's most successful silk merchants, these were the residences of the brothers Lukas and Jakob Sarasin. In 1777 the emperor Joseph II of Austria was a guest in the Blue House. But in 1814 even this was topped when Czar Alexander of Russia, Emperor Franz of Austria, and King Friedrich Wilhelm III of Prussia met in the Blue House for dinner. Compare the staggering, Bernini-esque excesses of the Blue House's ironwork gate to the simple majesty of it's neighbor's wooden counterpart. In addition, both rooflines, at first glance classically symmetrical, prove to be gracefully skewed to conform to old-town streets. ⊠ *Martinsgasse.*

⑰ Drei Könige (Three Kings) Hotel. Almost a millenium ago, in 1032 to be precise, Rodolphe II, king of Burgundy; Holy Roman emperor Konrad II; and the latter's son, the future Heinrich III, held a meeting here that joined Burgundy to the Holy Roman Empire. The statues on the facade depict the three wise men, and during the French Revolution the hotel's name was changed temporarily to the Three Moors. The young general Napoléon Bonaparte stayed here in 1797 (the suite has been named for him and redecorated in opulent Empire style), followed by other stellar guests: the kings of Italy, Princess Victoria, Charles Dickens, and Picasso. In 1887, the great Hungarian-born Jewish writer Theodor Herzl stayed here during the first Zionist Congress, which laid the groundwork for the founding of the state of Israel. A commemorative stamp showed him pondering the future from a Drei Könige balcony over the Rhine; 100 years later Chaim Herzog, then president of Israel, visited the balcony to relive the event. ⊠ *Blumenrain 8.*

Fasnacht-Brunnen. The so-called Carnival Fountain, created by Switzerland's internationally famous sculptor Jean Tinguely, is a witty, animated catchall commissioned by the city in 1977 to carry on Basel's tradition of fountain sculptures. It's composed of nine busy metallic figures, in Tinguely's trademark whimsical style. ⊠ *Theaterplatz.*

⑪ Haus zum Kirschgarten. The 18th-century Kirschgarten House was built as a palace for the young silk-ribbon manufacturer Johann Rudolf Burckhardt. Nowadays it contains the 18th- and 19th-century collections of the city's Historical Museum, displayed as furnishings in its period rooms. ⊠ *Elisabethenstrasse 27,* ☎ *061/271–13–33.* ⊠ *5 SF; 1st Sun. of month free.* ☼ *Daily 10–5.*

★ ⑫ Historisches Museum (Historical Museum). Housed within the **Barfüsserkirche** (Church of the Bare Feet), which was itself founded by the Franciscans in 1250 and built during the mid-14th century, the museum has an extensive collection of tapestries, wooden sculptures, coins, armor, and furniture, all displayed in a light and delicate interior. An underground gallery has been excavated to display fully reconstructed **medieval and Renaissance guild rooms,** complete with stained glass, ceramic stoves, and richly carved wood. Downstairs, in the back of the church, the **Münster treasury** contains priceless reliquaries in gold. Despite its status as one of the finest examples of Franciscan architecture north of the Alps, the Barfüsserkirche was deconsecrated in the 19th century and turned into a warehouse until it was rescued in 1894 and converted to the present-day museum. ⊠ *Barfüsserplatz, Steinenberg 4,* ☎ *061/271–05–05.* ⊠ *5 SF; 1st Sun. of month free.* ☼ *Wed.–Mon. 10–5.*

Holbeinbrunnen (Holbein Fountain). Created by an unknown 16th-century stonemason, this whimsical fountain depicts a group of dancing farmers—copied from a drawing by Holbein; above stands a bagpiper, copied from a Dürer engraving. The fountain itself is a copy, the original having been moved to the Historical Museum. ⊠ *Spalenvorstadt.*

★ ⑩ **Kunsthalle.** The first European gallery to show American abstract expressionists, the Kunsthalle (Basel Art Gallery) mounts some 10 exhibitions of contemporary art every year. Banners announce current exhibitions. ⊠ *Steinenberg 7,* ☎ *061/272–48–33.* ▢ *9 SF.* ☉ *Tues.–Sun. 11–5, Wed. 11–8:30.*

NEED A BREAK?	Have a drink or a light meal with the fashionable art crowd in the muraled restaurant of the Kunsthalle (Basel Art Gallery), open daily.

★ ⑨ **Kunstmuseum.** In a city known for its museums, the imposing Kunstmuseum (Museum of Fine Arts) is Basel's jewel. It was built in 1932–36 to house one of the oldest public collections of art in Europe, owned by the city since 1661, and includes the world's largest assemblage of paintings by Hans Holbein the Younger, an exceptional group of works by Konrad Witz, and, in fact, such a thorough gathering of the works of their contemporaries that the development of painting in the Upper Rhine is strikingly illuminated. You'll find a large representation of other Swiss artists as well, from the 18th-century Alpine landscapes of Caspar Wolf, through Klimt-like Hodler and sentimental Böcklin, to the contemporary works of Jean Tinguely, whose *Metaharmonie II,* an enormous mechanical musical sculpture, grinds into noisy action at 11 and 3:45 every day. The museum's other forte is its substantial international 20th-century collection, from Picasso and Braque to Jasper Johns. An entry ticket to this museum will also get you into the Museum für Gegenwartskunst (☞ *below*). ⊠ *St. Alban-Graben 16,* ☎ *061/271–08–28.* ▢ *7 SF (includes admission to Museum für Gegenwartskunst); 1st Sun. of month free.* ☉ *Tues.–Sun. 10–5.*

★ ② **Lällekönig.** When a famous gate tower on the Grossbasel side was destroyed, with it went the notorious Lällekönig, a 15th-century gargoyle of a king once mechanized by clockworks to stick out his tongue and roll his eyes at the Kleinbasel rivals across the river. Grossbasel didn't always have the last word, however: Every year during Kleinbasel's Vogel Gryff festival, a birdlike figure dances onto the bridge and gives the Lällekönig a flash of his backside. You can see a facsimile of the Lällekönig on the corner of what is now a chain restaurant (Churrasco) at Schifflände 1. The mechanized original still ticks away and sticks out his tongue in the nether regions of the Historical Museum. ⊠ *Schifflände.*

⑬ **Leonhardskirche.** Like virtually all of Basel's churches, this one was destroyed in the 1356 quake and rebuilt in the Gothic style, although its Romanesque crypt remains. Its High Gothic wooden pulpit is distinctive (the one in the Münster is stone). Free organ concerts are held on Friday evening. ⊠ *Heuberg.* ☉ *Daily 10–5.*

Marktplatz. Fruits, flowers, and vegetables are sold daily from open stands in this central square, Basel's historic and modern heart. In fall and winter passersby purchase bags of hot roasted chestnuts, the savory smoke of which fills the square.

③ **Martinskirche.** The acoustics inside make the Church of St. Martin popular for concerts, although it's rarely used for services anymore. The lower portions of the tower date from 1288, making it the oldest parish church in town; the greater part was rebuilt after the earthquake of 1356. The fountain outside, of a warrior dressed for battle, dates from the 16th century. ⊠ *Martinsgasse.*

★ ❶ **Mittlere Rheinbrücke.** The Middle Rhine Bridge is Basel's most historic and best-known. First built around 1225, the bridge made possible the development of an autonomous Kleinbasel and the consequent rivalry that grew between the two half-towns. It was replaced in stone at the turn of the 20th century, its 1478 chapel reconstructed at the center of the new bridge. ⊠ *Schifflände.*

NEED A   Stop at **Brauerei Fischerstube** (⊠ Rheingasse 45, ☎ 061/692–66–35),
BREAK?   on the Kleinbasel side of the Mittlere Rheinbrücke, for a pretzel and a
           home-brewed *Ueli Bier,* named for a Fasnacht clown.

★ ❻ **Münster.** On the site of a 9th-century Carolingian church and replacing a cathedral consecrated by Henry II in 1019, Basel's current cathedral was built during the 12th century in an impressive transitional style, late-Romanesque and pre-Gothic. The Münsterplatz square itself is one of the most satisfying architectural ensembles in Europe, its fine town houses set well back from the cathedral, the center filled with pollarded trees and, during the school year, with groups of obedient children on museum field trips.

Since much of the building was destroyed in the 1356 earthquake, the Romanesque and pre-Gothic influences diminished with the rebuilding of the church in Gothic style. But the facade of the north transept, called the **Galluspforte** (St. Gall's Door), dates back to the original structure and stands as one of the oldest carved portals in German-speaking Europe—and one of the loveliest. Slender, fine-tooled columns and rich, high-relief and freestanding sculpture frame the door. Each of the Evangelists is represented by his animated symbol: the angel for Matthew, an ox for Luke, a bulbous-chested eagle for John, a slim-limbed lion for Mark. Above, around the window, a wheel of fortune flings little men to their destiny.

Inside on the left, following a series of tombs of medieval noblemen, whose effigies recline with their feet resting on their loyal dogs, stands the strikingly simple **tomb of Erasmus.** Below the choir, you can see the delicately rendered death portraits on the double **tomb of Queen Anna of Hapsburg** and her young son Charles, from around 1285. The vaulted **crypt** dates from the original structure and still bears fragments of murals from 1202. ⊠ *Münsterplatz.* ☉ *Easter to mid-Oct., weekdays 10-6; Sat. 10–noon and 2-5; Sun. 1–5. Mid Oct. to Easter, Mon.–Sat. 10–noon and 2–4; Sun. 2–4.*

❽ **Museum für Gegenwartskunst.** Basel's Museum of Contemporary Art displays works of such artists as Frank Stella and Donald Judd from the 1970s and 1980s. The museum was a gift of Hoffman–La Roche heiress and arts patron Maja Sacher. ⊠ *St. Alban-Rheinweg 58,* ☎ *061/272–81–83.* ☑ *7 SF (includes admission to Kunstmuseum); 1st Sun. of month free.* ☉ *Tues.–Sun. 11–5.*

Museum für Völkerkunde (Museum of Ethnography). Home of one of the world's foremost ethnographic collections, including 32,000 non-European pieces collected from all over the world; the museum can display only a fraction of its holdings at any one time. Of particular interest are its Melanesian and Oceaniac pieces, a collection of Indonesian artifacts, and items from India and ancient America. This museum is housed within the same complex as the Naturhistorisches Museum (Natural History Museum) and the Schweizerisches Museum für Volkskunde (Swiss Museum of Folklife). ⊠ *Augustinergasse 2,* ☎

061/266–55–00. 🖼 *6 SF for all 3 museums; 1st Sun. of month free.* ⊙ *Nov.–Apr., Tues.–Sat. 10–noon and 2–5; Sun. 10-5; May–Oct., Tues.–Sun. 10–5.*

⑤ Naturhistorisches Museum. Located under the same monumental roof as the Schweizerisches Museum für Volkskunde (Swiss Museum of Folklife), and the Museum für Völkerkunde (Museum of Ethnography), the Natural History Museum outlines the history of the earth, indigenous minerals, mammals, mammoths, and insects. ⊠ *Augustinergasse 2,* ☎ *061/266–55–00.* 🖼 *6 SF for all 3 museums; 1st Sun. of month free.* ⊙ *Nov.–Apr., Tues.–Sat. 10–noon and 2–5; Sun. 10-5; May–Oct., Tues.–Sun. 10–5.*

⑭ Peterskirche. Living evidence of the late-Gothic heyday of Basel, the 13th-century St. Peter's Church sits in **Petersplatz**, a lovely park next to the Universität. Interesting 15th-century frescoes await you within. ⊠ *Petersplatz.*

⑮ Pharmazie-Historisches Museum. Though pharmaceuticals as the topic of an entire museum may not be everybody's medicine, in this instance unusual equals worthwhile (and one need only to glance up the Rhine's north bend to the headquarters of the pharmaceutical companies to be reminded of Basel's global prominence in that field to this day). The Museum of Pharmaceutical History is housed in Zum Vorderen Sessel, a home once frequented by Erasmus. ⊠ *Totengässlein 3,* ☎ *061/261–79–40.* 🖼 *Free.* ⊙ *Weekdays 9–noon and 2–5.*

★ **⑯ Rathaus.** This late-Gothic Town Hall, built to honor the city's entry into the Swiss Confederation in 1501, towers over the Marktplatz. (Only the middle portion actually dates from the 16th century; pseudo-Gothic work was added in 1900). A massive clock with figures of the Madonna, the emperor Henry II, and his wife, Kunegunde, adorns the center of the facade, while all around is a series of colorful frescoes, painted in 1608. Step into the courtyard, where the frescoes continue and one of several inscriptions declares: *Freiheit ist über Silber und Gold* (Freedom is greater than silver and gold)—not a sentiment likely to impress the Swiss banking community. ⊠ *Marktplatz.*

NEED A BREAK? | Choose a few jewel-like pastries and order loose-leaf–brewed tea in the carved-wood, clubby upstairs tearoom of the **Café Schiesser** (⊠ Marktplatz 19, ☎ 061-261-6077), open since 1870.

Rheinsprung. This steep little alley in Grossbasel is lined with 15th- and 16th-century houses and a handful of inkmakers' shops that reek of alchemy. No. 11 housed Basel's university when it was first founded, in 1460. The Rheinsprung is a nice vantage point for views of the old town, Mittlere Rheinbrücke and the Rhine.

⑦ St. Alban-Tor. This original medieval city gate, one of two, is set amid a lovely garden. Parts of the gate date from the 13th century. ⊠ *St. Alban-Berg.*

OFF THE BEATEN PATH | **LANGENBRUCK AND ENVIRONS** – In the German countryside south of Basel, known as the Baselbiet, a handful of stately little villages offer sturdy old guest houses and a range—from medieval to Roman—of historic sites to explore. Take the winding forest road (N12) west of the freeway between Liestal and Oensingen, watching for Balsthal, Holderbank, Oberer Hauenstein, and Langenbruck; the industrial stretch just south of Liestal is less attractive. Landgasthof Bären (☎ 062/60–14–14) in Langenbruck offers superb regional cooking, inexpensive fixed-price menus, and locally brewed beer, as well as attractive, moderately priced rooms.

VITRA DESIGN MUSEUM – Just 10 kilometers (6 miles) across the border in the German town of Weil am Rhein, this museum is a startling white geometric jumble designed by American architect Frank Gehry in 1987–89 as part of an avant-garde building complex associated with the Vitra furniture manufacturer. Here, witty and unexpectedly placed wall openings, asymmetrical skylights, and walkways compete for attention with the collection, some 1,200 items tracing the evolution of furniture design from 1850 to the present. Chair lovers will appreciate the soaring "wall of chairs" and the fact that visitors are encouraged to plop down on many of the pieces. In addition, temporary exhibitions display objects by artist or by themes of function, form, material, construction, and technique.

To get there by car, take A5/E35 north from Basel toward Karlsruhe; turn right just after German customs into Route 532, parallel to the parking lot, and turn left after exiting at Weil am Rhein. The museum is 1½ kilometers (about a mile) ahead on the right. Or from Badischer Bahnhof in Basel, take Bus 5 (toward Kandern) to the Vitra stop. ⊠ *Charles-Eames-Strasse 1, Weil am Rhein, Germany,* ☎ *(49) 7621/702–200.* ⊡ *DM 8.* ⊘ *Tues.–Fri. 2–6. Guided tours Wed.–Fri. at 2.*

Spalentor. Like St. Alban-Tor, Spalentor served as one of Basel's medieval city gates, beginning in the 14th century. Note Basel's coat of arms atop the gate. ⊠ *Spalenvorstadt.*

⑱ **Tinguely Museum.** Ticinese architect Mario Botta, creator of the Museum of Modern Art in San Francisco, designed this new museum, which is dedicated to the life and work of Switzerland's best-known 20th-century sculptor, Jean Tinguely; pharmaceutical giant Hoffman–La Roche presented the museum to Basel as a gift in October 1996. Incorporated within approximately 10,000 square feet is a collection of Tinguely's work, much of it the gift of his widow, artist Niki de Saint Phalle. Born in Fribourg—where another smaller Tinguely museum is currently being constructed—Tinguely is best known for his whimsical *metamecaniques* (mechanical sculptures), and his noisy car sculptures, which transform normally inhuman machinery into ironic and humorous statements about man and machine. The exhibition halls, with their individual lighting and moods, enhance the fine-limbed machine sculptures and show off the massive pandemoniac works' unique appeal. The "Barca," a wing projecting over the Rhine, offers a splendid river view of Basel. ⊠ *Grenzacherstrasse 210,* ☎ *061/681–93–20* FAX *061/681–93–21.* ⊘ *Wed.–Sun. 11-7.*

⟳ **Zoologischer Garten.** Famed for its armored rhinoceroses (it has had great luck breeding them) as well as its pygmy hippopotamuses, gorillas, and Javanese monkeys, this is no ordinary zoo. There are 5,000 animals here, the most beloved of which are the penguins. Especially for children, there's an arena for elephant-riding. The enormous restaurant-pavilion with its vast terrace in the center of the zoo serves child-friendly meals. Buy a booklet with a map to find your way, or you may end up wandering in circles. ⊠ *Binningerstrasse 40,* ☎ *061/295–35–35.* ⊡ *10 SF.* ⊘ *May–Aug., daily 8–6:30; Mar.–Apr. and Sept.–Oct., daily 8–6; Nov.–Feb., daily 8–5:30.*

Colonia Augusta Raurica (Augst)

Founded in 44–43 BC, Augst is the oldest Roman establishment on the Rhein. Although you can reach it from Basel in 10 minutes by car, Augst is most memorable if visited by boat. To view the different restoration sites scattered around the almost suburban neighborhood, be prepared to do some walking.

A Good Walk

A scenic, 1½-hour boat ride will take you to the old town of **Augst**. ★ From there, walk uphill to the ruins of **Augusta Raurica**, a 2,000-year-old Roman settlement that's been almost entirely rebuilt. The other main attraction here is the **Römermuseum** (Roman Museum), housed in a vividly reconstructed Roman House and containing countless ancient treasures.

TIMING

Augst merits at least a half day, slightly more if you go by boat. Boats (✉ Basler Personenschiffahrts-Gesellschaft, ☎ 061/261–24–00) leave up to three times a day in high season from the dock at Schifflände, behind the Three Kings Hotel. The 29 SF round-trip fare takes you slowly up the Rhine, passing the old town and the cathedral. Drinks and cold snacks are available on all cruises, hot meals on some. The last boat returning to Basel each day leaves Augst around 5 PM.

Sights to See

★ **Augusta Raurica.** The remains of this 2,000-year-old Roman settlement have been almost entirely rebuilt (one suspects the Swiss might have done the same had they gotten their hands on that rundown Colosseum in Rome), with substantial portions of the ancient town walls and gates, streets, water pipes, and heating systems all in evidence. The 2nd-century theater has been restored for modern use, and open-air plays and concerts are staged in summer.

Römermuseum. Housed in a vividly reconstructed Roman house, the Roman Museum contains a substantial treasure trove unearthed in 1962: The objects, dating mostly from the 4th century, are believed to have been buried by the Romans in 350 to protect them from the ravages of the Alemanni, the German tribes who drove the Romans out of Switzerland. Silver plates, bowls, goblets, spoons, statues, and toilet articles are all on display, as are coins thought to depict the emperor Constantine or one of his sons. To view the various restoration sites scattered around the almost suburban neighborhood, be prepared to do some walking. ✉ *Giebenacherstrasse 17, Augst,* ☎ *061/816–22–22.* 🖼 *5 SF.* ☉ *Mar.–Oct., Tues.–Sat. 10–5, Sun. 10–6; Nov.–Feb., Tues.–Sat. 10–noon, 1-4, Sun. 10–noon, 1–5, Mon. 1–4.*

DINING

CATEGORY	COST*
$$$$	over 70 SF
$$$	40 SF–70 SF
$$	20 SF–40 SF
$	under 20 SF

per person for a three-course meal (except in $ category), excluding drinks, tax, and 15% service charge

$$$$ ✕ **Stucki.** Hans Stucki remains one of the finest and most justly honored chefs in the world, rivaling Fredy Girardet, one of the other demigods in Switzerland's culinary pantheon (☞ Dining and Lodging *in* Chapter 12). Ambitious young chefs drop his name the way actors once mentioned Stanislavsky. Watch for such modern classics as pigeon in truffle *coulis* (liquid puree of cooked vegetables), or grilled lobster in tarragon sabayon. The service at this restaurant, in the green, residential neighborhood of the Bruderholz, is formal and the seating

competitive: Reserve as far ahead as possible. ⊠ *Bruderholzallee 42,* ☎ *061/361–82–22,* FAX *061/361–82–03. Reservations essential. AE, DC, MC, V. Closed Sun.–Mon. and late July–early Aug.*

$$–$$$$ ✕ **Teufelhof.** Owners Monica and Dominique Thommy have trans-
★ formed a grand old Heuberg mansion into a top gastronomic restau-
rant, a chic Weinstube, a trendy bar, two theaters, and guest rooms
decorated by artists. There are even medieval ruins in the basement.
The restaurant's decor is almost minimalist, showcasing a few artworks
and a star-pattern parquet floor. The menu changes daily under chef
Michael Baader's masterly guidance but always includes such inven-
tive dishes as beef in savoy cabbage with red-wine ice and gnocchi;
spinach-filled crepes with tomato-basil sauce and grilled mushrooms;
or savory pumpkin quiche. Wines by the glass come in astonishing va-
riety. The high-tech and warm-wood Weinstube serves the same wines
and a few inexpensive specialties (from the same kitchen) to a crowd
of low-key, upscale bohemians. The café-bar is tiny and usually crowded
with new-wave artists; try the locally brewed Ueli Bier. ⊠ *Leon-
hardsgraben 47/Heuberg 30,* ☎ *061/261–10–10,* FAX *061/261–10–
04. Jacket and tie in restaurant. AE, MC, V. Closed Sun. Restaurant
closed Mon.*

$$$ ✕ **Chez Donati.** This is where well-heeled Baslers gather, as if at a pri-
★ vate club, to feast on classic, old-school Italian cuisine, with sole and
rack of veal, among other fare, tantalizingly perfumed with black and
white truffles. Though the decor borders on kitsch, with its corny murals and abundance of gilt, the crowds pack in nightly, and Warhol and
Tinguely were once frequent guests. ⊠ *St. Johanns-Vorstadt 48,* ☎
061/322–09–19, FAX *061/322–09–81. AE, DC, MC, V. Closed
Mon.–Tues., mid-July to mid-Aug.*

$$$ ✕ **St. Alban-Eck.** This café, a five-minute walk behind the Museum of
Fine Arts, shows a glimpse of Basel's French blood. In a half-timbered
historic home, it's a real *petit coin sympa* (friendly little corner), with
plank wainscoting in natural wood, framed historic prints, and net cur-
tains. The cuisine gracefully mixes German and French favorites: grilled
entrecôte, sole, salmon, and *foie de veau à la Riehen* (liver with onions,
apple, and smoked bacon). ⊠ *St. Alban-Vorstadt 60,* ☎ *061/271–03–
20. AE, DC, MC, V. Closed weekends.*

$$$ ✕ **Schlüsselzunft.** This historic guildhall houses an elegant little restau-
rant with a ceramic stove and rustic appointments, as well as an in-
expensive open-atrium courtyard café, called the Schlüsselhöfli. The
restaurant, which draws business lunch crowds, serves upscale French
and *cuisine Bâloise,* meaning liver with onions and the local salmon
dish; the café serves shoppers cheap international plates. ⊠ *Freie
Strasse 25,* ☎ *061/261–20–46,* FAX *061/261–20–56. Reservations essential in restaurant. AE, DC, MC. Closed Sun.*

$$ ✕ **Safran-Zunft.** This clublike spot in a grand neo-Gothic hall built in
1900 has an old-downtown feel and draws businessmen lunching with
their wives and retirees. The food is basic and solid: grilled meats, lamb,
and trout. The daily three-course menus are a good deal. ⊠ *Gerber-
gasse 11,* ☎ *061/261–19–59,* FAX *061/261–18–37. AE, DC, MC, V.
Closed Sun.*

$$ ✕ **Zum Goldenen Sternen.** Dating from 1506, this Gasthof claims to
be the oldest restaurant in Switzerland, though the building has been
moved from the center of town to its current Rhine-side site. The impeccable restoration retains the antique beams, stenciled ceilings, and
unvarnished planks, yet without seeming contrived. Linens, flowers,
and stemware set the tone for discreet romance or impressive business
lunches. Though it could easily play a secondary role, the food almost
lives up to the setting: It's classic French, only slightly updated. Game

and seafood are specialties. ✉ *St. Alban-Rheinweg 70*, ☎ *061/272–16–66*, FAX *061/272–16–67. AE, DC, MC, V.*

$ ✗ **Café Pfalz.** This bookish little self-service café, down a narrow street below the Münster, dishes out veggie plates, *Muesli* (a Swiss cereal), sausage, and quiche in a trim beechwood-and-black contemporary setting. A salad bar, juicer, and one hot daily special add to the options. ✉ *Münsterberg 11*, ☎ *061/272–65–11. No credit cards.*

$ ✗ **Fischerstube.** If you're serious about local color, venture a few steps
★ beyond the tourist pale and try a home brew here. Established by a pubkeeper who refused the franchise of local brewers, the Fischerstube brews its own lagers and ales in the deep, frothing copper tanks behind the bar. The house label is Ueli Bier, named for a jesterlike Fasnacht clown; the timid can taste it at upscale Teufelhof (☞ Lodging, *below*). Pretzels hang on wooden racks on the sanded wooden tables, and the menu includes such local dishes as *Fleischkäse* (sausage loaf) with eggs and *frites* (french fries), rump steak, and just plain *Würstli* (sausage) from the grill. There's a beer garden in back. ✉ *Rheingasse 45*, ☎ *061/692–66–35. Reservations not accepted. AE, DC, MC, V. Closed Sun.*

$ ✗ **Löwenzorn.** This is a classic, comfortable gathering place for plain Germanic food, and though it offers a hodgepodge of fondues, fish, and Italian dishes as well as standard local fare, its regulars come here for beer, a full plate, and some laughs with the friendly staff. With high ceilings, woodwork, ceramic stoves, and a roof garden, it's a nice mix of bistro and beer hall. ✉ *Gemsberg 2*, ☎ *061/261–42–13*, FAX *061/261–42–17. AE, DC, MC, V. Closed Sun.*

$ ✗ **Zum Schnabel.** This dark-green and aged-wood *Wirtshaus* (inn) has a clubby, unpretentious feel, with motherly waitresses and multiple variations on Basel-brewed beer. Sausage, pork, and Rösti reign. ✉ *Trillengässlein 2*, ☎ *061/261–49–09. MC, V. Closed Sun.*

LODGING

With its industry, its banking, and its conference center, this is a business city first. As a result, hotel prices tend to be steep, bargains in short supply, and comforts—TV, minibar, phone—more important than atmosphere in the all-out competition for expense-account travelers. There are no guest houses here such as those in the country. When there's a conference in town, every bed for miles can be filled; book well ahead.

CATEGORY	COST*
$$$$	over 300 SF
$$$	200 SF–300 SF
$$	140 SF–200 SF
$	under 140 SF

All prices are for a standard double room, including breakfast, tax, and service charge.

Hotel reservations can be made through the **Basel Hotel Reservation Service** and the tourist office at the SBB train station (☞ Important Addresses and Numbers *in* Basel A to Z, *below*).

$$$$ 🏨 **Drei Könige.** An integral part of Basel history even before the first
★ bridges drew the distant banks of the Rhine together, this riverside hotel began in the 11th century as a small *relais*; it later became a coach stop, and today it's a landmark of the modern city. Expanded to its present form in 1835, it is now restored, and its opulent woodwork, paintings, and furnishings have all their 19th-century grandeur. Despite its regal history, the hotel is surprisingly intimate and understated. The reigning style is Empire; colors are cream, gilt, and powder blue, and

172

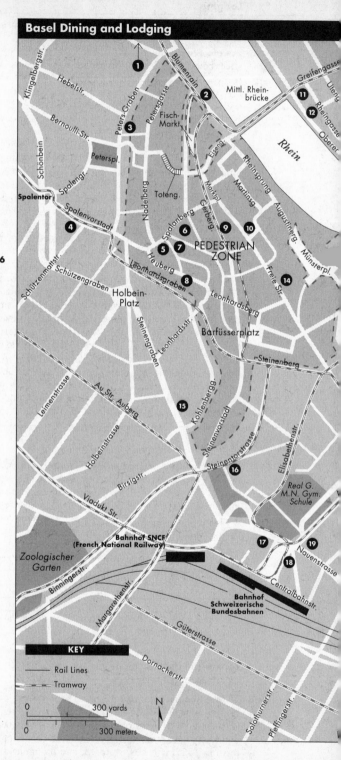

Basel Dining and Lodging

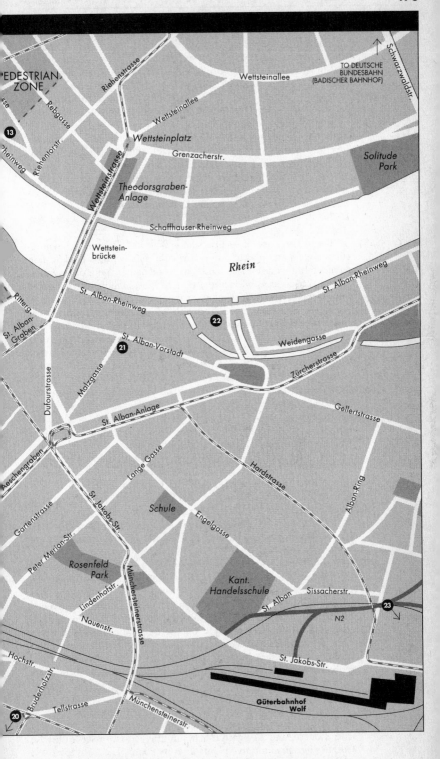

EDESTRIAN ZONE

Riehenstrasse

Rebgasse

Riehentorstr.

Rheinweg

13

Wettsteinstrasse

Wettsteinallee

Wettsteinallee

Wettsteinplatz

Grenzacherstr.

TO DEUTSCHE
BUNDESBAHN
(BADISCHER BAHNHOF)

Schwarzwaldstr.

Solitude
Park

Theodorsgraben-
Anlage

Schaffhauser-Rheinweg

Wettstein-
brücke

Rhein

St. Alban-Rheinweg

St. Alban-Rheinweg

Ritterg.

St. Alban-
Graben

22

21

St. Alban-Vorstadt

Weidengasse

Zürcherstrasse

Dufourstrasse

Malzgasse

St. Alban-Anlage

Gellertstrasse

Aeschengraben

Lange Gasse

Hardstrasse

Alban-Ring

Gartenstrasse

St. Jakobs-Str.

Schule

Engelgasse

Peter Merian-Str.

Rosenfeld
Park

Münchensteinerstrasse

Kant.
Handelsschule

St. Alban

Sissacherstr.

23

Lindenhofstr.

N2

Nauenstr.

Hochstr.

Bruderholzstr.

Tellstrasse

Münchensteinerstr.

St. Jakobs-Str.

**Güterbahnhof
Wolf**

20

all rooms have big, tile baths. Most rooms have air-conditioning; balconied rooms and rooms with serene Rhine views cost more. The formal French restaurant can serve meals on the broad, awning-shaded Rhine terrace, which is heated, well into fall. There's also a more casual brasserie. ⊠ *Blumenrain 8, CH-4001,* ☎ *061/261–52–52,* 𝔽𝔸𝕏 *061/261–21–53. 143 beds. 3 restaurants, bar. AE, DC, MC, V.*

$$$$ 🏨 **Euler.** An archetypal little Old World luxury hotel, this landmark
★   on the Centralbahnplatz draws a loyal business clientele, who mingle with local and international bankers over a *Cüpli* (glass of champagne) in the famous leather-and-red-velvet bar. Standard rooms are furnished in a classic but spare style, with antique-reproduction furnishings and plain chenille spreads; all have triple-glaze windows to cut out the Centralbahnplatz noise. (Back rooms, over an alley court, are quieter.) Ask for a peek at the Wiener salon, painted with extraordinary romantic landscapes. ⊠ *Centralbahnplatz 14, CH-4051,* ☎ *061/272–45–00,* 𝔽𝔸𝕏 *061/271–50–00. 100 beds. Restaurant, bar. AE, DC, MC, V.*

$$$$ 🏨 **Hilton.** There are no surprises here: Built in 1975, this anonymous cube of glass and plastic stands frozen in time, with its bold Scandinavian fabrics, marble slab, and slick wood panels. Yet it offers American-chain services and facilities no Old World landmark can touch: Full air-conditioning *and* windows that open, an entire floor of no-smoking rooms, rooms modified for people with disabilities, standard-size rooms for singles, and emergency exits marked by phosphorescent paint. The room decor is neutral, if uninspired. The restaurant and bar were upgraded in 1995. ⊠ *Aeschengraben 31, CH-4002,* ☎ *061/271–66–22,* 𝔽𝔸𝕏 *061/271–52–20. 380 beds. Restaurant, bar, coffee shop, pool, massage, steam room, meeting rooms. AE, DC, MC, V.*

$$$$ 🏨 **International Basel.** This downtown tower could be an airport terminal, and the noisy lobby and adjoining bar packed nightly with business types won't dissuade you from that initial impression. Yet the quiet, Euro-style guest rooms, as efficiently designed as ship staterooms, with streamlined built-in furniture and lots of light in all the right places, are warm and welcoming. The Burgundian restaurant, Charolaise, combines the rustic (stone arches, wooden beams, iron sconces) and the baronial (tapestry-covered high-back chairs and a chandelier); such side dishes as homemade Spätzle and Rösti remind you that you're in Switzerland, albeit right on the edge. ⊠ *Steinentorstrasse 25, CH-4001,* ☎ *061/281–75–85,* 𝔽𝔸𝕏 *061/281–76–27. 350 beds. 2 restaurants, bar, coffee shop, indoor pool, health club, massage, sauna, steam room. AE, DC, MC, V.*

$$$ 🏨 **Basel.** This all-modern hotel built in 1975 has the scale of the old town, where it has become part of the neighborhood, its bars and restaurants filling with locals after work. The newly renovated rooms have natural oak veneer, leather-and-chrome chairs, and some pine accents; the fifth-floor rooms have deep dormer windows. The clientele is almost exclusively businesspeople, but there's plenty of room on weekends. The Baslerkeller downstairs is an atmospheric, first-class restaurant; Münz is a coffee shop; and the dark and cozy bar Zum Sperber draws mobs of well-to-do workers for drinks and quick meals. ⊠ *Münzgasse 12, CH-4051,* ☎ *061/264–68–00,* 𝔽𝔸𝕏 *061/264–68–11. 84 beds. 2 restaurants, free parking. AE, DC, MC, V.*

$$$ 🏨 **Merian am Rhein.** Built in 1972 to blend with the landmark wa-
★   terfront Café Spitz, this has been renovated yet again; now the look is chic, modern, and airy with touches of gray wood, russet-leather Le Corbusier chairs, and live plants in every room. The Café Spitz is a study in postmodern beech, black lacquer, and halogen. Fish features prominently on the menu, and there's a lovely, sheltered terrace by the Mittlere Brücke and the Rhine. ⊠ *Rheingasse 2, CH-4005,* ☎ *061/681–*

00–00, FAX *061/681–11–01. 108 beds. Restaurant, café, in-room VCRs. AE, DC, MC, V.*

$$$ ▣ **Schweizerhof.** This bastion of the station area, once a luxury hotel,
★ now bestows on business travelers the proud, personal service once lavished on such stars as Toscanini, Menuhin, and Casals. Built in 1864 and in the same family since 1896, it is filled with antiques and faience, though its marble floors and wing chairs mingle with faded updates from the '50s and '60s. The most recently modernized rooms mix Biedermeier with beech and pine, though the big front bays feature rose plush and rosewood; half the rooms are air-conditioned. The traditional French restaurant offers terrace dining, and the bar is American-style. Staff cuts have cost this landmark its official fifth star, if not its five-star style. ✉ *Centralbahnplatz 1, CH-4002,* ☎ *061/271–28–33,* FAX *061/271–29–19. 110 beds. Restaurant, bar. AE, DC, MC, V.*

$$$ ▣ **Spalenbrunnen.** This is an unpretentious hotel in a historic building between the Holbein fountain and the Spalentor. Recently renovated rooms have built-in rosewood cabinets and taupe decor, with all-tile baths; older rooms are done in avocado and walnut. All windows are triple-glazed, and the solid halls are creak-free. The restaurant has an updated-rustic look and serves middle-class German and Italian fare. ✉ *Schützenmattstrasse 2, CH-4051,* ☎ *061/261–82–33,* FAX *061/261–00–37. 50 beds. Restaurant. AE, DC, MC, V*

$$$ ▣ **Teufelhof.** In addition to its bars, theaters, medieval ruins, and
★ restaurants (☞ *Dining, above*), this Basel bastion of style and gourmandise has a small guest house whose eight rooms are works of art in their own right: Each is decorated by a different artist and redesigned by another artist every other year. ✉ *Leonhardsgraben 47/Heuberg 30, CH-4051,* ☎ *061/261–10–10,* FAX *061/261–10–04. 16 beds. Restaurant, café, stübli, theaters. AE, MC, V.*

$$ ▣ **Krafft am Rhein.** A rare find in Swiss cities, this is an elegant little
★ mansion of an inn directly on the right-bank waterfront, with mosaic floors, elaborate moldings, chandeliers, and a sinuous atrium stairwell. The proud, accommodating management more than makes up for any wear and tear on the museum-quality architectural details. The views over the promenade, river, and the old-town skyline can't be overrated. Some higher-price Rhine-side rooms have been beautifully renovated, with polished wood floors, Biedermeier beds, and Oriental runners; others still have '50s mix-and-match. Those without bath fall into the $ category. There's a traditional dining room with peaceful Rhine views for breakfast and dinner, but the downstairs Zem Schnooggeloch (Mosquito's Den) is where everyone gathers for German-style food. The waterfront terrace café is justifiably popular. ✉ *Rheingasse 12, CH-4058,* ☎ *061/691–88–77,* FAX *061/691–09–07. 80 beds. Restaurant. AE, DC, MC, V.*

$$ ▣ **Rochat.** Built in 1898 across from the university, this modest but big, solid brownstone offers plain, if mildly institutional, comforts. Most rooms have a shower; those without cost less. ✉ *Petersgraben 23, CH-4051,* ☎ *061/261–81–40,* FAX *061/261–64–92. 80 beds. Restaurant (no alcohol served), café. AE, DC, MC, V.*

$ ▣ **Steinenschanze.** Despite its awkward, isolated position above the
★ busy highway, behind the nightlife district, this bargain hotel is clean, welcoming, and bright, with good-size rooms with linoleum floors, miniblinds, and tasteful Scandinavian furniture. The harsh parking-garage lines have been softened with a scattering of Oriental rugs, plants, posters, and knickknacks. Back rooms are quiet; there's a garden behind, visible from the spacious, informal breakfast room. ✉ *Steinengraben 69, CH-4051,* ☎ *061/272–53–53,* FAX *061/272–45–73. 75 beds. Breakfast room. AE, DC, MC, V.*

$$ ⊞ **Bad Schauenburg.** Ten kilometers (6 miles) southeast of Basel, this charming country inn has suites done in Biedermeier period antiques and a gourmet restaurant. There's also an informal bistro serving hearty fare. Take the main road to Liestal, then follow the signs after the turn-off in Frenkendorf. ⊠ *Schauenburgerstrasse, Liestal, CH-4410,* ☎ *061/901–12–02,* FAX *061/901–10–55. 45 beds. Restaurant. AE, DC, MC, V.*

NIGHTLIFE AND THE ARTS

For a complete listing of events in Basel, pick up a copy of *Basel Live*, a booklet published every two weeks. *Basel,* another listings publication, comes out every three months. Both are available at the tourist office and, usually, at hotel desks.

Nightlife

Bars and Lounges

The **Euler Bar** (⊠ Centralbahnplatz 14, ☎ 061/272–45–00), inside the Hotel Euler, draws a conservative business crowd after work. **Zum Sperber** (⊠ Münzgasse 12, ☎ 061/261–24–33), behind the Hotel Basel, fills tables and bar stools with well-heeled workers at happy hour; there's live music some evenings. **Campari Bar** (⊠ Steinenberg 7, ☎ 061/272–83–83), behind the Basel Art Gallery and the Tinguely-Brunnen, draws a young, arty crowd with pop-art paraphernalia, loud pop music, and a TGI-Friday mood all week. **Brauner Mutz** (☎ 061/261–33–69) is a big, landmark beer hall at Barfüsserplatz with long wooden tables and a beer in every hand.

Discos and Nightclubs

Le Plaza Club (⊠ Am Messeplatz, ☎ 061/692–32–06) has dancing. **Frisco-Bar** (⊠ Untere Rebgasse 3, ☎ 061/681–09–90) is an intimate nightclub with the oldest striptease show in town. **Hazy-Club** (⊠ Heuwaage, 061/261–99–82) has a top orchestra and show. **Singerhaus** (⊠ Marktplatz, ☎ 061/261–64–66) is a traditional nightclub with a good show; the bar opens at 5, dancing starts at 9; there is also old-time cheek-to-cheek dancing on Sunday afternoon from 4 to 7.

The Arts

Film

Movies in Basel are usually shown in the original language with subtitles. Newspaper listings can be deciphered, but most houses are along Steinenvorstadt in the old town, and times are prominently posted. Prices vary depending on how close to the screen you choose to sit.

Music

The **Stadtcasino** hosts the Basel Symphony Orchestra, the Basel Chamber Orchestra, and visiting performers as well. ⊠ *Steinenberg 14,* ☎ *061/272–66–57,* FAX *061/272–58–22. Advance bookings: Musikhaus au concert, Aeschenvorstadt 24,* ☎ *061/272–11–76. Tickets available at theater box office 1 hr before performance.*

The **Musik-Akademie der Stadt Basel** (⊠ Leonhardsgraben 4–6) is an important European academy with top-quality international performers. Book as for the Stadtcasino (☞ *above*).

Theater

The **Basel Stadttheater** hosts opera, operetta, dance, and plays (in German). Book in advance. ⊠ *Theaterstrasse 7,* ☎ *061/295–11–33, weekdays 10–1 and 3:30–6:45; Sun. by telephone only until 5. Box office opens 45 mins before performance.*

The **Komödie** (✉ Steinenvorstadt 63) offers light theater in an intimate atmosphere, in German. Book through the Stadttheater (☞ *above*) or at the box office 45 minutes before the curtain.

OUTDOOR ACTIVITIES AND SPORTS

Golf
Golf and Country Club Basel (✉ Hagenthal-le-Bas in France, ☎ 33/89–68–54–91) is one of the most beautiful golf courses in Europe, with attractive views of the Jura, Black Forest, and Vosges mountains. It is open to visitors; bring your passport.

Squash
Eglisee (✉ Riehenstrasse 315, ☎ 061/681–22–10) provides squash courts by reservation only. **Sportcenter Paradies** (✉ Bettenstrasse 73, ☎ 061/481–88–22), like Eglisee, has good squash facilities.

Tennis
Tennis-Center (☎ 061/361–95–95) has courts at Margarethenpark. **Sporthalle St. Jakob** (☎ 061/311–72–09) has courts to reserve.

SHOPPING

Though first impressions here may suggest yet another modern pedestrian shopping district, it's worth a closer look. There are still a lot of lone-wolf, private, quirky shops that contain extraordinary treasures.

Department Stores
The main department store chain is **Globus** (✉ Marktplatz 2, ☎ 061/261–55–00). **Jelmoli** (✉ Rebgasse 20, ☎ 061/681–00–11) is Globus' chief competitor. **Pfauen** at (✉ Freie Strasse 75, ☎ 061/261–60–60) has a large selection of goods. **Rheinbrücke** (✉ Greifengasse 22, ☎ 061/695–95–11) is on the Kleinbasel side of the Rhein.

Flea Markets
There's a large flea market at **Petersplatz** every Saturday from 9 to 4 (which draws serious watch sellers and watch repairmen, despite its garage-sale quality). A small flea market sets up shop on **Barfüsserplatz** every second and fourth Wednesday from 7 to 6:30. This square is also the site of a clothing market every Thursday from 1:30 to 6:30; it offers mostly bohemian batik and tie-dyed styles, though you may find cheap China silks.

Shopping Streets
The major, central shopping district stretches along **Freie Strasse** and **Gerbergasse,** though lower-priced shops along **Steinenvorstadt** cater to a younger crowd. Streets radiating left, uphill from the Gerbergasse area, feature more one-of-a-kind boutiques. Most antiquarian bookshops concentrate their business on **Klosterberg** through Elisabethenstrasse to Aeschengraben.

Specialty Stores
ANTIQUES
René Simmermacher (✉ Augustinergasse 7, ☎ 061/261–18–48) hides away his exquisite, if tiny, collection of European faience from the 17th and 18th centuries in a miniature shop across from the Folklife Museum.

ANTIQUE BOOKS

Among many fine competitors, **Erasmushaus/Haus der Bücher** (⊠ Bäumleingasse 18, ☎ 061/272–30–88) carries one of the largest collections of fine old and used books, mostly in German but including some multilingual art publications.

CALLIGRAPHIC PARAPHERNALIA

Though you may not have known you needed it, **Abraxas** (⊠ Rheinsprung 6, ☎ 061/261–60–70) offers not only its own fine writing work but the paraphernalia to go with it; luxurious sealing waxes and reproductions of antique silver seals are available too. **Scriptorium am Rhysprung** (⊠ Rheinsprung 2, ☎ 061/261–39–00) mixes its own ink and carries calligraphic pens.

CHINA AND GLASS

Füglistaller (⊠ Freie Strasse 23, ☎ 061/261–78–78) displays enormous quantities of top-quality crystal (Baccarat), china (Rosenthal, Villeroy & Boch), and kitchenware (Spring, Alessi) in its palatial, multitiered atrium showroom. There is a selection of upscale Basel souvenirs near the front door.

CIGARS

Oettinger (⊠ Aeschenvorstadt 4, ☎ 061/272–47–70; Centralbahnplatz 9, ☎ 061/272–11–52) sells Davidoff Havana cigars and their equals.

COINS

Münzen and Medaillen AG (⊠ Malzgasse 25, ☎ 061/272–75–44) carries coins and medals dating from antiquity to the mid-19th century.

CRAFTS AND GIFTS

Heimatwerk (⊠ Schneidergasse 2, ☎ 061/261–91–78) carries carefully selected and quality-controlled crafts from across Switzerland, from traditional ceramics to linen dish towels and children's wooden toys. Basel-made specialties include embroidered silk ribbons and terracotta cookie stamps, as well as wooden jigsaw puzzles of Switzerland. Highly specialized handiwork comes from **Johann Wanner** (⊠ Spalenberg 14, ☎ 061/261–48–26), who commissions hand-blown and hand-painted glass ornaments, tin Victorian miniatures, and tartan ribbons, all solely for Christmas.

FOOD SPECIALTIES

The famous **Läckerli-Huus** (⊠ Gerbergasse 57, ☎ 061/261–23–22) sells a variety of sweets but features the local specialty—*Leckerli,* a chewy spiced cookie of almond, honey, dried fruit, and kirsch. It also carries a large line of gift canisters and makes a business of shipping souvenir gifts. **Bachmann** (⊠ Gerbergasse 51, ☎ 061/261–35–83; Blumenrain 1, ☎ 061/261–41–52; and Centralbahnplatz 7, ☎ 061/ 271–26–27) carries the lovely little sweets that set Basel apart. **Schiesser** (⊠ Marktplatz, ☎ 061/261–60–77), a convivial tearoom, opened in 1870. **Käs Glauser** (⊠ Spalenberg 12, ☎ 061/261–80– 06) ages its own cheeses and offers a large assortment of fresh Swiss specialties.

LINENS

Caraco (⊠ Gerbergasse 77, Falknerstrasse entrance, ☎ 061/261–35– 77) sells handmade Swiss lace and embroidered goods as well as imports. **Langenthal** (⊠ Gerbergasse 26, ☎ 061/261–09–00) offers mostly Swiss products: tea towels, tablecloths, and folk-style aprons. **Sturzenegger** (⊠ Freie Strasse 62, ☎ 061/261–68–67) carries household linens made in St. Gallen, the Swiss textile capital.

LINGERIE

Sturzenegger (☞ Linens, *above*) also carries an extensive line of Hanro and Calida underwear in fine Swiss cottons. **Beldona** (⊠ Freie Strasse 103, ☎ 061/272–80–72) stocks Swiss cotton lingerie. **Fogal** sells its famous hosiery at two locations (⊠ Freie Strasse 44, ☎ 061/261–74–61; Freie Strasse 4, ☎ 061/261–12–20); both set out trays of clearance goods.

MEN'S CLOTHES

One of the best sources for men's designer apparel is the **Trois Pommes Uomo** branch at Freie Strasse 93 (☎ 061/272–92–57), which carries Armani, Ferre, Versace, Comme des Garçons, and Gaultier. **Ferre** (⊠ Freie Strasse 93, ☎ 061/272–92–57), under the same management as Trois Pommes Uomo, carries similar designers. For the smoking-jacket crowd, **Renz** (⊠ Freie Strasse 2a, ☎ 061/261–29–91) has a small but impeccable selection of fine Swiss-cotton pajamas, Hanro underwear, and classic Scottish cashmeres. **K. Aeschbacher** (⊠ Schnabelgasse 4, ☎ 061/261–50–58) carries unique Swiss silk ties, scarves, robes, and pajamas.

SHOES

Bally Capitol (⊠ Freie Strasse 38, ☎ 061/261–18–97) has a wide selection of these conservative Swiss-made shoes. **Bally Rivoli** (⊠ Falkenstrasse 8, ☎ 061/261–60–35) stocks the same shoes as Bally Capitol. **Bruno Magli** (⊠ Freie Strasse 44, ☎ 061/261–98–96) sells the well-known Italian brand. **Rive Gauche** (⊠ Schneidergasse 1, ☎ 061/261–10–80) carries top-quality shoes only. **Kropart** (⊠ Schneidergasse 16, ☎ 061/261–51–33) specializes in trendy, high-end styles. **Schatulle** (☞ Women's Clothes, *above*) has house-label shoes made in Italy.

TOYS

Slightly less folksy than Heimatwerk (☞ Crafts and Gifts, *above*), **Spielhuus** (⊠ Eisengasse 8, ☎ 061/264–98–98) is a good source for board games and reasonably priced children's toys. The large, mainstream **Dreamland** (⊠ Freie Strasse 17, ☎ 061/261–19–90) is Switzerland's answer to Toys "R" Us. **Bercher & Sternlicht** (⊠ Spalenberg 45, ☎ 061/261–25–50) has miniature trains and accessories.

WATCHES

The famous **Gübelin** outlet (⊠ Freie Strasse 27, ☎ 061/261–40–33) carries Baume & Mercier, Piaget, Rado, and Rolex. The well-known **Bucherer** (⊠ Freie Strasse 40, ☎ 061/261–40–00) sells Patek Philippe, Audemars Piguet, Ebel, and Tissot. The broad selection at **Kurz** (⊠ Freie Strasse 39, ☎ 061/261–26–20) ranges from Chopard to Tissot.

WOMEN'S CLOTHES

Trois Pommes (⊠ Freie Strasse 74, ☎ 061/272–92–55) dominates the high end, with Jil Sander, Versace, Armani, and Valentino. **Grieder** (⊠ Freie Strasse 29, ☎ 061/261–08–88) carries Gucci, Kenzo, Sonia Rykiel, and Max Mara. **La Boutique** (⊠ Falknerstrasse 33, ☎ 061/261–00–06) sells Krizia, Missoni, Thierry Mugler, and Mani. If you're not too proud to be seen in last year's Valentino, try **Check-out** (⊠ Schnabelgasse 4, ☎ 061/261–62–92), a bargain-bin outlet for Trois Pommes goods. **Fundgrube** (⊠ Steinenvorstadt 2, ☎ 061/281–88–58) has crowded racks of suits, cocktail dresses, shoes, and accessories at half-price.

Smaller and more individual selections can be found at several shops. **Crista Bis** (⊠ Schnabelgasse 4, ☎ 061/261–00–80) has Dorothee Bis and Olivier Strelli. **Schatulle** (⊠ Spalenberg/Rosshofgasse 15, ☎ 061/261–46–11) stocks Marimekko knits and privately commissioned silk-and-linen blends.

BASEL A TO Z

Arriving and Departing

By Car

The German autobahn A5 enters Basel from the north and leads directly to the Rhine and the center. From France, the autoroute A35 (E9) peters out at the frontier, and secondary urban roads lead to the center. As the most interesting and scenic portions of Basel are riddled with pedestrian-only streets, it is advisable to park your car for the duration of your visit.

By Plane

The **Euro Airport,** just across the border in France, is shared by Basel, Mulhouse, and Freiburg in Germany. Direct flights link Basel to most major European cities. The nearest intercontinental airport is **Kloten** in **Zürich,** approximately 80 kilometers (50 miles) southeast of Basel. There are connecting flights from Zürich into Basel's airport on **Crossair,** Switzerland's domestic airline.

BETWEEN THE AIRPORT AND DOWNTOWN

By Bus. Regular bus service runs between the airport and the train station in the city center. The trip takes about 15 minutes and costs 3 SF per person (☎ 061/325–25–11 for schedules and information).

By Taxi. One-way fare from the airport to Basel center costs approximately 20 SF; it takes about 15 minutes in light traffic and up to 30 minutes at rush hours (around noon, 2 PM, and between 5 and 7 PM). Taxi companies include **Mini Cab** (☎ 061/271–11–11), **33er Taxi** (☎ 061/66–66–66), and **Taxi-Zentrale** (☎ 061/271–22–22). To call Basel taxis from the airport (in France), you must dial two prefixes: 19 to get out of the country, then 4161, then the number; the cost is negligible.

By Train

There are two main rail stations in Basel, the **SBB** (**Schweizerische Bundesbahnen**) station (☎ 061/21–24–60), which connects to Swiss destinations as well as to France and its trains; and the **DB** (**Deutsche Bundesbahn**) station (☎ 061/690–11–11), north of the Rhine in Kleinbasel, which connects to Germany and to the SBB station. Arriving in Basel from France, you get off on the French side of the border, carry your bags through a small customs station, where your passport will be checked; then either continue into the open track area to find your connection or exit left into the city center. Arriving from Germany at the DB station, you walk through a customs and passport check as well.

Getting Around

By far the best way to see Basel is on foot or by tram, as the landmarks, museums, and even the zoo radiate from the old-town center on the Rhine, and the network of rails covers the territory thoroughly. Taxis are costly, less efficient, and less available than the ubiquitous tram.

By Tram and Bus

Most trams run every six minutes all day, every 12 minutes in the evening. Tickets must be bought at the automatic machines at every stop (most give change). As long as you travel within the central "zone 10," which includes even the airport, you pay 2.40 SF per ticket. If you are making a short trip—four stops or fewer—you pay 1.60 SF. *Mehrfahrtenkarten* (multijourney cards) allow you 12 trips for the price of 10 and can be purchased from the ticket office at Barfüsserplatz and from many of the tram-stop vending machines. *Tageskarten* (day cards)

allow unlimited travel all day within the central zone and cost 7.20 SF
for adults, 3.60 SF for children; those under six travel free of charge.
You can buy day cards at most hotels as well as through the above
sources. Holders of the Swiss Pass travel free on all Basel public transport systems.

Contacts and Resources

Emergencies
Police. ☎ 117.

Hospital. ✉ Kantonsspital, Petersgraben 2, ☎ 061/265–25–25.

Medical emergencies and late-night pharmacy referral. ☎ 061/261–
15–15.

English-Language Bookstores
Tanner Books. ✉ Streitgasse 5, ☎ 061/272–45–47.

Jäggi. ✉ Freie Strasse 32, ☎ 061/261–52–00, FAX 061/261-52–05.

Guided Tours
The **Basel Tourist Board** organizes daily tours of the city by bus, departing at 10 AM from the Hotel Victoria by the SBB train station. The
tours last about 1¾ hours (20 SF adults). They also offer two-hour walking tours on summer Sundays and Mondays (10 SF adults). **Basler Per-
sonenschiffahrt** (☎ 061/261–24–00) offers boat trips on the Rhine
to Augst, departing from Schifflände by Mittlere Brücke. The cost is
18 SF round-trip.

Travel Agencies
Thomas Cook. ✉ Freie Strasse 3, ☎ 061/261–50–55.

American Express. ✉ Aeschengraben 10, ☎ 061/272–66–90.

Visitor Information
The **Basel Tourist Office** is on the Rhine just left of the Mittlere Brücke,
at the Schifflände tram stop (✉ Schifflände 5, ☎ 061/261–50–50. The
SBB rail station center (☎ 061/157–33–33) will help you with hotel
reservations. **City Information,** in the Bahnhoff (☎ 061/271–36–84),
provides hotel and museum information.

8 Fribourg, Neuchâtel, and the Jura

Unself-conscious and largely undiscovered, the cantons of Fribourg, Neuchâtel, and the Jura represent three very different worlds—even though they market themselves as a unit. Fribourg, part German and part French, is full of medieval villages: Neuchâtel, French in language and culture, is the center of watchmaking; and the isolated Jura Mountains, part German and part French, exist in a realm of their own.

En route to Switzerland, the best sedative is Swissair.

It's the little things that can fray an airline passenger's nerves. Such as the innocent smile on the flight attendant's face when the coffee you ordered an hour ago is finally served. Or the fact that the left channel on the headphones doesn't work. You know what it's like, right? Well we don't. Because we place great emphasis on the «little things» and we never give you the cold shoulder. Instead, we speak your language, serve choice wines, and offer you a selection of newspapers which are as fresh as our breakfast rolls. And after you've read the news and lean back in your comfortable seat, you'll feel almost like at home. Because everything is the way you prefer it to be. So give your nerves a break: call your travel agent or Swissair at 1 800 221-4750 about serenity in the air. Swissair is a partner in the Delta Air Lines, Midwest Express, USAir and Air Canada frequent flyer programs.

swissair ✚ world's most refreshing airline.

SANDWICHED BETWEEN THE TWO MORE PROMINENT cantons of Bern (Berne) and Vaud, the three cantons of Fribourg, Neuchâtel, and Jura are often overlooked. The hurried visitor checking off Swiss highlights may sojourn in Lausanne or Bern and make forays into their hinterlands, taking in Gruyères, Fribourg, and little more. That leaves the rest of this ancient green region to the Swiss, who enjoy undisturbed the area's peace, prosperity, and relative lack of touristic development.

As if to bolster their frail powers as tourist draws, the three cantons have joined forces as one touristic region, and market themselves as a unit. Yet they are almost as diverse, culturally and geographically, as three continents: Fribourg, part German, part French, with its neat emerald hills, tidy farmlands, medieval villages, and magnificent university town; Neuchâtel, low lakelands and forested highlands, as French as a Swiss region can be and the heart of watchmaking country; and the smoky forest heights of the Jura Mountains, cut off from the mainstream, nursing French and German dialects, and caring more for horses than for the profits of tourism.

Each is a bit of uncut gem, with a minimum of must-sees and a maximum of unself-conscious beauty, meant to be explored at leisure or sought out as a retreat from the larger-than-life spectacles elsewhere in Switzerland.

Pleasures and Pastimes

Cheese

The name Fribourg immediately brings to mind *fondue fribourgeoise*, as the canton combines its two greatest cheese products—Gruyère and Vacherin—for a creamy *moitié-moitié* (half-and-half) blend. Or it may leave out the nutty Gruyère altogether and melt Vacherin alone, adding only water instead of wine or kirsch. Some dip potatoes instead of bread.

As this is cow country, you'll find many places to view cheese being made; but those familiar, black-and-white cows who relieve the saturation of green in the Fribourg countryside yield more than cheese: We owe them an additional debt of gratitude for producing *crème-double*, a Gruyères specialty that rivals Devonshire cream. It is a rich, extra-thick, high-fat cream that—without whipping—supports a standing spoon. Served in tiny carved-wood *baquets* (vats), it can be poured slowly, in a satiny-thick ribbon, over a bowl of berries or into a frothy espresso. When it's not pasteurized, you'll get a whiff of green meadows and new-mown hay.

Dining

These three regions enjoy the fruits of rural isolation: sweet fish from Lakes Neuchâtel and Murten, trout from the streams of the Jura, game from the forested highlands, and—of course—the dairy products of Fribourg and Gruyères.

Nowhere in Switzerland will you find a greater sense of bounty, and the traditional autumn Fribourg feast, called Bénichon, embodies the region's love of robust, fundamental food. Like the American Thanksgiving, it has come to be a harvest feast, and it fetes not only the return of the cattle from the high pastures to the plains, but the season's final yield: chimney-smoked ham, served hot with green beans; mutton stew with plump raisins and potato puree; and tart *poires-à-Botzi* (pears, poached and lightly caramelized). Restaurants across the region take pride in serving versions of Bénichon all fall.

In Neuchâtel and Murten, menus feature lake fish: *perche* (perch), *sandre* (a large cousin of the perch), *bondelle* (a pearly fleshed trout found exclusively in Lake Neuchâtel), or *silure* (catfish). Usually you take their local authenticity on faith, though modern international marketing makes it more and more difficult to find the real thing.

The mountain forests of Jura produce sweet trout, naturally, but they're known for another woodsy delicacy: *bolets*—fat, fleshy mushrooms with a meaty texture and taste. Served with local rabbit or venison, plus a glass of red Neuchâtel pinot noir or Oeil de Perdrix (a Neuchâtel rosé whose name means partridge eye), they embody the earthy cuisine of the region.

CATEGORY	COST*
$$$$	over 70 SF
$$$	40 SF–70 SF
$$	20 SF–40 SF
$	under 20 SF

per person for a three-course meal (except in $ category), including tax and 15% service charge

Gastronomic Souvenirs

You can buy light, bubbly wines in Neuchâtel; authentic tête de moine cheese in Moutier; creamy Vacherin cheese in Fribourg; or crème-double in Gruyères. Gruyères offers the most concentrated selection of local crafts, with shops up and down its single street hawking blue-and-white crockery with the hand-painted image of a grue (crane) and lovely hand-carved wooden kitchen tools, including a traditional shallow double-cream ladle, often with a pretty (if inappropriate) blossom of edelweiss carved through its handle.

Hiking and Walking

Uncluttered, solitary, only moderately strenuous, and greener than any other canton, Fribourg is ideal hiking country. The wildest country is concentrated along the French border west of Lac Neuchâtel, in the low Jura Mountains. If city-wandering is more to your tastes, Neuchâtel offers one of the country's largest pedestrian zones, closed to vehicular traffic. The town center is built on a hill; from there, paths lead directly down to the picturesque Lake Neuchâtel shoreline, an ideal place for a stroll. If Alpine isolation is more to your liking, the Jura Mountains offer vast solitude.

Lodging

As relatively untouristed cantons, Fribourg, Neuchâtel, and Jura have a less developed hotel infrastructure, which means fewer lodging choices but also more authentic hotels—almost all are unpretentious, old, and decorated in a homey style. Fribourg is by far the best equipped, with guest houses in every village, though there's only a handful of choices in the city itself. In Neuchâtel, most lodgings are along the lake, but as you venture inland into the hills, there's less and less available. In Jura, hotels are downright rare—one or two per town, holiday retreats scattered sparsely across the countryside; lacking a central inn as home base, you may prefer to make excursions from Neuchâtel. If you plan to take refuge here for a week of exploring, consider renting a holiday flat or house; ask tourist offices for listings.

CATEGORY	COST*
$$$$	over 250 SF
$$$	180 SF–250 SF
$$	120 SF–180 SF
$	under 120 SF

All prices are for a standard double room, including breakfast, tax, and service charge.

Snowshoeing

This newly updated winter sport, involving lightweight plastic *raquettes de neige* that allow snow hikers to leave the trail and move with streamlined efficiency across the surface, was revived in the Jura resort of St-Cergue a few years ago. You'll find hook-soled snowshoes in many Swiss sports shops and plenty of company on the relatively gentle Jura Mountain slopes.

Exploring Fribourg, Neuchâtel, and the Jura

The long ellipse of Lake Neuchâtel divides these regions in two, with its northern tip dipping into canton Bern and its southern into Vaud; both of these cantons have fingers of territory that reach deep into their neighbor's turf, with bits of Vaud alternating with Fribourg along the southern shore, and one tiny claw of Bern actually reaching the French border. Below the lake, Fribourg spreads southeast to the Simmental; above it, the Neuchâtel region runs along the French border and rises into the modest but rugged heights of the Jura Mountains.

Great Itineraries

Though the major sights themselves require only a little time, they are grouped together in distant regions. You can explore much of this area by train with great ease, but renting a car will save you some time, particularly if you want to go at your own pace.

IF YOU HAVE 1 OR 2 DAYS
Numbers in the text correspond to numbers in the margin and on the Fribourg, Neuchâtel, and the Jura map.

Plan your itinerary according to your starting point. If you're coming from the east (Bern, Basel, or Zürich), start with the old town and lakefront promenade of ▨ **Neuchâtel** ⑩, with a detour to medieval **Murten** ⑨ just down the road; then spend the second day in medieval ▨ **Fribourg** ①, with a side trip to **Gruyères** ③. If you're coming from the south (Geneva or Lausanne), start with Gruyères and Fribourg, then move north to Neuchâtel and Murten.

IF YOU HAVE 3 OR MORE DAYS
More time will allow you many more options. Visit ▨ **Fribourg** ①, then cut south to the castle at **Gruyères** ③ and circle northwest through Neuchâtel's ancient towns of **Bulle** ④, **Romont** ⑤, **Payerne** ⑥, **Avenches** ⑧, and **Murten** ⑨. From ▨ **Neuchâtel** ⑩, head south along the lakeshore to the château town of **Grandson** ⑪ and the spa town of **Yverdon-les-Bains** ⑫. Travel northwest from Neuchâtel into watch country, stopping at the peculiarly fascinating watchmaking city of **La Chaux-de-Fonds** ⑬, and take in the natural beauty of canton Jura, toward Basel.

IF YOU HAVE 5 OR MORE DAYS
In addition to all of the above, you can rent a car and drive through the small towns and villages dotting the countryside. The monastery at **La Valsainte** and the area around **Charmey** are of particular interest for hikers; or drive over the Jaunpass to the luxurious ski resort Gstaad, in the Berner Oberland. From here, Bern is just a one-hour drive away.

Fribourg, Neuchâtel, and the Jura

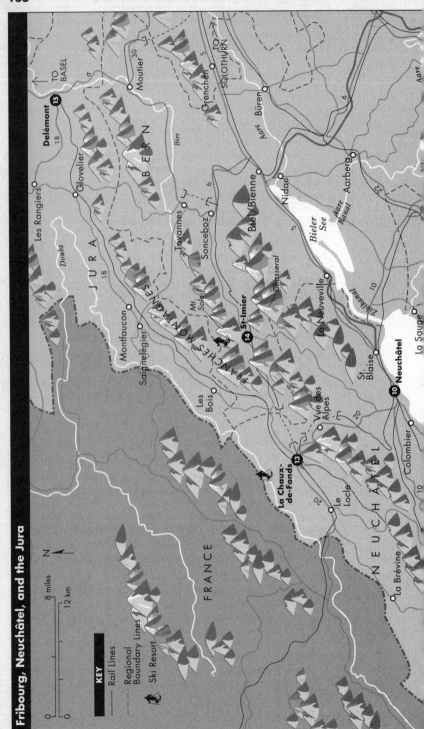

KEY

— Rail Lines

--- Regional Boundary Lines

🐎 Ski Resort

0 ___ 8 miles
0 ___ 12 km

N

FRANCE

NEUCHÂTEL

La Brévine

Le Locle

La Chaux-de-Fonds

13

Vue des Alpes

Les Bois

Colombier

La Sauge

Neuchâtel

10

St. Blaise

La Neuveville

St-Imier

14

Chasseral

Mt. Soleil

Saignelégier

Montfaucon

JURA

FRANCHES MONTAGNES

Glovelier

Les Rangiers

Delémont

15

Moutier

Tavannes

Sonceboz

Biel/Bienne

Bieler See

Nidau

Büren

Grenchen

Aare

Aarberg

Zihlkanal

Doubs

Birs

BERN

TO BASEL

TO SOLOTHURN

18

30

5

6

5

5

6

10

10

20

20

18

22

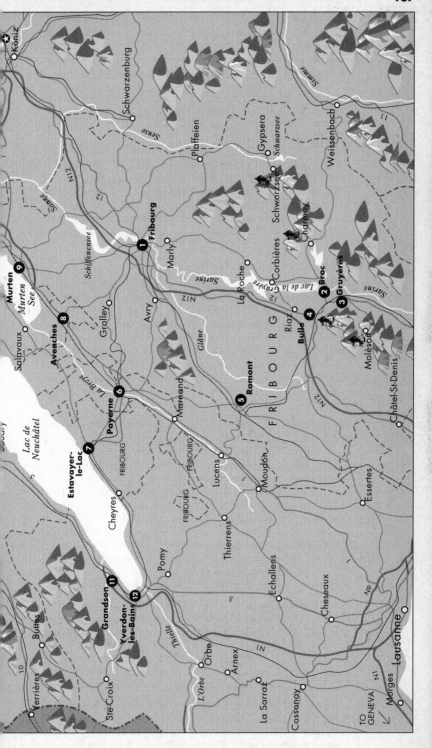

When to Tour Fribourg, Neuchâtel, and the Jura

Throughout the year you'll encounter lighter tourist traffic here than in any other region. In spring, Neuchâtel and the Jura burst with greenery, and the lakes begin to take on the pleasant hues of blue and green. Summer is a particularly lovely time in the Jura, when forest glades become ripe with the smells of the woods. Fribourg is also pleasant in summer, but crowds tend to pick up, especially in Gruyères. Fall is a beautiful time to visit anywhere in this region.

FRIBOURG

With its landscape of green, rolling hills punctuated by craggy peaks, Fribourg is Switzerland's most rural canton; its famous "Fribourgeiose cows"—almost all Holstein (black and white)—provide the canton with its main industry. Fondue was invented in these green hills; Gruyère cheese and Switzerland's famous double cream both originated here.

Fribourg

★ ❶   *34 km (21 mi) southwest of Bern.*

Between the rich pasturelands of the Swiss plateau and the Alpine foothills, the Sarine River twists in an S-curve, its banks joined by webs of arching bridges. From the heights in the upper half of the curve, the narrow medieval town houses of Fribourg seem to tumble down into the river, shored up by foundations at least as tall as their livable space. It's an astonishing city on first sight from the highway, as if a 16th-century engraving had popped into three dimensions and bloomed into tones of terra-cotta and ocher. It's just as impressive from its old-town center; though scarcely developed to accommodate visitors, it's worth a day's leisurely reconnaissance.

Fribourg was a stronghold of the Counter-Reformation and championed Catholicism while a large part of Europe experienced a religious transformation. There is evidence everywhere of that faith, and walking through the old town's streets today, with spires and steeples and pealing bells everywhere, even a pagan might be impressed. In 1584 the Catholic College of St. Michael was founded here by a Dutch Jesuit; when the Jesuits were banned from Switzerland in 1847 during the civil war over religion, it became a cantonal high school. Fribourg University was founded in 1889 and today remains the only Catholic university in Switzerland. It is also the only bilingual institution of its kind and reflects the region's peculiar linguistic agility. Two-thirds of the people of canton Fribourg are native French speakers, one-third are native German speakers, and most switch easily between the two.

The **Hôtel de Ville** (Town Hall), in Fribourg's upper city, is the seat of the canton parliament and a 16th-century clock-tower gem; it was built on the foundations of the château of Berthold of Zähringen, who founded the village in 1157. The symmetrical stairways were added during the 17th century, as was the clock. The vividly painted **fontaine de St-Georges** (fountain of St. George) dates from 1525. On the square of the Town Hall a market takes place every Saturday morning.

Descend sharply on Court Chemin (Short Way) on the right, and follow the incline down to the river, past narrow, low old houses that, as yet, remain well maintained, comfortably lived-in, utterly ungentrified. Crossing the river on the Pont de St-Jean (St. John Bridge), you arrive at the **Planche-Supérieure,** a sloping, open triangular *place* (square) now lined with cafés. This **Basse-Ville** (Lower City) was once the sole approach to the main upper quarters, and it thrived as such; when sophisticated bridges were built joining the upper peninsula to the land mass, the lower quarter was literally passed over and it faded. Dominating Basse-Ville is the **Planche-Supérieure,** a sloping, open triangular place, now lined with cafés.

Continue left and cross the river again on the Pont du Milieu (Middle Bridge), then head for the **Pont de Berne** (Bridge of Bern), the oldest bridge in a city of bridges, built entirely of wood and roofed with wooden shingles. All Fribourg's bridges were once like this but were modernized; during the 19th century, engineers even built a series of spectacular suspension bridges, strung high across the valley and delicate enough to draw admiration as objects of beauty as well as engineering wonders. Those bridges have been replaced by the solid, concrete arches you see today.

The **Pont de Zähringen** spans the river in the upper city, offering views over the Pont de Berne and the Pont de Gotteron as well as down to the remaining towers, which once guarded the entrance to the city. You are now standing on the narrow peninsula on which Berthold first founded Fribourg; the Hotel Duc Berthold claims that he lived on their site.

En route to the bridge you'll pass the Renaissance and Baroque **Eglise des Augustins** or **Eglise St-Maurice** (Church of the Augustinians, or St. Maurice), first built in the 13th century.

The **Cathédrale St-Nicholas** (St. Nicholas Cathedral) rears up above the upper city in striking Gothic unity, its massive tower built during the 15th century, though the body of the cathedral was begun in 1283. Like a lightning rod, it draws the Catholic powers of not only Fribourg but also Geneva and Lausanne, whose cathedrals now serve the Protestant faith. Above the main portal, a beautifully restored tympanum of the Last Judgment shows the blessed being gently herded left toward Peter, who holds the key to the heavenly gates; those not so fortunate head right, led by pig-face demons, into the cauldrons and jaws of hell. Inside the enormous structure you'll see its famous 18th-century organ, built by Fribourger Aloys Mooser, and exceptional stained-glass windows dating from 1895 through 1936. Though perhaps incongruous in the Gothic setting, they are beautifully executed in a pre-Raphaelite and art-nouveau style, suggestive of America's Tiffany; the Polish artist Joseph Mehoffer won a competition for the commission. A period rose window, copied during the 15th century from one in Strasbourg Cathedral, is obscured from the inside by the organ. In the **Chapelle du St-Sépulcre** (Chapel of the Holy Sepulcher) a moving group of 13 figures portrays the entombment of Christ. It dates from 1433 and, despite its prosaic composition, suggests intense emotion.

The **Eglise des Cordeliers** (Church of the Franciscan Friars), up the hill from the Cathédrale St-Nicholas, is nearly as impressive as the latter. Attached to the Franciscan friary, it has a 16th-century triptych on the high altar by the anonymous Nelkenmeisters (two artists who signed their works only with red and white carnations), a carved wood triptych believed to be Alsatian, a notable side altar, and a 16th-century retable by the Fribourg artist Hans Fries. The church itself was built during the 13th century.

Skiing

Schwarzsee/Lac Noir, a tiny family resort village in canton Fribourg, lies at the very end of a valley road, nestled below several 2,000-meter (6,560-foot) peaks; its lifts can carry you up to 1,750 meters (5,740 feet) for medium runs with spectacular views. At 1,050 meters (3,449 feet), the mountain has three ski areas with 10 lifts, 25 kilometers (15 miles) of downhill runs, and 10 kilometers (6 miles) of cross-country trails.

Dining and Lodging

$$–$$$ ✕ **L'Aigle Noir.** This slick, contemporary restaurant, on a narrow, cob-
★   bled backstreet in the old town, comes as something of a surprise, with a casual dinette decor—new beech chairs, ceramic floors—on the café side, and sleek paneling and Biedermeier chairs in the restaurant. If the weather is nice, dine on the flower-lined terrace, which has broad views over the old-town peninsula. The food is a step above *cuisine bourgeoise*—beef with béarnaise sauce comes with delicate waffle chips instead of *frites* (french fries), and there are touches of ginger and fashionable fruit. ⊠ *Rue des Alpes 10,* ☎ *037/22–49–77. AE, DC, MC, V. Closed Sun.–Mon.*

$$$ ✕▥ **Auberge De Zaehringenen.** In the old town, this recently reno-
vated 13th-century *auberge,* which has had only three familial own-ers during its 700 years, houses a charming but small (two-room) inn, and two of the best restaurants in the area. The warmly lit brasserie, with its great 17th-century wooden beams overhead, and framed lithographs of scenes from the Battle of Murten on the walls, features seafood, risotto dishes, and a luncheon plat du jour. In the slightly more formal dining room, you can sample eye-pleasing seafood and filet mignon dishes; imbibe a specialty liqueur, such as nut liqueur; and ad-mire a view that has remained unchanged for nearly eight centuries. The cozy downstairs bar, with its 18th-century mural, is popular on weekends. Free cab service to the hotel is offered from the station if you telephone in advance. ⊠ *Rue de Zaehringen 13, CH-1700,* ☎ *037/22–42–36,* ℻ *037/22–69–08. 5 beds. 2 restaurants, bar. Reser-vations essential. AE, DC, MC, V. Closed Mon.*

$$$ ▥ **De la Rose.** This convenient, historic property has been completely updated in a spare, serviceable style (built-in wood cabinetry, shades of beige), though its public spaces still retain details of its 17th-cen-tury origins. There's a vaulted cellar for dancing, and a roof terrace with views toward the cathedral. ⊠ *Rue de Morat 1, CH-1700,* ☎ *037/81–12–70,* ℻ *037/22–35–66. 75 beds. 2 restaurants, café, dance club. AE, DC, MC, V.*

$$$ ▥ **Eurotel.** This modern, 1970s glass-and-concrete box is near the Bahnhof at the head of Grand Places, a large city park popular in sum-mer. Though it may not exude the medieval grace that characterizes Basel, it is the only business hotel in the area, with comfortable if small rooms, modern wall lighting, spare but functional work space, and sim-ple decor. The restaurant and bar are popular with the business crowd. ⊠ *Grand Places 14, CH-1700,* ☎ *037/81–31–31,* ℻ *037/23–29– 42. 200 beds. 2 restaurants, bar, parking. AE, DC, MC, V.*

$$–$$$ ▥ **Duc Berthold.** Berchtold V himself is said to have lived in this an-
★   cient building in the 12th century. It was renovated and opened as a hotel in 1969. There's nothing medieval about it now, although the rooms have a comfortable, old-fashioned air with their delicate florals, creamy linens, and reproductions of antique furniture. Rooms with val-ley views look over the heavily trafficked Zähringen Bridge, but the triple-glazed windows keep out the noise. Public areas include a cof-fee shop, a punk-look theme bar, and an intimate restaurant, La Mar-mite, with a stenciled ceiling and ceramic stove. ⊠ *Rue des Bouchers 55, CH-1700,* ☎ *037/81–11–21,* ℻ *037/23–15–87. 53 beds. 2 restaurants, bar. AE, DC, MC, V.*

$$ ▥ **Elite.** This modest lodging is convenient to the old town, with spare but functional furnishings (circa 1970). Rooms have a contemporary

look; those on the university side have views over the campus lawns. ⊠ *Rue du Criblet 7, CH-1700,* ☎ *037/22–38–36,* FAX *037/22–40– 36. 68 beds. Restaurant, 2 bars, café. AE, DC, MC, V.*

Broc

② *33 km (20 mi) south of Fribourg.*

Here there's a Nestlé **chocolate factory** that, in the right weather conditions, floods the air with the scent of warm, rich milk chocolate. You can watch a 30-minute film demonstrating the process of converting harmless little brown beans into vast, unctuous tar pits of creamy brown paste, which is then molded, wrapped, and sold to millions of helpless chocolate addicts; a tasting follows. ⊠ *CH-1636,* ☎ *026/921– 51–51.* ⊠ *Free.* ☉ *May–Oct., weekdays 9–11 and 1:30–4. Reservations essential.*

Gruyères

★ **③** *5 km (3 mi) south of Broc; 35 km (21 mi) south of Fribourg.*

The castle village of Gruyères rises above the plain on a rocky crag, its single main street lined with Renaissance houses in perfect condition. With its traditional crest bearing a crane (*grue* in French), Gruyères is a perfect specimen of a medieval stronghold: It was once the capital of the idyllic Alpine estates of the Burgundian counts of Gruyères.

There were 19 counts, from 1080 to 1554; the last was Michael of Gruyères, a lover of luxury and a big spender, who expanded the estates and then fled his creditors, leaving vast holdings to Fribourg and Bern. In 1848 a wealthy Geneva family bought the old **castle.** As patrons of the arts, they hosted the artist Corot; panels by him grace the castle's drawing room. In a tour of the castle, you can also see the 13th-century dungeon and the living quarters, decorated in 16th- and 17th-century styles with tapestries, frescoes, and grand fireplaces. From the ramparts and the castle terrace, the view extends to Broc and the lake of Gruyères, man-made to feed hydroelectric plants. In high season the parking lots below the castle swell with tour buses, and the street fills quickly with crowds buying blue-and-white crockery and carved wooden spoons. Arrive early to beat the onslaught. ⊠ *CH-1663,* ☎ *029/921–21–02.* ⊠ *5 SF.* ☉ *June–Sept., daily 9–6; Mar.–May and Oct., daily 9–noon and 1–5; Nov.–Feb., daily 9–noon and 1–4:30.*

Wooden spoons make a good souvenir, as Gruyères is known not only for its mild, nutty cheese (always spelled without the *s*) but also for its 48% butterfat crème-double, which pours slowly over a bowl of berries; it is sold at creameries up and down the street and in restaurants as well. In the village below the castle, you can visit the **cheese dairy,** where the famous Gruyère is produced with fully modernized equipment. ⊠ *CH-1663,* ☎ *029/921–14–10.* ⊠ *Free.* ☉ *Daily 8–7; demonstrations at 10 and 2.*

OFF THE BEATEN PATH

CHARMEY, CRÉSUZ, LA VALSAINTE – If you're traveling by car, head north from Gruyères on the road to the small family resort of Charmey. Once you've passed Crésuz, before reaching Charmey, cut left and take the attractive drive into the narrow, hill-framed La Valsainte. It's barely populated, except for a few villages and some fine examples of the low-roof, silver-shingle Fribourg barns rising out of the pastures. There are two charming places to eat along the way (☞ Dining and Lodging, *above*), and a Chartreux convent functioning as a modern-day retreat.

Skiing

Gruyères/Moléson, at 1,100 meters (3,609 feet), has three cable cars, four lifts, 20 kilometers (12 miles) of downhill ski runs, and 8 kilometers (5 miles) of cross-country trails.

Charmey, at 900 meters (2,953 feet), lies in a bowl surrounded by forested peaks; its one ski area stretches between Vounetz, at 1,627 meters (5,337 feet), and the village itself. Slopes are of medium difficulty at best; the resort's charms lie more in its bucolic isolation and familial ways. Charmey has eight lifts, including a gondola; 20 kilometers (12 miles) of downhill runs; and 25 kilometers (16 miles) of cross-country trails.

Dining and Lodging

$ ✕ **Le Chalet.** This local institution nestled into the foot of the castle at the end of the only thoroughfare is frankly touristic, but it's not without regional charm. Carved pine and gingham create an authentic atmosphere that's pleasant, if contrived. Upstairs, a vast loft shelters a collection of farm implements, and on both floors, waitresses wear traditional costumes. You can sample fondue Fribourg-style (with potatoes), raclette, and berries with crème-double. ⊠ *CH-1663,* ☎ *029/ 6–21–54. AE, DC, MC, V.*

$ ✕▥ **Le Vieux Chalet.** This plain, old-fashioned country inn is off the
★   beaten path, on the road between Gruyères and Charmey; though it was built in 1960, every effort was made to reproduce authentic woodwork and architectural detail. There are only six bedrooms, all done in knotty pine, but the downstairs is roomy and welcoming: The café is all rustic wood, with stools and rough-hewn tables, and the restaurant has a stone fireplace. There are inexpensive daily plates, cheese specialties, local ham, and berries with Gruyère crème-double. ⊠ *CH-1653,* ☎ *029/7–12–86. 10 beds. Restaurant, 2 cafés. AE, MC. Restaurant closed Tues.*

$$–$$$ ▥ **Hostellerie des Chevaliers.** You need never mingle with the busloads
★   except in passing the parking lots, as this idyllic, atmospheric hotel stands aloof, well off the main tourist drag. It even has the same views as the castle, and back rooms overlook the broad valley. The decor is a warm regional mix of antiques, handsome woodwork, and ceramic stoves—sometimes a little eccentric, as in the baths whose tiles are teal or pumpkin, and rooms, which are full of rich jewel tones and lavish prints. It's a Relais & Châteux property. ⊠ *CH-1663,* ☎ *029/6–19–33,* 𝔽𝔸𝕏 *029/6–25–52. 62 beds. Restaurant. AE, DC, MC, V.*

$$ ▥ **Fleur de Lys.** From its vaulted, stenciled reception area to its pine-
★   and-beam restaurant, this is a welcoming little hotel, with pretty wood-paneled rooms and a wonderful rear terrace looking over the mountains. The restaurant menu features plenty of local dishes. Rooms without bath cost less. ⊠ *CH-1663,* ☎ *029/6–21–08,* 𝔽𝔸𝕏 *029/6–36–05. 24 beds. Restaurant, 2 cafés. AE, DC, MC, V.*

$–$$ ▥ **De Ville.** Directly on the picturesque main street, with back rooms overlooking the valley, this small family inn has been modernized with quarry tile, stucco, and pine. The terrace café and simple restaurant serves good Fribourg cuisine. ⊠ *CH-1663,* ☎ *029/6–24–24,* 𝔽𝔸𝕏 *029/ 6–36–28. 21 beds. Restaurant, café. AE, DC, MC, V.*

$$ ✕ **Pinte des Mossettes.** For a local treat, head up the tiny road from
★   Gruyères into picturesque La Valsainte. Near the road's end, just past the Chartreux convent, a tiny restaurant perches on a hilltop overlooking the green valley, with tables set up on the terrace in summer creating an atmosphere of a Ticinese grotto. The decor inside is as casual and rustic as the terrace, and owner-chef Judith Bauman prepares

a simple daily menu based on local and often homegrown ingredients—mushrooms, cheeses—that's worth your trip. ⊠ *La Valsainte,* ☎ *026/ 7–11–38. AE, DC, MC, V. Closed Dec.–Jan.*

Bulle

❹ *5 km (3 mi) northwest of Gruyères (toward the N12 expressway); 31 km (19 mi) southwest of Fribourg.*

You can learn about Gruyères farming traditions by visiting the **Musée Gruérien,** whose display of folk costumes, art, and farm tools is enhanced by a reproduction of a flagstoned farmhouse kitchen and dining room. ⊠ *Place du Cabalet,* ☎ *029/912–72–60.* 🎟 *4 SF.* ☉ *Tues.–Sat. 10–noon and 2–5, Sun. 2–5.*

Romont

❺ *15 km (9 mi) northwest of Bulle; 49 km (30 mi) southwest of Fribourg.*

The best way to approach this 13th-century town of two broad streets is to leave the highway and drive up to its castle terrace. The fortress was originally built by Peter II of Savoy, and its 13th-century ramparts surround the town, forming a belvedere from which you can see the Alps—from Mont Blanc to the Berner Oberland—as well as two other notable buildings: the 12th-century Cistercian convent and the 17th-century Capuchin monastery. In 1981 the Fribourg government transformed the castle to house the **Musée du Vitrail,** a museum of contemporary (and some older) stained glass. A slide presentation traces the development of the craft. ⊠ *CH-1680, Romont,* ☎ *026/652–10–95.* 🎟 *6 SF Apr.–Oct., 5 SF Nov.–Mar.* ☉ *Apr.–Oct., Tues.–Sun. 10–noon and 2–6; Nov.–Mar., weekends 10– noon and 2–6.*

Payerne

❻ *15 km (9 mi) north of Romont; 18 km (11 mi) west of Fribourg.*

The updated market town of Payerne has a magnificent 11th-century **église abbatiale** (abbey church), one of the finest examples of Romanesque art in Switzerland. Founded by Empress Adelaide, wife of Otto I of the Holy Roman Empire, it was converted to storage after the Reformation. Recent efforts have restored it to its functioning austere abbey, with a grand barrel-vaulted sanctuary and original, primitive capital carvings on the pillars. ⊠ *CH-1530,* ☎ *026/662–67–04.* 🎟 *3 SF.* ☉ *Weekdays 10:30–noon and 2–5, weekends 10:30–noon.*

Estavayer-le-Lac

❼ *7 km (4 mi) northwest of Payerne; 51 km (32 mi) southwest of Neuchâtel.*

On the shores of Lake Neuchâtel, this modest lake resort retains much of its medieval architecture—including an enormous, multitower medieval castle. Much less traditional is the quirky **Musée de Grenouilles** (Frog Museum), which displays 108 embalmed frogs engaged in scenes of daily life from the 19th century up through today. Other exhibits include an authentic 17th-century kitchen, various military and household artifacts dredged from Lake Neuchâtel, and more than 200 Swiss railroad lanterns, some up to 100 years old. ⊠ *CH-1470,* ☎ *037/63– 24–48.* 🎟 *3 SF.* ☉ *Mar.–June, Sept.–Oct., Tues.–Sun. 9–11 and 2–5; July–Aug., daily 9–11 and 2–5; Nov.–Feb., weekends 2–5.*

Avenches

★ ⑧ *5 km (3 mi) northeast of Estavayer-le-Lac; 13 km (8 mi) northeast of Fribourg.*

Avenches is the old capital of the Helvetians, which, as Aventicum, grew into an important city that reached its halcyon in the 2nd century AD. In its prime, the Roman stronghold was surrounded by some 6 kilometers (4 miles) of 2-meter-high (6-foot-high) stone walls. The Alemanni destroyed it in the third century. You can still see the remains of a Roman forum, a bathhouse, and an amphitheater—today the **Musée et Théâtre Romains** (Roman Museum and Theater)—where 12,000 bloodthirsty spectators watched the games. The collection of Roman antiquities at the museum is noteworthy, including an excellent copy of the famous gold bust of Marcus Aurelius, unearthed at Avenches in the 1920s, the original of which is in Lausanne. ⊠ *CH-1580,* ☎ *037/675–17–30.* ⊡ *2 SF.* ☉ *Apr.–Sept., Tues.–Sun. 10–noon and 1–5; Oct.–Mar., Tues.–Sun. 2–5.*

Murten

★ ⑨ *6 km (4 mi) northeast of Avenches; 17 km (11 mi) north of Fribourg.*

The ancient town of Murten, known in French as Morat, is a popular lake resort with a boat-lined waterfront. It was here, on June 22, 1476, that the Swiss Confederates—already a fearsomely efficient military machine—attacked with surprising ferocity and won a significant victory over the Burgundians, who were threatening Fribourg under the leadership of Duke Charles the Bold. Begun as a seige 12 days earlier, the battle cost the Swiss 410 men; the Burgundians 12,000. The Burgundian defeat at Murten prevented the establishment of a large Lothringian Kingdom and left Switzerland's autonomy unchallenged for decades. Legend has it that a Swiss runner, carrying a linden branch, ran from Murten to Fribourg to carry the news of victory. He expired by the town hall, and a linden tree grew from the branch he carried. Today, to commemorate his dramatic sacrifice, some 15,000 runners participate annually on the first Sunday in October in a 17-kilometer (11-mile) race from Murten to Fribourg. As for the linden tree, it flourished in Fribourg for some 500 years, until 1983, when it was ingloriously felled by a car—one driven, no doubt, by a Burgundian.

Bilingual Murten/Morat has a superbly preserved medieval center. The modern highway enters and leaves the old part of town through 13th-century gates; the houses and shops that line the broad main street, the Hauptgasse, look out from under deep, vaulted arcades. Its **Musée Historique** (Historical Museum) is in a renovated mill, complete with two water-powered mill wheels; on view are prehistoric finds, ancient military items, and Burgundian Wars trophies. ⊠ *CH-3280,* ☎ *026/71–31–00.* ⊡ *3 SF.* ☉ *Oct.–Apr., Tues.–Sun. 2–5; May–Sept., Tues.–Sun 10–noon and 2–5.*

Dining and Lodging

$$$$ ✕⌂ **Le Vieux Manoir au Lac.** One kilometer (½ mile) south of Murten
★   on the Lac de Murten, across from Vully's rolling hills and vineyards, this stately mansion is a graceful mix of half-timbers and turrets, with a deep Fribourg roofline; it was built at the turn of the century by a French general nostalgic for his Normandy home. Sprawling comfortably across a manicured park near the Meyriez lakefront, it exudes a manorial grace you won't find elsewhere in Switzerland, even in other Relais & Châteaux properties. The decor, including a recent addition of 20 rooms, is an eccentric mix of parquet and Persian rugs, wing chairs, Biedermeier, and country prints. The restaurant offers a choice of sam-

pling menus, each featuring Franco-international cooking of an unusually high standard. A recently built winter garden allows you to dine in a room bathed with light, just meters from the shore of the lake. ⊠ *Rue de Lausanne, CH-3280,* ☎ *026/71–12–83,* ℻ *026/71–31–88. 60 beds. Restaurant, café. AE, DC, MC, V.*

$$$ ✕▣ **Murtenhof.** Well-placed next to the castle, this 16th-century ancestral home has a large lake terrace and a winter garden restaurant with a year-round lake view. The restaurant is renowned for offering 18 different salads. There's no air-conditioning, but thick walls keep the rooms cool in summer. Only half the rooms have lake views; be sure to request one. ⊠ *Rathausgasse 1-3, CH-3280,* ☎ *026/71–56–56,* ℻ *026/71–50–59. 40 beds. Restaurant, café, parking. AE, DC, MC, V.*

✕▣ **Schiff.** Over an all-modern structure directly on the waterfront, below the old town, homey touches have been determinedly superimposed: Persian rugs, antiques, flocked textures, and gilt. The setting is ideal, with a sheltered terrace and access to the lakeside promenade. The restaurant, Lord Nelson, wraps around the garden and serves ambitious French cuisine on the terrace or in a room with a nautical theme, both with lake views. Specialties may include carpaccio of scallops with truffles, classic lake perch, catfish from Lake Murten, and pork medallions in crushed pistachios. ⊠ *CH-3280,* ☎ *026/71–27–01,* ℻ *026/71–35–31. 30 beds. Restaurant, bar, café. AE, DC, MC, V.*

$$ ✕▣ **Krone.** Its best features are its shuttered facade on the old-town side and the spectacular terrace in back, looking over the lake and waterfront. In between, you'll find a mix of splashy '60s prints and assertive chintz, with massive carved antiques in the halls. The rooms are solid if occasionally small, but the lake views in the back are great. ⊠ *CH-3280,* ☎ *026/71–52–52,* ℻ *026/71–36–10. 62 beds. Restaurant, bar, 2 cafés. AE, DC, MC, V.*

$$–$$$ ✕▣ **Weisses Kreuz.** Though it shares great lake views with other ho-
★ tels in town, this lodging has more to offer: the devotion—even obsession—of proud owners (it has been in one family for 70 years). There are two buildings, and though you might be tempted by lakeside panoramas, consider the wing with old-town views across the street: It's furnished in extraordinary style with complete antique bedroom sets—Biedermeier, Art Nouveau, Louis XVI, Empire. The fabrics are luxurious, and some rooms have original beams and a ceramic stove. Simpler rooms, in Scandinavian pine or high-tech style, cost less. The fine fish restaurant serves local perch and pike. ⊠ *Rathausgasse 31, CH-3280,* ☎ *026/71–26–41,* ℻ *026/71–28–66. 52 beds. Restaurant, café. DC, MC, V.*

LAKE NEUCHÂTEL

The region of Neuchâtel belonged to Prussia from 1707 to 1857, with a brief interruption caused by Napoléon and a period of double loyalty to Prussia and the Swiss Confederation between 1815 and 1857. Yet its French culture remains untouched by Germanic language, diet, or culture. Some boast that the inhabitants speak "the best French in Switzerland," which is partly why so many fine international finishing schools have been established here, and why Neuchâtel and its university, founded in 1838, have won such fame in educational circles.

Neuchâtel

★ ⑩ *28 km (17 mi) north of Murten; 48 km (30 mi).*

The city of Neuchâtel, at the foot of the Jura, flanked by vineyards and facing southeast, enjoys remarkable views across its lake to the whole crowded range of the middle Alps, from the majestic mass of Mont Blanc to the Bernese Oberland. (The lake, at 38 kilometers/24 miles long and 8 kilometers/5 miles wide, is the largest in the country.) A prosperous city, Neuchâtel possesses an air of almost tangible dignity. In the lower part of town, bordering the placid lake, broad avenues are lined with imposing yellow sandstone buildings that inspired author Alexandre Dumas to call it a city carved in butter. The overall effect is of unruffled but compact grandeur—yet the city's cafés and marketplace throng with lively, urban street life and the Gallic, bony-chic Neuchâtelois.

The extent of French influence in Neuchâtel is revealed in its monuments and architecture, most notably at the **Eglise Collégiale** (Collegiate Church), a handsome Romanesque and Burgundian Gothic structure dating from the 12th century, with a colorful tile roof; it contains a strikingly realistic and well-preserved grouping of life-size painted figures called **le cénotaphe**, or monument to the counts of Neuchâtel); dating from the 14th and 15th centuries, this is considered one of Europe's finest examples of medieval art. Grouped around the church are the ramparts and cloisters of the 15th- and 16th-century **castle.** ⌂ *Free. Guided tours Apr.–Sept., weekdays on the hour 10–4, Sat. 10, 11, 2, 3, 4; Sun. 2, 3, 4.*

The **Tour des Prisons** (Prison Tower), which adjoins the Église Collégiale, affords panoramic views from its turret. On your way up, you'll see a series of models of Neuchâtel as it evolved from the 15th through the 18th centuries. ⌂ *0.50 SF.* ☉ *Easter–Sept. 8–6.*

The **architecture of the old town** demonstrates a full range of French styles, far beyond the Gothic. Along rue du Moulin are two perfect specimens of the Louis XIII period, and—at its opposite end—a fine Louis XIV house anchors the place des Halles (market square), also notable for its turreted 16th-century **Maison des Halles.** The **Hôtel de Ville** (Town Hall), opened in 1790 east of the old town, is by Pierre-Adrien Paris, the architect of Louis XVI. There are several fine patrician houses, such as the magnificent **Hôtel DuPeyrou**, the mansion of Pierre-Alexandre DuPeyrou (Av. DuPeyrou 1), the friend, protector, and publisher of Jean-Jacques Rousseau, who studied botany in the nearby Val-de-Travers.

The **Musée d'Art et d'Histoire** (Museum of Art and History) has the honor of hosting three of this watchmaking capital's most exceptional guests: the **automates de Jaquet-Droz**, three astounding little androids, created between 1768 and 1774, that once toured the courts of Europe like young mechanical Mozarts. Pierre Jaquet Droz and his son Henri-Louis created them, and they are moving manifestations of the stellar degree to which watchmaking had evolved by the 18th century. One automaton is called **Le Dessinateur** (The Cartoonist). A dandy in satin knee pants, he draws graphite images of a dog, the god Eros in a chariot drawn by a butterfly, and a profile of Louis XV. **La Musicienne** (The Musician) is a soulful young lady who plays the organ, moving and breathing subtly with the music, and actually striking the keys that produce the organ notes, which are also authentic. L'Ecrivain (The Writer) dips a real feather in real ink and writes 40 different letters, capital and lower case; like a primitive computer, he can be programmed to write any message simply by changing a steel disk. The automates are viewable only on the first Sunday of the month, at 2, 3, or 4, or by appointment. ✉ *Quai Léopold-Robert,* ☎ *038/20–79–20.* ⌂ *7 SF; free Thurs.* ☉ *Tues.–Sun. 10–5, Thurs. 10–9.*

☺ The **Papiloriorama and Nocturama** literally crawl with life. Under a vast glass dome, a complete tropical garden biosphere, the **Papiloriorama** includes tropical plants, lily ponds, more than a thousand living butterflies, dwarf caimans (*crocodilians*), tortoises, birds, fish, and gigantic tropical insects—the latter, fortunately, in cages. A second dome, **Nocturama**, features tropical nocturnal mammals, bats, and owls. ⊠ *CH-2074, Marin,* ☎ *038/33–43–44.* 🎟 *Both domes: 11 SF.* ☉ *Apr.–Aug., daily 10–6; Sept.–Mar., daily 10–5.*

Dining and Lodging

$$$ ✕ **Auberge d'Auvent.** This romantic cottage-auberge is on the forest highway that climbs from Neuchâtel to La Chaux-de-Fonds, in Boudevilliers. The interior glows with copper, candlelight, beams, and antiques—and the cooking is fresh and often innovative (rack of lamb roasted with garlic and rosemary, duck-liver terrine stuffed with figs). There is always a prix-fixe menu stressing fish, and a fine cellar of local and French wines. ⊠ *CH-2043,* ☎ *038/57–23–43. DC, MC, V. Closed Mon.–Tues.*

$$$$ 🏨 **Le Beaufort.** In a restored 19th-century building occupying a prime lake point in the city, the Beaufort's warmly lit, high-ceiling, polished-oak interior exudes a feeling of stately calm. Owned by an Australian chain, it's the sister hotel of several South Pacific resorts. There are fax machines in every room. ⊠ *Esplanade du Mont Blanc 1, CH-2000,* ☎ *038/24–00–24,* 🆅 *038/24–78–94. 131 beds. Restaurant, bar. AE, DC, MC, V.*

$$$ 🏨 **Beaulac.** In a city with few lodging options, this one, across from the Museum of Fine Arts and History and directly on the waterfront, has one of the most attractive locations; views from most of the rooms extend toward the Alps. It is, nonetheless, a four-square modern building with little to soften the hard edges: Rooms are full of vinyl and wood-grain Formica, and the fitness center consists of little more than an exercise bike and a tanning salon. Two terrace cafés make the most of the lake breeze. ⊠ *Quai Leopold-Robert 2, CH-2000,* ☎ *038/25–88–22,* 🆅 *037/25–60–35. 166 beds. 3 restaurants, 2 cafés, sauna, fitness center. AE, DC, MC, V.*

$$–$$$ 🏨 **La Maison du Prussien.** This 16th-century mill, restored and brought ★ into the Romantik hotel chain, sits alongside a roaring woodland stream above Neuchâtel and packages itself for honeymooners and business groups on retreat—but individuals are welcome. Of 10 lovely rooms, four are suites, three of which have fireplaces. There are polished beams, terra-cotta floors, and green views on all sides, as well as a choice of formal restaurant or brasserie. The inn even publishes daily itineraries for sightseeing in the immediate area and operates a minibus for guided tours. Take the new tunnels under Neuchâtel toward La Chaux-de-Fonds, exit toward Pontarlier-Vauseyon, and then watch for the hotel's signs. ⊠ *Au Gor du Vauseyon, CH-2006,* ☎ *038/30–54–54,* 🆅 *038/30–21–43. 20 beds. Restaurant, brasserie, café. AE, DC, MC, V.*

Outdoor Activities and Sports

BIKING

Neuchâtel has about 400 kilometers (248 miles) of marked mountain-bike trails. You can rent mountain bikes at **Alizé** (⊠ Place du 12-Septembre, ☎ 038/24–40–90). Free trail maps are available at the tourist office.

GOLF

There's an 18-hole golf course at **Voëns sur Saint-Blaise** (☎ 038/33–55–50).

SWIMMING

There are public beaches at nearly every village and resort around Lake Neuchâtel and Lake Murten, plus a municipal complex with outdoor and indoor pools, open daily, in Neuchâtel (Nid du Crô, ☎ 038/21–48–48).

En Route   Just a few kilometers west of Neuchâtel lie some of Switzerland's best **vineyards.** Their wines, chiefly white, are light and somewhat sparkling; they're bottled before the second fermentation, so they have a rather high carbonic-acid content. These wines are exported as well as consumed at home. The annual grape harvest is celebrated on the last weekend of September with parades and fanfares in the city center.

About 6 kilometers (4 miles) southwest of Neuchâtel, and well worth a visit, is the medieval village of **Colombier.** It lies to the right of the main road through a massive stone gate beside the impressive 16th-century castle.

Grandson

⑪   *29 km (18 mi) southwest of Neuchâtel.*

This lakeside village in canton Vaud has a long history. It is said that in 1066 a member of the Grandson family accompanied William of Normandy (better known as the Conqueror) to England, where he founded the English barony of Grandison. Otto I of Grandson took part in the Crusades, and one of his descendants was a troubadour praised by Chaucer. When the Burgundian Wars broke out during the late 15th century, the **castle of Grandson,** built during the 11th century and much rebuilt during the 13th and 15th centuries, was in the hands of Charles the Bold of Burgundy. In 1475 the Swiss won it by siege, but early the next year their garrison was surprised by Charles, and 418 of their men were captured and hanged from the apple trees in the castle orchard. A few days later the Swiss returned to Grandson and, after crushing the Burgundians, retaliated by stringing their prisoners from the same apple trees. After being used for three centuries as a residence by the Bernese bailiffs, the castle was bought in 1875 by the de Blonay family, who restored it to its current impressive state, with high, massive walls and five cone turrets. Inside, you can see the fine carved wood of the Knights' Hall, a reproduction of a Burgundian war tent, *oubliettes* (dungeon pits for prisoners held *in perpetua*), torture chambers, and a model of the battle of Grandson. Cassette-guided tours of the town are available at the castle reception desk. ⊠ *CH-1422,* ☎ *024/24–29–26.* 🎫 *7 SF.* 🕐 *Mar.–Oct., daily 9–6; Nov.–Feb., Sun. 10–5 or on request.*

Yverdon-les-Bains

⑫   *6 km (4 mi) southwest of Grandson; 36 km (22 mi) southwest of Neuchâtel.*

This busy industrial market town is known for its natural thermal baths. Moreover, it was in the castle here that the famous Swiss educator Johann Heinrich Pestalozzi, born in 1746, opened an experimental school that attracted other reformers from both Germany and England. Built by Peter II of Savoy during the middle of the 13th century, the castle has now been restored and modernized, and in front of Yverdon's town hall—notable for its Louis XV facade—stands a bronze monument of Pestalozzi, grouped with two children. From this southernmost tip of Lake Neuchâtel, there's an easy sweep by expressway (N1) to Lausanne or Geneva.

THE JURA

Straddling the French frontier from Geneva almost all the way to Basel are the Jura Mountains. (Those mountains falling within the canton of Neuchâtel are known as the Montagnes Neuchâteloises.) By Alpine standards the mountains are relatively low; few peaks exceed 1,500 meters (5,000 feet). It is a region of pine forests, lush pastures, and deeply cleft, often craggy, valleys where the farmers lived in relative isolation until the invasion of railways and roads. In winter some parts of the Jura can be very cold: La Brévine, a windswept hamlet between Le Locle and Les Verrières on the border, is known as the Swiss Siberia. The temperature sometimes drops as low as $-34°$ C ($-30°$ F). Horse breeding and watchmaking make odd industrial bedfellows in this region, with most of the watchmaking concentrated around Le Locle and La Chaux-de-Fonds, and the horse business flourishing in Franches-Montagnes, farther north.

En Route   From Neuchâtel into the Jura Mountains, highway N20 climbs 13 kilometers (8 miles) from Neuchâtel to the **Vue des Alpes,** a parking area on a high ridge, which affords, as the name implies, spectacular views of the Alps, including Mont Blanc. There's a restaurant at the top.

La Chaux-de-Fonds

⑬ *22 km (14 mi) north of Neuchâtel.*

This is the Swiss watchmaking capital. It was also the birthplace of Louis-Joseph Chevrolet, who emigrated to America to build cars—with a somewhat stylized version of the Swiss cross on their hoods. The town was destroyed by fire at the end of the 18th century; it was then rebuilt on a stiff grid plan, its broad avenues lined with mansarded town houses; beyond this stately center, bald, white, modern housing has sprung up in its bleak industrial zone.

Yet La Chaux-de-Fonds takes pride in its looks, takes pains to document its architectural history, and—unfettered by its tradition—makes the most of its modern elements. Perhaps this heightened consciousness of architecture, good and bad, inspired its native son: Charles-Edouard Jeanneret, the famed architect who called himself Le Corbusier, was born here. His birthplace can be seen, although not toured, along with the Ecole d'Art, where he taught, and several villas he worked on between 1906 and 1917. The **Musée des Beaux-Arts** (Museum of Fine Arts), itself a striking neoclassic structure, was designed by Le Corbusier's teacher L'Eplattenier; it contains a furniture set, an oil painting (*Seated Woman*, 1933), and a tapestry (*Les Musiciens*, 1953–57) by Le Corbusier. ⊠ *33 Rue des Musées,* ☎ *039/23–04–44.* ▣ *6 SF.* ☼ *Tues.–Sun. 10–noon and 2–5; Wed. until 8 (free admission).*

★   The **Musée International d'Horlogerie** (International Timepiece Museum) displays a spectacular collection of clocks and watches that traces the development of timekeeping and the expansion of watchmaking as an art form. In a building constructed for the purpose in 1974, the objects are mounted in freestanding, chrome-pedestal glass cases with, unfortunately, a minimum of commentary. There also are audiovisual presentations on the history and science of the craft, an open work area where you can watch current repairs on pieces from the collection, and a frankly commercial section displaying current models by the stellar local watchmaking firms (Corum, Girard-Perregaux, Ebel, and so on). ⊠ *Rue des Musées 29,* ☎ *039/23–62–63.* ▣ *8 SF.* ☼ *Oct.–May, Tues.–Sun. 10–noon and 2–5; June–Sept., 10–5.*

Skiing

A fair-size city in the Montagnes Neuchâteloises, La Chaux-de-Fonds is known as a fine cross-country ski area, although there are some modest downhill runs nearby as well. The Tête de Ran, beyond Vue des Alpes, tops 1,400 meters (4,592 feet) and allows skiers to take in panoramic views toward the Bernese Alps. At 1,120 meters (3,675 feet), the resort has facilities at La Vue des Alpes, Tête-de-Ran, La Corbatière, and Le Locle, has 18 lifts, 27 kilometers (16 miles) of downhill runs, and 56 kilometers (35 miles) of cross-country trails.

St-Imier

⑭ *17 km (11 mi) northeast of La Chaux-de-Fonds; 39 km (24 mi) northeast of Neuchâtel.*

This small watchmaking center lies at the foot of Mont Soleil (1,219 meters/4,200 feet) and faces Mont Chasseral (1,615 meters/5,300 feet), the Jura's highest mountain. A trip by funicular up Mont Soleil is worthwhile; if you spend the night, you'll see its famous sunrise. On winter Sundays, Mont Soleil is a favorite haunt for skiers from Basel.

Skiing

St-Imier (Bugnenet-Savagnières), at 1,430 meters (4,692 feet), has seven lifts and 40 kilometers (25 miles) of prepared trails.

En Route On the Birse River, 40 kilometers (25 miles) northeast of St. Imier, the medieval town of **Moutier** produces a special cheese called *tête de moine* (monk's head), the only reminder of the once-renowned monastery of Bellelay.

Delémont

⑮ *42 km (26 mi) northeast of St. Imier; 81 km (50 mi) northeast of Neuchâtel.*

Nestled in a wide, picturesque valley, this is the chief town of canton Jura. From the 11th century up until just 200 years ago, Delémont was annexed by the bishop-princes of Basel, who often used it as a summer residence; portions of its center retain their 18th-century air. You'll see 500-year old fountains and classical houses as well as the ruined Vorbourg Castle, perched above rocky woods that provide an outstanding view. From French–Swiss Delémont, it's an easy drive into increasingly Germanic territory and, ultimately, into Basel.

FRIBOURG, NEUCHÂTEL, AND THE JURA A TO Z

Arriving and Departing

By Car

An important and scenic trans-Swiss artery, the N12 expressway, cuts from Bern to Lausanne, passing directly through Fribourg; a parallel northwestern route approaches from Basel by expressway (N1) to Solothurn, then changes to a secondary highway and follows the northwestern shore of Lake Neuchâtel, with brief sections of expressway at Neuchâtel itself and from Yverdon on down to Lac Léman. A slow but scenic route cuts from Basel through the Jura by way of Delémont.

By Plane

Cointrin airport at **Geneva,** the second-busiest international airport in Switzerland, brings in frequent flights from the United States and the United Kingdom by **Swissair** as well as by other international carriers; it lies about 138 kilometers (86 miles) from Fribourg, on a major rail route. The airport at **Bern** is only 34 kilometers (21 miles) from Fribourg.

By Train
The main train route between Basel, Zürich, and Geneva passes through Fribourg between Bern and Lausanne. Trains generally arrive twice an hour.

Getting Around

By Boat
There are boat trips on the lakes of Neuchâtel, Murten (Morat), and Biel (Bienne), as well as on the Aare River and the Broye Canal, a natural wildlife sanctuary. Schedules vary seasonally, but in summer are frequent and include evening trips.

By Bus
Postbus connections, except in the principal urban areas, can be few and far between; plan excursions carefully using the bus schedules available at the train station.

By Car
The charms of this varied region can be seen best by car, and there are scenic secondary highways throughout.

By Train
Secondary connections are thin, but they allow visits to most towns. To visit Gruyères, you must take a bus out of Broc.

Contacts and Resources

Emergencies
Police: ☎ 117; in Fribourg ☎ 117 or 037/23–12–12. For ambulance or medical emergency ☎ 037/24–75–00 in Fribourg; Neuchâtel ☎ 117.

Medical and dental referrals: Fribourg (☎ 037/22–33–43). Neuchâtel (☎ 038/25–10–17).

Guided Tours
Guided walks of Neuchâtel depart from in front of the Tour de Dièsse (⊠ Rue du Châteaux) in July and August (⊡ 8.50 SF adults). The tour lasts about two hours.

Visitor Information
The regional office for canton Fribourg is based in Fribourg (⊠ Rte. de la Glâne 107, ☎ 037/24–56–44).

Local tourist offices include those in **Fribourg** (⊠ Av. de la Gare, CH-1700, ☎ 026/321–31–75, FAX 037/22–35–27), **Gruyères** (⊠ CH-1663, ☎ 029/6–10–30), **La Chaux-de-Fonds** (⊠ Rue Neuve 11, CH-2302, ☎ 039/28–13–13), **Murten** (⊠ Franz-Kirchgasse 6, CH-3280, ☎ 026/71–51–12), and **Neuchâtel** (⊠ Rue de la Place d'Armes 7, CH-2001, ☎ 038/25–42–42).

9 Bern

Humble and down-to-earth, Bern is a city of broad medieval streets, farmers' markets, and friendly, slow-spoken people. It is also the federal capital of Switzerland and, more remarkably, a World Cultural Heritage city known for its sandstone arcades, fountains, and thick, sturdy towers.

THOUGH BERN (BERNE IN FRENCH) is the Swiss capital, you won't find much cosmopolitan nonsense here: The *cuisine du marché*, based on the freshest ingredients available in the local market, features fatback and sauerkraut; the annual fair fetes the humble onion; and the president of the Swiss Confederation often takes the tram to work. It's fitting, too, that a former Swiss patent office clerk, Albert Einstein, began developing his theory of relativity in Bern. Warm, friendly, down-to-earth, the Bernese are notoriously slow-spoken; ask a question, and then pull up a chair while they formulate a judicious response. Their mascot is a common bear; they keep some as pets in the center of town. Walking down broad medieval streets past squares crowded with farmers' markets, past cafés full of shirt-sleeve politicos, you might forget that Bern is the geographic and political hub of a sophisticated, modern, and prosperous nation.

Although Bern is full of patrician houses and palatial hotels, there is no official presidential residence: The seven members of the coalition government, each of whom serves a year as president, have to find their own places to live when in Bern.

Bern wasn't always so self-effacing. It earned its pivotal position through a history of power and influence that dates from the 12th century, when Berchtold V, duke of Zähringen and one of the countless rulers within the Holy Roman Empire, established a fortress on this gooseneck in the River Aare. An heir to the German Alemanni tribes, whose penetration into Switzerland can roughly be measured by the areas where Swiss German is spoken today, he chose Bern not only for its impregnable location—it's a steep promontory of rock girded on three sides by the river—but also for its proximity to the great kingdom of Burgundy, which spread across France and much of present-day French-speaking Switzerland.

By the 14th century Bern had grown into a strong urban republic, a powerful force in the land. When the last Zähringens died, the people of Bern defeated their would-be replacements and, shedding the Holy Roman Empire, became the eighth canton to join the rapidly growing Swiss Confederation. It was an unlikely union: aristocratic, urban Bern allied with the strongly democratic farming communities of Central Switzerland. But it provided the Bernese with enough security against the Hapsburg Holy Roman Empire to continue westward expansion.

Despite a devastating fire that laid waste to the city in 1405, by the late 15th century the Bernese had become a power of European stature—a stature enhanced exponentially by three decisive victories over the duke of Burgundy in 1476 and 1477. Aided by the other cantons and prompted by Louis XI, king of France and bitter enemy of the Burgundians, the Bernese crushed Charles the Bold and drove him out of his Swiss lands. Not only did the Bernese expand their territories all the way west to Geneva but they also acquired immense wealth—great treasures of gold, silver, and precious textiles—and assumed the leading role in Switzerland and Swiss affairs.

Bern stayed on top. Through the 17th and 18th centuries, the city's considerable prosperity was built not so much on commerce as on the export of troops and military know-how. The city and her territories functioned essentially as a patrician state, ruled by a nobility that saw its raison d'être in politics, foreign policy, the acquisition of new lands, and the forging of alliances. At the same time, her landed gentry continued to grow fat on the fruits of the city's rich agricultural lands.

Napoléon seized the lands, briefly, from 1798 until his defeat in 1815, but by the 1830s the Bernese were back in charge, and when the Swiss Confederation took its contemporary, democratic form in 1848, Bern was a natural choice for its capital.

Yet today it's not the massive Bundeshaus (Houses of Parliament) that dominates the city but instead its perfectly preserved arcades, fountains, and thick, sturdy towers—all remnants of its heyday as a medieval power. They're the reason UNESCO granted Bern World Cultural Heritage status, along with the pyramids of Egypt, Rome, Florence, and the Taj Mahal.

Pleasures and Pastimes

Arcades

Like a giant cloister, Bern is crisscrossed by arcades (*Lauben*) that shelter stores of every kind and quality. Sturdy 15th-century pillars support the low, vaulted roofs, which extend to the edge of the pavement. At the base of many arcades, nearly horizontal cellar doors lead down into interesting underground eateries and businesses. Combined with Bern's sturdy towers and narrow cobbled streets, the arcades distinguish the city as one of the country's best-preserved medieval towns. Best of all, you'll never get rained (or snowed) upon.

Flowers

Geranium-filled window boxes are as common a sight in Bern as ruins are in Rome. In 1897 Bern formed a preservation society to encourage the population to (florally) decorate their houses, even appointing a jury to award the best-decorated residences in the old town. In 1902 this society began to decorate the public fountains and then a few years later, the windows of buildings in the old town. In 1984 Bern won the title of Europe's most floral city, with the geranium as the city's official flower. The hillside Rosengarten (Rose Garden), with its 150-plus types of roses, and the city's flower market have added to Bern's renown as a floral city.

Fountains

Throughout Bern, scores of brilliantly colored and skillfully carved fountains—their bases surrounded by flowers—provide relief from the structural severity of the medieval houses that form their background. Like the stela of Athens, these fountains remind the Bernese of their moral forbears: Witness the Anna Seilerbrunnen, an ode to temperance and moderation, and the Gerechtigkeitsbrunnen (Justice Fountain) whose statue depicts the godess Justice standing over several severed heads. Most of the fountains are the work of Hans Gieng, who created them between 1539 and 1546.

Markets, Old and New

In the Middle Ages, Bern was a great marketing center, and markets are still an integral part of daily life. The lone surviving market from medieval Bern is the Zibelemärit (Onion Market), which takes place on the fourth Monday in November. Draped from scores of stalls are long strips of onions woven into the shapes of dolls, animals, and even alarm clocks. The Onion Market dates from the 1405 fire: In gratitude for assistance given by Fribourg, Bern granted farmers the right to sell their onions in the city's market square.

Every Tuesday and Saturday morning, more mundane but no less colorful farmers' markets (fruits, vegetables, and flowers) take place in front of the Bundeshaus on Bundesplatz, where buskers perform pantomime and music. There's a meat and dairy market on Münstergasse, and a general market on Waisenhausplatz. From May through October, a flea market sets up shop every third Saturday on Mühleplatz, behind the cathedral. On the first Saturday of the month, Münsterplatz is the site of an arts-and-crafts fair; and mid-May brings a geranium market to the Münsterplatz.

EXPLORING BERN

Because Bern stands on a high, narrow peninsula formed by a goose-neck in the Aare, its streets seem to follow the river's flow, running in long parallels to its oldest, easternmost point; from afar, its uniform red-tile roofs seem to ooze like glowing lava down the length of the promontory. The old town was founded on the farthest tip and grew westward; its towers mark those stages of growth like rings on a tree.

Great Itineraries

IF YOU HAVE 1 OR 2 DAYS

You can visit Bern's old town in a single day; but two days will allow you a more leisurely pace, with plenty of time for museums and shopping. Starting at the Bahnhof, you can move eastward through the towers, fountains, and arcades of the old town to the founding site of Bern at Nydeggkirche. Across the Aare are more museums, the Rosengarten (Rose Garden), and the embassy row of Thunstrasse. Back on the north side of the river to the west and south, the Münster and the Bundeshaus (Houses of Parliament) are not to be missed.

IF YOU HAVE 3 TO 5 DAYS

If you're making an extended stay in Bern, head into the Berner Oberland mountains, one hour away. You can visit the Jungfrau region by train, taking the Interlaken–Grindelwald–Klein Scheidegg–Jungfraujoch route (and, weather permitting, Wengen) in a single, long day. (☞ Chapter 10).

The Old Town

Now a pedestrian zone, the old city center retains a distinctly medieval look—thanks to the 1405 fire that destroyed its predominantly wooden structures. The city was rebuilt in sandstone, with arcades stretching on for some 6 kilometers (4 miles).

As medieval as it may look, the old town of Bern is decidedly modern, with countless shops concentrated between the train station and the Clock Tower—especially on Spitalgasse and Marktgasse. Beyond, along Kramgasse and Gerechtigkeitsgasse and, parallel to them on the north, Postgasse, there are quirkier, artier spots and excellent antiques stores. You may hear the Bernese calling this easternmost part of town the "old town," as its 800 years of commerce give it seniority over the mere 15th-century upstarts to the west. Junkerngasse and Münstergasse have plenty of shopping options as well, with galleries featuring avant-garde fashion.

A Good Walk

Numbers in the text correspond to numbers in the margin correspond and on the Bern exploring map.

Start on the busy Bahnhofplatz in front of the grand old Schweizerhof hotel, facing the station. To your left is the **Heiliggeistkirche** ① (Church of the Holy Spirit), finished in 1729. Beyond the church, turn left and walk down Spitalgasse *outside* the arcades (keeping an eye out for trams) to see some of the city's stunning architecture; if you walk inside the sheltered walkways, you'll be seduced by modern shops and cafés.

Head for the Pfeiferbrunnen (Bagpiper Fountain), the first of the city's many sculptured fountains. Beyond the Bagpiper, at the edge of the Barenplatz, stands the **Käfigturm** ② (Prison Tower), once a medieval city entrance and now a small cultural museum. Continue down Marktgasse past the Anna Seilerbrunnen, an allegory on temperance and moderation, and the Schützenbrunnen (Marksman Fountain), a tribute to a troop commander from 1543.

Just beyond and spreading to your left lie the Kornhausplatz and the imposing 18th-century **Kornhaus** ③ (Granary), now a popular restaurant (☞ Dining, *below*). In the Kornhausplatz, the Kindlifresserbrunnen (Ogre Fountain) is worth a second look: He's enjoying a meal of small children.

The mighty **Zytgloggeturm** ④ (Clock Tower), built in 1191 as a gate to the then smaller city, dominates the town center, with an hourly mechanical puppet performance as an added attraction. From the Clock Tower continue down Kramgasse, a lovely old street with many guild houses, some fine 18th-century residences, more arcades, and, of course, more fountains: first the Zähringerbrunnen (Zähringen Fountain), a monument to Bern founder Berchtold V; then the powerful Simsonbrunnen (Samson Fountain).

Turn left at the next opening and make a brief diversion to the Rathausplatz and, at its north end, the **Rathaus** ⑤ (Town Hall) itself, seat of the cantonal government. Across from it stands the Vennerbrunnen (Ensign Fountain), of a Bernese standard-bearer.

Return as you came and turn left on the main thoroughfare, now called Gerechtigkeitsgasse. You'll pass the Gerechtigkeitsbrunnen (Justice Fountain). Beyond are some lovely 18th-century houses; two are now hotels. Hospiz zur Heimat, at No. 50, was constructed between 1760 and 1762 and has the best Louis XV facade in Bern. At No. 7 is the Gasthaus zum Goldenen Adler. Built between 1764 and 1766, it has a particularly captivating coat of arms by locksmith Samuel Rüetschi.

A left turn at the bottom of Gerechtigkeitsgasse will take you steeply down Nydegg Stalden through one of the oldest parts of the city; the church on your right is the **Nydeggkirche** ⑥ (Nydegg Church). Down the hill stands the Läuferbrunnen (Messenger Fountain), the image of a city herald. Take the Untertorbrücke (Bridge under the Gate) across the Aare.

From here, it's a short, steep climb to the east end of the high Nydeggbrücke. If you're feeling energetic, however, it's well worth crossing the road and either climbing a small path to the left, turning right at the top; or turning right and then left to walk up the broader Alter Aargauerstalden, where you'll turn left. Either will bring you to the entrance (free) of the splendidly arranged and kept **Rosengarten** ⑦ (Rose Garden), where more than 160 varieties of roses bloom from June to October. There are panoramic views from here over the snaking sprawl of the old town.

Head back down to the Nydegg Bridge but don't cross it yet: On your left, facing the old town, you'll find the famous **Bärengraben** ⑧ (Bear Pits). Here live the city's mascots: fat brown bears who clown and beg for carrots, which vendors provide for tourists and loyal townsfolk.

Cross the bridge and turn left up Junkerngasse, notable for its fine old houses. No. 59 is the elegant Béatrice von Wattenwyl house, where the Swiss government gives receptions for its famous guests; the facade of the building dates from the mid-15th century. At the top of Junkerngasse, you come to the pride of the city: the magnificent Gothic **Münster** ⑨ (cathedral), which you'll want to explore at length. On leaving

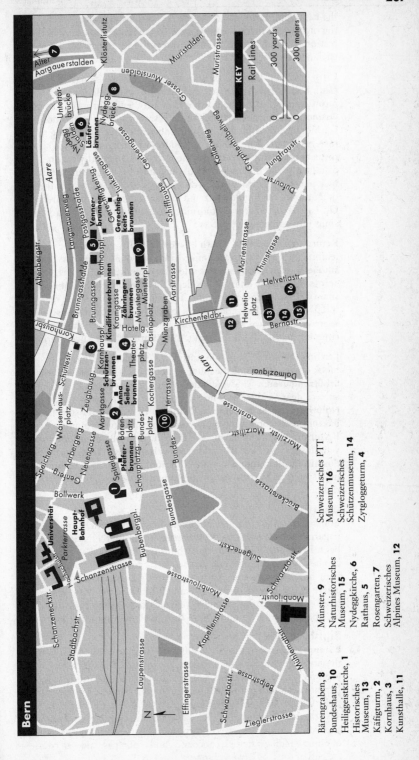

Bern

KEY
— Rail Lines

300 yards
300 meters

Bärengraben, 8
Bundeshaus, 10
Heiliggeistkirche, 1
Historisches
Museum, 13
Käfigturm, 2
Kornhaus, 3
Kunsthalle, 11

Münster, 9
Naturhistorisches
Museum, 15
Nydeggkirche, 6
Rathaus, 5
Rosengarten, 7
Schweizerisches
Alpines Museum, 12

Schweizerisches PTT
Museum, 16
Schweizerisches
Schützenmuseum, 14
Zytgloggeturm, 4

the cathedral, head left to the terrace on its south side, where, from the high walls, there is a good view to the river. Look east, in the direction from which you've come, and you'll see the gardens of the patrician Junkerngasse houses.

Cross the Münsterplatz, passing by the Mosesbrunnen (Moses Fountain). Follow Münstergasse past chic shops and galleries and turn left into Casinoplatz: At the north end of Kirchenfeldbrücke, a so-called **Casino** houses a concert hall and a restaurant, but no casino. From Casinoplatz, turn left down Münzgraben and then right along the terrace behind the **Bundeshaus** ⑩ (Houses of Parliament). This spot affords another fine view across the river and, in good weather, to the distant Alps. At the bridge end of the parapet is a diagram to help you pick out the principal peaks. You can walk around the end of the Bundeshaus into the Bundesplatz and then into the traffic-free Bärenplatz. On Tuesday and Saturday mornings, a colorful and lively market here spills into surrounding streets.

Return to Casinoplatz. South of the Clock Tower, cross the Kirchenfeldbrücke to Helvetiaplatz. Immediately on your left you'll see the **Kunsthalle** ⑪, which houses a fine selection of contemporary art. Directly across the square, on its west side, is the **Schweizerisches Alpines Museum** ⑫ (Swiss Alpine Museum), for armchair climbers and real ones, too. Dominating Helvetiaplatz on its south side is the **Historisches Museum** ⑬ (Historical Museum), where armor and arms, tapestries, and church treasures illustrate Bern's 15th-century victory over Burgundy.

Leaving the history museum, turn left and follow Bernastrasse a half block down. Adjoining the museum at the back is the **Schweizerisches Schützenmuseum** ⑭ (Swiss Rifle Museum), a thorough treatment of a subject dear to the Swiss heart. Continue down Bernastrasse to the **Naturhistorisches Museum** ⑮ (Museum of Natural History), which has unusually convincing dioramas of animals from around the world. If you turn right on leaving the Historical Museum and follow Helvetiastrasse, you'll find the striking **Schweizerisches PTT Museum** ⑯ (Swiss Postal and Telecommunications Museum), tracing the evolution of the mail system in Switzerland, from Roman messengers to telegraph and radio.

TIMING

You can tour the old town in a single day, leaving extra time for Bärenagarten, the Münster, and Rosengarten (if the weather's clear). If you'll be in Bern longer, indulge your whims in the arcaded shops. Crowds can be considerable on weekends, so plan accordingly. If necessary, leave your hotel early to tour, particularly if it's a Saturday. Make sure to arrive at the Zytgloggeturm five minutes before the hour, at the very latest: The mechanical figures spring into action at precisely four minutes before, and it's best to leave time to claim a spot on the street.

Sights to See

★ ☺ ❽ **Bärengraben.** Since the late 1400s, the Bear Pits have been home to the city's mascots: fat brown bears who clown and beg for carrots, which vendors provide for tourists and loyal townsfolk. According to legend, Berchtold announced to fellow hunters that he would name the new city after the first animal he killed. It was a bear, of course; in those days the woods were full of them. The German plural for *bears* is Bären, and you'll see their images everywhere in Bern: on flags, the city coat of arms, buildings, statues, chocolates, and umbrellas, and—of course— as stuffed toys. ✉ *Nydeggbrücke.*

★ ❿ **Bundeshaus.** This hulking, domed building is the beating heart of the Swiss Confederation and meeting place of the Swiss National Council. Free guided tours include entry to the parliamentary chambers. ⊠ *Bundesplatz,* ☎ *031/322–85–22.* ⊘ *Varies according to when Parliament is in session.*

Casino. Despite its name, the Casino in Casinoplatz houses an important concert hall, a restaurant, and banquet rooms—but no casino. That is north of the old town, in the Jackpot Casino of the Kursaal—with the usual 5 SF legal limit.

❶ Heiliggeistkirche. The Church of the Holy Spirit, completed in 1729, adds a bit of Baroque flamboyance to the otherwise medieval old town. It's across from the Bahnhof. ⊠ *Spitalgasse.*

★ ⓭ Historisches Museum. Bern's Historical Museum displays an enormous and enlightening collection from Bern's colorful past. Much of it was booty from victories over Burgundy, including magnificent tapestries "acquired" in 1476–77, when the Bernese pushed Charles the Bold back into France. There are armor and arms, lavish church treasures (including 15th- and 16th-century stained-glass windows), and the original Last Judgment sculptures from the cathedral's portal. Don't miss the novel three-way portrait of Calvin, Zwingli, and Luther. Among the significant exhibitions about the outside world is an exceptional Islamic collection. ⊠ *Helvetiaplatz 5,* ☎ *031/351–18–11.* ☞ *5 SF.* ⊘ *Tues.–Sun. 10–5.*

⓫ Kunsthalle. A very good contemporary art gallery that has taken successful risks in the past, the Kunsthalle has staged early one-man shows of Donald Judd, Sol LeWitt, Richard Long, and Cy Twombly. It features only temporary exhibitions. ⊠ *Helvetiaplatz 1,* ☎ *031/351–00–31,* FAX *031/352–53–85.* ☞ *6 SF.* ⊘ *Tues. 10–9, Wed.–Sun. 10–5.*

★ ❷ Käfigturm. A city entrance from the 13th and 14th centuries (later restored in the 18th century), when the limits of Bern extended only this far west, the Käfigturm served as a prison until 1897. Now it houses a small museum that charts the economic and cultural life of Bern, including a permanent multiscreen slide show. ⊠ *Marktgasse 67,* ☎ *031/311–23–06.* ☞ *Free.* ⊘ *Tues.–Fri. 9–1 and 2–6.*

OFF THE
BEATEN PATH

KUNSTMUSEUM BERN – Although it's far from the Helvetiaplatz cluster of museums and not convenient to your old-town walking tour, the Bern Museum of Fine Arts merits a visit. The museum's pride—and its justified claim to fame—is its unparalleled collection of more than 2,000 works by Paul Klee, who lived for many years in Bern. Striking allegories (some enormous), landscapes, and portraits by Berner Ferdinand Hodler, one of this century's most important Swiss artists, also are a highlight. But the Kunstmuseum's concentration is not entirely Swiss, as early Bern masters mingle with Fra Angelico, and Böcklin and Anker share space with artists of the caliber of Cézanne, Rouault, and Picasso. ⊠ *Hodlerstrasse 8–12,* ☎ *031/311–09–44.* ☞ *6 SF.* ⊘ *Tues. 10–9; Wed.–Sun. 10–5.*

---

❸ Kornhaus. Now a popular Bernese restaurant (☞ Dining, *below*), the imposing 18th-century Kornhaus, or Granary, has a magnificent cellar, which once held wine brought to town by farmers as a tribute to the patrician city government. ⊠ *Zeughausgasse 2.*

Matte. In the narrow row houses below the patrician residences of Junkerngasse, laborers once lived along the banks of the Aare. In those days as today, the neighborhood was called *Matte* and was the most sociable, raucous part of town, with many inns. There developed a bizarre dialect—*Mattenenglisch*—that can still be heard today, though it has grown so rare that its proponents have formed a club to keep it alive.

Spotted with Yiddish and Gypsy terms, the dialect derives its name from *Matten* (lowland) and *Englisch* (unintelligible). Even if you don't hear the local tongue, Matte is a lovely old neighborhood to wander. From the cathedral terrace, a little funicular (0.80 SF) whisks visitors down to the river. There's a flea market here on Mühleplatz, every third Saturday from May through October.

★ ❾ **Münster.** Started in 1421 by master mason Matthäus Ensinger on a site formerly occupied by an older church, Bern's famous cathedral was planned on lines so spacious that half the population could worship in it at one time. Its construction went on for centuries. Even the Reformation, the impact of which converted it from a Catholic to a Protestant church, did not halt the work. Daniel Heinz directed construction for 25 years (from 1573 to 1598), completing the nave and the tower. The finishing touch, the tip of the 100-meter (328-foot) steeple (the highest in Switzerland), was not added until 1893. Today you can ascend it by stairs to enjoy a panorama of red roofs, the Aare, and if the weather's clear, the Bernese Alps off in the distance.

The cathedral has two outstanding features, one outside and one in. Outside is the **main portal,** with a magnificent sculptured representation of the Last Judgment (1490) composed of 234 carved figures—on the left is heaven and on the right, hell. This work was completed immediately before the Reformation, but it escaped destruction by the iconoclasts who emptied the niches of the side portals. The main portal was recently restored and painted in vivid—some may say jarring—colors. Green demons with gaping red maws and ivory-skin angels with gilt hair appear with technicolor intensity.

Inside the church, while the elaborately carved pews and choir stalls are worth attention, of particular interest is the **stained glass,** especially the detailed 15th-century windows of the choir, dealing as much with local heraldry as with Christian iconography. ⊠ *Münsterplatz 1,* ☎ *031/311–05–72,* ⏲ *10–noon, 2–5:30. Closed Sunday afternoon.*

👆 ⓯ **Naturhistorisches Museum.** Bern's Museum of Natural History has an unusually evocative selection of animal displays covering an exotic range of species. Even more interesting (to non-dog-lovers only) is the stuffed body of Barry, a St. Bernard who saved more than 40 people in the Alps during the last century. In response to children's awkward questions, there's a slide show on modern taxidermy techniques. There's also a splendid collection of Alpine minerals. ⊠ *Bernastrasse 15,* ☎ *031/350–71–11.* ▣ *3 SF, free Sun.* ⏲ *Mon. 2–5, Tues.–Sat. 9–5, Sun. 10–5.*

OFF THE BEATEN PATH
TIERPARK DÄHLHÖLZLI – Here is a zoo with a difference: It's open 24 hours a day, so you can watch nocturnal animals while they're awake and diurnal animals while they sleep. In addition to some exotic species and a vivarium full of reptiles and fish, the majority of the zoo's creatures are European: bison, wolves, owls, chamois, moose, lynx, seals, and—of course—bears. They live in natural woodlands. The zoo is an easy trip south on Bus 18. ⊠ *Tierparkstrasse 1,* ☎ *031/351–06–16.* ▣ *Zoo, free; vivarium, 6 SF.* ⏲ *Zoo: daily 24 hrs; Vivarium: Apr.–Sept., daily 8–6:30; Oct.–Mar., daily 9–5.*

❻ **Nydeggkirche.** Built in 1341–46, the Nydegg Church stands on the ruins of Berchtold V's first fortress (destroyed in 1295), the founding place of Bern. ⊠ *Nydeggasse,* ☎ *031/311–61–02.* ⏲ *10–noon, 2–5:30. Closed Sunday afternoon.*

★ ❺ **Rathaus.** Bern's stately town hall is the seat of the cantonal government. Along with the city's arcades, it was built after the great fire of 1405, and still retains its simple Gothic lines. ⊠ *Rathausplatz 2.*

❼ **Rosengarten.** At the splendidly arranged and kept Rose Garden, some 160 varieties of roses bloom from June to October. One of Bern's most popular gathering places, this is a great vantage point for the Jungfrau, Eiger and Mönch—on clear days only. ⊠ *Alter Aargauerstalden.* ⌚ *Free.* ☉ *Daily sunrise–sunset.*

⓬ **Schweizerisches Alpines Museum.** The unusual Swiss Alpine Museum has topographical maps and reliefs—their own evolution fascinating—illustrating the history of mountain climbing, alongside epic art and fine old photos. There's an enormous model of the Berner Oberland. ⊠ *Helvetiaplatz 4,* ☎ *031/351–04–34.* ⌚ *4 SF.* ☉ *Mid-May–mid-Oct., Mon. 2–5, Tues.–Sun. 10–5; mid-Oct.–mid-May, Mon. 2–5, Tues.–Sun. 10–noon and 2–5.*

⓰ **Schweizerisches PTT Museum.** The Swiss PTT Museum, housed in a striking building behind the Historical Museum, has detailed documents, art objects, and early artifacts that trace the history of the mail system in Switzerland. There's also a fine stamp collection, one of the largest and most valuable in the world. ⊠ *Helvetiastrasse 16,* ☎ *031/338–77–77.* ⌚ *2 SF.* ☉ *Tues.–Sun. 10–5.*

⓮ **Schweizerisches Schützenmuseum.** The Swiss Rifle Museum, run by the Swiss Marksmen's Association, pays homage to this very Swiss art. Through a large collection of guns in every imaginable form, the museum traces the evolution of firearms from 1817; through trophies, it celebrates centuries of straight shooting, as Swiss men have always measured themselves against the apple-splitting accuracy of archer William Tell. ⊠ *Bernastrasse 5,* ☎ *031/351–01–27.* ⌚ *free.* ☉ *Tues.–Sat. 2–4, Sun. 10–noon and 2–4.*

★ ❹ **Zytgloggeturm.** The mighty Clock Tower, Bern's oldest building, was built in 1191 as the west gate to the then smaller city. Today it dominates the town center with its high copper spire and a massive astronomical clock and calendar, built on the eastern side in 1530. As an added attraction, a delightful group of mechanical puppets performs every hour. To see the puppet show it's best to take up position at the corner of Kramgasse and Hotelgasse at least five minutes before the hour: You won't be the only one there. For photographs, the best time in summer is 10 or 11 AM.

At about four minutes to the hour, heralded by a jester nodding his head and ringing two small bells, the puppet show begins. From a small arch on the left, a couple of musically inclined bears—a drummer and a piper—appear, leading a procession of a horseman with a sword, a proud bear wearing a crown, and lesser bears, each carrying a gun, a sword, or a spear. When the procession comes to an end, a metal cockerel on the left crows and flaps his wings, a knight in golden armor above hammers out the hour, and Father Time, on a throne in the middle, beats time with a scepter in one hand and an hourglass in the other. ⊠ *Kramgasse.*

DINING

While Bern strikes a diplomatic balance in heading French-Swiss and German-Swiss politics, its Teutonic nature conquers Gaul when it comes to cuisine. Dining in Bern is usually a down-to-earth affair, with Italian home cooking running a close popular second to the local standard fare: German-style meat and potatoes. The most wide-spread specialty is the famous *Bernerplatte,* a meaty version of Alsatian *choucroûte*—great slabs of salt pork, beef tongue, smoky bacon, pork ribs, and mild pink pork sausages cooked down in broth and heaped on a broad platter over juniper-scented sauerkraut, green beans, and boiled potatoes. When a waitress eases this wide load onto the table before you, you may glance around to see who's sharing: One serving can seem enough for four. Another meaty classic is the Berner version of *Ratsherrtopf,* traditionally enjoyed by the town councilors: veal shank cooked in white wine, butter, and sage. (A version with cabbage, pork, turnips, and potatoes originated in Zürich.) The busy market brings in plenty of local produce, so hearty soups are abundant, and everyone looks forward to a fat pastry and coffee in the late afternoon.

CATEGORY	COST*
$$$$	over 80 SF
$$$	50 SF–80 SF
$$	20 SF–50 SF
$	under 20 SF

*per person for a three-course meal (except in $ category), including sales tax and 15% service charge

$$$$ ✕ **Bellevue-Grill.** When Parliament is in session, this haute-cuisine
★   landmark is transformed from a local gourmet mecca to a political clubhouse where the movers and shakers put their heads together over healthy portions of such updated classics as veal liver *Geschnetzeltes* with raspberries, and grilled beef with orange butter and Grand Marnier. The culinary standard is exceptionally high, the decor modern, and the wine selection broad. ⊠ *Kochergasse 3–5,* ☎ *031/320–45–45. AE, DC, MC, V.*

$$$$ ✕ **Schultheissenstube.** The intimate, rustic dining room, with a club-
★   like bar and an adjoining, even more rustic, all-wood *stübli* (taverncafé), looks less like a gastronomic haven than a country pub; folksy piped-in music furthers the illusion. Yet the cooking is sophisticated, international, and imaginative—consider duck breast with hazelnut vinaigrette, oyster-and-champagne risotto, seafood lasagna with saffron, or quail breast with lentil sprouts—and the wine list encyclopedic. ⊠ *Hotel Schweizerhof, Bahnhofplatz 11,* ☎ *031/311–45–01. Jacket and tie in dining room. AE, DC, MC, V. Closed Sun.*

$$$ ✕ **Jack's Brasserie.** Sometimes referred to by locals as "Stadt Restaurant" (City Restaurant), this dining room at street level, with high ceilings, wainscoting, and roomy banquettes is airy, bustling, urbane, and cosmopolitan. Enjoy a drink here by day at bare-top tables or settle in at mealtime for smartly served Swiss standards, French bistro classics, or a hefty Wiener schnitzel. ⊠ *Hotel Schweizerhof, Bahnhofplatz 11,* ☎ *031/311–45–01. AE, DC, MC, V.*

$$$ ✕ **Zimmermania.** This very simple bistro, with plank floors, lace curtains, and white linen, is a local favorite for French bourgeois cooking *à la Bernaise.* It has been serving wine, beer, and rich meals (asparagus in puff pastry, beef with chanterelle mushrooms and cream) for 150 years. ⊠ *Brunngasse 19,* ☎ *031/311–15–42. No credit cards. Closed Sun.–Mon.*

$$$ ✕ **Zum Rathaus.** Across from the Rathaus in the old town, this atmospheric landmark has been a restaurant since 1863, though the row house dates from the 17th century. Downstairs, it's casual and comfortable, with dark wood banquettes, pine tables, and lead glass, while the upstairs Marcuard-Stübli is considerably more formal ("solemn" according to its own advertisements), with a heavy beam ceiling and severe dark wood. The cooking ranges from local meat basics to game, salmon, and hearty pastries. In summer, you can eat on the terrace in the

Rathausplatz. ✉ *Rathausplatz 5,* ☎ *031/311–61–83. AE, DC, MC, V. Closed Sun.–Mon.*

$$ ✗ **Beaujolais.** Don't be fooled by the name. The French veneer on this popular local restaurant is only pigskin-deep: Down in the kitchen there lurks a Swiss-German chef. The menu lists all the right names—onion soup, *aiguillettes de boeuf* (thin strips of sautéed beef), profiteroles—but the sauces are salty-brown, distinctively Swiss-German; the profiteroles, Germanically oversize; and the setting, pure Bern. It's popular and appealing as such, and local couples come on dates or baby-sitter nights for a little French romance. There's a complete selection of Beaujolais, both open and in bottles. ✉ *Aarbergergasse 52,* ☎ *031/311–48–86. AE, DC, MC, V. Closed Sun.*

$$ ✗ **Brasserie zum Bärengraben.** Directly across from the Bear Pits, this
★ popular, easygoing little local institution serves up lunch specials and local standards to shoppers, tourists, businesspeople, and retirees, who settle in with a newspaper and a *Dezi* (deciliter) of wine. Arched windows and lace curtains open onto the Nydegg Bridge, and back windows overlook the downward slope toward the old town. You'll find old-style basics—*Kalbskopf an vinaigrette* (chopped veal head in vinaigrette), pigs' feet, stuffed cabbage—as well as French-accented brasserie fare (lamb with rosemary, for instance) and wonderful pastries. Stick to daily specials and one-plate meals; dining à la carte can be expensive here. ✉ *Muristalden 1,* ☎ *031/331–42–18. No credit cards.*

$$ ✗ **Della Casa.** You can stay downstairs in the steamy, rowdy stübli,
★ where the necktied businessmen roll up their sleeves and play cards, or head up to the linen-and-silver restaurant, where they leave on their jackets. An unofficial Parliament headquarters, the restaurant has a solid Italian menu and generous platters of local specialties as well; it's a good place to try the Bernerplatte. In a country where local beer is light and forgettable, Czech-brewed Pilsner Urquell on tap is a treat. ✉ *Schauplatzgasse 16,* ☎ *031/311–21–42. DC, MC, V. No credit cards downstairs. Closed Sat. eve. and Sun.*

$$ ✗ **Harmonie.** Run by the same family since 1900, this lead-glass and old-wood café-restaurant serves basics: sausage and *Rösti* (hash brown potatoes), *Käseschnitte* (cheese toast), *Bauern* omelettes (farm-style, with bacon, potatoes, onions, and herbs), and fondue. Full à la carte dinners are pricier, of course. It's lively and a little dingy, very friendly, and welcoming to foreigners. ✉ *Hotelgasse 3,* ☎ *031/311–38–40. No credit cards.*

$$ ✗ **Il Grissino.** In a busy Bernese square, this popular haunt specializes in wood-oven-cooked pizzas—26 colorful varieties—and such traditional pastas as *fettucine nere Stefano* (black noodles with salmon and broccoli). Run by a Swiss-Italian family, it has a modern Italian interior and an all-Italian wine list. The outdoor terrace is great for summer dining. ✉ *Waisenhausplatz 28,* ☎ *031/311–00–59. AE, DC, MC, V.*

$$ ✗ **Lorenzini.** After a few days of Bern's rib-sticking cooking, plain and
★ simple Italian food may sound more appealing than ever: This hip, bright spot is a breath of fresh Tuscan air. Delicious homemade pastas and specialties of various Italian regions—say, Alba truffles—are served with authentic, contemporary flair. The clientele is an attractive mix of voguish yuppies. The café-bar downstairs draws the young and the chic. ✉ *Theaterplatz 5,* ☎ *031/311–78–50. DC, MC, V.*

$$ ✗ **Zunft zu Webern.** Founded as a weavers' guild house and built in 1704, this classic building has been renovated on the ground floor to slick but traditional style, with gleaming fresh wood and bright lighting. The upgraded standards on the menu (lamb stew with saffron, for example), while generously portioned, reflect a light, sophisticated

214

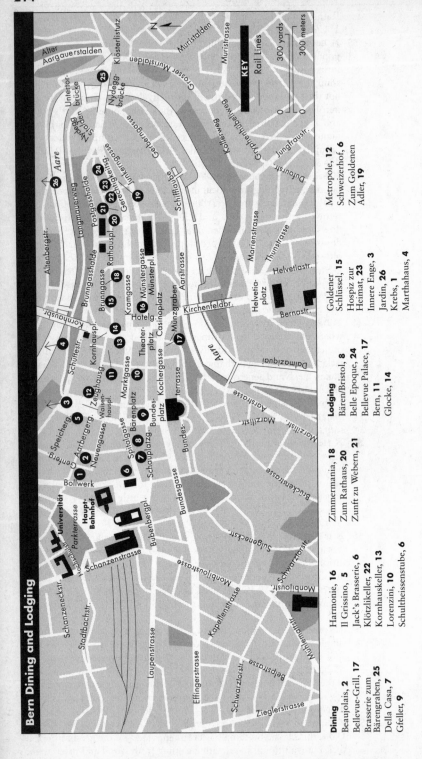

Bern Dining and Lodging

Dining
Beaujolais, **2**
Bellevue-Grill, **17**
Brasserie zum Bärengraben, **25**
Della Casa, **7**
Gfeller, **9**

Harmonie, **16**
Il Grissino, **5**
Jack's Brasserie, **6**
Klötzlikeller, **22**
Kornhauskeller, **13**
Lorenzini, **10**
Schultheissenstube, **6**

Zimmermania, **18**
Zum Rathaus, **20**
Zunft zu Webern, **21**

Lodging
Bären/Bristol, **8**
Belle Epoque, **24**
Bellevue Palace, **17**
Bern, **11**
Glocke, **14**

Goldener Schlüssel, **15**
Hospiz zur Heimat, **23**
Innere Enge, **3**
Jardin, **26**
Krebs, **1**
Marthahaus, **4**

Metropole, **12**
Schweizerhof, **6**
Zum Goldenen Adler, **19**

KEY
━━━ Rail Lines

0   300 yards
0   300 meters

In case you want to see the world.

At American Express, we're here to make your journey a smooth one. So we have over 1,700 travel service locations in over 120 countries ready to help. What else would you expect from the world's largest travel agency?

do more ®

http://www.americanexpress.com/travel   **Travel**

In case you want to be welcomed there.

We're here to see that you're always welcomed at establishments everywhere. That's why millions of people carry the American Express® Card – for peace of mind, confidence, and security, around the world or just around the corner.

do more ®

Cards

In case you're running low.

We're here to help with more than 118,000 Express Cash locations around the world. In order to enroll, just call American Express before you start your vacation.

do more

Express Cash

And just in case.

We're here with American Express® Travelers Cheques and Cheques *for Two*.® They're the safest way to carry money on your vacation and the surest way to get a refund, practically anywhere, anytime.
Another way we help you...

do more ®

Travelers Cheques

touch in the kitchen. ✉ *Gerechtigkeitsgasse 68,* ☎ *031/311–42–58. MC, V. Closed Sun. and Mon.*

$ ✕ **Gfeller.** This Bern-style luncheonette on the Bärenplatz, with outdoor tables drawing sun seekers, has laminate decor and pastries in a glass display carousel. Have a cheap plate lunch or a slice of the tasty fruit pie. ✉ *Bärenplatz 21,* ☎ *031/311–69–44. No credit cards.*

$ ✕ **Klötzlikeller.** This cozy, muraled wine cellar, tucked in below
★ Gerechtigkeitsgasse in the old town, is worth a visit for the atmosphere alone. More intimate than the Kornhauskeller and just as lovely, it dates from 1635, when Bern was home to some 250 wine cellars. Try the Bern wine, which is sold by the glass. ✉ *Gerechtigkeitsgasse 62,* ☎ *031/311–74–56. AE, MC, V. Closed Sun. and Mon.*

$ ✕ **Kornhauskeller.** This spectacular vaulted old wine cellar under the
★ Granary is now a popular beer hall with music on weekends. Drinkers and revelers take tables up in the galleries, while diners sit in the main hall, gazing up at the frescoed ceiling. The menu, pure Swiss, satisfies the healthiest of appetites. ✉ *Kornhausplatz 18,* ☎ *031/311–11–33. AE, DC, MC, V. Closed Sun. and Mon.*

LODGING

As a frequent host to conventioneers, tourists, and visiting members of Parliament, Bern is well equipped with hotels in all price ranges. Rooms are hard to find when Parliament is in session; this is one town where you need to book well ahead. All but the bargain hotels are concentrated around the old-town center.

CATEGORY	COST*
$$$$	over 300 SF
$$$	180 SF–300 SF
$$	140 SF–180 SF
$	under 140 SF

All prices are for a standard double room, including breakfast, tax, and service charge.

$$$$ 🏨 **Bellevue Palace.** As the name implies, this 1864 landmark, set on the high bank above the river, is considerably more palatial than the Schweizerhof, its friendly rival. There are a sweeping staircase and a spectacular Belle Epoque stained-glass ceiling in the lobby; the rooms are up to the same standard, discreetly colored in shades of powder blue, cream, and orchid. The chief advantage over the Schweizerhof is the view, which is best from the back rooms; these face the river and the snow-capped Alps, including the Eiger and the Jungfrau. The Restaurant La Terrasse is lavish, but it's the Bellevue-Grill that draws crowds of nonguests, many of them politicos from the Parliament building next door. (☞ Dining, *above*). ✉ *Kochergasse 3–5, CH-3001,* ☎ *031/320–45–45 or 800/223–68–00,* ℻ *031/311–47–43. 230 beds. 2 restaurants, bar, café, grill. AE, DC, MC, V.*

$$$$ 🏨 **Schweizerhof.** This landmark just across from the Hauptbahnhof and next to the liveliest part of the Spitalgasse is decidedly nonpalatial: The lobby is tiny, though deluxe, and the broad corridors are lined with an impressive collection of antiques and objets d'art of the Gauers, the hotel's founding family. Each room's decor is different in an original, quirky way. You might be assigned to one of four rooms designed by young Bernese artists representing the ultramodern streak in Swiss design; or you might find a Sheraton chair keeping company with a pair of giant porcelain Dalmatians. Countless thoughtful touches (next day's weather report on your pillow beside the requisite truffle, for instance) make this a definite rival to the Bellevue Palace. And you won't go hungry: In addition to the luxury deli near the lobby, there's the

Schultheissenstube, Jack's Brasserie (☞ Dining, *above*), and Yamato—a pretty Japanese restaurant (and one of only two in Bern). ⊠ *Bahnhofplatz 11, CH-3001,* ☎ *031/311–45–01,* FAX *031/312–21–79. 160 beds. 3 restaurants, bar, deli, nightclub. AE, DC, MC, V.*

$$$ ⊞ **Bären/Bristol.** These adjoining twin Best Western properties are dependable business-class hotels, with all-modern interiors and first-class comforts. The Bärenbar serves drinks and snacks, and days figure heavily in the decor. ⊠ *Bären: Schauplatzgasse 4–10, CH-3011,* ☎ *031/311–33–67 or 800/528–12–34,* FAX *031/311–69–83, 85 beds; Bristol:* ☎ *031/311–01–01,* FAX *031/311–94–79, 136 beds. Both hotels: Snack bar, sauna. AE, DC, MC, V.*

$$$ ⊞ **Belle Epoque.** Its historic theme has nothing to do with Bern's me-
★   dieval background, but this relatively new hotel has made itself into a period museum nonetheless, more suggestive of Gay Paris than Berchtold's lair. Every inch of the arcaded row house has been filled with authentic art nouveau or Jugendstil antiques, from the stylized wooden vines on the reception desk to the Hodlers and Klimts hung over the beds. Despite the aged opulence of the furnishings, the amenities are state-of-the-art, with white-tile baths, electric blinds, and a no-smoking floor. Downstairs, a pianist livens up the antiques-filled bar. The manager came over from the Schweizerhof, bringing the Gauer name with her, so standards are appropriately high. ⊠ *Gerechtigkeitsgasse 18, CH-3011,* ☎ *031/311–43–36,* FAX *031/311–39–36. 33 beds. Breakfast room, piano bar. AE, DC, MC, V.*

$$$ ⊞ **Bern.** Behind a spare and imposing neoclassic facade, this former
★   theater and once-modest hotel has been transformed into a slick, business-class lodging, with an air-shaft garden "courtyard" lighting the better rooms. Avoid the cheaper rooms, which are dark and stuffy. The restaurant, "Seven Stuben," consists of seven rooms—each with its own motif—within one restaurant. The piano bar is cozy and well-stocked. ⊠ *Zeughausgasse 9, CH-3011,* ☎ *031/312–10–21,* FAX *031/312–11–47. 170 beds. 2 restaurants, café, piano bar. AE, DC, MC, V.*

$$$ ⊞ **Innere Enge.** In 1992 this early 18th-century inn was transformed into a slick deluxe-business hotel. Spacious, light, and airy—thanks to generous windows that take in views toward the Bernese Alps—it's outside the city center, with trees and lawns to compensate for the bus or cab ride into town. Marian's Jazzroom, in the Louis Armstrong Bar, features top jazz acts. Take Bus No. 21 ("Bremgarten") from the train station. ⊠ *Engestrasse 54, CH-3012,* ☎ *031/309–61–11,* FAX *031/309–61–12. 52 beds. Restaurant, bar, café. AE, DC, MC, V.*

$$ ⊞ **Zum Goldenen Adler.** Built, like Hospiz zur Heimat, in a magnifi-
★   cent patrician town house in the old town, this now-simple guest house has been lodging travelers since 1489, though the current structure dates from 1764. The interiors are modest and modern, with linoleum baths and severe Formica furniture, but the ambience is comfortable and welcoming nonetheless: One family has run it for 100-odd years. The simple restaurant is homey, with parquet floors and plaid linens. ⊠ *Gerechtigkeitsgasse 7, CH-3006,* ☎ *031/311–17–25,* FAX *031/311–37–61. 30 beds. Restaurant, café. AE, DC, MC, V.*

$$ ⊞ **Krebs.** A classic small Swiss hotel being steadily upgraded under the
★   rigorous direction of the Buri family, the Krebs is solid and impeccable, thanks to the ownership's eye for detail. The rooms are spare but pristine, and there's a good ground-floor restaurant. A handful of inexpensive rooms without bath offer excellent value. ⊠ *Genfergasse 8, CH-3001,* ☎ *031/311–49–42,* FAX *031/311–10–35. 80 beds. Breakfast room. AE, DC, MC, V.*

$$ ⊞ **Metropole.** Centrally located between the old town and the station, Metropole buzzes with activity in its tiny lobby. Interiors and rooms are clean but plain. The Brasserie, on street level, serves moderately priced Swiss fare and is always crowded. ⊠ *Zeughausgasse 28, CH-3011.* ☎ *031/311–50–21,* FAX *031/312–11–53. 100 beds. 3 restaurants, bar. AE, DC, MC, V.*

$ ⊞ **Glocke.** Although it's very plain, there's a young, friendly management here and two lively restaurants—one a Swiss chalet, with dancing and folklore shows, and the other Italian. The few rooms without baths cost less. ⊠ *Rathausgasse 75, CH-3011,* ☎ *031/311–37–71,* FAX *031/311–10–08. 38 beds. 2 restaurants. AE, DC, MC, V.*

$ ⊞ **Goldener Schlüssel.** This bright, tidy little hotel in the heart of the old town has been scrupulously maintained, with fresh linens and tile baths. As the building looks over the Rathausgasse, you'll find the back rooms quieter. The good, inexpensive restaurant on the ground floor serves home-cooked meat-and-Rösti favorites in a dinette with paper-place-mat ambience; or you can have the same menu in the atmospheric stübli. Rooms without bath are a bargain. ⊠ *Rathausgasse 72, CH-3011,* ☎ *031/311–02–16,* FAX *031/311–56–88. 48 beds. Restaurant, stübli. DC, MC, V.*

$ ⊞ **Hospiz zur Heimat.** The elegant 18th-century exterior belies the dormitory gloom inside, but the baths and rooms are immaculate. It's in an excellent old-town location, and some bargain rooms without bath are available. ⊠ *Gerechtigkeitsgasse 50, CH-3011,* ☎ *031/311–04–36,* FAX *031/312–33–86. 70 beds. Breakfast room. AE, DC, MC, V.*

$ ⊞ **Jardin.** In a commercial neighborhood far above the old town, this
★ is a solid, roomy, middle-class hotel, with friendly management, fresh decor, and baths in every room. It's easily reached by Tram 9 to Breitenrainplatz. ⊠ *Militärstrasse 38, CH-3014,* ☎ *031/333–01–17,* FAX *031/333–09–43. 34 beds. Restaurant, bowling. AE, DC, MC, V.*

$ ⊞ **Marthahaus.** This cheap, cheery hotel stands at the end of a quiet
★ cul-de-sac in a residential neighborhood north of the old town. All the rooms have been freshly decorated in white, and the squeaky-clean look is reinforced with hospital-style metal beds. Most rooms have sinks with baths down the hall; several have in-room baths or showers. It's an easy ride over the Kornhaus bridge on Bus 15 or via Lorrainebrucke on Bus 20. ⊠ *Wyttenbachstrasse 22a, CH-3013,* ☎ *031/332–41–35,* FAX *031/333–33–86. 40 beds. Breakfast room. MC, V.*

NIGHTLIFE AND THE ARTS

This Week in Bern, edited every week by the tourist office, carries listings on concerts, museums, and nightlife.

Nightlife

Bars and Lounges

On the ground floor of the little hotel **Belle Epoque** (⊠ Gerechtigkeitsgasse 18, ☎ 031/311–43–36), there's a lovely small bar where you can drink surrounded by art nouveau treasures. For a nightcap in a formal setting, go to the **Hotel Bellevue Palace** (⊠ Kochergasse 3–5, ☎ 031/320–45–45). The **Hotel Schweizerhof** (⊠ Bahnhofplatz 11, ☎ 031/311–45–01) has a small American-style bar. **Arlequin** (⊠ Gerechtigkeitsgasse 51, ☎ 031/311–39–46) is a cozy wine bar where small meals are served. For history, head for **Klötzlikeller,** said to be the oldest wine bar in Bern (☞ Dining, *above*).

Casinos

Bern's **Kursaal** (⊠ Schänzlistrasse 71–77, ☎ 031/333–10–10) has a disco with live music as well as gambling in the Jackpot Casino, within the 5 SF limit.

Dancing

The popular **Mocambo** (⊠ Aarbergergasse 61, ☏ 031/311–50–41) has dancing to recorded music until 3 AM on weeknights, 3:30 AM on Saturday. **Babalu** (⊠ Gurtengasse 3, ☏ 031/311–08–08) draws crowds for dancing with live music.

Jazz Clubs

Marian's Jazzroom (⊠ Engestrasse 54, ☏ 031/309–61–11) in the Innere Enge hotel offers top live acts nightly from 7:30 PM to 1 AM, with a "Concert Apéro" every Saturday from 4 to 6:30 PM.

The Arts

Film

Bern's 23 movie theaters show films in the original language. Current listings can be found in hotels, the daily newspaper, and the tourist office.

Music

The **Bern Symphony Orchestra,** under conductor Dmitrij Kitajento, is the city's most notable musical institution. Concerts take place at the Casino (Casinoplatz) or Stadttheater (⊠ Kornhausplatz 20), tickets (☏ 031/311–42–42). There also is a five-day **International Jazz Festival** every April or May, with tickets available at the Schweizerischer Bankverein (Swiss Bank Corporation) on Bärenplatz, ☏ 031/336–25–39.

Opera

Bern's resident company is famous for its adventurous production standards. Performances are at the **Stadttheater** (⊠ Kornhausplatz 20, ☏ 031/311–07–77). Tickets are sold next door (⊠ Kornhausplatz 18; Mon.–Sat. 10–6:30 and Sun. 10–12:30).

Theater

Although you can see traditional and modern plays presented in the **Stadttheater** (Kornhausplatz 20, ☏ 031/311–07–77), a characteristic of Bern is its range of little theaters, mostly found in the cellars in the old town.

Avant-garde plays, satires, and burlesques (in German or dialect), plus pantomime and modern dance, are performed at **Theater am Käfigturm** (⊠ Marktgasse 67, ☏ 031/311–61–00). **Kleintheater** (⊠ Kramgasse 6, ☏ 031/311–30–80) has a modern repertoire; buy tickets at Da Capo (⊠ Münstergasse 42, ☏ 031/311–00–35). **Berner Puppentheater** (⊠ Gerechtigkeitsgasse 31, ☏ 031/311–95–85) produces funny, action-packed puppet shows that are enjoyable even if you don't speak the language.

OUTDOOR ACTIVITIES AND SPORTS

Bicycling

There are about 300 kilometers (185 miles) of marked trails around Bern; ask for routes at the tourist office. Bikes can be rented at the main train station.

Golf

The **Golf and Country Club Blumisberg** (⊠ 18 kilometers/11 miles west of town, ☏ 037/36–34–38) has 18 holes and a clubhouse with a restaurant, a bar, showers, and a swimming pool. The club admits visitors, provided they are members of any golf club with handicaps, on weekdays. Only local members and their guests are admitted on weekends.

Riding

The riding school **Reitsportanlage Eldorado** (⊠ Gurtentäli, ☎ 031/971–48–40) is easily reached by Bus 17.

Swimming

Hallenbad Hirschengraben (⊠ Maulbeerstrasse 14, ☎ 031/381–36–56) is a central indoor swimming pool. Below the Parliament Building you can swim in the river at the **Marzili** river bath (⊠ Marzilistrasse 29, ☎ 031/311–00–46). **Aarebad Eichholz** (☎ 031/963–26–02), in the town of Wabern, is a river bath facility. The river bath at **Aarebad Lorraine** (⊠ Uferweg, ☎ 031/332–29–50) is on the right bank northwest of the Kursaal.

SHOPPING

Department Stores

EPA (⊠ Marktgasse 24, ☎ 031/311–24–22) is an inexpensive department store with a supermarket. **ABM** (⊠ Spitalgasse 3, ☎ 031/311–75–11) has a broad range of reasonably priced goods. **Migros** (⊠ Marktgasse 46, ☎ 031/311–23–77) has one of the city's best supermarkets in its basement. **Globus** (⊠ Spitalgasse 17–21, ☎ 031/311–88–11), one of the city's largest department stores, has a wide variety of designer labels. **Loeb** (⊠ Spitalgasse 47–57, ☎ 031/320–71–11) is known for its high-quality clothes.

Shopping Streets

The old town of Bern is one big shopping center, and its 6 kilometers (4 miles) of arcades shelter stores of every kind and quality. Many of the modern, mainstream shops are concentrated between the train station and the Clock Tower, especially on **Spitalgasse** and **Marktgasse.** Beyond, along **Kramgasse** and **Gerechtigkeitsgasse** and, parallel to them on the north, **Postgasse,** there are quirkier, artier spots and excellent antiques stores. You may hear the Bernese calling this area, the farthest east, the "old town," as its 800 years of commerce give it seniority over the mere 15th-century upstarts to the west. Junkerngasse and Münstergasse have good shopping as well, with galleries and avant-garde fashion.

Specialty Stores

ANTIQUES

The best antiques shops line Gerechtigkeitsgasse and Postgasse; their wares range from cluttery *brocante* (collectibles) to good antiques from all over Europe. The **Puppenklinik** (⊠ Gerechtigkeitsgasse 36, ☎ 031/312–07–71) is just this side of a museum, with its shelves and window densely packed with lovely (if slightly eerie) old dolls and toys.

CHOCOLATE

Tschirren (⊠ Kramgasse 73, ☎ 031/311–17–17) has been making chocolates and sweets for more than 40 years. **Abegglen** (⊠ Spitalgasse 36, ☎ 031/311–21–11) is a local favorite. **Eichenberger** (⊠ Bahnhofplatz 5, ☎ 031/311–33–25) has a fine selection of chocolates and candies. **Beeler** (⊠ Spitalgasse 29, ☎ 031/311–28–08) is another top chocolatier.

SOUVENIRS/GIFTS

Heimatwerk Bern (⊠ Kramgasse 61, ☎ 031/311–30–00), a branch of this excellent Swiss chain of handicraft stores, offers a broad and high-quality line of ceramics, jewelry, wood carvings, linens, and woolens—all Swiss made. **Alscher** (⊠ Gerechtigkeitsgasse 59, ☎ 031/312–19–15) displays an enormous stock of Reuge music boxes (Swiss made), including tiny, detailed wooden chalets; if you're in the market, you can also buy street organs. **Galerie Trag-art** (⊠

Gerechtigkeitsgasse 9, ☎ 031/311–64–49) has credible reproductions of art nouveau pewter pieces.

Kunsthandwerk Anderegg (✉ Kramgasse 48, ☎ 031/311–02–01) carries trendy, colorful wooden toys from all over the world.

BERN A TO Z

Arriving and Departing

By Car
Bern is connected conveniently by expressway to Basel via N1, to the Berner Oberland via N6, and to Lac Léman and thus Lausanne, Geneva, and the Valais via N12.

By Plane
Belp (☎ 031/961–21–11) is a small airport 9 kilometers (6 miles) south of the city in a suburb called Belpmoos that has flights to Amsterdam, Brussels, Frankfurt, and most other major European airports connecting through **Crossair,** Switzerland's domestic airline. Now **Air Engiadina,** a regional airline, offers direct flight connections with Munich and Vienna. For reservations with Crossair or Air Engiadina, call 031/961–55–33.

A city bus runs regularly between Belp and the city's Bahnhof (the main train station). The fare each way is 14 SF.

A taxi from the airport to the Hauptbahnhof (Main Train Station) costs about 35 SF and takes about 15 minutes.

By Train
Bern is a major link between Geneva, Zürich, and Basel, and fast trains run almost every hour from the enormous central station. Bern is the only European capital to have three high-speed trains: the ICE, the TGV, and the Pendolino. The ICE from Berlin takes 9 hours; the TGV from Paris takes 4½ hours; the Pendolino from Milan takes 3 to 4 hours.

Getting Around

By Bus and Tram
The best of Bern is concentrated in a relatively small area, and it's easy to get around on foot. Bus and tram services are excellent, however, with fares ranging from 1.50 SF to 2.40 SF. Buy individual tickets from the dispenser at the tram or bus stop; the posted map will tell you the cost. Tourist cards for unlimited rides are available at 7.50 SF per day. Buy them at the Bahnhof tourist office or from the public-transportation ticket office in the subway leading down to the train station (take the escalator in front of Loeb's department store and turn right through the Christoffel Tower). A Swiss Pass lets you travel free.

By Limousine
Heinz Sollberger (✉ Sonnenhofweg 28, CH-3006, ☎ 031/352–63–63) rents limos by the day.

By Taxi
Taxis are actually a cumbersome alternative to walking, especially when streets are dominated by trams. It costs between 6 SF and 15 SF to cross town.

Opening and Closing Times

Banks
Banks are open Monday–Wednesday 8–4:30, Thursday 8–6, and Friday 8–4:30; they are closed weekends.

Museums
Museums are usually open Tuesday–Sunday 10–5, but it's safest to check before you visit one.

Stores
Commercial hours are generally Monday–Friday 8:15–6:30, Thursday to 9 PM, and Saturday 8:15–4; Sunday most stores are closed, and many remain closed Monday morning.

Contacts and Resources

Bookstore
Stauffacher (⊠ Neuengasse 25, ☎ 031/311–24–11) has the broadest selection of books in English.

Embassies
United States (⊠ Jubiläumstrasse 93, ☎ 031/357–70–11). **Canada** (⊠ Kirchenfeldstrasse 88, ☎ 031/352–63–81). **United Kingdom** (⊠ Thunstrasse 50, ☎ 031/352–50–21).

Emergencies
Police (☎ 117). **Ambulance** (☎ 144). **Hospital** (⊠ Insel Spital, Freiburgstrasse, ☎ 031/632–21–11). **Medical and dental referrals** (☎ 031/311–92–11). **All-night pharmacy referrals** (☎ 031/311–22–11).

Guided Tours
ORIENTATION TOURS
A two-hour bus tour around the old town, covering all the principal sights, is offered by the tourist office, where you meet. *Cost: 22 SF.*

Personal Guides
To arrange for a private guide, contact the tourist office (☎ 031/311–66–11).

Travel Agency
Wagons-Lits (⊠ von Werdt-Passage 3-5, ☎ 031/328–28–28).

Visitor Information
The tourist office is at Bahnhofplatz, at the train station. ⊠ Postfach, CH-3001, ☎ 031/311–66–11.

10 The Berner Oberland

The Bernese Alps concentrate the very best of rural Switzerland: panoramas of the treble peaks of the Eiger, Mönch and Jungfrau mountains; crystalline lakes, gorges, and waterfalls; and emerald slopes dotted with gingerbread chalets and cows with bells—not to mention world-class skiing. It's no secret, though: The Berner Oberland is the most touristic canton in Switzerland.

THERE ARE TIMES WHEN THE REALITY OF Switzerland puts postcard idealization to shame, surpassing tinted-indigo skies and advertising-image peaks with its own astonishing vividness. Those times happen often in the Berner Oberland. Though the Valais and Graubünden areas offer stiff competition, this rugged region concentrates the very best of rural Switzerland: mountain panoramas that can't be overrated, massive glaciers, crystalline lakes, gorges and waterfalls, chic ski resorts, and emerald slopes scattered with gingerbread chalets.

It was the Romantics who first beat a path to this awe-inspiring region. After contemplating the Staubbach Falls in 1779, the great German writer Johann Wolfgang von Goethe was moved to write one of his most celebrated poems, *Gesang der Geister über den Wassern* (*Song of the Spirits over the Waters*). Rousseau spread word of its astounding natural phenomena to Paris society. Then Lord Byron came to investigate; it's said he conceived *Manfred* in barren, windswept Wengernalp. Shelley followed, then William Thackeray, John Ruskin, and Mark Twain; the landscape master painter J. M. W. Turner took in the views, and the composer Johannes Brahms; finally, Queen Victoria herself came, beginning a flood of tourism that changed the Berner Oberland's—and Switzerland's—profile forever.

Before the onslaught of visitors inspired the locals to switch from farming to innkeeping, agriculture was the prime industry—and is still much in evidence today. As if hired as props to style a photo opportunity, Swiss-brown cows pepper the hillsides wherever rock gives way to grass, and the mountains echo with their bells. The houses of the Berner Oberland are classics, the definitive Swiss chalets: The broad, low, deep-eaved roofs cover gables that are scalloped, carved, and painted with the family dedication; the wood weathers to dark siena after generations of harsh cold and clear sun. From early spring through autumn, every window box spills torrents of well-tended scarlet geraniums, and adjacent woodpiles are stacked with mosaiclike precision.

The region is arranged tidily enough for even a brief visit. Its main resort city, Interlaken, lies in green lowlands between the gleaming twin pools of the Brienzersee and the Thunersee, linked by the River Aare. Behind them to the south loom craggy, forested foothills with excellent views, and behind those foothills stand some of Europe's noblest peaks, most notable the snowy crowns of the Eiger (3,970 meters/13,022 feet), the Mönch (4,099 meters/13,445 feet), and the fiercely beautiful Jungfrau (4,158 meters/13,638 feet). Because nature laid it out so conveniently, the region has become far and away the most popular for tourism, with its excursion and transportation systems carrying enormous numbers of visitors to its myriad viewpoints, overlooks, and wonders of the world. The railroad to the Jungfraujoch transports masses of tour groups to its high-altitude attractions, and on a peak-season day its station can resemble the Sistine Chapel in August or the Chicago Board of Trade. But the tourist industry can handle the onslaught, offering such an efficient network of boats, trains, and funiculars; such a variety of activities and attractions; and such a wide range of accommodations, from posh city hotels to rustic mountain lodges, that every visitor can find the most suitable way to take in the marvels of the Bernese Alps.

Pleasures and Pastimes

Dining

Meals in the Berner Oberland tend to be down-to-earth, starting with hearty soup or a mixed-slaw salad, followed by lake fish or meat and potatoes, and then a sizable dessert. Fried or broiled *Egli* (perch), or *Felchen* or *Fera* (two kinds of whitefish), are frequently local and lake-fresh; waterfront resorts like Spiez, Brienz, and Iseltwald specialize in fish. Meat dishes represent Bernese and Zürich cuisines: *Ratsherren-topf* is a mixed grill, *geschnetzeltes Kalbsfleisch* or *-leber* is veal or calves' liver in cream sauce. Colorful mixed salads showcase crisp shredded celery root, beet, carrot, cabbage, and sometimes sauerkraut. Because the Alpine experience demands it, the Oberland has adopted the French territories' cheese fondue and *raclette* (melted cheese with potatoes and pickles) as winter-night staples.

The valley town of Meiringen claims to have invented meringue; whether or not this is true, its region consumes enough to corner the market. Enormous crisp, ivory meringue puffs may be served with or without vanilla ice cream; regardless, they are buried under mounds of heavy piped whipped cream. You may find a half-portion more than adequate.

CATEGORY	COST*
$$$$	over 70 SF
$$$	40 SF–70 SF
$$	20 SF–40 SF
$	under 20 SF

per person for a three-course meal (except in $ category), including sales tax and 15% service charge

Hiking

Partly because of its spectacular ski transport network woven throughout the region, the Berner Oberland offers a wealth of highly developed walking and hiking options. The scenery is spectacular—what can surpass the views from the Mürren plateau toward the Jungfrau, Eiger, and Mönch?—and the options varied, from rough trails toward glaciers to smooth postbus roads. From May through October you'll be unlikely to find yourself alone for long on any given trail. A wide variety of topographical maps and suggested itineraries is available at local tourist offices, especially the Jungfrau region central office on the Höheweg in Interlaken.

Lake Cruises

Steamers crisscross the lakes of Brienz and Thun, trailing leisurely across crystal waters past rolling panoramas of forested hills and craggy, snow-capped peaks. They provide an alternative to high-speed car cruises and limited train runs, and, with their buslike schedule, allow passengers to step off at any port for a visit; they need only choose the best boat to catch next. Drinks and meals in the glassed-in cafés (both first and second class) offer respite on windy days.

Lodging

The Berner Oberland tradition mandates charming chalet-style exteriors replete with scalloped-wood balconies, steeply sloped roofs, and cascades of scarlet geraniums, no matter what architectural era a hotel dates from. In fact, many hotels in the region have interiors that reflect their roots in the '60s ski boom, with their no-nonsense, Scandinavian-spare, avocado-beige and walnut-grain Formica furnishings. Some of the most recently renovated have softened the '60s edge with folksy touches like carved knotty pine, and a few landmarks have preserved charming interiors that reflect their lovely facades.

CATEGORY	COST*
$$$$	over 250 SF
$$$	200 SF–250 SF
$$	120 SF–200 SF
$	under 120 SF

*All prices are for a standard double room, including breakfast, tax, and service charge.

Shopping

The Berner Oberland is known for its spindle-made *torchon* (dishrag) lace from Lauterbrunnen and the wood carvings of Brienz, especially fine nativity scenes. Traditional hand-painted pottery from around Steffisburg is gaining popularity. Winter resorts like Grindelwald, Mürren, and Wengen have their share of state-of-the-art ski boutiques, with Gstaad adding international designer shops as well.

Skiing

As one of Switzerland's capitals of winter sports, the Berner Oberland provides a dazzling variety of choices to skiers. Each resort offers its own style of transit and its own peculiar terrain, from the nursery slopes at Bodmi to the deadly narrow pistes of the Schilthorn.

Exploring the Berner Oberland

The central, urban-Victorian resort of Interlaken makes a good base for excursions for visitors who want to experience the entire Jungfrau region, which includes the craggy bluff-lined Lauterbrunnen Valley and the opposing resorts that perch high above it: Mürren and Wengen. Both busy, sporty Grindelwald, famous for scenic rides and sports, and isolated Kandersteg, ideal for hiking and cross-country skiing, can be visited out of Interlaken, but make good home bases themselves; they both lie at the dead-end of gorge roads that climb into the heights. Spreading east and west of Interlaken are the Brienzersee and the Thunersee, both broad, crystalline, and surrounded by forests, castles, and picturesque waterfront resorts, including Brienz and Thun. From Spiez on the Thunersee, you may head west through the forest gorge of the Simmental to the Saanenland and glamorous Gstaad. Connections by rail or car keep most highlights within easy reach.

Great Itineraries

Ten days in the Berner Oberland gives you the luxury of exploring each of the valleys and lakes of this varied region, but you can experience it en passage as well, depending on your travel pace and your capacity for excursions.

IF YOU HAVE 3 DAYS
Numbers in the text correspond to numbers in the margin and on the Berner Oberland map.

Base yourself in 🚉 **Interlaken** ①, one day taking a boat trip across the Thunersee to **Thun** ⑪, the next day a driving tour around the Brienzersee to **Brienz** ⑧ and the Freilichtmuseum Ballenberg. The third day (or best-weather day) head up the Lauterbrunnen Valley and take the famous rail trip from **Wengen** ⑤ to the **Jungfraujoch** ④, returning via **Grindelwald** ⑥.

IF YOU HAVE 5 DAYS
Take in the tours above, and, while in the Lauterbrunnen Valley, take the cable cars or cogwheel rail up to **Mürren** ③ and the Schilthorn. On day five, drive up to **Kandersteg** ⑭ to hike to the Oeschinensee, or wind through the forest to visit famous **Gstaad** ⑮.

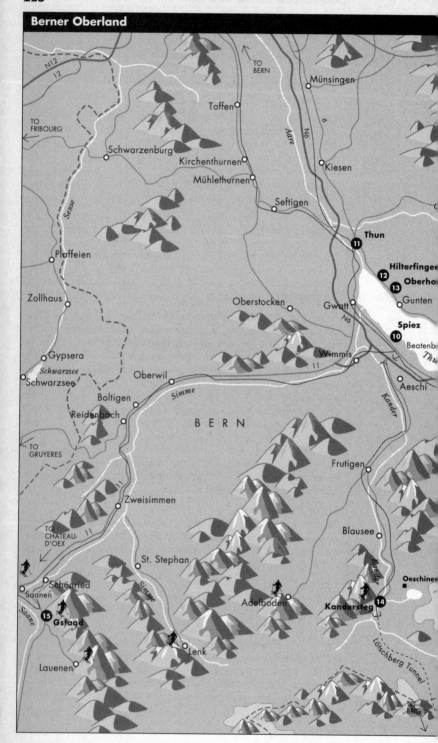

TO BERN

Münsingen

Toffen

N12

12

TO FRIBOURG

Schwarzenburg

Kirchenthurnen

Mühlethurnen

Kiesen

Sense

Aare

N6

Seftigen

Plaffeien

Thun ⑪

Hilterfingen

⑫

Zollhaus

Oberstocken

Gwatt

Oberho

⑬

Gunten

N6

Spiez

⑩

Gypsera

Wimmis

Beatenb

Schwarzsee

Oberwil

11

Thu

Schwarzsee

Simme

Kander

Aeschi

Boltigen

Reidenbach

B E R N

TO GRUYERES

Frutigen

11

Zweisimmen

Blausee

TO CHATEAU-D'OEX

11

St. Stephan

Kander

Oeschiner

Schönried

Simme

Adelboden

Kandersteg ⑭

Saanen

⑮

Gstaad

Saane

Lenk

Lötschberg Tunnel

Lauenen

TO BRIG

TO
BERN

10

TO
LUZERN

Wiggen

Flühli

Marbach

TO
LUZERN

Oberei

Kleinteil

Glaubenbüelenpass

chwarzenegg

Brienzer
Rothorn

Lungern

4

Niederhorn

6–11

Brienz

8

Freilichtmuseum
Ballenberg

9

eatenberg

Harder
Kulm

Brienzer
See

Giessbach

Meiringen

St. Beatus-
höhlen

Iseltwald

7

cht

r See

Unterseen

Bönigen

Interlaken

1

First

Heimwehfluh

Matten

Schynige Platte

Wilderswil

Gundlischwand

Zweilütschinen

Grindelwald

6

Wengen

5

Lauberhorn

OBERER GRINDELWALD GLETSCHER

Lauterbrunnen

2

Staubbachfälle

Kleine Scheidegg

Eiger

Trümmelbachfälle

Mönch

Schilthorn

Mürren

3

Jungfraujoch

4

Mürrenbachfälle

Jungfrau

ALETSCH GLACIER

nsee

BLÜMLISALP

Breithorn

KEY

——— Rail Lines
••••••• Funicular/
Cable Car
– – – Regional
Boundary Line
Ski Resort

N

0   6 miles

0   9 km

IF YOU HAVE 10 DAYS

Rent an apartment or settle in on a half-board plan in one of the cozier hotels of Itnerlaken or any crossroads resort (Grindelwald and Lauterbrunnen also offer easy access to sights), taking in the lesser sights as you cruise around the varied region. Visit the Trümmelbach Falls in the Lauterbrunnen Valley, see the castles at **Hilterfingen** ⑫ and **Oberhofen** ⑬ on the Thunersee, and take another high-altitude excursion out of Interlaken to Harder Kulm, Heimwehfluh, or Schynige Platte. You might even hop on a train and make a day trip into the capital city of Bern, only an hour away (☞ Chapter 9).

When to Tour

In high summer, the Berner Oberland is the most popular tourist area in Switzerland and can feel overrun, so aim for the cusp—early June, late September—while the weather still holds but the crowds thin. May and November are low season, and prices drop—but some hotels and cable cars shut down for maintenance. Ski season begins in mid-December and runs through Easter vacation.

THE JUNGFRAU REGION

The charming resort town of Interlaken holds forth between two spectacularly sited lakes, the Brienzersee and the Thunersee, and is the gateway to two magnificent mountain valleys, one leading up to the popular sports resort of Grindelwald, the other into Lauterbrunnen and the famous car-free resorts of Wengen and Mürren. Rearing over both valleys, the Jungfrau and its partner peaks the Eiger and Mönch can be viewed to advantage from various high-altitude overviews.

Interlaken

❶ *58 km (36 mi) southeast of Bern.*

The name "Interlaken" has a Latin source: *interlacus* (between lakes); as a gateway to the Berner Oberland, this bustling Victorian resort town is the obvious home base for travelers planning to visit the region's two lakes and the mountains towering behind them. At 570 meters (1,870 feet), Interlaken dominates the Bödeli, the branch of lowland between the lakes that Interlaken shares with the adjoining towns of Unterseen, Wilderswil, Bönigen, and Matten. There are unlimited excursion options, and it's a pleasant, if urban, place to stay put as well, as its setting is spectacular and its ambience genteel.

East of the high-rise (and highly visible) Hotel Metropole, at the center of town, the **Höheweg** is the city's main promenade, its tree- and flower-lined walkways on the right cutting through the edge of the broad green parklands of the **Höhematte**. This 35-acre park once pastured the herds of the Augustinian monastery.

The **Grand Hotel Victoria-Jungfrau** (☞ Dining and Lodging, *below*), on the left side of the Höheweg, was conceived to take in the view of the snowy Jungfrau that towers above town. The hotel originated as two humbler inns, the Jungfrau (1864) and the Chalet Victoria (1865); these were merged and expanded in 1895, and the facade redesigned and landmark tower added in 1899. Mark Twain sojourned here.

Between the Höheweg and the River Aare, you'll find the landscaped **Kursaal** grounds, complete with a floral clock. Built in 1859 in a dramatic combination of Oberland chalet and Victorian styles, the Kursaal was renovated in 1968 and has become once again a social focal point for the city. Plays and concerts are presented here, and there are folklore evenings in the adjoining *Spycher* (the Swiss name for a farm storage barn). The **Casino** here has gambling nightly, but with bets limited by federal law to 5 SF; 120 slot machines were recently added.

At the end of the Höhematte south of the Hotel du Nord is the **Schlosskirche** (Reformed Church), once the chapel for the Augustinian monastery. Though founded in 1133, the monastery and the convent that shared its grounds during the 13th century have left only a 14th-century chancel and a branch of the cloister. The rest of the convent was built into a private castle in 1745, which, attached behind the church, now provides office space to the community.

On the north side of the River Aare is the town of **Unterseen,** with its picturesque little old town and Marktplatz. Founded in 1279 on lands rented from the Augustinians, Unterseen retains some of the region's oldest buildings, including the 17th-century **Stadthaus** and the 14th-century **church,** whose steeple dates from 1471. The Schloss Unterseen (Unterseen Castle), built in 1656 for the reigning Bernese nobleman, stands at the opposite end of the square, where an arched gateway separates Unterseen from the modern world.

Fronting on the Unterseen Marktplatz is the **Touristik-Museum der Jungfrau Region** (Museum of Tourism of the Jungfrau Region), which traces the history of tourism and excursions in the Jungfrau region with models of early transportation and examples of primitive mountain-climbing and skiing equipment. ⊠ *Obere Gasse 26,* ☎ *033/822–98–39.* ✍ *3 SF.* ☉ *May–mid-Oct., Tues.–Sun. 2–5.*

In central Interlaken, between 2 and 4 PM, you can visit the **Chäs-Dörfli,** a model cheese dairy tucked back behind the Burri dairy. In a reconstructed herdsman's hut, you can watch Swiss-style cheese being made over a wood fire. Various cheeses and paraphernalia are for sale. ⊠ *Centralstrasse 3,* ☎ *033/822–30–12.* ✍ *Free.* ☉ *May–Sept., Tues. and Fri. 2–4.*

NEED A BREAK?	Have a coffee and pastry at the top of the **Hotel Metropole** (☎ 036/21–21–51), on the Höheweg. From the café on the 18th floor you can see all over the city and the surrounding peaks.

OFF THE BEATEN PATH	**HEIMWEHFLUH** – An old-fashioned red funicular railway leads to the top of this 669-meter (2,194-foot) mountain, where you will get views over both lakes and an elevated peek at the Jungfrau, the Eiger, and the Mönch. A restaurant and playground have been built at the top, and there's a show of model trains every 30 minutes. Catch the funicular (14 SF; open Apr.–Oct.) at a station five minutes south of Interlaken West.
	HARDER KULM – North of the River Aare near Interlaken East, take the 12-minute funicular ride up Harder Kulm (1,310 meters/4,297 feet); from there, hike uphill to views south over the city, the lakes, and the whole panorama of snowy peaks. A turreted Gothic "chalet" restaurant offers Friday-evening visitors more than food: From mid-June through September, there are folk music and dancing, too—and not only the tourists participate. ☎ *033/822-34-44.* ✍ *Round-trip transit: 20 SF.* ☉ *June–Oct., Fri. entertainment: 6 SF music charge.*

Dining and Lodging

$$ ✕ **Im Gade.** This welcoming hybrid of carved-wood coziness and sleek
★ formality, in the Hotel du Nord, fills up night after night with appreciative locals who recognize fresh, fine cooking and alert service. Details count here: Even that dab of smoky sauerkraut in your crisp mixed salad is homemade. Seasonal specialties (game, mushrooms) stand out. Fondues are available but not the restaurant's forte: Stick to the

hearty veal dishes, the lovely lake fish, or the generous daily specials. ⊠ *Höheweg 70,* ☎ *033/822–26–31. AE, DC, MC, V. Closed mid-Nov.–mid-Dec. and Apr.*

$$ ✕ **Krebs.** The sunny front-porch serving area looks over the street, but head for the more formal dining room, glassed-in yet still opening onto the main promenade. You may feel you've forgotten your parasol: This is a classic Old World resort spot and serves its upscale Swiss classics and homey daily plates with starched-collar style. It has been in Interlaken—and the Krebs family—since 1875. ⊠ *Bahnhofstrasse 4,* ☎ *033/822–71–61. AE, DC, MC, V. Closed Nov.–Apr.*

$$ ✕ **Stella.** This unusual hotel dining room offers aggressively modern, highly flavored cuisine, including several vegetarian options, with organically grown ingredients (say, curried rice with fruit), and an extraordinary variety of salads—from 40 to 50 kinds at the Thursday salad buffet. Order the "surprise" menu in advance, and you'll be served five courses of unexpected delights on pretty, mismatched china. Service is friendly, and the owners supervise the staff. An attractive terrace, complete with fountain, turns summer dining into a garden idyll. ⊠ *Waldeggstrasse 10,* ☎ *033/822–88–71. Reservations essential. AE, DC, MC, V.*

$–$$ ✕ **Schuh.** With a luxurious shady terrace spilling into the Höhematte in summer, and cocktail piano enhancing the dated elegance inside, this sweet shop and café-restaurant serves everything from tea to rich, hot meals. Leave room for the showcase pastries, which you'll find in the adjoining shop. ⊠ *Höheweg 56, across from Metropole,* ☎ *033/822–94–41. AE, DC, MC, V.*

$ ✕ **Laterne.** You'll find this unpretentious, local favorite a bit off the tourist
★ track, east of the center near the N8 ring road (10 minutes' walk from Interlaken West). With a sports-bar ambience and a rustic, woody setting, it offers good Swiss specialties: six kinds of *Rösti* (hash brown potatoes) served in iron skillets, mixed salads, and fondue at reasonable prices. ⊠ *Obere Bönigstrasse 18,* ☎ *033/822–11–41. AE, DC, MC, V.*

$$$$ 🏨 **Beau Rivage.** Its Belle Epoque grandeur glossily restored, this Inter-
★ laken old-timer offers more intimate luxury and isolation than the Victoria-Jungfrau (☞ *below*). There are lovely mountain views in front and the quiet Aare behind, and it's a stone's throw from Interlaken East, departure point for many excursions. Delicate *cuisine du marché* (based on the freshest ingredients available) is served in the hearth-warmed restaurant, La Bonne Fourchette. ⊠ *CH-3800,* ☎ *033/821–62–72,* 𝕱𝕬𝕏 *033/823–28–47. 170 beds. 2 restaurants, 2 bars, indoor pool, sauna, fitness center. AE, DC, MC, V.*

$$$$ 🏨 **Metropole.** As the Berner Oberland's only skyscraper, this 14-story concrete high-rise gobbles up the scenery and ruins everyone's view but its own—which is spectacular. If you turn your back on the picture windows, you'll think you're in the United States: It's slick, airtight, dependable, and banal; there's even an atrium lobby-lounge. The rooftop restaurant has a sharp new look and serves up soups, salads, and sandwiches along with staggering views. ⊠ *CH-3800,* ☎ *033/821–21–51,* 𝕱𝕬𝕏 *033/822–84–87. 160 beds. Restaurant, snack bar, indoor pool, massage, sauna. AE, DC, MC, V.*

$$$$ 🏨 **Victoria-Jungfrau.** Follow in Mark Twain's footsteps to this 1865
★ landmark, a splendid, block-long, wedding-cake sprawl that dominates the Höheweg. Its restoration has taken it firmly into the 20th-century, with a glitzy postmodern black-and-burled-wood entry, and the flashy formal restaurant La Terrace, a vision of marble and glass, which overlooks the promenade and the Höhematte. ⊠ *CH-3800,* ☎ *033/827–11–11 or 800/223–6800,* 𝕱𝕬𝕏 *033/827–37–37. 400 beds. Restaurant*

(jacket and tie), 2 bars, stübli, indoor pool, beauty salon, spa, tennis, cabaret, dance club. AE, DC, MC, V.

$$$ 🏨 **Du Lac.** Don't be put off by the views over the tracks of Interlaken East: The trains run only in the day. Moreover, the waterfront restaurant and pricier back rooms have one of the most peaceful situations in town—a wide, woodsy bank of the Aare. The hotel's musty grandeur has been maintained by a single family for more than 100 years. The stübli has a casual buffet. ✉ *CH-3800,* ☎ *033/822–29–22,* FAX *033/822–29–15. 70 beds. Restaurant. AE, DC, MC, V.*

$$$ 🏨 **Interlaken.** When they pronounce this the oldest hotel in town, they don't fool around: It's been hosting overnight guests since 1323—first as a hospital, then as a cloister, and by the early 15th century as a tavern-hotel. Although its original walls are visible in the restaurant, the structure nowadays is a standard-issue Victorian, well renovated during the late 1980s and filled with (occasionally irrelevant) antiques. Byron and Mendelssohn slept here. ✉ *CH-3800,* ☎ *033/821–22–11,* FAX *033/823–31–21. 100 beds. 2 restaurants, bar, sauna. AE, DC, MC, V.*

$$$ 🏨 **Royal–St. Georges.** If you are a fan of Victoriana, this impeccably restored gem is a dream come true, with original moldings, built-in furnishings, and fantastical bath fixtures reproduced in gleaming Jugendstil–Art Nouveau. A few rooms were done in ho-hum modern, as some guests object to bathtubs with feet, but you can ask for a period version. The streetside rooms—the ones with Jungfrau views—are noisier. ✉ *CH-3800,* ☎ *036/22–75–75,* FAX *033/823–30–75. 170 beds. Restaurant. AE, DC, MC, V.*

$$ 🏨 **Chalet Oberland.** A vacation-intensive combination of rustic decor and city-crossroads position, this downtown lodge attracts the young with music, dancing, and pizza in its all-wood stübli. The rooms are sleek but minimal; the art deco–style 1988 wing is slicker. ✉ *CH-3800,* ☎ *033/821–62–21,* FAX *033/822–13–88. 230 beds. Stübli, pizzeria, live music. AE, DC, MC, V.*

$$ 🏨 **Hirschen.** This dark-beam 17th-century guest house, in one family
★ since 1666 and now completely renovated, has old, deep-shingle eaves and rooms with private baths, fresh knotty-pine walls, and built-in furniture. The stübli, paneled in aged pine, and the restaurant, scattered with antiques, serve local specialties; veal, beef, cheese, vegetables, and even honey come from the owner's farm. There's a sheltered terrace and balcony overlooking a lovely garden. The hotel's location on an outskirts crossroad makes it convenient for drivers who are covering the region rather than staying in town. ✉ *CH-3800,* ☎ *033/822–15–45,* FAX *033/823–37–45. 32 beds. Restaurant, stübli. AE, DC, MC, V.*

$$ 🏨 **Splendid.** Location is key here: You can't get more central to shopping and nightlife. Renovations have ironed out the wrinkles in this modest little Victorian palace, and now you'll find new baths, sleek beige decor, and cozy spindle beds. The back rooms overlook a quiet backstreet; the corner bays are prettiest. The proprietor is a hunter, so game in season is fresh and local. ✉ *CH-3800,* ☎ *033/822–76–12,* FAX *033/822–76–79. 60 beds. Restaurant, pub. AE, MC, V.*

$$ 🏨 **Toscana.** This former downtown pizzeria has evolved into a sleek, sizable hotel. The stress on technical perfection (intercom, elevators, cable TV, indoor parking, angled mountain views) belies the personal touch of good Tuscan cooking, prepared by the Italian owners. ✉ *CH-3800,* ☎ *033/823–30–33,* FAX *033/823–35–51. 42 beds. Restaurant, café. V.*

$ 🏨 **Aarburg.** Many of the freshly renovated rooms in this homey, gera-
★ nium-brightened guest house look over a stunning curve of the River Aare on the edge of the old town. The owners are warm, the blond-wood stübli welcoming, and there's front-porch dining over the waterfront. Some rooms have no bath. ✉ *CH-3800,* ☎ *033/822–26–15. 14 beds. Stübli. AE, MC, V.*

$ 🏨 **Alp Lodge.** Part of the historic building that now houses the Belle-
★ vue Park Plaza, this separate enterprise is possibly the best bargain in
town. The tiny, cheery rooms have bunk beds, doubles, or twins, and
murals painted by local art students. Though breakfast is not included,
you won't find a better deal. ⊠ CH-3800, ☎ 033/822–47–48, FAX
033/822–92–50. 30 beds. Bar. AE, DC, MC, V.

$ 🏨 **Balmer's.** A democratic institution, this popular private youth hos-
★ tel is a quick bus ride from either rail station, and it offers families and
young travelers bare-bones bedrooms at rock-bottom prices. Kitchen access, washers and dryers, videos, two fireplaces, and self-service suppers,
and an English-speaking staff make guests feel at home in this lively, collegiate international ambience. Rooms are available with one to five beds,
all with sinks. Check-in is required by 5 PM, check-out by 9 AM; there
are no lockers or day storage. There's even a massive group tent pitched
at the edge of town. ⊠ Hauptstrasse 23–25, CH-3800, ☎ 033/822–
19–61, FAX 033/823–32–61. 200 beds. Kitchens, coin laundry. MC, V.

$ 🏨 **Pilgerruhe.** This charming Victorian guest house, on a quiet side street
between Interlaken West and the Heimwehfulh, offers a quintessen-
tially middle European pristine stuffiness—waxed parquet, brocade,
and heavy florals—and an equally typical, impeccable garden. ⊠ Ru-
genaustrasse 8, CH-3800, ☎ 033/822–30–51, FAX 033/823–30–69.
35 beds. Breakfast room. AE, DC, MC, V.

Nightlife and the Arts

BARS

In Interlaken the **Edelweiss** in the Victoria-Jungfrau (☎ 033/827–11–
11) offers live, easy-listening Tyrolean-style background music for
your steak and salad. **Riverside East** and **Riverside West** in the Hotel
Bellevue (☎ 033/822–44–31) offer live blues and New Orleans–style
music. **Buddy's Pub** (⊠ Hotel Splendid, ☎ 033/822–76–12) is a popular conversation spot where locals and visitors actually mingle. **Sternen** (☎ 033/822–34–25), on the pedestrian stretch of the
Jungfraustrasse, offers a good selection of wines by the glass and summer seating on the sidewalk.

CASINOS

Interlaken's Casino/Kursaal (☎ 033/822–25–21) has a 5 SF gambling
limit and 120 new slot machines.

DANCING

The new **Hollywood** (⊠ Hotel Central, ☎ 033/823–10–33) has up-
to-date sound equipment. **Barbarella,** the most popular disco, features
some live bands (⊠ Victoria-Jungfrau, ☎ 033/821–21–71). **High-life**
near Interlaken West specializes in easygoing oldies. **Johnny's Club** (⊠
Hotel Carlton, ☎ 033/822–38–21) draws a rougher crowd. The
newest disco, **Black and White,** is in the Hotel Metropole (☎ 033/821–
21–51) and attracts an upscale crowd.

FOLKLORE

Folklore shows, yodeling and all, are presented at Interlaken's **Folk-
lore-Spycher** in the Casino/Kursaal, with admission including meals or
not, as space allows; you can choose from one of four typical menus.
⊠ off Höheweg, ☎ 033/822–25–21. 🍽 3-course menu 44 SF, up to
54 SF for 4 courses; admission without dinner 16 SF. Priority is given
to diners. Meals 7:30, shows 9.

At the restaurant at **Harder Kulm,** reached by funicular, you can hear
typical ländler (traditional dance) music and try a little regional dancing. ☎ 033/822–34–44. 🍽 4 SF for the music; food, drinks, and the
ride up not included. ☉ June–Sept., Fri.

THE ARTS

For a real introduction to the local experience, don't miss the **Tellfreilichtspiele**, an outdoor pageant play presented in Interlaken every summer by a cast of Swiss amateurs. Wrapped in a rented blanket—which you'll need, since the show goes on regardless of weather, June through September—and seated in a 2,200-seat sheltered amphitheater that opens onto illuminated woods and a permanent village-set, you'll see 250 players in splendid costume acting out the epic tale of Swiss hero William Tell. The text is Schiller's famous play, performed in German with the guttural singsong of a Schwyzerdütsch accent—but don't worry; with galloping horses, flower-decked cows, bonfires, parades, and, of course, the famous apple-shooting climax, the operatic story tells itself. Tickets are available through the **Tellbüro** (✉ Bahnhofstrasse 5, ☎ 033/822–37–22 or 033/822–37–23), travel agents, and some hotel concierges; prices range from 12 SF to 32 SF.

Outdoor Activities and Sports

GOLF

The 18-hole **Unterseen** golf course (☎ 033/822–60–22) along Lake Thun has a new clubhouse and restaurant (handicap card and club membership required).

HORSEBACK RIDING

The area between the Thunersee and Brienzersee offers a number of scenic marked bridle paths through woods, over fields, and by streams. Guided rides and classes are available from **E. Voegeli** (✉ Scheidgasse 66, Unterseen, ☎ 033/822–74–16).

MOUNTAIN CLIMBING

Contact **Alpinenzentrum Jungfrau** (✉ Postgasse 16, Interlaken, ☎ 033/823–43–63) for placement with accredited mountain guides.

SAILING

The Thunersee provides the area's most beautiful sailing; Interlaken's **Swiss Sailing School** offers courses and boat rental (☎ 033/822–83–30; open Apr.–mid-Oct.).

TENNIS

In Interlaken, there are four outdoor courts on the **Höhematte** (☎ 033/822–14–72), plus three outdoor and four indoor courts at **Tennis-Center Interlaken** (☎ 033/822–54–22).

Shopping

An excellent central source for handicrafts and goods typical of the region as well as throughout Switzerland is **Heimatwerk** (☎ 033/822–16–53), on Interlaken's Höheweg past the Casino.

OFF THE BEATEN PATH

SCHYNIGE PLATTE – An ambitious trip yields the most splendid overview in the region: Take a six-minute ride on the Bernese Oberland Railway from Interlaken East to Wilderswil and then a 50-minute cogwheel train ride to this 1,965-meter (6,445-foot) peak for a picnic, a wander down any of numerous footpaths, or a visit to the Alpine Botanical Garden, where more than 500 varieties of mountain flowers grow. You may opt to walk either up or (more comfortably) down: Specify when you buy your ticket (round-trip 50 SF).

Wilderswil

2 km (1 mi) south of Interlaken.

Visitors who like a base for excursions but who hope to avoid the tourist crowds and commercialism of Interlaken may opt for Wilderswil, as conveniently placed as Interlaken (at the crossroads to Grindelwald and Lauterbrunnen, with swift access to either lake highway) but offering tranquil isolation and the ambience of a small village. In the old-fashioned **Oberdorf** (Upper Village), a few blocks from the main throughway, there are beautiful old carved-wood chalets, complete with flower boxes, fountains and gardens.

Dining and Lodging

$–$$$$ ✕🏨 **Alpenblick.** With arguably the best restaurant in the Berner Ober-
★   land (competing with Grindelwald's Fiescherblick) on the premises, this carved-wood-and-shingle 17th-century landmark in the quiet old Oberdorf serves a varied clientele, from loyal gastronomes who make a pilgrimage to try chef Richard Stöckli's adventurous international cuisine, to families who take hearty demipension fare in the stübli after a day's excursions. Locals dine here regularly, too, seeking out old-style classics (Rösti with wild mushrooms) and upscale bistro fare (marinated lakefish tartare, duck liver pâté with onion confit). The large chestnut-shaded dining terrace makes for lovely summer dinners. There's a maze of creaky, comfortable rooms upstairs; rooms in modern annex-chalets cost slightly more. ✉ CH-3812, ☎ 033/ 822–07–07. 🗚 033/822–80–07. 65 beds. Restaurant, bistro, stübli. AE, MC, V.

Lauterbrunnen

★ ❷ 8 km (5 mi) south of Wilderswil; 9 km (6 mi) south of Interlaken.

Below Interlaken the mountains seem to part like the Red Sea into the awesome, bluff-lined Lauterbrunnen Valley. Around the village of Lauterbrunnen, grassy meadows often lie in shadow, as 460-meter (1,508-foot) rocky shoulders rise on either side. This tidy town of weathered chalets serves as a starting point for the region's two most spectacular excursions: to the Schilthorn and to the Jungfraujoch. Lauterbrunnen's airportlike, superefficient car park and rail terminal allows long- and short-term parking for visitors heading for Wengen, Mürren, the Jungfraujoch, or the Schilthorn. Consider choosing this valley as a home base for day trips by train, funicular, or cable, thereby saving considerably on hotel rates.

Magnificent **waterfalls** adorn the length of the Lauterbrunnen Valley, the most famous being the 300-meter (984-foot) **Staubbachfälle** (Staubbach Falls) and, just beyond, the spectacular **Trümmelbachfälle**, a series of seven cascades hidden deep inside rock walls at the base of the Jungfrau, which you can access by underground funicular. Approach the departure point via a pretty, creek-side walkway and brace yourself for some steep stair-climbing. ☎ 033/855–32–32. 🗐 10 SF; June–Aug., ☉ daily 8:30–6; Apr.–May and Sept.–Oct., daily 9–5:30.

Dining and Lodging

$ ✕🏨 **Stechelberg.** At the very end of the Lauterbrunnen Valley, where the road peters out into a beautiful foot trail, this isolated old lodging offers unspoiled comforts with a hard-core local touch: heavy smoke, muddy boots, and yodeling on Saturday night. Rooms upstairs are creaky, cozy, and all-wood, with balconies that open to the sound of the roaring river. Stick to simple sausage-and-Rösti specials; more ambitious attempts fall short. ✉ CH-3824, ☎ 033/855–29–21, 🗚 033/855–44–38. 25 beds. Restaurant, café. MC, V.

$ ✕🏨 **Sternen.** In Lauterbrunnen center, near the parking and rail complex, this century-old, weathered-wood hotel has rooms that show some wear, but clean, sociable public spaces, dramatic views, and low prices compensate. Rooms are available with or without bathrooms. Rates go down daily, the longer you stay. ✉ *CH-3822,* ☎ *033/855–12–31,* FAX *033/855–44–31. 16 beds. Restaurant, café. AE, MC, V.*

$ ✕▦ **Waldrand.** If you really want to get away from it all but still take in Jungfrau/Eiger/Mönch views, drive or take the postbus up a narrow, winding mountain road from Lauterbrunnen to Isenfluh, the poor man's Mürren. Its sole, tiny pension provides contemporary knotty-pine rooms and flower-lined balcony views as well as plain, hot café food downstairs. The hiking possibilities are endless. On request, the owners will pick you up at the rail station in Lauterbrunnen. ✉ *CH-3822,* ☎ *033/855–12–27,* FAX *033/855–13–92. 22 beds. Restaurant. No credit cards.*

Shopping

A good source of Lauterbrunnen lace is **Handwarch Lädeli** (by the old schoolhouse, ☎ 033/855–35–51).

Mürren

★ ❸   *7 km (4 mi) southwest of Lauterbrunnen; 16 km (10 mi) south of In- terlaken, plus a 5-minute cable-car ride from Stechelberg.*

The most popular way to reach this lofty sports mecca (elevation 1,000 meters/3,280 feet) is by cable car (☞ *below*) from Stechelberg, but if you can't stomach (or afford) that route, you may approach Mür- ren by funicular out of Lauterbrunnen's train station, then connect by cogwheel rail from Grütschalp, following the track along the run of the cliff and looking toward magnificent views of the Big Three. The whole trip takes about 30 minutes and drops you at the Mürren rail station, at the opposite end of town from the cable-car stop. If you're not settling in to stay in a Mürren hotel, this is an ideal takeoff point for a day hike along the bluff-top. Pointing your binoculars at the gleam- ing dome on the Jungfraujoch across the valley, you can almost hear the winds howling off the Aletsch glacier.

Mürren's primary attractions are panoramic hiking trails in summer and unrivaled views toward the Jungfrau, the Mönch, and the Eiger. Skiers may want to settle here for daredevil year-round skiing at the top; hikers may combine staggering views and bluff-top trails with ex- traordinarily peaceful mountain nights.

Mürren is one of the stops along the ride down the south side of the **Schilthorn** (2,970 meters/9,742 feet), famed for its role in the James Bond thriller, *On Her Majesty's Secret Service.* The peak of this icy go- liath is accessed by a four-stage cable-lift ride past bare rock cliffs and stunning slopes. At each level, you step off the cable car, walk across the station, and wait briefly for the next cable car up. At the top is a revolving restaurant, Piz Gloria. ☎ *033/855–21–41.* ✉ *Round-trip cable car Stechelberg–Schilthorn, 78.40 SF (60.20 SF between 7:25 AM and 8:55 AM). Departures twice hourly 6:25 AM–11:25 PM; last departure from the top 6:03 PM in summer, 5:03 PM in winter.*

The cable-car station that accesses the Schilthorn actually has its base in Stechelberg, site of the **Mürrenbachfälle,** which at 250 meters (820 feet) are among the tallest in Europe.

Skiing

Mürren provides access to the Schilthorn (2,970 meters/9,742feet)— start of 15-kilometer (9-mile) run that drops all the way through Mür- ren to Lauterbrunnen. At 1,650 meters (5,413 feet), the resort has one funicular railway, two cable cars, seven lifts, and 65 kilometers (40 miles) of downhill runs. A one-day pass covering the entire Jungfrau region costs 52 SF; a six-day pass costs 232 SF.

Lodging

$$ ☷ **Alpenblick.** This simple, comfortable modern pension is in a spec-
tacular setting and offers balconies with astonishing views. It's just be-
yond the center, near the train (not the cable-car) station, so you may
choose to take the funicular up if you have loads of luggage. ⊠ CH-
3825, ☎ 033/855–13–27, ℻ 033/855–13–91. 35 beds. Restaurant,
café. DC, MC, V.

$$ ☷ **Bellevue-Crystal.** Distinguished from surrounding chalets by its
sturdy brick-and-shutter construction, this older landmark presents it-
self as a traditional ski lodge with full modern comforts. Each room
has a tiny balcony with fine views, and there is fresh new pine-and-
gingham decor. ⊠ CH-3825, ☎ 033/855–14–01, ℻ 033/855–14–
90. 30 beds. Restaurant, café, sauna. AE, DC, MC, V.

The Jungfraujoch

★ ❹ *Half-day cog-railway excursion out of Interlaken, Lauterbrunnen, or
Grindelwald.*

The granddaddy of all high-altitude excursions: the famous journey
to the Jungfraujoch, site of the highest railroad station in the world.
From the station at Lauterbrunnen you take the green cogwheel Wenger-
alp Railway nearly straight up the wooded mountainside as the valley
and the village shrink below. From the hilltop resort of **Wengen** (☞
below) the train climbs up steep grassy slopes past the timberline to
Kleine Scheidegg, a tiny, isolated resort settlement surrounded by vertiginous scenery. Here you change to the Jungfraubahn, which tunnels
straight into the rock of the Eiger, stopping briefly for views out enormous picture windows blasted through its stony face.

Forty minutes from the station at Lauterbrunnen, the **Jungfraujoch terminus** stands at an elevation of 3,475 meters (11,400 feet). You may
feel a bit light-headed from the altitude. Follow signs to the **Top of Europe** restaurant, a gleaming white glass-and-steel pavilion built in 1987
to replace a 1924 structure on the site, which burned in 1972. The expanse of rock and ice you see from here is simply blinding.

If you're not sated with the staggering views from the Jungraujoch terminus, you can reach yet another height by riding a 90-second elevator up 111 meters (364 feet) to the **Sphinx Terrace:** To the south crawls
the vast Aletsch Glacier, to the northeast stand the Mönch and the Eiger,
and to the southwest—almost close enough to touch—towers the tip
of the Jungfrau herself. Note: Even in low season, you may have to
wait in long lines for the elevator up.

More than views are offered to the hordes that mount daily to the
Jungfraujoch. You can take a beginner's **ski lesson** or a **dogsled ride,**
or tour the chill blue depths of the **Ice Palace,** a novelty attraction on
the order of a wax museum, full of incongruous and slightly soggy sculptures. Admission is included in the price of the excursion.

A few things to keep in mind for the Jungfraujoch trip: Take sunglasses,
warm clothes, and sturdy shoes; even the interior halls can be cold and
slippery at the top. Return trains, especially toward the end of the day,
can be standing room only. A round-trip ticket from Interlaken East
to the Jungfraujoch via Lauterbrunnen and Wengen, then back to Interlaken via Grindelwald, takes 2½ hours and costs 153.20 SF. To save
money take the 6:30 train first thing in the morning; the trip costs only
120 SF at this unpopular hour. Guided tours with escort and commentary
(they're called "Jungfrau Tour" as opposed to "Jungfrau individuell")
cost less (139 SF) and leave daily May through October from Interlaken East around 8:30 AM. You also can get to Lauterbrunnen or

Grindelwald (☞ *below*) on your own steam (or using your Swiss Pass) and then buy a ticket to the top; if you've driven, of course, you'll have to return the way you came and miss the full round-trip tour. Inquire at the Jungfraubahn offices (☎ 033/826–41–11). Call ahead for Jungfraujoch weather information (☎ 033/855–10–22).

Wengen

❺ *½-hour cog-railway ride from Lauterbrunnen.*

This south-facing hilltop resort perched on a sunny plateau over the Lauterbrunnen Valley has magnificent panoramas down the valley toward the Breithorn. It rivals Mürren for its quiet, its chic, and its challenging skiing, which connects with the trail network at Grindelwald; loyalists prefer Wengen for its memorable sunsets. You can aim for central, upscale hotels, near resort shopping and active bars, or head downhill to pleasant, more isolated lodgings, all artfully skewed toward the view.

Skiing

Just over the ridge from Grindelwald, the sunny resort of Wengen (1,300–3,450 meters/4,265–11,316 feet) nestles on a sheltered plateau high above the Lauterbrunnen Valley; from there, a complex lift system connects to Grindewald, Kleine Scheidegg, and Männlichen. Wengen has six funicular railways, one cable car, 13 lifts, and 250 kilometers (155 miles) of downhill runs.

Dining and Lodging

$$–$$$ ✕🖼 **Beausite Park Hotel.** As Wengen's only grand hotel, the Beausite
★ Park has spacious, traditional rooms with windows overlooking the town and the valley below. Service is efficient and geared more toward couples than families: Pampering is encouraged. A 10-minute walk from the village, the hotel is near the cable-car station. ✉ CH-3823, ☎ 033/856–51–61, 📠 033/855–30–10. *53 rooms with bath. Restaurant, indoor pool, massage, sauna. MC, V.*

$$–$$$ ✕🖼 **Silberhorn.** Its 19th-century origins evident only in the roofline, this all-modern resort lodge has a young, lively staff and ambience. Newly decorated rooms are full of pine and chintz; the simple digs in the older wing are excellent value. ✉ CH-3823, ☎ 033/856–51–31, 📠 033/855–22–44. *140 beds. Restaurant, hot tub, sauna, dance club, nursery. AE, DC, MC, V.*

$$–$$$ ✕🖼 **Victoria Lauberhorn.** Since 1895, this gabled bastion of mountain
★ tourism has offered knee-buckling views to its guests—especially those paying slightly more for the southern panorama that put Wengen on the map, though north and west village-and-hillside views are nothing to sniff at, either. The public spaces mix rustic with funeral-parlor swank, but the new room decor has discreet regional flair with its pretty painted furniture. ✉ CH-3823, ☎ 033/856–51–51, 📠 033/855–33–77. *120 beds. Restaurant, bar. AE, DC, MC, V.*

$$ ✕🖼 **Alpenrose.** Run by one family for more than 100 years, this wel-
★ coming inn has fresh new decor, all knotty pine and painted wood. Rooms with south-facing balconies are only slightly more expensive, and worth it. It's downhill and away from the center, with an emphasis on good half-board food. ✉ CH-3823, ☎ 033/855–32–16, 📠 033/855–15–18. *80 beds. Restaurant (for guests only). AE, DC, MC, V.*

$$ ✕🖼 **Regina.** Guests can ski to the door of this hotel and then walk five minutes to the village center for a cup of hot chocolate. The Victorian-style decor is cozy, and every room is different. Ask for a corner room; these overlook the valley. The restaurant is reasonable, and the Italian maitre d' is especially attentive. ✉ CH-3823, ☎ 033/855–15–12, 📠 033/855–15–74. *95 rooms with bath. Restaurant, bar, nightclub. AE, DC, MC, V. Closed Nov.*

$–$$ ✕▣ **Eden/Eddy's Hostel.** A Victorian shingled jewel box joins forces with an unpretentious crash pad—the Eden hotel providing marvelous southern views, rooms with or without bathrooms, and pretty gardens and a terrace, and Eddy's hostel providing a no-frills bed, a shower, and a breakfast buffet across the street at the Eden. There are plenty of occasions to mix at barbecues, over aperitifs on the terrace or stone-grilled meats in the restaurant, or at one of many live music events. ⊠ CH-3823, ☎ 033/855–16–34, ᴾᴬˣ 033/855–39–50. 26 beds. Restaurant, café. MC, V.

$ ✕▣ **Schweizerheim.** It's worth the hike to this old-fashioned family-
★   run pension nestled well below the beaten path: The full-valley views are flawless, the gardens pristine, and the terrace picnic tables precariously balanced over the Lauterbrunnen Valley. The good restaurant, once frequented by locals, now serves pension guests only. The adjacent chalet, dating from 1930, offers rock-bottom prices for simple, old-style rooms with running water. There's live folk music Wednesday night. ⊠ CH-3823, ☎ 033/855–11–12, ᴾᴬˣ 033/855–23–27. 58 beds. Restaurant. MC, V.

$–$$ ▣ **Bären.** This lodging just past the center is straightforward and modern, with good views and low rates. Each balcony room has a bath and toilet; others have only running water. There are a pleasant terrace café and a good family restaurant. Demipension is not available. ⊠ CH-3823, ☎ 033/855–14–19. 26 beds. Restaurant. AE, DC, MC, V.

Outdoor Activities and Sports

SKATING

Wengen has a natural rink (Natureisbahn) and a partially sheltered indoor rink (Kunsteisbahn); for hours, contact the tourist office (☎ 033/855–14–14).

TENNIS

Five public courts are available for rental through the tourist office (☎ 033/855–14–14).

Nightlife and the Arts

DANCING

There's dancing Monday through Saturday at **Le Carrousel** (⊠ Hotel Regina, ☎ 033/855–15–12) and at **Tiffany** (⊠ Hotel Silberhorn, ☎ 033/856–51–31). Tuesday through Sunday, **Paradise** (⊠ Hotel Belvédère, ☎ 033/855–24–12) has a nightclub with cabaret.

Grindelwald

❻ *27 km (17) mi east of Interlaken.*

Strung along a mountain highway and offering two convenient train stations, Grindelwald (1,050 meters/3,445 feet) is the most easily accessible of the region's high resorts. It makes an excellent base for skiing and hiking, shopping and dining—if you don't mind a little traffic.

★ From Grindelwald you can drive, take a postbus, or hike up to the **Oberergletscher,** a craggy, steel-blue glacier you can admire from a distance while comfortably seated at the Hotel Wetterhorn's outdoor café (☞ Dining and Lodging, *below*)—or approach at the base along wooded trails. (There's an instrument at the base to measure the glacier's daily movement.)

Also out of Grindelwald, you can take the **Firstbahn,** a 30-minute gondola ride to the lovely views and pistes of the **First** ski area (2,163 meters/7,095 feet). A recently planted **Alpine garden** now flourishes within easy walking distance (it's even wheelchair-accessible) of the first cable car. Without hiking into the heights, you can see gentian, edelweiss, anemones, and Alpine aster in their natural habitat.

Skiing

An ideal base camp for the Jungfrau ski area, Grindelwald (1,050 meters/3,445 feet) provides access to the varied trails of Grindelwald First and Kleine Scheidegg/Männlichen. Grindelwald has eight funicular railways, three cable cars, 22 lifts, and 165 kilometers (103 miles) of downhill runs.

Dining and Lodging

$$$$ ✕⊞ **Schweizerhof.** Behind a dark-wood Victorian chalet facade dat-
★ ing from 1892, this big, comfortable, homelike hotel has attracted a loyal clientele for more than 30 years. A 1995 renovation brightened up the lobby lounge and dining rooms, all scrubbed pine and hand-painted (and carved) trim, with inviting wingbacks and bookcases for rainy days. Rooms are decorated in fabrics and cozy carved pine and have tile baths, along with luxurious bathrobes. The emphasis here is on half pension, and the generous nightly smorgasbord includes entrée, soup, meat course from an open grill, salad (grown in the hotel's own garden), cheese, and fruit; the breakfasts are big, too. The à la carte Schmitte stübli is lovely for fondue. Reserve well in advance, and keep in mind that there's a slight surcharge for stays of less than three nights. ⊠ *CH-3818,* ☎ *033/853–22–02,* 𝔽𝔸𝕏 *033/853–20–04. 96 beds. Restaurant, stübli, indoor pool, beauty salon, sauna, bowling, fitness center. AE, MC, V.*

$$$ ✕⊞ **Fiescherblick.** This is the place to eat in Grindelwald, whether as
★ a pension hotel guest or day-tripper: The serious cuisine in the intimate restaurant continues to draw kudos and devoted food lovers, and the low-priced Swiss Bistro in the adjoining Stöckli bar allows casual lunchers to enjoy the talents of the same chef. Sample *tête de veau bouilli* (a rugged head-scrap stew with vinaigrette), potato pancakes with farm cheese and chives, wild garlic sausage with onion sauce, or lamb *geschnetzeltes* (fine-sliced lamb in cream-and-wine mushroom sauce), all served on naive-patterned china. The fresh, new-pine decor carries into the guestrooms, too. ⊠ *CH-3818,* ☎ *033/853–44–53,* 𝔽𝔸𝕏 *033/853–44–57. 50 beds. Restaurant, stübli. AE, DC, MC, V.*

$$$ ✕⊞ **Gletschergarten.** In the same family for three generations, this atmospheric pension radiates welcome, from the heirloom furniture and paintings (by the grandfather) to the tea roses cut from the owner's garden. There's heraldry in the stained-glass windows, a ceramic stove with built-in seatwarmer, and every amenity, including a piano, a solarium, and a ski drying room. All rooms have balconies, some with glacier views, others overlooking the emerald green hills. Simple home-cooking is served to guests only; demipension is de rigueur. ⊠ *CH-3818,* ☎ *036/53–17–21,* 𝔽𝔸𝕏 *033/853–29–57. 50 beds. Restaurant, bar, sauna, Ping-Pong, billiards, coin laundry. No credit cards.*

$–$$ ✕⊞ **Wetterhorn.** Overlooking the magnificent ice-blue upper glacier—as well as the sprawling parking lot where hikers leave their cars—this modest inn offers generous lunches outdoors, with full glacier views, and unusually good regional dining inside its comfortable restaurant. Portions of veal favorites are large and delicious, and there is a good selection of Swiss wines. The adjoining Gletscherstübli attracts locals as well as the hordes of tourists and hikers who come to marvel at its namesake. Up the creaky old stairs, there are simple aged-pine rooms—some have glacier views—with sink and shared bath. An adjoining dormitory provides budget accommodation. ⊠ *CH-3818,* ☎ *036/53–12–18. 15 beds. Restaurant, café, stübli. No credit cards.*

$ ✕⊞ **Säumertaverne.** Outside Gündlischwand, in the forested gorge be-
★ tween Interlaken and Grindelwald, the Stoller family runs an impec-

cable little country inn, with rustic room decor (painted cabinetry, farm implements), modern baths, forest-and-valley views, and cowbells thunking outside the windows. There are a sunny terrace café and a comfortable family restaurant that offers cheese specialties. It's convenient only if you're traveling by car. ⊠ *CH-3815,* ☎ *033/855–32–76,* 𝔽𝔸𝕏 *033/855–23–51. 18 beds. Restaurant, café. AE, DC, MC, V.*

$$$$ 🏨 **Regina.** Although its turreted exterior dates from the turn of the century, Grindelwald's pricey establishment became a hotel in 1953 and exudes '50s glamour; its spare beige-and-avocado sprawl is packed with a boggling array of wing chairs, baroque antiques, and Swiss kitsch, all from the founder's collection. The views are flawless, however, the location central, and the tennis courts may be the most spectacularly sited in the world. ⊠ *CH-3818,* ☎ *033/854–54–55 or 800/223–6800,* 𝔽𝔸𝕏 *033/853–47–17. 180 beds. Restaurant, indoor and outdoor pools, beauty salon, massage, sauna, 2 tennis courts, nightclub. V.*

$$$ 🏨 **Alpina.** The cinder-block construction of this vacation lodging, built in 1973 and renovated 15 years later, is stone-cold to all appearances. But its lofty location makes for sensational views from its front balconies—and the edges are softened within and without by parlor-plush public areas, geraniums below every window, and warm, personal service. Tile bathrooms, most with showers, accompany no-nonsense rooms. It's a five-minute walk straight uphill from the station. ⊠ *CH-3818,* ☎ *033/853–33–33,* 𝔽𝔸𝕏 *033/853–33–76. 60 beds. Restaurant. AE, DC, MC, V.*

Nightlife and the Arts

DANCING

There's dancing at the **Challi Bar** in the Hotel Kreuz (☎ 033/854–54–92), **Herbie's Bar-Dancing** (Grand Hotel Regina, ☎ 033/854–54–55), and at the **Cava Bar** (Hotel Derby Bahnhof, ☎ 033/854–54–61).

Outdoor Activities and Sports

MOUNTAIN CLIMBING

The **Bergsteigerzentrum** (☎ 033/853–20–20), in the center of Grindelwald, offers daily and weekly courses to mountain and glacier hikers.

SKATING

The **Sportzentrum Grindelwald** (☎ 033/853–33–66) has indoor and natural rinks.

TENNIS

Grindelwald has six public courts; for permits, call the tourist office (☎ 033/853–12–12).

THE BRIENZERSEE (LAKE BRIENZ)

Reputedly the cleanest lake in Switzerland—which surely means one of the cleanest in the world—this magnificent bowl of crystal-clear water mirrors the mountainscape and forests, cliffs, and waterfalls that surround it. You can cruise along it at high-speed on the N8 freeway, or crawl along its edge on secondary waterfront roads; or you can cut a wake across it on a steamer, gliding quietly from port to port, exploring each stop on foot, then cruising to your next destination.

Iseltwald

❼ *9 km (6 mi) northeast of Interlaken.*

This isolated peninsula juts out into the lake, its small hotels, cafés, and rental chalets clustered picturesquely at water's edge. Every restaurant prides itself on its lake fish, of course. From the village edge, you may want to take off on foot; a lovely forest walk of about 1½ hours brings you to the falls of the **Giessbach** (Giess Brook), which tumbles in several stages down through the rocky cliffs to the lake. The most scenic route to Iseltwald from Interlachen is via the south-shore road; follow the black-and-white "Iseltwald" signs. You can also take the N8 expressway, following the autoroute signs for Meiringen.

Brienz

★ ⑧ *12 km (7 mi) northeast of Iseltwald; 21 km (13 mi) northeast of Interlaken.*

The romantic waterfront village of Brienz, world renowned as a wood-carving center, is a favorite stop for boat-tourists as well as drivers. Several artisan shops display the local wares, which range in quality from the ubiquitous, winningly naive figures of spotted cows to finely modeled nativity figures and Hummel-like portraits of William Tell. Brienz is also a showcase of traditional Oberland architecture, with some of its loveliest houses (at the west end of town, near the church) dating from the 17th century. Once an important stage stop, Brienz hosted Goethe and Byron at its landmark Hotel Weisses Kreuz (☞ Dining and Lodging, *below*); their names, along with the 1688 date of construction, are proudly displayed on the gable.

At Brienz you may want to try your own hand at wood carving: In one lesson at the atelier of **Paul Fuchs** you can learn to carve the typical Brienzer cow. ⊠ *Scheidweg 19D, in Hofstetten, between Brienz and Ballenberg,* ☎ *033/951–14–18.* ⊡ *22 SF. 2-hr workshops Apr.–Oct., Tues. 2:15 and Thurs. 6:15.*

Switzerland's last steam-driven cogwheel train runs from the center of Brienz, from the waterfront up to the summit of **Brienzer-Rothorn**, 2,346 meters (7,700 feet) above the town; the round-trip cost is 62 SF.

OFF THE BEATEN PATH

FREILICHTMUSEUM BALLENBERG – Just east of Brienz, a small road leads to this child-friendly, outdoor museum-park, where 80 characteristic Swiss houses from 18 cantons have been carefully dismantled and transported to the site. Linen weaving, basket making, and baking are demonstrated throughout the summer. ⊠ *Case postale,* ☎ *033/951–11–23.* ⊡ *12 SF.* ☉ *Mid-Apr.–Oct., daily 10–5.*

Dining and Lodging

$–$$ ✕ **Steinbock.** Whether you dine on the broad flower-lined terrace or
★ inside the wonderful old (1787) carved-wood-and-homespun chalet, you'll feel the atmosphere of this proud local institution. Choose from no less than nine presentations of Lake Brienz whitefish, regional pastas, or veal classics. ⊠ *CH-3855,* ☎ *033/951–40–55. AE, DC, MC, V. Closed Tues.*

$$ ✕⊞ **Lindenhof.** In a 1787 lodge high above the touristic lakefront, dis-
★ cerning German and Austrian families settle in for a week or two of evenings by the vast stone fireplace, dinners in the panoramic winter garden (or on the spectacular terrace), and nights in dressed-up theme rooms with such evocative names as Marmot Cave and Hunter's Hut. The grounds are vast and beautifully manicured, the atmosphere familial and formal at once. Families with small children dine together by the fire, apart from other guests. ⊠ *CH-3855,* ☎ *033/951–10–72.* 🅵🅰🆇 *033/951–40–72. 100 beds. Restaurant, café, kitchenettes, indoor pool. AE, DC, MC, V.*

$$ ✕⊞ **Weisses Kreuz.** Generic modern improvements have erased some of the fine old origins of this structure, which was built in 1688 and ac-

commodated Goethe and Byron in their prime, but the current version has a tidy, cozy charm of its own. Yes, the location is across the highway from the waterfront, close to Rothorn railway excursion crowds. But if you are a history buff, the idea of its antiquity and the hallowed names on the gable may be allure enough, and the woody stübli draws loyal locals for a chat and a daily paper. The pine and homespun-linen restaurant offers omelettes and *käseschnitte* (cheese and bread baked in its own whey) as well as lake fish, steaks, and strudel. Some rooms have lake views, and the sunny, lake-view terrace café draws locals as well as tourists fresh off the boat. ⊠ *CH-3855,* ☎ *033/951–17–81,* ☎ *033/951–41–17. 30 beds. Restaurant, café. AE, DC, MC, V.*

$$ ⊞ **Bären.** The modern construction and 1960s room decor are happily upstaged by the gracious dining room, flower-framed terrace café, and private waterfront promenade. Lakeside rooms, which have serene water views, are considerably pricier in high season; back rooms open over the main road. There is also a small beach giving access to the crystalline water. ⊠ *CH-3855,* ☎ *033/951–24–12,* ☎ *033/951–40–22. 50 beds. Restaurant, café, lake, beach. AE, DC, MC, V.*

$ ⊞ **Schönegg und Spycher.** Clinging to a steep, garden-covered hillside over town, this tidy little pension is run by house-proud Christine Mathyer, who sees to it that all three small lodgings maintain their old-fashioned charm. There's a 1957 fireplace lounge, with flagstone floors and wood carvings, and rooms with rustic painted furniture. There are flower-sprigged duvets, checked bedspreads, and chocolates on the pillow at night. Guests can play Ping-Pong and lounge in the sunny garden overlooking the lake, and it's an easy walk up to the Lindenhof or down to the Steinbock restaurant (☞ *above*) for dinner. ⊠ *CH-3855,* ☎ *033/951–11–13. 29 beds. Breakfast room, bar, Ping-Pong. MC, V.*

Shopping
In Brienz, **H. Huggler-Wyss** (⊠ Fischerbrunnenplatz, ☎ 033/951–16–79), **Walter Stahli AG** (⊠ Hauptstrasse 41, ☎ 033/951–14–71), and **Ed Jobin** (⊠ Hauptstrasse 111, ☎ 033/951–14–14) all offer good selections of local wood carvings.

Meiringen

🟑 *12 km (7 mi) east of Brienz; 35 km (22 mi) northeast of Interlaken.*

Set apart from the twinned lakes and saddled between the roads to the Sustenpass and the Brünigpass, Meiringen is a resort town with 300 kilometers (186 miles) of marked hiking trails and 60 kilometers (37 miles) of ski slopes. Its real claim to fame, though, is **Reichenbach Falls**, where Sherlock Holmes was supposedly thrown by Professor Moriarty—his archenemy—into the "cauldron of swirling water and seething foam in that bottomless abyss above Meiringen." Visitors can now view the dramatic fall where Conan Doyle intended to end his series of mysteries. A nearby hotel bears the detective's name, and in the center of town, the **Sherlock Holmes Museum** offers an "authentic" replica of Holmes's front room at 221b Baker Street. ☎ 033/971–41–41. ☎ 3.50 SF. 🕐 *May–Sept., daily 3–7; Oct.–Apr., Wed.–Sun. 3–6.*

The private, 20-kilometer (12-mile) **road to Grindelwald** permits no cars, but makes for a beautiful seven-hour alpine hike.

Dining and Lodging
$$ ✕⊞ **Sporthotel Sherlock Holmes.** This sports-oriented hotel is ideal for hikers and skiers. Though the building is modern and unspectacular, most rooms look out on Reichenbach Falls. Rooms are functional and simple, but wood cabinetry gives them a cozy, Alpine feel. The restaurant

serves wholesome Swiss food. ⊠ *CH-3860,* ☎ *033/972–98–89,* 🅵🅰🅇
033/972–98–88. 110 beds. Restaurant, sauna, fitness center. MC, V.

THE THUNERSEE (LAKE THUN)

If you like your mountains as a picturesque backdrop and prefer a re-
laxing waterfront sojourn, take a drive around the Thunersee—or
crisscross it on a leisurely cruise boat. More populous than the Brien-
zerzee, it offers both the marina town of Spiez and the large market
town of Thun, spread at the feet of the spectacular Schloss Zähringen
(Zähringen castle). There are more castles along the lake as well, and
yet another high-altitude excursion for rising above the waterfront to
take in Alpine panoramas.

Spiez

❿ *19 km (11¾ mi) west of Interlaken.*

The town of Spiez is a summer lake resort with marinas for anyone who
loves water sports. Its enormous waterfront **castle** was home to the family Strättligen and, in the 13th century, its great troubadour, Heinrich.
The structure spans four architectural epochs, starting with the 11th-
century tower; its halls contain beautiful period furnishings, some from
as long ago as Gothic times. The early Norman church on the grounds
dates from the last millennium. ☎ *033/654–15–06.* 🖭 *4 SF.* ☯
Apr.–Oct., Tues.–Sun. 10–5, Mon. 2–5; July–mid.-Sept. 10–6.

Dining and Lodging

$$–$$$ ✕🏨 **Seegarten Hotel Marina.** With a pizzeria corner in one wing and
two dining rooms that stretch comfortably along the marina front, this
is a pleasant, modern family restaurant, and its lake-fish specialties are
excellent, served in generous portions. The Spiez castle looms directly
behind you, unfortunately out of sight. The rooms upstairs are spare
and modern. ⊠ *CH-3700,* ☎ *033/654–67–61,* 🅵🅰🅇 *033/654–67–07.*
70 beds. Restaurant, café. AE, DC, MC, V.

$$$ 🏨 **Strandhotel Belvedere.** A member of the Hotel Suisse Silence chain,
this graceful old mansion-hotel has beautiful lawns and gardens, and
its manicured waterfront on the Thunersee offers secluded swimming.
Corner and lakeside rooms are worth the higher price. Belvedere guests
have free access to the city's heated outdoor pool, 100 meters (328 feet)
away. ⊠ *CH-3700,* ☎ *033/654–33–33,* 🅵🅰🅇 *033/654–66–33. 59 beds.*
Restaurant, beach. AE, DC, MC, V.

Outdoor Activities and Sports

TENNIS
Spiez has municipal tennis courts at the bay, by the municipal pool (☎
033/654–49–17).

Thun

⓫ *10 km (6 mi) north of Spiez; 29 km (18 mi) northwest of Interlaken.*

Built along an island on the River Aare as it leaves the Thunersee, the
picturesque market town of Thun is laced with rushing streams crossed
by wooden bridges, and its streets are lined with arcades. The main
shopping thoroughfare of the old town may be unique in the world:
Pedestrians stroll along flowered terrace sidewalks built on the roofs
of the stores' first floors, and climb down stone stairs to visit the
"sunken" street-level shops.

From the charming medieval Rathaus square, a covered stair leads up
★   to the great **Schloss Zähringen** (Zähringen Castle), its broad donjon
cornered by four stout turrets. Built in 1191 by Berchtold V, duke of
Zähringen, it houses a fine historical museum and provides magnificent views from its towers. The knights' hall has a grand fireplace, an
intimidating assortment of medieval weapons, and tapestries, one from
the tent of Charles the Bold. Other floors display local Steffisburg and
Heimberg ceramics, 19th-century uniforms and arms, and Swiss household objects, including charming Victorian toys. ☎ *033/623–20–01.*
🎫 *5 SF.* ⊙ *Apr.–May and Oct., daily 10–5; June–Sept., daily 9–6.*

Dining and Lodging

$$ ✕🏨 **Krone.** Positioned directly on the lovely Rathausplatz in the old
town, this landmark has some fine bay-window tower rooms and river
views. Despite its historic setting and classic exterior, the slick new in-
terior is tile-and-wood modern. The Chinese restaurant Wong-Kun has
a cross-cultural menu, and an upscale bistro offers chic versions of re-
gional dishes. ⊠ *CH-3600,* ☎ *033/222–82–82,* 🆅 *033/222–45–87.*
60 beds. Restaurant. MC, V.

$ ✕🏨 **Zu Metzgern.** This grand old shuttered and arcaded *Zunfthaus*
(guild house), at the base of the castle hill, provides fresh pastel rooms
(bathrooms down the hall) with Rathausplatz views. There's atmospheric
dining, too, whether in the wood-and-linen restaurant or on the inti-
mate little terrace, which is tucked behind an ivy-covered trellis. It's
ideally placed for a castle climb and old-town shopping and touring.
⊠ *CH-3600,* ☎ *033/222–21–41,* 🆅 *033/222–21–82. 15 beds.*
Restaurant, café. MC, V.

Shopping

A Thun branch of **Heimatwerk** (⊠ Obere Hauptgasse 66, ☎ 033/222–
34–41) offers a wide variety of Swiss handicrafts—good pottery, fine
embroidery, music boxes, pressed flowers. Swiss Army knives, linens,
and general gifts are also widely available.

In addition to Heimatwerk, a good spot for traditional and artisanal
pottery in Thun is **Töpferhaus** (⊠ Obere Hauptgasse 3, ☎ 033/222–
70–65). Just outside Thun, **Töpferei Howald** in Heimberg (⊠ Bern-
strasse 272, ☎ 033/237–14–72) has a good selection of traditional
pottery.

Hilterfingen

⓬   *4 km (2½ mi) southeast of Thun; 18 km (11 mi) northwest of Interlaken.*

Hilterfingen's castle, **Schloss Hünegg,** was built in 1861 and furnished
over the years with a bent toward Jugendstil and Art Nouveau. ☎
033/243–19–82. 🎫 *4 SF.* ⊙ *Mid-May–mid-Oct., Mon.–Sat. 2–5,*
Sun. 10–noon and 2–5.

Oberhofen

⓭   *2 km (1 mile) southeast of Hilterfingen; 16 km (10 mi) northwest of*
Interlaken.

Oberhofen boasts its own **castle,** this one a hodgepodge of towers and
spires on the waterfront. Begun during the 12th century, it spans 700
years. Inside, the Historical Museum of Bern has a display on the
lifestyle of Bernese nobility. ☎ *033/243–12–35.* 🎫 *4 SF.* ⊙ *Mid-
May–mid-Oct., Tues.–Sun. 10–noon and 2–5, Mon. 2–5.*

....

OFF THE   **NIEDERHORN** – Thirteen kilometers (8 miles) east of Oberhofen, the town
BEATEN PATH   of Beatenbucht has a shore terminal that sends funiculars to Beatenberg.

From there you can either walk up a trail or catch a chairlift to the Niederhorn (1,919 meters/6,294 feet), from which an astonishing panorama unfolds: the Thunersee and the Brienzersee, the Jungfrau, and even, on a fine day, Mont Blanc.

ST. BEATUSHÖHLEN – Just west of Beatenberg, the illuminated St. Beatushöhlen (caves) have been heavily developed, complete with a wax figure of Irish missionary St. Beatus himself, isolated in his cell as he was during the 6th century. This is less a center for pilgrimage than a simple cave tour with stalactites and stalagmites in dripping grottoes. 🎟 *10 SF.* ⊙ *Apr.–Oct., daily 9:30–5:30. Guided tours every 30 mins.*

THE KANDER VALLEY

Easily reached by car or the Lötschberg rail line from Interlaken via Spiez, the spectacular, high-altitude Kander Valley leads up from the Thunersee toward Kandersteg, an isolated resort strewn across a level plateau. From Kandersteg, you can make a hiker's pilgrimage to the silty-blue Oeschinensee. And en route to the lakes below, you may want to visit the touristy but pleasant Blausee.

Kandersteg

⑭ *45 km (28 mi) southwest of Interlaken.*

At 1,176 meters (3,858 feet), Kandersteg stands alone, a quiet resort spread across a surprisingly broad, level—and thus walkable—plateau. Lofty bluffs, waterfalls, and peaks—including the **Blümlisalp**, at 3,664 meters (12,018 feet), and the **Doldenhorn**, at 3,643 meters (11,949 feet)—surround the plateau, and at the end of its 4-kilometer (2½-mile) stretch the valley road ends abruptly.

Exploration above Kandersteg must be accomplished by cable or on foot, unless (depending on Swiss Army training schedules and weather) you find the tiny paved road into the magnificent **Gastern Valley** open: Carved into raw rock, portions of the road are so narrow that cars must take turns coming and going.

Don't miss the **Oeschinensee,** an isolated, austere bowl of glacial silt at 1,578 meters (5,176 feet); you can walk there in about 1½ hours, and it's also accessible by chairlift to the Oeschinen station with a downhill walk of approximately 30 minutes through peak-ringed meadowlands. You also may choose to hike back down to Kandersteg from the Oeschinensee, but be prepared for the severe downhill grade. Less ambitious hikers can circle back to the chairlift at the end of a relatively level walk.

Although it's a dead-end valley for cars confining themselves to the Berner Oberland, Kandersteg is the source of one of Switzerland's more novel modes of transit: the rail-ferry tunnel through the **Lötschenpass.** Having driven your car onto a low-slung railcar, you will be swept along piggyback through a dark and airless tunnel to Brig, at the east end of the Valais region (☞ Chapter 11). Travel time is 15 minutes; the cost is 23 SF.

Dining and Lodging

$$$ ✕🏨 **Waldhotel Doldenhorn.** Nestled into a forest hillside far from the
★   road through the center, this retreat—a member of the Relais du Silence group, inns specializing in peace and quiet—offers several options: large rooms with balconies and mountain views, smaller rooms opening onto the woods, or modest lodging in a separate budget chalet. For the active, a cross-country ski trail starts at the hotel's door. There's

a formal Swiss-French restaurant and a casual stübli, too. The rooms combine modern and rustic style gracefully. Some apartments have kitchens. ✉ *CH-3718,* ☎ *033/675–18–18,* FAX *033/675–18–28. 50 beds. Restaurant, stübli. AE, DC, MC, V.*

$$ ✕🏨 **Ruedihus.** This beautifully, painstakingly restored all-wood chalet,
★ set in a meadow beyond the village center, is the best hotel to open in Switzerland in years. With bulging lead-glass windows, authentically low ceilings and doors (watch your head), and raw, aged woodwork throughout, this re-creates the atmosphere of the 1753 original. Antique beds with bleached homespun linens are counterbalanced by modern baths, and every corner has its waxed cradle, pewter pitcher, or crockery bowl. Upstairs, the Biedermeier restaurant offers excellent meat specialties, but eat downstairs at least once: The Käse- und Wystuben serves nothing but Swiss products—Vaud and Valais wines, greens and sausages, and a variety of fondues. It's a proud, tasteful, informed effort to serve travelers in search of a true regional experience; the Maeder family, owners of the Doldenhorn (across the road) and this one, are to thank. As the hotel has only nine rooms, reservations are key. ✉ *CH-3718,* ☎ *033/675–15–80,* FAX *033/675–18–28. 18 beds. 2 restaurants, café. AE, DC, MC, V.*

$ ✕🏨 **Edelweiss.** Built in 1903 by the current owner's grandfather, this cozy old inn has sleek, impeccable rooms and a welcoming, personal atmosphere, complete with low ceilings and burnished wood. There's good Swiss fare in the checkered-cloth restaurant, and the pretty garden makes you forget you're on the main road, five minutes from the train station. ✉ *CH-3718,* ☎ *033/675–11–94. 12 beds. Restaurant. No credit cards.*

OFF THE
BEATEN PATH
BLAUSEE – Traveling with a family, you may want to visit the much-vaunted Blausee, a naturally blue pool 4 kilometers (2½ miles) north of Kandersteg, above Frutigen. Be warned: It's privately owned and so developed, with a restaurant, boat rides, and a shop, that you may think the lake itself is artificial. Admission includes a boat ride, a visit to the trout nursery, and use of the picnic grounds. ☎ *033/671-16-41.* 📧 *4.30 SF.* ⊙ *Late Apr.–mid-Oct., daily 8–5.*

THE SIMMENTAL AND GSTAAD

Separate in spirit and terrain from the rest of the Berner Oberland, this craggy forest gorge follows the Lower Simme into a region as closely allied with French-speaking Vaud as it is with its Germanic brothers. Here the world-famous winter resort of Gstaad has flexed the muscle of its famous name to link up with a handful of neighboring ski resorts, creating the almost limitless sports opportunities of the Gstaad "Super-Ski" region. From Gstaad, it's an easy day trip into the contrasting culture of Lac Léman and the waterfront towns of Montreux and Lausanne.

En Route From Interlaken, take N8 toward Spiez, then cut west on N11 toward Gstaad. The wild forest gorges of the Simmental Valley lead you through **Zweisimmen,** the principal sporting center of the surrounding area, to the Saanenland. The total distance from Spiez is about 40 kilometers/25 miles.

Gstaad

⑮ *49 km (30 mi) southwest of Spiez; 67 km (42 mi) southwest of Interlaken.*

Your passport around the world.

- Worldwide access
- Operators who speak your language
- Monthly itemized billing

MCI   Calling Card

415 555 1234 2244
J.D. SMITH

Use your MCI Card® and these access numbers for an easy way to call when traveling worldwide.

Austria (CC)♦†	022-903-012
Belarus	
From Gomel and Mogilev regions	8-10-800-103
From all other localities	8-800-103
Belgium (CC)♦†	0800-10012
Bulgaria	00800-0001
Croatia (CC)★	99-385-0112
Czech Republic (CC)♦	00-42-000112
Denmark (CC)♦†	8001-0022
Finland (CC)♦†	9800-102-80
France (CC)♦†	0800-99-0019
Germany (CC)†	0130-0012
Greece (CC)♦†	00-800-1211
Hungary (CC)♦	00▼800-01411
Iceland (CC)♦†	800-9002
Ireland (CC)†	1-800-55-1001
Italy (CC)♦†	172-1022
Kazakhstan (CC)	1-800-131-4321
Liechtenstein (CC)♦	155-0222
Luxembourg†	0800-0112
Monaco (CC)♦	800-90-19

Netherlands (CC)♦†	06-022-91-22
Norway (CC)♦†	800-19912
Poland (CC)✛†	00-800-111-21-22
Portugal (CC)✛†	05-017-1234
Romania (CC)✛	01-800-1800
Russia (CC)✛♦	747-3322
For a Russian-speaking operator	747-3320
San Marino (CC)♦	172-1022
Slovak Republic (CC)	00-42-000112
Slovenia	080-8808
Spain (CC)†	900-99-0014
Sweden (CC)♦†	020-795-922
Switzerland (CC)♦†	155-0222
Turkey (CC)♦†	00-8001-1177
Ukraine (CC)✛	8▼10-013
United Kingdom (CC)†	
To call to the U.S. using BT■	0800-89-0222
To call to the U.S. using Mercury■	0500-89-0222
Vatican City (CC)†	172-1022

To sign up for the MCI Card, dial the access number of the country you are in and ask to speak with a customer service representative.

http://www.mci.com

(CC) Country-to-country calling available. May not be available to/from all international locations. (Canada, Puerto Rico, and U.S. Virgin Islands are considered Domestic Access locations.) ♦ Public phones may require deposit of coin or phone card for dial tone. † Automation available from most locations. ★ Not available from public pay phones. ▼ Wait for second dial tone. ✛ Limited availability. ■ International communications carrier.

It helps to be pushy in airports.

Introducing the revolutionary new TransPorter™ from American Tourister®. It's the first suitcase you can push around without a fight. TransPorter's™ exclusive four-wheel design lets you push it in front of you with almost no effort–the wheels take the weight. Or pull it on two wheels if you choose. You can even stack on other bags and use it like a luggage cart.

Stable 4-wheel design.

TransPorter™ is designed like a dresser, with built-in shelves to organize your belongings. Or collapse the shelves and pack it like a traditional suitcase. Inside, there's a suiter feature to help keep suits and dresses from wrinkling. When push comes to shove, you can't beat a TransPorter™. For more information on how you can be this pushy, call 1-800-542-1300.

Shelves collapse on command.

Making travel less primitive.®

©1996 American Tourister®

The peak-ringed valley called the Saanenland is anchored by this, the Oberland's most chic resort. Linking the Berner Oberland with the French-accented territory of the Pays-d'Enhaut (Highlands) of canton Vaud, Gstaad blends the two regions' natural beauty and their cultures as well, upholding such Pays-d'Enhaut folk-art traditions as *papier découpé* (paper cutouts) as well as decidedly Germanic ones (cowbells, wood carving). Even Rösti and fondue cohabit comfortably on heavy tooled-pine tables—which are here decked in delicate French-style linens.

But in Gstaad, neither local culture wins the upper hand: The folksy Gemütlichkeit of the region gives way to jet-set international style, and while the architecture still tends toward weathered-wood chalets, the main street is lined with designer boutiques, which seem oddly out of context. Prince Rainier of Monaco, Julie Andrews, Roger Moore, and Elizabeth Taylor have all owned chalets in Gstaad, rubbing elbows at local watering holes, and Yehudi Menuhin founded his annual summer music festival here as well. (The Menuhin festival takes place every August, and hotels fill quickly then—as they do for the Swiss Open Tennis tournament, held here every July.)

This is a see-and-be-seen spot, with less emphasis on its plentiful but moderate skiing than on the scene—après-ski, après-concert, or après-match. The Christmas–New Year season brings a stampede of glittering socialites to rounds of international dinner parties, balls, and elite soirees. Occasionally, the jet-setters even ski. Despite a few family-style hotels, the number of deluxe lodgings is disproportionate, and prices tend to be high, on the scale of those at St. Moritz. Yet Gstaad's setting defies its socialite pretensions: Richly forested slopes, scenic year-round trails, and, for the most part, stubbornly authentic chalet architecture keep it firmly anchored in tradition.

Skiing

Gstaad does not hesitate to call itself a "Super Ski Region," and the claim is not far from the truth. It has become increasingly popular since the beginning of the century, both for its ideal situation at the confluence of several valleys, and for the warmth of its slopes, which—at 1,100 meters (3,608 feet), stay relatively toasty compared to other resorts.

Skiing in Gstaad is, in terms of numbers, the equivalent of Zermatt: 69 lifts can transport more than 50,000 skiers per hour to its network of 250 kilometers (155 miles) of marked runs. In fact, these lifts are spread across an immense territory, 20 kilometers (12 miles) as the crow flies, from Zweisimmen and St. Stefan in the east (where German is spoken, as in Gstaad) to Château-d'Oex, a Vaud town where French is spoken; to understand one another, people sometimes use English.

Gstaad's large area means that most of its lifts are not reachable by foot: Since parking is in short supply, public transport is the best option. The flip side is that except in very high seasons (Christmas, February, Easter) and in certain places, such as the lift for the Diablerets Glacier, or the Pillon, the crowds are not heavy, and lift line waits are tolerable. A one-day ticket costs 46 SF; a six-day pass costs 233 SF.

Dining and Lodging

$$$$ ✕ **Chesery.** This lively late-night dining scene, complete with piano bar, manages to combine the height of upscale chic with summits of culinary excellence—all at 1,100 meters (3,608 feet). Chef Robert Speth marries exotic details (ginger, mango) with market-fresh ingredients: Watch for veal and salmon in pastry with spinach, or duck in kumquat sauce. Crowds pack in, ordering dinner until midnight, so book well ahead in high season. ✉ *Lauenenstrasse,* ☎ *030/473–03. AE, DC, MC, V. Closed Tues.*

$$$$ ✕🏨 **Bernerhof.** This modern chalet-style inn, in the center of town a half-block from the station, was built on the site of an older hotel dating from 1904. The crowds of young couples, families, and singles who came during its opening season, in 1974, are still returning and stay in touch by means of the hotel's newsletter. It's simple, solid, and surprisingly cozy, with tile baths, lots of natural pine, and a balcony for every room. There are good play facilities for children. Though considerably lower than those at the Park, prices remain very expensive by Berner Oberland standards. Homemade pasta is the highlight of the restaurant, while local and Asian dishes are served in the café. ⊠ *CH-3780*, ☎ *033/748–88–44*, ⅡAX *033/748–88–40. 90 beds. 2 restaurants, café, indoor pool, sauna, fitness center. AE, DC, MC, V.*

$$$$ ✕🏨 **Palace.** Towering over tiny Gstaad like Mad Ludwig's castle, this
★ fantasyland burlesque is one of the most expensive hotels in Switzerland—and thus in the world. Cozily referring to itself as a "family pension," it features an indoor swimming pool with underwater music and water-jet massage, chauffeured Rolls-Royces, and oxygen cures, among other amenities. The rooms are lavished with appropriately rustic touches, though you could play hockey in the sprawling tile baths. Be prepared for the steep 15-minute walk uphill. And bring cash—preferably gold bullion—as management turns up its nose (already at a healthy cant) at credit cards. ⊠ *CH-3780*, ☎ *033/748–31–31, or 800/223–6800*, ⅡAX *033/744–33–44. 207 beds. 4 restaurants, piano bar, 2 pools (1 indoor), 2 saunas, steam room, 4 tennis courts, fitness center, squash, ice-skating. No credit cards.*

$$$$ ✕🏨 **Park.** A little bit of Vail comes to the Alps in this enormous modern hotel, which opened in 1990 and seems bent on helping wealthy Americans make a seamless transition between two cultures. Its 1910 predecessor on the site destroyed, this structure refers to the old style in its deep mansard roofs and rows of arched windows, and some furniture and woodwork were transplanted, but there the homage ends: The interiors create a look that's a heavy mix of chalet-modern and Spanish grandee. The facilities are state-of-the-art, right down to the antistress program and indoor saltwater pool. Built in cooperation with the neighboring (and nearly twice as expensive) Palace (☞ *above*) but now on its own, the Park insists the two are not in competition. This one, however, takes credit cards. ⊠ *CH-3780*, ☎ *033/748–33–77*, ⅡAX *033/744–44–14. 180 beds. 3 restaurants, 3 bars, 2 pools (1 indoor), beauty salon, tennis court, squash. AE, DC, MC, V. Closed mid-Nov.–mid-Dec. and Apr.–May.*

$$$ ✕🏨 **Olden.** In the middle of downtown, this charming Victorian inn
★ has artisan woodwork in every niche and an air of cozy-chic. The rooms are fresh, folksy, and atmospheric but have slick, modern baths. The adjoining chalet wing, slightly pricier, is lovely; the views from the pretty dormer window in room 39 are worth a bribe. See and be seen at the sidewalk café. ⊠ *CH-3780*, ☎ *033/744–34–44*, ⅡAX *033/744–61–64. 25 beds. 4 restaurants, café. AE, DC, MC, V.*

$$$ ✕🏨 **Posthotel Rössli.** This comfy, modest pension-style inn, the oldest
★ inn in town, combines down-home knotty-pine decor with soigné style: Despite the mountain-cabin look, its staff and clientele are young and chic, and the café, a local-landmark watering hole, draws crowds. The restaurant, full of linens and candlelight, serves simple daily menus at reasonable prices. ⊠ *CH-3780*, ☎ *033/744–34–12*, ⅡAX *033/744–61–90. 36 beds. Restaurant, café. AE, DC, MC, V.*

$ ✕🏨 **Gasthof Alte Post/Weissenburg.** This graceful, isolated old coach
★ stop is on the magnificent forested Simmen Valley road between Spiez and Gstaad, about 45 minutes outside Gstaad. Dating from 1808, it has been restored and decorated with loving respect. You'll find much carved and painted wood, many antiques, and good home cooking.

The back rooms look over the Simmen River. Like its fellow family pension, the Gstaad Palace, it takes no credit cards. It's about 45 minutes outside Gstaad. ⊠ *CH-3764*, ☎ *033/783–15–15. 20 beds. Restaurant. MC, V.*

Outdoor Activities and Sports

GOLF

Gstaad-Saanenland (☎ 030/4–26–36) in Saanenmöser has 18 holes in an idyllic setting.

HORSEBACK RIDING

In Gstaad, the **M.J. Lieber Reitzentrum** (☎ 030/4–24–60) offers guided outings for experienced riders only.

MOUNTAIN CLIMBING

For day climbs in Gstaad, contact **Bergführerbüro Glacier Sport** (☎ 030/4–17–75). For more ambitious ventures, contact **Armin Oehrli** (☎ 030/4–54–77) in Saanenmöser.

TENNIS

Gstaad's Tenniscenter (☎ 030/4–10–90) has three indoor and two outdoor courts.

Nightlife and the Arts

DANCING

There are dance clubs at the lavish **Gstaad Palace** (☎ 030/8–31–31), the **Olden** (☎ 030/4–34–44), and the **Sporthotel Victoria** (☎ 030/4–14–31).

CONCERTS

The **Gstaad Musiksommer** brings violinist-conductor Yehudi Menuhin to the Alps to head a summer music school and lead a few world-class concerts; after his departure, the concerts continue as part of the **Alpengala.** To reserve seats in advance, write to the Festivalbüro, (⊠ Verkehrsverein, CH-3780 Gstaad, ☎ 030/4–88–66). Information on the next summer's programs is generally available in December.

THE BERNER OBERLAND A TO Z

Arriving and Departing

By Car

There are swift and scenic roads from both Bern and Zürich to Interlaken. From **Bern,** the autoroute N6 leads to Spiez, then N8 continues as the highway to Interlaken. From **Zürich,** the planned autoroute link with Luzern (Lucerne) is incomplete; travel by highway E41 south, then pick up the autoroutes N4 and N14 in the direction of Luzern. From **Geneva,** the autoroute leads through Lausanne and Fribourg to Bern, where you catch N6 south, toward Thun. A long, leisurely, scenic alternative: Leave the autoroute after Montreux, and head northeast on N11 from Aigle through Château-d'Oex to Gstaad and the Simmental.

By Plane

Belpmoos airport in **Bern** brings you within an hour's train ride of Interlaken, the hub of the Berner Oberland; the airport at **Basel** is within 2¼ hours by train. The **Zürich** airport is within 3 hours; and the one at Geneva, almost 2¾ hours.

By Train

Trains from **Bern** to Interlaken run once an hour between 6 AM and 11 PM, some requiring a change at Spiez. From **Zürich,** a direct line leads through Bern to Interlaken and takes about 2½ hours, departing hourly;

a more scenic trip over the Golden Pass route via Luzern takes about two hours. From **Basel** trains run twice an hour via Olten (approximately a 2½-hour trip). Trains run hourly from **Geneva** (a 2¾-hour ride). Trains stop at Interlaken West station first, then Interlaken East. West is the more central, but check with your hotel if you've booked in advance: Some fine hotels are clustered nearer the East station, and all Brienzersee boat excursions leave from the docks nearby. For train information in Interlaken, ask at Interlaken West.

Getting Around

By Boat

Hourly round-trip boat cruises around the Thunersee and the Brienzersee provide an ever-changing view of the craggy foothills and peaks. The round-trip from Interlaken to Thun takes about four hours; the trip to Spiez takes about two hours and includes stop-offs for visits to the castles of Oberhofen, Spiez, and Thun. A round-trip from Interlaken to Brienz takes around 2½ hours, to Iseltwald about 1¼ hours. These boats are public transportation as well as pleasure cruisers; just disembark whenever you feel like it, and check timetables when you want to catch another. Tickets are flexible and coordinate neatly with surface transit: You can cruise across to Thun and then take a train home for variety. Buy tickets and catch boats for the Thunersee at Interlaken West station; for the Brienzersee, go to Interlaken East.

By Bus

Postbuses travel into much of the area not served by trains, including many smaller mountain towns. In addition, a number of private motorcoach tours cover points of interest. Schedules are available from tourist offices or the PTT (post, telephone, and telegraph office).

By Cable Car

More than 30 major cableway and lift systems climb Bernese Oberland peaks, including the largest cableway in the world, which stretches up to the Schilthorn above Mürren.

By Car

Driving in the Berner Oberland allows you the freedom to find your own views and to park at the very edges of civilization before taking off on foot or by train. If you are confining yourself to the lakefronts, valleys, and lower resorts, a car is an asset. But there are several lovely resorts beyond the reach of traffic, and train, funicular, and cable-car excursions take you to places ordinary tires can't approach (☞ *below*); sooner or later, you'll leave the car behind and resort to public transportation. Rent a car in Bern if you fly into Belpmoos, or take a train into Interlaken and rent a car there for maximum flexibility.

On Foot

You can cover a lot of ground without wheels, as this region (like most others in Switzerland) has highly developed, well-groomed walking trails leading away from nearly every intersection. Most are comfortably surfaced and are marked with distances and estimated walking times. Several itineraries are available from the Berner Oberland tourist office; these combine hikes with lodging along the way. The less ambitious walker may take advantage of postbus rides uphill and a leisurely stroll back down—though descents prove more taxing for calf muscles and knees than novice hikers imagine.

By Train

The Berner Oberland is riddled with federal and private railways, funiculars, cogwheel trains, and cable lifts designed with the sole purpose of getting you closer to its spectacular views. A **Swiss Pass** lets you travel free on federal trains and lake steamers, and it gives reductions on many private excursions. If you're concentrating only on the Berner Oberland, consider a 15-day **Regional Pass,** which offers 450 kilometers (279 miles) of rail, bus, and boat travel for any five days of your visit, with half fare for the remaining 10 days, as well as discounts on some of the most spectacular (and pricey) private excursions into the heights. For adults, the price is 185 SF (second class) and 235 SF (first class); children pay 92 SF and 122 SF, respectively. To travel first-class (upper deck) on the boat and second class on the train, adults pay 195 SF, children 105 SF. A new seven-day pass starts at 140 SF. With a **Family Card** (20 SF), children up to 16 accompanied by at least one parent travel free. Discount passes pay for themselves only if you're a high-energy traveler; before you buy, compare the price à la carte for the itinerary you have in mind.

Contacts and Resources

Car Rental
Interlaken (Avis, ⊠ Waldeggstrasse 34a, ☎ 033/822–12–14; Hertz, ⊠ Harderstrasse 44, ☎ 033/822–61–72).

Emergencies
Police (☎ 117). **Hospital** (☎ 033/826–26–26). **Doctor referral** (☎ 033/823–23–23). **Dentist and pharmacist referral** (☎ 111).

Guided Tours
Auto AG Interlaken offers guided coach tours and escorted excursions within the Berner Oberland. There are bus tours to Mürren and the Schilthorn (including cable car), to Grindelwald and Trummelbach Falls, to Kandersteg and the Blausee, and to Ballenberg. Guests are picked up at either Interlaken West or East station or at the Metropole or Interlaken hotel (reservations ☎ 033/822–15–12). The tourist office is the best source for tour information.

If you're traveling without either a Swiss Pass or a Regional Pass, note that guided tours to the Jungfraujoch or to the Schilthorn, arranged through the railway and cable companies themselves, cost less than independent round-trip tickets.

For a nostalgic tour of the streets of greater Interlaken by **horse-drawn carriage,** line up by the Interlaken West station (⊠ Ernst Voegeli Kutschenbetrieb, ☎ 033/822–74–16).

Travel Agencies
Interlaken (Kuoni, ⊠ Höheweg 3, ☎ 033/822–13–32; Jungfrau Tours, ⊠ Höheweg 12, ☎ 033/822–85–85; Vaglio, ⊠ Höheweg 72, ☎ 033/822–07–22).

Visitor Information
The **Verkehrsverband Berner Oberland** dispenses tourist information for the entire region, though it's not oriented toward walk-ins, so write or call (⊠ Jungfraustrasse 38, CH-3800, Interlaken, ☎ 033/822–26–21).

The **Interlaken Tourist Office,** at the foot of the Hotel Metropole Höheweg (☎ 033/82–21–21), offers information on Interlaken and the Jungfrau region. Arrange your excursions here.

Other tourist offices can be found in **Brienz** (⊠ CH-3855, ☎ 033/951–32–42), **Grindelwald** (⊠ CH-3818, ☎ 033/854–12–12), **Gstaad** (⊠ CH-3780, ☎ 033/4–10–55), **Kandersteg** (⊠ CH-3718, ☎ 033/675–12–34), **Lauterbrunnen** (⊠ CH-3822, ☎ 033/855–19–55), **Mürren** (⊠ CH-3825, ☎ 033/856–86–86), **Spiez** (⊠ CH-3700, ☎ 033/654–21–38), **Thun** (⊠ CH-3600, ☎ 033/222–23–40), and **Wengen** (⊠ CH-3823, ☎ 033/855–14–14).

11 Valais

Alpine villages, verdant vineyards, world-class resorts, and that rocky celebrity the Matterhorn—all are good reasons to visit the valley (valais) of the Rhône. This is wilderness country, where tumbledown huts and state-of-the-art sports facilities share steep green hillsides and forests. Long isolated from the world by mountains, it remains a land apart.

THIS IS THE VALLEY OF THE MIGHTY Rhône, a river born in the heights above Gletsch (Glacier), channeled into a broad westward stream between the Bernese and Valais Alps, lost in the depths of Lac Léman (Lake Geneva), and then diverted into France, where it ultimately dissolves in the marshes of the Camargue. Its broad upper valley forms a region of Switzerland that is still wild, remote, beautiful, and slightly unruly, its architecture romantically tumbledown, its highest slopes peopled by nimble farmers who live at vertiginous angles.

The birthplace of Christianity in Switzerland, the Valais was never reformed by Calvin or Zwingli, nor conquered by the ubiquitous Bernois—one reason, perhaps, that the western end of the Valais seems the most intensely French of the regions of the Suisse Romande.

Its romance appeals to its fellow Swiss, who, longing for its rustic atmosphere, build nostalgic Valais theme-huts in their modern city centers to eat raclette under mounted pitchforks, old pewter pitchers, and grape pickers' baskets. On holiday, the Swiss come here to play: to escape, to hike, and, above all, to ski. Zermatt, Saas-Fee, Crans-Montana, and Verbier—renowned resorts for serious sports lovers—are all in the Valais, some within yodeling distance of villages barely touched by modern technology.

Pleasures and Pastimes

Dining
Though the French influence in the western portion of this region means a steady diet of cuisine bourgeoise, leading newcomers to think entrecôte with peppercorn sauce is a native dish, the elemental cuisine of the Valais is much simpler. In a word: cheese.

Fondue, of course, is omnipresent. Often it is made with the local *Bagnes* or *Orsières,* mild cheeses from near Martigny. But the noblest application for these regional products is *raclette* (melted cheese with potatoes and pickles), an exclusive invention of this mountain canton (though the French of Haute-Savoie embrace it as their own). Ideally, the fresh-cut face of a half-wheel of raclette is melted before an open wood fire, the softened cheese scraped onto a plate and eaten with potatoes (always in their skins), pickled onions, and tiny gherkins. Nowadays, even mountain *carnotzets* (cellar pubs) with roaring fires depend on electric raclette-heaters that grip the cheese in a vise before toasterlike elements. The beverage: a crisp, bubbly, fruity Fendant.

The Valais rivals the Graubünden in its production of *viande séchée* (air-dried beef), a block of meat marinated in herbs, pressed between planks until it takes on its signature bricklike form, and then dried in the open air. Shaved into thin, translucent slices, it can be as tender as a good *prosciutto crudo*—or as tough as leather. The flavor is concentrated, the flesh virtually fat-free.

CATEGORY	COST*
$$$$	over 70 SF
$$$	40 SF–70 SF
$$	20 SF–40 SF
$	under 20 SF

*per person for a three-course meal (except in $ category), including sales tax and 15% service charge

Hiking

As skiing is to winter, hiking is to summer in the Valais, and the network of valleys that radiate north and south of the Rhône provide almost infinite possibilities. Sociable hikers can follow trails out of the big resorts—especially outside Saas-Fee and Zermatt, where the mountains' peaks and glaciers are within tackling distance—but don't overlook wilder, more isolated alternatives in the less-developed Val d'Hérens and Val d'Anniviers. Good maps and suggested itineraries are available through the Valais regional tourist office in Sion (rue Pré-Fleuri 6, CH-1951, ☎ 027/322–31–61).

Lodging

The most appealing hotels in the Valais seem to be old. That is, historic sites have maintained their fine Victorian ambience; postwar inns, their lodgelike feel. Most of those built after about 1960 popped up in generic, concrete-slab, balconied rows to accommodate the masses who arrived with the 1960s ski boom. They are solid enough but, for the most part, anonymous, depending on the personality and dedication of their owners.

Valais is home to some of Switzerland's most famous resorts, and prices vary widely between top-level Zermatt lodgings and those in humbler towns. To indicate the relationship between resort prices and simple, wayside *auberges* (inns), the price categories below have been equally applied, so remember: A hotel in Zermatt given a $$$ rating may be moderate for such a pricey town. When you write for information, check prices carefully. Demipension is often included, and rates may be listed per person. And when planning a vacation in fall or spring, research your itinerary carefully: Many of the resorts shut down altogether during the November and May lulls and schedule their renovations and construction projects for these periods. That means that while some places offer low-season savings, others simply close their doors.

CATEGORY	COST*
$$$$	over 250 SF
$$$	180 SF–250 SF
$$	120 SF–180 SF
$	under 120 SF

All prices are for a standard double room, including breakfast, tax, and service charge.

Skiing

With plateaus and cavernous gorges radiating out from the valley, the Valais has nurtured ski resorts since the sport was invented. Historic Zermatt, with its rustic, historic atmosphere, contrasts sharply with its high-tech peers to the west: Verbier, Crans-Montana and Anzères are virtually purpose-built, with every amenity and connection—and considerably less focus on charm. You can find all ranges of difficulty, and all kinds of snow—even, above Crans, in July.

Exploring the Valais

The Valais is an L-shape valley with Martigny at its angle; the eastern, or long, leg of the L is the most characteristic and imposing. This wide, fertile riverbed is flanked by bluffs and fed from north and south by remote, narrow valleys that snake into the mountains. Some of these valleys peter out in desolate Alpine wilderness; some lead to its most famous landmarks—including that Swiss superstar, the Matterhorn. Not all of the Valais covers Alpine terrain, however: The western stretch—between Martigny and Sierre—comprises one of the two chief sources of wine in Switzerland (the other is in Vaud, along Lake Geneva). Valais wines, dominated by round, fruity Fendant and light, ruby Dole, come from verdant vineyards that stripe the hillsides flanking the Rhône.

The Val d'Entremont leads southward down an ancient route from Lac Léman to the Great St-Bernard Pass, traversing the key Roman crossroads at Martigny. Up the valley, past the isolated, eagles-'nest village of Isérables, two magnificent castle-churches loom above the historic old town at Sion. From Sion, the Val d'Hérens winds up into the isolated wilderness past the stone Pyramides d'Euseigne and the Brigadoonlike resorts of Evolène and, even more obscure, Les Haudères. The Val d'Anniviers, the valley winding south from Sierre, leads to tiny, isolated skiing and hiking resorts such as Vissoie and Grimentz. The most famous southbound rib of Valais valleys leads from Visp to the stellar resort of Zermatt and its mascot mountain, the Matterhorn. The fork in that same valley leads to spectacular Saas-Fee, another car-free resort in a magnificent glacier-bowl. Back at the Rhône, the valley mounts southward from Brig to the Simplonpass and Italy, or northeastward to the glacier-source Gletsch and the Furka Pass out of the region.

Great Itineraries

It's not necessary to explore every wild valley that ribs out from the Rhône in order to experience the Valais; better to choose one region and spend a few days hiking, driving, or skiing. However, you will want to see the sights of the main river valley: Martigny, Sion, and at least one of the great Alpine passes, depending on your next travel goal.

IF YOU HAVE 2 DAYS
Numbers in the text correspond to numbers in the margin and on the Valais map.

If you're using the Rhône Valley highway as a means to cover ground scenically, enter from Lac Léman and cruise directly to ⌘ **Sion** ⑦, where you'll walk through the old town and climb up to the church fortress of Valére. While you won't have time to cut north or south into a radiating valley, any pass you use to exit the region will cover magnificent terrain: either the climb from **Martigny** ② to the **Col du Grand St-Bernard** ⑤ into Piedmont in Italy, the dramatic ascent from Brig over the **Simplon Pass** ⑱, or the slow, isolated approach to **Gletsch** ⑳ and the **Furka Pass** ㉑. Whenever time and road conditions permit, opt for the slow switchback crawl over the mountain passes rather than more efficient tunnels.

IF YOU HAVE 5 DAYS
Enter from Lac Léman and visit the museums of **Martigny** ②. Spend the night and next day exploring ⌘ **Sion** ⑦, then make your selection: If you have never seen the Matterhorn, head directly to ⌘ **Zermatt** ⑭ and spend three nights shutter-snapping, riding cable cars for better views, and shopping for state-of-the-art sports equipment. Other Alpine resort options are magnificently sited ⌘ **Saas-Fee** ⑯, glamorous ⌘ **Verbier** ③, or trendy ⌘ **Crans-Montana** ⑪. If you prefer wilderness and old-fashioned retreat, shun the famous spots and head up the Val d'Hérens to pretty little ⌘ **Evolène** ⑧, up the Val d'Anniviers to ⌘ **Grimentz** ⑫, or up the Mattertal to charming ⌘ **Grächen** ⑮, teetering on a high plateau.

IF YOU HAVE 10 DAYS
En route to the mountains, take time to visit **St-Maurice** ① and **Martigny** ②, then head directly into the mountains and spend four quiet days wandering up the Val Hérens to ⌘ **Evolène** ⑧, with side trips to see the Grande Dixence Dam and the Pyramides d'Euseigne, and time for wilderness walks or cross-country skiing. Set aside a full day for

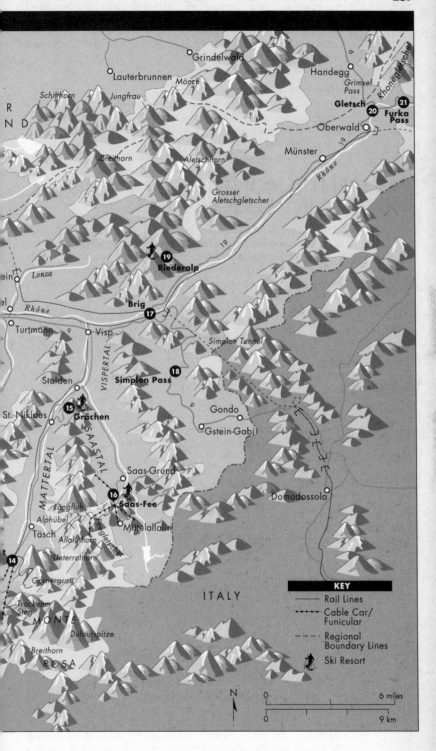

Grindelwald

Lauterbrunnen

Handegg

Schilthorn

Mönch

Grimsel Pass

Rhonegletscher

Jungfrau

Gletsch

21

20 **Furka Pass**

R N D

Oberwald

Breithorn

Aletschhorn

Münster

Grosser Aletschgletscher

Rhône

19

ein

Lonza

19

Riederalp

el

Rhône

Brig

17

Turtmann

Visp

Simplon Tunnel

VISPERTAL

Stalden

18

Simplon Pass

St.-Niklaus

15

Grächen

Gondo

Gstein-Gabi

SAASTAL

MATTERTAL

Saas-Grund

16

Längfluh

Saas-Fee

Alphübel

Mittelallalin

Täsch

Allalinhorn

Feegletscher

t

14

Unterrothorn

ITALY

Domodossola

Gornergrat

Trockener Steg

M O N T E

Dufourspitze

Breithorn

KEY

R O S A

Rail Lines

Cable Car/ Funicular

Regional Boundary Lines

Ski Resort

N

0 _____ 6 miles

0 _____ 9 km

the monuments and museums of ⌑ **Sion** ⑦ before heading back into the heights. You'll feel the contrast when you reach highly-developed, Germanic ⌑ **Zermatt** ⑭, where another four nights will give you time to exploit its facilities. From Zermatt, you can exit the Valais via the Simplon or Furka passes.

When to Tour

The Valais is at its sunny best in high summer and mid-winter, with foggy dampness overwhelming the region in late autumn (its low season). Mid-December to Easter is peak ski season in the resorts. As Europeans vacation here for weeks at a time, book well ahead if you want to compete for lodging in August or at Easter time.

VAL D'ENTREMONT TO THE
GREAT SAINT-BERNARD PASS

The Rhône River at Villeneuve broadens, deltalike, into a flat valley that pours into Lake Geneva. But heading south, up the valley, the mountains already begin to crowd in on either side. Once you cross the Rhône and officially enter the canton of Valais, leaving Vaud behind, the valley and the river begin to change character. The mountains—the Dents du Midi in the west and the Dents de Morcles to the east—come closer; the Rhône no longer flows placidly but gives a foretaste of the mountain torrent it will become as you approach its source. This most ancient of Alpine routes leaves the Rhône at the Martigny elbow and ascends due south to 2,469 meters (8,098 feet) before descending into Italy's Val d'Aosta.

St-Maurice

❶ *46 km (28 mi) west of Sion.*

The **St-Maurice abbey** is an important stop on this ancient route to the Grand St-Bernard Pass. Here, at the end of the 3rd century, a Theban leader named Maurice was massacred, with most of his men, for refusing to worship the pagan gods of Rome. (Christianity was first established in Switzerland here in the Valais, and its fierce Catholicism—at both the French and the German ends—reflects this early zeal.) The abbey was built in AD 515 to commemorate the martyrdom, and excavations near the Baroque **église abbatiale** (abbey church) have revealed the foundations of this original building. The abbey treasury contains an exceptionally precious collection of Romanesque and Gothic objects. ☎ *025/65–11–81.* ▨ *Free. Guided tours July–Aug., Tues.–Sat. 9:30, 10:30, 2:30, 3:30, 4:30 and Sun. 2:30, 3:30, 4:30; May–June and Sept.–Oct., Tues.–Sat. 10:30, 3, 4:30 and Sun. 3, 4:30; Nov.–Apr., Tues.–Sun. 3, 4:30.*

Martigny

❷ *17 km (11 mi) south of St-Maurice; 23 km (14 mi) southwest of Sion.*

This valley crossroads, once used as a Roman camp, is still on the map today thanks to the Foundation Pierre Gianadda, which sponsors a cluster of world-class museums. Leonard Gianadda created the foundation in 1976 after the death of his brother, Pierre, in an airplane accident. Its first application: To develop Gallo-Roman ruins discovered during a building project. This became the **Musée Gallo-Romain,** which displays relics excavated from a 1st-century temple: striking bronzes, statuary, pottery and coins. A marked promenade leads visitors through the antique village, baths, drainage systems, and foundations to the fully-restored, 5,000-seat amphitheater, which dates from the 2nd century.

Temporary art exhibitions—say, a recent Manet retrospective—often take place in the museum. Hours vary with the temporary show; you'll see posters throughout Swiss capitals. And don't be surprised if you see posters for a concert by an international classical star—the Roman museum not only doubles as an art gallery but as a concert hall as well. ✉ CH-1920, ☎ 027/722–39–78. ☒ 12 SF. ☉ Mid-June–Oct., daily 9–7; Feb.–June, daily 10–6; Nov.–Jan., daily 10–12, 1:30–6.

The Foundation Pierre Gianadda also sponsors a sizable **Musée de l'Automobile,** which contains some 50 antique cars, including an 1897 Benz, the Delauneay-Belleville of Czar Nicholas II of Russia, and a handful of Swiss-made models—all in working order. ✉ CH-1920, ☎ 027/722–39–78. ☒ 12 SF. ☉ Mid-June–Oct., daily 9–7; Feb.–June, daily 10–6; Nov.–Jan., daily 10–12, 1:30–6.

In the gracefully landscaped garden surrounding the Foundation Pierre Gianadda's museums, a wonderful **Parc de Sculptures** displays works of Rodin, Brancusi, Miró, Calder, Moore, Dubuffet and Segal.

Verbier

❸ *29 km (18 mi) east of Martigny (exit at Sembrancher); 58 km (36 mi) southwest of Sion.*

It's the skiing, not the social life, that draws Diana Ross, Björn Borg and thousands of other committed sports lovers to Verbier, a high-tech, state-of-the-art sports complex that connects to several nearby resorts (including Thyon and Nendaz). Verbier has the biggest aerial cableway in Europe, with two cabins accommodating 150, and some 86 smaller transportation installations. Summer sports are equally serious: Hang gliding and its variations compete with golf as the principal sun sports. Though it's perched on a sunny shelf high above the Val de Bagnes, with the 3,023-meter (9,915-foot) Mont Gelé towering behind and wraparound views, Verbier is one of Switzerland's least picturesque resorts architecturally (Davos competes for the title), having been purpose-built by developers in the '60s and '70s in a jarringly modern style.

Skiing

At 1,500 meters (4,921 feet), Verbier is the center of Switzerland's most famous transit network, Televerbier—which consists of 12 gondolas, seven cable cars, 34 chairlifts, and 47 ski lifts giving access to 400 kilometers (247 miles) of marked pistes. From this resort an immense complex of resorts has developed—some more modest—others more exclusive, covering four valleys in an extended ski area whose extremities are 15 or so kilometers (9 miles) apart as the crow flies and several dozen kilometers apart by way of winding mountain roads.

Les Ruinettes gives access to Verbier's entire upper ski area, which culminates at Mont-Fort, at 3,300 meters (10,825 feet). This is reached by an aerial tram, Le Jumbo, equipped with a cab that accommodates 150, the largest in Switzerland. This entire sector is crisscrossed by a dense network of astonishingly varied pistes. Remember the names of several strategic passages if you don't want to get lost: Les Attelas, Mont-Gelé, Col des Gentianes, Lac des Vaux, Tortin; some of these are reserved for experienced skiers. One-day lift tickets cost 59 SF; six-day passes cost 297 SF.

Dining and Lodging

$$$$
★
X☷ Rosalp. The honey-gold pine, rustic-chic decor makes a surprisingly warm and comfortable setting for one of Switzerland's great meals. Chef Roland Pierroz continues to earn the highest gastronomic kudos and an international following for his prawn bisque, pigeon with truffles, and apple tarts, as well as for the variety of fine local cheeses he presents. A glorious finish to a day on the slopes: Dine here, then roll upstairs to the fine little hotel, a member of the Relais & Châteaux chain. Built in 1946, it has been renovated several times since then; ask for the newer rooms, which have marble baths. The upper rooms are smaller but quieter, and have better views. ☒ CH-1936, ☎ 027/771–63–23, FAX 027/771–10–59. 50 beds. Restaurant (reservations essential), café, hot tub, sauna. AE, DC, MC, V.

$$$–$$$$
☷ Grand Combin et Golf. As modern and central as most of its Verbier rivals, this chalet hotel, which recently increased its rates, is a bit softer around the edges thanks to some knotty pine, some overstuffed chairs, a fireplace, and a clublike ambience, particularly in Jacky's Bar. In summertime, barbecues and raclette dinners promote mingling. Guests may enjoy free rounds of golf on the 18-hole golf course with magnificent views. The hotel runs private buses to the cable cars. ☒ CH-1936, ☎ 027/771–65–15, FAX 027/771–14–88. 52 beds. Restaurant, bar, sauna, steam room, 18-hole golf course, fitness center. AE, DC, MC, V.

$$$
☷ Rhodania. Built, like its peers, in the mid-1960s, and renovated in the late '80s, this generic, centrally located property is coolly chic with its carved wood fixtures and the occasional cozy accent. South balconies have the famous view. There's a spaghetteria and a "rustic" discotheque. ☒ CH-1936, ☎ 027/771–61–21, FAX 027/771–52–54. 72 beds. 2 restaurants, bar, dance club. AE, DC, MC, V.

$$
☷ Ermitage. Right in town, its best views to the south (though taking a parking lot and other hotels into the panorama), this modern chalet is simple, serviceable, and central. The interior is all beige, tile, and blond pine. ☒ CH-1936, ☎ 027/771–64–77, FAX 027/771–52–64. 44 beds. Restaurant, café. MC, V.

$
☷ Les Touristes. If you're here for the world-class skiing and want to pass on the anonymous comforts of chic but pricey Verbier, head for this old-style pension. Built in the 1940s in a dark-wood roadhouse style, it's in the village below the main resort, where a few traditional chalets are still evident. The rooms are spare, and the bare-bones shower and toilet are down the hall, but the stübli-restaurant attracts locals disenchanted with the uptown scene. Staying here means one more connection to get you to the slopes—a brief bus ride—but you save a bundle. ☒ CH-1936, ☎ 027/771–21–47. FAX 027/771–21–47. 22 beds. Restaurant, stübli. AE, aa MC, V.

Outdoor Activities and Sports

BICYCLING
Jet Sports (☎ 027/731–20–67) rents mountain bikes.

GOLF
The **Golf Club** (☎ 027/771–62–55) has two 18-hole courses.

MOUNTAIN CLIMBING
Les Combins (☎ 027/771–68–25) and **École d'Alpinisme de Verbier** (☎ 027/771–22–12) offer guides and training.

PARAGLIDING
The **Centre Parapente** gives paragliding lessons and sells equipment (☎ 027/771–68–18). **L'Envol** paragliding school offers training and rentals (☎ 027/771–51–31).

OTM (☎ 027/38–33–23), in Haute-Nendaz, near Verbier, arranges private *raquettes de neige* (snowshoe) hiking expeditions and trains individuals in this surface-skimming sport.

SPORTS CENTERS
The **Centre Polysportif** in **Verbier** (☎ 027/771–66–01) has indoor skating as well as a swimming pool, saunas, whirlpools, a solarium, curling, tennis courts, and squash.

TENNIS
The **Centre Polysportif** (☎ 027/771–66–01) has nine courts. There are three private courts available for rental through **Gérard Pesson** (☎ 027/771–23–33).

Champex

4 *31 km (19 mi) south of Martigny; 51 km (32 mi) southwest of Sion.*

Clinging high above the Orsières Valley (famous for its raclette cheese), this delightful little family resort lies wrapped around a tiny mirror of a lake and surrounded by forested peaks, concentrating some of the prettiest scenery in the region—including views dominated by the massive Combin (4,314 meters/14,150 feet).

Dining and Lodging

$$ ✕🏨 **Belvedere.** This is the prototypical *relais de campagne* (country
★   inn): full of warm wood, cozy old-style rooms with balconies, creaky pine-panel halls hung with historic photos, and doilies everywhere, crocheted by the owner herself. Set on a wooded hill above the lake and town, it offers breathtaking views all the way down to the Val d'Entremont. The café attracts local workers, and the restaurant serves the owners' fresh, straightforward cuisine bourgeoise as well as a variety of fondues. Watch for garlic-sautéed porcini mushrooms on toast, lamb filet in sage with Rösti, and muscat mousse with grape compote. Vegetables are local and organically grown. The list of local wines includes some rare bargains. ⊠ CH-1938, ☎ 027/783–11–14, FAX 027/783–25–76. 16 beds. Restaurant, café. MC, V.

$ ✕🏨 **Auberge de la Forêt.** On a quiet street facing the lake, this place has a few lake-view rooms with a comfortable, modern look. The fireplace and grill turn out authentic raclette. ⊠ CH-1938, ☎ 027/783–12–78, FAX 027/783–21–01. 30 beds. Restaurant, café. MC, V.

Col du Grand St-Bernard

★ **5** *40 km (25 mi) south of Martigny; 69 km (43 mi) southwest of Sion.*

The Great St-Bernard Pass, breasting the formidable barrier of the Alps at 2,069 meters (6,786 feet), is the oldest and most famous of the great Alpine crossings, and the first to join Rome and Byzantium to the wilds of the north. Known and used for centuries before the birth of Christ, it has witnessed an endless stream of emperors, knights, and simple travelers—think of Umberto Eco's *The Name of the Rose*, with two friars crossing on donkeyback in howling winter winds. Napoléon took an army of 40,000 across it en route to Marengo, where he defeated the Austrians in 1800.

You'll have an easier time crossing today: If you simply want to get to Italy quickly, you can take the swift tunnel that opens out on the other side, above the Val d'Aosta. But by skipping the tiny winding road over the top, you'll miss the awe-inspiring, windswept moonscape at the summit and the hospice that honors its namesake. In 1038, the story goes, Bernard of Menthon, bishop of Aosta, came to clear the pass of brigands. When he reached the top he found a pagan temple, which he covered with his chasuble. The shrine immediately crumbled to dust and, by the same power, the brigands were defeated. There Bernard established his hospice.

The hospice of St. Bernard served international travelers throughout the Middle Ages. Kings and princes rewarded the hospice by showering estates upon the order. By the 12th century, it owned 79 estates in England, including the site of the present-day Savoy Hotel in London. Nowadays its residents—Augustinian canons—train as mountain guides and ski instructors and accommodate young groups.

Behind the hospice, there's a kennel full of the landmark's enormous, furry namesakes: the famous St. Bernard dogs, who for centuries have helped the monks find travelers lost in the snow. They supposedly came to Switzerland with silk caravans from Central Asia and were used by Romans as war dogs; nowadays they're kept more for sentimental than functional reasons. The most famous was Barry, who saved more than 40 people in the 19th century and today stands stuffed in the Bern Museum of Natural History. Souvenir stands sell plush versions of St. Bernards on either side of the pass.

ISÉRABLES, SION, AND THE VAL D'HÉRENS

The Rhône Valley just east of Martigny is at its most fertile, its flatlands thick with fruit orchards and vegetable gardens, its south-facing slopes striped with vineyards. The region nurtures a virtual market basket of apples, pears, and carrots and delicate white asparagus, a specialty of early spring. The blue-blood crop of the region is grapes: This is one of the primary wine-producing regions in the country, and the fruity Fendant and hearty red Dôle (a blend of pinot noir and gamay grapes) appear on every region's lists. (Once Valais wines were poured from hinged-lid tin or pewter pitchers or *channes*; reproductions are displayed and sold throughout the region.) Also from the orchards come potent but intensely perfumed eaux-de-vie (or schnapps), especially *abricotine* (from apricots) and *williamine* (from pears).

This patch of the Valais concentrates the contrasts of this dramatic region: Over the fertile farmlands looms the great medieval stronghold of Sion, its fortress towers protecting the gateway to the Alps. Yet jutting sharply up into the bluffs to the south are the once-primitive, isolated mountain villages of Isérables and Evolène.

Isérables

★ ⑥ *24 km (15 mi) southwest of Sion.*

This is a rare opportunity to visit one of the scores of eagle's-nest towns you'll glimpse as you pass through the region's valleys. Set on a precarious slope that drops 1,000 meters (3,280 feet) into the lowlands, it has narrow streets that weave between crooked old stone-shingled *mazots*, the typical little Valais barns balanced on stone discs and columns to keep mice out of winter food stores.

Since the arrival of the cable car in recent times, Isérables has prospered and modernized itself considerably. Yet the inhabitants of this village still carry the curious nickname Bedjuis. Some say it is derived from "Bedouins" and that the people are descended from the Saracen hordes who, after the battle of Poitiers in 732, overran some of the high Alpine valleys. Certainly some of the people here—stocky, swarthy, and dark-eyed—seem different from most in the canton.

Sion

★ ⑦ *158 km (98 mi) south of Bern.*

Rearing up spookily in the otherwise deltalike flatlands of the western Valais, two otherworldly **twinned hills** flank the ancient city of Sion. Crowning the first, **Tourbillon**, is a ruined castle that was built as a bishop's residence at the end of the 13th century and destroyed by fire in 1788. On the other, **Valère**, is an 11th-century church. The two together are a powerful emblem of the city's 1,500-year history as a bishopric and a Christian stronghold. Valère offers dramatic views of Tourbillon; the views from Tourbillon itself are splendid as well, but redundant if you've climbed to Valère.

Sion can be comfortably explored on foot in an afternoon, unless you lose yourself in one of its museums or labyrinthine antiques shops. Coming out of the city tourist office on the rue de Lausanne with a map in your hand, turn left and walk toward the **old town,** a comfortable blend of shuttered 16th-century houses and modern shops.

Tucked into a passageway off rue Supersaxo stands the grand old **Maison Supersaxo** (House of Supersaxo). Built in 1505 by Georges Supersaxo, the local governor, to put his rivals to shame, this extravagantly decorated building features a Gothic staircase and a grand hall whose painted wood ceiling is a dazzling work of decorative art. ⊠ *Free.* ☉ *Weekdays 8–noon and 2–6.*

The imposing **Hôtel de Ville** (Town Hall), at the intersection of rue de Conthey and rue du Grand-Point, has extraordinary historic roots: Though it was built in the 1650s, there are transplanted stones in the entrance bearing Roman inscriptions, including a Christian symbol from the year 377. The 17th-century doors are richly carved wood, and the tower displays an astronomical clock. Upstairs the Salle du Conseil (Council Hall) is adorned with more ornate woodwork. ☉ *Daily 8–noon and 2–6.* ⊠ *Free interior visits only with guided walking tour (6 SF) from the Sion tourist office.*

The **Musée Cantonal d'Archéologie** (Museum of Archaeology) displays a cantonal collection of excavated pieces, including fine Roman works found in the Valais. The narrow old cobbled rue des Châteaux leading up toward the twin fortifications passes graceful old patrician houses, among them the museum. ⊠ *Rue des Châteaux 12,* ☎ *027/21–69–16.* ⊠ *4 SF.* ☉ *Tues.–Sun. 10–noon and 2–6.*

★ In the **Eglise-forteresse de Valère** (Church-fortress), high above the town and valley, you'll observe a striking example of sacred and secular power combined, as in the church's heyday it often subjugated rather than served its parishioners. Built on Roman foundations, massive stone walls enclose both the château and the 12th-century **Eglise Notre Dame de Valère** (Church of Our Lady of Valère). This structure stands in a relatively raw form, rare in Switzerland, where monuments are often restored to Disneyland perfection: Over the engaging Romanesque carvings, 16th-century fresco fragments, and 17th-century stalls, painted with scenes of the Passion, there hangs a rare jewel of an **organ** in "swallow's nest" form, its cabinet painted with two fine medieval Christian scenes. Dating from the 14th century, it is the oldest playable organ in the world, and an organ festival celebrates its musical virtues annually (☞ Nightlife and the Arts, *below*). The church also houses the **Museum of History and Ethnology**, which displays a wide array of medieval

chests and sculptures, as well as objects from popular culture. ⊠ *5 SF.
⊙ Tues.–Sun. 10–noon and 2–6. Guided tours 1st Tues. of month,
12:30–1:30.*

The cathedral **Notre-Dame du Glarier** (Our Lady of Glarier) is dominated by its Romanesque tower, built in the Lombard or Italian style
and dating from the 12th century; the rest of the church is late-Gothic.
Just up from the cathedral grounds, the **Tour des Sorciers** (Sorcerers'
Tower), is the last remnant of the walls that once ringed the town.

Dining and Lodging

$$ ⌕ **Du Rhône.** This spare, cinder-block urban property could be an Amer-
ican motel if it weren't for the illuminated antiquities visible from the
north windows. At the edge of the old town and handy to the castle
walks, it makes a comfortable, no-frills base for your explorations. ⊠
CH-1950, ☎ *027/22–82–91,* FAX *027/23–11–88. 80 beds. Restaurant.
AE, DC, MC, V.*

$ ⌕ **Du Midi.** On the corner of the old town, and now absorbed into the
upper floors of a downtown shopping block, this was once a freestanding
roadhouse, a loner in the shadow of the city's twin citadels. Its small
rooms are sparkling and attractive despite their vibrant pink color
scheme. There's a popular brasserie on the first floor, adjoining a fussy
French restaurant. ⊠ *CH-1950,* ☎ *027/23–13–31,* FAX *027/23–61–
73. 25 beds. Restaurant, café. AE, DC, MC, V.*

Nightlife and the Arts

Sion attracts world-class musicians and scholars to its festivals cele-
brating the medieval organ in its fortress-castle Valère (☞ *Exploring,
above*). The **Festival International de l'Orgue Ancien Valère** (CH-1950
Sion, ☎ 027/22–85–93) takes place in July, August, and the begin-
ning of September.

OFF THE **GRANDE DIXENCE DAM** – Veer right past Vex up the narrow mountain
BEATEN PATH road that leads about 16 kilometers (10 miles) up the Val d'Hérémence
to the Grande Dixence Dam, a gargantuan monolith of concrete built in
the mid-1960s at the improbable altitude of 2,364 meters (7,754 feet).
Only the Swiss could have accomplished such a feat of Alpine engineer-
ing—an achievement that brings them millions on millions of kilowatt-
hours every year. The potential energy is impressively apparent as the
now-vast Lac des Dix backs up some 4 kilometers (2½ miles) into the bar-
ren, abandoned valley.

En Route South of Sion, the Val d'Hérens is a valley lined with improbably high
mountain farms and pastures. Here you will find the **Pyramides d'Eu-
seigne,** a group of bizarre geological formations: stone pillars, formed
by the debris of glacial moraines, that were protected by peculiar hard-
rock caps from the erosion that carved away the material around
them. The effect is that of enormous, freestanding stalagmites wear-
ing hats. Through the base of three of them, a car tunnel has been carved.

Evolène

❽ *23 km (14 mi) southeast of Sion (cross the main highway and head
south toward Vex).*

In a broad, fertile valley, Evolène is a town of beflowered wood
houses and ramshackle mazots that provide a picturesque setting for
vacationers—mostly French—and mountaineers, who tackle nearby
Mont-Collon and the Dent-Blanche. If you're lucky, you'll see some
of the older women villagers in the traditional dress—kerchiefs, flow-

ered cottons—they still favor. Evolène is known for its rough home-spun wool.

NEED A
BREAK? Have a drink, raclette, or the plat du jour (special of the day) in the wood-panel pub of **Café Central** (☎ 027/831–132), a quaint landmark on the main street of Evolène.

Les Haudères

❾ *5 km (3 mi) south of Evolène; 28 km (17 mi) southeast of Sion.*

This tiny but popular vacation retreat south of Les Haudères is little more than a scattering of chalets in a spectacular, isolated mountain valley. Farther on, the little skiing and mountaineering resort of **Arolla** (2,010 meters/6,593 feet) is custom-made for those seeking a total retreat in Alpine isolation.

CRANS-MONTANA AND THE VAL D'ANNIVIERS

Spiking north and south of the market crossroads of Sierre, you'll find polar extremes: The sunny, open plateau that is home to the glamorous resorts of Crans and Montana, and the wild, craggy Val d'Anniviers that leads to the isolated forest retreat of Grimentz.

Sierre

❿ *15 km (9 mi) northwest of Sion.*

This main market town is distinguished by its hilly setting among the remains of a prehistoric rock slide. Sierre claims the most hours of sunshine in Switzerland.

Crans-Montana

⓫ *12 km (7 mi) north of Sierre; 19 km (11¾ mi) northwest of Sion.*

This well-known twinned sports center rises above the valley on a steep, sheltered shelf at 1,495 meters (4,904 feet), and commands a broad view across the Rhône Valley to the peaks of the Valais Alps; its grassy and wooded plateau shares the benefits of Sierre's sunshine. Behind it, the **Rohrbachstein** (2,953 meters/9,686 feet), the **Gletscherhorn** (2,943 meters/9,653 feet), and the **Wildstrubel** (3,243 meters/10,637 feet) combine to create a complex of challenging ski slopes, including the 3,000-meter (9,840-foot) **Plaine Morte**, which has snow year-round. Every September, the 18-hole golf course is the site of the annual Swiss Open. The most direct route to Crans-Montana is from Sierre, either by car or funicular.

The resort towns themselves are highly developed, cookie-cutter-modern, and lacking the regional color and grace of Zermatt. The streets are lined with new shops and hotels, and car traffic can be heavy. The crowds are young, wealthy, and international.

Skiing

The pearl of the region is the **Plaine Morte**, a flat glacier 5–6 kilometers (3–3½ miles) long, perched like a pancake at an elevation of 3,000 meters (9,840 feet); a cross-country ski trail (watch out for your lungs at this altitude) of 10–12 kilometers (6–7½ miles) is open and maintained here seven months of the year. You can also downhill ski on the gentle slopes here in summer; in winter the descent from the Plaine Morte

follows wide and relatively easy pistes as far as one or two chutes. The
ascent on the **gondola from Violettes Plaines-Morte,** which is virtually
under assault during the high season and in good weather, will in itself justify your stay in Crans-Montana. Expert skiers may prefer the
Nationale piste (site of the 1987 world championships) or the incredibly steep-pitched **La Toula.** A one-day lift ticket costs 52 SF; a six-
day pass costs 235 SF.

Dining and Lodging

$$$ ✕ ⊞ **Aïda-Castel.** In a resort that mushroomed in the 1960s and seems
★   to be frozen in time, this warm and welcoming complex is refreshingly
     au courant. The public areas are rustic-chic, with carved or aged wood,
     terra-cotta, and stucco; the rooms have hand-painted furniture and some
     stenciled ceilings. The new wing, full of knotty pine, is especially fresh
     and inviting. The amenities are all top-quality. The very popular pub-
     lic restaurant, La Hotte, serves Italian fare, some prepared on the open
     grill, as well as real raclette made at fireside. The hillside location is
     moderately isolated, with great southern views from nearly every bal-
     cony. ⊠ CH-3962, ☎ 027/40–11–11, FAX 027/41–70–62. 100 beds.
     3 restaurants (reservations essential in La Hotte), 2 pools, hot tub, sauna,
     tennis court, fitness center. AE, DC, MC, V.

$$$$ ⊞ **Crans-Ambassador.** A stylized château with a three-peak roofline and
      direct access to the slopes, this dramatic modern structure stands apart
      from the twin towns and offers some of the resorts' finest views south.
      (The back rooms look onto shaggy pine forests.) Each room has a bal-
      cony or terrace. The interiors are anonymously sleek, warmed up by
      occasional touches of wood; all the baths sparkle. The classic French
      restaurant also has a terrace. ⊠ CH-3962, ☎ 027/41–52–22, FAX 027/
      41–91–55. 135 beds. 2 restaurants, indoor pool, sauna, fitness center.
      AE, DC, MC, V.

$$$$ ⊞ **Grand Hôtel du Golf.** This is the blue blood of the lot, a grand, gen-
★   teel old resort oasis with urbane good taste and every amenity. Built
      by English golfers in 1907 and owned by the same family since 1914,
      it's been postmodernized outside and carefully tended within, right down
      to the lovely marble baths. In addition to a formal restaurant and a
      rustic café, there's a fine bar completely paneled in oak. Manicured
      grounds adjoin a 9- and an 18-hole golf course. ⊠ CH-3963, ☎
      027/41–42–42, FAX 027/41–97–58. 130 beds. Restaurant, bar, café,
      in-room VCRs, indoor pool, beauty salon, sauna, tennis courts. AE,
      DC, MC, V.

$$$ ⊞ **Le Green.** What was once a rustic, welcome alternative to Crans glitz
     has succumbed: Completely renovated and redecorated in jazzy, bright
     style golf, and with a new floor constructed on top, this has become
     another pricey four-star option. There are a Chinese restaurant, a
     brasserie, two bars (one of them still in rustic pine), and sauna-solar-
     ium facilities to boot. ⊠ CH-3963, ☎ 027/41–32–56, FAX 027/41–17–
     81. 62 beds. Restaurant, 2 bars, brasserie, sauna. AE, DC, MC, V.

$$$ ⊞ **Mirabeau.** Completely redone in pastels straight out of suburbia,
     this attractive midtown property offers views of the street—or of other
     hotels. It's at the hub, however, of the downtown restaurant and shop-
     ping scene. ⊠ CH-3962, ☎ 027/40–21–51, FAX 027/41–39–12. 90
     beds. Restaurant, bar, sauna, fitness center. AE, DC, MC, V.

$$ ⊞ **La Prairie.** Wally Cleaver might have stayed here on a school ski trip:
    There's rustic wood and fireplaces everywhere, and the young, rec-room
    atmosphere is downright wholesome. Built in the 1930s, the updated
    rooms glow with pine, and the baths are very modern. The hotel is away
    from the noisy center but conveniently placed. ⊠ CH-3962, ☎ 027/41–

44–21, FAX *027/41–85–86. 60 beds. Restaurant, bar, pool. AE, DC, MC, V.*

$$ 🖼 **Regina.** On the main shopping street in Montana, this is a spare, tidy city inn with the rare option of inexpensive rooms (bathrooms are down the hall). Although their decor is dated (wood paneling, all-weather carpet), some rooms have balconies that overlook the valley. There's a cozy lounge downstairs as well as a wonderful bakery—so breakfasts are homemade and fresh. ⊠ *CH-3962,* ☎ *027/41–35–22,* FAX *027/40–18–68. 40 beds. Breakfast room. MC, V.*

Outdoor Activities and Sports

BICYCLING

Alex Sports (☎ 027/41–40–61) rents mountain bikes by the day and week.

GOLF

Crans and Montana have one 18-hole golf course and two 9-hole courses (☎ 027/41–21–68).

PARAGLIDING

Contact the **Ecole de Parapente du Valais** (☎ 077/28–62–49).

TENNIS

The Centre de Tennis Au Lac Moubra (☎ 027/41–50–14) has seven indoor courts.

En Route   East of the city limits of Sierre and south of the Rhône, follow signs southward for Vissoie. Here you will enter the **Val d'Anniviers,** a wild and craggy valley said to derive its name from its curious and famous (among anthropologists, at least) nomads, known in Latin as *anni viatores* (year-round travelers). Some claim they are descended from the Huns who straggled into the area in the 5th century. Since the development of modern roads, the Anniviards no longer follow their ancient pattern: to migrate down into the valley around Niouc in spring, move to Sierre in summer to cultivate collectively owned vineyards, and return to their isolated villages to hole up for the winter. The ancient practice disappeared in the 1950s, but many residents are the nomads' descendants.

Grimentz

⑫   *20 km (12 mi) of Sierre.*

With a population of 370, this ancient little 13th-century village has preserved its weathered-wood houses and mazots in its tiny center, although anonymous new hotels have sprung up near the ski facilities above.

NEED A
BREAK?

Warm your feet by the central fireplace, open on all sides, in the old, all-wood **Le Mélèze** (☎ 027/65-12-87), a café and restaurant on the edge of Grimentz that serves raclette, crepes, and generous hot meals.

Skiing

Grimentz shares transit facilities with Zinal (☞ *below*) and Chandolin in the Val d'Anniviers. Though they're separated by wilderness, each can provide a day's skiing, with easy access for variety the next day. Grimentz's trails, while limited, should meet everyone's needs: There's a hair-raising expert run from Pointe de Lona (at 2,900 meters/9,512 feet) all the way back down to the parking lot (at 1,570 meters/5,150 feet); beginners can enjoy equally spectacular sweeps from Orvizal, starting at 2,780 meters (9,118 feet), back to town. The upper runs are reached by ski tows only; a cable car has been added to the first level. Grimentz, at 1,570 meters (5,150 feet), has eight tows, one chair-lift, one cable car, 50 kilometers (31 miles) of downhill runs, and 22 kilometers (14 miles) of cross-country trails. A ski pass, which costs 36 SF for one day, 172 for six days, offers access for all Val d'Anniviers facilities, including 46 lifts and 250 kilometers (155 miles) of down-hill runs.

Zinal

⑬ *25 km (16 mi) south of Sierre.*

Summer travelers can cut down a tiny forest road from Grimentz to-ward Zinal, with the Weisshorn dominating the views. Zinal (1,675 meters/5,494 feet) is another isolated mountaineering center with well-preserved wood houses and mazots. It is worth building enough time into your itinerary to stop over in one of these windswept mountain aeries and walk, climb, ski, or relax by the fire.

ZERMATT AND SAAS-FEE

Immediately east of Sierre, you'll notice a sharp change: *vals* become *-tals,* and the sounds you overhear at your next pit stop are no longer the throaty, mellifluous tones of Suisse Romande but the lilting, gut-tural Swiss-German dialect called Wallisertiitsch, a local form of Schwyzerdütsch. Welcome to Wallis (*vahl*-is), the Germanic end of the Valais.

This sharp demographic frontier can be traced back to the 6th cen-tury, when Alemannic tribes poured over the Grimsel Pass and pene-trated as far as Sierre. Here the middle-class cuisine changes from *steak-frites* (steak with french fries) to veal and *Rösti* (hash brown pota-toes), though the basics of the mountain peasants—cheese, bread, and wine—are found throughout.

Zermatt

★ **⑭** *29 km (18 mi) south of Visp, plus a 10-kilometer (6-mile) train ride from Täsch.*

Despite its fame—which stems from that mythic mountain, the Mat-terhorn, and from its excellent ski facilities—Zermatt is a resort with its feet on the ground, protecting its regional quirks along with its wildlife and its tumbledown mazots, which crowd between glass-and-concrete chalets like old tenements between skyscrapers. Streets twist past weathered-wood walls, flower boxes, and haphazard stone roofs until they break into open country sloping, inevitably, uphill. Despite the crowds, you are never far from the wild roar of the silty river and the peace of a mountain path.

Hordes of package-tour sightseers push shoulder to shoulder to get yet
★ another shot of the **Matterhorn** (4,477 meters/14,685 feet). Called one of the wonders-of-the-Western-world, the mountain deserves the title: Though it has become an almost self-parodying icon, like the Eiffel Tower or the Empire State Building, its peculiar snaggle-tooth form, free on all sides of competition from other peaks, rears up over the village, larger than life and genuinely awe-inspiring. Leaving the train station and weav-ing through the pedestrian crowds, aggressive electric taxi carts, and aromatic horse-drawn carriages, you are assaulted on all sides by Mat-terhorn images: On postcards, on sweatshirts, on calendars, on beer steins, on candy wrappers, it looms in multiples of a thousand, the orig-inal obscured by resort buildings (except from the windows of pricier hotel rooms). But breaking past the shops and hotels onto the main

road into the hills, visitors seem to reach the same slightly elevated spot and stop dead in their tracks: There it is at last, up and to the right, its twist of snowy rock blinding in the sun, mink-brown weathered mazots scattered romantically at its base. Surely more pictures are taken from this spot than from anywhere else in Switzerland.

It was Edward Whymper's spectacular—and catastrophic—conquering of the Matterhorn, on July 14, 1865, that made Zermatt a household word. Whymper stayed at the Hotel Monte Rosa (☞ *below*) the nights before his departure and there revealed the names of his party of seven for the historic climb: Michel Croz, a French guide; old Peter Taugwalder and his son, young Peter, local guides; Lord Francis Douglas, a 19-year-old Englishman; Douglas Hadow; the Reverend Charles Hudson; and Whymper himself. They climbed together, pairing "tourists," as Whymper called the Englishmen, with experienced locals. They camped at 11,000 feet and by 10 AM had reached the base of the mountain's famous hook. Wrote Whymper of the final moments:

The higher we rose the more intense became the excitement. The slope eased off, at length we could be detached, and Croz and I, dashing away, ran a neck-and-neck race, which ended in a dead heat. At 1:40 PM, the world was at our feet, and the Matterhorn was conquered!

Croz pulled off his shirt and tied it to a stick as a flag, one that was seen in Zermatt below. They stayed at the summit one hour, then prepared for the descent, tying themselves together in an order agreed on by all. Croz led, then Hadow, Hudson, Lord Douglas, the elder Taugwalder, then the younger, and Whymper, who lingered to sketch the summit and leave their names in a bottle.

I suggested to Hudson that we should attach a rope to the rocks on our arrival at the difficult bit, and hold it as we descended, as an additional protection. He approved the idea, but it was not definitely decided that it should be done.

They headed off, "one man moving at a time; when he was firmly planted the next advanced," Whymper recalled.

Croz . . . was in the act of turning around to go down a step or two himself; at this moment Mr. Hadow slipped, fell against him, and knocked him over. I heard one startled exclamation from Croz, then saw him and Mr. Hudson flying downward; in another moment Hudson was dragged from his steps, and Lord Douglas immediately after him. All this was the work of a moment. Immediately we heard Croz's exclamation, old Peter and I planted ourselves as firmly as the rocks would permit; the rope was taut between us, and the jerk came on us both as on one man. We held; but the rope broke midway between Taugwalder and Lord Francis Douglas. For a few seconds we saw our unfortunate companions sliding downward on their backs, and spreading out their hands, endeavoring to save themselves. They passed from our sight uninjured, disappeared one by one, and fell from precipice to precipice on to the Matterhorn glacier below, a distance of nearly 4,000 feet in height. From the moment the rope broke it was impossible to help them. So perished our comrades!

A "sharp-eyed lad" ran into the Hotel Monte Rosa to report an avalanche fallen from the Matterhorn summit; he had witnessed the deaths of the four mountaineers. The body of young Lord Douglas was never recovered, but the others lie in the grim little cemetery behind the Zermatt church, surrounded by scores of other failed mountaineers, including a recent American whose tomb bears the simple epitaph: "I chose to climb."

In summer, the streets of Zermatt fill with sturdy, weathered climbers, state-of-the-art ropes and picks hanging at their hips. They continue to tackle the peaks, and climbers have mastered the Matterhorn literally thousands of times since Whymper's disastrous victory.

In Zermatt it's quite simple to gain the broader perspective of high altitudes without risking life or limb; the Gornergrat train trip functions as an excursion as well as ski transport. Part of the rail system completed in 1898 and the highest open-air rail system in Europe (the tracks to the Jungfraujoch, though higher, bore through the face of the Eiger), it connects out of the main Zermatt train station and heads sharply left, at right angles with the track that brings you into town. Its first stop is the **Riffelberg**, which, at 2,582 meters (8,469 feet), offers wide-open views of the Matterhorn. Farther on, from **Rotenboden,** at 2,819 meters (9,246 feet), a short downhill walk leads to the **Riffelsee,** which obligingly provides photographers with a postcard-perfect reflection of the famous peak. At the end of the 9-kilometer (6-mile) line, the train stops at the summit station of **Gornergrat** (3,130 meters/10,266 feet), and passengers pour onto the observation terraces to take in the majestic views of the Matterhorn, Monte Rosa, Gorner glacier, and an expanse of scores of peaks and 24 other glaciers. *Round-trip fare: 58 SF. Train departure every 24 mins, 7–7. One-way fare (34 SF) makes for a relatively easy hike down . Bring warm clothes and sunglasses.*

Skiing

Zermatt's skiable terrain lives up to its reputation: The 73 lift installations are capable of moving more than 50,000 skiers per hour to reach its 230 kilometers (143 miles) of marked pistes—if you count those of Breuil in Italy. Among the lifts are the cable car that carries skiers in several minutes up to an elevation of 3,820 meters (12,532 feet) on the Klein Matterhorn, a small train that creeps up to the Gornergrat (3,100 meters/10,170 feet), and a subway through an underground tunnel that gives more pleasure to ecologists than it does to sun-loving skiers.

This royal plateau has several less-than-perfect features, however, not least of which is the separation of the skiable territory into three sectors: Sunegga-Blauherd-Rothorn, which culminates at an elevation of 3,100 meters (10,170 feet); Gornergrat-Stockhorn (3,400 meters/11,155 feet); and the region dominated by the Klein-Matterhorn—to go from this sector to the others you must return to the bottom of the valley and lose considerable time crossing town to reach the lifts to the other elevations. The solution is to ski for a whole day in the same area, especially during high season (mid-December to the end of February, or even until Easter if the snow cover is good). On the other hand, thanks to snowmaking machines and the eternal snows of the Klein Matterhorn, Zermatt is said to guarantee skiers 2,200 meters (7,216 feet) of vertical drop no matter what the snowfall—an impressive claim. A one-day lift ticket costs 60 SF; a six-day pass costs 292 SF.

OFF THE
BEATEN PATH

MONTE ROSA – Zermatt lies in a hollow of meadows and trees ringed by mountains—among them the broad Monte Rosa (4,554 meters/14,937 feet) and its tallest peak, the **Dufourspitze** (at 4,634 meters/15,200 feet, the highest point in Switzerland)—of which visitors hear relatively little, so all-consuming is the cult of the Matterhorn. In the mid-19th century, Zermatt was virtually unheard-of; the few visitors who came to town stayed at the vicarage. It happened, however, that the vicar had a nose for business and a chaplain named Seiler. Joseph Seiler convinced his little brother Alexander to come to this spectacular mountain valley and start an inn. Opened in 1854 and named the Monte Rosa, it remains as one of five Seiler hotels in Zermatt. In 1891, the cog railway between Visp and Zermatt took its first summer run and began disgorging tourists with profitable regularity—though it didn't plow through in wintertime until 1927.

Dining and Lodging

$$ ✕ **Findlerhof.** Managers Franz and Heidi Schwery have maintained the
★ stylishness and popularity of this high-altitude institution, formerly the beloved Enzo's Hitte. Whether for long lunches between sessions on the slopes or for the traditional après-ski wind-down, this mountain restaurant, in tiny Findeln between the Sunnegga and Blauherd ski areas, is still de rigueur, especially with hip young English and Americans. The Matterhorn views are astonishing and the food surprisingly fine. Traditional hot dishes such as Rösti and *Käseschnitte* (toasted cheese sandwiches), share billing with more fashionable specialties, including homemade pastas and salads fresh from the Schwery's garden, just over the balcony railing. The nice wine list makes for a lazy descent back to town. The restaurant is also accessible on foot in summer. ☎ *027/967–25–88. MC, V. Closed May–mid-June, Oct.–Nov.*

$$ ✕ **Zum See.** This alternative to Findlerhof, beyond Findeln in a tiny
★ village (little more than a cluster of mazots) of the same name, serves up light meals of a quality and inventiveness that would merit acclaim even if it weren't in the middle of nowhere at 1,766 meters (5,792 feet). In summer, its shaded picnic tables draw hikers rewarding themselves at the finish of a day's climb; in winter, its cozy, low-ceiling log dining room gives skiers a glow with an impressive assortment of brandies. Regional specialties are prepared with masterly care, from wild mushrooms in pastry shells to rabbit, Rösti, and *foie de veau* (calves' liver). The hand-formed tortellini, with garlic, basil, and rich cream, are worth the trek—as is the variety of homemade ice creams. ⊠ *Zum See,* ☎ *027/967–20–45. Reservations essential après-ski. AE, MC, V. Closed May–June and Oct.–mid-Dec.*

$ ✕ **Elsie's Bar.** This tiny log cabin of a ski haunt, directly across from the church, draws an international crowd for cocktails, American-style. Light meals include cheese dishes and snails. ☎ *027/967–24–31. AE, DC, MC, V.*

★ ✕▥ **Mont Cervin.** One of the flagships of the Seiler dynasty, which founded and still dominates the hotel business in Zermatt, this sleek, luxurious, and urbane mountain hotel is never grandiose, in either scale or attitude. First built in 1852, it's unusually low-slung for a grand hotel, with dark beams and a color scheme of burnished jewel tones that enhances the womblike impression. The newest wing is subdued and classic, with a few rooms in rustic stucco and carved blond wood; across the street, connected by tunnel, the chic Résidence offers luxury apartments. Jacket and tie are required in the guests' dining hall, and for the Friday gala buffet, it's black-tie only. There's an attractive stübli-style *dancing* (dance bar) with live music and a grill and a sparkling sports center. ⊠ *CH-3920,* ☎ *027/966–88–88,* ℻ *027/967–28–78. 267 beds. Restaurant, grill, sauna, indoor pool, fitness center, dance club. AE, DC, MC, V.*

$$$$ ✕▥ **Monte Rosa.** Alexander Seiler founded his first hotel in the core
★ of this historic building, expanding it over the years to its current scale. Behind the Monte Rosa's graceful shuttered facade you find an ideal balance between modern convenience and history in the abundance of brass, stained and beveled glass, and burnished pine, the fine old flagstone floors, the original ceiling moldings, the fireplaces, and the candlelit Victorian dining hall. The room decor, while impeccably up-to-date, favors prim Victorian prints and gleaming cabinetry. South-

ern views go quickly and cost more. The bar is an après-ski must. ⊠ *CH-3920,* ☎ *027/766–11–31,* FAX *027/967–11–60. 88 beds. Restaurant, bar, sauna. AE, DC, MC, V.*

$$–$$$ ✕⊞ **Julen.** The 1937 chalet architecture, the local *Arvenholz* (Alpen ★ pine) within, and the impeccable 1981 renovation qualify this second-generation lodge for membership in the Romantik chain, which assures guests of authentic regional comforts. The rooms are simple, with carved pine beds, beige carpet, and warm brown ceramic-tile baths; those on the south have balconies with Matterhorn views. The cozy but elegant main restaurant offers French cooking—the daily menu is an excellent value—but downstairs the welcoming stübli, all pine, beams, and cowbells, serves unusual dishes prepared with lamb from local, family-owned herds. ⊠ *CH-3920,* ☎ *027/967–24–81,* FAX *027/967–14–81. 71 beds. Restaurant, café, sauna. AE, DC, MC, V.*

$$–$$$ ✕⊞ **Riffelalp.** If you want to experience all the beauty of Zermatt's ★ spectacular setting and none of the bustle of a popular, urbanized resort, consider staying partway up the Gornergrat cogwheel run on a sunny, isolated plateau. This Victorian inn was burned and rebuilt from the ground up in 1988, and now is a trim, solid, airy structure with pretty rooms and stunning views. The restaurant has a terrace that's popular with day-trippers and offers unusual local specialties such as *Walliser noodle gratin,* (noodle and cheese casserole), and ravioli with morel cream sauce. It's a 400-meter (1,312-foot) walk through the woods from the cog-rail stop; if you have luggage and equipment, the owners will meet you. ⊠ *CH-3920,* ☎ *027/966–46–46,* FAX *027/967–51–09. 40 beds. Restaurant, sauna, tennis court. AE, DC, MC, V.*

$ ✕⊞ **Touring.** Its reassuringly traditional architecture and snug, sunny rooms full of pine, combined with an elevated position apart from town and excellent Matterhorn views, make this an appealing choice for travelers avoiding the chic downtown scene. Built in 1958, with subsequent updates studiously blended in, it's family-run, and rooms with Matterhorn views cost only 2 SF extra. Hearty daily menus are served to pension-guests in the cozy dining room, and a sunny enclosed playground has lounge chairs for parents. ⊠ *CH-3920,* ☎ *027/967–11–77,* FAX *027/967–46–01. 38 beds. Restaurant, stübli, fitness center. MC, V.*

$$$$ ⊞ **Pollux.** This modern hotel is simple and chic, with its straightforward rooms trimmed in pine and leatherette. It's small-scale, and none of its windows look onto the Matterhorn, but its position directly on the main pedestrian shopping street puts guests at the heart of resort activities. There's a French restaurant and an appealing old-fashioned stübli that draws locals for its low-price lunches, snacks, and Valais cheese dishes; its terrace café sits directly on the busy street. Children in adjoining rooms, complete with toilet and shower, get a 60% reduction. ⊠ *CH-3920,* ☎ *027/967–19–46,* FAX *027/967–54–26. 70 beds. Restaurant, stübli, sauna, dance club. AE, DC, MC, V.*

$$$$ ⊞ **Schweizerhof.** Despite its location on Zermatt's main pedestrian street and the ranks of storefronts on its ground floor, this member of the Seiler group is surprisingly tranquil, and some of its angled windows have Matterhorn views. A solid building, it has been warmed with tooled pine and cozy fabrics, and its facilities are top-quality, including a terrace garden in back. As a Seiler hotel, it participates in the Dine-Around plan, which allows pension guests to eat in any of the Seiler restaurants, including Mont Cervin, Monte Rosa, and others. ⊠ *CH-3920,* ☎ *027/966–11–55,* FAX *027/967–31–21. 180 beds. Restaurant, indoor pool, sauna, fitness center. AE, DC, MC, V.*

$$$$ ⊞ **Zermatterhof.** The Cervin's rival for five-star luxury dates back almost as far—it was built in 1879—and is decorated with a stylistic nod to its more rustic beginnings: Most rooms are dominated by carved and inlaid knotty pine, others by classic dark wood and brass. There's an informal grill and a pricey, formal restaurant, beautifully detailed with fine woodwork. ✉ *CH-3920,* ☎ *027/967–01–01,* FAX *027/967–48–42. 145 beds. 2 restaurants (one for guests only), bar, indoor pool, hot tub, sauna, tennis court, fitness center. AE, DC, MC, V.*

$$$ 🏨 **Parnass.** Across the street from the roaring river, with views east and south to the Matterhorn, this simple '60s construction offers a cozy, clublike lounge, knotty-pine rooms, and private pension dining with unusually adventurous and successful cooking. In winter, annual regulars rub shoulders by the fireplace. ✉ *CH-3920,* ☎ *027/967–11–79,* FAX *027/967–45–57. 50 beds. Restaurant. MC, V.*

$$ 🏨 **Alphubel.** Although it's surrounded by other hotels and is close to the main street, this modest, comfortable pension built in 1954 feels off the beaten track—and it offers large, sunny balconies to lodgers on the south side. The interiors are a little institutional, but there's a sauna in the basement, available to guests for a small charge. ✉ *CH-3920,* ☎ *027/967–30–03,* FAX *027/967–66–84. 51 beds. Restaurant, sauna. AE, MC, V.*

$$ 🏨 **Romantica.** Among the scores of anonymously modern hotels cloned all over the Zermatt plain, this modest structure—unremarkable at first glance—offers an exceptional location directly above the town center, no more than a block's walk up a narrow mazot-lined lane. Its tidy, bright gardens and flower boxes, its game trophies, and its old-style granite stove give it personality, and the plain rooms—in beige, white, and pine—benefit from big windows and balconies. Views take in the mountains, though not the Matterhorn, over a graceful clutter of stone roofs. ✉ *CH-3920,* ☎ *027/967–15–05,* FAX *027/967–58–15. 24 beds. Bar. AE, DC, MC, V.*

$ 🏨 **Mischabel.** One of the least, if not *the* least, expensive hotels in this pricey resort town, this slightly stuffy old inn was run by one family for 40 years; since the death of the proud owner in 1994, it's gone downhill a bit, lacking her house-proud management. Still, Mischabel provides comfort, atmosphere, and a central situation few places can match at twice the price: Southern balconies frame a perfect Matterhorn view—the higher the better. Creaky, homey, and covered with Arvenholz aged to the color of toffee, its rooms have sinks only and share the linoleum-lined showers on every floor. A generous daily menu caters to families and young skiers on the cheap. ✉ *CH-3920,* ☎ *027/967–11–31,* FAX *027/967–65–07. 55 beds. Restaurant. MC, V.*

Outdoor Activities and Sports

BICYCLING

Mountain biking is severely limited by Zermatt authorities to prevent interference with hiking on trails. About 25 kilometers (15 miles) have recently been set aside, however; a new map is available at the tourist office. Bikes can be rented at **Slalomsport** (☎ 027/967–11–16).

MOUNTAIN CLIMBING

For guides and instruction, contact the **Bergführerbüro** (☎ 027/967–34–56).

TENNIS

The **Tennisstar/Club** (☎ 027/967–13–64) has three courts, and the **Gemeinde** (☎ 027/967–36–73) has nine.

Shopping

At the top of the list for most first-time visitors to Switzerland, Zermatt may be the country's souvenir capital, offering a broad variety of watches, knives, and logo clothing. Folk crafts and traditional products you'll find include large, **grotesque masks** of carved wood and lidded **wine pitchers** (*channes*) in pewter or tin, molded in graduated sizes; they are sold everywhere, even in the grocery stores of tourist-conscious resorts.

Zermatt's streets are lined with stores offering state-of-the-art **sports equipment and apparel,** from collapsible grappling hooks for climbers to lightweight hiking boots in psychedelic colors. You'll see plenty of the new must-have walking sticks—pairs of lightweight, spiked ski poles for hikers to add a bit of upper-body workout to their climb and a touch of neon flash as well. While prices are consistently high, the array of choices is dazzling.

Bayard, which has branches at the Bahnhofplatz (☎ 027/967–45–55) and on Bahnhofstrasse (☎ 027/967–22–55), heads the long list of sporting-goods stores. **Glacier Sport** (☎ 027/967–21–67) specializes in ski equipment and accessories. **La Cabane** (☎ 027/967–20–33) is the best source for trendy sports clothing.

Grächen

⑮ *28 km (17 mi) south of Visp.*

From the valley resort village of St. Niklaus, a narrow, winding road crawls up to this small, tame family resort nestled comfortably on a sunny shelf at 1,617 meters (5,304 feet). Little more than a picturesque scattering of small hotels, chalets, and mazots, it concentrates its business near a central parking lot and closes the rest of its streets to car traffic. Small and isolated as it is, there are butchers, grocers, and enough shops and cafés to keep visitors occupied on a foggy day. This is a place to escape tourist crowds, hike high trails undisturbed by the traffic you find near the larger resorts, or ski a variety of fine trails on the Hannigalp. Grächen makes a heroic effort to keep families happy, offering a staffed and supervised winter sports area, with ski and toboggan lifts, playgrounds, and even igloos, for children under six years old, free of charge.

Dining and Lodging

$$ ✕▥ **Désirée.** Though the rooms are institution-modern, the balconies take in valley views, and the restaurant-stübli downstairs is rich in smoky, meaty, local atmosphere. It's in the center but above traffic; access is by electric cart. ⊠ *CH-3925,* ☎ *027/956–22–55,* FAX *027/956–20–70. 40 beds. Restaurant, stübli, fitness center. MC, V.*

$$ ✕▥ **Hannigalp.** The oldest hotel in town, this welcoming landmark
★   built in 1909 and run by the same family for 80 years has been completely modernized without losing its regional character. The rooms have been updated to spare, blond-wood simplicity; most have balconies. The amenities are remarkable for the price. Headed by the owner himself, the kitchen creates straightforward French cuisine for the restaurant and regional specialties to serve in the cozier bar. It is in a quiet, car-free zone. ⊠ *CH-3925,* ☎ *027/956–25–55,* FAX *027/956–28–55. 50 beds. Restaurant, bar, indoor pool, hot tub, sauna, fitness center. AE, MC, V.*

$$ ✕▥ **Walliserhof.** Directly in the center of town, this eye-catching dark-wood Valais-style chalet is ringed with balconies; in summer geraniums spill from every window. The interior is bright and elegant, and rooms glow with warm knotty pine. The south-side suites hog the magnificent views. The restaurant, serving basic French fare, has a formal air, with candles and linens. ⊠ *CH-3925,* ☎ *027/956–11–22,* FAX *027/956–29–22. 50 beds. Restaurant, café, dance club. AE, DC, MC, V.*

$ ▦ **Alpha.** A no-nonsense alternative for bargain hunters, this spare dorm-style hotel *garni* (serving breakfast only) offers some rooms with kitchenettes. Built in 1973, it has retained that period's unmistakable decor (orange, scarlet, splashy tiles) but offers balconies and good Swiss views to all. It's slightly downhill from the center of town and has a small sunning lawn. ✉ CH-3925, ☎ 027/956–13–01. *30 beds. No credit cards.*

Saas-Fee

⑯ *36 km (22 mi) south of Visp.*

At the end of the switchbacking road to **Saas-Grund** (1,559 meters/5,114 feet) lies a parking area where visitors must abandon their cars for the length of their stay in Saas-Fee. It might be enough to simply stay in the parking lot, for the view even on arriving at this lofty (1,790 meters/5,871 feet) plateau is humbling. Saas-Fee lies in a deep valley that leaves no doubt about its source: It seems to pour from the vast, intimidating **Fee glacier,** which oozes like icy lava from the broad spread of peaks above. *Fee* can be translated as fairy, and Saas-Fee is indeed fairylike: It's at the heart of a cirque of mountains, 13 of which tower to more than 4,000 meters (13,120 feet), among them the **Dom** (4,545 meters/14,908 feet), the highest mountain entirely on Swiss soil.

Saas-Fee offers skiers and hikers facilities competitive with Switzerland's best, and the new **Metro Alpin** is the highest underground cableway in the world. The village itself, draped along the valley floor, combines the modern resort look with its weathered chalets with some success; the 1963 church at the center is a stylized and inoffensive homage to the shingled steeples all across the country.

Skiing
The first glacier to be used for skiing here was the **Langfluh** (2,870 meters/9,414 feet), accessed by gondola, then cable car. The run is magnificent, sometimes physically demanding, and always varied.

From Langfluh you can take the new ski lift to reach *the* ski area of Saas-Fee, the **Felskinn-Mittelallalin** sector (3,000–3,500 meters/9,840–11,480 feet). Felskinn harbors its own surprise: In order to preserve the land and landscape, the Valaisans have constructed a subterranean funicular, the **Metro alpin,** which climbs through the heart of the mountain to Mittelallalin, that is, halfway up the Allalinhorn (4,027 meters/13,210 feet); tourists debark in a rotating restaurant noted more for the austere grandeur of its natural surroundings than for the quality of its food. Felskinn-Mittelallalin's exceptional site, its high elevation, its runs (15 kilometers/9 miles), and its ample facilities (cable car, funicular, and 5 ski lifts), have made Saas-Fee the number-one summer-skiing resort in Switzerland. A one-day lift ticket costs 55 SF; a six-day pass costs 255 SF.

Dining and Lodging
$$$$ ✕▦ **Waldhotel Fletschhorn.** High on a forested hillside above the re-
★ sort, this quiet *Landgasthof* (country inn) is a sophisticated retreat for gourmets who like to rest undisturbed after an excellent meal. The baths are sizable, and the ultramodern rooms have pine paneling, antiques, and serene views. Half board includes innovative French cuisine that features local products and specialties: reindeer with wild mushrooms, stuffed quail with polenta in pinot noir, straw-roasted chicken. Manager Hansjörg Dütsch provides transportation from town. ✉ CH-3906, ☎ 027/957–21–31, ℻ 027/957–21–87. *30 beds. Restaurant (reservations essential), sauna. AE, DC, MC, V.*

$$$$ ★ **Ferienart Walliserhof.** Offering a refreshing break from the '60s decor that dominates the region, this bright, spacious new inn, while pricey enough, is not in the luxury range. Meticulously carved blond wood, Euro-style furnishings, and view-glorifying windows combine the best of Saas-Fee, indoors and outdoors. The hotel's location in the town's very center doesn't deprive it of great panoramas on all sides. ✉ CH-3906, ☎ 027/957–20–21, FAX 027/957–29–10. 108 beds. Restaurant, bar, café, indoor pool, beauty salon, massage, sauna. AE, DC, MC, V.

$$$$ **Saaserhof.** Renovation in 1994 brought the dated decor of this Saas-Fee institution up to date attractively, and the location near the best lift facilities is excellent. Facilities (including a fitness center) dovetail with those of the Hotel Schweizerhof and Europa. ✉ CH-3906, ☎ 027/957–35–51, FAX 027/957–28–83. 100 beds. Restaurant, bar, hot tub, sauna. AE, DC, MC, V.

$$$ ★ **Allalin.** Families especially will appreciate the flexibility and up-to-date design of the apartment quarters available here, all with kitchen equipment as well as balconies. (In high season, guests must pay half pension and eat one meal per day in the restaurant—no great punishment, as the kitchen is surprisingly sophisticated.) Built in 1928, the hotel has been completely renovated and expanded, and the look is warm, bright, and natural. It's on the hill just east of the center and a block from the main parking, and all doubles have a spectacular southern or southeastern view. ✉ CH-3906, ☎ 027/957–18–15, FAX 027/957–31–15. 80 beds. Restaurant, bar, café, kitchenettes. AE, DC, MC, V.

$$$ **Britannia.** Compensating for its brand-new architecture with light carved pine in every corner, this tidy, fresh, simple lodging is in the heart of town, near resort shopping on the main pedestrian street. The best balconies face south and east. ✉ CH-3906, ☎ 027/957–16–16, FAX 027/957–19–42. 37 beds. Restaurant. AE, MC, V.

Outdoor Activities and Sports

MOUNTAIN CLIMBING
The **Swiss Mountaineering School** conducts daily guided forays (☎ 027/957–44–64).

SPORTS CENTERS
The **Bielen Recreation Center** has a four-lane swimming pool, a children's pool, whirlpools, steam baths, a sauna, a solarium, fitness, and games (☎ 027/957–24–75).

TENNIS
Kalbermatten Sports Ground (☎ 027/957–24–54) and **Bielen Indoor Tennis Courts** (☎ 027/957–24–75) are both private tennis sites.

BRIG AND THE ALPINE PASSES

This region is the Grand Central Station of the Alpine region; all mountain passes lead to Brig, and traffic pours in (and through) from Italy, the Ticino, Central Switzerland, the Berner Oberland—and, via the latter, from Paris, Brussels and London and on to Rome.

Brig

⑰ 209 km (129 mi) south of Bern.

A rail and road junction joining four cantons, this small but vital town has for centuries been a center of trade with Italy. It guards not only the Simplon route but also the high end of the Rhône Valley, which leads past the Aletsch Glacier to Gletsch and the Grimsel Pass (toward Meiringen and the Berner Oberland) or the Furka Pass (toward Andermatt and Central Switzerland).

Brig's most distinctive tourist attraction is the fantastical **Stockalper-schloss,** a massive Baroque castle built between 1658 and 1678 by Kaspar Jodok von Stockalper, a Swiss tycoon who made his fortune in Italian trade over the Simplon Pass. Topped with three gilt onion domes and containing a courtyard wrapped by elegant Italianate arcades, it was once Switzerland's largest private home and is now completely restored. ☎ 028/23–19–01. ⊠ 4 SF. ⊙ May–Oct., Tues.–Sun., with guided tours at 10, 11, 2, 3, 4, and 5.

En Route   Above the eastern outskirts of Brig is the entrance to the **Simplon Tunnel,** which carries trains loaded with passive cars nearly 20 kilometers (12 miles) before emerging into Italian daylight. The first of the twin tunnels—the world's longest railway tunnels—was started in 1898 and took six years to complete.

Simplon Pass

18   *23 km (14 mi) southeast of Brig.*

Beginning just outside Brig, this historic road meanders through deep gorges and wide, barren, rock-strewn pastures to give increasingly beautiful views back toward Brig. At the summit (2,010 meters/6,593 feet), the Simplon-Kulm Hotel shares the high meadow with the **Simplon Hospice,** built 150 years ago at Napoléon's request and now owned by the monks of St. Bernard. Just beyond stands the bell-towered **Alt Spital,** a lodging built in the 17th century by Kaspar Jodok von Stockalper.

From the summit you can still see parts of the old road of the tradesmen and Napoléon, and it is easy to imagine the hardships travelers faced at these heights. Look north toward the Bernese Alps and a portion of the massive Aletsch Glacier. Beyond the pass, the road continues through Italy, and it's possible to cut across the Italian upthrust and reenter Switzerland in the Ticino, near Ascona.

Riederalp and the Val de Conches

19   *13 km (8 mi) north of the Brig.*

The bleak and stony ascent of the Val de Conches follows the increasingly wild, silty Rhône to its source, with mountain resorts threading into the flanking heights.

Within the Val de Conches, **Riederalp** is best known as the home of Art Furrer, who became famous in the United States as one of the pioneers of freestyle skiing. On his return to Switzerland, he came to this resort and established a freestyle ski school accessible to nearly every good skier. On a rugged, treeless plateau, the resort is accessible only by cable car from Mörel, and its views over the Italian Alps are rivaled only by the secondary ascent by cable car up to **Moosfluh** for staggering views over the Aletsch glacier. A swift new (1995) gondola up to Moosfluh, reputedly the fastest in Europe, holds 12 people. Riederalp borders the preserved pine stands of the **Aletsch forest,** one of the highest in Europe.

From Fiesch, just up the valley from Mörel, you can ascend by cable car all the way to the top of the **Eggishorn** (2,927 meters/9,600 feet). This extraordinary vantage point looks over the entire sweep of the Aletsch and its surrounding peaks.

Skiing

At 1,900 meters (6,232 feet), with a peak of 2,700 meters (8,856 feet), **Riederalp** has seven lifts and 30 kilometers (19 miles) of downhill runs, a third of which are expert. A one-day lift ticket (including access to the whole Aletsch ski area) costs 43 SF; a six-day pass costs 203 SF.

Stretching from Münster to Oberwald, the **Val de Conches** offers superior snow conditions and villages straight out of the Middle Ages, as well as the most beautiful cross-country skiing trails in the Alps, with the exception of those in the Upper Engadine (St. Moritz) at 1,300 meters (4,265 feet), with a peak of 1,450 meters (4,757 feet), has 85 kilometers (53 miles) of trails and an ice-skating rink.

Gletsch

20 *48 km (30 mi) northeast of Brig.*

Summer travelers may want to travel the distance to the tiny resort of Gletsch, named for its prime attraction: the glacier that gives birth to the Rhône. The views over the Bernese and Valais Alps are magnificent. From Gletsch, you can drive over the Furka Pass directly, or over the scenic **Grimsel Pass** (2,130 meters/7,101 feet) to the Bernese Oberland.

Furka Pass

★ **21** *11 km (7) mi east of Gletsch; 59 km (37 mi) northeast of Brig.*

Making the final ascent of the Valais, drivers arrive at Oberwald, source of the train tunnel through the Furka Pass, which cuts over the heights and leads down to Central Switzerland. Spectacular views and stark moonscapes are punctuated by Spielbergesque military operations–white-clad soldiers melting out of camouflaged hangars carved deep into solid-rock walls. The sleek, broad highway that snakes down toward Andermatt shows Swiss Alpine engineering at its best.

VALAIS A TO Z

Arriving and Departing

By Car
The Valais is something of a dead end by nature: A fine expressway (N9) carries you in from Lac Léman, but to exit—or enter—from the eastern end, you must park your car on a train and tunnel through the Furka Pass to go north, the Simplon Pass to go southeast. (The serpentine roads over these passes are open in summer.) You also may cut through from or to Kandersteg in the Berner Oberland by taking a car train to Goppenstein or Brig. A summer-only road twists over the Grimsel Pass as well, heading toward Meiringen and the Berner Oberland or, over the Brünig Pass, to Luzern.

By Plane
The **Geneva** international airport is nearest the west (French) end of the Valais; it's about two hours away by train or car. **Zürich**'s airport brings you closer to the east (German) side, but the Alps are in the way; you must connect by rail tunnel or drive over one of the passes. The small airport at **Sion** is served by **Crossair,** Switzerland's domestic airline.

By Train
There are straightforward rail connections to the region by way of Lausanne to the west and Brig to the east. The two are connected by one clean rail sweep that runs the length of the valley.

Getting Around

By Car

If you want to see the tiny back roads—and there's much to be seen off the beaten path—a car is the only means. The N9 expressway from Lausanne shrinks, at Sion, to a well-maintained highway that continues on to Brig. Distances in the north and south valleys can be deceptive: Apparently short jogs are full of painfully slow switchbacks and distractingly beautiful views. Both Zermatt and Saas-Fee are car-free resorts, though you can drive all the way to a parking lot at the edge of Saas-Fee's main street. Zermatt must be approached by rail from Täsch, the end of the line for cars. Car ferries over mountain passes, either to Kandersteg or over the Simplon and Furka passes, can be claustrophobic and time-consuming: Think of them as the world's longest car wash.

On Foot

This is one of the hiking capitals of Switzerland, and it's impossible to overstate the value of getting away from wheeled transit and setting off on a mountain path through the sweet-scented pine woods and into the wide-open country above timberline. The trails are wild but well maintained here, and the regional tourist office publishes a thorough map with planned and timed walking tours. Ask for *Sentiers valaisans;* it's written in English, French, and German.

By Train

The main rail service covers the length of the valley from Lausanne to Brig, but routes into the tributary valleys are limited.

Guided Tours

Air-Glaciers in Sion (☎ 027/322–64–64) proposes several itineraries out of Sion for groups of four who want a bird's-eye view of the Valais—from a helicopter. Prices range from 290 SF for 10 minutes on up into the thousands for personalized itineraries. Groups of one to seven can save a bit by choosing a Cessna 206 or Pilatus Porter airplane; prices for these start at 519 SF per hour.

Three packages are available through travel agents or appropriate tourist offices: the **Palm Express** combines rail and coach travel from St. Moritz to Zermatt via Ascona and Lugano in canton Ticino. The **Glacier Express** runs by rail from St. Moritz to Zermatt via Andermatt and the Furka Pass. The **Swiss Romantic Tour** starts at Grindelwald in the Berner Oberland, crosses the Grimsel Pass, and follows the Glacier Express route to Zermatt.

Guided coach tours of the Valais are offered by **Valais Incoming,** a tour company based in Sion (⊠ av. de Tourbillon 3, ☎ 027/322–54–35), including lodging and dining packages. Wine lovers can trace the best Valais vineyards firsthand by following a list provided by the **OPAV** (⊠ Office de Promotion des Produits de l'Agriculture Valaisanne, av. de la Gare 5, ☎ 027/322–22–47), which promotes agriculture in the region; you must arrange the visits yourself.

Contacts and Resources

Emergencies

Police: Crans-Montana (☎ 027/41–24–50); Sion (☎ 027/60–56–56); Verbier (☎ 026/36–12–56); Zermatt (☎ 027/60–56–56). **Medical assistance:** Crans-Montana (ambulance, ☎ 027/55–17–17); Sion (ambulance, ☎ 027/23–33–33); Verbier (☎ 026/31–66–77); Zermatt (ambulance, ☎ 027/967–20–00). **Late-night pharmacies** (☎ 111).

Visitor Information

The main tourist office for the Valais region is in **Sion** (⊠ 6 rue Pré-Fleuri, CH-1951, ☎ 027/322–31–61). It's open from 8 until noon and from 2 until 6 weekdays and closed on weekends.

The main sources of **local information** are in **Crans-sur-Sierres** (⊠ CH-3963, ☎ 027/4854–04–04), **Montana** (⊠ av. de la Gare, CH-3962, ☎ 027/485–04–04), **Saas-Fee** (⊠ CH-3906, ☎ 027/959–11–11), **Sion** (⊠ place de la Planta, CH-1950, ☎ 027/322–85–86), **Verbier** (⊠ CH-1936, ☎ 027/771–62–22), and **Zermatt** (⊠ CH-3920, ☎ 027/966–11–81).

12 Vaud

The verdant vineyards of La Côte and Lavaux, the rugged Vaudoise Alps, and two graceful waterfront cities—Lausanne and Montreux—comprise one of Switzerland's most diverse regions. Centered around Lac Léman (also known as Lake Geneva), this French-speaking canton harbors some of the country's most famous cathedrals and castles, as well as Alpine retreats, balmy lake resorts, and picturesque coastal wine villages.

FORCED TO CONCENTRATE ON JUST ONE region of
Switzerland, a visitor could do worse than choose Vaud
(pronounced "Voh"). Its cultural and geographic di-
versity covers the spectrum: It has a world-class Gothic cathedral (Lausanne) and one of Europe's most evocative castles (Chillon), Edwardian
mansions and weathered-wood chalets, sophisticated culture and ancient folk traditions, snowy Alpine slopes and balmy lake resorts, simple fondue and the legerdemain of Fredy Girardet, one of the world's
great chefs. And everywhere there are the roadside vineyards that
strobe black-green, black-green, as the luxurious rows of vines alternate with the rich, black loam.

This is the region of Lac Léman, known to some as Lake Geneva, a
grand and romantic body of water crowned by Lausanne's cathedral
and the castle of Chillon. Its romance—Savoy Alps looming across the
horizon, steamers fanning across its surface, palm trees rustling along
its shores—made it a focal point of the budding 19th-century tourist
industry, an object of literary fancy, an inspiration to the arts. In a Henry
James novella, the imprudent Daisy Miller made waves when she
crossed its waters, unchaperoned, to visit Chillon; Byron's Bonivard
languished in chains in its dungeons. From their homes outside Montreux, Stravinsky wrote *The Rite of Spring* and Strauss his transcen-
dent *Four Last Songs*. Yet at the lake's east end, romance and culture
give way to wilderness and farmlands, in mountains with some peaks
so high they grow grazing grass sweet enough to flavor the cheese. There
are resorts, of course—Leysin, Villars, Château-d'Oex—but none of
them so famous as to upstage the region itself.

Throughout the canton, French is spoken, and the temperament the
Vaudoise inherited from the Romans and Burgundians sets them apart
from their Swiss-German countrymen. It's evident in their humor, their
style, and—above all—their love of their own good wine.

Pleasures and Pastimes

Castles
Home to magnificently restored Chillon, arguably the best castle in
Switzerland, Vaud offers a variety of smaller draws as well, including
Coppet, Nyon, Rolle, Allaman, Aubonne, and Château-d'Oex, among
others. Most house museums and offer baronial views.

Dining
Because of its fortuitous position, draped along a sloping, sunny coast
facing a sparkling lake and the looming peaks of the French Alps, the
Lac Léman coast draws weekenders and car tourists who speed along
the waterfront highway, careening through cobbled wine towns, tops
down, gastronomy guides on the dashboard, in search of the perfect
lunch. As in all great wine regions, *dégustation* and *haute-gastronomie*
go hand in hand, and in inns and auberges throughout La Côte and
Lavaux (the two stretches of vineyard-lined coast) you'll dine beside
ascoted oenophiles who lower their half-lenses to study a label and order
a multi-course feast to complement their extensive tastings.

The culinary delights of Vaud range from the universally worshiped *cuisine du marché* (cuisine based on fresh market produce) of chef Fredy
Girardet (in Crisier, outside Lausanne) to the simplest fare: *papet Vaudois,* a straightforward stew of leeks, potatoes, and cream served with
superb local sausages; delicate *filets de perche* (local perch filets, sautéed
in butter and served by the dozen with steamed potatoes); and even

Malakoffs, egg-and-Gruyère fritters, that trace back to soldiers of La Côte fighting in the Crimean wars.

Though nowadays fondue is de rigueur in any Alpine setting, Vaud is the undisputed capital of the Swiss national dish and one of its most loyal custodians. In the Pays-d'Enhaut and on the slopes of the Jura Mountains, the cattle head uphill every summer and production of the local cheese soars—the nutty hard cheese known as Gruyère, whether or not it comes from that Fribourgeois village. It is sold at various stages of its production: young and mild, ripe and savory, or aged to a heady tang.

The concept of fondue is elementary: Grated cheese is melted in a pot with white wine, garlic, and a dash of kirsch, and diners sit in a circle around the pot, dipping chunks of bread into the bubbling cream with slender forks. Many restaurants prefer to serve it in an adjoining *carnotzet* or *stübli* (the French and German versions of cozy drinking parlors)—not only to re-create a rustic Alpine experience but also to spare fellow diners the heavy fumes of Sterno, which is used to keep the cheese warm and liquid.

It is a dish at its best when the windows are thick with frost, its flickering fuel dish creating its own, private *coin de feu* (hearth; literally, corner of fire). To wash it down, you drink fruity white wine or plain black tea—never red wine, beer, or (shudder) cola. And, halfway through, you down a stiff shot of kirsch—the reviving blast called the *coup du milieu* (shot in the middle). A mixed salad of winter crudités—grated carrots, celery root, cabbage—is indispensable to digestion.

Another Alpine cheese specialty of Vaud is *tomme,* mild white pressed patties of fresh, raw cow's-milk cheese, often breaded and fried and served whole, piping hot and oozing through the golden crust.

To experience Vaud's best international cuisine, look for *déjeuners d'affaires* (business lunches) and prix-fixe lunch menus, which can offer considerable savings over à la carte dining.

CATEGORY	COST*
$$$$	over 70 SF
$$$	40 SF–70 SF
$$	20 SF–40 SF
$	under 20 SF

per person for a three-course meal (except in $ category), including sales tax and 15% service charge

Lodging

It's a pleasure unique to Vaud to wake up, part floor-length sheers and look out over Lac Léman to the Mont Blanc; a series of 19th-century grand hotels with banks of balconied lake-view rooms were created to offer this luxury to Grand-Tourists such as Strauss, Twain, Stravinsky and Henry James. Yet there's no shortage of charming little inns that offer similar views on an intimate scale. Up another 1,200 meters (3,936 feet) you'll find the antithesis to an airy lakefront inn: the cozy, honey-gold Alpine chalet, with down quilts in starched white envelopes, homespun doilies, balustrade balconies with potted geraniums, and panoramic views.

The hotels of Lausanne and Montreux are long on luxury and grace, and low prices are not a strong suit, though they do offer an occasional bargain. Especially at peak periods—Christmas–New Year's and June, July, and August—it's important to book ahead. Plenty of small auberges (inns) in the villages along the lake offer traditional dishes and simple comforts. Up in the Pays-d'Enhaut and the Alps southeast of the lake, there are comfortable mountain hotels in all price ranges—though rates are naturally higher in the resorts themselves. Charges are generally not as steep as those in the Alpine resorts of Graubünden or Valais.

CATEGORY	COST*
$$$$	over 300 SF
$$$	200 SF–300 SF
$$	120 SF–200 SF
$	under 120 SF

All prices are for a standard double room, including breakfast, tax, and service charge.

Museums

Lausanne is a city of museums and galleries, not only covering history, science, and the Beaux-Arts, but eclectic subjects as well—the Olympics and Art Brut, for example. And all along the coast you'll find tiny, atmospheric museums covering local history, from the strong local influence of the Romans to winemaking, the military, and, at Nestlé's Alimentarium, the history of food.

Skiing

The Alpes Vaudoises are home to lovely, not-overdeveloped high-altitude resorts—Leysin, Villars, Les Diablerets, Château-d'Oex—where you can experience all levels of skiing difficulty and all the Swiss-Alps atmosphere you could wish for.

Wine

As one of the main wine production regions in Switzerland, Vaud can't be experienced without sampling the local wares. If you're only tangentially interested, check the blackboard listings in any café for local names on open wines, sold by the deciliter: the fruity whites of Epesses and St-Saphorin of Lavaux (between Lausanne and Montreux); the flinty Luins, Vinzel, and La Côte variations between Lausanne and Geneva. If you want to experience more detail and atmosphere, plan a drive worthy of Albert Finney and Audrey Hepburn in *Two for the Road,* steering that rent-a-car through narrow, fountain-studded stone streets in tiny wine villages, stopping at inns and vignobles' *degustations* to contrast and compare. (Do designate a driver.) And head for a market Saturday in Vevey, where vendors sell wine wholesale and tasters carry a glass from booth to booth.

Exploring Vaud

Lac Léman is a graceful swelling in the River Rhône, which passes through the northern hook of the Valais, channels between the French and Vaudoise Alps, then breaks into the open at Bouveret, west of Villeneuve. Its northern shore hosts three of Switzerland's great French cities, grandes dames of the Suisse Romande: Lausanne, Montreux, and Geneva (☞ Chapter 13). The southern shore falls in France's Haute-Savoie, providing those famous shore cities with magnificent mountain views of the French Alps. The north portion of the lake and the cluster of nearby Alps that loom over its eastern end, as well as the green hillsides to its north, make up the canton of Vaud.

Great Itineraries

You could easily spend a full Swiss vacation in Vaud, flying directly in and out of Geneva Cointrin without setting toe in Geneva: By rail or car, you could head straight for such coastal villages as Coppet, Nyon and Morges, dig into Lausanne's urban graces, crawl through even lovelier wine towns en route to Montreux, then head straight up into those mountains that have been looking over your shoulder. In three days' time, you could visit the exquisite wine towns of Lavaux, also taking in Lausanne and Montreux's Chillon castle. In five, you could slow your pace to explore La Côte as well. In 10 days, you could expand your castle-touring along the lake, see more museums in Lausanne, and head into the Pays-d'Enhaut for a few days' mountain walking.

IF YOU HAVE 3 DAYS

Numbers in the text correspond to numbers in the margin and on the Vaud and Lausanne maps.

Drive the coastal highway through **Coppet** ① to 🔄 **Nyon** ② to visit the Roman museum and medieval castle that juts over the lake. Spend a day exploring a few select sights in the charming waterfront town of 🔄 **Lausanne** ⑥–⑱, then set out for the winding Corniche road, visiting a vignoble or two at Epesses or St-Saphorin. You'll end up at the lakefront town of 🔄 **Montreux** ㉑, with its fabled Château de Chillon ㉒.

IF YOU HAVE 5 DAYS

After a drive through **Coppet** ① and a trip to the château and Roman museum at 🔄 **Nyon** ②, spend a leisurely day cruising the Route du Vignoble to **Rolle, Aubonne, Allaman** ③, **Morges** ④, and **St-Sulpice** ⑤; then spend two days exploring 🔄 **Lausanne** ⑥–⑱. On your last day, explore the Corniche road en route to 🔄 **Montreux** ㉑ and **Chillon** ㉒.

IF YOU HAVE 10 DAYS

Spend a night in 🔄 **Nyon** ②, tour the Route du Vignoble to Rolle, Aubonne, **Allaman** ③, **Morges** ④, and **St-Sulpice** ⑤; then spend three nights in 🔄 **Lausanne** ⑥–⑱, allowing time for a leisurely tour of museums and waterfront sights. Spend a day winding along the Corniche road, with stops to wander Epesses and St-Saphorin, tasting the local wines and eating a waterfront meal. Then drive into 🔄 **Vevey** ⑳, the genteel sister to honkey-tonk **Montreux** ㉑; its old town, museums, and Saturday wine market merit an overnight stop, with an evening run to the casino. A half-day allows you to take in the magic of the **Château de Chillon** ㉒ before you leave Lac Léman to head into the Alpes Vaudoises. Two nights in 🔄 **Leysin** ㉖ or 🔄 **Villars** ㉔ will allow you to hike, ski, or sit on a sunny balcony, enjoying spectacular views. Then cross the Col des Mosses and the Gorges du Pisson into 🔄 **Château-d'Oex** ㉘, where two more nights allow you to breathe the pure air, walk the mellow hills, and study the rustic, folkloric chalets that link the region culturally to Gstaad and the Berner Oberland (☞ Chapter 10).

When to Tour Vaud

The lake sparkles and clouds lift from the Mont Blanc from spring through fall; November tends to be drizzly-gray, then winter brightens up. Crowds monopolize Montreux and Chillon year-round but overwhelm it in July (jazz festival time) and August (Europe-wide vacations). It's worth aiming for concert–dance season in Lausanne: September through May. Prime ski time in the Alpes Vaudoises is late December through Easter, and prices go up accordingly. Early spring is daffodil season in Les Avants, over Montreux, where the hillsides come alive with the wild yellow flowers.

LA CÔTE AND LAUSANNE

Just northeast of Geneva, La Côte (the Coast) of Lac Léman has been settled since Roman times, and its south-facing slopes cultivated for wine. It is thus peppered with ancient waterfront and hillside towns, castles, and Roman remains. A car is a must if you want to wind through tiny wine villages, but do get out and walk—if only to hear the trickling of any number of Romanesque trough-fountains. Be willing to zigzag a few times from the slopes to the waterfront and back if you're determined to cover all the region's charms; sticking exclusively to either

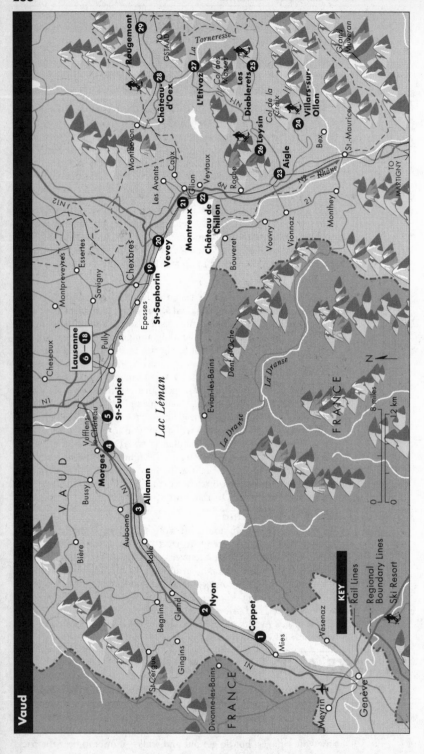

Vaud

the diminutive Route du Vin or the coastal highway deprives you of some wonderful sights. You'll end your rural tour in the sophisticated city of Lausanne.

Coppet

❶ *10 km (6 mi) south of Nyon; 46 km (28 mi) southwest of Lausanne.*

Its pretty, arcaded main street, with occasional peeks through to the waterfront, would make Coppet a pleasant stop for a stroll, but it is the **Château de Coppet** that puts this pretty lake village on the map. Gracefully symmetrical and enclosed within vast iron gates, the château has been kept in its original 18th-century form, with luxurious Louis XVI furnishings arranged in a convincingly lived-in manner; its grounds, with grand old trees, hidden courtyards and stone stairs, are equally evocative.

The château was built by Jacques Necker, a Genevan banker who served as financial minister to France's Louis XVI. The turmoil of the French Revolution and Necker's opposition to Napoléon led him into exile in this splendid structure, where, with his remarkable wife Madame de Staël, he created the most sought-after salon in Europe. The daughter of Suzanne Curchod, Madame de Staël had been jilted by the youthful historian Edward Gibbon in 1756; her own intellectual sparkle and concern for the fiery issues of the day attracted the company of the giants of the early Romantic period: Lord Byron, the French writer Benjamin Constant, the Swiss historian Jean-Charles Sismondi, the German writer August Schlegel, and the faithless Edward Gibbon himself. ⊠ *CH-1296,* ☎ *022/776–10–28.* 🎫 *7 SF. Guided tours Apr.–Oct., Tues.–Sun. 10–noon and 2–6; July–Aug., daily 10–12:30 and 2–6; last tours depart 11:30 and 5:30.*

For the house-tour hound, the small **Musée Régional du Vieux-Coppet** holds forth in a 15th-century residence on the arcaded Grand-Rue, displaying its collection of lace and faience among the restored furnishings of a local 19th-century bourgeois family. There's a noteworthy instrument in the music room, part piano, part violin. ⊠ *Grand-Rue 30,* ☎ *022/776-36-88.* 🎫 *2.50 SF.* ⊙ *Apr.–Oct., Tues.–Sat. 2–5. Guided tours by request.*

Dining and Lodging

$$$$ ✕🏨 **Hôtel du Lac.** First classed a "Grand Logis" in 1628 to distinguish it from a common roadhouse, this historic inn still caters to serious business-lunchers and well-heeled travelers without tipping the scales toward luxury. It fronts on the main road but opens directly onto the water, with a sycamore-shaded terrace, an lake-view porch with awning for diners, and rooms with beams, niches, and antiques. Its classic French restaurant features grilled meats and fish. ⊠ *CH-1296,* ☎ *022/776-15-21,* 🖹 *022/776-53-46. 40 beds. Restaurant. AE, DC, MC, V.*

Nyon

❷ *9 km (4 mi) north of Coppet; 27 km (17 mi) southwest of Lausanne.*

This lovely lakeside market town, with a waterfront drive, shops, museums, and a castle dominating its cliff-top old town, was founded by Julius Caesar around 56 BC as a camp for war veterans. The Romans called it Noviodunum, and developed the entire region for miles around, charting, building, and developing sophisticated systems.

★ Flanked by a statue of Caesar himself, the Basilique et Musée Romain (Basilica and Roman Museum) contains an attractively mounted collection of sumptuously detailed architectural stonework, fresco fragments, statuary, mosaics, and earthenware. A pristine miniature model inside, and an excellent trompe-l'oeil artist's impression of the basilica on the outside wall of the museum make clear the original structure's remarkable size and sophistication. ⊠ *Rue Maupertuis,* ☎ *022/361–75–91.* ⊡ *5 SF (good for all three of Nyon's museums).* ☉ *Apr.–Oct., daily 10–noon and 2–6; Nov.–Mar., Tues.–Sun. 2–5. Guided tours by request.*

Dominating Nyon's hilltop over the waterfront, the **Château de Nyon** is a magnificent multispire 12th-century fortress with a terrace that takes in sweeping views of the lake and Mont Blanc. Only the exterior can be viewed throughout 1997, as renovations are underway.

After the French Revolution, Nyon became a great porcelain center, creating flower-sprigged tea sets, vases, and bowls; today a fine collection of its products is displayed in the **Musée de la Porcelaine,** which will soon set up quarters within the château (contact the tourist office for its temporary location). ⊠ *CH-1260,* ☎ *022/361–58–88.* ⊡ *5 SF (good for all three of Nyon's museums).* ☉ *Apr.–Oct., daily 10–noon and 2–6; closed Nov.–Mar. Guided tours by request.*

There are outstanding views of the lake and Mont Blanc from the château-museum's terrace, but don't miss the town's waterfront promenade below, where boats bob in the waves. Nestled in a charming floral park that parallels the water, the **Maison du Léman** features models of Lac Léman boats through the ages as well as sizable lake-water aquariums, housed in a shuttered 18th-century hospital. ⊠ *Quai Louis Bonnard 8,* ☎ *022/361–09–49.* ⊡ *5 SF (good for all three museums).* ☉ *Apr.–Oct., Tues.–Sun. 10–noon and 2–6; Nov.–Mar., Tues.–Sun. 2–5.*

Dining

$ ✕ **Auberge du Château.** Just behind the cathedral and steps from the Musée Romain, this cozy, simple restaurant serves straightforward French fare and reasonable *plats du jour,* including game in season. In summer, a big terrace lets diners study the château over lunch; in winter, broad windows take in the view. ⊠ *place du Château 8,* ☎ *022/361–63–12. AE, DC, MC, V.*

$ ✕ **Au Coeur de la Côte.** Whether you lunch on steak and salad, taste the commune's Vinzel in slim stemless glasses, or fill up on two or three hot, rich Gruyère-based malakoffs, served with pickles and mustard, stop for local atmosphere at this simple village inn. Plain and homey inside, it has a pretty flower-framed terrace looking over the rolling vineyards and Lac Léman. Malakoffs are served nonstop from 11:30 AM to 9:30 PM. ☎ *021/ 824–11–41. No reservations. MC, V. Closed Mon.*

OFF THE BEATEN PATH **ST-CERGUE** – From Nyon you can take a beautiful ride into verdant Jura-range resort country on the little mountain railway Nyon–St-Cergue–Morez up to St-Cergue, 20 kilometers (12 miles) to the north, and beyond. Note the contrast between the old rolling stock, museum pieces in themselves, and the brand-new coaches. St-Cergue is a charming little resort in both summer and winter, with good ski facilities for children, modest skiing for adults, and fine cross-country trails. It's also the birthplace of snowshoeing, the winter sport that involves lightweight, plastic *raquettes de neige,* which allow snow hikers to leave the trail and move with streamlined efficiency across the surface.

ROUTE DU VINGNOBLE – Parallel to the waterfront highway, threading through the steep-sloping vineyards between Nyon and Lausanne, the Route du Vignoble unfolds a rolling green landscape high above the lake, punctuated by noble manor-farms and vineyards. **Luins,** home of the flinty, fruity white wine of the same name, is a typical, pretty village.

Just up the road, the tiny, picturesque village of **Vinzel** develops its own white wines on sunny slopes and sells them from the wine cellars that inspired its name (vin-cellier). It is also the best source for a very local specialty, the *malakoff*. These rich, steamy cheese-and-egg beignets have always been a favorite of the Vaudois, but after the Crimean Wars were renamed after a beloved officer who led his army of Vaud-born mercenaries to victory in the siege of Sebastopol. The Route du Vignoble continues through Bursins, home of an 11th-century Romanesque church; drivers can choose to follow it all the way to Morges, or to cross under the autoroute to view lakefront castles.

En Route Twelve kilometers (7 miles) northeast of Nyon, the lakefront village of **Rolle** merits a detour for a look at its dramatic 13th-century **château**, built at the water's edge by a Savoyard prince.

Allaman

❸ *17 km (10 mi) northeast of Nyon; 20 km (12 mi) west of Lausanne.*

You can actually wander the interior of the stately 16th-century **château d'Allaman,** built first during the 12th century by the barons of Vaud, then rebuilt by the Bernois after a 1530 fire: It's been converted to an antiques mall, its atmospheric halls and stairwells lined with beeswaxed armoires and historic portraits, all for sale through private entrepreneurs who rent space within. The château's vaulted crypt offers wine *dégustations* for potential buyers as well. ⊠ *CH-1165, Allaman,* ☎ *021–807–38–05.* ☎ *Free.* ☉ *Wed.-Sun. 2-6.*

Morges

❹ *9 km (5 mi) northeast of Allaman; 8 km (5 mi) west of Lausanne.*

On the waterfront just west of the urban sprawl of Lausanne, Morges is a pleasant lake village popular with sailors. Its castle, built by the duke of Savoy around 1286 as a defense against the bishop-princes of Lausanne, now houses the **Musée Militaire Vaudois** (Vaud Military Museum), which displays weapons, uniforms, models, and a collection of 10,000 miniature lead soldiers. In the Général Henri Guisan hall, you'll find memorabilia of this beloved World War II general, much honored for keeping both sides happy enough to leave Switzerland safely alone. ⊠ *CH-1110,* ☎ *021/801–26–16.* ☎ *5 SF.* ☉ *Feb.–mid-Dec., weekdays 10–noon and 1:30–5, weekends 1:30–5. July–Aug., daily 10-5.*

One of Vaud's principal wine-producing centers, Morges hosts an exuberant three-day **wine festival** every year on the last weekend in September. The whole town throws itself into the merrymaking with folklore shows, parties, and—naturally—more than a little serious wine tasting.

Dining

$$$$ ✕ **L'Ermitage.** With a growing reputation that dares to challenge the unchallengeable Fredy Girardet, Bernard Ravet now offers visitors to the Lausanne area a once unthinkable alternative at half the price. Branching out with bold visuals and confident combinations—say, rabbit tartare with caviar, fried cracklings of sweetbreads and frogs' legs, or lightly smoked Bavarian salmon—and enriching his sophisticated *cave*, he continues to offer a warm, even casual welcome, from the glass of local St-Saphorin by the fire downstairs to the frankly homey double-crème with cinnamon. This is a chef and restaurant to be reckoned with. It's 15 kilometers (9 miles) west of the city, in a graceful, shuttered former wine maker's home, with beams and fireplaces inside and grand

old trees in the garden. ✉ *Vufflens-le-Château*, ☎ *021/802–21–91. Reservations required. DC, MC, V. Closed Sun.–Mon.*

OFF THE BEATEN PATH	**VUFFLENS-LE-CHÂTEAU** – Two kilometers (1 mile) northwest of Morges, this village is known for its namesake château, a 15th-century Savoyard palace with a massive *donjon* (fortified tower) and four lesser towers, all trimmed in fine Piedmont-style brickwork.

St-Sulpice

❺   *5 km (3 mi) east of Morges; 3 km (1¼ mi) west of Lausanne.*

Just outside Lausanne, turn toward the waterfront to visit St-Sulpice, site of one of the best-preserved 12th-century Romanesque churches in Switzerland, **l'Eglise de St-Sulpice.** Severe but lovely, it was built by monks from the Cluny Abbey in Burgundy; its painted decoration softens the spare purity of its lines. Three original apses remain, although the nave has disappeared; the short bell tower is built of small stone blocks that were probably brought from the ruined Roman township at nearby Vidy. The adjoining priory was converted into a private residence during the 16th century.

Lausanne

❻–⓲   *66 km (41 mi) northeast of Geneva.*

"Lausanne is a block of picturesque houses, spilling over two or three gorges, which spread from the same central knot, and are crowned by a cathedral like a tiara. . . . On the esplanade of the church . . . I saw the lake over the roofs, the mountains over the lake, clouds over the mountains, and stars over the clouds. It was like a staircase where my thoughts climbed step by step and broadened at each new height," wrote Victor Hugo of this grand and graceful tiered city, which does reign like a tiaraed queen over the lake and surrounding mountains. Voltaire, Rousseau, Byron, and Cocteau all waxed equally passionate about Lausanne—and not only for its visual beauty. It has been a cultural center for centuries, the world drawn first to its magnificent Gothic cathedral and the powers it represented, then to its university, and finally, during the 18th and 19th centuries, to its vibrant intellectual and social life.

Lausanne's importance today stems from its several disparate roles in world affairs. Politically, it is important as the site of the Tribunal Fédéral, the highest court of appeals in Switzerland. Commercially, while it is by no means in the same league as Zürich or Bern, it figures as headquarters for a great many multinational organizations and corporations. On a major international rail route and an important national junction, Lausanne serves as a trade center for most of the surrounding agricultural regions and the expanding industrial towns of the Vaud. Prosperity nurtures the arts, and Lausanne is home to a surprising concentration of dance companies—including that of Maurice Béjart—as well as small theaters and the Orchestre de la Suisse Romande. Pride of place in Lausanne is reserved for the city's role as the Olympic capital. The International Olympic Committee has been based here since 1915, steering the Olympic movement through times of crisis and success alike. Ironically, the citizens of Lausanne voted against hosting the 1994 Winter Olympics, afraid, in part, of upsetting the delicate balance of old and new they cautiously sustain.

The balance has not always been kept. The first 20 years after World War II saw an immense building boom, with old buildings and whole neighborhoods pulled down to make way for shining new office blocks and apartment buildings—an architectural exuberance that has given Lausanne a rather lopsided air. Rising in tiers from the lakeside at Ouchy (360 meters/1,181 feet) to more than 600 meters (2,000 feet), the city covers three hills, which are separated by gorges that once channeled rivers; the rivers have been built over, and huge bridges span the gaps from hilltop to hilltop. On one hillside in particular, modern skyscrapers contrast brutally with the beautiful proportions of the cathedral rising majestically from its crest. For the sake of hygiene, atmospheric alleys and narrow streets have mostly been demolished, yet the old town clustered around the cathedral has been painstakingly and attractively restored. Yet Lausanne continues to develop its assets: Two slick new museum complexes have been opened, one devoted to the city's Roman roots, the other to the worldwide glories of the Olympics.

For walking in Lausanne you should bring comfortable shoes, as the city's steep hills and multiple layers add considerable strain to getting from neighborhood to neighborhood. There are plenty of buses, but to see the concentrated sights of the old town, it's best to tackle the hills on foot.

❻ The commercial hub of the city is the **Place St-François,** nicknamed "Sainfe" by the Lausannois. It is dominated by the massive post office and the former Franciscan **Eglise St-François** (Church of St. Francis), built during the 13th and 14th centuries. From 1783 to 1793, Edward Gibbon lived in a house on the site of the post office and there finished work on *The Decline and Fall of the Roman Empire.* In those days, the place was a popular riding circuit.

Behind the Eglise St-François, the pedestrian shopping street leading
❼ up to the right is the ancient **rue de Bourg,** once a separate village isolated on this natural ridge, now densely packed with upscale, modern shops. At the top of rue de Bourg, rue Caroline leads you left and over the **Pont Bessières,** where you can see the city's peculiar design spanning gorges and covered rivers.

❽ The Ancien-Evêché (Old Bishopric) now houses the **Musée Historique de Lausanne,** a sophisticated museum with a permanent collection and temporary exhibitions on the history of the city. Don't miss the 250-square-foot scale model of 17th-century Lausanne, with its lighted commentary illuminating the neighborhoods' histories. ⊠ *Place de la Cathédrale 4,* ☎ *021/312–13–68.* ▱ *4 SF.* ☉ *Tues., Wed., and Fri.–Sun. 11–6, Thurs. 11–8.*

At the top of rue St-Etienne and above the place de la Riponne tow-
★ ❾ ers the **Cathédrale de Notre-Dame,** a Burgundian-Gothic architectural treasure on par with some of France's and England's best, and certainly the finest in Switzerland. Begun during the 12th century by Italian, Flemish, and French architects, it was completed in 1275; Viollet-le-Duc restored portions to Victorian-Gothic perfection in the 19th century. (His repairs are visible as paler stone, not weathered local sandstone; his self-portrait appears in the face of King David, harp and scroll in hand, to the right of the main portal.) Streamlined to the extreme, without radiating chapels or the excesses of later Gothic trim, it wasn't always so spare: When zealous Reformers plastered over florid paintwork, they unwittingly preserved it for modern visitors, who can see portions of brilliant color restored in the right transepts. The dark and delicate choir contains the 14th-century tomb of Othon I of Grandson (☞ Chapter 8) and exceptionally fine 13th-century choir stalls, unusual for their age alone, not to mention their beauty.

When this architectural milestone was dedicated, Pope Gregory X came expressly to perform the historic consecration ceremony—of double im-

292

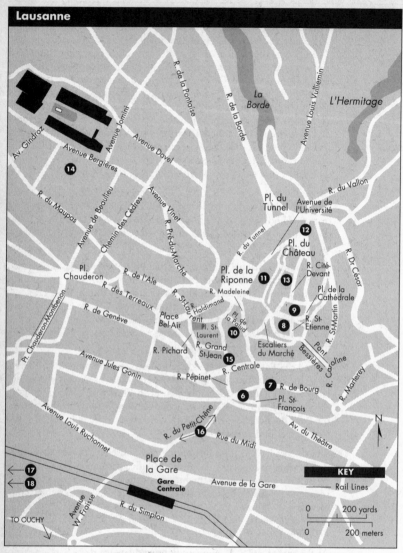

Lausanne

Ancienne-
Académie, **13**
Cathédrale de Notre-
Dame, **9**
Château St-Maire, **12**
Collection de l'Art
Brut, **14**

débarcadère, **16**
Hôtel de Ville, **10**
Musée Historique de
Lausanne, **8**
Musée
Olympique, **17**

Musée Romain, **18**
Ouchy, **15**
Palais de Rumine, **11**
Place St-François, **6**
Rue de Bourg, **7**

portance, as it also served as a coronation service for Rudolph of Haps-burg as the new emperor of Germany and of the Holy Roman Empire. Emperor Rudolph brought his wife, 8 children, 7 cardinals, 5 archbishops, 17 bishops, 4 dukes, 15 counts, and a multitude of lesser lords, spiri-tual and temporal, who must have crowded the church's exquisitely pro-portioned nave. Protestant services (the cathedral was Reformed in the 15th century) exclude non-worshiping visitors Sunday from 10 to 11:30. ⊠ *Rue Pierre Viret.* ⊙ *Closes daily at 7 (5:30 in winter).*

Near the entrance to the cathedral, a flight of wooden steps leads down to the second, more dramatic **Escaliers du Marché,** a wooden-roof medieval staircase. At the bottom of the stairs, the **Place de la Palud** ⑩ is dominated by the 15th- and 17th-century **Hôtel de Ville** (Town Hall), the seat of the municipal and communal councils. A painted medieval **Fontaine de la Justice** (Justice Fountain) draws social strollers to lounge on its heavy rim. Across from the Town Hall, you can watch the **ani-mated clock,** a modern work with moving figures that was donated to the city by local merchants. A market is held here every Wednesday and Saturday.

Just up rue Madeleine from the Place de la Palud, the **Place de la** ⑪ **Riponne** is home to the neo-Renaissance **Palais de Rumine,** built at the turn of the century. This enormous structure houses the **Musée Can-tonal d'Histoire Naturelle** (Cantonal Museum of Natural History), with geological and zoological sections, and the **Musée Cantonal d'Archéolo-gie et d'Histoire** (Cantonal Museum of Archaeology and History), with exhibits of relics from the Bronze and Iron ages and the gold bust of Marcus Aurelius discovered at Avenches in 1939. The **Musée Can-tonal des Beaux-Arts** (Cantonal Museum of Fine Arts) also holds forth in the Palais de Rumine, offering an enlightening collection of Swiss art, not only by the Germanic Hodler and Anker but also by artists of Vaud—especially Bocion, whose local landscapes are well worth study during a visit to this region. ⊠ *Palais de Rumine, pl. de la Riponne 6,* ☎ *021/312–83–36 (Museum of Natural History); 021/312–83–34 (Museum of Archaeology); 021/312–83–32 (Museum of Fine Arts).* 🖅 *free for Museum of Natural History and Museum of Archaeology; 6 SF for Museum of Fine Arts.* ⊙ *Daily 10–noon and 2–5 for Mu-seum of Natural History and Museum of Archaeology; Tues.–Wed. 11–6, Thurs. 11–8, Fri.–Sun. 11–5 for Museum of Fine Arts.*

Up l'Avenue de l'Université from the place de la Riponne towers the ★ ⑫ **Château St-Maire,** a formidable castellated stone cylinder built during the 15th century for the bishops of Lausanne. Its fortresslike structure was functional: The citizens wearied of ecclesiastic power in the 16th century and allied themselves with Bern and Fribourg, against the bishops protected within. Before long, however, Bern itself marched on Lausanne, put a bailiff in this bishops' castle, and stripped the city fathers of their power. The Bernese imposed Protestantism on the Lau-sannois, and their Catholic churches and cathedral were ransacked to fill the coffers of Bern. Today the Château St-Maire is the seat of the cantonal government.

⑬ The **Ancienne-Académie,** early home of the university, stands halfway between the château and the cathedral, on rue Cité-Devant.

A hike up avenue Vinet (or Bus 2 from St-Laurent, in the direction of Le Désert) takes you to the **Palais de Beaulieu,** the city's convention center and one of its main performance spaces, seating 2,000. Across ★ ⑭ the avenue is the **Collection de l'Art Brut,** housed in the Château de Beaulieu, a former mansion of Madame de Staël. This is a world-class museum devoted to the slightly bizarre world of fringe or "psychopathological" art, dubbed *art brut* in the 1940s by French artist Jean Dubuffet. His own collection forms the base of this chilling ensemble of works created by prisoners, schizophrenics, or the merely obsessed. ⊠ *Château de Beaulieu, 11 av. des Bergières,* ☎ *021/647– 54–35.* ▣ *6 SF.* ☾ *Tues.–Fri. 10–noon and 2–6, weekends 2–6.*

⑮ Completely separate from the old town on the hilltop, the waterfront community of **Ouchy** can be easily reached by the steep funicular Metro across from the Gare Centrale (train station). Officially a separate township, Ouchy serves as Lausanne's port; its main boat traf-
⑯ fic comes from the white steamers that land at the **débarcadère** (wharf) on rue du Petit-Chêne. The town is dominated by the **Château d'Ouchy**, now a hotel; its tower dates from the Middle Ages. In fine weather, the waterfront buzzes with nightlife—strollers, diners, drinkers in cafés, roller skaters and mimes, craftspeople selling their wares. It's as if sedate Lausanne lifts her skirts a bit at the shoreline.

Just east of Ouchy, on a hillside overlooking the lake, a dramatic museum complex is dedicated to the history and disciplines of the Olympic
⑰ Games: The **Musée Olympique** pays tribute to the athletic tradition in ancient Greece, to the development of the modern Games, to the evolution of the individual sports, and to the athletes themselves. There are art objects (an Etruscan torch from the 6th century BC, Rodin's *The American Athlete*), 7,000 hours of archival films and videos, interactive displays, photographs, coins and stamps, and medals from various eras throughout Olympic history; you'll even see the running shoes Carl Lewis wore to win the 200-meter gold medal at Los Angeles in 1984. A museum shop, stocked with books, posters, and Olympic-logo clothes, a lovely café overlooking the lake and sculpture park, and occasional Sunday afternoon classical concerts complete this ambitious, world-class endeavor. Cynics may find the high-tech, top-budget displays short on substance (despite the emotional *Chariots of Fire*–style music throbbing in the background) and some of the video archives skimpy, if technologically intriguing. Video viewings are limited to two selections at a time to keep zealots from commandeering a machine for the afternoon. ⊠ *Quai d'Ouchy 1,* ☎ *021/621–65–11.* ▣ *12 SF.* ☾ *May–Sept., Tues.–Sun. 10–7, Thurs. until 9:30; Oct.–Apr., Tues.–Sun. 10–6.*

West of Ouchy at Vidy (and just off the Lausanne-Maladière exit from
⑱ E25/N1) is the **Musée Romain** (Roman Museum), the current incarnation of the restored remains of a late Roman community, Lousonna, that flourished here from 15 BC into the 4th century. A private home, complete with a well and painted murals, has been reconstructed and used as the centerpiece for a permanent exhibition on the ancient civilization; a small treasure trove of coins, votive figures, and objects from daily life—carved combs, toga pins, jewelry—is displayed. ⊠ *Chemin du Bois-de-Vaux 24,* ☎ *021/625–10–84.* ▣ *4 SF.* ☾ *Tues.–Sun. 11– 6, Thurs. until 8. Guided tours of museum on the 1st Sun. of the month, an additional 3 SF; guided tour of neighboring archaeological sites on the last Sun. of the month, an additional 3 SF.*

Dining and Lodging

$$$$ ✕ **Girardet.** It's often said that the world's greatest French chef lives
★   in Switzerland: Fredy Girardet has been granted virtually every culinary award and has been earnestly named chef of the century by his Parisian peers. Thus it's no surprise that travelers must be organized well in advance to gain an audience, approaching not only by telephone on the first working day of the month—when the line is predictably busy—but also in writing, preferably enclosing a $100 deposit for two. H.R.H. Girardet has been burned too often by no-shows, so for the sake of others who want to experience his masterworks, honor your

reservations. Should you gain access to this hallowed ground, you might sample artichoke Bavarian with lobster, preserved duckling in lemon and spices, or glazed sweetbreads with wild mushrooms; or lean back and opt for one of the artfully orchestrated prix-fixe menus: Your choice, fish or fowl, will be carved tableside and consumed in hushed, even reverent appreciation. Leave room for selections from the immense cheese cart and for the celestial desserts. Service and presentation are spectacular. It's 7 kilometers (4 miles) east of Lausanne's center in a suitably palatial former *hôtel de ville* (town hall). Note: Don't save the splurge for your next trip to Vaud, as rumors of retirement fly. ✉ *Rue d'Yverdon 1,* ☎ *021/634–05–05. Reservations essential. No credit cards. Closed Sun.–Mon.*

$$$$ ✕ **La Grappe d'Or.** In this relaxed but classic firelit French restaurant,
★ imaginative modern cooking of a high standard is prepared to order by Bavarian chef Peter Baermann and served under the discreet supervision of his wife, Angelika. Try the monkfish with olive juice, scallops with potato gnocchi, saddle of veal with lentils, or the hearty *cardons* (cousins to the artichoke) in foie gras. Pastries are extraordinary. ✉ *Cheneau de Bourg 3,* ☎ *021/323–07–60. Reservations essential. AE, MC, V. Closed Sat. noon, Sun.*

$$–$$$ ✕ **Café Beau-Rivage.** As if turning its back on the aristocratic splen-
★ dor of the Beau-Rivage Palace that shelters it, this young, lively brasserie-café faces the lake and the Ouchy waterfront scene. At lunch and for late dinners, its flashy brass-and-Biedermeier dining area and bar fill with smart Lausannois and Grand-Tour internationals enjoying upscale, trendy cuisine du marché, duck with wild mushrooms, salmon tartare. Despite the brasserie atmosphere, there are no paper placemats: Linen, silver, and monogrammed damask set the BCBG (*bon chic, bon genre*) tone. Summers, the pillared terrazzo terrace is the place to be seen. ✉ *Pl. du Général-Guisan, Ouchy,* ☎ *021/613–33–30. Reservations essential. AE, DC, MC, V.*

$$ ✕ **A la Pomme de Pin.** In the pretty restored old town behind the cathedral, this graceful shuttered *pinte* (wine pub) offers simple French food and reasonable *plats du jour,* served both in the casual café and the adjoining linen-decked restaurant. ✉ *Rue Cité-Derrière 11-13,* ☎ *021/323–46–56. Credit cards AE, MC, V. Closed Sat. lunch, Sun.*

$$ ✕ **Café du Grütli.** Tucked in between the place de Palud and the covered stairs to the cathedral, this is a typical, old-style French-Swiss restaurant, with a bentwood-and-net-curtained café on the ground floor and a simple, more formal dining room upstairs. There are several fondues as well as brasserie classics—*steak de cheval* (horsemeat steak), boiled beef vinaigrette, rabbit in mustard sauce, profiteroles, and *tarte tatin* (upside-down apple tart). Have one of several open Vaud wines or a *café pomme* (coffee with a side shot of apple eau-de-vie) with the locals, who unwind here with the daily papers. There are a handful of tables outdoors if you want to make the American in Paris–style street scene. ✉ *Rue de la Mercerie 4,* ☎ *021/312–94–93. DC, MC, V. Closed Sat. night, Sun.*

$ ✕ **Bleu Lezard.** A complete cross-section of Lausanne urbanites—hip
★ artists, yuppies, shoppers, university students—fight for tables at this laid-back, stylish restaurant, where you can sample aubergine carpaccio, duck breast in violet vinegar sauce, a salad of bacon, marrow crisps and grapes, or cod baked lightly in olive oil with capers and tomato, all for remarkably low prices. A tongue-in-cheek decor of found-object art and easygoing waiters dressed in whatever khakis and flannels they found near the bed that morning adds to the New Age ambience. Mixed drinks and live jazz draw a night clientele. ✉ *Rue Enning 10,* ☎ *021/312–71–90. AE, MC, V. Open daily.*

$ ✕ **Café Romand.** All the customers seem to know each other at this
★   vast, smoky, parqueted dining institution, where shared wooden tables
and clattering china create the perfect ambience for fondue feasts,
smoked fish platters, mussels, choucroute, or a sausage plate. Prominent members of Lausanne's arts community swarm here after re-
hearsals and concerts, and are known to toast each other loudly across
the crowded room. ⊠ *Place St-Francis 2,* ☎ *021/312–63–75. MC, V.
Closed Sun.*

$ ✕ **Manora Crocodile.** If you're fed up with heavy Vaud cheese dishes
and local sausage, this cheery self-service chain offers startlingly inexpensive options, fresh-chopped and cooked before your eyes in huge
woks under silent no-smoke hoods. The light, bright, woody decor increases the greening effect of iced pitchers of fresh-squeezed fruit juices,
four sizes of salad, a fruit bar with almonds and pomegranates, and a
daily risotto. Hot food is served nonstop from 10:45 AM to 10 PM, and
no one dish costs more than 14 SF. A no-smoking dining room is a life-
saver in this city of chain-smokers. ⊠ *Place St-Francois 17,* ☎ *021/320–
92–93. Reservations not accepted. No credit cards. Open daily.*

$ ✕ **Pinte Besson.** Through the dense smoke and fondue fumes in this
old-fashioned barrel-vaulted drinking parlor, you'll discern crowds of
friendly, rowdy Vaudois enjoying cheese specialties, cheap plates
mounded high with slabs of ham and potato salad, horsemeat grilled
on a stone slab, and *deci* after *deci* of open local wine, syphoned into
recycled bottles. In summer, a handful of outdoor tables spare you the
smoke. ⊠ *Rue de l'Ale 4,* ☎ *021/312–72–72. No credit cards. Closed
Sat. night, Sun.*

$$$$ ⊞ **Beau-Rivage Palace.** Of the scores of deluxe hotels in Switzerland,
★   this gleaming grande dame stands apart, its neoclassic structure seamlessly restored to period opulence, its vast waterfront grounds as gracefully manicured as the estate of a country manor. It opened in 1861 as
the Beau-Rivage (the Palace wing and Renaissance cupola were added
in 1908), but every inch of marble, crystal, and polished mahogany
sparkles like new. The Palace was renovated from the roots up in 1994
(to the tune of 25 million francs): Rooms now have remote light controls, doorbells, maid lights, towel heaters, piped-in music over the tub
and walk-in shower, and phones sprouting from every surface—as
well as classic comforts: wing chairs, Oriental rugs, and balconies
with lake views. Among the facilities are a variety of first-class restaurants, including the gourmet La Rotonde, and both a disco and a
dance bar in the nightclub Janus. ⊠ *Chemin de Beau-Rivage, CH-1000
Ouchy 6,* ☎ *021/613–33–33,* ⅎⅩ *021/613–33–34. 340 beds. 3 restaurants (jacket and tie in La Rotonde), 3 bars, pool, beauty salon, sauna,
2 tennis courts, exercise room, jogging, dance club, piano, playground.
AE, DC, MC, V.*

$$$$ ⊞ **Lausanne Palace.** There are two Palaces in town: This Edwardian
landmark—considerably smaller than the Beau-Rivage and distinctly
urban in setting and style—stands on a hill high over the lake, with
layers of city scenery draped behind. It faces a city street, so to take
advantage of its views you need a back room—though three-quarters
of the rooms have balconies. The room decor varies from Empire reproduction to cool modern, and a few rooms retain such fine architectural details as inlaid wood and marble fireplaces. The restaurant,
Le Tinguley, serves ambitious French cuisine. ⊠ *Rue du Grand Chêne
7–9, CH-1002,* ☎ *021/331–31–31,* ⅎⅩ *021/323–25–71. 260 beds.
Restaurant, bar, beauty salon, sauna, fitness center. AE, DC, MC, V.*

$$$–$$$$ ⊞ **Royal Savoy.** Guests here not only stay in an enormous Victorian
★   castle but also enjoy a broad, private landscaped garden and park, with
outdoor swimming pool, terrace restaurant, and strolling musicians.

The rooms themselves are lovely—something more expensive hotels often seem unable to achieve—with discreet florals and jewel tones, delicate period reproduction desks and chairs, and French doors that open onto balconies over the lawns and lake. ☒ *Av. d'Ouchy 40, CH-1000,* ☎ *021/614–88–88,* ℻ *021/614–88–78. 170 beds. 2 restaurants (reservations advised), bar, pool. AE, DC, MC, V.*

$$$ ⊞ **Agora.** Certainly one of the most novel lodgings in Lausanne—and
★ in Switzerland—this hotel seems a vision, almost a hallucination. Built from scratch in 1987, it sits like a landed spaceship on an otherwise ordinary city block. From its sculptural marble facade to its high-tech bathrooms, it is decked in metallic tones and cool blues; even the vinyl upholstery has a silvery glow. All rooms have air-conditioning, videos in four languages, windows that open, and wet bars—and the light fixtures are Michael Graves–cum–Jetsons. The cool-tone restaurant features contemporary, market-fresh cuisine. ☒ *Av. du Rond-Point 9, CH-1006,* ☎ *021/617–12–11,* ℻ *021/616–26–05. 180 beds. Restaurant, bar, minibars, in-room VCRs. Restaurant closed Sat. and Sun; in winter, Sat.–Mon. AE, DC, MC, V.*

$$$–$$$$ ⊞ **La Résidence.** Within three graceful 18th- and 19th-century villas
★ near the waterfront at Ouchy, this gracious and polished small hotel complex has been modernized without ruffling its gentility or disturbing its graceful stone arches, marble floors, or discreet gardens. You may think you're in a country manor—especially in the rooms that overlook the Beau-Rivage's park. Room decor was brought up to state-of-the-art in 1993, with fresh chintz and plush. There's an outdoor pool tucked into the arbored garden. Fresh flowers and personal service from the small staff make this the pleasant antithesis of a grand-hotel experience. ☒ *Pl. du Port 15, CH-1006,* ☎ *021/617–77–11,* ℻ *021/617–06–67. 87 beds. Restaurant, pool. AE, DC, MC, V.*

$$$ ⊞ **Alpha.** Under the same management as the Agora, this is another architectural statement, all exposed concrete, walnut-grain Formica, and orange Scandinavian patterns. As the Agora will in a few years, this hotel shows its age—but the baths are fresh nonetheless, and there are VCRs available, as well as outlets for fax machines and computers. It's close to the train station and the place St-François. ☒ *Rue du Petit-Chêne 34, CH-1003,* ☎ *021/323–01–31,* ℻ *021/323–01–45. 250 beds. 2 restaurants, no-smoking rooms. AE, DC, MC, V.*

$$$ ⊞ **Château d'Ouchy.** Here, you pay for the privilege of staying in a 12th-century castle that was converted into a pseudo-medieval hotel during the 19th century. The interiors are dated-modern and a little faded, and the glassed-in terrace restaurant is like most others on the waterfront. If you really want medieval atmosphere, spring for the deluxe $$$$ top tower room, which has wraparound views through Romanesque windows. There's a Parisian-style brasserie and a popular waterfront veranda with pasta and pizzas. ☒ *Pl. du Port 2, CH-1006,* ☎ *021/616–74–51,* ℻ *021/617–51–37. 76 beds. 2 restaurants, bar, café, dancing. AE, DC, MC, V.*

$$$ ⊞ **De la Paix.** This business-class hotel in the center of town has all the amenities of a Best Western property and wonderful lakeside views. The rooms on the lake are done in warm shades of pumpkin and terra-cotta; those on the backstreet side are considerably humbler. ☒ *Av. Benjamin-Constant 5, CH-1002,* ☎ *021/320–71–71,* ℻ *021/323–02–07. 214 beds. Restaurant, bar, café. AE, DC, MC, V.*

$$$ ⊞ **Mövenpick Radisson.** This is a pleasant business-style hotel across the street from a new marina built along Lac Léman. It's one of the nicer and newest of several hotels that stretch along the lake in Ouchy and is a five-minute drive from city center. Rooms, styled by Laura Ashley, are spacious for a European hotel, but those facing the lake can be noisy. A generous buffet breakfast in one of the three restaurants is included in the price. ✉ *Av. de Rhodanie 4, CH-1000*, ☎ *021/617–21–21*, FAX *021/616–15–27. 470 beds. 3 restaurants, bar, no-smoking rooms, sauna, fitness center. AE, MC, V.*

$$ ▦ **Angleterre.** A plaque by the door says Lord Byron wrote *The Prisoner of Chillon* here, and it looks as if it hasn't been kept up since. Behind the classic symmetry of the 18th-century facade, you'll find chipped mix-and-match furniture, rumpled carpet, and postwar bathrooms. Nevertheless, the terrace café is popular, and above, each shuttered window opens directly onto the lake. The view might inspire you to poetry, too. ✉ *Pl. du Port 9, CH-1006*, ☎ *021/616–41–45*, FAX *021/616–80–75. 55 beds. Restaurant, café. AE, DC, MC, V.*

$$ **City.** Under the same management as the Agora and the Alpha, this once-faded urban hotel, at the hub of downtown crossroads, has undergone a profound and daring renovation, transforming itself from a steam-heated dump into a spectacular architectural showcase with curving chrome planes, a two-way escalator, and breathtaking views of the city, especially from the glassed-in breakfast room. Slick and soundproof, with fresh duvets, pink tile baths, videos, hair dryers, and room service, the City is a model for its peers. ✉ *Rue Caroline 5, CH-1007*, ☎ *021/320–21–41*, FAX *021/320–21–49. 105 beds. Restaurant, bar, in-room VCRs. AE, DC, MC, V.*

$$ ▦ **Des Voyageurs.** In a narrow town house in the old town, this is a comfortable, friendly hotel, with fresh decor and impeccable maintenance. Although it was renovated in 1994 to provide more modern services (copy machines, fax machines, VCRs), Victorian details are still in evidence; the oak stairways, stained glass, and Victorian breakfast room are just enough to keep you interested in what could have been an anonymous urban space. ✉ *Rue Grand-St-Jean 19, CH-1003*, ☎ *021/323–19–02*, FAX *021/323–69–33. 62 beds. Breakfast rooms, no-smoking rooms. AE, DC, MC, V.*

$$ ▦ **Elite.** Directly uphill from the train station on a surprisingly quiet ★ street, this hotel is a tranquil little enclave, and most rooms have a view of fruit trees and a garden. Ask for a fourth-floor room for a spectacular lake view. The hotel has been in one family for 50 years, and it shows—from the solid renovation and proud modern touches (electric doors, piped-in music) to the squeaky-clean maintenance. There are kitchenettes available. ✉ *Av. Ste-Luce 1, CH-1003*, ☎ *021/320–23–61*, FAX *021/320–39–63. 55 beds. Breakfast room, no-smoking rooms. AE, DC, MC, V.*

$ ▦ **Regina.** This tiny old lodging in the middle of the old town has spruced up its public areas, although room decor is still mix-and-match and fabrics are unrelated. The back rooms are quiet, with roofline views, and the management is friendly. Rooms without bath here are among the cheapest in town. ✉ *Rue Grand-St-Jean 18, CH-1003*, ☎ *021/320–24–41*, FAX *021/320–25–29. 55 beds. Breakfast room. MC, V.*

Outdoor Activities and Sports

SAILING

La Nautique has a clubhouse, changing rooms, and a crane (☎ 021/616–00–23). Vidy, a port just west of Ouchy, has the **Ecole de Voile de Vidy,** a sailing school with rentals (☎ 021/617–90–00).

SKATING

Five open-air skating rinks in Lausanne stay open from October to March: **Patinoire de Monchoisi** (✉ Av. du Servain 30, ☎ 021/616–10–62), which has 35,000 square feet of surface, **Patinoire de la Pontaise** (✉ Rte. Plaines-du-Loup 11, ☎ 021/646–81–63), and the three rinks operated by **Centre Intercommunal de Glace de Malley** (✉ Chemin du Viaduc 14, ☎ 021/624–21–22).

SWIMMING

In Lausanne, the **Piscine de Monchoisi,** a swimming pool (⊠ Av. du Servan 30, ☎ 021/616−10−62) has artificial waves; it's open from May through August. **Bellerive Beach** (⊠ Av. de Rhodanie 23, ☎ 021/617−81−31) has access to the lake and three pools, one Olympic-size, plus generous lawns and a self-service restaurant. The covered pool at **Mon-Repos** (⊠ Av. du Tribunal-Fédéral 4, ☎ 021/323−45−67) stays open year-round.

Nightlife and the Arts

Lausanne is one of the arts capitals of Switzerland, sharing with Geneva the **Orchestre de la Suisse Romande** and hosting the great ballet company of **Maurice Béjart** since his exodus from Brussels. Tickets to arts events are generally sold through the Lausanne Convention and Tourist Office (⊠ Av. de Rhodanie 2, ☎ 021/617−18−50); the tourist office's calendar of monthly events, as well as the publication *Reg'art* (published bimonthly), offers information on upcoming activities. Check out the daily newspaper *24 Heures* for listings as well.

BARS AND LOUNGES

One of the most chic and lively gathering spots in Lausanne is the **Café Beau-Rivage** (☎ 021/613−33−30), in the luxury hotel of the same name; there's an American-style bar with stools, the wicker-and-marble decor of a Parisian brasserie, and live music nightly. The Lausanne Palace serves drinks in its lobby-bar **Le Relais** (☎ 021/320−37−11). The Royal Savoy serves drinks at one end of its bowered garden restaurant, **La Terrasse** (☎ 021/616−64−00), throughout the warm season, with guitarists or small ensembles; its interior bar is an intimate, armchaired lounge.

CLASSICAL MUSIC

Théâtre-Municipal Lausanne (⊠ Av. du Théâtre 12, ☎ 021/312−64−33), like a tattered bomb shelter deep underground in the heart of Lausanne, is one of the city's central performance venues for concerts, operas, and ballets, including the riveting experiments of Maurice Béjart. The **Beaulieu** (⊠ Av. des Bergières 10, ☎ 021/643−21−11) hosts full-scale performances of orchestral music, opera, and dance in its larger hall.

DANCING

The Beau-Rivage Palace in Ouchy has two rooms at **Janus** (☎ 021/613−33−38): a slick discotheque with a DJ and a video screen, and a more subdued dance room with live music. **Le Paddock** (⊠ Hotel Victoria, Av. de la Gare 46, ☎ 021/320−57−75) is a popular discotheque. The discotheque **La Griffe** (⊠ Pl. de la Gare 2, ☎ 021/311−02−62) has a disc jockey, video screen and light show. **Grand Café** (⊠ Casino de Montbenon, Allée E.-Ansermet 3, ☎ 021/323−82−51) offers reggae, rock, and punk music live. In summer, **Voile d'or** (⊠ Av. Emile-Jacques Dalcroze 9, Vidy, ☎ 021/617−80−11) offers open-air dancing by the lake, with the twinkling lights of Evian in full view.

JAZZ

Au Boulevard 1900 (⊠ Blvd. de Grancy 51, ☎ 021/616−54−43) has jazz Friday and Saturday after 9 PM. There's weekend jazz at **Grizzly** (⊠ Hotel de l'Ours, Rue du Bugnon 2, ☎ 021/320−49−71). **Le Chorus** has a jazz cellar (⊠ Av. Mon Repos 3, ☎ 021/323−22−33).

NIGHTCLUBS

La Belle Epoque (⊠ Rue de Bourg 17, ☎ 021/312−11−49) has "sexy table dance" and girls, girls, girls. The Lausanne Palace's upscale **Brummell** (⊠ Rue du Grand-Chêne 7, ☎ 021/312−09−20) has dancing and a cabaret.

THEATER

Théâtre Vidy-Lausanne (⊠ Av. Emile-Jacques-Dalcroze 5, ☎ 021/617–45–45), west of Lausanne's center, presents classical and contemporary theater in French. **Théâtre Kléber-Méleau** (⊠ Chemin de l'Usine-à-Gaz 9, Renens, ☎ 021/625–84–00) at Vidy, offers a variety of French-language theater, old and new.

Shopping

DEPARTMENT STORES

In Lausanne, **Bon Génie** (⊠ Pl. St-François, ☎ 021/320–48–11) carries a broad and varied line of upscale goods. **Innovation** (⊠ Rue Centrale at rue du Pont, ☎ 021/320–19–11) has a supermarket and a restaurant. **Placette** (⊠ Rue St-Laurent, ☎ 021/320–67–11) is a large chain with a variety of inexpensive goods. **Jemoli** (⊠ Rue du Pont 5, ☎ 021/320–19–11) is a mid-priced department store.

DISTRICTS

The main shopping circle centers on place St-François, rue St-François, rue de Bourg, and rue du Grand-Pont. Less expensive shopping is along rue St-Laurent and rue de l'Ale.

MARKETS

There are fruit-and-vegetable markets in Lausanne along rue de l'Ale, rue de Bourg, and place de la Riponne every Wednesday and Saturday morning. Place de la Palud adds a flea market to its Wednesday and Saturday produce market and is the site of a handicraft market the first Friday of the month from March through December.

BOOKS

Librairie Payot (⊠ Pl. Pépinet 4 and Rue de Bourg 1, ☎ 021/341–33–31) carries mass-market French books and a good assortment in English.

LINENS

Langenthal (⊠ Rue de Bourg 8, ☎ 021/323–44–02) is the central source for towels, sheets, and embroidered handkerchiefs, mainly Swiss made. **Drafil** (⊠ Pl. St-Laurent, ☎ 021/323–50–44) carries a lovely line of trousseau goods, all made in Suisse Romande. **Coupy** (⊠ Madeleine 4, ☎ 021/321–78–66) has a large selection of duvets, pillows, and linens.

TOBACCO

For Davidoff cigars and fine smokers' novelties, go to **Besson** (⊠ Rue de Bourg 22, ☎ 021/312–67–88).

TOYS

Franz Carl Weber is the main Swiss source for international toys (⊠ Rue de Bourg 23, ☎ 021/320–14–71). **Davidson Formation** (⊠ Rue Grand St-Jean 20, ☎ 021/323–25–22) has a unique collection of educational toys and English-language books.

WATCHES

The place St-François has most of the watch shops. **Bucherer** (⊠ Pl. St-François 5, ☎ 021/320–63–54) sells Rolex and Piaget. **Junod** (⊠ Pl. St-François 8, ☎ 021/312–27–45) carries Blancpain. **Grumser** (⊠ Rue St-François 11, ☎ 021/312–48–26) specializes Baume & Mercier. **Roman Mayer** (⊠ Pl. St-François 12 bis, ☎ 021/312–23–16) carries Audemars Piguet, Ebel, and Omega.

WOMEN'S CLOTHES

Naphta Line (⊠ Rue Curtat, below the cathedral, ☎ 021/312–62–24) carries a novel line of exotic print fabrics, made-to-measure clothing and bead jewelry. **Kathleen Davidson** (⊠ Rue de la Mercerie 5, ☎ 021/311–06–66) carries old-Austrian wools by Geiger, plus English woolens and Scottish cashmeres.

LAVAUX VINEYARDS AND MONTREUX

To the east of Lausanne stretches the **Lavaux,** a remarkably beautiful region of vineyards that rise up the hillsides all the way from Pully, on the outskirts of Lausanne, to Montreux—a distance of 24 kilometers (15 miles). Brown-roofed stone villages in the Savoy style, old defense towers, and small baronial castles stud the green-and-black landscape. The vineyards, enclosed within low stone walls, slope so steeply that all the work there has to be done by hand. Insecticides, fungicides, and manures are carried in baskets, and containers are strapped to men's backs. Harvest in mid-October is a time for real rejoicing, with the women picking the heavy, round fruit and the men carrying the loads to the nearest road, emptying them into vats, and driving them by tractor to the nearest press. Some Lavaux vintages are excellent and in great demand, but unfortunately, as with so much of Switzerland's wine, the yield is small and the product is never exported. In summer, especially on weekends, you'll find some of the private châteaux-vignobles open for tastings and, of course, sales.

En Route The scenic **Corniche road** stretches some 17 kilometers (10 miles) through Lavaux, threading above the waterfront from Lausanne to Vevey, between the autoroute and the lakeside Route 9. This is Switzerland at its most Franco-European, reminiscent in its small-scale, humble way of the Riviera or the hilltowns of Alsace. You'll careen around hairpin turns through villages' narrow cobbled streets, with the Savoy Alps glowing across the sparkling lake and the Dents du Midi looming ahead, hand-painted signs beckoning you to stop and taste the wines from the vine-rows that stripe the hills above and below the road.

Stop to gaze at roadside overlooks, or wander down a side lane into the fields of **Riex, Epesses, Rivaz,** or the Dézaley, the sources of some of Switzerland's loveliest white wines, and typically magical little Vaudois villages. Toward the end of the road is **Chexbres,** a spick-and-span summer lake resort about 600 meters (2,000 feet) above sea level.

St-Saphorin

⑲ *15 km (9 mi) southeast of Lausanne.*

At the end of the Corniche Road just east of Vevey, St-Saphorin is perched just above the water. With its impossibly narrow, steep cobbled streets and ancient wine makers' houses crowded around fountains and crooked alleys, this is a village that merits a stop.

Dining

$$ ✕ **Auberge de l'Onde.** Once the main stagecoach *relais* between the
★ Simplon and Geneva, this is a vineyard inn out of central casting, groaning with history and heady with atmosphere: Igor Stravinsky and Charlie Chaplin were among the artists loyal to its charms. The ambiance is equally seductive in its tiny wood-panel café, where locals read the papers over a chipped pitcher of "St-Saph" and a cheap plate of butter-fried lake perch, or in its dainty beamed dining room lined with ancient crockery and lit with grape-wood sconces. The latter is worth the splurge, with silver-platter service (two helpings) of very local *omble chevalier* (salmon trout) in sorrel sauce and bubbling hot fruit gratins, served by white-bloused waitresses who hover with a good bottle of the local *recolte* (vintage) while day-tripping connoisseurs sniff and roll the almond-perfumed wine over their tongues. ⊠ *CH-1813,* ☎ *021/921–30–83. AE, DC, MC, V.*

Vevey

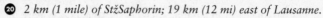

② *2 km (1 mile) of StžSaphorin; 19 km (12 mi) east of Lausanne.*

This atmospheric waterfront town was the setting for Anita Brookner's evocative 1985 novel *Hotel du Lac,* about a woman retreating to a lake resort to write; her heroine was attracted to the site, in part, because of its slightly stuffy 19th-century ways. In the 1870s, Henry James captured this mood of prim grace while writing (and setting) *Daisy Miller* in the Hotel des Trois Couronnes. Indeed, despite its virtual twinning with glamorous Montreux, Vevey retains its air of isolation, of retirement, of Old World gentility. Loyal guests have been returning for generations to gaze at the **Dent d'Oche** (2,222 meters/7,288 feet) across the water in France and make sedate steamer excursions into Montreux and Lausanne. Yet Vevey offers more atmosphere in its shuttered old town, better museums and landmarks, and more native activity in its wine market than cosmopolitan Montreux can muster.

Vevey is a marketing center for wines of the region, and the local white is sold at its Saturday market on the waterfront alongside fruits and vegetables; you buy your own glass and taste *à volonté* (at will). Vevey is also the hometown of Nestlé, which dominates the world market in chocolate and milk products; its laboratories and main factory are based here.

Among the notables attracted to live or sojourn in Vevey were numbered Graham Greene, Victor Hugo, Jean-Jacques Rousseau (who set much of *La Nouvelle Heloise* here), Dostoyevsky, the French artist Gustave Courbet, Oskar Kokoschka, Charlie and Oona Chaplain (buried in the cemetery at Corsier), and Swiss native Edouard Jeanneret "Le Corbusier."

★ Le Corbusier's **Villa le Lac,** a low-slung, one-story white house built directly on the Vevey waterfront, was constructed for his parents in 1923; it remains unaltered, with his original furnishings and details preserved within. Shingled in corrugated sheet metal, with white-metal railed balcony looking over the water and a "birdhouse" chimney in molded concrete, it is typically sculptural, and, in a modest way, visionary. ⊠ *On the western outskirts of Vevey, just west of the marina, directly opposite its official sign,* ☎ *021/923–53–63.* ۞ *Guided tours Wed. 2– 5; closed mid-Nov.–mid-Mar.*

A dominant financial power in the region, Nestlé sponsors an unusual museum in Vevey, the **Alimentarium.** This well-funded, unusually presented exhibition addresses three aspects of food and food production: science (the food chain), ethnology (food in different world cultures), and history (eating habits through the ages). Displays are in a grand 19th-century mansion; in addition, there are films, computers, and— if the subject matter makes you feel a bit peckish—a snack bar. Though many of the displays are esoteric and even unfocussed, the downstairs interactive exhibits on nutrition—based on museum goers' personal statistics—are straightforward and informative. ⊠ *Quai Perdonnet,* ☎ *021/924–41–11.* ⊡ *5 SF.* ۞ *Tues.–Sun. 10–noon and 2–5.*

The **Musée Jenisch** owes its considerable inventory of the works of the Expressionist Oskar Kokoschka to his retirement on Vevey's shores. ⊠ *Av. de la Gare 2,* ☎ *021/921–29–50,* ⊡ *9 SF–12 SF,* ۞ *Tues.–Sun 10:30–noon and 2–5:30.*

The **Musée historique du Vieux Vevey** occupies a grand 16th-century manor house, briefly home to Charlotte de Lengefeld, wife of Friedrich von Schiller. It retains some original furnishings as well as collections of arms, art, keys, and wine makers' paraphernalia. ⊠ *Rue du Château 2,* ☎ *021/921–07–22.* ⊡ *4 SF.* ۞ *Tues.–Sun. 10:30–noon and 2–5:30.*

Dining and Lodging

$–$$$$ ✕ **Café/Restaurant du Raisin.** This genial dining spot facing the ani-
★ mated marketplace, where wine makers and wine lovers share the
local wares, offers two diverse experiences. You can lounge on the ar-
bored terrace or in the snug tile café, enjoying a light blackboard-menu
lunch—tomme pannée and a big mixed salad—or a plat du jour that's
a notch above the usual café fare (duck à l'orange, cassoulet of kid-
neys in mustard sauce). Or you can head upstairs to the hushed, ex-
clusive restaurant, for pricier, more ambitious cuisine du marché.
There's an encyclopedic wine list, with plenty of local choices. ⊠ *Pl.
du Marché,* ☎ *021/921–10–28. AE, MC, V. Closed Sun. dinner, Mon.*

$$$$ 🏨 **Des Trois Couronnes.** Honeycombed by dramatic atrium stairwells
and thick with alabaster and *faux marbre* (fake marble), this regal land-
mark was Henry James's home base in writing (and setting) the novella
Daisy Miller. (The antiheroine, on her grand tour of Europe's finest,
strayed unchaperoned to Chillon and, having thus flown in the face
of Victorian propriety, met a richly deserved demise.) In filming his ver-
sion of the story, Peter Bogdanovich cast the hotel as itself: Its halls
are indeed evocative of an era of grand tours, and even guest rooms
still exhibit period sensibility. A vast lakefront terrace overlooks the
pollards, the promenade, and the steamers that still carry their cargo
of headstrong women toward Chillon. ⊠ *Rue d'Italie 49, CH-1800,*
☎ *021/921–30–05,* 🖷 *021/922–72–80. 109 beds. Restaurant (reser-
vations essential), bar, café, beauty salon. AE, DC, MC, V.*

$$$ 🏨 **Du Lac.** Anita Brookner wrote and set her novel *Hotel du Lac* in
this subdued relative of the Trois Couronnes, and its readers may be
disappointed to find the Best Western Swiss property lacking the dis-
cretion and refinement but still flaunting the stuffiness she so precisely
described. Though some rooms are newly done up with prim florals
or chic burled wood, others retain the kelly-green carpet and mustard
chenille of another era in decorating. The lakeside facilities are the hotel's
greatest attraction, as there's a graceful sheltered restaurant, a garden,
and a pool, all just across the street from the waterfront. ⊠ *Rue d'I-
talie 1, CH-1800,* ☎ *021/921–10–41,* 🖷 *021/921–75–08. 100 beds.
Restaurant, café, pool. AE, DC, MC, V.*

$–$$ 🏨 **Des Negociants.** Handy to the market, in the old town by the lake,
this is a comfortable, no-nonsense lodging. Its arcaded, shuttered facade
is in sharp contrast to the laminated, four-square interiors, but the top
floor has a dormer room of knotty pine that is suitable for families, and
all baths are tiled. The restaurant serves standard brasserie fare, cooked
by the owner himself. ⊠ *Rue du Conseil 27, CH-1800,* ☎ *021/922–
70–11,* 🖷 *021/921–34–24. 45 beds. Restaurant. AE, DC, MC, V.*

Outdoor Activities and Sports

Pedal boats for splashing along the sunny waterfront can be rented from
José Justo (⊠ Pl. du Marché, ☎ 021/921–38–80).

Montreux

㉑ *4 km (2 mi) northwest of Vevey; 21 km (13 mi) northwest of Lausanne.*

Petite Montreux could be called the Cannes of Lac Léman—though it
might raise an eyebrow at the slur. Spilling down steep hillsides into a
sunny south-facing bay, its waterfront thick with magnolias, cypress,
and palm trees, the historic resort earns its reputation as the capital of
the Swiss Riviera; unlike the French Riviera, it has managed, despite
overwhelming crowds of conventioneers, to keep up appearances. Its
Edwardian-French dignity has survived considerable development,
and though there are plenty of harsh new high-rises with parking-garage

aesthetics, its mansarded landmarks still unfurl orange awnings to shield millionaires from subtropical sun.

The site where Stravinsky composed *Petrouchka* and *Le Sacre du Printemps,* and where Vladimir Nabokov resided in splendor, Montreux and its suburbs have attracted artists and literati for 200 years: Byron, Shelley, Tolstoy, Hans Christian Andersen, and Flaubert were drawn to its lush shoreline. When its **casino** opened in 1883, tourism began in earnest. (For trivia fans: When the casino caught fire during a Frank Zappa concert in 1971, Deep Purple commemorated the event with the song "Smoke on the Water.") Today, Montreux is best known for its history-making **jazz festival,** which takes place each July; with Vevey, it also sponsors a **classical music festival** in September.

★ ㉒ Certainly the greatest attraction at Montreux and one of Switzerland's must-sees is the **Château de Chillon,** the awe-inspiring 12th-century castle that rears out of the water at Veytaux, less than 3 kilometers (1¾ miles) down the road from and within sight of Montreux. On Roman foundations, Chillon was built under the direction of Duke Peter of Savoy with the help of military architects from Plantagenet England. For a long period it served as a state prison, and one of its shackled guests was François Bonivard, who supported the Reformation and enraged the Savoys. He spent six years in this prison, chained most of the time to a pillar in the dungeon, before being released by the Bernese in 1536.

While living near Montreux, Lord Byron visited Chillon and was so transported by its atmosphere and by Bonivard's grim sojourn that he was inspired to write his famous poem *The Prisoner of Chillon.* Like a true tourist, he carved his name on a pillar in Bonivard's dungeon; that graffito is protected under a plaque today.

Visitors to Chillon now must file placidly from restored chamber to restored turret, often waiting at doorways for entire busloads of fellow tourists to pass. Yet the restoration is so evocative and so convincing, with its tapestries, carved fireplaces, period ceramics and pewters, and elaborate wooden ceilings, that even the jaded castle hound may become as carried away as Byron was. While you're waiting your turn, you can gaze out the narrow windows over the sparkling, lapping water and remember Mark Twain, who thought Bonivard didn't have it half bad. ⊠ *CH-1820,* ☎ *021/963–39–12.* ⊡ *5.50 SF.* ☉ *Nov.–Feb., daily 10–noon and 1:30–4; Mar., daily 10–noon and 1:30–4:45; Apr.–June and Sept., daily 9–5:45; July–Aug., daily 9–6:15; Oct., daily 10–4:45.*

Dining and Lodging

$$ ✕ **Du Pont.** In the old town high on the hill over Montreux's honky-
★ tonk waterfront, this quiet, old local restaurant-café takes its food and its customers seriously. Guests may either let their hair down with jean-clad friends in the smoky café or enjoy full-service and pink linens in the lovely dining room upstairs. Suit your whim: The menu and the prices are exactly the same, including a cheap daily special—and whether you order them upstairs or down, the German-born chef (who spent years in Italy) will personally grate your white Alba truffle. There are big portions and definitive versions of veal piccata, pastas, steaks and game, and toothesome risotto. ⊠ *rue du Pont 12,* ☎ *021/963–22–49. AE, DC, MC, V.*

$$$$ ▥ **L'Ermitage.** Freestanding on its own waterfront-garden grounds, this
★ genteel, intimate retreat offers top-drawer *haute gastronomie* and a few luxurious rooms upstairs. Broad windows take in full lake views, and a summer terrace allows diners to enjoy their meal *alfresco.* Chef Eti-

enne Krebs's exceptional cuisine may include ray-wing in saffron-potato emulsion with oil and smoked tomato bouillon, breast of duck in a celery-root casserole, or hot chestnut soufflé with kirsch ice cream. The ultimate splurge: his seven-course *laissez-faire* menu, a parade of delicately orchestrated surprises. ✉ CH-1815, ☎ 022/964–44–11. AE, DC, MC. V. ☾ *Main restaurant closed Sun., Mon.; garden restaurant open daily in summer.*

$$$$ 🏨 **Le Montreux Palace.** Dominating the hillside over the Grand-Rue and the waterfront, the silver mansards and yellow awnings of this vast institution flag the Palace as a landmark, though its aristocratic origins have been compromised considerably in an era of business-convention crowds. It was first opened in 1906, a colossal Belle Epoque folly of stained glass, frescoes, and flamboyant molded stucco; much of that excess has been tempered with age and updated with touches of modern glitz, including a glossy, modern shopping arcade, a pavilion across the street (accessible by tunnel) with two nightclubs, and Switzerland's first Harry's New York Bar. The florid, formal Restaurant du Cygne serves from separate Swiss and seafood menus. Lakeside rooms are appropriately posh; mountainside rooms, in the back, miss out on the hotel's raison d'être: a commanding Lac Léman view. ✉ *Grand-Rue 100, CH-1820,* ☎ *021/962–12–12,* 🖷 *021/962–17–17. 500 beds. 5 restaurants (reservations essential), 3 bars, no-smoking rooms, pool, beauty salon, tennis court. AE, DC, MC, V.*

$$$ 🏨 **Suisse et Majestic.** Despite its grand Victorian facade, this is a business-class hotel, offering standard services to groups and conferences. Renovation has revived some of its fin de siècle appeal, even imposing period details to enhance the vaguely ice-cream-parlorish theme. The results: a comfortable lodging that might have popped up anywhere—though it's in the heart of old Montreux. ✉ *Av. des Alpes 43, CH-1820,* ☎ *021/963–51–81,* 🖷 *021/963–35–06. 250 beds. Restaurant, bar, café. AE, DC, MC, V.*

$$ 🏨 **Hostellerie du Lac.** This broad, quirky old Swiss-Victorian house
★ stands directly on the waterfront promenade and offers smashing lake views from the front rooms. The decor is eccentric, with fussy, flocked Victoriana jumbled in with mixed-'60s styles; some rooms have a fireplace or a balcony. The ambience is casual and personal. Downstairs, the popular restaurant and front-porch terrace café serve solid renditions of old favorites and cheap daily plates. ✉ *Rue du Quai 12, CH-1820,* ☎ *021/963–32–71,* 🖷 *021/963–18–35. 18 beds. Restaurant, café. MC, V.*

$$ 🏨 **Masson.** If you're traveling by car or you enjoy being away from
★ the downtown resort scene, look up this demure little inn on a hillside in Veytaux, between Chillon and Montreux. Since it was built in 1829, it's had only four owners, and the current family takes pride in its genteel period decor and up-to-date technology, including color television with remote headphones so one guest won't disturb another. There are floral prints, pristine linens, buffed parquet, and expansive lake views from the numerous balconies. The breakfast buffet is generous, with homemade jams. A simple evening meal is served for half-board guests. ✉ *Rue Bonivard 5, CH-1820,* ☎ *021/963–81–61,* 🖷 *021/963–81–66. 60 beds. Restaurant (for guests and evenings only; reservations essential). AE, MC, V.*

Outdoor Activities and Sports

BOATING

Pedal boats are popular along Montreux-Vevey's waterfront; rentals are available at **Albert Morisod** (✉ by the convention center, ☎ 021/963–39–36) and **Jean Morisod** (✉ at the quai du Casino, ☎ 021/963–31–60).

SAILING

At Montreux, **Cercle de la Voile de Montreux,** the local sailing club, is located in nearby Clarens (☎ 021/964–38–98).

SWIMMING

In Montreux, **La Maladaire** (☎ 021/964–57–03) in adjoining Clarens has an Olympic-size indoor pool. The **casino** (⊠ Rue du Théâtre 9, ☎ 021/963–53–31) has a pool on an outdoor terrace with a bar.

WATER SPORTS

Montreux offers guests of its hotels free and supervised use of its waterfront facilities for windsurfing and waterskiing; afternoons, there's a fee at the **Ski-nautique Club** (☎ 021/963–44–56).

Nightlife and the Arts

Montreux's famous festivals and arts events are listed in a seasonal booklet published by the tourist office; tickets are sold from its booth at the waterfront. The renowned **Festival International de Jazz** takes place every July; its more sedate, classical **Festival International de Musique** shares venues with Vevey from August through October. For tickets to these popular events, contact the Montreux tourist office (⊠ rue du Théâtre, CH-1820) as far in advance as possible. In summer, Montreux offers a variety of free outdoor concerts from its bandstand on the waterfront near the landing stage.

BARS

In Montreux, the Montreux Palace (⊠ Grand-Rue 100, ☎ 021/962–12–12) now has a **Harry's Bar** with a pianist after 5. The **Royal Plaza** (⊠ Grand-Rue 97, ☎ 021/963–51–31) has a piano bar with jazz in the summer and an American-style bar in the lobby.

CASINOS

The **Casino** (⊠ Rue du Théâtre 9, ☎ 021/963–53–31) at Montreux, established in 1883, was burned in 1971 and rebuilt in 1975; now you'll find dancing, strip shows, live country music (in a Western saloon), and a new billiards room. The usual 5 SF gambling limit applies.

DANCING

In Montreux, you can dance on the **Bateau Dansant,** which departs from the landing stage on Wednesday at 7:25 and 9, throughout July and August. **Museum** (⊠ Rue de la Gare 40, ☎ 021/963–16–62) is a discotheque in the old town. **Caesar's** (⊠ Grand-Rue 55, ☎ 021/963–75–59) offers dancing by the lakefront.

NIGHTCLUBS

In Montreux, **Hungaria** (⊠ Av. Nestlé 19, ☎ 021/963–40–74) has striptease shows next door to its all-night restaurant. **The Casino** (⊠ Rue du Théâtre 9, ☎ 021/963–53–31) has a cabaret.

OFF THE BEATEN PATH

BLONAY-CHAMBY RAILROAD – The allure for travelers to Montreux is not limited to the shoreline scene. Out of Montreux, a number of railways climb into the heights, which, in late spring, are carpeted with an extravagance of wild narcissi. If you like model railroads, you will especially enjoy a trip on the Blonay-Chamby railroad, whose real steam-driven trains alternate with electric trains on weekends only between Blonay and Chamby above Montreux, with a stop at a small museum of railroad history in between. You can depart from either end; the trip takes about 20 minutes each way, not including a browse in the museum. ⊠ *Case Postale 366, CH-1001, Lausanne,* ☎ *021/943–21–21. Round-trip ticket: 12 SF. Trains run May–Oct., Sun. 9:40–6 and Sat. 2–6.*

LES AVANTS – The Montreux–Oberland–Bernois railway line (MOB) leads to the resort of Les Avants (970 meters/3,181 feet)—and then on to Château-d'Oex, Gstaad, and the Simmental (☞ Les Alpes Vaudoises, *below*). Noel Coward built his 1958 dream house in Les Avants; Ernest Hemingway wrote to family and friends of its magnificent daffodil show.

THE ALPES VAUDOISES

At the eastern tip of Lac Léman, the Alps on the French and Swiss sides close in on the Rhône, and the lakefront highways begin a gradual, ear-popping ascent as the scenery looms larger and the mountains rise around you. The high-altitude Alpine resorts of Villars, Leysin and Les Diablerets each have their charms for winter sports fans and summer hikers; a visit to any one of the three would suffice for a mountain retreat. On the other hand, the Pays-d'Enhaut, over the Col des Mosses, is a rustic, lower-altitude region surrounded by rocky ridges and velvet hillsides, flecked with snow and sprinkled with ancient carved-wood chalets; either Château-d'Oex or Rougemont would serve well as home base for a sojourn in this gentle resort area. You can make a beeline from one to another, but rail connections are limited and driving often torturous; you'd do well to choose one dreamy spot and stay put—by the fireplace, on the balcony—for as many days as your itinerary allows.

The resorts of the Vaud Alps, while anything but household words to most ski buffs, offer the bonus of a linkup with the sprawling Gstaad "Super Ski Region" (☞ Chapter 10), which takes in the entire Saanen Valley from Zweisimmen to Château-d'Oex and even dovetails with the parallel valley resorts of Adelboden and Lenk, justifying a visit for skiers who want to cover a lot of territory during their stay.

En Route   At **Roche,** on the highway between Villeneuve and Aigle, there's a massive 15th-century stone barn that was built by the monks of Grand St-Bernard, on a scale as big as an airplane hangar, and divided into three great pillared naves. The building itself would be worth the detour, but today—after extensive restorations—it houses the **Musée Suisse de l'Orgue** (Swiss Organ Museum), a vast collection of instruments that had been without the cathedral-scale space required for display until it arrived in this gargantuan barn. There's an ornate Louis XVI organ case, an 18th-century pedal-board, a neo-Gothic harmonium, and even an Emmental home organ. The curator leads three one-hour tours a day and demonstrates the instruments. ⊠ *Association des Amis du Musée Suisse de l'Orgue, Pl. St-François 5, CH-1003, Lausanne,* ☎ *021/320–02–77.* ▦ *Free.* ☉ *May–Oct., Tues.–Sun. 10–noon and 2–5.*

Aigle

❷❸ *17 km (10 mi) south of Montreux; 38 km (24 mi) southeast of Lausanne.*

On a smooth plain flanked by the sloping vineyards of the region of **Le Chablais,** Aigle is a scenic wine center with a museum devoted to wine. Its spired and turreted Savoy **castle,** originally built during the 13th century, was almost completely destroyed—and was then rebuilt—by the 15th-century Bernese.

The **Musée de la Vigne et du Vin** has a collection of casks, bottles, presses, and wine makers' tools attractively displayed within its wood-beam chambers. Some living quarters are reproduced, and there's even a collection of costumes worn over the centuries for the local Fête des Vignerons. ⊠ *CH-1860,* ☎ *025/26–21–30.* ▦ *6 SF.* ☉ *Apr.–Oct., daily 9–12:30 and 2–6; Nov.–Mar., tours by appointment.*

OFF THE
BEATEN PATH

SWISS VAPEUR PARC – Where the Rhône empties into Lac Léman, between Vaud and France, families may want to visit the Swiss Vapeur Parc (Swiss Steam Park), a miniature railway circuit laid out in a green park. There you can straddle the tiny models and cruise around a reduced-scale landscape. ⊠ CH-1897, Le Bouveret, ☎ 025/81–44–10. 🖃 8.50 SF (includes ride). ⊘ Mid-May–late Sept., weekdays 1:30–6, weekends 10–6; late Apr.–May and late Sept.–Oct., Wed. and weekends 1:30–6.

Villars-sur-Ollon

★ ㉔ *15 km (9 mi) southeast of Aigle; 53 km (33 mi) southeast of Lausanne.*

At 1,300 meters (4,264 feet), this welcoming ski center spreads comfortably along a sunny terrace, the craggy peaks of Les Diablerets (3,210 meters/10,528 feet) behind it, and before it a sweeping view over the Rhône Valley all the way to Mont Blanc. Balanced along its ridge and open to the vast space below, its busy little downtown—sports shops, cafés, resort hotels—tapers off quickly into open country. Though it's thriving with new constructions, Villars has a sense of tradition, and some of its family-owned hotels retain an air of mountain lodges rare these days in Switzerland. A network of lifts connecting with Les Diablerets make this a good choice for skiers or hikers who want to experience Suisse Romande relatively unspoiled.

Skiing

For serious skiers, Villars combines a pleasant balance of sophistication and Alpine isolation, offering some of the best-developed options and including a reasonably accessible link to Les Diablerets glacier. The main ski area over the village can be reached easily either by cable car to Roc d'Orsay (2,000 meters/6,560 feet) or by cog railway from the center to Bretaye; either site allows access to the lifts that fan out over a sunny bowl riddled with intermediate runs and off-trail challenges. From Bretaye, you also can take lifts up to Grand Chamossaire (2,120 meters/6,954 feet) for gentle, open runs or to Petit Chamossaire for a more taxing expert descent. Trails from Chaux Ronde and Chaux de Conches are easy enough for beginners, but the more advanced can find jumps and trees enough to keep them more than alert. Just beyond Villars, the linking resort of **Gryon** presents a few more options and a change of scenery, again with trails for all levels of skill. Villars, at 1,300 meters (4,264 feet), has 45 lifts, 120 kilometers (75 miles) of downhill runs, and 44 kilometers (27 miles) of cross-country trails.

Lodging

$$$–$$$$ 🏨 **Le Bristol.** This resort hotel rose from the ashes of an older landmark and—despite the Colorado-condo exterior and the jutting balcony for every room—is now furnished with a light, bright, and convincingly regional touch. The interiors are all-white with carved blond pine, and picture windows are angled to take in the views. There are good health facilities and a choice of attractive restaurants, including a terrace above the valley. Activities and theme events abound. ⊠ CH-1884, ☎ 025/36–11–36, 📠 025/35–10–36. 220 beds. 2 restaurants, bar, indoor pool, hot tub, sauna, exercise room, squash. AE, DC, MC, V.

$$ 🏨 **Alpe Fleurie.** From the minute you check in, you'll know this is a fam-
★ ily-run, family-oriented hotel: There are snapshots of kids and dogs over the reception desk. Launched in 1946 and maintained by the second generation, who live on the top floor, the hotel has been updated steadily, and the rooms show a thoughtful mix of modern textures and classic pine. It stands on the main street along the valley side, and south-facing

rooms have terrific views. ✉ *Av. Centrale, CH-1884,* ☎ *025/35–34–64,* ℻ *025/35–13–17. 30 beds. Restaurant, bar, café. AE, DC, MC, V.*

$$ ⚑ **Ecureuil.** Although there's a restaurant downstairs and a carnotzet
★ for fondue, nearly every room in this welcoming, family-run inn has
a kitchenette, so you can make yourself at home, mountain cabin–style.
Opened in 1947 and run by the son of the founder, the hotel has lots
of homey touches: books and magazines, swing sets, and a piano par-
lor. An older, stone-base chalet on the grounds offers bigger rooms; both
buildings stand across the street from the Bristol and therefore don't
have direct access to those Villars views. ✉ *Av. Centrale, CH-1884,*
☎ *025/35–27–95,* ℻ *025/35–42–05. 54 beds. Restaurant, café,*
kitchenettes, Ping-Pong. MC, V.

$$ ⚑ **La Renardière.** This group of three traditional chalets, set back
★ from the resort center and surrounded by tall firs, was opened as a hotel
in 1957 and still looks like a '50s mountain lodge, with its warm pine,
plaid curtains, and log bar. The lounges and sitting areas have fireplaces;
the rooms are simple and warm, done in pine and chenille. In the traditional restaurant, linens, crystal, and fresh flowers soften the rustic
edges, and there's a pleasant terrace café that serves good lunches
under the firs. ✉ *CH-1884,* ☎ *025/35–25–92,* ℻ *025/35–39–15.*
40 beds. Restaurant, bar, café. AE, DC, MC, V.

Outdoor Activities and Sports

GOLF

The precipitously sited **Golf Alpin** (☎ 025/35–42–14) has 18 holes.

SKATING

Non-skiers can amuse themselves at a centrally-located indoor **skating rink** (☎ 025/35–12–21).

SWIMMING

In the same building as the skating rink in Villars, there's an indoor
pool (☎ 025/35–21–28). There's an outdoor pool at the **Centre Sportif**
(☎ 025/35–19–69).

OFF THE **MINE DU SEL** – Children inured to the thrill of cable cars, narrow-gauge
BEATEN PATH railroads, and steam trains might brighten at a journey to the center of
the earth in the Mine de Sel (Salt Mine) at Bex, just off the southbound
Route 9. First dug in 1684, this ancient underground complex bores into
the mountain as far as Villars and covers some 50 subterranean kilometers (30 miles). After an introductory audiovisual show, you ride a narrow-gauge train into the depths and take a guided walk through the
works. Wear sturdy shoes and warm clothing, as the temperature stays
at 63° F year-round. ✉ *CH-1880, Bex,* ☎ *025/63-24-62.* ▣ *15 SF.
Prior booking essential, even for individuals.* ☉ *Apr.–mid-Nov., with 2¼-
hr-long tours leaving promptly at 10, 2, and 3.*

Les Diablerets

㉕ *19 km (12) mi northeast of Aigle; 59 km (37 mi) southwest of Lausanne.*

In summer, car travelers can cut along spectacular heights on a tiny
13%-grade road over the **Col de la Croix** (1,778 meters/5,832 feet) to
get from Villars to the small neighboring resort of Les Diablerets
(1,160 meters/3,806 feet). (Train travelers will have to descend to Bex
and backtrack to Aigle.) Les Diablerets lies at the base of the 3,209-
meter (10,525-foot) peak of the same name—which sheds the dramatic
3,000-meter (9,840-foot) glacier of the same name.

Skiing

The ski facilities at Les Diablerets are only moderately developed, though it offers fairly dependable summer-ski options on the glacier itself, some dramatic intermediate peak-top runs at Quille du Diable and Scex Rouge, and one gravity-defying expert slope, directly under the gondola, from Pierre-Pointes back to the valley. (From Scex Rouge, a popular run carries you around the top of the Oldenhorn and down to Oldenegg, a wide-open intermediate run through a sheltered valley.) At 1,250 meters (4,100 feet), Les Diablerets has six cable cars, 16 lifts, 120 kilometers (75 miles) of downhill runs, 30 kilometers (19 miles) of cross-country trails, and 7 kilometers (4 miles) of prepared tobogganing trails. A one-day lift ticket, valid at Villars, Gryon, and Les Diablerets, costs 38 SF; a six-day pass costs 210 SF.

Leysin

26 *16 km (10 mi) northeast of Aigle; 54 km (33 mi) southeast of Lausanne.*

From the switchback highway N11, a small mountain road leads up to this family resort with easy skiing and a spectacular sunny plateau setting, looking directly onto the Dents du Midi.

Skiing

Small-scale and cozy, Leysin offers a widespread network of lifts that allow you to cover a lot of varied ground on easy-to-medium slopes. From Berneuse, you can top up your courage in the revolving restaurant and head for the **Chaux de Mont** (2,200 meters/7,216 feet), where an expert run winds along a razorback and back through the forests to town. At 1,250 meters (4,100 feet), has two cable cars, 17 lifts, a shuttle train, and 60 kilometers (37 miles) of ski runs, as well as skating, curling, ski bob, and 36 kilometers (22 miles) of cross-country trails. A one-day lift ticket costs 34.50 SF; a six-day pass costs 162 SF.

THE PAYS D'ENHAUT

Separated from the high-altitude Alpine resorts by the modest **Col des Mosses** (1,445 meters/4,740 feet), and isolated, high-altitude family ski centers (Les Mosses, La Lécherette), the Pays d'Enhaut (Highlands) offers an entirely different culture from its Vaud cousins. Here the architecture begins to resemble that of the Berner Oberland, which it borders: Deep-eave wooden chalets replace the Edwardian structures of the lakelands, and the atmosphere takes on a mountain-farm air. The Pays d'Enhaut once belonged to Gruyères, then was seized by Bern; when Vaud was declared a canton, the Pays d'Enhaut went with it. A stone's throw up the valley, you cross the Sarine/Saanen and the so-called "Rösti Border," where the culture and language switch to Bernese German. This is still Gruyère cheese country, and also the source of one of Switzerland's most familiar decorative arts: *papier découpé*, delicate, symmetrical paper cutouts, an ornate and sophisticated version of America's grade-school snowflakes. They are cut in black, often with naive imagery of cattle and farmers, and fixed on white paper for contrast. The real thing is a refined craft and is priced appropriately, but attractive prints reproducing the look are on sale at reduced prices throughout the region.

L'Etivaz

27 *21 km (13 mi) northeast of Aigle; 59 km (37 mi) southeast of Lausanne.*

Visitors to the Pays d'Enhaut who cross the Col des Mosses first pass through the village of L'Etivaz, where a Gruyère-style cheese is made from milk drawn exclusively from cows grazed on pastures between 1,000 and 2,200 meters (3,280–7,216 feet) elevation; the sweet, late-blooming flowers they eat impart a flavor that lowland cheeses can't approach. The very best L'Etivaz cheese—*Rebibes*—is aged for three years in the cooperative here until it dries and hardens to a Parmesan-like texture; then it's shaved into curls and eaten by hand. Feel free to stop in at the cooperative; one of the workers in cream-color rubber boots will be happy to sell you brick-size chunks of both young and old cheeses at prices well below those at resort groceries.

Dining and Lodging

$ ✕⌂ **Du Chamois.** For four generations, one family has coddled guests
★ in this weathered-wood chalet. Its bookcases are full of rainy-day reading, and its meals simple, impeccable presentations of trout, cheese, omelettes, and steaks marvelously prepared and garnished by the current generation's man of the house. Warm gold pine planking covers nearly every surface, and historic photos, lace curtains, and local paper cutouts add the grace notes. The baths are up-to-date, while the rooms are simple and genuinely homey. ⌧ CH-1831, ☎ 029/4–62–66, FAX 029/4–60–16. 30 beds. Restaurant, café, tennis court, playground. AE, DC, MC, V.

En Route   Clinging to a precarious cliffside road between L'Etivaz and Château-d'Oex, drivers penetrate the canyon wilderness of the **Gorges du Pis-son,** where sports lovers in wet suits "canyon"—literally, hike the river bottom—the white waters of the Torneresse River.

Château-d'Oex

㉘ *33 km (20 mi) northeast of Aigle; 64 km (40 mi) east of Lausanne.*

At the crossroads between the Col des Mosses highway to Aigle and the Valais and the route to the Berner Oberland lies Château-d'Oex (pronounced "day"), a popular sports resort that connects, in these days of sophisticated ski transit, with the greater Gstaad ski region. Its perhaps even greater claim to fame these days: ballooning, with periodic hot-air-balloon competitions that draw mobs of international enthusiasts and fill hotels throughout the region. Mixing Edwardian architecture with weathered-wood chalets, the town spreads over a green, forest-top hillside above the highway and heads the French end of the valley of the Sarine River—also known, in the Berner Oberland, as Saanenland.

★   In Château-d'Oex's small center, the **Musée Artisanal du Vieux Pays d'Enhaut** (Artisan and Folklore Museum of the Old Highlands) gives you real insight into life in these isolated parts, with complete interiors evocatively reproduced: two kitchens, a farmer's home, a cheese maker's house, and a carpenter's studio. There's marvelous woodwork and ironwork, along with a variety of ceramics. There also are displays of old papier découpé, furniture, and popular art. ⌧ CH-1837, ☎ 029/4–65–20. ⌸ 3 SF. ☉ Tues., Thurs., and Fri. 10–noon and 2–4:30; weekends 2–4; closed Oct.

Le Chalet is a rather commercialized reproduction of a mountain cheese maker's place, with afternoon demonstrations over an open fire. Visitors sit at café tables (and are sold drinks or cheese dishes) while they watch the hot labor of stirring milk in a vast copper vat. Regional crafts and dairy products are on sale downstairs. ⌧ CH-1837, ☎ 029/4–66–77. ⌸ Free (though some purchase or consumption is expected). ☉ Sat.–Thurs. 9–6, Fri. 9 AM–11 PM; demonstrations Tues.–Sun.

Skiing

Château-d'Oex itself has cable-car links to La Braye and the expert and intermediate trails that wind back down. At 1,000 meters (3,280 feet), it has one cable car, one chairlift, 10 lifts, 50 kilometers (31 miles) of downhill runs, and 30 kilometers (19 miles) of cross-country trails. A one-day lift ticket costs 36 SF; a six-day pass costs 171 SF.

Dining and Lodging

$ ✕ **Buffet de la Gare.** Though you'd be better off driving five minutes up to L'Etivaz for equivalent (but better prepared and served) middle-class cuisine, this comfortable and convenient train-station café draws a regular local crowd for light meals and a dependable plat du jour (daily special). Stick with *croûtes* (rich toasted-cheese sandwiches) and salads, and opt for the casual (smoky) café rather than the more formal restaurant, though it's fun to watch the trains roll in from the latter. ⊠ *CH-1837,* ☎ *029/4–77–17. MC, V.*

$$ ✕🏨 **Bon Accueil.** Occupying a beautifully proportioned, weathered-wood
★   chalet that has been sitting on a green hillside looking over the valley since the 18th century, this is the quintessential French-Swiss country inn. The rooms mix aged pine planking, spindle furniture, and antiques, and under the old low-beam ceilings the floors creak agreeably. Up-to-date amenities, immaculate appointments, pastel accents, and fresh flowers—inside and out—keep standards at a well-above-rustic level. The restaurant is even more civilized, and the menu offers a range of specialties, from simple lake fish to such intricate creations as freshwater fish flash-fried and artfully served in tarragon-shallot sauce. Meals are served in a warm dining room with a brick fireplace, much waxed wood, and pewter accents. For winter nights, there's a firelit stone cellar bar with low-key jazz. ⊠ *CH-1837,* ☎ *029/4–63–20,* 🅵🅰🆇 *029/4–51–26. 40 beds. Restaurant (reservations essential), bar. AE, DC, MC, V.*

$$ 🏨 **De L'Ours.** Built in 1801, this old, central inn now follows the ubiquitous post-renovation format: standard, dependable beige and Formica. The rooms on the top floor have more character, with their attic timbers and touches of fresh pine. There's a shady courtyard and an inexpensive, understated restaurant that serves regional specialties. ⊠ *CH-1837,* ☎ *029/4–63–37,* 🅵🅰🆇 *029/4–51–48. 86 beds. Restaurant, café. AE, DC, MC, V.*

$$ 🏨 **Ermitage.** This 1965 chalet-style hotel on the highway is full of bright colors and splashy prints and aspires to the rustic Victorian look. All baths were updated attractively in 1992. The restaurant mixes French and Ticinese specialties. ⊠ *CH-1837,* ☎ *029/4–60–03,* 🅵🅰🆇 *029/4–50–76. 44 beds. Restaurant, café. AE, DC, MC, V.*

$$ 🏨 **Richmont.** The exterior is authentic (weather-blackened wood, flower boxes on the balconies), but the interior is a study in florid Victorian excess—the colors intense, the upholstery heavy, and the half-timbering an apparent afterthought. There are a lively pizzeria and a steak house downstairs. ⊠ *CH-1837,* ☎ *029/4–52–52,* 🅵🅰🆇 *029/4–53–84. 23 beds. Restaurant, bar, café, pizzeria. AE, DC, MC, V.*

$ 🏨 **Printannière.** This creaky old cottage offers simple, cheap lodging without bathrooms, just beyond the town center. The linens are fresh, the decor straightforward, and the windows frame astonishing views. There's a pretty garden terrace behind. ⊠ *CH-1837,* ☎ *029/4–61–13. 18 beds. Restaurant for guests (reservations advised). No credit cards.*

Outdoor Activities and Sports

BALLOONING

Château-d'Oex is a hot-air-ballooning center, offering accompanied flights. To arrange one, contact the tourist office (☎ 029/4–77–88). There's also an annual festival in January.

BICYCLING

In this graceful region of rolling hills and steep, verdant climbs, mountain bikes can be rented through **Roch Sports** (☎ 029/4–72–51) and **Château Sports** (☎ 029/4–58–58).

RAFTING

Several gorges near Château-d'Oex offer excellent rafting, as well as two unusual white-water sports: "Hydrospeed" involves floating the waters in flippers and wet suit; "canyoning" has you hiking the river bottom in wet suit, life jacket, and helmet. Arrange supervised initiations into these sports through the tourist office (☎ 029/4–77–88).

SKATING

In Château-d'Oex, there's an outdoor rink at the **Parc des Sports** (☎ 029/4–67–00).

SWIMMING

In summer, Château-d'Oex opens a heated, 50-meter open-air pool with restaurant (☎ 029/4–62–34).

Rougemont

29 *40 km (25 mi) northeast of Aigle; 71 km (44 mi) east of Lausanne.*

Though this historic village is now being encroached on by sporty Gstaad—its beautiful wooden barns and ornately decorated chalets crowded out by modern resort lodgings—it retains its ancient monuments. The striking Romanesque **church,** built between 1073 and 1085, with its deeply raked roof and needle-sharp spire, forms a lovely group with the 16th-century **château**: Its exterior wall is emblazoned with the *grue* (crane) of Gruyères, harking back to the Pays d'Enhaut's earliest loyalties.

Skiing

Rougemont has La Vidamanette, a cable run that drops you off for leisurely, moderate skiing back to the village, or on up to trails that wind over toward Gstaad, the glamour resort across the invisible German-language frontier.

VAUD A TO Z

Arriving and Departing

By Car

There are two major arteries leading to Lac Léman, one entering from the north via Bern and Fribourg (N12), the other arcing over the north shore of Lac Léman, from Geneva to Lausanne (N1), then to Montreux and on south through the Alpes Vaudoises toward the Grand St. Bernard Pass (N9) in canton Valais. They are swift and often scenic expressways, and the north-shore artery (N1 and N9) traces a route that has been followed since before Roman times. Secondary highways parallel the expressways, but this is one case where, as the larger road sits higher on the lakeside slopes, the views from the expressway are often better than those from the highway. Be sure, however, to detour for the Corniche Road views between Lausanne and Montreux.

By Plane

Cointrin airport at **Geneva** is the second-busiest international airport in Switzerland, receiving frequent flights from America and the United Kingdom on **Swissair** as well as on other international carriers; it lies about 55 kilometers (34 miles) southwest of Lausanne. From Cointrin, **Crossair**—Switzerland's domestic line—connects to secondary airports throughout the country.

By Train

Lausanne lies on a major train route between Bern and Geneva, with express trains connecting from Basel and Zürich. From Geneva, trains take about 30 minutes and arrive in Lausanne up to four times an hour; from Bern, they take a little more than an hour and arrive twice an hour. TGVs (high-speed trains) run from Paris four times a day and take 3 hours and 40 minutes.

Getting Around

By Boat

Like all fair-size Swiss lakes, Lac Léman is crisscrossed with comfortable and reasonably swift **steamers.** They carry you scenically from port to port, and sometimes run more often than the trains that parallel their routes. With a Swiss Pass you travel free.

By Bus

A useful network of **postbus routes** covers the region for the resourceful traveler with plenty of time; some routes are covered only once or twice a day. Schedules are available from tourist offices and rail stations. Lausanne has a good bus and tram network; if you have a Swiss Pass, you can travel free on city buses and trams in Montreux-Vevey and Lausanne.

By Car

A web of **secondary highways** cuts north into the hills and winds east of the southbound expressway into the Alpine resorts, giving the driver maximum flexibility.

By Train

Trains along the waterfront, connecting major Lac Léman towns, are swift and frequent. There also are several **private rail systems** leading into small villages and rural regions, including the Montreux–Oberland–Bernois line, which climbs sharply behind Montreux and cuts straight over the pre-Alps toward Château-d'Oex and the Berner Oberland.

Lausanne itself has a tiny but essential **Metro** that, every seven minutes, connects the waterfront at Ouchy to the train station and the place St-François above.

Guided Tours

Orientation

The **Lausanne tourist office** sponsors a two-hour coach trip into the old town, including a visit to the cathedral and an extended city coach tour that takes in the Lavaux vineyards. There also are three general tours during the summer: one to Gruyères; one to Chamonix and Mont Blanc; and one to the Alps by coach and the Montreux–Oberland–Bernois line *Panoramic Train* to Les Diablerets and Château-d'Oex.

Special-Interest

The **Office des Vins Vaudois** (✉ Chemin de la Vuachère 6, CH-1005, Lausanne, ☎ 021/729–61–61) offers carefully marked walks—not personally guided—through the vineyards, passing production centers, wine growers' homes, and *pintes* (pubs) for tasting along the way. Write for the *Guide du Vignoble Vaudois* for itineraries, hours, and addresses of suggested stops.

Contacts and Resources

Emergencies

Throughout Vaud (☎ 117). **Police:** Château-d'Oex (☎ 029/4–44–21); Villars (☎ 025/35–22–21); Montreux (☎ 021/963–22–22). **Ambulance:** Château-d'Oex (☎ 029/4–75–93); Montreux (☎ 021/963–22–22); Villars (☎ 025/35–15–37). **Hospitals:** Aigle (☎ 025/26–15–11); Lausanne (Centre Hospitalier Universitaire Vaudois emergency services, ☎ 021/314–11–11); Montreux (☎ 021/963–53–11); Pays d'Enhaut (☎ 029/4–75–93). **Medical and dental referrals** for Lausanne (☎ 021/652–99–32). **Late-night pharmacies** (☎ 111). **Auto breakdown:** Touring Club of Switzerland (☎ 140).

Visitor Information

The **Office du Tourisme du Canton de Vaud** (⊠ Av. d'Ouchy 60, CH-1006, Lausanne, ☎ 021/617–72–02) has general information on the region.

Other tourist offices are in **Château-d'Oex** (⊠ CH-1837, ☎ 029/4–77–88), **Lausanne** (⊠ Av. de Rhodanie 2, ☎ 021/617–14–27), **Leysin** (⊠ CH-1854, ☎ 025/34–22–44), **Montreux** (⊠ Pl. du Débarcadère, CH-1820, ☎ 021/963–12–12), and **Villars** (⊠ CH-1884, ☎ 025/35–32–32).

13 Geneva

As the headquarters of the United Nations, the World Health Organization, and the International Red Cross; an international mecca for writers and thinkers of every stripe; and a stronghold of luxurious stores and extravagant restaurants, Geneva is Switzerland's most cosmopolitan city. This is a city of wealth and influence, where the rustic chalets of hilltop villages seem worlds away.

DRAPED AT THE FOOT OF THE JURA and the Alps on the westernmost tip of Lake Geneva, or Lac Léman (as the natives know it), Geneva (Genève in French) is the most cosmopolitan and graceful of Swiss cities and the soul of the French-speaking territory. Prodding into France as though dipping a delicate toe into Gallic waters—bordered on the north by the Pays de Gex and the south by Haute-Savoie, and lying little more than 160 kilometers (100 miles) from Lyon—the city emits an aura of Gallic hauteur. Grand mansarded mansions stand guard beside the River Rhône, where yachts bob, gulls dive, and Rolls-Royces purr past manicured promenades. The combination of Swiss efficiency and French savoir faire gives Geneva a chic polish, and the infusion of international blood from the UN adds a heterogeneity rare in a population of only 167,000. The canton has a population of 378,487, many of whom work in Geneva; still others commute by the thousands from the relatively cheap housing in St-Julien, to the south, in France.

Geneva has long been a city of humanity and enlightenment, offering refuge to the writers Voltaire, Victor Hugo, Alexandre Dumas, Honoré de Balzac, and Stendhal, as well as the religious reformers John Calvin and John Knox. Lord Byron, Percy Bysshe Shelley, Richard Wagner, and Franz Liszt all fled scandals into Geneva's sheltering arms.

While many left Geneva to escape the narrow austerity and bigotry of 16th-century Calvinism—whose namesake reformed the city that sheltered him, preaching fire and brimstone from the *auditoire* and stripping the Cathedral of its papist icons—masses of Protestants fled *to* it nonetheless. The English fled Bloody Mary, Protestant Italians the wrath of the pope, Spaniards the Inquisition, French Huguenots the oppressive French monarchy—and Geneva flourished, inevitably expanding its horizons once more.

Yet to this day the conservative Genevois seem to hear Calvin tsk-tsking in their ears as they do a little *lèche-vitrines* (literally "window-licking" or window-shopping) at some of the world's most expensive stores and most excessive restaurants; it's the cosmopolitan foreign population that seems to indulge itself the most. Some say that during the 1970s, there was more Middle Eastern oil money in Geneva than in the Middle East, and stories abound of sheiks taking over half a hotel for monthlong shopping sprees.

Nowadays, Geneva lets down her discreet chignon only once a year, to celebrate the Escalade. On the night of December 11–12, 1602, the duke of Savoy—coveting Geneva and hoping to restore it to Catholicism—sent his men to scale the city walls with ladders. They were ignominiously defeated when a housewife, seeing the Savoyards clambering up the walls, emptied a *marmite* (pot) of hot soup over their heads and gave the alarm. The event is commemorated every year by the Festival of the Escalade, when uniforms come out of museums to be worn in reenactments of the battle, chocolate versions of the marmite are filled with marzipan vegetables for the children, and throughout the old town the usually decorous Genevois take to the streets in costume.

Pleasures and Pastimes

Antiquing
Catering to the public that frequent auctions at Sotheby's and Christie's, Geneva's old town and Pacquis neighborhood are chock full of atmospheric shops bulging with 16th-century books, ancient engravings, carved picture frames, and fine old jewelry and silver.

Churches

The Gothic and neoclassic cathedral St-Pierre, with its early Christian excavations, and the Temple de l'Auditoire, where Jean Calvin preached and taught, offer an illuminating overview of Geneva's catholic and reformed personae.

Dining

Connoisseurs of *haute gastronomie* will not be disappointed by a city that seduces great French chefs to cross the border with a wealthy, discerning clientele. But budget diners can experience earthy Geneva cuisine—sausage, pigs' feet, chicken fricasée—in unpretentious bistros, too. With only 160 kilometers (100 miles) separating it from France's true culinary capital, Geneva is a blood brother to Lyon: Its traditional cuisine is earthy and rich, with much emphasis placed on *abats* (organ meats), *andouillettes* (chitterling sausages), potatoes, and onions. And like that of Lyon, its haute cuisine rivals the best in the world.

Not only is the food French but the style of dining is as well—late, leisurely, with seasonal specialties celebrated like the annual visit of an old friend. Brasseries and bistros are social centers, and open-air cafés spill into every square.

There are some dishes to watch for: *Cardon* is an artichokelike vegetable cultivated in Geneva and Lyon, often baked with cream and Gruyère in rich gratins; *omble chevalier,* a kind of salmon trout, is native to Geneva's Lac Léman. The city's two most traditional dishes are even more down-to-earth: *pieds de cochon* (pigs' feet), served in a variety of ways; and *fricassée* (savory wine-based stew) of chicken or pork. *Longeole*—a novel sausage blending spinach, cabbage, and leeks with pork by-products—is a specialty of Geneva and Haute Savoie. At bistros where these not-so-delicate treats are served, you may find *petit salé* (salt pork) with lentils, tripes, or *boudin*—rich, rosy-brown blood pudding.

Yet for all its robust, old-fashioned favorites, Geneva cultivates an astonishing number of great restaurants—many of them headed by chefs imported from across the French border. Prices at these gastronomic meccas can be dry-mouth high, but—as in most Swiss cities—you can save considerably by choosing a lunchtime prix-fixe menu. If you want to splurge, starting with tiers of briny oysters and finishing with chocolate truffles and good *vieille prune* (a plum-based eau-de-vie), and plumbing the depths of great French-Swiss wine lists, there's no limit to what you can spend (and enjoy) in this, Switzerland's culinary cosmopolis.

Museums

Not only are there grand, world-class public museums of art and natural history here; you'll also find privately sponsored, eclectic collections—of new sculpture, primitive art, Oriental ceramics, musical instruments, and more. The Palais des Nations, while fully functional as home to the UN, serves as a living museum, with its radio-age translation devices and Socialist-Realist murals; the International Red Cross Museum puts the horrors of the modern age into uncomfortable perspective.

Neighborhoods

In addition to its beautifully preserved and atmospheric Vielle Ville, there are various residential and commercial areas to wander, many with strong personalities: the honky-tonk sleaze behind the gare/rue des Pâcquis, the stately homes above the Parc des Bastions, the Sardinian architecture in Carouge across the River Arve, the glittering shops on the rue du Rhone, the avant-garde galleries west of Plainpalais.

EXPLORING

Geneva lies between the southwestern end of Lac Léman and the canton of Geneva, which bulges even farther west into France. The city itself crowds along the tapering shores of Lac Léman, which, at the Pont du Mont-Blanc, narrows back into the Rhône. Thus Geneva is as much a river town as a lake town, and its Rive Droite (Right Bank, on the north side) and Rive Gauche (Left Bank, on the south side) have strong identities. Most of the central city's best is concentrated on the Rive Gauche, but the Rive Droite is where the waterfront and many handsome hotels are located.

Great Itineraries

IF YOU HAVE 2 DAYS

Allow yourself an hour to stroll the Right Bank before crossing to the Left Bank and entering the old town. Save time for the Gothic–neo-classic hybrid Cathédrale-St-Pierre and its fascinating early Christian excavations (Site archéologique). Then window-shop your way through ancient streets to the Musée d'Art et d'Histoire, where such Swiss masterworks as Ferdinand Hodler's Impressionist landscapes are on view. The next day, head for the international area and spend the morning at the Palais des Nations, the afternoon at the Musée internationale de la Croix Rouge. Nights are for concerts and hearty dinners with a beaker or two of Lac Léman wines.

IF YOU HAVE 3 DAYS

Museum hounds will want to devote their first day to walking the Right Bank, then heading for the Musée Rath for a world-class temporary exposition—say, "1945: the Faces of Liberty," featuring European works created in post-crisis transition. Visit the Monument de la Reformation, then climb up into the old town to visit the Cathedral and its excavations, the Temple de l'Auditoire (where Jean Calvin preached), the 14th-century Maison Tavel, and any number of bookstores and antiques shops. The next day, concentrate on museum country behind the old town: There's the Musée d'Art et d'Histoire, the Baur Collection of Oriental art, the Musée d'Histoire Naturelle, and the Musée d'Horlogerie et de l'Emaillerie. On your third day, head for the international area and spend the morning at the Palais des Nations, the afternoon at the Musée internationale de la Croix Rouge. If time remains, there's also the Musée Ariana, devoted to ceramics and glass.

IF YOU HAVE 4 DAYS

Art lovers will want to devote a fourth day to all the art museums mentioned above—plus a morning at the Musée Barbier-Mueller, studying primitive and ancient art from Oceana, as well as an afternoon at the new, cutting-edge Musée d'Art Moderne et Contemporain.

The Right Bank, Left Bank, and Old Town

This is the heart of Geneva. On the Right Bank, grand hotels line the banks of the Rhône and monuments, with parks and fountains relieving the big-city modernity. Once you climb into the ancient and peaceful heights of the *vielle ville*, or old town, cosmopolitan, world-class museums pepper the neighborhoods—though walkers may be so seduced by the stores and sidewalk cafés that they may not have time to explore them all.

A Good Walk

Numbers in the text correspond to numbers in the margin and points of interest on the Geneva exploring map.

Begin your walk from Cornavin, the long rail station. As it's awkward to cross the **place de Cornavin** ① directly, take the pedestrian underpass from the shopping center below the station. You'll emerge above rue du Mont-Blanc, a partially pedestrian shopping street that slopes down to the lake. If you venture into the neighborhood to the north (Les Pâquis), you may be surprised at the prevalence of daytime red-light life, a source of not-so-Calvinist (and not-so-original) sin. To the south, rue du Mont-Blanc opens onto the Pont du Mont-Blanc, a broad bridge that spans the last gasp of Lac Léman as it squeezes back into the Rhône. From the middle of the bridge you can see the snowy peak of Mont Blanc itself, and from March to October you'll have a fine view of the **Jet d'Eau** ②, Europe's highest fountain, gushing 145 meters (475 feet) high.

Heading back on the bridge toward land, turn right onto quai du Mont-Blanc and walk along the pollard-lined waterfront promenade toward the *débarcadères,* the docks used by Swissboat, Mouettes, and the CGN steamers. Across the quai stands the elaborate neo-Gothic **Monument Brunswick** ③, the tomb of a duke of Brunswick who left his fortune to the city. Across the street at the Hotel Beau-Rivage, you'll see the discreet sign for **Sotheby's,** the famous international auction house. Some of the city's most glamorous hotels stand beyond the hotel; just past them you'll reach the Pâquis-Plage, a swimming area with changing rooms, restaurants, and plenty of space to swim and sunbathe.

Back at the Pont du Mont-Blanc, continue southwest along the Right Bank waterfront on quai des Bergues. Here you'll find a novelty that shows Geneva's Swiss accent: Beneath the water alongside the opposite (left) bank is a four-story, electronically controlled parking lot that holds 1,500 cars. In the center of the river, off the Pont des Bergues, is **Ile Rousseau** ④, whose namesake is memorialized with a statue.

The next bridge along the quai is the Pont de la Machine, where the crystal-clear Rhône—its waters having lost the mud they carried when entering the eastern end of the lake—tumbles in a tumult of foam over the dam that regulates the level of the lake. By crossing the river at yet the next bridge, the Pont de l'Ile, you will pass the **Tour de l'Ile** ⑤, a onetime prison.

On the right bank, cross the place Bel-Air, the center of the business and banking district; Geneva is home to the second-largest banking community in Switzerland. Follow the rue de la Corraterie, during the 17th century the riding circuit of the best Geneva horsemen, to the **place Neuve** ⑥. This imposing crossroads holds several landmarks. On the northern end, opposite the entrance to the park, stands the Grand Théâtre, which hosts opera, ballet, and sometimes the Orchestre de la Suisse Romande, whose usual venue is nearby Victoria Hall. To its right is the Conservatoire de Musique; where an important solo competition is held annually. To its left is the **Musée Rath** ⑦, noted for its excellent temporary exhibitions.

Behind imposing gates, the Parc des Bastions is the site of the Geneva University, founded as an academy in 1599 by Calvin himself. Enter the park and keep to your left. Almost immediately, at the foot of the ramparts, you will come to Geneva's most famous monument, the **Monument de la Réformation** ⑧, an enormous international memorial to the Reformation; it is worth sitting down on the terrace steps—made of Mont Blanc granite—which face the wall, to take it all in. Afterwards, walk on to the back of the park and exit by a gate on the left; then turn left onto rue St-Léger, passing under an ivy-hung bridge.

As you climb the winding street, the present quickly falls away, and thick-walled houses with weathered shutters take you into the atmospheric old town. You'll soon reach the tiered plateau of the historic **place du Bourg-de-Four** ⑨, where stores and restaurants attract an eclectic crowd. From the *place,* angle uphill on rue de l'Hôtel-de-Ville, past the chic shops and *antiquaires* (antiques shops). Then cut right into place de la Taconnerie, past **Christie's,** one of the world's foremost auction houses. Calvin certainly would not have approved of such a material establishment being so near his turf: Just beyond lies the small Gothic church that served as his **Temple de l'Auditoire** ⑩—the lecture theater where he taught missionaries his doctrines of reform.

Just past the Auditoire rises the magnificent mongrel **Cathédrale-St-Pierre** ⑪, where Calvin galvanized the faltering souls of Geneva. After exploring its austere interior, take the stairs on the left side to the **site archéologique** ⑫ where you can spend an hour or so exploring the restored remains of the churches that once stood on the site of the present-day cathedral. From there, head to the ancient rue du Puits-St-Pierre, where the **Maison Tavel** ⑬, now a historical museum, stands as the oldest house in town.

Turn left on rue Jean-Calvin. Number 11, now a stately neoclassic facade, was the address of John Calvin himself. (Just beyond, a plaque commemorates George Sand's sojourn here from 1849 to 1859.) Next door, the **Musée Barbier-Mueller** ⑭ has a private collection of African, Oceanique, and Southeast Asian art in permanent rotation.

Head back up rue du Puits-St-Pierre past the Maison Tavel, passing some ancient cannons from the Swiss Republic under vaulted arcades of the old arsenal. Beyond stands the imposing facade of the **Hôtel de Ville** ⑮ (Town Hall), where the Geneva Convention was signed in 1864. From here you can make short half-block jaunts to see the site of John Calvin's house, now rebuilt (rue Jean-Calvin 11, beyond the Tavel House and to the left), and, just down the Grande-Rue, the birthplace of Rousseau (No. 40). Ferdinand Hodler, the Swiss Impressionist, lived at No. 33 from 1881-1902; you'll see his works at the Musée d'Art et d'Histoire (☞ *below*).

If you continue down the steep Grande-Rue, you'll see shops selling a pleasant mix of antiques and luxury goods, and—after the Grande-Rue becomes rue de la Citée—you'll arrive at the modern shopping district and rue de la Confédération. You can shop up and down this street, whose name changes from rue de la Confédération to rue du Marché to rue de la Croix-d'Or to rue de Rive in a matter of blocks. From there you can either head back to the river to the centrally positioned place Longmalle, cross the quai Général-Guisan, and relax in the Jardin Anglais (English Garden), famous for its floral clock; or turn right at the Rond-Point de Rive and follow boulevard Jaques-Dalcroze to rue Ferdinand-Hodler, turn right, then turn left at rue Théodore. There, at an open crossroads, you'll find the Collège Calvin, which was sponsored by the stern reformer in 1559 and is now the Cantonal Secondary School. Cross the bridge and continue straight on rue Charles-Galland. On the right the vast **Musée d'Art et d'Histoire** ⑯ (Museum of Art and History) spreads before you, its broad corridors packed with international paintings and sculpture.

Leaving the museum, turn right and follow rue Charles-Galland to rue Le-Fort; turn left and look for the spiraling cupolas of the late-19th-century Eglise Russe (Russian Church), completely decorated within in neo-Byzantine styles. Take rue Le-Fort to rue Munier-Romilly and

322

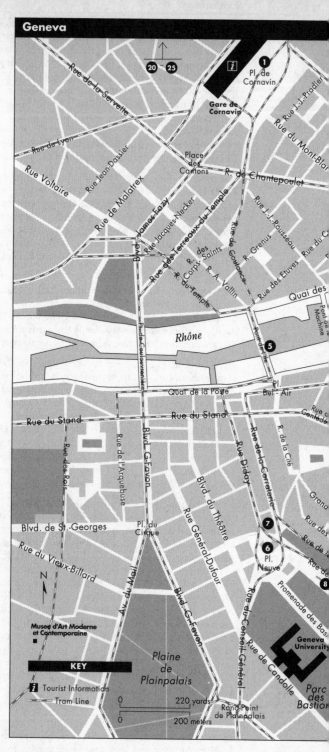

Geneva

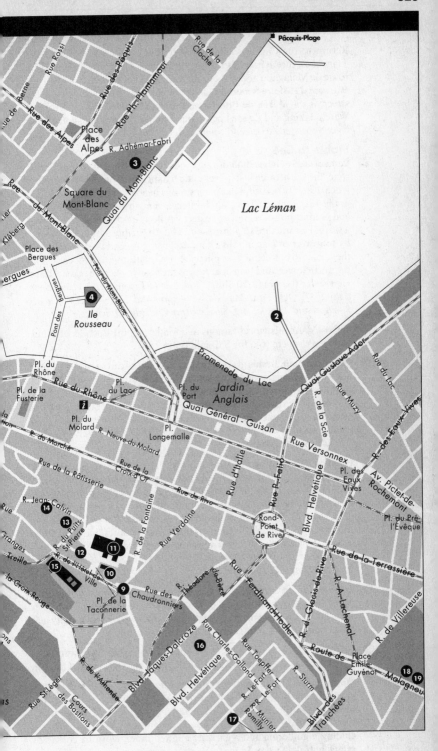

Pâcquis-Plage

Rue de la Cloche

Rue Rossi

Rue des Pâcquis

Rue Ph.-Plantamour

Rue de Berne

Rue des Alpes

Place des Alpes

R. Adhémar-Fabri

3

Rue de

Rue du Mont-Blanc

Square du Mont-Blanc

Quai du Mont-Blanc

Kléberg

Place des Bergues

Bergues

Pont du Mont-Blanc

Pont des Bergues

4

Ile Rousseau

Lac Léman

2

Pl. du Rhône

Rue du Rhône

Pl. du Lac

Promenade du Lac

Quai Gustave-Ador

Rue du Lac

Pl. de la Fusterie

i

Pl. du Port

Jardin Anglais

Quai Général - Guisan

Rue Muzy

R. de la Scie

R. des Eaux-Vives

Pl. du Molard

R. Neuve-du-Molard

Pl. Longemalle

la

Rue du Marché

Rue de la Rôtisserie

Rue de la Croix-d'Or

Rue de Rive

Rue d'Italie

Rue Versonnex

Pl. des Eaux-Vives

Av. Pictet-de-Rochemont

R. Jean-Calvin

14

13

R. du Puits-St-Pierre

Rue de la Fontaine

Rue Verdaine

R. P.-Fatio

Bld. Helvétique

Pl. du Pré l'Évêque

Rue de la Terrassière

ranges

Treille

12

11

Rond-Point de Rive

R. A.-Lachenal

R. de l'Hôtel-de-Ville

15

10

9

Rue des Chaudronniers

Pl. de la Taconnerie

R. Théodore-de-Bèze

Rue Ferdinand-Hodler

R. Glacis-de-Rive

R. de Villereuse

la Croix-Rouge

R. de l'Athénée

Bld. Jacques-Dalcroze

Rue Charles-Galland

16

Rue Toepffer

Route de

Place Emile-Guyénot

18 **19**

Malagnou

Rue St-Léger

Cours des Bastions

Bld. Helvétique

R. Sturm

R. Le-Fort

R.P. Le-Fort

R. Munier-Romilly

Bld. des Tranchées

17

turn left. On the right is the **Collection Baur** ⑰, an elegantly mounted collection of Japanese and Chinese art objects.

Return to rue Charles-Galland and follow it right to boulevard des Tranchées; turn left and head for place Emile-Guyénot. Veer right on route de Malagnou and walk to the varied and even occasionally lively **Muséum d'Histoire Naturelle** ⑱. Just beyond it, on the same side of the street, is the **Musée de l'Horlogerie et de l'Emaillerie** ⑲ (Museum of Watchmaking and Enameling), a bijou in itself. From here you can re-trace your steps to the old town or catch Bus 6 back to place Bel-Air.

Sights to See

★ ⑪ **Cathédrale St-Pierre.** Built during the 12th and 13th centuries in Gothic style, the Cathédrale lost its aesthetic balance and some of its grandeur when a sternly beautiful but incongruous neoclassic portico was added in the 18th century. The church interior remains wholly Romanesque and Gothic, however, and its austerity reflects its change of role—from a Catholic cathedral to a Protestant church, stripped of its ornaments by followers of Calvin. His chair, according to tradition, remains on the left, in front of the last pillar before the transept. You can climb the **north tower** (and from it across to the south tower) to take in grand views over Geneva (2.50 SF). ⊠ *Place de la Taconnerie.* ☉ *June–Sept. daily 9–7; Oct., Apr.–May daily 9–noon and 2–6; Nov.–Mar. daily 9–noon and 2–5. Closed Sun. morning during services.*

Christie's. At this world-famous auction house, the duchess of Windsor's jewels were sold for $50 million in 1987.

★ ⑰ **Collection Baur.** In this graceful mansion, visitors can peruse the broad and exquisite array of Japanese and Chinese art objects collected by businessman Alfred Baur. Over a period of 50 years, Baur acquired rose and celadon porcelains from China, smooth-lined medieval Japanese stoneware, ceramics and jade, Samurai swords, lacquer boxes, lovely printed textiles, and more. ⊠ *Rue Munier-Romilly 8,* ☎ *022/346–17–29.* ☒ *5 SF.* ☉ *Tues.–Sun. 2–6.*

⑮ **Hôtel de Ville.** Dating from the 16th century but restored and enlarged in later years, this still-active Town Hall shelters the **Alabama Hall,** where, on August 22, 1864, the Geneva Convention was signed by 16 countries, laying the foundation of the International Red Cross. Eight years later, in 1872, a court of arbitration was convened in this same room to settle the Alabama dispute between Great Britain and the United States, which was unhappy over British support to the Confederacy during the Civil War. ⊠ *Rue de l'Hôtel de Ville,* ☎ *022/319–22–09.* ☉ *Individual visits by request.*

❹ **Ile Rousseau.** In the center of Rhône, off the Pont des Bergues, this small island is known for its statue of the Geneva-born French philosopher Jean-Jacques Rousseau, who did much to popularize both the city and Switzerland during the 18th century.

★ ❷ **Jet d'Eau.** Europe's tallest fountain, gushing 145 meters (475 feet) high, is visible from the Pont du Mont-Blanc from March through October.

★ ⑬ **Maison Tavel.** Dating from the 14th century, Geneva's oldest house has been studiously restored. Several rooms are furnished as they would have been during the period, while others house collections of architectural details, arms, and arcane souvenirs of Geneva's past—including a guillotine and a garishly painted miter, worn by convicted pimps in Calvin's day. In the large attic, there's a relief map of the city as it was around 1850; a recorded commentary with timed lights moves from site to site. Good temporary expositions occasionally focus on details of local lore. ⊠ *Rue du Puits-St-Pierre 6,* ☎ *022/310–29–00.* ☎ *Free.* ☉ *Tues.–Sun. 10–5.*

③ Monument Brunswick. This tomb of a duke of Brunswick who died in Geneva in 1873 and left his fortune to the city is modeled on the Scaglieri monument in Verona.

★ ⑧ Monument de la Réformation. Built between 1909 and 1917, this gigantic wall—more than 90 meters (295 feet) long—is as impressive for its simplicity and clean lines as for its sheer size. The central group consists of four statues of the great leaders of the Reformation—Bèze, Calvin, Farel, and Knox—each more than 15 feet high. On either side of these giants are smaller statues (a mere 9 feet tall) of other personalities, such as Oliver Cromwell. Between the smaller figures are bas-reliefs and inscriptions that tell the story of important events connected with the Reformation. Carved in the wall to the right of Cromwell is the presentation by the English Houses of Parliament of the Bill of Rights to King William III, in 1689. Above it, in English, are listed the bill's main features—the guiding principles of democracy. To the left of Cromwell is a bas-relief of the Pilgrim fathers praying on the deck of the *Mayflower* before signing the Mayflower Compact; farther left another relief shows John Knox preaching with obvious passion in Edinburgh's St. Giles Cathedral. At the far ends of the work stand two memorials, one on the left to Martin Luther, one on the right to Ulrich Zwingli.

OFF THE
BEATEN PATH

MUSÉE D'ART MODERNE ET CONTEMPORAIN – This is the gritty new venue for a collection of stark, profound, mind-stretching art works, none dating from before 1965. Opened in September 1994 and funded by a private foundation of seven Genevois, the museum occupies a former factory whose original concrete floors and fluorescent lighting remain. Its spare, bleak lines serve as a foil to the sometimes stark, often over-scaled art works it houses: Paintings, sculptures, and structures by Gordon Matta-Clark, Jenny Holzer, Sol Lewitt, Nam June Paik, Dennis Oppenheim, and Jean Basquiat, among others. Of particular interest is a permanent reconstruction of art collector Ghislain Mollet-Viéville's Paris apartment, where he lived in a state of pure modernism among works of Sol Le Witt and Carl André. A walking commentary on the museum's contents takes place every Tuesday evening at 6:30 (4 SF). To get here from the city center, take tram 12 toward Plaine de Plainpalais; at its main stop, get off and walk straight across the park. Head up rue des Vieux-Grenadiers and turn right into the entrance. (Note: Don't go in the front door, which is the separate Centre d'art, but enter the "court" and pass through the massive metal doors.) ⊠ *Rue des Vieux-Grenadiers 10,* ☎ *022/320–61–22.* ☎ *9 SF.* ☉ *Tues.–Sun. noon–6.*

★ ⑯ Musée d'Art et d'Histoire. A massive mother lode of world culture that administrates several other museums, including the Maison Tavel and the Rath, this 1910 landmark houses an enormous Beaux-Arts collection: Among its gems, you'll find the famous 14th-century *The Fishing Miracle* by Swiss painter Konrad Witz, which shows Christ walking on the waters of a recognizable Lac Léman; several masterworks of Maurice-Quentin de la Tour; and a full room of Alpine landscapes by Swiss impressionist Ferdinand Hodler. In addition, there are six rooms furnished in various period styles, and large collections on archaeology (including Genevan pre-history), arms, and porcelain. ⊠ *Rue Charles-Galland 2,* ☎ *022/311–43–40.* ☎ *Free.* ☉ *Tues.–Sun. 10–5.*

⑭ Musée Barbier-Mueller. Since Josef Mueller began collecting so-called "primitive" art in 1907, his family has amassed a staggering quantity of fine pieces from Africa, Oceania, Southeast Asia, and the Americas. Only a small but exquisite selection is on view at any given time in this new, private museum—but each is exquisitely lighted, framed, labeled, and juxtaposed with similar and contrasting works. English labels guide visitors from ivory fly-whisk handles from Zaire to massive carved masks from New Ireland, explaining their origins and illuminating their symbolism. The museum building, a restored old-town vault of scrubbed terra cotta and halogen-lit stone, is a work of art itself. ⊠ *Rue Calvin 10,* ☎ *022/312–02–70.* 🎟 *5 SF.* ☺ *Daily 11–5.*

⑱ Musée d'Histoire Naturelle. Among natural history museums, this landmark stands out, with aquariums full of living fish and animals, and fine displays of mammals, birds, and dinosaurs; you can even trace the history of humankind. There's also an illuminating display on Swiss geology. ⊠ *Rte. de Malagnou 1,* ☎ *022/735–91–30.* 🎟 *Free.* ☺ *Daily 9:30–5.*

⑲ Musée de l'Horlogerie et de l'Emaillerie. At the Museum of Watchmaking and Enameling, you'll find not only several centuries' worth of timepieces—many of them made in Geneva—but also music boxes, elaborately enameled watchcases, and even a collection of art nouveau jewelry. They're mounted in a mansion as impressive as its contents. Try to be there on the hour, as the chiming of the clocks produces quite a show. ⊠ *Rte. de Malagnou 15,* ☎ *022/736–74–12.* 🎟 *Free.* ☺ *Wed.–Mon. 10–5.*

❼ Musée Rath. Opened in 1825, Geneva's first art museum is now a high-profile venue for eclectic, international, temporary art exhibits. It also houses the collection of paintings and sculpture that once belonged to Simon Rath, a Russian lieutenant general. ⊠ *Pl. Neuve,* ☎ *022/310–52–70. Admission and hrs depend on the exposition (up to 10 SF); check local listings.*

★ ❾ Place du Bourg-de-four. This atmospheric, sprawling old-town "square" was once the crossroads of some important routes leading to southern France via Annecy and Lyon, to Italy, to the Chablais, and beyond. Before that, it served as a Roman forum and as a cattle and wheat market. Today it's a crossroads still, where shoppers, workers, and students meet in open cafés and lounge around its fountain. The old town's merchants and restaurateurs have struck a delicate and charming balance, a mix of scruffy bohemia, genteel tradition, and slick gentrification.

NEED A BREAK? Have a coffee or *apero* (aperitif) at the lively **La Clémence** (⊠ 20, place du Bourg-de-Four, ☎ 022/312-24-98) a sidewalk café whose tables spill out into the middle of the place du Bourg-de-Four. You can people-watch or read for hours, Paris-style.

❻ Place Neuve. From this imposing crossroads you'll see a high rock wall, part of the city's ancient ramparts, towering over all surrounding landmarks. The noble old houses at the top of the wall are home to some of Geneva's wealthiest families.

⑫ Site archéologique. In the 1980s the floors of the Cathédrale St-Pierre (☞ *above*) were lifted and the foundations of previous churches excavated. Today, walkways allow visitors to examine the different levels of these excavations. Portions remain of an early Christian baptistery that dates from the late 300s—when the Roman Empire was still vacillating about its conversion to the new faith. Especially striking is a 5th-century room, from which an ornate mosaic floor remains. There also are remains of several early cathedrals as well as the first Romanesque cathedral on this site, dating from 1000; its ruins serve as the foundation for the cathedral today. There are markers and charts to guide you through the different eras and a collection of sculptures from the site. ☎ 022/738–56–50. ⬚ 5 SF. ☉ Tues.–Sun. 10–1 and 2–6.

Sotheby's. In 1995 the wife of the Aga Khan sold some of her jewelry at this famous auction house for $54,000,000.

⑩ **Temple de l'Auditoire.** In this former Catholic chapel built on the foundations of a 5th-century predecessor, Jean Calvin taught missionaries his doctrines of radical, puritanical reform. (From 1556 to 1559, the Scots reformer John Knox also preached here.) During the heat of the Reformation battles, the temple became a haven of worship for Protestant refugees, whom Calvin encouraged to hold services in their native English, Italian, Spanish, and Dutch; today it is a multinational center of worship, with Sunday services in English and Dutch. The austerity is striking, the period furniture still in use. Printed information and historic documents are also on display. ⬚ Pl. de la Taconnerie, ☎ 022/738–56–50. ⬚ Free. ☉ Oct.–May, Tues.–Sat. 2–5; June–Sept., hrs extended until 6.

NEED A BREAK?	Have an exotic, elegantly served tea, an exquisite hot snack, or a hot plat du jour in the **Darjeeling Salon de Thé** (⬚ place du Bourg-de-Four 9 at Etienne Dumont, ☎ 022/311–29–79), an intimate, upscale postmodern corner tearoom with sculptural, if uncomfortable, leather chairs.

⑤ **Tour de l'Ile.** Dating from the epoch of the bishops' rule, this one-time prison off the Pont de l'Ile is today almost swallowed up by modern buildings on either side.

The International Area

Well north of the city center, a modern area of open grassland and hills hosts a handful of museums, embassies, and landmarks. Graceful estates surround most, and a serene botanical garden is a good place to digest the heavy historical and political fare you will encounter within.

A Good Walk

To visit the **Palais des Nations** ⑳, an architecturally unusual building created to house the well-intentioned League of Nations, take Bus 8 to the place des Nations. On weekends, get off here and enter directly past the guard gates. On weekdays, when security is in full swing in front, stay on the bus for another stop, getting off at Appia. In addition to the Palais des Nations, the Appia bus stop gives you access to the palatial Italianate **Musée Ariana** ㉑, a subsidiary of the Museum of Art and History housing the Musée Suisse de la Ceramique et du Verre (Swiss Museum of Ceramics and Glass). Consider a brief stop, but if you're pressed for time, forge ahead to the Red Cross Museum (☞ below).

Past the parklands of the Palais des Nations—which do not belong to Geneva but have their own territorial rights—head back uphill on avenue de la Paix, which becomes route de Pregny, and turn right on chemin de l'Impératrice to the Château de Penthes. This 1852 mansion has been converted to house the **Musée des Suisses à l'Etranger** ㉒ (Museum of Swiss Citizens Abroad), a permanent exhibition addressing Switzerland's relations with the outside world—many of them military. It neighbors the **Musée militaire genevois,** which focuses exclusively on local history.

Head back down route de Pregny and right into a cut in the hill. You'll arrive at the **Musée Internationale de la Croix-Rouge** ㉓ (International

Red Cross Museum), a fiercely moving and important permanent exhibition tracing the history of people helping people. You may want to follow this with a 20-minute contemplative stroll down the length of avenue de la Paix, heading toward the lake and the peaceful **Jardin Botanique** ㉔.

If you are traveling by car or have on your walking shoes, continue toward the lake and cross the Parc Mon Repos to the **Musée d'Histoire des Sciences** ㉕ (Museum of the History of Science) in the lovely Villa Bartholoni (1826). Bus 4-44 will carry you back to the center.

TIMING

You could easily devote a full day to this area, spending the morning in the International Museum of the Red Cross, the early afternoon in the Musée des Etrangers, and touring the Palais des Nations after. You might even hike home via the Jardins Botanique if your feet hold out, but take note: The International Area's suburban landscape stretches over the equivalent of many city blocks—the grounds of the Palais des Nations covers more surface than the entire old town—so prepare for a lot of walking. This neighborhood's museums and the Palais (off-season) are closed on Tuesday.

Sights to See

㉔ **Jardin Botanique.** Fans of living flora and fauna will enjoy this botanical garden, with its deer park, exotic hothouses, rose garden, and collection of Alpine rock plants. There's even a section devoted to scent and touch. ⊠ *North of av. de la Paix, east of International Complex.* ☎ *022/732–69–69.* ▣ *Free.* ☉ *Daily 8–7:30.*

㉑ **Musée Ariana.** Home to the **Musée Suisse de la Ceramique et du Verre** (Swiss Museum of Ceramics and Glass) and recently restored to mint condition, this grand 1884 edifice displays a massive collection, spanning seven centuries, of pottery, porcelain, and faience, from Europe, Asia, and the Near East, as well as from regions of Switzerland. The exchange of style and techniques between East and West is emphasized. Downstairs, a 20th-century hall showcases Art Nouveau and Art Deco ceramics and glass; another area illuminates production and firing techniques. ⊠ *Av. de la Paix 10,* ☎ *022/734–29–50.* ▣ *Free.* ☉ *Wed.–Mon. 10–5.*

㉕ **Musée d'Histoire des Sciences.** A collection of scientific instruments, with videos demonstrating their use, illustrates the evolution of modern science, giving viewers a glimpse of Geneva's role as intellectual capital of Europe during the 18th century. The building alone is worth visiting. ⊠ *Villa Bartholoni, Rue de Lausanne 128,* ☎ *731–69–85.* ▣ *Free.* ☉ *Wed.–Mon. 1–5.*

★ ㉓ **Musée Internationale de la Croix-Rouge.** (International Red Cross Museum). In a country that, despite its neutrality, seems sometimes to idealize warfare, where military museums are as prevalent as mountains, this painstakingly nonjudgmental museum sends a different message to the world. Housed in a grim glass-and-concrete structure designed to reflect the contents' sobering themes, it uses state-of-the-art technology in several media to illuminate human kindness in the face of disaster, both natural and man-made. Good deeds are dramatized, from the proverbial Samaritan's to Clara Barton's, and, through film, you not only learn how Henry Dunant was inspired by the battle of Solferino to found the Red Cross but also see for yourself the post-battle horrors that moved him to action. Every effort is made to project the telling image, since mere dates and numbers might leave you unmoved. The sometimes grim displays include endless, monolithic aisles of file boxes containing records of World War I prisoners—recorded on 5 million cards—and a reconstruction of a 3-by-2-meter (10-by-6½-foot) concrete prison cell, reported by a Red Cross observer, that once contained 17 political prisoners—34 footprints make the inhumanity instantly, poignantly clear. And then you learn what people did to help: The Red Cross alerted families of the World War I prisoners to their sons' and husbands' moves, and lodged formal protests that resulted in improved conditions for the cell's inhabitants.

The masterpiece of the exhibition is the astonishing **Mur du temps**, a simple time line that traces, year by year, wars and natural disasters that have killed 100,000 people or more. At first the list starts short, with earthquakes, volcanoes, and plagues dominating; as you enter the modern age the lists stretch long and heavy with wars—even the natural disasters seem to increase, as if the sophisticated man-made devastation had unleashed evil into the atmosphere.

Though it seems no expense has been spared in creating this exhibition and its building, no funds were drawn from the Red Cross itself; the project relied on corporate donors. ⊠ *Av. de la Paix 17,* ☎ *022/733–26–60.* ⊠ *8 SF.* ☉ *Wed.–Mon. 10–5. Commentaries and captions are in English, French, and German.*

Musée Militaire Genevois. The Geneva Military Museum features, among other highlights in the city's history, the Geneva hero Général Henri Guisan, who rallied the Swiss to unity during World War II. ☎ *022/733–53–81.* ⊠ *Free.* ☉ *Wed.–Sun. 2–5.*

★ ㉒ **Musée des Suisses à l'Etranger.** Since Swiss neutrality began during the early 16th century, the Swiss have remained consummate soldiers—for other countries' wars. Sometimes they were even hired to fight on opposing sides in the same war. So impressive was their reputation as mercenary soldiers that the pope himself hired them as bodyguards—and they continue to serve at the Vatican today. This museum, housed inside the circa-1852 **Château de Penthes,** sheds light on Swiss military history with documents, models, prints, and a multitude of flags and uniforms. There are also displays on nonmilitary topics, from the Swiss postal system to Swiss participation in the California Gold Rush. ⊠ *Chemin de l'Impératrice 8,* ☎ *022/734–90–21.* ⊠ *5 SF.* ☉ *Tues.–Sun. 10–noon and 2–6.*

NEED A BREAK?	Have a prix-fixe meal, a plat du jour (daily special), or a slice of home-made fruit tart at **Cent Suisses** (⊠ 19, Chemin de l'Imperatrice, ☎ 022/734–48–65), a simple, comfortable lunch-only spot adjoining the Museum des Suisses à l'Etranger.

★ ⑳ **Palais des Nations.** To create a home for the League of Nations, the Palais des Nations was built between 1929 and 1937; it was inaugurated in 1938 but dissolved in 1940, when the former Soviet Union withdrew. In 1945, when the United Nations was formed in the United States, the Palais des Nations took on the European branch of the organization. The original wing was built according to plans selected in an architectural competition: Le Corbusier's modernist designs were rejected in favor of those of a group of international architects who followed a style that has, ironically, come to be known as Fascist. Indeed, this is a superb example of the severe blend of Art Deco and stylized classicism that Mussolini and Hitler idealized, and its details, both architectural and decorative, have been preserved practically untouched—the bronze torchéres, the gleaming cold marble, and the exaggerated stylistic references that foreshadow the postmodernism of the 1980s. You can visit the **Assembly Hall,** where the original system for simultaneous translation, including earpieces that must surely qualify as antiques, remains virtually as it was in 1937. Here, in 1988, Yassir Arafat met with the remaining UN delegates when he was denied a U.S. visa. In the **Council Chamber** you'll see splendid allegorical murals in heroic style painted by Catalan artist José Maria Sert in 1934; in shades of gold and sepia, they depict humankind's progress in health, technology, freedom, and peace. In the corridors, you'll see rows of delegates' overcoats, which, while their owners negotiate global disarmament, hang trustingly under signs marked *vestiaire non gardé* (coat rack unsupervised). Buy your ticket at the booth outside, and wait in the lobby, where you can watch videos on world hunger or browse through the bookstore, which is full of literature on international issues and demographics. The tour lasts about an hour, not including the initial wait. ⊠ *Palais des Nations,* ☎ *022/907–45–60.* ⚐ *8.50 SF.* ☉ *Apr.–June and Sept.–Oct., daily 10–noon and 2–4; July–Aug., daily 9–6; Jan.–Mar. and Nov.–mid-Dec., weekdays 10–noon and 2–4. By appointment only, last 2 weeks in December.*

DINING

Many restaurants close on weekends, especially Sunday night.

CATEGORY	COST*
$$$$	over 90 SF
$$$	50 SF–90 SF
$$	30 SF–50 SF
$	under 30 SF

per person for a three-course meal (except in $ category), excluding drinks, sales tax, and 15% service charge

$$$$ ✕ **Le Béarn.** Directed by precocious young French chef Jean-Paul Goddard, this elegant, intimate little place done in Empire style and dressed up with pretty porcelain and crystal features modern, light, and creative cuisine: ravioli stuffed with Scotch salmon and oysters, preserved rabbit in green mustard sauce, and any number of truffle specialties, including a spectacular truffle soufflé. The clientele tends toward somber diplomats and politicians. Both the dessert cart and the wine list, which has mostly Swiss and French vintages, are remarkable. ⊠ *Quai de la Poste 4,* ☎ *022/321–00–28. Reservations required. AE, DC, MC, V. Closed Sun. Oct.–April; no lunch Sat. Closed weekends May–Sept.*

$$$$ ✕ **Les Continents.** Though chef Tommy Byrne is Irish, his touch with
★   seafood is inventive, colorful, and more French than international: There's sole sautéed in pistou, cannelloni of langoustines and truffles, pigeon pie, and veal kidney with shallots and sweetbreads, as well as lovely desserts and a full wine list. As this restaurant is in the Intercontinental Hotel in the international area of north Geneva, it functions as a branch of the UN in spirit if not in fact, and all the U.S. presidents and international heads of state have met here during the peace conferences of the past 25 years. ⊠ *Chemin du Petit-Saconnex 7–9,* ☎ *022/919–33–50. Reservations essential. AE, DC, MC, V. Closed weekends.*

$$$$ ✕ **Le Cygne.** This handsome and luxurious restaurant of the Noga-
★   Hilton, all sleek lacquered wood and modern architectural style, offers splendid views over the bay, the Jet d'Eau, and, in the distance, Mont Blanc. It features Parisian chef Philippe Jourdin's exotic creations, including such rare fish as wolf eel and turbot. There's a fabulous cellar of French wines (including some little-known ones), as well as Swiss, Italian, and American vintages. The real show: the caravan of six constantly changing dessert carts. The clientele is a mix of chic natives and international gastronomes. ⊠ *Quai du Mont-Blanc 19,* ☎ *022/731–98–11. Reservations essential. AE, DC, MC, V.*

$$$$ ✕ **Le Lion d'Or.** On the lakeside bluff of Cologny—the Beverly Hills
★ or Neuilly of Geneva—the summer terrace of this culinary landmark
is a little paradise, with an overwhelming view of the bay and the UN.
Though the chic decor is strictly Louis XV–Louis XVI, the cuisine is
modern, light, sophisticated, and glories in seafood. Chef Henri Large,
a Frenchman, creates refined dishes that complement his cellar of great
Bordeaux and Burgundies. Watch for a mixed-seafood grill with Greek
artichokes, turbot in Meursault, and pheasant-and-truffle sausage—
but don't miss the famous bouillabaisse, enormous, savory, and reflecting
chef Large's years in St-Tropez. (He occasionally breaks forth in an opera
aria, having also attended a conservatory.) Jet-setters, artists, writers,
and celebrities often pass through. Take Bus G or A in the direction of
Corsier Village, or take a cab—it's not far beyond quai Gustave-Ador.
⊠ *Pl. Gauthier 5,* ☏ *022/736–44–32. Reservations essential. AE, DC,
MC, V. Closed weekends.*

$$$ ✕ **La Cassolette.** In the heart of Carouge, the picturesque *ville Sarde*
★ of old houses, tiny streets and ancient courtyards, this modern and col-
orful upscale bistro features the imaginative cuisine of young chef
Réné Fracheboud, nicknamed "the Pink Panther" because he wears a
pink chef's uniform and has chosen a vivid pink, rose, and russet color
scheme for the restaurant. Equally vivid culinary experiments—salmon
and zucchini with dried tomatoes and curry oil, or veal sweetbreads
with duck liver in bitter cocoa and Arabian coffee—are served on tri-
angular Miami-bright platters. This little café is the favorite rendezvous
of artists, the privileged, and, occasionally, tourists. There's an unusual
list of lesser-known wines that are available by the glass with each course;
the list of bottled wines is prestigious and pricey. ⊠ *Rue Jacques-Dal-
phin 31,* ☏ *022/342–03–18. MC, V. Closed weekends.*

$$$ ✕ **La Glycine/Chez Jipek'à.** This is a classic *caboulot* (downscale
cabaret-bistro), and a picturesque *caf' conc'* (café-concert) complete
with a little Italian-style terrace under the *glycine* (hanging wisteria).
Jipek'à—a Czech turned Swiss—is the soul of the popular spot, which
is always smoky, noisy, and full to bursting. The clientele is cosmopolitan and draws many of its regulars from the nearby UN. The
food is only average, but you come here for the ambience, to sing or
laugh with the pianist and *les bohèmes* who frequent the place. People have been known to dance between tables here. ⊠ *Rue de Mont-
brillant 21,* ☏ *022/733–62–85. No credit cards. Closed weekends.*

$$$ ✕ **La Mère Royaume.** Only in Geneva could you find good, classic French
cooking served in a pseudo-historic setting under the careful direction
of a charming Italian couple. Even the name is Genevois: La Mère Roy-
aume was a kind of Genevois Joan of Arc who in 1602 repulsed the
attack of the troops of the duke of Savoy by dumping hot soup on their
heads. The main restaurant serves haute cuisine—foie gras sautéed in
raspberry vinegar, rack of lamb with garlic confit—but inexpensive plats
du jour are available in the rustic bistro. ⊠ *Rue des Corps-Saints 9,*
☏ *022/732–70–08. AE, DC, MC, V. Closed Sat. lunch, Sun.*

$$$ ✕ **Roberto.** The "Commendatore" Roberto Carugati, a young man of
★ 70-plus, and his daughter, Marietta, have made this spot the meeting
point and the melting pot of Genevans, Italians from Milan and Rome,
and Parisian artists and political stars. You'll find classic Italian dishes—
gnocchi (potato-based dumplings), *bollito misto* (boiled meat with
herb sauce), osso buco (veal shank in tomato and white-wine sauce),
and grilled sole—as well as great Italian wines, a lively ambience, and
swift service. ⊠ *Rue Pierre-Fatio 10,* ☏ *022/311–80–33. AE, MC,
V. Closed Sat. dinner, Sun.*

$$–$$$ ✕ **La Perle du Lac.** This grand wooden chalet, set alongside a swan-
populated lake in a vast, romantic park-promenade, has a lovely summer terrace where you can order simple grilled meats and salads, and

an elegant but intimate panoramic restaurant called L'Orangerie, the rendezvous of the gentry, which serves more sophisticated cuisine: *rouget barbet* (lean, delicate Mediterranean fish) on zucchini spaghetti with saffron, *dorade* (white flaky fish) on rhubarb compote with orange butter, duckling with honey and spices, puff pastry with seasonal berries. The view over the lake is magnificent. After your meal, you can take a walk through the flower gardens in one of Geneva's prettiest landscapes. ✉ *Rue de Lausanne 128,* ☎ *022/731–79–35. AE, DC, MC, V. Closed Mon.*

$$ ✕ **Aux Halles de l'Ile.** This island in the middle of the flowing waters of the Rhône was once occupied by a permanent market, as important to the region as Les Halles in Paris. Now it is an artists' center, with galleries selling paintings and a vast arcaded café. On the open terrace, with the river rippling by, you might think you're on a boat. The menu mixes bistro and brasserie specialties, and evenings are enhanced by jazz concerts. The clientele is young and casual. Inside, a small panoramic restaurant directly overlooks the river. ✉ *Pl. de l'Ile 1,* ☎ *022/311–52–21. AE, DC, MC, V. Closed Sun.*

$$ ✕ **Boeuf Rouge.** Despite the contrived decor—a send-up of a Lyonnais
★ bistro, jam-packed with kitschy ceramics and art nouveau posters—this cozy, popular spot delivers the real thing: rich, unadulterated Lyonnais cuisine, from the bacon-egg-and-greens *salade Lyonnaise* and hand-stuffed pistachio-studded sausage to the *boudin noir* (blood sausage) with apples, andouillettes in mustard sauce, tender *quenelles de brochet* (pike dumplings), and authentic *tarte tatin* (caramelized apple tart). While the ambience is relaxed, the service—by the couple who own the place and the chef himself—is flamboyant: All dishes are presented on a flower-crowded tray before they're served at tableside. Dine late to avoid crowds of sauce-on-the-side Americans and their political chatter; chic Genevois slum for comfort food after 10. ✉ *Rue Alfred-Vincent 17,* ☎ *022/732–75–37. MC, V. Closed weekends.*

$$ ✕ **Brasserie Lipp.** As popular since it came to Geneva in 1986 as its counterpart has always been in Paris, this slick, synthetic brasserie plunges you into the belle epoque, with its *garçons de café* (waiters), its mirrors, its ceramics, and its retro style. Lipp draws Swiss and foreigners alike, in part because of its prime position in the deluxe supermall called Confédération-Centre. Lines form day and night as chic clients vie to take part in the noise and animation and to eat herring salad, *pot-au-feu, choucroûte* (sauerkraut), *petit salé aux lentilles* (salted pork with lentils), andouillettes in white wine, platters of seafood, entrecôte, and good beer. There are more sophisticated menu items as well, including oysters in winter. A choice of small or large portions on many dishes, as well as a cheap daily lunch plate, help keep prices down. ✉ *Rue de la Confédération 8,* ☎ *022/311–10–11. AE, DC, MC, V.*

$$ ✕ **Buffet Cornavin.** This grand train-station restaurant complex, with its pleasantly passé old-brasserie decor, shows Geneva's Swiss roots. The several rooms range in style from a shabby one downstairs to a full-service *restaurant français.* The liveliest hall is just outside the French restaurant, where a pianist accompanies the clatter of the open kitchen and you can enjoy sandwiches, sausages, oysters, game, and Lyonnais specialties while watching travelers in transit. ✉ *Gare Cornavin,* ☎ *022/732–43–06. AE, DC, MC, V.*

$$ ✕ **Chez Bouby.** At the corner of rue Grenus, this popular, modernized bistro serves a mixed and arty crowd until 1 AM. The cooking is earthy, with an emphasis on *abats* (organ meats), game, mussels, and good wine by the glass. ✉ *Rue Grenus 1,* ☎ *022/731–09–27. MC, V. Closed Sun.*

$$ ✕ **Chez Jacky.** Despite the predictable wood-and-copper bistro look, the seafood cooking in this restaurant is a cut above average, exhibiting a nouvelle influence in the sauces and combinations but not in the portions, which are sizable. Try the *omble chevalier* (local salmon trout), which comes in a sauce made of Swiss red wine, or the *cuisson de lapin* (rabbit thigh) with cabbage and mustard sauce. Be sure to leave room for a sampling from the overloaded dessert cart. ⊠ *Rue Jacques-Necker 9–11,* ☎ *022/732–86–80. AE, MC, V. Closed weekends.*

$$ ✕ **La Coupole.** This is a vast culinary theme park, with several lounges, bars, wine bars, a cozy restaurant, and a small brasserie, all extravagantly decorated in dark plush, mirrors, and etched glass. There's a pianist evenings after 9:30; and crowds gather for drinks, red-meat meals (mixed grill, entrecôte, lamb chops), and quick indulgences (caviar, smoked salmon, oysters), the latter served until 1 or 2 AM. ⊠ *Rue du Rhône 116,* ☎ *022/735–65–44. AE, DC, MC, V. Closed Sun.*

$$ ✕ **L'Entrecôte Couronnée.** At the edge of the Pâquis quarter and the red-light district and run by a retired chanteuse, this exclusive, clubbish little bistro merits its name (meaning "The Crowned Steak"). The entrecôte is excellent, and so are the frites and salad, which is a blessing: The house specialty is the only menu choice. It's not just the steaks that are "crowned"—the elite clientele has included the Archduke of Hapsburg and Marie-Astrid de Luxembourg. ⊠ *Rue des Pâquis 5,* ☎ *022/732–84–45. V. Closed weekends.*

$$ ✕ **La Favola.** Run by a young Ticinese couple from Locarno, this
★ quirky little restaurant may be the most picturesque in town. The tiny dining room, at the top of a vertiginous spiral staircase, strikes a delicate balance between rustic and fussy, with its lace window panels, embroidered tablecloths, polished parquet, and rough-beam ceiling sponge-painted in Roman shades of ocher and rust. The food echoes this style, part country-simple and part city-chic: Try carpaccio with olive paste or white truffles, bollito of venison in Barolo, ravioli with asparagus, or rabbit in Gorgonzola. Lunch menus offer excellent value. ⊠ *Rue Jean-Calvin 15,* ☎ *022/311–74–37. MC, V. Closed weekends.*

$$ ✕ **Griffin's Café.** This café of the well-known international nightclub, Griffin's, draws privileged and often glamorous young people, who come to eat chic bistro dishes—perch filets, entrecôte Paris-style, grilled scampi in anise—amid belle epoque beveled glass and carved oak. A jazz pianist plays every night. ⊠ *Blvd. Helvétique 36,* ☎ *022/735–42–06. Reservations advised. AE, DC, MC, V. Closed Sun.*

$$ ✕ **Harry's New York Bar.** Geneva's establishment mingles with its young internationals here, gathering around the pianist for high-style, lively evenings, live jazz trios, and light meals: endive salad with Roquefort and walnuts, onion soup, pasta, grilled steaks, even American spareribs and chili. ⊠ *Confédération-Centre, rue de la Confédération 8,* ☎ *022/311–42–06. Reservations advised. AE, MC, V. Closed Sun.*

$$ ✕ **Le Jardin.** This is another local favorite among bankers, artists, and
★ the Geneva intelligentsia. Businesspeople choose light lunch menus here, while elegant *bourgeoises* order salads and salmon carpaccio. The well-prepared daily plates and local specialties are served in an agreeable—if a little snobbish—setting: The ambience is impeccably BCBG (*bon chic, bon genre*). The summer terrace is lovely, and the whole place hops when Christie's, located in the hotel, has an auction. ⊠ *Hotel Richemond, rue Adhémar-Fabri 8,* ☎ *022/731–14–00. AE, DC, MC, V.*

$$ ✕ **Le Pied-de-Cochon.** While visiting antiques shops and art galleries
★ in old town, stop for lunch or supper in this old bistro, which retains its ancient beams and original zinc-top bar, rarely seen nowadays. Crowded, noisy, smoky, and lively, it faces the Palais de Justice and welcomes famous lawyers who plead celebrated causes; there are artists and workers as well. The good, simple cooking includes pieds de cochon, of course—grilled, with mushrooms, with lentils, or *désossés* (boned)—as well as simple Lyonnais dishes, including petit salé, ham,

Dining

Aux Halles de l'Ile, **28**
Boeuf Rouge, **8**
Brasserie Lipp, **31**
Buffet Cornavin, **16**
Café du Grütli, **35**
Chez Bouby, **26**
Chez Jacky, **21**
Chez Léo, **49**
Griffin's Café, **46**
Harry's New York Bar, **30**
La Cassolette, **38**
La Coupole, **47**
La Favola, **39**
La Glycine/Chez Jipek'à, **17**
La Mère Royaume, **22**
La Perle du Lac, **1**
Le Béarn, **29**
Le Cygne, **3**
Le Jardin, **5**
Le Lion d'Or, **45**
Le Pied-de-Cochon, **37**
Le Saint-Germain, **33**
L'Echalotte, **32**
L'Entrecôte Couronnée, **7**
Les Armures, **36**
Les Continents, **12**
Mirador, **18**
Roberto, **48**
Taverne de la Madeleine, **40**

Lodging

Ambassador, **25**
Beau-Rivage, **4**
Beau-Site, **34**
Bernina, **13**
Central, **41**
D'Allèves, **24**
De Berne, **9**
De la Cigogne, **44**
De la Cloche, **2**
Des Tourelles, **27**
Intercontinental, **12**
International et Terminus, **11**
Le Richemond, **6**
Les Armures, **36**
Lido, **20**
Metropole, **43**
Moderne, **19**
Montana, **10**
Savoy, **14**
St-Gervais, **23**
Strasbourg-Univers, **15**
Touring-Balance, **42**

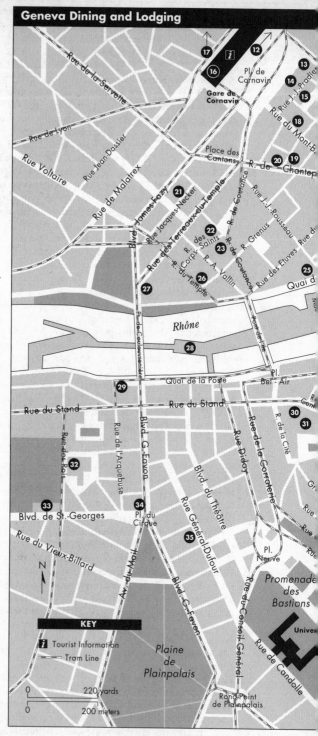

Geneva Dining and Lodging

KEY

🛈 Tourist Information
Tram Line

0 ___ 220 yards
0 ___ 200 meters

grilled andouillettes, tripe, and salads. ⊠ *Pl. du Bourg-de-Four 4,* ☎ *022/310–47–97. AE, DC, MC, V. Closed Sun. May–Sept.*

$$ ✕ **Le Saint-Germain.** In this intimate little establishment near the place du Plainpalais the specialty is seafood: delicate raw fish salad, poached St-Pierre (John Dory). The *patronne* welcomes you with a smile and presents the fish whole before serving. The prices are reasonable for such high quality. ⊠ *Blvd. de St-Georges 61,* ☎ *022/328–26–24. AE, DC, MC, V. Closed weekends.*

$ ✕ **Les Armures.** In the picturesque and historic hotel at the summit of
★   the old town, just steps from the cathedral, this atmospheric restaurant offers several dining halls, all decorated with authentic arms from the Middle Ages. There's a broad menu of pan-Swiss specialties, from fondue to choucroûte to *Rösti* (hash brown potatoes), but some of the dishes are pure Genevois: *longeole* (sausage), fricasée. In addition, there are inexpensive pizzas, shellfish in winter, and a good selection of salads. Everyone comes here, from workers to politicians, if only for a slab of homemade fruit tart. ⊠ *Rue du Puits-St-Pierre 1,* ☎ *022/310–34–42. AE, DC, MC, V.*

$ ✕ **Café du Grütli.** This is a high-tech, high-style student canteen in the postmodernized Maison Grütli, where Geneva offers creative space to its painters, sculptors, photographers, and filmmakers. The light nouvelle lunches (Gruyère carpaccio with dried fruit, grilled duck, preserved lamb stew) and late snacks (quiches, melted-cheese salads) are as hip as the clientele, which spills out into the atrium lobby. ⊠ *Rue Général-Dufour 16,* ☎ *022/329–44–95. No credit cards.*

$ ✕ **Chez Léo.** This tiny, charming bistro, on the corner next door to Roberto, features the simple Italian cuisine of Roberto's son, Léo. Here you'll find veal piccata (in lemon sauce), homemade tortellini; and fresh-fruit tarts in an old-fashioned bentwood-and-posters setting. Fans of father and son line up at the door for good, honest, simple meals. ⊠ *Rue Pierre-Fatio 12,* ☎ *022/311–53–07. MC, V. Closed Sat. dinner, Sun.*

$ ✕ **L'Echalotte.** Big and brightly lit, with warm polished wood banquettes and paper place mats, this casual, comfortable spot draws Genevois of all social levels. Offering a choice of no fewer than six first courses and three seconds, the fixed-price menu is generous, and the cooking is eclectic and homey. Such dishes as scallop casserole with asparagus tips, snails in puff pastry, and lemon-meringue pudding are all highly flavored and served with casual flair. There are good carafe wines as well as a modest list of bottles. ⊠ *Rue des Rois 17,* ☎ *022/320–59–99. No credit cards. Closed weekends.*

$ ✕ **Mirador.** Opened in the 1960s by an Italian family and still run by the second generation, this typical Geneva bistro near the train station draws a diverse clientele who spill out onto the pavement in summer, when much of rue du Mont-Blanc becomes a pedestrian street. The fare is fresh, well-prepared traditional French, featuring entrecôte, fish, salads, and such specialties as *pierrade*—meat cooked on hot stones. ⊠ *Rue du Mont-Blanc 24,* ☎ *022/732–98–60. AE, DC, MC, V. Closed Sun. Sept.–June.*

$ ✕ **Taverne de la Madeleine.** Tucked into the commercial maze between
★   rue de la Croix-d'Or and the old town, overlooking l'Eglise de la Madeleine, this casual café claims to be the oldest eatery in Geneva. Run by the city's temperance league, it serves no alcoholic beverages and thus loses the business-lunch crowd, who insist on a pitcher of Fendant with meals. That means that there's all the more room for you to relax over homemade choucroûte, perch, or fresh-baked fruit tarts in the charming Victorian dining room upstairs. There are big, fresh salads, vegetarian plates, and a variety of loose-leaf teas. In summer, the terrace—overlooking the *place*—is in demand. The kitchen closes

at 7 in summer, at 4 in winter. ⊠ *Rue Toutes-âmes 20,* ☎ *022/310–60–70. No credit cards.*

LODGING

Spending the night in Geneva is as financially taxing as eating a meal: This is a sophisticated European city, and the prices reflect its stature. It is also a popular convention center, and rooms can sell out in blocks, whole groups of hotels snatched up at a time. Book well in advance and brace yourself: You will have to pay more than 400 SF a night for posh lodgings and more than 120 SF simply to have a toilet in your room.

CATEGORY	COST*
$$$$	over 300 SF
$$$	200 SF–300 SF
$$	120 SF–200 SF
$	under 120 SF

All prices are for a standard double room, including breakfast, sales tax, and service charge. Luxury hotels start at 500 SF.

$$$$ ★ **Les Armures.** In the heart of old town, this archaeological treasure dates from the 17th century, but its original stonework, frescoes, and stenciled beams are now complemented with impeccable modern comforts. Its few, intimate rooms embellish appropriate Old World furnishings with slick marble baths. Despite the luxury, prices are lower than grand hotels on the Rive Droite. The casual restaurant is an old-town must (☞ Dining, *above*). Approach by car can be difficult: from the Place Neuve, head into the old town via rue de la Tertasse. ⊠ *Rue du Puits-St-Pierre 1, CH-1204,* ☎ *022/310–91–72,* FAX *022/310–98–46. 48 beds. Restaurant, bar, in-room VCRs. AE, DC, MC, V.*

$$$$ ★ **Beau-Rivage.** Hushed and genteel, this grand old Victorian palace has had much of its original 1865 decor restored: It's all velvet, parquet, and fresco splendor, and there's a marble fountain in the lobby. The bar and some suites are particularly florid, and most rooms, though updated, retain fine old architectural details. The front rooms take in Right Bank views, as does the terrace restaurant on the first floor, over the prestigious French restaurant Le Chat Botté. Mme. Mitterrand stays here when in town, and the empress Elizabeth of Austria died here after being shot only 100 meters away. This landmark and its rival, the Richemond, really create their own price category, with doubles starting at more than 500 SF. ⊠ *Quai du Mont-Blanc 13, CH-1201,* ☎ *022/731–02–21,* FAX *022/738–98–47. 168 beds. 2 restaurants, bar, café, no-smoking rooms, in-room VCRs. AE, DC, MC, V.*

$$$$ **De la Cigogne.** Offbeat and slightly fantastical, this is an eccentric hotel. Every room showcases a different decorative style, sometimes with questionable taste. Still, it's a great place to enjoy antiques, some working fireplaces, and lovely slate-roof-and-chimney views in the heart of the luxury shopping area, steps from the old town. It's a Relais & Châteaux property. ⊠ *Pl. Longmalle 17, CH-1204,* ☎ *022/818–40–40,* FAX *022/818–40–50. 100 beds. Restaurant, bar, in-room VCRs. AE, DC, MC, V.*

$$$$ **Intercontinental.** This massive, modern high-rise is as big as an airport terminal, with every amenity amassed on floor after solidly constructed floor. The older rooms, last renovated during the late '60s, are surprisingly warm, even homey; the new ones have glossy faux bird's-eye paneling and brass. Rooms with lake views are magnificent, no more expensive than rooms without them, and much in demand. As it's located in the international neighborhood, the hotel draws a diplomatic crowd to its restaurant, Les Continents (☞ Dining, *above*), but caters

to large groups as well. ⊠ *Chemin du Petit-Saconnex 7–9, CH-1211,* ☎ *022/919–39–39,* FAX *022/919–38–38. 406 beds. 2 restaurants, bar, snack bar, pool, beauty salon, fitness center, free parking. AE, DC, MC, V.*

$$$$ 🖬 **Metropole.** Built in 1855, lent to the city of Geneva to house the
★ Red Cross prisoners-of-war archives, and now restored by its management of more than a quarter of a century, the Metropole has as much riverside splendor as its Right Bank sisters—and at a lower price. The ambience is relaxed and unfussy despite the grand scale, with leather and hunting prints mixed in with discreet pastels. The riverside rooms are noisier, because of traffic, but the view is superb. Request the quieter third or fourth floors. The restaurant L'Arlequin draws gastronomic kudos, and the spacious lobby lounge, with pianist, attracts an elegant local clientele. It's seconds from the best shopping and minutes from the old town. ⊠ *Quai Général-Guisan 34, CH-1204,* ☎ *022/311–13–44,* FAX *022/311–13–50. 202 beds. 2 restaurants, bar, café. AE, DC, MC, V.*

$$$$ 🖬 **Le Richemond.** Managed by the Armleder family since 1875, this
★ luxury Right Bank landmark maintains the opulence of its Victorian origins without looking like a museum. Nor does it feel like one: This is a lively, thriving contemporary inn, proud of recent guests (Michael Jackson) as well as past ones (Colette, Miró, Chagall). The decor makes much of scarlet and leather. Only the restaurant, Le Gentilhomme, indulges in museumlike conservatism. Amid its pompous red velvet, crystal, and gilt, you can indulge in a meal Escoffier or Dolly Levi would have enjoyed: classic but showy French cuisine, old wines, fine brandy, rare cigars, and your share of the eight kilos of caviar served here each day. For transportation, choose your Rolls: Will it be a Silver Wraith II or a Phantom V? ⊠ *Rue Adhémar-Fabri 8–10, CH-1211,* ☎ *022/731–14–00,* FAX *022/731–67–09. 163 beds. 2 restaurants, bar, café, beauty salon, fitness center. AE, DC, MC, V.*

$$$ 🖬 **Ambassador.** On the Right Bank directly over the roaring torrents of the Pont de la Machine, this business-class lodging has recently updated its rooms with sleek, new wood and soft colors. Double-window corner rooms are especially desirable. ⊠ *Quai des Bergues 21,* ☎ *022/731–72–00,* FAX *022/738–90–80. 126 beds. Restaurant, bar, free parking. AE, DC, MC, V.*

$$$ 🖬 **De Berne.** Despite its unfortunate position on the fringe of the prostitutes' district, this is a solid business-class hotel, spacious and well maintained. It was built during the mid-'60s, but most of its harshest edges have been softened with spindled wood, touches of brass, and a warm cocoa color scheme. Rooms on the rue Sismondi side are quietest. ⊠ *Rue de Berne 26, CH-1201,* ☎ *022/731–60–00,* FAX *022/731–11–73. 160 beds. Restaurant, bar. AE, DC, MC, V.*

$$$ 🖬 **Touring-Balance.** This Best Western Swiss hotel has a sharp new lobby
★ and old-style but gracious lower floors with French doors; the higher floors are slick, solid, and high tech. There are gallery-quality lithos in every room, a lovely belle epoque breakfast room, a chic ground-floor restaurant, and professional service. The location, in the midst of Left Bank luxury shopping, is ideal. ⊠ *Pl. Longemalle 13, CH-1204,* ☎ *022/310–40–45,* FAX *022/310–40–39. 100 beds. Restaurant, café, coffee shop. AE, DC, MC, V.*

$$ 🖬 **Bernina.** Directly across from the train station, this mildly gloomy city hotel offers several combinations to suit your budget, from cheap double beds with sink and bidet to full doubles with the works. Most rooms have neutral colors and tile baths; the oldest rooms are done in florid prints. Breakfasts are served with some of the niceties you find in fancier hostelries, like jam in bowls rather than in little plastic packages and sugar in cubes rather than in paper packets. ⊠ *Pl. de Cor-*

navin 22, CH-1211, ☎ 022/731–49–50, FAX 022/732–73–59. *145 beds. Breakfast room. AE, DC, MC, V.*

$$ 🏨 **D'Allèves.** This simple hotel on a quiet square between the station and the Right Bank is crowded with the owner's art and antique collection and decorated with a kind of dark elegance (velvet, red carpet, chenille) no longer quite in vogue. There's a modest but good restaurant and a coffee shop. ✉ *Rue Kléberg 13, CH-1211, ☎ 022/732–15–30, FAX 022/738–32–66. 77 beds. Restaurant, coffee shop, AE, DC, MC, V.*

$$ 🏨 **International et Terminus.** Although it's in the busy station district, this bargain lodging has made an effort to warm its public areas with antiques and to freshen the rooms with clean, neutral decor. There are an Italian restaurant and a terrace café. Rooms without bath fall into the $ category. ✉ *Rue des Alpes 20, CH-1201, ☎ 022/732–80–95, FAX 022/732–18–43. 83 beds. Restaurant, bar, café. AE, DC, MC, V.*

$$ 🏨 **Moderne.** This is a no-nonsense urban hotel. The brass-and-pastel decor is what you notice first, not the old Formica; all the baths are tiled. The courtyard-side rooms are quiet, and some no-smoking rooms are available. It's between the station and the Right Bank. ✉ *Rue de Berne 1, CH-1201, ☎ 022/732–81–00, FAX 022/738–26–58. 70 beds. Restaurant. AE, DC, MC, V.*

$$ 🏨 **Montana.** This station-area property offers sharp rooms with a
★ taupe-and-salmon color scheme, new double-glazed windows, and all-tile baths. ✉ *Rue des Alpes 23, CH-1201, ☎ 022/732–08–40, FAX 022/728–25–11. 70 beds. Restaurant. AE, DC, MC, V.*

$$ 🏨 **Savoy.** For the train traveler with heavy luggage, this is a good station-area stop in the business-class range. Despite the steady traffic, rooms are fairly quiet; double-glazed windows keep noise at bay. The decor, plumbing, and heating are dated, but the amenities are at the Best Western level. ✉ *Pl. de Cornavin 8, Ch-1201, ☎ 022/731–12–55, FAX 022/738–46–08. 100 beds. Restaurant, bar. AE, DC, MC, V.*

$$ 🏨 **Strasbourg-Univers.** Though this station-area hotel has a slick
★ wood-and-marble look, its prices remain well below those of much shabbier competitors. The new rooms have glossy burled-wood details and chic pastels, and there's a freshly furnished restaurant as well as a bar in the style of a *carnotzet* (pub). ✉ *Rue Jean-Jacques Pradier 10, CH-1201, ☎ 022/732–25–62, FAX 022/738–42–08. 100 beds. Restaurant, bar, café. AE, DC, MC, V.*

$ 🏨 **Beau-Site.** While the flea-market furniture and creaky parquet, exposed wiring, and thick paint may be grim, the prices in this hotel are rock-bottom, and some rooms have showers, though all toilets are down the hall. Room 11 has a fireplace. Rooms on the courtyard side are quietest. ✉ *Pl. du Cirque 3, CH-1204, ☎ 022/328–10–08, FAX 022/329–23–64. 50 beds. Breakfast room. No credit cards.*

$ 🏨 **Central.** Despite its location at the top of an anonymous urban
★ building on a back shopping street, this bargain hotel merits the elevator ride: Most rooms are freshly decorated with grass-cloth wallpaper and carpet, and all have tile bathrooms. Prices are the lowest in town for rooms with bath. ✉ *Rue de la Rôtisserie 2, CH-1204, ☎ 022/818–81–00, FAX 022/818–81–01. 40 beds. Breakfast in room only. AE, DC, MC, V.*

$ 🏨 **De la Cloche.** This once-luxurious walk-up flat has a tidy, tasteful
★ new look that hasn't altered its period details, and the courtyard setting is so quiet that you can hear birds in the garden. Good-size rooms with high ceilings share baths down the hall. ✉ *Rue de la Cloche 6, CH-1201, ☎ 022/732–94–81. FAX 022/738–16–12. 18 beds. Breakfast room. No credit cards.*

$ 🏨 **Des Tourelles.** Once worthy of a czar, now host to backpackers, this
★ fading Victorian vision offers enormous bay-window corner rooms, many

with marble fireplaces. French doors open over the Rhône. The furnishings are scarce and strictly functional, but the staff is young and friendly. Bring earplugs: The location is extremely noisy, over roaring bridge traffic, not to mention the pop radio playing in the reception-breakfast nook. Half the rooms share bathrooms. ⊠ *Blvd. James-Fazy 2, CH-1201,* ☎ *022/732–44–23,* FAX *022/732–76–20. 36 beds. Breakfast room. AE, DC, MC, V.*

$ 🏠 **Lido.** Despite the red linoleum and black-and-white tile baths that show this hotel's age, rooms have fresh, pale carpet, wood veneer furnishings, and double-glazed windows; those over the square are quietest, and those in the 33–43 series are largest. Most rooms have a bath. ⊠ *Rue de Chantepoulet 8, CH-1201,* ☎ *022/731–55–30,* FAX *022/731–65–01. 60 beds. Breakfast room. AE, DC, MC, V.*

$ 🏠 **St-Gervais.** On a historic block in the Right Bank town center, this
★ low-budget inn offers garretlike rooms that are neat, tidy, quaint, and well maintained, with fresh linens and framed prints. Families should ask for the large, old room with ancient beams. A tiny pub on the ground floor serves snacks. Two rooms have baths. ⊠ *Rue des Corps-Saints 20, CH-1201,* ☎ *022/732–45–72,* FAX *022/738–43–69. 26 beds. Café. AE, MC, V.*

NIGHTLIFE AND THE ARTS

Geneva Agenda, which has weekly listings of films, concerts, museum exhibitions and galleries, is available free of charge in most hotels.

The Arts

Theater

The leading Geneva theaters include the **Théâtre le Caveau** (⊠ av. Ste-Clotilde, ☎ 022/328–11–33); **Théatre de Grütli** (⊠ rue Général-Dufour 16, ☎ 022/328-98-78); **Théâtre de Carouge** (⊠ rue Ancienne 57, ☎ 022/343–43–43); **Comédie de Genève** (⊠ blvd. des Philosophes 6, ☎ 022/320–50–01); and **Nouveau Théâtre de Poche** (⊠ rue de Cheval Blanc 7, ☎ 022/328–37–59). Performances are mostly in French, but during the summer, amateur companies of a high standard present plays in English as well. Children will enjoy shows with the **Marionettes de Genève** (⊠ 3 rue Rodo, ☎ 022/329–67–67).

Music

Victoria Hall (⊠ rue Général-Dufour 14, ☎ 022/328–81–21) is the main venue of L'Orchestre de la Suisse Romande, which was conducted for 50 years by Ernest Ansermet and through him had close links with Stravinsky. For information on the orchestra's season, call 022/311–25–11. The **Grand-Théâtre de Genève** (⊠ pl. Neuve, ☎ 022/311–23–11) burned down in 1951 when a rehearsal of *Die Walküre*'s fire scene became too realistic. It reopened in 1962 and now features concerts of classical music as well as opera, operetta, and dance; watch for listings of Sunday-morning chamber music recitals in the foyer. **Radio-Suisse Romande** (⊠ blvd. Carl-Vogt 66, ☎ 022/708–77–11) has a concert hall, and audiences are welcome at some of the live broadcasts. Various concerts take place in the **Conservatoire de Musique** (⊠ pl. Neuve, ☎ 022/311–76–33).

Film

Most movies are dubbed in French; to see English-language films in English, watch listings in the local newspapers or *Geneva Agenda* for the initials *v.o.,* meaning *version originale.* They are often shown in late afternoon and after 10 PM.

Nightlife

Bars and Lounges

If you want a cocktail with piano music in the background, go to one of the luxury hotels and sink into an armchair. The **Hotel Metropole** (⊠ Quai Général Guisan 34, ☎ 022/311–13–44) is particularly comfortable; you can sit in the lobby or in the bar itself. **La Coupole** (⊠ rue Pierre-Fatio 16, ☎ 022/735–65–44) has piano music from 7 PM. **Griffin's Café** (⊠ blvd. Helvétique 36, ☎ 022/735–12–18) has a singer-pianist. Visitors homesick for a southwestern drawl will hear plenty at the **Cactus Club** (⊠ rue Chaponnière 3, ☎ 022/732–63–98); it specializes in margaritas and other often tequila-based "southwestern" cocktails. Upstairs from the Cactus Club is **Mañana** (☎ 022/732–21–31), which has guitarists. Many Genevois drink in cafés, bistros, and brasseries; you'll see a different local scene by joining them (☞ Dining, *above*).

Cabaret/Nightclub

Griffin's (⊠ blvd. Helvétique 36, ☎ 022/735–12–18) is a chic, exclusive nightclub with dancing. **Velvet** (⊠ rue du Jeu-de-l'Arc 7, ☎ 022/735–00–00) and **Pussy-Cat-Saloon** (⊠ rue des Glacis-de-Rive 15, adjoining Club 58, ☎ 022/735–15–15) have strip shows. **Moulin Rouge** (⊠ av. du Mail 1, ☎ 022/329–35–66) offers shows and dancing. **La Garçonnière** (⊠ rue de la Cité 15, ☎ 022/310–21–61) has an all-male revue. **Chez Maxim's** (⊠ rue Thalberg 2, ☎ 022/732–99–00) features revues, live dance orchestras, and the occasional dog act.

Casinos

Geneva has its own casino in the **Grand Casino** complex (⊠ quai du Mont-Blanc 19, ☎ 022/732–63–20), but there's a 5 SF gambling limit.

Discos

Le Petit Palace (⊠ rue de la Tour-de-Boël 6, ☎ 022/311–00–33), **Blue Chip** (⊠ quai du Mont-Blanc 19, ☎ 022/731–57–35), **Club 58** (⊠ rue des Glacis-de-Rive 15, ☎ 022/735-15-15), **L'Interdit** (⊠ 18, quai du Seujet, ☎ 022/738-90-91), and **Arthur's** (⊠ rte. de Prè-Bois 20, ☎ 022/788–16–00) are popular. Just over the French border, St. Julien-en-Genêvois claims to have the biggest disco in Europe, **La Macumba;** cross the border at Perly (⊠ rte. d'Annecy, ☎ 023/50–49–23–50).

Jazz

Halles de l'Ile (⊠ pl. de l'Ile, ☎ 022/311–52–21) features jazz and views over the Rhône. **Sud des Alpes** (⊠ rue des Alps 10, ☎ 022/732–30–95) is a jazz club frequented by true aficionados.

SHOPPING

Shopping Streets and Malls

The principal streets for luxury shopping are **rue du Rhône** and the neighboring street that changes names: **rue de la Confédération, rue du Marché, rue de la Croix-d'Or,** and **rue de Rive;** the two run parallel along the Left Bank. The **Grande-Rue** in the old town, as well as other streets radiating down from **place du Bourg-de-Four,** are lined with interesting boutiques. **Rue du Mont-Blanc** on the Right Bank has less expensive watch and souvenir shops. The **Centre-Confédération** is a glitzy three-story shopping center that opens at the bottom onto place Bel-Air and from the top leads into the old town. **Les Cygnes,** a small, glossy urban mall just north of the train station on rue de Lausanne, has everything from shoes to gourmet food.

Department Stores

Au Grand Passage (⌧ rue du Rhône 50, ☎ 022/310–66–11) is the granddaddy of Geneva department stores, with a full line of upscale goods. **Bon Génie** (⌧ rue du Marché 34, ☎ 022/310–82–22) has attentive service to match its luxurious goods. **Placette** (⌧ rue Rousseau 27, ☎ 022/231–83–00), on the Right Bank, offers cheaper goods than most other department stores, with nearly as wide a selection. The central branch of **Migro** (⌧ rue des Pâquis 41, ☎ 022/731–79–50) offers a wide variety of goods and clothes, in addition to groceries. The **SupercentreCoop** (⌧ rue de la Confédération, ☎ 022/310–77–11) is another all-purpose megastore, with clothes, groceries, and more.

Flea Markets

There is a flea market in the **plaine de Plainpalais** with plenty of brocante (one man's junk, another man's antiques) every Wednesday and Saturday. An arts-and-crafts market on the **place de la Fusterie** holds forth every Thursday in summer. A clothing and book market takes place daily on **place de la Madeleine.**

Auctions

As a jewelry capital rivaled only by New York, Geneva is home to the world's two most famous auction houses. **Christie's** (⌧ pl. Taconnerie 8, ☎ 022/311–17–66), often has wines and ornaments to complement its jewelry collection. **Sotheby's** (⌧ quai du Mont-Blanc 13, ☎ 022/732–85–85), at the Hotel Beau-Rivage, has exquisite collections on display.

Specialty Stores

ANTIQUES

Antiquorum (⌧ rue du Mont-Blanc 2, ☎ 022/909–28–50) deals exclusively in the sale of antique watches. **Ars Nova** (⌧ rue Jean-Calvin 6, ☎ 022/311–86–60) has a gallery-quality selection of treasures from the early 20th century, including Art Deco jewelry. **Au Vieux Canon** (⌧ Grande-Rue 40, ☎ 022/310–57–58) offers an extravagant selection of English silver. **Buchs** (⌧ Grande-Rue 34–36, ☎ 022/311–74–85) sells beautifully restored antique frames of Old Master vintage and quality. **Jadis** (⌧ Grande-Rue 21, ☎ 022/781–24–02) sells an unusual selection of antique watches and jewelry. **Rue des Belles Filles** (⌧ rue Etienne-Dumont 6 bis, ☎ 022/310–31–31) offers a crowded treasure hunt for vintage clothing, jewelry, and knickknacks.

BOOKS

Librairie Jullien (⌧ pl. du Bourg-de-Four 32, ☎ 022/310–36–70) has sold new and antique books since 1839. **Librairie Payot** (⌧ rue Chantepoulet 5, ☎ 022/731–89–50; ⌧ rue de la Confédération 5, ☎ 022/310–92–66; ⌧ rue du Conseil-Général 11, ☎ 022/320–27–33; ⌧ rue de Candolle 6, ☎ 022/320–26–23) carries English as well as French titles. **A Montparnasse** (⌧ 39, Grande Rue, ☎ 022/311–67–19) carries lovely old books and prints. **Galerie Bernard Letu** (⌧ rue Calvin 2ter, ☎ 022/310–47–57) carries an inspired collection of art and photography books. **Oreille Cassé** (⌧ pl. Grenus 8, ☎ 022/732–40–80) sells hardcover French comic books (*bandes dessinées*) and children's books.

CHOCOLATE

Arn (⌧ 12 pl. du Bourg-de-Four, ☎ 022/310–40–94) is an old-town institution for handmade chocolates, pastries, and sweets. **Du Rhône** (⌧ rue de la Confédération 3, ☎ 022/311–56–14) has an excellent, expensive selection of its famous chocolates. **Jenny** (⌧ rue Kléberg 8, ☎ 022/731–48–11) has fine sweets and a tearoom to sample them in. **Rohr** (⌧ pl. de Molard 3, ☎ 022/311–63–03; and in the covered passageway at rue du Rhône 42, ☎ 022/311–68–76) has its loyal devotees.

CHILDREN'S CLOTHES
One Benetton (⊠ rue du Rhone 19, ☎ 022/311–36–72) specializes in fashions for babies under 2, while a second store (⊠ rue du Marché 12–14, ☎ 022/311–76–67) caters to children between the ages of 3 and 14. **Jacadi** (⊠ rue du Port 8, ☎ 022/311–01–86) carries goods for children up to 16 years.

MEN'S CLOTHES
Lanvin (⊠ rue du Rhône 62, ☎ 022/310–81–43) carries a full men's line. **Hoffstetter Sports** (⊠ rue de la Corraterie 12, ☎ 022/311–85–11) sells Ungaro, Valentino, New Man, and Polo. **Savile Row** (⊠ rue du Vieux-Collège 10 bis, ☎ 022/311–37–64) has Daks of London suits, plus Burberry, Swiss-made Zimmerli underwear, and Church shoes.

WOMEN'S CLOTHES
Anita Smaga owns a block of boutiques (⊠ rue du Rhône 21, ☎ 022/311–12–90) representing Yves Saint-Laurent, Christian La Croix, Claude Montana, Genny, and Valentino. **Chanel** (⊠ rue du Rhône 43, ☎ 022/311–08–62) carries a complete line of the great couture house's prêt-à-porter. **Chacok** (⊠ rue Verdaine 12, ☎ 022/311–94–74) sells brilliantly colored "ethnic" knits by a designer from the Midi in France. **Les Créateurs** (⊠ rue du Rhône 100, ☎ 022/311–51–42), under the same direction, carries Alaïa and Angelo Tarlazzi. **Charles Jourdain** (⊠ rue de la Croix-d'Or 10, ☎ 022/311–28–38) is known for its clothing and shoes. **Olivia** (⊠ rue du Rhône 15, ☎ 022/310–60–88) carries such upscale labels as Armani, Etro, and Fontana. **Fendi** (⊠ Confédération-Centre 8, ☎ 022/310–85–84) has accessories and leather goods. **Céline** (⊠ rue du Rhône 31, ☎ 022/312–14–60) is known for ready-to-wear, leather goods, and accessories.

FOOD
Caviar House (⊠ rue du Rhône 30, ☎ 022/781–02–37) stocks international indulgences, most of them easy to carry.

JEWELRY
L'Arcade (⊠ rue de la Corraterie 20, ☎ 022/311–15–54) offers Edith Moldaschl's unique selection of "real" costume jewelry, fine old pieces and unique new works. **Ludwig Muller** (⊠ rue des Chaudronniers 5, ☎ 022/310–29–30) makes fine jewelry and gold pieces to order. There's no ceiling on the price of world-famous baubles—the real thing—at **Chopard** (⊠ rue de la Confédération 8, ☎ 022/311–37–28), **Cartier** (⊠ rue du Rhône 35, ☎ 022/311–80–66), **Boucheron** (⊠ rue du Rhône 23, ☎ 022/310–13–11), **Tabbah** (⊠ rue du Rhône 25–27, ☎ 022/310–18–60), and **Bulgari** (⊠ rue du Rhône 30, ☎ 022/310–15–00).

LINENS
Descamps (⊠ pl. Longemalle, ☎ 022/310–98–40) sells the house line of French sheets and towels in chic, bold colors and prints. **Frette** (⊠ rue Céard 5–7, ☎ 022/310–85–23) carries luxurious household linens. **Langenthal** (⊠ rue du Rhône 13, ☎ 022/310–65–10) carries pretty, practical Swiss goods.

LINGERIE
Fogal (⊠ rue du Marché 8, ☎ 022/311–51–36) sells fine Swiss hosiery.

RECORDED MUSIC
Au Ménestrel (⊠ quai de l'Ile 15, ☎ 022/310–42–65) has a large selection of classical CDs, demonstrated in the effete atmosphere of a rare-books shop.

SHOES

The most popular Swiss-made line is **Bally** (⊠ rue du Rhône 62, ☎ 022/310–10–66; ⊠ rue du Marché 18, ☎ 022/310–22–87; ⊠ rue du Cendrier 28, ☎ 022/732–29–11.

TOBACCO

Davidoff & Cie. (⊠ rue de Rive 2, ☎ 022/310–90–41) is the original source of these world-famous Havana cigars. **Grisel** offers its own Havana cigars (⊠ pl. Longemalle 2, ☎ 022/311–97–40).

TOYS

Pinocchio (⊠ rue Etienne-Dumont 10, ☎ 022/310–40–47) has chic, colorful wooden toys, including Bauhaus blocks for adults. **Weber** (⊠ rue Crois-d'Oriz, ☎ 310–42–55) is Switzerland's main chain for international toys.

WATCHES

Of Geneva's myriad watchmakers, three are known for unparalleled excellence. **Piaget** (⊠ rue du Rhône 40, ☎ 022/310–73–88) has high prices to match its high-quality timepieces. **Vacheron-Constantin** (⊠ rue des Moulins 1, ☎ 022/310–32–27), opposite the Jardin Anglais, is a Geneva tradition. **Patek Philippe** (⊠ quai Général-Guisan 22, ☎ 022/781–24–48), on the Right Bank overlooking the place de l'Ile, needs no introduction.

Larger chains offer selections of several makes. **Bucherer** (⊠ quai Général-Guisan 26, ☎ 022/311–62–66) carries Rolex, Baume & Mercier, and Rado. **Gübelin** (⊠ pl. de Molard 1, ☎ 022/310–86–55) has Audemars Piguet. **Les Ambassadeurs** (⊠ rue du Rhône 39, ☎ 022/310–55–66) carries Omega, Tissot, and Audemars Piquet. **Columna** (⊠ rue du Marché 8, ☎ 022/311–45–42) carries Longines.

OUTDOOR ACTIVITIES AND SPORTS

Golf

The **Golf Club de Genève** (⊠ rte. de la Capite 70, Cologny, ☎ 022/735–75–40) welcomes visitors and rents equipment.

Sailing

The **Ecole Club Migros** (⊠ rue du Prince 3, ☎ 022/310–65–55) offers sailing courses. The **Centre Culturel Coop** (⊠ rue des Pâquis 35, ☎ 022/731–26–50) gives instruction. **Bateaux Ecole Léman** (⊠ across from quai Gustave-Ador 44, ☎ 022/735–22–63) has rentals and classes.

Skating

There are two skating rinks open from October to March: **Patinoire des Vernets** (⊠ quai des Vernets, ☎ 022/343–88–50) indoors, and **Patinoire de Meyrin,** outdoors (⊠ chemin Louis Rendu, ☎ 022/782–13–00).

Skiing

Though Geneva is not a ski destination, those in need of a quick fix should head for the **Gare Routière de Genève** (⊠ bus station, ☎ 022/732–02–30), which provides daily trips to many local French resorts, including Chamonix. The trip takes an hour to an hour and a half, and the 50 SF fare includes a ski-lift pass.

Swimming

The skating rink at Meyrin becomes an outdoor pool in summer. As for swimming in Lac Léman, Geneva residents are divided: Some have been swimming in it for years, while others offer dire predictions that you'll catch cystitis, strep throat, and worse from its polluted waters. There are two access points close to the center: **Pâquis-Plage** (☎ 022/732–29–74), a sheltered area above quai Mont-Blanc, with a restaurant and changing rooms; and **Genève-Plage** (☎ 022/736–24–82), on quai Gustave-Ador beyond the Jet d'Eau.

Tennis

Visitors are welcome at the **New Sporting Club** (✉ rte. de Collex 51, Bellevue, ☎ 022/774–15–14), the **Tennis du Bois Carré** (✉ rte. de Veyrier 204, Carouge, ☎ 022/784–30–06), and the **Tennis Club des Eaux-Vives** (✉ Parc des Eaux-Vives, ☎ 022/735–53–50).

GENEVA A TO Z

Arriving and Departing

By Bus

Bus tours generally arrive at and depart from the **Gare Routière de Genève** (✉ bus station, ☎ 022/732–02–30), at place Dorcière, just off rue du Mont-Blanc, behind the English church in the city center.

By Car

Approaching Geneva by car is straightforward enough, as a major expressway (N1) enters from the north via Lac Léman's northern shore, connecting through Lausanne by way of either Bern (N12) or Martigny in the Valais (N9). It's easy to enter from France, either from Grenoble to the south or Lyon to the southwest, as border controls are minimal. From the Valais, you also can approach Geneva from the scenic southern shore of Lac Léman, via Evian-les-Bains. (You will, of course, need your passport and vignette—Swiss road-tax sticker—no matter how brief the foray.)

By Plane

Cointrin (☎ 022/799–31–11), Geneva's airport and the second-largest international airport in Switzerland, is served by several airlines that fly directly to the city from New York City, Toronto, and London. **Swissair** serves the airport most frequently. **Crossair,** the domestic airline, connects from Cointrin to Bern, Zürich, Lugano, and other Swiss cities—as well as to several European capitals.

BETWEEN THE AIRPORT AND THE CITY CENTER
There is regular bus service from the airport to the center of Geneva. The bus takes about 20 minutes, and the fare is 2.20 SF. Some of the city's hotels also have their own shuttle system. Cointrin has a direct rail link with **Cornavin** (☎ 022/731–64–50), the city's main train station, in the center of town. Trains run about every 10 minutes, from 5:30 AM to midnight. The trip takes about six minutes, and the fare is 5 SF.

By Taxi. Taxis are plentiful but very expensive and charge at least 25 SF to the city center. Tips are expected for luggage only.

By Limousine. Ambassador Cab Service (☎ 022/732–31–32) and **Executive Car Service** (☎ 022/732–79–77) rent private limousines; some luxury hotels either keep their own fleet or will arrange one through the concierge.

By Train

Cornavin (✉ pl. de Cornavin, ☎ 022/731–64–50) is an important terminus for the Swiss Federal Railroads, with direct expresses coming from most Swiss cities every hour.

Getting Around

By Boat

The **Compagnie Générale de Navigation (CGN) sur le Lac Léman** (✉ Jardin-Anglais, CH-1204 Genève, ☎ 022/311–25–21) offers steamer transportation between most lake ports, including those of France as well as Lausanne and Montreux. Holders of the Swiss Pass travel free; those with a Swissboat Pass receive a 50% discount. Boat excursions onto the lake are offered by several smaller private firms, including **Mouettes Genevoises** (☎ 022/732–29–44) and **Swissboat** (☎ 022/732–47–47).

By Taxi

Taxis (☎ 022/321–22–23, 022/794–71–11, or 022/331–41–33) can be immaculate and the drivers are polite, but there's a 5 SF charge per passenger plus 2 SF per kilometer (about a half mile), and you may find yourself waiting in slow traffic while pedestrians flow by. There's a surcharge on evening and Sunday fares as well.

By Tram and Bus

Geneva has an excellent network of trams, buses, and trolleybuses, extremely efficient and remarkably inexpensive; the schematic maps are relatively easy to follow. Every bus stop has a machine selling tickets, and for 2.20 SF you can use the system for one hour, changing as often as you like. Children 6 to 16 years, women over 62, and men over 65 travel half price. A trip limited to three stops, with return within 30 minutes, costs 1.50 SF. If you plan to travel frequently, buy a *carte journalière*, a ticket covering unlimited travel within the city center all day for 5 SF; it's available at newsstands that display a TRANSPORTS PUBLICS GENEVOIS (TPG) sign near the stop. Holders of the Swiss Pass can travel free on Geneva's public transport system.

Contacts and Resources

Bookstores

Librairie Payot (✉ rue Chantepoulet 5, ☎ 022/731–89–50; rue de la Confédération 5, ☎ 022/310–92–66; rue du Conseil-Général 11, ☎ 022/320–27–33; rue de Candolle 6, ☎ 022/320–26–23) has a stock of English-language books.

Consulates

Canada (✉ rue du Pré de la Bichette 1, ☎ 022/733–90–00). **United Kingdom** (✉ rue de Vermont 37, ☎ 022/734–38–00). **United States Mission** (✉ rte. de Pregny 11, ☎ 022/749–41–11).

Emergencies

Police (☎ 117). **Ambulance** (☎ 144). **Hospital** (✉ Hôpital Cantonal, rue Micheli-du-Crest 24, ☎ 022/372–33–11). **Doctor referral** (☎ 022/320–25–11); emergency house calls (☎ 022/348–49–50). **Pharmacies** (☎ 111).

Guided Tours

BOAT TOURS

Swissboat (✉ quai du Mont-Blanc 4, ☎ 022/732–47–47) offers guided excursions along the shores of Lac Léman, with views of famous homes and châteaux. Departures are from the quai du Mont-Blanc; times vary with the season. **Mouettes Genevoises** tours (✉ quai du Mont-Blanc 8, ☎ 022/732–29–44) are not guided in person, but you're given a printed and numbered commentary with map to guide yourself on tours of the Geneva end of the lake.

ORIENTATION

Bus tours around Geneva are operated by **Key Tours** (☎ 022/731–41–40). They leave from the bus station in place Dorcière, behind the English church, daily at 2; during high season (May–Oct.) there is also a tour departing at 10. The tours (27 SF) last approximately two hours and include an overview of the international area and a walk through the old town.

Key Tours also offers bus excursions into the countryside, the Jura, and Montreux/Chillon, as well as all-day trips to outlying attractions, including the Jungfraujoch and Chamonix, in the French Alps; lunch and guide are included.

PERSONAL GUIDES
The **Geneva tourist office** provides private guided tours of the city by day or evening for fees starting at 30 SF for two hours (minimum two persons). Reserve in writing.

SPECIAL INTEREST
The **United Nations** organizes tours around the Palais des Nations. Enter by the Pregny Gate in the avenue de la Paix; if you take Bus 8 from Cornavin, don't get off at Nations: Wait for the smaller Appia stop. Tours last about an hour. ✉ *8.50 SF.*

WALKING TOURS
The tourist office will provide you with an audio-guided tour (in six languages, including English) of the old town that covers 26 points of interest, complete with map, cassette, and player. Rental is 10 SF, and a deposit of 50 SF is required.

Travel Agencies
American Express (✉ rue du Mont-Blanc 7, ☎ 022/731–76–00). **Thomas Cook** (✉ rue de Lausanne 64, ☎ 022/732–45–55). **Automobile Club Suisse** (✉ Fontenette 21, CH-1227 Carouge, ☎ 022/342–22–33). **Touring Club Suisse** (✉ rue Pierre Fatio 9, ☎ 022/737–12–12).

Visitor Information
The city has an excellent and well-organized tourist office, the **Office du Tourisme de Genève** (☎ 022/738–52–00, FAX 022/731–90–56), located in the Cornavin rail station. There is another tourist information booth at place du Molard 4, on the left bank. For information by mail, contact the administration at route de l'Aèroport 10, Case Postale 1215, Genève 15, ☎ 022/788–08–08, FAX 022/788–81–70.

14 Portraits of Switzerland

Cheese: The Swiss Cure

The View from the Trail

Skiing Switzerland

Books and Videos

CHEESE: THE SWISS CURE

Grandfather sat himself down on a three-legged stool and blew up the fire with the bellows till it was red and glowing. As the pot began to sing, he put a large piece of cheese on a toasting fork and moved it to and fro in front of the fire until it became golden yellow all over. . . . Heidi took up the bowl of milk and drained it thirstily. . . . She ate her bread with the toasted cheese, soft as butter, which tasted delicious, and every now and then she took a drink. She looked as happy and contented as anyone could be.

—Heidi, by Johanna Spyri*

IT WAS SWISS CHEESE that put the apples in the cheeks of the hardy little mountain girl named Heidi, the heroine earth-child who inspired Victorians to leave dark city streets for clear Alpine air; to climb in high, flower-carpeted meadows; to rise early, work hard, and—first and foremost—eat cheese three times a day.

A creature of fiction but set by her creator in the very real verdant heights above Maienfeld, near the borders of Liechtenstein and Austria, Heidi grew strong, wise, and honest under her reclusive grandfather's bushy-browed gaze and his steady diet of goat's milk, black bread, and great slabs of cheese. She drank milk for breakfast, packed a fat chunk of cold cheese for lunch (with an occasional helping of cold meat), had fire-toasted cheese at supper, and drank more bowls of creamy milk, warm from the goat, before she climbed into the hayloft to sleep.

One wonders that she didn't waddle instead of climb. Despite the conspicuous absence of fruit and vegetables—even, say, a jar of canned cabbage from the pantry—Heidi flourished like the green bay tree. She even seduced her crippled friend Clara to leave dank, beshadowed Frankfurt and take an Alpine cure. The daily cheese and

goat's milk worked a mountain miracle on Clara as well, and when her father came to take her home, she walked down the hillside to greet him.

It is the elements of freshness and purity in plain, wholesome cheese that captured the imagination of the Victorians—a true, untreated *cuisine du marché* carried from barn to table with all nature's goodness intact. Butterfat was a virtue; cholesterol, a concept unborn.

Cheese is still a way of life in Switzerland, eaten in dishes of such simplicity that they may seem uninspired to a palate grown used to trendy international cuisine. Raclette, the famous cheese specialty of canton Vaud, is nothing more than a great wheel of cheese cut in half, its exposed side held to an open fire and the softening semiliquid scraped onto a plate; this plain yellow puddle is enhanced only by a couple of crisp pickles and potatoes roasted in their jackets. Alples Maggrone, found in variation throughout the mountain regions but particularly around Appenzell, makes America's macaroni and cheese (the national dish of the 1950s) seem sophisticated by comparison: The Swiss version simply tosses boiled macaroni and potatoes in melted butter and grated cheese, a few curls of butter-fried onions providing its sole textural contrast.

In German regions you'll find *Käseschnitte* (the French Swiss call it *croûte*), closest to Heidi's own toasted cheese: Slabs of bread are topped with grated cheese and butter, then baked in a casserole until the whey and butterfat saturate the bread and the cheese turns golden brown. (Variations may combine wine, ham, mushrooms, or eggs.) Chäschüchli from the Valais region are ramekins of baked cheese, egg, and bread crumbs. *Käseknopfli* are chewy little fingers of noodle dough—*Spätzle* to Germans—served in a creamy mountain cheese sauce so pungently aromatic that you may

---

*From translations by Helen B. Dole (New York: Grosset & Dunlap, 1927) and Eileen Hall (London: Penguin Books, 1956).

rear back from the steamy plate. The flavor, though, is surprisingly sweet, fresh, and mild.

AND OF COURSE FONDUE (from *fondre*—"to melt"), though it went in and out of vogue in America with the '60s ski rage, remains a winter fixture here: With its pungent crushed garlic and sting of kirsch stirred through the creamy molten mass, its flavors are relatively complex. Different regions press the subtlety further by demanding specific blends of the local cheese to create the only *true* fondue: Proportions of aged Gruyère and milder Emmental vary, and in Fribourg, it's made with creamy Vacherin. (The convivial system of sharing fondue around a table dates back to the ancient peasant tradition of circling around a common pot for the family meal. It is rendered all the more convivial today by the tradition of downing a shot of 90-proof kirsch halfway through the pot: the *coup du milieu*.)

Cheese is available around the clock, today as in Heidi's time. A good Swiss breakfast, especially in German cantons, won't be served without a fan of brown-skinned slices of Gruyère, Emmental (the one with the holes that gave "Swiss cheese" its name), or Appenzeller. Cubed cheese may show up in your lunch salad (*Käsesalat*), along with nuts, potatoes, and greens. And after a French-style meal, there's always the cheese course: In addition to the usual array of aged hard cheeses, there's usually a token *tomme* (a creamy-white fresh cheese from cow, sheep, or goat's milk) and the mild but novel *tête de moine* from the Jura, shaved off in spiraling ruffles with a crank. The best L'Etivaz, an Alpine Gruyère-style cheese from near Château-d'Oex, is aged three years and then scraped across a wooden plane: Its grainy sheets, nutty as a good Reggiano Parmesan, are rolled into tight curls (*rebibes*), which are eaten by hand. In the Italian canton of Ticino, you may end a simple meal in a mountain grotto with a squeaky-fresh mold of goat cheese, called *formaggini*.

In Heidi's world, cold meat—yet another source of animal fats—seems to provide the only relief from her dairy diet. The meat she packed off to eat high in the goats' grazing meadows was probably air-dried beef, an Alpine delicacy that fills the role of Italy's *prosciutto crudo* as a first-course cold meat. Its texture—at best, tender and sliced paper thin; at worst, cut crudely and taking on the texture of bookbinding—reflects the simple process of its creation: It is dried outdoors in the mountain breeze. (A much rarer, though tastier, variation—and worth looking out for—is Appenzeller *Mostbröckli,* which is marinated in cider before being dried in air.)

Had Heidi not lived alone on a mountaintop, her diet might have been richer still—indeed, it might have killed her. Today as in Heidi's day, hot meat dishes in Switzerland are served from large chafing dishes containing portions enough for two healthy farm boys. Often, two or more cutlets will be offered. When one heaping dinner plate has been cleared and the diner is ready to sigh in relief, the server reappears with a clean plate—and fills it completely again. The pan-Swiss dish called *geschnetzeltes Kalbfleisch* or *emincé de veau* appears in nearly every middle-class dining room, its mounds of cut veal wallowing in rich, buttery cream. This ribsticking mainstay inevitably comes with *Rösti,* an oil-crisped patty of hash browns often more than 8 inches in diameter.

And that's not all. Many of the simple stews and meaty *plats du jour* (daily specials) come swimming in a savory brown gravy, a distant cousin of *sauce bordelaise*. Frequently—even usually—its basic flavor has been given a boost with the ubiquitous brown condiments that stock all but the most enlightened Swiss kitchens. They are made by the soup magnates Maggi and Knorr, and their primary ingredients are salt and monosodium glutamate (*Geschmackverstärker* or *exhausteur de goût*). If the gravy hasn't been boosted enough already, chances are you can season it to taste from the handy MSG shakers on your table, standing by in baskets made to fit with the salt, pepper, and toothpicks.

At least Heidi's diet, though heavy in fats, was chemically pure. And when she climbed up to pasture the goats every day, she did carry hard black bread with her cheese. She coveted the aristocratic white rolls of Frankfurt and hoarded them during her urban sojourn—but only to smuggle them back to her friend Peter's grandmother, whose aged teeth couldn't handle a proper chunk of bread. Nowadays, though the countries that surround Switzerland still prize refined flour (Styrofoamlike baguettes in France are that country's weakest culinary link these days), it is coarse, crusty brown loaves that the Swiss offer with even their finest foods, especially in the German cantons. More generously leavened than in Heidi's day but chewy nonetheless, it is served simply fresh-sliced or, at breakfast buffets, as a whole loaf wrapped in a snowy linen napkin to be sawed at the last possible moment. In Heidi's time and until the turn of the century, these whole-grain breads offered the only cereal roughage in a diet that was relentlessly high in animal fats. They were often, of course, heaped with cheese and sweet butter.

It was in reaction, in part, to Swiss cheese that Dr. R. Bircher-Benner, at a clinic in Zürich, developed the antidote that changed Swiss eating habits for good: Bircher-Müsli. A simple cereal blend of soaked raw oats, nuts, and whole apples (skins, pips, and all), it is eaten for breakfast or as a light supper—the latter, in fact, a throwback to the modest plate of evening gruel Swiss peasants once faced before tapping into the wealth of protein-rich cheese in their own backyard.

With one foot on the farm, the other in the factory, the cheese industry today reveals much about Switzerland's perpetually split personality, from its humble mountain huts that produce one cheese a day to its high-tech, high-volume, steel-and-tile factories. At L'Etivaz in canton Vaud, independent farmers graze their family's few cows on green Alpine slopes only during summer months, when the snow at elevations above 1,000 meters (3,280 feet) recedes enough for sweet grass to break through. In old copper pots over wood fires, each family stirs its own daily milk, gathers up the thick curd in broad cheesecloth, squeezes out excess whey with a wooden press, and molds the cheese into a round wheel to drain. Each cheese is stamped with the family brand and carried down to the village, where a modern cooperative *affineur* carefully supervises its aging until the farmer reclaims the finished product to sell or keep as he likes.

The directness of the process is striking. A family Subaru, manure spattered on its fenders, backs up to the co-op door; a wiry, sunburned farmer opens the hatch and rolls out a pale, waxy new cheese wheel; a worker wades in rubber boots through the puddles of pungent whey, greets the farmer, takes a bacterial sample, and rolls the cheese onto a rack. It joins the ranks of similar cheeses, all bearing family brands, on long wooden shelves that stretch on and on like library stacks, each cheese to be washed and turned according to a schedule well tested over the centuries.

THE GREAT COMMERCIAL cheese factories of Emmental and Gruyères still stir their cheeses in vast copper cauldrons, and their fires are still fueled by wood. The difference, of course, is in volume. At the *Schaukäserei* (demonstration factory) in Affoltern, outside Bern, 10,000 kilos (22,000 pounds) of milk a day (2,900,000 kilos a year) pour in from 59 suppliers throughout the Emmental valley. In pots as big as smelters, it is heated over fires fueled by a steady conveyor-belt flow of wood chips gleaned from Swiss lumber mills—250 tons a year. The storage racks—the stacks, as it were—could rival those of the Library of Congress.

It is Swiss science and industry in action. It may be disappointing to the romantic to learn that even the holes in Emmentaler cheese—the type Americans call "Swiss cheese"—no longer swell naturally from the internal gases of fermentation but are carefully controlled by the addition of bacteria known to produce holes of a dependable size.

Yet a traveler, cruising Switzerland's emerald hills and villages far from industrial turf, can't help but notice the damp, fresh, earthy ephemera of the dairy that hangs in the air—a mild, musky tang that scents the cream, thickens the chocolate, and wafts through cool, muddy farmyards. That essence, mingled with crystalline mountain air, worked miracles in *Heidi*. It is the essence of Swiss cheese itself.

—Nancy Coons

THE VIEW FROM THE TRAIL

FOR ALL THE CABLE CARS weaving their steel webs across the mountainsides, and all the cogwheel trains lugging shutter-clicking tourists up 45° slopes, and all the panoramic buses with their wraparound bubble windows (and distracting TV screens) idling in château parking lots, and all the refurbished period steamers that offer up water-level views from plush banquettes and brass-railed decks—despite every effort made by this most accommodating, pampering host of a country to keep sightseers comfortably settled on their Rösti-padded bottoms, the only *real* way to see Switzerland is on foot. For the Swiss experience is a multisensory one that can't be appreciated from a ringside seat but must be participated in, encountered, drunk in and savored like a mouthful of complex wine—crystalline air, jewel-tone meadow flowers, crushed pine needles, damp stone, muffled cowbells, fresh-chewed wintergreen, the trebles of birdsong, and the subsonic rumble of the mountains themselves, primordial and inexplicable: Is it a distant avalanche? A storm? Can you hear a glacier moving?

Certainly not from an idling bus. From the moment you leave your state-of-the-art transportation, cross the immaculate parking lot, and confirm your route on tidy signposts—a virtual index of timed and measured footpaths, arrayed for your convenient selection—you'll begin to enter the terrain, like Alice passing through the looking glass. The improbable blues and greens of postcard views will begin, suddenly, to pop into three dimensions, and as you succumb to the sensory experience, your perceptions will intensify, your mind will clear, your blood will course clean. The immensity of the panorama grows rather than recedes with exposure, and the massive peaks and cliffs around you take on a splendor only a live performance can offer. They're alive with waterfalls, cuckoos, masses of living clouds that shift and evolve as you stride past. Eventually you'll settle into a meditative rhythm, responding to the sound of your own two feet crunching down the trail, your heightened breathing pattern, the swish of Gore-Tex—a rhythm broken only by the occasional counterbeat of a "*Grüezi!*", or "Greetings!"

Because you are never alone on a Swiss footpath: As the natives gather for their ritual coffee and cake at 4 or their glass of Luins over cards, so do they hit the trails every weekend, every holiday, every summer vacation. Add to that loyal faction the waves of visitors who pour over Swiss borders every year, and your average isolated mountain trail can become a virtual thoroughfare, as sociable as a pub, as busy as a highway, and as varied and fascinating in its array of human fauna as a sidewalk café.

The German-Swiss dominate, earth-loving, pragmatic, wearers of practical shoes. With their lead-heavy Raichle boots and woolly knee socks, they are enthusiastic traditionalists, walking briskly, chins up, their *Wanderstäbe* (walking sticks) stabbing the ground in marchlike rhythm. Arrive at a trail base for what you think is an early start on an all-day hike, and you're liable to meet the loden-set stretching out at the end of a hard dawn's walk, their rosy cheeks and ice-blue eyes glowing from the fresh air as they load their gear back into the car.

As you head off at a more reasonable hour, you may be followed by the German and Austrian families, inordinately tall, blond fathers in short shorts carrying towheaded toddlers in backpacks while the straw-haired mothers prod on the gradeschoolers. The next wave to arrive will be ivory-skinned English retirees in leather walking shoes and tweed, and tawny American students in featherweight, hightech, fluorescent boots, already stripped down to tank tops. (You may even spot along the way a few Americans strapped into Walkmen; what are they listening to, drowning out the birdsong: Mahler's *Songs of the Wayfarer*?) All are committed to a day's hard hiking, with snacks and picnics packed for the midday meal.

But as the groups are gathering up their litter from a long lunch stop in an emerald-green meadow, a low din of voices approaches: These are the Italians, lean, aristocratic, olive-skinned northerners dressed head to toe in fresh-pressed white, navy sweaters tied around their necks, 6, 8, 10 of them at a time sauntering, laughing, and cuffing each other up the trail. You'll find them mid-afternoon, sleeping off their lunch in the sun on woollen blankets, still smiling, still impeccably wrinkle-free.

By late afternoon, the families look weary, carrying used Pampers, flattened juice packs, and whining children back toward the car; the English are ready for their tea, the Americans their beer. Yet they may be greeted on their return by a party of sultry French, just now hitting the trail after a decent lunch, dressed (in defiance of blinding primary-color trail fashion) in dark leather and espadrilles, smoking. They will walk until sunset, stopping frequently to sit and read, talk, and smoke some more. By the time they return to their hotels, the kitchen, staffed by the early-bird Swiss, will be closed.

With all this talk of cosmopolitanism on the trail, social codes that dictate passing politely if your pace exceeds that of the wanderer ahead, greeting comers and goers like colleagues in an office corridor, you may wonder where the wilderness is. It's there, all around you, the spectacle of waterfalls dissolving in mist, and snowfields glittering in sun, the hoofprints of cows and deer mingled in the streamside mud testimony to Switzerland's comfortable symbiosis between domesticated countryside and wilderness, between the social convention of nature appreciation and its intensely personal counterpart. It's the natural beauty of Switzerland that attracts all hikers to the trail and unites them, and as you share the view with them, you'll see it, perhaps, with heightened appreciation. But your encounter never resembles that of the crowds on the buses or in the lines for the cable cars: You and your fellow hikers share something a little more intimate, each of you drawn to the same unadulterated experience, the same hands-on, feet-on-the-ground adventure.

—Nancy Coons

SKIING SWITZERLAND

TWO CABLE-CAR RIDES and thousands of feet above the resort village of Verbier, we sit in a mountain restaurant. On the table in front of us are one café renversé, two cups of hot chocolate, one tiny glass of bubbly white *Fendant* wine from Sion. Our legs tired from a long day of skiing, we catch our breath before the evening run, while the slopes and pistes below empty themselves of skiers and fill up with evening light. Outside, the sun hovers only inches above the horizon. Mont Blanc is an island of ice rising out of a sea of summits along the Franco-Swiss border. Peaks and passes stretch as far as the eye can see, an art director's Alpine fantasy in late light.

Verbier skiing is one reason I've returned to Switzerland in winter, faithfully, for the past 25 years. This is a giant of a ski area in a region of giant ski areas, perched high in the French-speaking, southwest corner of Switzerland, draped over four mountain valleys, embracing six villages, a labyrinth of interconnected lifts (more than 100), interlaced slopes (too many to count)—a ski area one can't explore in a week or even exhaust in a season.

For passionate skiers every trip to Switzerland is a homecoming. All our skiing archetypes originate here. White sawtooth horizons point to the sky, picture-postcard chalet roofs poke up under great white hats of snow, necklaces of lifts and cable cars drape themselves over the white shoulders of fairy-tale mountains, and runs go on forever.

These are big mountains, with vertical drops twice the length of those of the Rockies. In the Alps you can often drop four, five, or six thousand vertical feet in one run. Here runs are so long that halfway down you need a break—which you'll find at a little chalet restaurant in the middle of nowhere, where the views are as exhilarating as the schnapps that's so often the drink of choice.

These are pure white mountains, too, whiter than we're used to. In the Alps, the tree line is low, often only 1,000 meters

(3,000 feet) above sea level, and ski areas stretch upward from there. The skier's playing field is white on white; marked pistes are white rivers of groomed snow snaking down equally white but ungroomed flanks of Alpine peaks. There are more treeless bowls than you can count, than you can hope to ski in several skiers' lifetimes.

When European skiers tell you that the western Alps are higher and more glaciated, more likely to have good snow in a dry year, and that the eastern Alps are lower in elevation but full of charm, with more intimate, more richly decorated villages, they are usually referring to the difference between the French Alps and Austria. In fact, they could just as well be talking about the mountains and ski resorts of southwest Switzerland versus those of eastern Switzerland, Graubünden, and the Engadine; for Switzerland, with its many cantons, is a microcosm that mirrors the diversity of skiing all across the greater Alps. You can test your credit-card limits at the Palace Hotel in worldly St. Moritz, hear the Latin echoes of Romansh as you ride the cog railways of modest Kleine Scheidegg, or ponder the hearty existence of hearty mountain farmers among the peaks of French-speaking Valais—but always, the local mountain culture will be part of your ski experience.

As varied as the regions are the people who ski them. Depending on which canton you ski, you may hear the lilting singsong French of Vaud and the western Valais, the incomprehensible Swiss German of the Berner Oberland and eastern Wallis, or the haunting Latin echoes of Romansh in the high valleys of Graubünden. The ski pistes of Switzerland are the polyglot crossroads of Europe, where stylish Parisians in neon outfits rub elbows with Brits in navy blue, Munich businessmen in Bogner suits, and Swedish students with punk haircuts. And yet, when you're surrounded by mountains that will outlast fashions, lifetimes, and languages, such differences fade, and the mountains are all you can see.

We walk uphill through knee-deep powder toward the summit of the Allalinhorn—the friendliest of canton Wallis's many 4,000-meter (13,120-foot) peaks. Early morning sunshine rakes the corniced ridges around us; the village of Saas-Fee still hides in shadow below. With climbing skins glued to the bottom of our skis, we've shuffled up the Feegletscher to earn a morning's bliss in deep untracked snow. This glacier highway is taking us above the domain of passes and ski lifts and groomed slopes, into a world of icy north walls, pure knife-edge ridges, undulating mile-long coverlets of fresh powder, summits of whipped meringue, and snow crystals sparkling at our feet. Munching cheese and chocolate as we climb, thinking that we must look like silhouettes in one of Herbert Matter's prewar Swiss travel posters, breathing deeply, climbing slowly, we daydream our way to the top. Our tracks, like zippers in the snow, stretch up to a vanishing point in the midnight-blue sky above.

It's a soft April morning at Les Diablerets, a ski area on the frontier between francophone Vaud and the German canton of Bern. It's already 11 AM and the frozen corn snow is only now softening up on the wide glacier beneath the dark, thumblike peak of the Oldenhorn. From the topmost lift we can see west toward Lake Geneva, south toward the giant peaks of the Valais, and east toward the dark brooding peaks of the Berner Oberland. An observation deck on the roof of the Alps reveals mountains filling space to its farthest corners, to the hazy horizon, waves on a wind-tossed sea, frozen white, as far as one can see. On the deep valley flanks below Les Diablerets, winding west toward the Rhône Valley, another winter's worth of cow manure has performed its annual alchemy: The slopes are greening up with no respect for common-sense color—pastures of eye-dazzling kelly green under dark forests and crags. Only a few miles away, down the eastern German-speaking side of the mountains, the chic resort of Gstaad seems deserted; its jet-set winter guests have already hung up their skis and headed for the Mediterranean. The mountains are ours for a day.

At the top of the lift we break through the clouds. A sea of fog fills the Rhône Valley below us, a fluffy false plain, punctured only by snowy peaks, stretching to the horizon. Somewhere under these clouds is Lake Geneva, and far across, Les Dents du Midi ("The Teeth of Noon") rise out of the clouds like ice-sheathed knuckles. Villars sur Ollon is a ski resort so small most American skiers have never heard of it, even though it's bigger than half the ski areas in Colorado. Alone, we ski along the edge of the piste, where the slope steepens and drops away in a succession of rocky ledges. Just over the border that separates the skier's world from the mountaineer's, we see a lone ibex, posing on a rock outcrop against the clouds, scimitar-shape horns swept back in wide twin arcs. We christie to a stop, stand in awe wishing we had cameras, and realize eventually that the ibex is not going to bolt. These are its Alps, its domain; we are the newcomers, birds of passage, intruders. It feels like a privilege to share the roof of Europe with this ibex, a privilege that our Swiss hosts have slowly earned over 700 years by farming basically unfarmable mountainsides, by making this land their domain. We push off, the cold winter snow squeaking under our skis. Behind our backs the ibex still stares off into the distance.

THESE IMAGES STAY WITH ME, indelible as the Alps themselves. Say the word Switzerland and I see the gentle slopes of the Plateau Rosa above Zermatt, perforated by the dotted lines of T-bars, peppered with tiny, bright-color skiers, slopes lapping in white waves against the base of the Matterhorn. Near St. Moritz, I see the blue-green crevasses of the Morteratsch glacier, a frozen white-water rapid spilling down from the Diavolezza ski area: ice walls, blue ice caves, a labyrinth of ice. I see the three giants of the Berner Oberland, the Eiger, the Mönch, and the Jungfrau—the Ogre, the Monk, and the Virgin—shadowy 13,000-foot-high northern faces that loom above the toy skiers and runs of Grindelwald and Wengen.

That Switzerland has some of the best skiing in the world goes without saying. In the end, though, it's not the skiing I remember, or the runs, or the trails, or my turns. It's the mountains I remember. And so will you.

—Lito Tejada-Flores

Resort	Lift-Ticket Cost (SF) (one day/six day)	Elevation (m/ft)	Number of Lifts	Lift Capacity (number of riders per hour)	Maintained Trails (km/mi)	Snowmaking
Arosa	52/219	1,800–2,650 m 5,900–8,700 ft	16	21.7	70/43	❄
Crans-Montana	52/235	1,500–3,000 m 4,920–9,843 ft	42	41	160/100	❄
Davos-Klosters	56/259	1,560–2,844 m 5,118–9,330 ft	55	55.0	317/197	❄
Flims-Laax	55/270	1,160–3,292 m 3,808–10,798 ft	31	41	225/140	❄
Gstaad-Saanenland	46/232	1,100–3,000 m 3,600–9,843 ft	69	50.0	257/160	❄
La Vallée de Conches (cross-country)		1,300–1,450 m 4,265–4,757 ft				
Le Val d'Anniviers	36/172	1,350–3,000 m 4,430–9,843 ft	46	25.0	250/155	❄
Les Portes du Soleil (Champery and 14 linked Swiss and French areas)	46/210	1,000–2,500 m 3,280–8,200 ft	228	228.8	650/400	❄
Verbier (including 6 linked areas of Quatre-Vallées)	59/297	820–3,330 m 2,690–10,925 ft	100	80.1	400/248	❄
Saas-Fee	55/255	1,800–3,600 m 5,900–11,800 ft	25	20.0	80/50	❄
St. Moritz	54/258	1,856–3,060 m 6,100–10,000 ft	60	16.2	55/34	❄
Wengen	52/232	1,300–3,450 m 4,265–11,330 ft	44	36.5	182/113	❄
Zermatt	60/292	1,260–3,820 m 4,132–12,530 ft	73	70.7	245/152	❄

† depending on type and quality of snow, as well as grooming of slopes

Average Annual Snowfall (cm/in)	Difficulty of Terrain: % Beg/Int/Exp	Cross-Country (km/mi of trails)	Glacier Skiing	Heli-Skiing	Para/Hang Gliding	Ice-Skating	Luge Runs	Skibob Runs	Ballooning	Accommodations (beds in hotels, chalets, and apartments)
692/272	31/57/12	26/16			❄	❄	❄		❄	7,800
518/204	40/50/10	52/32	❄	❄	❄	❄	❄	❄	❄	40,000
427/168	30/40/30	50/31			❄	❄	❄	❄		8,500
440/173	50/30/20	60/37	❄	❄	❄	❄	❄		❄	10,800
627/247	40/40/20	127/75	❄	❄	❄	❄	❄	❄	❄	12,300
522/206	n/a	85/53				❄				7,000
348/137	30/40/30	47/29		❄	❄	❄	❄	❄		20,000
619/244	25/40/35	250/155		❄	❄	❄				93,000
491/193	46/58/18	51/32	❄	❄	❄	❄	❄	❄		50,000
357/141	30/45/25	8/5	❄		❄	❄		❄		8,500
368/145	10/70/20	12/8	❄	❄	❄	❄	❄	❄	❄	12,500
389/153	25/50/25	n/a		❄	❄	❄	❄	❄		5,700
334/131	30/40/30	10/6	❄	❄	❄	❄				13,500

BOOKS AND VIDEOS

Books

Wilhelm Tell, by Friedrich von Schiller, is the definitive stage version of the dramatic legend. *The Prisoner of Chillon,* by Lord Byron, is an epic poem inspired by the sojourn of François Bonivard in the dungeon of Chillon. *A Tramp Abroad,* by Mark Twain, includes the author's personal impressions—and tall tales—derived from travels in Switzerland. *Arms and the Man,* by G. B. Shaw, was the source of Oscar Straus's Viennese operetta *The Chocolate Soldier;* both are about a Swiss mercenary with a sweet tooth. Novels set at least partially in Switzerland include *Heidi,* by Johanna Spyri (Maienfeld); *Daisy Miller,* by Henry James (Lac Léman, Chillon); *Tender is the Night,* by F. Scott Fitzgerald; *A Farewell to Arms,* by Ernest Hemingway; and *Hotel du Lac,* by Anita Brookner (Vevey).

La Place de la Concorde Suisse, by John McPhee, was developed from a series of *New Yorker* pieces the author wrote after traveling with members of the Swiss Army. *Heidi's Alp,* by Christine Hardyment, a first-person account of a family traveling in a camper-van in search of the Europe of fairy tales, includes an adventure with a latter-day Alm-Uncle in a cabin above Maienfeld. *A Guide to Zermatt and the Matterhorn,* Edward Whymper's memoirs of his disastrous climb up the Matterhorn, is now out of print, but it may be available in a library (excerpts appear in Chapter 11, Valais). Thomas Mann's *The Magic Mountain* is set in the ski resort town of Davos, while *Terminal,* by Colin Forbes, is a murder-mystery tale containing fantastic descriptions of Swiss cities.

Videos

Heidi is undoubtedly the best-known film to be shot in Switzerland. Make sure you see the 1937 version directed by Allan Dulan, starring Shirley Temple. *On Her Majesty's Secret Service,* the 1969 James Bond thriller, shows dazzling ski scenes of the Schilthorn in central Switzerland; *The Eiger Sanction* (1975) has Bond climbing the Eiger. *Trois Couleurs Rouge (Three Colors Red),* the last in director Krzysztof Kieslowski's trilogy, and a big hit in Europe, is set in Geneva's old town, while Peter Greenaway's 1993 *Stairs* shows Geneva through the director's unique artistic vision. The moving *Reise der Hoffnung (Journey of Hope),* directed by Xavier Koller in 1990, centers on a Kurdish family fleeing Turkish persecution to seek sanctuary in Switzerland.

INDEX

Index   361

Fodor's Travel Publications

Available at bookstores everywhere, or call 1–800–533–6478, 24 hours a day.

Gold Guides

U.S.

Alaska

Arizona

Boston

California

Cape Cod, Martha's
Vineyard, Nantucket

The Carolinas & the
Georgia Coast

Chicago

Colorado

Florida

Hawai'i

Las Vegas, Reno,
Tahoe

Los Angeles

Maine, Vermont,
New Hampshire

Maui & Lāna'i

Miami & the Keys

New England

New Orleans

New York City

Pacific North Coast

Philadelphia & the
Pennsylvania Dutch
Country

The Rockies

San Diego

San Francisco

Santa Fe, Taos,
Albuquerque

Seattle & Vancouver

The South

U.S. & British Virgin
Islands

USA

Virginia & Maryland

Washington, D.C.

Foreign

Australia

Austria

The Bahamas

Belize & Guatemala

Bermuda

Canada

Cancún, Cozumel,
Yucatán Peninsula

Caribbean

China

Costa Rica

Cuba

The Czech Republic
& Slovakia

Eastern &
Central Europe

Europe

Florence, Tuscany
& Umbria

France

Germany

Great Britain

Greece

Hong Kong

India

Ireland

Israel

Italy

Japan

London

Madrid & Barcelona

Mexico

Montréal &
Québec City

Moscow, St.
Petersburg, Kiev

The Netherlands,
Belgium &
Luxembourg

New Zealand

Norway

Nova Scotia, New
Brunswick, Prince
Edward Island

Paris

Portugal

Provence &
the Riviera

Scandinavia

Scotland

Singapore

South Africa

South America

Southeast Asia

Spain

Sweden

Switzerland

Thailand

Tokyo

Toronto

Turkey

Vienna & the Danube

Fodor's Special-Interest Guides

Caribbean Ports
of Call

The Complete Guide
to America's
National Parks

Family Adventures

Gay Guide
to the USA

Halliday's New
England Food
Explorer

Halliday's New
Orleans Food
Explorer

Healthy Escapes

Kodak Guide to
Shooting Great
Travel Pictures

Net Travel

Nights to Imagine

Rock & Roll Traveler
USA

Sunday in New York

Sunday in
San Francisco

Walt Disney World,
Universal Studios
and Orlando

Walt Disney World
for Adults

Where Should We
Take the Kids?
California

Where Should We
Take the Kids?
Northeast

Worldwide Cruises
and Ports of Call

Special Series

Affordables

Caribbean
Europe
Florida
France
Germany
Great Britain
Italy
London
Paris

Fodor's Bed & Breakfasts and Country Inns

America
California
The Mid-Atlantic
New England
The Pacific Northwest
The South
The Southwest
The Upper Great Lakes

The Berkeley Guides

California
Central America
Eastern Europe
Europe
France
Germany & Austria
Great Britain & Ireland
Italy
London
Mexico
New York City
Pacific Northwest & Alaska
Paris
San Francisco

Compass American Guides

Arizona
Canada
Chicago
Colorado
Hawaii
Idaho
Hollywood
Las Vegas

Maine
Manhattan
Montana
New Mexico
New Orleans
Oregon
San Francisco
Santa Fe
South Carolina
South Dakota
Southwest
Texas
Utah
Virginia
Washington
Wine Country
Wisconsin
Wyoming

Fodor's Citypacks

Atlanta
Hong Kong
London
New York City
Paris
Rome
San Francisco
Washington, D.C.

Fodor's Español

California
Caribe Occidental
Caribe Oriental
Gran Bretaña
Londres
Mexico
Nueva York
Paris

Fodor's Exploring Guides

Australia
Boston & New England
Britain
California
Caribbean
China
Egypt
Florence & Tuscany
Florida

France
Germany
Ireland
Israel
Italy
Japan
London
Mexico
Moscow & St. Petersburg
New York City
Paris
Prague
Provence
Rome
San Francisco
Scotland
Singapore & Malaysia
Spain
Thailand
Turkey
Venice

Fodor's Flashmaps

Boston
New York
San Francisco
Washington, D.C.

Fodor's Pocket Guides

Acapulco
Atlanta
Barbados
Jamaica
London
New York City
Paris
Prague
Puerto Rico
Rome
San Francisco
Washington, D.C.

Mobil Travel Guides

America's Best Hotels & Restaurants
California & the West
Frequent Traveler's Guide to Major Cities
Great Lakes
Mid-Atlantic

Northeast
Northwest & Great Plains
Southeast
Southwest & South Central

Rivages Guides

Bed and Breakfasts of Character and Charm in France
Hotels and Country Inns of Character and Charm in France
Hotels and Country Inns of Character and Charm in Italy
Hotels and Country Inns of Character and Charm in Paris
Hotels and Country Inns of Character and Charm in Portugal
Hotels and Country Inns of Character and Charm in Spain

Short Escapes

Britain
France
New England
Near New York City

Fodor's Sports

Golf Digest's Best Places to Play
Skiing USA
USA Today The Complete Four Sport Stadium Guide

Fodor's Vacation Planners

Great American Learning Vacations
Great American Sports & Adventure Vacations
Great American Vacations
Great American Vacations for Travelers with Disabilities
National Parks and Seashores of the East
National Parks of the West

NOTES

NOTES

NOTES

CNN✈
Airport Network

Your
Window
To The
World
While You're
On The
Road

Keep in touch when you're traveling. Before you take off, tune in to CNN Airport Network. Now available in major airports across America, CNN Airport Network provides nonstop news, sports, business, weather and lifestyle programming. Both domestic and international. All piloted by the top-flight global resources of CNN. All up-to-the minute reporting. And just for travelers, CNN Airport Network features two daily Fodor's specials. "Travel Fact" provides enlightening, useful travel trivia, while "What's Happening" covers upcoming events in major cities worldwide. So why be bored waiting to board? TIME FLIES WHEN YOU'RE WATCHING THE WORLD THROUGH THE WINDOW OF CNN AIRPORT NETWORK!

WHEREVER
YOU TRAVEL,
*H*ELP IS NEVER
FAR AWAY.

From planning your trip to providing travel assistance
along the way, American Express® Travel Service Offices
are always there to help.

Switzerland

Reisebuero WM Mueller
& Co. Ltd. (R)
Steinnenvorstadt 33
Basel
61/281 3380

American Express Travel Service
Schweizerhofquai 4
Lucerne
41/410 0077

Kehrli & Oeler (R)
Bubenbergplatz 9
Berne
31/311 0022

VIP Travels SA (R)
Via Al Forte 10
Lugano
91/923 8545

American Express Travel Service
7 Rue du Mont Blanc
Geneva
22/731 7600

Valais Incoming, Sion (R)
Avenue Tourbillon 3
Sion
27/224 822

American Express Ltd.
c/o United Nations
16 Ave. Jean Trembley
Geneva
22/798 2391

American Express Travel Service
Bahnhofstrasse 20
Zurich
1/211 8370

Travel

http://www.americanexpress.com/travel